The Editor

MICHAEL NEILL is Emeritus Professor of English at the University of Auckland and Professor in Early Modern Literature at the University of Kent. He is the author of *Issues of Death: Mortality and Identity in English Renaissance Tragedy* (1997) and *Putting History to the Question* (2000). His editions include Thomas Kyd's *The Spanish Tragedy* (2014) for Norton, *Antony and Cleopatra* (1994) and *Othello* (2006) for the Oxford Shakespeare, Thomas Middleton's *The Changeling* (2006) for New Mermaids, and Massinger's *The Renegado* (2010) for Arden Early Modern Drama.

Norton Critical Editions
Renaissance

For a complete list of Norton Critical Editions, visit
wwnorton.com/nortoncriticals

A NORTON CRITICAL EDITION

John Webster

THE DUCHESS OF MALFI

AN AUTHORITATIVE TEXT
SOURCES AND CONTEXTS
CRITICISM

Edited by

MICHAEL NEILL
UNIVERSITY OF KENT

W. W. NORTON & COMPANY · *New York* · *London*

W. W. Norton & Company has been independent since its founding in 1923, when William Warder Norton and Mary D. Herter Norton first published lectures delivered at the People's Institute, the adult education division of New York City's Cooper Union. The firm soon expanded its program beyond the Institute, publishing books by celebrated academics from America and abroad. By midcentury, the two major pillars of Norton's publishing program—trade books and college texts—were firmly established. In the 1950s, the Norton family transferred control of the company to its employees, and today—with a staff of four hundred and a comparable number of trade, college, and professional titles published each year—W. W. Norton & Company stands as the largest and oldest publishing house owned wholly by its employees.

Manufacturing by Maple Press
Book design by Antonina Krass
Production manager: Vanessa Nuttry

Library of Congress Cataloging-in-Publication Data

The Duchess of Malfi : an authoritative text, sources and contexts, criticism / edited by Michael Neill, University of Kent. — First edition.
    pages cm. — (A Norton critical edition)
Includes bibliographical references.

ISBN 978-0-393-92325-4 (pbk. : alk. paper)

1. Webster, John, 1580?–1625? Duchess of Malfi.   I. Neill, Michael, 1942– editor.
PR3184.D83D8255 2015
822'.3—dc23

                                        2015010169

W. W. Norton & Company, Inc., 500 Fifth Avenue, New York, N.Y. 10110
www.wwnorton.com

W. W. Norton & Company Ltd., 15 Carlisle Street, London W1D 3BS

3   4   5   6   7   8   9   0

Contents

Criticism

Illustrations

Abbreviations

Bevington	David Bevington et al., eds., *English Renaissance Drama* (New York: Norton, 2002).
Brennan	Elizabeth M. Brennan, ed., *The Duchess of Malfi* (London: A&C Black, 1964).
Brown	John Russell Brown, ed., *The Duchess of Malfi*, Revels Plays, 2nd ed. (Manchester: Manchester University Press, 2009).
Cambridge	David Gunby et al., eds., *Complete Works of John Webster*, 4 vols. (Cambridge: Cambridge University Press, 1995–2012).
conj.	conjectured.
Dent	R. W. Dent, *John Webster's Borrowing* (Berkeley: University of California Press, 1960).
Donne, *Ignatius*	*Ignatius His Conclave* (London, 1611).
Dyce 1	Alexander Dyce, *The Works of John Webster*, 4 vols. (London, 1830).
Dyce 2	Alexander Dyce, *The Works of John Webster*, 4 vols., 2nd ed., (London, 1857).
ed.	edition.
Gibbons	Brian Gibbons, ed., *The Duchess of Malfi* (London: A&C Black, 2001).
Goulart	Simon Goulart, *Admirable and Memorable Histories Containing the Wonders of Our Time,* trans. Edward Grimeston (London, 1607).
Hazlitt	William Hazlitt, ed., *The Dramatic Works of John Webster* (London, 1857).
Lucas	*The Complete Works of John Webster*, ed. F. L. Lucas, 4 vols. (London: Chatto & Windus, 1927).
Marcus	Leah Marcus, ed., *The Duchess of Malfi* (London: Arden, 2009).

Matthieu	Pierre Matthieu, *The Heroic Life and Deplorable Death of the Most Christian King Henry IV*, trans. Edward Grimeston (London, 1612).
McIlwraith	A. K. McIlwraith, ed., *The Stuart Tragedies* (Oxford: Oxford University Press, 1953).
Middleton	Thomas Middleton, *Collected Works*, ed. Gary Taylor et al. (Oxford: Clarendon Press, 2007).
Montaigne	Michel de Montaigne, *Essays*, 3 vols., trans. John Florio (London: Dent, 1910).
ms.	manuscript.
OED	*Oxford English Dictionary.*
Painter	William Painter, *The Second Tome of the Palace of Pleasure* (London, 1567).
Plutarch	*The Lives of the Noble Grecians and Romans*, trans. Sir Thomas North (London, 1579).
Q	quarto.
Sampson	Martin W. Sampson, ed. *The White Devil and The Duchess of Malfi* (New York: D. C. Heath, 1904).
SD	stage direction.
Sidney	Sir Philip Sidney, *The Countess of Pembroke's Arcadia* in *Works*, ed. A. Feuillerat, 4 vols. (Cambridge: University of Cambridge Press, 1912–26).
sig.	signature.
subs.	substantially.
Thorndike	Ashley H. Thorndike, ed., *Masterpieces of the English Drama* (New York, 1912).
Tilley	Morris Palmer Tilley, *Dictionary of the Proverbs in England in the Sixteenth and Seventeenth Centuries* (Ann Arbor: University of Michigan Press, 1950).
Whetstone	George Whetstone, *Heptameron of Civil Discourses* (London, 1582).
Williams	Gordon Williams, *A Glossary of Shakespeare's Sexual Language* (London: Athlone Press, 1997).

Acknowledgments

It is impossible to complete an edition of this kind without the help of numerous individuals and institutions. I am particularly grateful to the various friends and colleagues who have offered help and advice, especially Mac Jackson, David Gunby, David Carnegie, Leah Marcus, Rory Loughnane, and Louise Noble. I am indebted to Keyvan Allahyari for bibliographic assistance; to Faith Cu and Kube Jones-Neill for transcription work; to April-Rose Geers and Gregory Lauzon for invaluable assistance with proofreading; and to Carol Bemis, Rivka Genesen, Thea Goodrich, and Rachel Goodman at Norton for their thoughtful editorial assistance. The Universities of Auckland and Kent have both given invaluable material support. It goes without saying that I have profited enormously from the work of previous editors.

Introduction

After two centuries of relative neglect, *The Duchess of Malfi* has become the most frequently performed play of its period, outside the Shakespearean canon.[1] The tragedy's current popularity mirrors its early success: first performed by the King's Men in 1613–14, it probably had its debut at the Blackfriars, the more exclusive "private" playhouse reserved for their winter performances, before being transferred to the splendidly refurbished Globe, the arena theater on the Bankside for which Shakespeare had written his greatest plays. Over the next quarter century *Malfi* went on to enjoy an unusual number of revivals. We know that the company staged it again in 1617–18, when its treatment of the Cardinal attracted the indignation of the Venetian ambassador's chaplain, Horatio Busino, who saw it as an anti-Catholic libel (see p. 187 in this volume); and there must have been a second production before the play's first publication in the quarto of 1623, since the list of the actors' names printed in that text includes, as the alternative casting for Ferdinand, Richard Robinson, who did not join the company until 1619. Theatrical records for the period are spotty, but we know that the King's Men restaged Webster's tragedy in the early 1630s—perhaps at about the same time as it was honored with a performance at the Cockpit-in-Court (December 26, 1630). Despite the changing theatrical tastes on which contemporary prologues often remark, it was still sufficiently admired to justify a reprinting in 1640.

The Duchess of Malfi's popularity continued through the Restoration into the early eighteenth century with two more editions and a number of revivals—two of which were seen by Samuel Pepys. However, the increasing dominance of neoclassical theory ensured that, like most early modern plays, it was then banished from the stage for a century and a half, with the exception of an unsuccessful rewriting by Lewis Theobald, titled *The Fatal Secret* (1733); but its theatrical fortunes began to revive with a sympathetic adaptation by R. H. Horne, which was directed by Samuel Phelps at Sadler's

---

1. The scope of this introduction does not allow for a full performance history; readers who wish for a more complete account are referred to Leah Marcus's edition in the Arden Early Modern Drama series (London: Arden Shakespeare, 2009), pp. 91–113.

Wells in 1850. By the middle of the twentieth century revivals that were much more faithful to the original text had become relatively frequent.

The extensive critical literature on *The Duchess of Malfi* should by now have guaranteed the play a canonical status on a par with some of Shakespeare's best work, and its increasing prominence in the stage repertory has no doubt had something to do with its growing academic reputation. But this has not always been reflected in the more ambivalent response of theater reviewers, which can still be colored by the older view of Webster as an author of sensational melodramas. Despite the signal success of a number of productions since the 1960s—notably those by Clifford Williams with Judi Dench as the Duchess and Geoffrey Hutchings as Bosola (RSC 1971), Adrian Noble with Helen Mirren and Bob Hoskins (Manchester Royal Exchange, 1980), and Dominic Dromgoole with Gemma Arterton and Sean Gilder (Shakespeare's Globe, 2014)—the popular view of the playwright continues to be the one extravagantly burlesqued by Tom Stoppard in the 1998 film *Shakespeare in Love*, where Webster appears as an unpleasant small boy who delights in feeding live mice to cats and whose favorite play is Shakespeare's notoriously gory *Titus Andronicus* ("I like it when they cut the heads off. And the daughter mutilated with knives. . . . Plenty of blood. That's the only writing!"). Indeed it was precisely in this light that the Globe's Duchess invited her audiences to view the play, when she told the *Radio Times:* "It's like Tarantino. There's mass bloodshed, incest, violence, lots of kick-arse kind of stuff—and everybody dies in the end."[2] The origins of such views are to be found in the well-known attacks of G. H. Lewes and Bernard Shaw on the waxwork extravagance of Act 4, Scene 1. Reviewing Phelps's production Lewes declared that "instead of 'holding the mirror up to nature', this drama holds the mirror up to Madame Tussaud's and emulates her Chamber of Horrors."[3] Of course, a fully sympathetic response to the scene would not only pay attention to the powerful rendering of the Duchess's grief, which provides its dramatic focus; it would notice the metatheatrical wit of a display that parodically remembers the numerous scenes in revenge tragedy, from Thomas Kyd's *The Spanish Tragedy* (ca. 1587) to Henry Chettle's *Hoffman* (1602), in which audiences themselves are "plagued in art" (4.1.118), when they are persuaded to accept similarly "*artificial figures*" (1.63 SD) as actual corpses.[4]

2. Gemma Arterton, interview, *The Radio Times*, May 25, 2014.
3. G. H. Lewes, review, *The Leader*, November 30, 1850, p. 86.
4. See Rory Loughnane, "The Artificial Figures and Staging Remembrance in Webster's *The Duchess of Malfi*," in *The Arts of Remembrance in Early Modern England: Memorial Cultures of the Post Reformation*, ed. Andrew Gordon and Thomas Rist (Farnham:

Webster was at all times a self-conscious dramatic artist, and it will be the purpose of this introduction to show—without denying the theatrical excitements of which he (like Shakespeare, it should be said) was an unembarrassed master—that *The Duchess of Malfi* is a much more serious work than Shaw's disdainful gibe at the "Tussaud laureate" would imply:[5] one that engages in a provocative and potentially dangerous way with social and political issues of its own day, and does so with a poetic intensity unmatched by any of its immediate rivals.

The Dramatist in His Own Time

"I do not altogether look up at your title, the ancientest nobility being but a relic of time past, and the truest honor indeed being for a man to confer honor on himself." With these words, John Webster addresses the young nobleman to whom *The Duchess of Malfi* is dedicated and whose litany of pompous titles he has duly recited: "*the Right Honorable George Harding, Baron Berkeley of Berkeley Castle and Knight of the Order of the Bath to the Illustrious Prince Charles.*" Of course the notion that individual honor is of more significance than mere aristocratic lineage was a recurrent theme of moral philosophy, but there is a truculence about Webster's tone that will be immediately apparent if his dedicatory epistle is set beside others of the genre, whose authors typically strive to outdo one another in expressions of abject regard for the patron each desires to serve. In this, as we shall see, the epistle resonates with the play's own subversive commentary on the vanities of rank and worldly power and with its complementary insistence on "integrity of life" as the foundation of true fame. At the same time the epistle invites the reader to recognize in poetry itself a source of immortal renown for author and patron alike, "for by such poems as this, poets have kissed the hands of great princes and drawn their gentle eyes to look down upon their sheets of paper when the poets themselves were bound up in their winding-sheets. The like courtesy from your lordship shall make you live in your grave and laurel spring out of it."

The terminology here is important: rather than being simply a script for performance, Webster's tragedy is presented as a "poem"

Ashgate, 2013), pp. 211–28. Loughnane complicates the scene's metatheatricality by suggesting that, since actual waxworks were expensive to produce, the scene would have been mounted by players pretending to be the artificial figures that in turn imitate actual corpses. The foundational commentary on the figures is David Bergeron's "The Wax Figures in *The Duchess of Malfi*," *SEL* 18 (1978), 331–39. See also Brian Chalk's essay, on pp. 335–53 in this volume.

5. George Bernard Shaw, "Our Theatres in the Nineties," in *Collected Works* (New York: Wise, 1930–32), Vol. XXV, p. 332.

that has its most important life upon "sheets of paper." Whereas most Elizabethan dramatists, including Shakespeare, appear to have taken little interest in publishing their plays, their Jacobean successors were increasingly keen to claim priority for the printed text—and thereby to bring about a change in the cultural status of playwriting. Earlier plays often appeared anonymously, publishers thinking it more important to advertise the acting companies who performed and owned a piece than to identify its mere writer. By contrast, works like *The Duchess of Malfi*, as they mount their claim to the prestige of "dramatic poetry," insist on the primary importance of authorship.

For all these lofty claims, the actual circumstances of Webster's career seem to have forced him to spend much of his time as a hack writer, working in (frequently anonymous) collaboration with other playwrights. Nevertheless the author of the *Malfi* dedication clearly thinks of himself, in the fashion of such writers as Ben Jonson and George Chapman, as above all a literary dramatist: the title page of the tragedy's first edition, while promising that it appears "*As it was Presented privatly, at the Blackfriars and publiquely at the Globe, by the* Kings Maiesties Servants," is at pains to emphasize the superiority of the printed version, containing as it does "diverse *things . . . that the length of the Play would* not beare in the Presentment." All the evidence suggests that Webster was keenly involved in the preparation of the printed text, where a determination to assert the integrity of his own authorship is evidenced by the marginal note inserted at 3.4.8–9, dissociating him from the doggerel sung at the Cardinal's military "instalment": "The author disclaims this ditty to be his."

Webster's dedicatory epistle, then—along with the sets of encomiastic verses contributed by his fellow dramatists Thomas Middleton, William Rowley, and John Ford—is part of the apparatus with which *The Duchess of Malfi* seeks to promote its literary credentials. Publication did not occur until 1623, a decade after the play was launched on the stage, but Webster had already made his authorial ambitions clear in the address "To the Reader" attached to his first tragedy, *The White Devil*, which had gone to print in the immediate wake of its initial production in 1612. That epistle aimed to separate the lasting virtues of his play from the deficiencies of its performance, acted as it had been "in so dull a time of winter, [and] in so open and black a theatre," before an audience of "ignorant asses."[6] Proud of the "labour" and "industry" necessary to the production of a true "dramatic poem," Webster boldly compares himself with Euripides, then the most widely admired of Greek tragedians:

6. John Webster, *The White Devil*, ed. John Russell Brown, The Revels Plays (London: Methuen, 1960), p. 2, lines 4–8. All citations from the earlier tragedy are to this edition.

To those who report I was a long time in finishing this tragedy . . . I must answer them with that of Euripedes to Alcestides, a tragic writer: Alcestides objecting that Euripedes had
only in three days composed three verses, whereas he himself
had written three hundred: "Thou tell'st truth . . . but here's the
difference,—thine shall be read for three days, but mine shall
continue three ages."

lines 25–33

At the same time, Webster insists on his affiliation with a distinguished lineage of contemporary dramatists, Shakespeare and Jonson among them, "wishing that what I write may be read by their
light," and insisting, with a favorite epigram from Martial, on the eternizing power of the written word: *non norunt, haec monumenta
mori* (these monuments do not know how to die).[7]

Webster would use the same tag as a motto for *Monuments of
Honor,* the city pageant he produced in memory of King James's
eldest son, the Protestant hero Prince Henry, in 1624. Martial himself had borrowed the conceit of poetry-as-monument from Horace,
whose *Exegi monumentum aere perennius* (I have built a monument
more lasting than bronze; *Odes* III, 30, 1–5) provided the inspiration for Shakespeare's time sonnets: "Not marble, nor the gilded
monuments / Of princes, shall outlive this powerful rhyme" (Sonnet 55, lines 1–2); but where Shakespeare characteristically attached
the idea of artistic immortality to his nondramatic poetry, Webster
used it to elevate the status of a form that for many contemporaries
was still tainted by its association with popular entertainment. For
him the *"ancient dignity"* that Heywood's *Apology for Actors* (1612)
had recently claimed for the players and their theaters belonged
more properly to tragic poetry itself; so it was no coincidence that
the conceit of poetry-as-monument should have been picked up by
both Middleton and Ford in their verses on the play. For Middleton,
the play becomes a figure for the same separation of worth and rank
on which Webster's epistle insists:

Thy monument is raised in thy lifetime.
And 'tis most just; for every worthy man
Is his own marble, and his merit can
Cut him to any figure and express
More art than Death's cathedral palaces,
Where royal ashes keep their court.

lines 8–13

Middleton was no doubt remembering Webster's own lines from *A
Monumental Column* (1613), his funeral elegy for Prince Henry,

---

7. Ibid., pp. 3–4, lines 27–47.

which contrasts the evanescent pomp of *"Henry* the sevenths Chappell" and its royal tombs with the transcendant artifice of poets: "For they shall live by them, when all the cost / Of gilded Monuments shall fall to dust" (sig. C2). The customs of a deferential society may require that poets offer "service" to their aristocratic and princely patrons, but there is to be no doubt as to where lasting authority will reside—in the eternizing potential of art.

This insistence on the vanity of worldly power and rank is a recurrent motif in the play itself, exemplified in its tragic conclusion by the fate of "the Aragonian brethren" (5.1.2), members of a Spanish royal house notorious among Webster's audience for its overweening pride. As he contemplates the mortally wounded carcass of the Cardinal, Bosola, remembering the decayed monuments of ancient Egypt, glories "That thou, which stood'st like a huge pyramid / Begun upon a large and ample base, / Shalt end in a little point, a kind of nothing" (5.5.74–76); and the theme is elaborated by Delio, even as he celebrates the Duchess's triumphant *"Integrity of life"* in the choric oration that ends the play (5.5.110–14).

The other face of such moralizing reflection is to be found in the satirical raillery through which Bosola finds a vent for his malcontent humor earlier in the play: in Act 2, Scene 1, he is confronted by Antonio, the Duchess's steward, to whom she has been secretly married; urged to abandon his "out-of-fashion melancholy" (line 84), Bosola launches an outright assault on the pretensions of inherited rank:

> Oh, sir, you are lord of the ascendant, chief man with the Duchess; a duke was your cousin-german removed . . . : what of this? Search the heads of the greatest rivers in the world, you shall find them but bubbles of water. Some would think the souls of princes were brought forth by some more weighty cause than those of meaner persons. They are deceived: there's the same hand to them; the like passions sway them. The same reason that makes a vicar go to law for a tithe-pig and undo his neighbours makes them spoil a whole province and batter down goodly cities with the cannon.

> lines 93–103

At such moments Bosola becomes a choric inquisitor, as Hamlet sometimes is, or Vindice in *The Revenger's Tragedy,* serving as a kind of mask for the dramatist himself. Bosola's speech is closely modeled on a passage in Montaigne,[8] but its tone, marked by the contemptuous reference to a vicar's tithe pig, is authentically Websterian

---

8. See "An Apology of Raymond Sebond," in *Montaigne's Essays,* intro. L. C. Harmer (London: Dent, 1910), II.xii., pp. 125–326 (170–1). All citations from Montaigne are to this edition.

and, in its colloquial directness, reminiscent of the unabused language of popular revolt, exemplified by the Lollard John Ball's famous challenge: "When Adam delved and Eve span, / Who was then the gentleman?"

Interestingly enough, the character of Bosola was the most substantial of Webster's additions to the story as he found it in William Painter's *Palace of Pleasure* (1567). There Daniel de Bozola is barely more than a name, a thuggish soldier who appears only at the very end of the tale when the Duchess's brothers hire him to murder Antonio. But in *The Duchess of Malfi* "[t]his new *Judas* and assured manqueller"[9] becomes an altogether more significant figure: introduced in the opening scene as the brothers' tool villain, hired to spy on their sister and later suborned by Ferdinand to kill her, he nevertheless emerges as a psychologically complex and oddly sympathetic character whom the play's carefully structured double ending allows to vie with the Duchess herself for the role of tragic protagonist. He is, moreover, given a backstory that offers some clues as to why Webster might have chosen to place him at the center of his tragedy. He is first introduced as a former convict, sentenced to "seven years in the galleys / For a notorious murder" (1.1.67–68) committed at the behest of the Cardinal; but it was evidently need that drove him to undertake this corrupt service, for (as we later hear from Delio) his original ambition had been to pursue a life of recondite learning:

> I knew him in Padua—a fantastical scholar, like such who study to know how many knots was in Hercules' club, of what color Achilles' beard was, or whether Hector were not troubled with the toothache. He hath studied himself half blear-eyed to know the true symmetry of Caesar's nose by a shoeing-horn; and this he did to gain the name of a speculative man.
>
> 3.3.41–47

Bosola conforms, that is to say, to a type entirely familiar to the Jacobean audience, resembling one of those "alienated intellectuals" identified by the social historian M. H. Curtis as a source of social disaffection in the decades leading up to the English Civil War: products of the rapid expansion of education under the Tudors, they were bright young graduates whose ambitions were focused on offices in church and state but who found themselves doomed to disappointment by the impoverished condition of James's exchequer.[1]

---

9. All citations of Painter, Grimeston, and Beard refer to the modernized texts printed in this volume.
1. M. H. Curtis, "The Alienated Intellectuals of Early Stuart England," *Past and Present* 23 (1962), 25–43. An abbreviated version of Curtis's classic article appears on pp. 191–99 in

Addressing the bishops and judges of the realm before the Privy Council in 1611, Lord Chancellor Ellesmere had warned that "learning without living doth but breed traitors as common experience too well showeth."[2] Bosola, the frustrated scholar and malcontent hireling who murders his royal mistress before turning on her brothers, killing them both, is a creature of precisely such dangerous breeding—as, in a less lurid fashion, Webster himself seems to have been.

Born in about 1580, a decade and a half after Shakespeare, John Webster was the son of a prosperous coach builder and senior member of the Merchant Taylors Company. He seems to have been educated at the prestigious grammar school established by his father's guild and to have been admitted to legal study at the Middle Temple, one of the Inns of Court that made up the so-called third university of England, in 1598. While there is no evidence of his ever proceeding into the legal profession, this extensive educational history helps account for the breadth of learning in his plays, and his legal training was of particular use in the composition of his last surviving independent play, the tragicomedy titled *The Devil's Law-case* (ca. 1617). Moreover, Webster maintained important personal links with the Inns of Court, especially the Middle Temple, where his fellow dramatists John Marston—whose play *The Malcontent* he revised for the King's Men (1604)—and John Ford—with whom he collaborated on *Keep the Widow Waking* (1624) and *The Fair Maid of the Inn* (1626)—had also studied. But his most important social ties were to the affluent middle class into which he was born, the city world whose habitual suspicion of the court is so often reflected in his writing. Webster became a freeman of the Merchant Taylors Company after his father's death in 1614; and it was for a distinguished member of this guild, John Gore, Lord Mayor of London, that he wrote his civic pageant *Monuments of Honor* (1624), celebrating Gore's promotion to the office of Lieutenant of the Royal Chamber: on its title page he is proudly named as "John Webster Merchant-Taylor." *The Duchess of Malfi* even seems to offer its own tribute to the company's charitable history through the ambiguous guise chosen by Bosola in the murder scene, where he presents himself to the Duchess as "the common bellman," whose role it is to prepare the souls of condemned prisoners (4.2.160–62). The detail belongs not to sixteenth-century Amalfi, but to early-seventeenth-century London; for in 1606 a group of Merchant Taylors, Webster's father prominent among them, had endowed just such an office at the notorious Newgate prison.

---

this volume. *Malfi*'s radicalism probably helps to account for its republication in 1640, in the midst of the political crisis that would issue in the Civil War—see Marcus, p. 95.
2. Cited in Curtis, "The Alienated Intellectuals," p. 28.

The full extent of the dramatist's involvement with his father's business remains, however—despite Henry Fitzgeffrey's famous sneer at "the playwright-cartwright"[3]—a matter for speculation. It is entirely possible that Webster drew his principal income from this source, because his dramatic and literary endeavors on their own could hardly have provided him with an adequate living. No matter how materially advantageous Webster's other attachments may have been, however, his lofty ambitions as a writer must have left him frustrated. Despite collaborative work on at least eight plays, he never achieved the secure connection with an acting company enjoyed by dramatists like Shakespeare, Fletcher, Massinger, or even Shirley; nor did he enjoy the popular cachet of the most successful jobbing playwrights like Dekker and Middleton. His surviving independent works were performed by leading companies—*The White Devil* and *The Devil's Law-case* by Queen Anne's Men and *The Duchess of Malfi* by Shakespeare's old colleagues, the King's Men—but he seems to have written only one other independent play, the lost tragedy of *The Guise* (ca. 1616) for which no performance records survive. This must have seemed a somewhat meager achievement for the playwright who had aspired to inherit the mantle of Euripides, and it may have been disappointed ambition, as much as the contemporary vogue for snarling satire, that produced the sometimes bilious tone of Webster's writing. A deep disillusionment with the world of courts and aristocratic patronage energizes the two great tragedies of the man whom Fitzgeffrey dubbed "crabbed [fractious, bad-tempered] *Websterio*."

One thing we do know about Webster's political allegiance: as David Gunby has shown, the dramatist—like many of the urban middle class from which he came—was strongly influenced by Calvinist doctrine,[4] and so it is not entirely surprising that he should have become a fervent admirer of King James's eldest son, Prince Henry, who, before his untimely death in 1612, had become a focus for the rapidly accruing discontents of his father's reign, especially among the faction of more militant protestants hostile both to the court and to the king's self-proclaimed role as *rex pacificus* (the king of peace). In 1604 Webster had contributed verses to *Arches of Triumph*, the lavishly illustrated volume celebrating James's coronation, but his view of the court had undergone a radical transformation by the time he sat down to write the fiercely satiric *White Devil*, eight years later. The villain-hero, Flamineo, descants on the frustrations of a world governed by the caprice of "Courtly reward, / And

---

3. Henry Fitzgeffrey, "Notes from Blackfriars," in *Satires and Satirical Epigrams* (London, 1617), reprinted on p. 187 in this volume.
4. See D. C. Gunby, "*The Duchess of Malfi*: A Theological Approach," in *John Webster*, ed. Brian Morris (London: Ernest Benn, 1970), pp. 178–204, reprinted on pp. 219–39 of the present volume.

punishment" (*White Devil*, 1.1.3–4): "'tis just like a summer bird-cage in a garden—the birds that are without, despair to get in, and the birds that are within despair and are in a consumption for fear they shall never get out" (1.2.43–46).

In that same year, Prince Henry was carried off by typhoid fever at the age of eighteen, prompting Webster to write an elegy for the dead hero whose passing he never ceased to lament. The language of *A Monumental Column* is repeatedly echoed in *The Duchess of Malfi* itself, making it feel at times like a coded tribute to Henry and the dissident ideals for which he had come to stand. In the tragedy's opening scene Antonio's paean to the Duchess repeats a striking line from the elegy, when he declares that this paragon of women "stains the time past, lights the time to come" (1.1.202). In *A Monumental Column*, Henry is hailed as a "Young, grave *Mæcenas* of the noble Arts, / Whose beams shall break forth from thy hollow tomb, / Stain the time past, and light the time to come" (sig. C1), and this passage is even more vividly remembered in *Malfi*'s last act when Antonio and Delio visit the ruined abbey where, unbeknown to them, the Duchess has been buried. The entire episode seems to have been inspired by a passage in George Wither's elegy *Prince Henry's Obsequies*, where the spirit of Britain interrogates the dead hero who answers from the grave as Echo. In *Malfi* the friends' melancholy reflections on the scene of worldly decay are interrupted by an Echo "*from the Duchess's grave*" (5.3.19) that sounds to the grieving Antonio uncannily "like my wife's voice" (line 26); and then "on the sudden a clear light [shows him] a face folded in sorrow" (lines 45–46). In performance this moment will have been especially striking because it seems to have involved the reuse of an elaborate property that the King's Men had acquired three years earlier for Middleton's *The Lady's Tragedy* (*The Second Maiden's Tragedy*). In that play the protagonist visits his wife's tomb, where, as it suddenly opens, "*a great light appears [showing] his Lady, as went out, standing just before him*" (4.4.42.3–4).[5] Middleton's play was licensed on October 31, 1611, just a week before Prince Henry's death, and it was probably this unusual stage effect that inspired Webster's own vision of the light of fame bursting from the prince's tomb, while in *Malfi* it once again serves to animate the idea of a moral force capable, in the words of Delio's final speech, of surviving "*beyond death* [to] *crown the end*" (5.5.118). In turn, Webster's use of the device would

---

5. Cited from Julia Briggs in *Thomas Middleton: The Collected Works*, ed. Gary Taylor et al. (Oxford, 2007). For further discussion of this property, see John Russell Brown's introduction to his Revels edition, p. xxxv; Michael Neill, "Monuments and Ruins in *The Duchess of Malfi*," in *Drama and Symbolism*, Themes in Drama 4, ed. James Redmond (Cambridge: Cambridge University Press, 1982), pp. 71–87; and Michael Neill, "'Fame's best friend': The Endings of *The Duchess of Malfi*," *Issues of Death: Mortality and Identity in English Renaissance Tragedy* (Oxford: Clarendon Press, 1997), pp. 328–53.

provide an occasion for Middleton's own (ingeniously reflexive) tribute at the end of his encomiastic verses: "*Ut lux ex tenebris ictu percussa Tonantis, / Illa (ruina malis) claris fit vita poetis*" ("As light springs from darkness at the stroke of the Thunderer, so may she [Tragedy] bring life to illustrious poets, and ruin to bad ones").

Webster carefully sets Delio's celebration of the Duchess's "integrity of life" against the "great ruin" of her brothers—"*diamonds cut with* [their] *own dust*" or "huge pyramid[s] . . . end[ing] in a little point, a kind of nothing" (5.5.70, 74–76). In his elegiac vision of "Henry the Seventh's Chapel," by contrast, the poet finds that "The dust of a rich diamond's there enshrined," while, just as the Duchess's grave is placed in a prospect of ruins (5.3.9–19), so Henry's death reduces the architecture of worldly pride to collapse:

> As if our loftiest palaces should grow
> To ruin, since such highness fell so low.
> And angry Neptune makes his palace groan,
> That the deaf rocks may echo the land's moan.
>
> sig C1v

Significantly, both play and poem continued to haunt Webster's imagination long after they were written: *Monuments of Honour,* the civic pageant he wrote for the Merchant Taylors a decade later, concludes with a tribute to Henry whose imagery not only remembers the mysteriously illuminated tombs that link elegy and play but also recalls Delio's concluding couplet in *Malfi* with its celebration of the protagonist's "*Integrity of life*":

> Such was the Prince, such are the noble hearts;
> Who when they die, yet die not in all parts,
> But from the integrity of a brave mind,
> Leave a most clear and eminent fame behind.
> Thus hath this jewel not quite lost his ray,
> Only cased up 'gainst a more glorious day.
>
> sig. C2v

The Play and Its Sources

John Webster was, in some respects, the most derivative of poets, making it unusually difficult to determine which of the many texts that fed into his work should be privileged as sources. In his classic study of the playwright's borrowing, R. W. Dent was able to demonstrate that much of Webster's text, including some of its most celebrated speeches, had been adapted from the work of other writers.[6]

6. R. W. Dent, *John Webster's Borrowing* (Berkeley: University of California Press, 1960).

A case in point is the Duchess's emotionally charged account of her suffering as Ferdinand's prisoner:

> I'll tell thee a miracle:
> I am not mad yet, to my cause of sorrow.
> Th'heaven o'er my head seems made of molten brass,
> The earth of flaming sulphur, yet I am not mad.
> I am acquainted with sad misery
> As the tanned galley-slave is with his oar—
> Necessity makes me suffer constantly,
> And custom makes it easy.
>
> 4.2.22–29

Webster must have found the initial inspiration for this passage in Painter, where the Duchess rails against her brothers' refusal to countenance her marrying again:

> I think we be the daily slaves of the fond and cruel fantasy of those tyrants which say they have puissance over us; and that, straining our will to their tyranny, *we be still bound to the chain like the galley slave.* [emphasis added]

Perhaps because he had already invented the story of Bosola's years in the galleys (1.1.34–36, 67–69, 207), the figure of the chained galley slave lodged itself in Webster's imagination, where it resonated with the lament of an imprisoned noblewoman in Edward Grimeston's translation of Jean de Serres's *General Inventory of the History of France:* "I am inured to my afflictions, as a galley slave to his oar. Necessity teacheth me to suffer constantly, and custom makes my sufferance easy."[7] This in turn he combined with a passage from Deuteronomy concerning God's punishments for disobedience: "thy heaven that is over thy head shall be brass, and the earth that is under thee shall be iron" (28:23).

This magpie method of composition—no doubt dependent on one of those commonplace books in which contemporaries jotted down favorite quotations—probably helps explain the laboriousness for which Webster was sometimes mocked. But in a culture that prized a writer's command of the art of imitation above any notion of originality, such incorporation of borrowed material was not in itself exceptional: Webster may have used it more extensively than other playwrights, but it is worth remembering that one of Shakespeare's most celebrated rhetorical *tours de force*, Enobarbus's lyrical

---

7. Jean de Serres, *A General Inventory of the History of France from the Beginning of That Monarchy,* trans. Edward Grimeston (London, 1607), p. 817. Webster's interest in this work may have been stimulated by reading the version of the Malfi story contained in Grimeston's translation of Goulart, published in the same year.

description of Cleopatra's arrival at Cydnus ("The barge she sat in, like a burnished throne, burned on the water . . ." *Anthony and Cleopatra*, 2.2.198–99), was itself substantially lifted from his main source, Plutarch's "Life of Antony." In each case, however, the borrowed material is reshaped by delicate rhetorical and rhythmic adjustments that serve to produce a voice unmistakably the playwright's own.

If the verbal details of *Malfi's* borrowing are transformed by Webster's poetic alchemy, the same is true of the larger story he had to tell. The broad outline of his plot, as he found it in Painter, was historical: Giovanna d'Aragona (ca. 1478–ca. 1513) was a member of the Spanish house of Aragon, belonging to the branch that ruled Naples from 1442 to 1501; she was married at the age of twelve to Alfonso Piccolomini, who became Duke of Amalfi in 1493. Giovanna bore him a daughter in 1490 and a son in 1498, the same year in which both daughter and husband died. In about 1506 the widowed Duchess contracted a secret marriage to her majordomo, Antonio da Bologna, with whom she soon produced two more children. By 1510, she was again pregnant; fearing discovery by her jealous brothers—Lodovico, Cardinal of Santa Maria in Cosmedin, and Carlo, Marquis of Gerace—Antonio fled with the children to Ancona, where the Duchess, by feigning a pilgrimage to the shrine of Our Lady in Loreto, subsequently managed to join them. In Ancona the couple made their marriage defiantly public, only to be forced to flee once more. Seeking refuge in Siena, they were expelled at the behest of the Cardinal, and then set off for Venice; along the way, they were overtaken by a party of horsemen: Antonio managed to make his escape with their elder son, but Giovanna and the two younger children were taken prisoner and escorted back to her palace in Amalfi. They were never heard from again. Antonio found safe haven in Milan until 1514, when he was stabbed to death by a Lombard captain, Daniele de Bozolo, and three other assassins, presumably in the pay of the Cardinal.

The story was first recounted by a man who had himself witnessed this murder, Matteo Bandello, Bishop of Agen. The version included in Bandello's *Novelle* (1554) includes his self-portrait, in the guise of Delio, Antonio's friend and confidant, and it is generally sympathetic to the transgressive couple, whose fate is chosen to illustrate the iniquity of what would nowadays be called "honor killings." But the tale was given a different complexion by the moralizing commentary that accompanied François de Belleforest's French translation in his *Histoires Tragiques* (1565): despite occasional expressions of sympathy for the Duchess, Belleforest makes it plain that her tragedy is a consequence of her surrender to lecherous desires. This view is fully endorsed in Painter's English translation of Belleforest, *The Palace of Pleasure:* here, once again, the Duchess is presented as a warning to all princes, and especially to powerful women, about the danger of indulging their private appetites:

> The greater honor and authority men have in this world, and the greater their estimation is, the more sensible and notorious are the faults by them committed, and the greater is their slander. . . . Wherefore it behoveth the noble, and such as have charge of common wealth, to live an honest life, and bear their port upright, that none have cause to take ill example upon discourse of their deeds and naughty life. And above all that modesty ought to be kept by women, whom as their race, noble birth, authority, and name maketh them more famous, even so their virtue, honesty, chastity, and continency more praiseworthy. . . . Thus I say, because a woman being as it were the image of sweetness, courtesy and shamefastness, so soon as she steppeth out of the right tract and leaveth the smell of her duty and modesty, besides the denigration of her honor, thrusteth herself into infinite troubles and causeth the ruin of such which should be honored and praised, if women's allurement solicited them not to folly.

Painter's Duchess is "a fine and subtle dame" who yields to "her follies and shameless lusts" by "taking a husband more to glut her libidinous appetite than for other occasion":

> [she] waxed very weary of lying alone, and grieved her heart to be without a match, specially in the night, when the secret silence and darkness of the same presented before the eyes of her mind, the image of the pleasure which she felt in the lifetime of her deceased lord and husband . . . [and] pressed with desire of match, to remove the ticklish instigations of her wanton flesh . . . she did set her mind on [Antonio, the master of her household].

Painter may blame the Duchess's brothers for the "choler and . . . deadly fury" that makes Duke Carlo denounce his sister as a "false and vile bitch" and for the excessive pride in "the royal blood of Aragon and Castile" that drives them to murder, but he is fundamentally in sympathy with their scorn for the Duchess's weakness and their outrage at her marriage of disparagement:

> Behold here (O ye foolish lovers) a glass of your lightness, and ye women, the course of your fond behaviour. It behoveth not the wise suddenly to execute their first motions and desires of their heart, for so much as they may be assured that pleasure is pursued so near with a repentance so sharp to be suffered, and

hard to be digested, as their voluptuousness shall utterly dis-content them. True it is, that marriages be done in heaven, and performed in earth; but that saying may not be applied to fools, which govern themselves by carnal desires, whose scope is but pleasure, and the reward many times equal to their folly. Shall I be of opinion that a household servant ought to solicit, nay rather suborn, the daughter of his lord without punishment, or that a vile and abject person dare to mount upon a prince's bed? No, no! Policy requireth order in all, and each wight ought to be matched according to their quality, without making a pas-time of it to cover our follies. . . . A goodly thing it is to love, but where reason loseth his place, love is without his effect, and the sequel rage and madness. . . . And yet you see this great and mighty duchess trot and run after the male like a female wolf or lioness when they go to salt,[8] and forget the noble blood of Aragon whereof she was descended, to couple herself almost with the simplest person of all the trimmest gentlemen of Naples.

It is telling that, virtually without exception, the writers who bor-rowed from Belleforest and Painter endorsed their censorious account of the Duchess's behaviour. George Whetstone, in his *Hep-tameron of Civil Discourses* (1582), though critical of the Cardinal's extreme tyranny, nevertheless condemns the Duchess for betray-ing her own honor, which "doth injury to her whole house" (p. 160 in this volume). Edward Grimeston, in his translation of Simon Gou-lart's *Admirable and Memorable Histories* (1607), denounces not only the "lascivious eye" that compromises her estate, but the Duchess's irreligious willingness to "cover her fault [under] the colour of mar-riage," while he holds Antonio equally to blame for yielding to her "unchaste looks," thereby "forgetting the respect which he ought [owed] unto his lady and her house."[9] If these writers seem mainly concerned with the lovers' offence against the proprieties of rank and gender, the Puritan cleric Thomas Beard sees her trespass as a mor-tal sin inviting divine chastisement. In his *Theatre of God's Judge-ments* (1597)—best known for its gleeful account of Christopher Marlowe's death—Beard invokes the Duchess's story to illustrate the inevitable punishment "*Of Whoredoms committed under colour of Marriage*": the Cardinal is exposed as a vicious Catholic hypocrite, but in his killing of the Duchess and her family he becomes the "instrument" of "God's justice . . . to punish those who under the veil of secret marriage thought it lawful to commit any villainy."[1]

8. Sexual excitement.
9. Simon Goulart, *Admirable and Memorable Histories*, trans. Edward Grimeston (London, 1607), pp. 364–65. An excerpt from Goulart is printed on pp. 161–66 of this volume.
1. Thomas Beard, *The Theatre of God's Judgements: Revised, and Augmented* (London, 1631), Chap. XIV, p. 379. An excerpt from Beard is printed on pp. 166–67 of this volume.

"Infected Blood": The Aragonian Brothers

Webster's take on the story is quite opposite: indeed it is as if he
deliberately set out to confound the social and doctrinal pieties that
frame the standard English accounts of the Duchess's fate. It is true
that Antonio's long speech at the beginning of the play at first seems
designed to prepare the way for a conventional narrative in which
the Duchess's capitulation to her own lustful desires provokes a
wider storm of "rage and madness":

> a prince's court
> Is like a common fountain, whence should flow
> Pure silver drops in general. But if't chance
> Some cursed example poison't near the head
> Death and diseases through the whole land spread.
>   1.1.11–15

And her brothers' admonitory duet later in the scene develops this
theme, leaving no doubt that, in their minds at least, the Duchess
is poised to become just such a "cursed example": "You live in a rank
pasture here, i'th'court. / There is a kind of honeydew that's deadly; /
'Twill poison your fame" (lines 298–300); but their tirade has already
been framed by Antonio's paean of praise for his mistress's "noble
virtue" (lines 180–202), by his acerbic "characters" of the brothers
themselves (lines 150–79), and (perhaps most tellingly of all) by
Bosola's bitter denunciation of the very men upon whose patronage
he depends:

> Some fellows, they say, are possessed with the devil, but this
> great fellow were able to possess the greatest devil and make
> him worse. . . . He and his brother are like plum trees that grow
> crooked over standing pools; they are rich and o'erladen, stag-
> nant with fruit, but none but crows, pies, and caterpillars feed
> on them.
>
>   lines 43–51

The "poison" and "disease" foreshadowed by Antonio's anatomy
of courtly corruption will become running motifs in the play; and
they are ones that the action increasingly associates not with the
Duchess but with her brothers and with the principal instrument of
their villainy whose own "foul melancholy" serves to "poison all his
goodness" (1.1.73–74). Bosola tempts his lady with "poisoned pills"
wrapped in the "gold and sugar" of hypocrisy (4.1.19–20), while the
Cardinal and Ferdinand preside over a world where, in the words of
the Duchess's lunatic tormentors, the law itself has become "a corrosive [that] will eat to the bone" (4.2.92–93). These metaphoric tox-
ins become shockingly literal when the Cardinal despatches his

mistress with a devotional book he has smeared with venom (5.2.278, 5.5.81)—a wicked surrogate for the secrets that he threatened would destroy her "like a ling'ring poison" (5.2.265).

In much the same way, Antonio's metaphor of sickness is made real in the "pestilent disease . . . lycanthropia" (5.2.5–6) that possesses the Duke after his sister's murder. Earlier in the play Bosola has identified "the ulcerous wolf" (i.e., lupus) as a figure for the morbid decay hidden beneath the "rich tissue" of the court (2.1.54–58). Painter had imagined his Duchess as a sexual predator "like a female wolf"—a comparison that presumably underlies Ferdinand's contemptuous dismissal of the Duchess's children as "cubs" or "young wolves [whose death] is never to be pitied" (4.1.33; 4.2.243–44); but it is the brothers themselves whose vulpine "howling," echoed in the "deadly dogged howl" of the madmen's masque, haunts the imaginations of both the Duchess and Bosola (4.1.39, 106; 4.2.61; 5.5.12), and his sister is barely dead before Ferdinand, in uncanny anticipation of his own madness, begins to imagine his guilty conscience as just such a creature: "The wolf shall find her grave and scrape it up— / Not to devour the corpse, but to discover / The horrid murder" (4.2.293–95). Sure enough, his next appearance is ushered in by the Doctor's symptomology of lycanthropia, whose sufferers

> imagine
> Themselves to be transformed into wolves,
> Steal forth to churchyards in the dead of night
> And dig dead bodies up
>
> 5.2.9–12

And so it is with Ferdinand, who has been seen

> 'bout midnight in a lane
> Behind Saint Mark's Church, with the leg of a man
> Upon his shoulder; and he howled fearfully,
> Said he was a wolf—only the difference
> Was, a wolf's skin was hairy on the outside,
> His on the inside—bade them take their swords,
> Rip up his flesh, and try.
>
> 5.2.13–19

Ripping up his flesh to discover his wolfish secret becomes the equivalent of the imaginary wolf's scraping at the Duchess's grave to uncover the secret of her murder.

From the beginning, of course, *Malfi* has been a play obsessed with secrets: in the opening scene, when the Duchess appeals to Cariola's "known secrecy" regarding her love for Antonio, the lady-in-waiting promises, in a loaded simile, to "conceal this secret from the world / As warily as those that trade in poison / Keep poison from their children" (1.1.341–44). Later the Duchess identifies Antonio's "bosom [as] the treasury of my secrets" (1.1.485–86), conflating his official roles as "treasurer" (1.1.363) with that of "secretary"—the appointed keeper of secrets whose discretion Julia promises to emulate (5.2.233). Ironically enough, Bosola, having at last discovered the identity of the Duchess's lover, pledges similar discretion regarding "the secret of my prince, / Which I will wear on th'inside of my heart!" (3.2.287–88).

But, as the Cardinal sarcastically reminds Julia, the only safe place for secrets is their proverbial repository, the grave:[2] "Think you your bosom / Will be a grave dark and obscure enough / For such a secret?" (5.2.271–73). The play's language constantly reminds us of the "rotten purposes" concealed, as though in some ostentatious tomb, beneath the "fair marble colors" of the court (5.2.297–98); while the pathology of concealment turns the body itself into a kind of burial place. Bosola has used the same metaphor of the Cardinal and his brother: "You have a pair of hearts are hollow graves, / Rotten and rotting others" (4.2.303–04); in Ferdinand's case, however, the hidden infection that risks discovery is not so much the murder itself as the more obscure and intimate secret that motivates it— one hidden even from himself.

In the brothers' first confrontation with their sister, Ferdinand warns the Duchess that "your darkest actions—nay, your privat'st thoughts— / Will come to light" (1.1.306–07); while his own are to remain hidden in the darkness to which he commits himself at the end of his nocturnal visit in 3.2 (lines 136–40) and which is rendered literal at their last encounter ("'Cause once he rashly made a solemn vow / Never to see you more, he comes i'th'night," 4.1.23–24). In fact it is not she, but he who must not be seen. Bosola's intelligencing makes of him "a very quaint invisible devil" (1.1.253), whom the Cardinal persuades Ferdinand to hire in order to keep himself out of view: "I would not be seen in't" (line 217); but it is Ferdinand who, at the psychological level, most craves invisibility. Telling Bosola of his determination to thwart his sister's remarriage, he quickly forestalls any questioning of his motives: "Do not you ask the reason, but be satisfied / I say I would not" (1.1.250–51). Such an interdict necessarily invites scrutiny, however: the phallic innuendo of Ferdinand's threats to the Duchess with that symbol of patriarchal power, "my father's poniard" (1.1.321–27, 3.2.70), and the jealous excitements of his fantasies in 2.5, where he imagines her fornicating with "some strong-thighed bargeman, / Or one o'th'woodyard . . . or else some lovely squire" (lines 42–44), have led

---

2. Theobald's choice of a title for his unlucky adaptation, *The Fatal Secret*, testifies to the conspicuousness of this motif.

critics to conjecture a hidden incestuous motive. His tormented longing both to see and not to see when he begs the Cardinal to distract him lest "my imagination . . . carry me / To see her in the shameful act of sin" (2.5.40–41) certainly suggests some deeply conflicted emotion—one that is again apparent in the strangely contradictory explanations he gives for needing to kill her (4.2.267–71) and in his desperately fluctuating reaction to the sight of his dead sister: "Cover her face. Mine eyes dazzle. . . . Let me see her face again . . . I have cruel sore eyes" (4.2.249, 256; 5.2.62). It is as if the "clear light" that Antonio witnesses emanating from his wife's grave had become, for Ferdinand, the glare of an unbearable illumination.

The Spirit of Greatness or of Woman

Contemplating the "great ruin" that lies about him in the play's final scene, Delio returns to the imagery of light, this time associating it with the transcendant truth that exposes the vanity of worldly greatness:

> These wretched eminent things
> Leave no more fame behind 'em than should one
> Fall in a frost and leave his print in snow—
> As soon as the sun shines, it ever melts
> Both form and matter. I have ever thought
> Nature doth nothing so great for great men
> As when she's pleased to make them lords of truth.
> 5.5.111–17

As this introduction has already suggested, questions about the nature of true greatness lie at the heart of the play's moral and political concerns. Even Delio, we might notice, speaks of "great men" as though he instinctively thought of greatness as a masculine attribute, and to begin with, *great* is an adjective that attaches exclusively to the Cardinal, the Duke, and their male entourage (1.1.44, 84, 86, 233). But one reason the play has attracted the sympathy of feminist critics lies in its challenge to such conventionally gendered notions: as the Duchess prepares to confront the hierarchical prerogatives of both gender and rank, she imagines her courtship of Antonio in the heroic masculine language of chivalric romance:

> as men in some great battles,
> By apprehending danger, have achieved
> Almost impossible actions—I have heard soldiers say so—
> So I, through frights and threat'nings, will assay
> This dangerous venture. . . .

Figure 1. Biographical portrait of Sir Henry Unton by an unknown artist (ca. 1596), showing his funeral rites and his tomb, in Faringdon, All Saints Church. © National Portrait Gallery, London.

Figure 2. Effigy of Francis Manners with his two wives, illustrating the traditional posture of "seeming to pray up to heaven with their eyes fixed upon the stars" (4.2.146–49). © travelib europe / Alamy.

> Wish me good speed,
> For I am going into a wilderness
> Where I shall find nor path nor friendly clew
> To be my guide.
> 1.1.334–51

The climax of the wooing scene comes at the moment when the Duchess, boldly asserting the autonomy of her own desire, repudiates the symbolism of female deference: "This is flesh and blood, sir; / 'Tis not the figure cut in alabaster / Kneels at my husband's tomb" (1.1.441–43). In the vocabulary of such monuments the living widow is frozen forever in her posture of submissiveness by the fact of her husband's death (Figure 1). In theatrical terms, this repudiation of authority is set against the gesture with which the Duchess goes on to undo the hierarchical relationship that commands Antonio's own deference to his mistress:

> Sir,
> This goodly roof of yours is too low built;
> I cannot stand upright in't, nor discourse,
> Without I raise it higher. Raise yourself,
> Or, if you please, my hand to help you: so.   [*Raises him.*]
> lines 403–07

To undo the symbolism of obedience in these kneeling figures is to engage in an act of iconoclasm that helps account for Cariola's fearful anxiety: "Whether the spirit of greatness or woman / Reign most in her, I know not" (lines 487–88). But the ensuing action will progressively erase this seemingly absolute difference by redefining the very notions of greatness on which it depends.

As we have seen, it is Bosola who is the play's most conspicuous vehicle for questioning such notions: "Search the heads of the greatest rivers in the world, you shall find them but bubbles of water" (2.1.96–97). His satire may be compromised by temperamental melancholy, but it finds a significant echo in Antonio's "*The great are like the base; nay, they are the same*" (2.3.51). Initially fearful of ambition as "a great man's madness" (1.1.408), by the time of his death Antonio has come to scorn it as a childish male fantasy: "In all our quest of greatness, / Like wanton boys, whose pastime is their care, / We follow after bubbles blown in th'air" (5.4.62–64). But it is the Duchess herself who is given the most extended reflection on this theme: responding to Bosola's sneer at Antonio as "this base low fellow" (3.5.112), she offers to prove "who is greatest" by her parable of the salmon and the dogfish: "So to great men the moral may be stretched: / *Men oft are valued high when they're most wretch'd*" (3.5.118–39).

This claim will be put to the test in Act 4 when, as the disguised Bosola reminds the Duchess of "the small compass of [her] prison"

(4.2.122–23), she does indeed find herself trapped in "the fisher's basket." Instinctively appealing to the authority of inherited rank ("Am I not thy Duchess . . . I am Duchess of Malfi still," lines 124, 131), she is met with a grimly sardonic response from her adversary:

> Thou art some great woman, sure, for riot begins to sit on thy forehead, clad in grey hairs, twenty years sooner than on a merry milkmaid's. . . .
> *Glories, like glow-worms, afar off shine bright,*
> *But looked to near have neither heat nor light.*
>
> lines 125–34

In a passage that must have inspired Middleton's encomiastic verses, with their reflection on the empty pomp of "death's cathedral palaces," the pretended tomb-maker then moves on to a mocking account of the "fashion in the grave" favored by adherents of worldly greatness:

> Princes' images on their tombs do not lie as they were wont, seeming to pray up to heaven [see Figure 2], but with their hands under their cheeks as if they died of the toothache [Figure 1]. They are not carved with their eyes fixed upon the stars, but as their minds were wholly bent upon the world, the self-same way they seem to turn their faces [see Figure 1].
>
> lines 145–50

Just as this satire sends us back to the Duchess's iconoclastic description of her own husband's monument, so it may also remind us of Cariola's earlier description of her imprisoned mistress as resembling "some reverend monument / Whose ruins are even pitied" (4.2.32–33). But the gesture with which the Duchess at last acquiesces in her own death returns to the language of tombs in a different way, utterly redefining what is meant by greatness: simultaneously remembering the alabaster figure of the kneeling widow and that defiant moment when she raised the abject Antonio from his knees, it creates a stage picture whose emotional force depends on its conscious reversal of both images:

> Pull, and pull strongly, for your able strength
> Must pull down heaven upon me.
> Yet stay—heaven gates are not so highly arched
> As princes' palaces: they that enter there
> Must go upon their knees. [*Kneels.*]
>
> 4.2.216–20

Dual Protagonists: Bosola and the Ideals of Service

Occurring at the end of the fourth act, the Duchess's death has often been regarded, even by sympathetic critics, as a flaw in Webster's design. With the elimination of its nominal protagonist, it is some-times argued, the tragedy can end only in anticlimax; and while it has been suggested that the effect is to a show a world that, robbed of the Duchess's presence, descends into chaos,[3] that contention serves only to explain the anticlimax not to eliminate it. But a more attentive examination of Webster's dramaturgy suggests a different way of looking at the last act, and one that is generally borne out in performance. For the play, despite the precedence accorded to the Duchess by its title, is actually built around the fortunes of twin pro-tagonists: worked up from a bare couple of sentences in Painter, Bosola is elevated to structural parity with the Duchess, being given approximately the same number of lines,[4] while his name is placed at the head of the original cast list, as hers heads the list of female characters. Webster's decision to rearrange his source narrative so as to focus the action on a pair of tragic heroes necessarily pushed him to devise a structure that would build toward two discrete catas-trophes. For this he had precedent in a tragedy that the King's Men had performed seven years earlier: Shakespeare's *Anthony and Cleopatra*[5] brings its fourth act to a close with the death of Anthony, and leaves its fifth act denouement to Cleopatra. Upsetting the con-ventionally masculine style of tragic heroism,[6] it contrasts the male protagonist's humiliatingly botched suicide with the superb theat-ricality of his female counterpart's self-immolation. Webster's tragedy takes over the double ending but reverses Shakespeare's arrange-ment, so that the female hero's death, now a ceremonious exercise

3. On this aspect of the play's structure, see, e.g., Lee Bliss, *The World's Perspective: John Webster and the Jacobean Drama* (New Bruswick, NJ: Rutgers University Press, 1983), pp. 159–66. An excerpt from Bliss's book is printed on pp. 273–97 of this volume.
4. An exact count is difficult because of the large numbers of shared lines and especially the unusual amount of prose in the play, but the Duchess and Bosola are each allotted approximately 530, significantly more than either Ferdinand (ca. 470) or Antonio (ca. 450). The Cardinal, whose usual taciturnity corresponds to his desire "not to be seen in't," gets approximately 280, more than two-thirds of them in the last act.
5. The structural parallel with *Anthony and Cleopatra* is also noted by Bliss, *The World's Perspective*, pp. 141, 155, 168.
6. For general discussion of the relationship between gender and genre see Linda Bamber, *Comic Women, Tragic Men* (Stanford, CA: Stanford University Press, 1982); on gender issues in *The Duchess of Malfi*, see Kate McLuskie, "Drama and Sexual Politics: The Case of John Webster's Duchess," in *Drama, Sex and Politics*, Themes in Drama 7, ed. James Redmond (Cambridge: Cambridge University Press, 1985), 77–91; Christina Luckyj, "'Great Women of Pleasure': Main Plot and Subplot in *The Duchess of Malfi*," *Studies in English Literature* 27 (1987), 267–83; and Theodora A. Jankowski, "Defin-ing/Confining the Duchess: Negotiating the Female Body in John Webster's *The Duch-ess of Malfi*," *Studies in Philology* 87 (1990), 221–45. The last two are printed in this volume, on pp. 297–312 and 313–34.

in humility, is allowed to frame the male protagonist's self-annihilating despair. In place of the ritual with which Cleopatra asserts the eternizing symbolism of her monument ("Give me my robe, put on my crown, I have / Immortal longings in me," *Anthony and Cleopatra,* 5.2.279–80), the Duchess's persistence "beyond death" may be represented only by an echo and the mysterious "clear light" from her grave; but these are set against Bosola's "deep pit of darkness" and the grim silence of the burial place to which he sees himself consigned: "We are only like dead walls, or vaulted graves / That, ruined, yields no echo" (5.5.94–96).

Despite their utterly opposed endings, there are important parallels in the treatment of these two figures. If Webster's version of the Duchess's life involves a radical critique of the hierarchical assumptions on which the early modern "society of orders" was founded, the same is true of the story he invents for Bosola; and the relationship between the Duchess and her Provisor of the Horse becomes the vehicle for a profoundly questioning approach to the ideals of service that governed virtually all social relations in this period. In appealing to Baron Berkeley for his patronage, Webster formally associates himself with those who "owe to your honor their clearest service" (lines 8–9), protesting that he is "your lordship's in all duty and observance"; yet, as we have seen, the general tone of his epistle is a long way from the servility expected of such entreaties,[7] tacitly anticipating the play's sceptical account of "what 'tis to serve / A prince with body and soul" (3.2.205–06). If the Duchess and her brothers begin as the masters of the play world, Bosola and Antonio represent those who are bound to serve them. If Bosola, the former galley slave, sees himself as Ferdinand's "creature" (1.1.280), a mere artifact of princely power, the same is effectively true of Antonio whom Ferdinand may grant the lofty title of "great master of [the Duchess's] household" (1.1.86), but whom he really thinks of as

> A slave that only smelled of ink and counters,
> And ne'er in's life looked like a gentleman
> But in the audit time.
>
> 3.3.72–74

And if Antonio's "brave horsemanship" (1.1.136) seems to be a mark of aristocratic prowess ("noble action," line 139–40), it nevertheless implicitly links him once again to Bosola as Provisor of the Horse— the man whose "corruption / Grew out of horse dung" (lines 279–80).

---

7. The subdued wordplay of Middleton's superscription to his encomiastic verses ("*In the just worth of that well-deserver, Mr.* [i.e. Master] *John Webster, and upon this masterpiece of tragedy*"), when combined with his rhetorical emphasis on *merit, fame,* and *honor* and the conceit of the author's plain style as constituting his "richest coat [of arms]," show Webster's fellow dramatists responding to this motif.

Both are initially defined by their function as servants; but it is Bosola, above all, who becomes Webster's vehicle for exposing the hollowness of the ideology to which both are subjected. He is introduced in the first scene railing against the fraudulence of "courtly reward" and the Cardinal's betrayal of the mutual obligations on which the master–servant relationship was supposed to be based:[8]

> I have done you
> Better service than to be slighted thus.
> Miserable age, where only the reward
> Of doing well is the doing of it! . . .
> I fell into the galleys in your service, where, for two
> years together, I wore two towels instead of a shirt.
>   1.1.29–35

> Who would rely upon these miserable dependences in expectation to be advanced hopes of appointment tomorrow? . . . There are rewards for hawks and dogs, when they have done us service.
>   lines 53–58

With cruel irony, the recompense Bosola finally receives is an office in the Duchess's household that will further reduce him to Ferdinand's abject "creature," thereby compelling him to reject the very ideals of mutual obligation upon which the institution of service was ostensibly founded: accepting the Provisorship of the Horse, he reflects ruefully that his "corruption / Grew out of horse dung"—a conceit that he will render wittily concrete in the apricots that he uses to expose his mistress's pregnancy: "the knave gard'ner— / Only to raise his profit by them the sooner— / Did ripen them in horse dung" (2.1.135–37). This mockery of Bosola's high-sounding office is carefully placed against the more benign irony that governs Antonio's elevation: insisting that the performance of his duty is not something to be bartered for profit, he is immediately answered by a reward he could never have imagined, one that, as the Duchess's wordplay has foreshadowed, transforms him from servant to "sovereign"(1.1.396), making him "master of her household" in a quite different sense from the one denoted by his office (line 86):

> ANTONIO   Were there nor heaven nor hell,
> I should be honest. I have long served virtue,
> And ne'er ta'en wages of her.
> DUCHESS   Now she pays it . . .

8. See, e.g., Michael Neill, "Servant Obedience and Master Sins: Shakespeare and the Bonds of Service," in *Putting History to the Question* (New York: Columbia University Press, 2000), pp. 13–48; David Evett, *Discourses of Service in Shakespeare's England* (New York: Palgrave Macmillan, 2005), Chaps. 1 and 6; and David Schalkwyk, *Shakespeare Love and Service* (Cambridge: Cambridge University Press, 2008), Chap. 1.

> I do here put off all vain ceremony,
> And only do appear to you a young widow
> That claims you for her husband.
> > 1.1.426–46

These intertwining ironies are further complicated in Act 3, when the device chosen by the Duchess to provide cover for Antonio's flight gives him occasion to lament "the inconstant / And rotten ground of service" (3.2.196–97) in terms that echo Bosola's own cynical opinions. Antonio's pretended banishment incites a group of time-serving officers to denounce him to their mistress, provoking Bosola into a bitter tirade against these "flatt'ring rogues" who "Would have prostituted their daughters to his lust; / Made their firstborn intelligencers; thought none happy / But such as . . . wore his livery" (3.2.228–31). His reference to "intelligencers" and "livery" is enough to reveal the self-contempt that underlies Bosola's scorn, and it is that which renders him vulnerable to the Duchess's continuing show of anger, prompting him to a paean of praise for her disgraced steward:

> Let me show you what a most unvalued jewel you have, in a wanton humor, thrown away. . . . Will you make yourself a mercenary herald, rather to examine men's pedigrees than virtues? You shall want him: for know, an honest statesman to a prince is like a cedar planted by a spring: the spring bathes the tree's root; the grateful tree rewards it with his shadow.
> > lines 242–55

Ironically, the effect of this unaccustomed outburst of feeling is to induce the Duchess to lay bare the very secret that all of Bosola's patient intelligencing has so far failed to uncover—"This good one that you speak of is my husband" (line 263)—thereby turning on their heads all of the cynical assumptions by which this creature of "courtly reward" has lived his life:

> Do I not dream? Can this ambitious age
> Have so much goodness in't as to prefer
> A man merely for worth, without these shadows
> Of wealth and painted honors? Possible?
> > lines 264–67

The simplicity of Bosola's language makes it hard to mistake the incredulous sincerity of this speech, which marks a turning point in the play. The florid extravagance of his succeeding oration only shows him trying to recover his poise though an exaggerated parody of his real emotions (and of the play's own resolutely anti-aristocratic stance):

No question but many an unbeneficed scholar
Shall pray for you for this deed, and rejoice
That some preferment in the world can yet
Arise from merit. The virgins of your land
That have no dowries shall hope your example
Will raise them to rich husbands. Should you want
Soldiers, 'twould make the very Turks and Moors
Turn Christians, and serve you for this act.
Last, the neglected poets of your time,
In honor of this trophy of a man,
Raised by that curious engine, your white hand,
Shall thank you in your grave for't, and make that
More reverend than all the cabinets
Of living princes. For Antonio,
His fame shall likewise flow from many a pen,
When heralds shall want coats to sell to men.

lines 271–85

From this point on Bosola's interactions with the Duchess, not least when he is forced to assume the role of her tormentor and murderer, will be marked by the agonised ambivalence that leads to his ultimate despair. No wonder that he ends the scene with a sour reflection on "this base quality / Of intelligencer," even as he struggles to console himself with the thought that "for this act I am certain to be raised" (lines 313–14, 316).

Bosola begins the fourth act by reporting to Duke Ferdinand on the noble bearing of the imprisoned Duchess (4.1.2–10), and he does so with a lyricism that is strangely reminiscent of Antonio's homage in the opening scene—only for him to act as his master's stage manager in the cruel piece of waxwork theater that persuades their victim that her husband and her children are dead. But while Ferdinand's confessed aim is "To bring her to despair" (line 113), Bosola, in lines oddly poised between sarcasm and tender concern, urges her to avoid that mortal sin (lines 72–73), offering her "comfort" and "pity" (lines 83, 86), and reminding her, in a famously ambivalent phrase, that "the stars shine still" (4.1.97). On Ferdinand's return, Bosola urges him to furnish the Duchess with the instruments of redemption, "a penitential garment . . . beads and prayer-books" (lines 115–17), insisting that "When you send me next, / The business shall be comfort" (lines 131–32). It will not be, of course: when he does next come to her, his business will be strangling; yet the murder is prefaced by what amounts to an extended sermon, shared by his twin personae of tomb-maker and bellman, on the vanity of worldly things—a spiritual exercise whose avowed purpose is to bring her "By degrees to mortification" (4.2.164). Even here, however, the meaning of *mortification* is disconcertingly poised between

that "mortifying of the flesh," which is understood to be a preparative to salvation (*OED* n. 1), and that fearful "state of torpor and
insensibility that precedes death" (*OED* n. 3).

His murderous service discharged with the strangling of the
Duchess, her children, and Cariola, Bosola rounds on his master to
denounce his lack of pity:

> Do you not weep?
> Other sins only speak; murder shrieks out.
> The element of water moistens the earth,
> But blood flies upwards and bedews the heavens.
>   4.2.245–48

Even as this language seems to acknowledge Bosola's own damnability, however, Ferdinand's self-preoccupied response drives the
intelligencer back to a mercenary insistence on "The reward due to
my service" (line 278). And even as he angrily recognizes his hopes
of advancement as the fictions of "a sweet and golden dream" (line
308), he continues to rail against his master's failure to recognize
the mutual compact of service:

> Let me know
> Wherefore I should be thus neglected. Sir,
> I served your tyranny, and rather strove
> To satisfy yourself than all the world;
> And, though I loathed the evil, yet I loved
> You that did counsel it, and rather sought
> To appear a true servant than an honest man.
>   lines 311–17

As the opposition between apparent synonyms suggests, to be honest (trustworthy and honorable) in the world of courtly reward and
punishment cannot be reconciled with what it means to offer true
(actual, as opposed to honest) service—just as the "painted honor"
of Bosola's high-sounding office is incompatible with the "peace of
conscience" for which he now yearns (line 320). Momentarily tempted
by the Duchess's seeming revival into the belief that "mercy" is still
possible for him (line 333), he is left to the despair of a "perspective /
That shows us hell: that we cannot be suffered / To do good when
we have a mind to it" (lines 343–45). In theological terms, as Gunby
has argued, the lesson enforced here is Calvinistic, but there is also a
politics to it, one that has everything to do with the play's sceptical
attitude toward the pretensions of rank and the ideology of service—a
scepticism for which, ironically enough, Bosola's has been the principal voice.

In the last act, with a grim symmetry appropriate to what has now
become a species of revenge tragedy, Bosola uses the rhetoric of

service only to beguile others, whether it is the promise of erotic "service" with which he persuades the lustful Julia to become his own intelligencer (5.2.211, 217) or the mimicry of his earlier abjection with which he persuades the Cardinal of his need to "find a great man like yourself. . . . To remember my service" (lines 290–92). Driven by his "manly sorrow" (4.2.346) to act in a fashion that will make his "dejection" worth its extreme cost, the servant learns too late what it might mean to act as his own master: "I will not imitate things glorious, / No more than base; I'll be mine own example" (5.4.79–80). Ironically this determination, along with his inadvertent killing of Antonio ("The man I would have saved 'bove mine own life," 5.4.51), his coldly offhand murder of Antonio's innocent servant (5.5.33–35), and his savage revenge on the Aragonian brothers, only mires Bosola deeper in damnation. This, however, is what cements his claim to be a tragic hero—albeit of a very different kind from the Duchess—one whose claim to the audience's sympathy is perfectly exemplified in the contradictions of his dying speech, oscillating as it does between wry acknowledgment of the benighted human condition, despair at his own damnability, and a defiant assertion of self in the face of annihilation:

> We are only like dead walls or vaulted graves
> That, ruined, yields no echo. Fare you well:
> It may be pain, but no harm to me to die
> In so good a quarrel. Oh, this gloomy world!
> In what a shadow, or deep pit of darkness,
> Doth womanish and fearful mankind live!
> Let worthy minds ne'er stagger in distrust
> To suffer death or shame for what is just—
> Mine is another voyage.
>
> lines 95–103

The Text of
THE DUCHESS OF MALFI

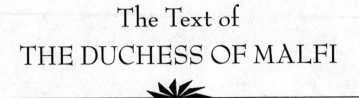

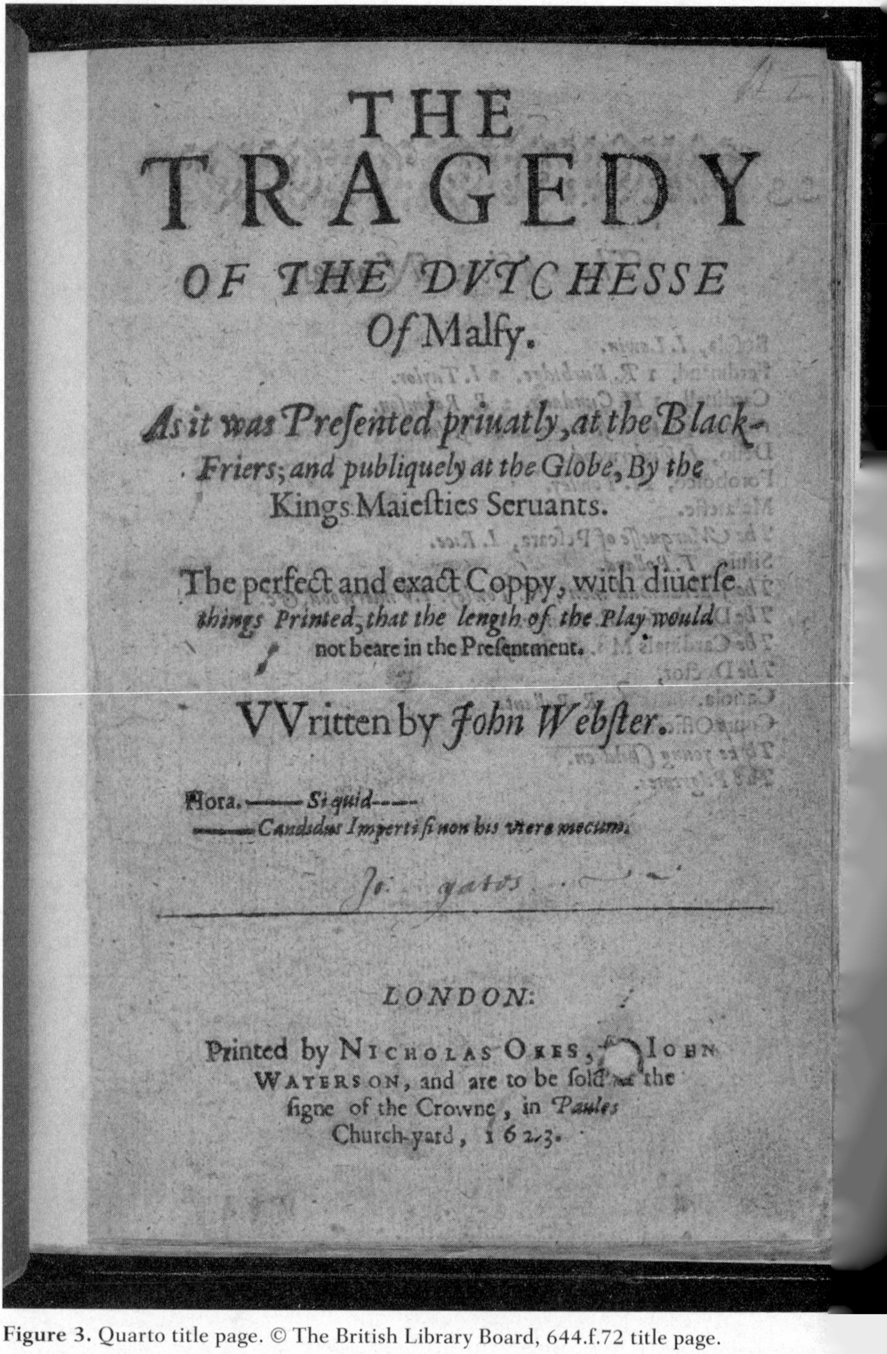

THE
TRAGEDY

OF THE DVTCHESSE
Of Malfy.

As it was Presented priuatly, at the Black-Friers; and publiquely at the Globe, By the Kings Maiesties Seruants.

The perfect and exact Coppy, with diuerse things Printed, that the length of the Play would not beare in the Presentment.

VVritten by *John Webster.*

Hora.——— *Si quid——*
——— *Candidus Impertis si non his vtere mecum.*

Jo: gates

LONDON:

Printed by NICHOLAS OKES, for IOHN WATERSON, and are to be sold at the signe of the Crowne, in *Paules* Church-yard, 1 6 2 3.

Figure 3. Quarto title page. © The British Library Board, 644.f.72 title page.

4. 1623 dramatis personae with list of actors' names. © The British Library Board, 22.

[Dedication]

TO THE RIGHT HONORABLE GEORGE HARDING, BARON BERKELEY
OF BERKELEY CASTLE, AND KNIGHT OF THE ORDER OF THE BATH
TO THE ILLUSTRIOUS PRINCE CHARLES.

My noble lord,

That I may present my excuse why, being a stranger to your
lordship, I offer this poem to your patronage, I plead this
warrant: men who never saw the sea, yet desire to behold
that regiment of waters, choose some eminent river to guide
them thither, and make that, as it were, their conduct or   5
postilion. By the like ingenious means has your fame arrived
at my knowledge, receiving it from some of worth who, both
in contemplation and practice, owe to your honor their
clearest service. I do not altogether look up at your title, the
ancientest nobility being but a relic of time past, and the   10
truest honor indeed being for a man to confer honor on
himself, which your learning strives to propagate and shall
make you arrive at the dignity of a great example. I am confident this work is not unworthy your honor's perusal; for
by such poems as this, poets have kissed the hands of great   15
princes and drawn their gentle eyes to look down upon their
sheets of paper when the poets themselves were bound up
in their winding-sheets. The like courtesy from your lordship shall make you live in your grave and laurel spring out
of it, when the ignorant scorners of the Muses (that, like   20
worms in libraries, seem to live only to destroy learning)
shall wither, neglected and forgotten. This work and myself

Harding: The grandson, on his mother's side, of Lord Hunsdon, patron of the King's
Men in their former incarnation as the Lord Chamberlain's Men, Harding (1601–1658)
succeeded to his ancient title in 1613, shortly before the likely first performance of Webster's tragedy, becoming eighth Baron Berkeley. He was made a Knight of the Bath in
1616. Berkeley studied at Oxford (1619–23) and subsequently at Gray's Inn. "An amiable
nonentity," according to the family historian, "bent for the most part on peacefully
administering the estates left to him by his grandfather," he seems, nevertheless, to have
been something of a literary and theatrical patron: he found a living for Robert Burton,
who dedicated *The Anatomy of Melancholy* to him in 1621; and he received further dedications from both Philip Massinger (*The Renegado*, 1630), and James Shirley (*The
Young Admiral*, 1637). There are striking parallels between Webster's and Massinger's
dedications, especially in their emphasis on the superior distinction conferred on Harding by Harding's generous patronage as opposed to his hereditary titles—a theme echoed
in Burton's epistle.
4. regiment: kingdom (*OED* n. 7).
5. conduct: escort.
6. postilion: guide.
9. clearest: most absolute, pure (*OED* adj. 17).
9–12. I do . . . himself: cf. Bosola 2.1.93–103, and *Devil's Law Case*, 1.1.40–1. The sentiment and tone contrast with the conventionally obsequious style of most dedicatory
epistles.
13. arrive . . . example: earn you the honor of becoming a great example to others.
13–18. I am . . . sheets: echoed in Webster's dedicatory epistle for *The Devil's Law Case*.

5

I humbly present to your approved censure—it being the
utmost of my wishes to have your honorable self my weighty
and perspicuous comment; which grace so done me, shall   25
ever be acknowledged.

By your lordship's, in all duty and observance,

John Webster

[*Commendatory Verses*]

IN THE JUST WORTH OF THAT WELL-DESERVER, MR. JOHN WEBSTER,
AND UPON THIS MASTERPIECE OF TRAGEDY

In this thou imitat'st one rich and wise
That sees his good deeds done before he dies.
As he by works, thou by this work of fame
Hast well provided for thy living name.
5   To trust to others' honorings is worth's crime;
Thy monument is raised in thy lifetime.
And 'tis most just; for every worthy man
Is his own marble, and his merit can
Cut him to any figure and express
10   More art than Death's cathedral palaces,
Where royal ashes keep their court. Thy note
Be ever plainness: 'tis the richest coat.
Thy epitaph only the title be:
Write "Duchess"—that will fetch a tear for thee;
15   For whoe'er saw this duchess live and die
That could get off under a bleeding eye?

In Tragediam.
Ut lux ex tenebris ictu percussa Tonantis,

---

23. **approved censure:** well-tried judgment.
25. **comment:** embodied exposition (of my ideas).
[**Commendatory Verses**]: By three prominent fellow dramatists, all of whom collaborated
with Webster (as well as with one another) at various points in their careers. As Brown
notes, Ford wrote in commendation of several plays, but *Malfi* is the only play that Middleton and Rowley praised in this way. Like Webster's dedication, all three sets of verses
self-consciously echo the play's own preoccupation with reputation and posthumous
fame.
6–11. [**Middleton**]. **Thy monument . . . court:** cf. 5.5.115–19.
10–11. **cathedral . . . court:** Middleton is no doubt thinking particularly of Westminster
    Abbey—not technically a cathedral, but the site of Henry VII's monumental chapel and
    many of England's royal tombs, including that of Webster's personal hero, Prince
    Henry, the subject of his poem *A Monumental Column* (1612).
12. **coat:** The context of royal tombs, with their elaborate heraldic displays, suggests that
    coat must here mean "coat-of-arms" (*OED* n. 4).
17–19. *In Tragediam . . . poetis*: "To Tragedy. As light springs from darkness at the stroke
    of the Thunderer, so may she (Tragedy) bring life to illustrious poets, and ruin to bad
    ones." In conjunction with *lux* (light), *clarus* (clear, bright/illustrious, famous), the pas-
    sage probably plays on the clear light that illuminates the Duchess's tomb (5.3.45).

Illa, (ruina malis) claris fit vita poetis.
20   *Thomas Middletonus,*
         Poeta & Chron: Londinensis

TO HIS FRIEND MR. JOHN WEBSTER UPON HIS *DUCHESS OF MALFI*

I never saw thy Duchess till the day
That she was lively bodied in thy play.
Howe'er she answered her low-rated love,
Her brothers' anger did so fatal prove;
5   Yet my opinion is, she might speak more,
But never in her life so well before.
                              William Rowley

TO THE READER OF THE AUTHOR AND HIS *DUCHESS OF MALFI*

Crown him a poet, whom nor Rome nor Greece
Transcend in all theirs for a masterpiece;
In which, whiles words and matter change, and men
Act one another, he, from whose clear pen
5   They all took life, to memory hath lent
A lasting fame, to raise his monument.
                              John Ford

The Actors' Names

Bosola,   *I. Lowin.*
Ferdinand,   1. *R. Burbidge.* 2. *J. Taylor.*

21. *Chron: Londinensis*: Middleton was appointed London's City Chronologer in 1620.
3–4. [Rowley]. Howe'er . . . prove: "However eloquently in her real life the Duchess
may have defended that misalliance *which* her brothers' anger made so fatal" (Lucas).
3–4. [Ford]. whiles . . . another: "While literature has its fashions and the theatre
lasts" (Brown).
The Actors' Names: *The Duchess of Malfi* was the first English play to be published with
a full list of the characters and the actors who played them.
Bosola: As Brown notes, lists of *dramatis personae* in this period are normally arranged
with strict regard for hierarchy: this elevation of a household servant to the head of the
list cannot even be explained by casting, since Richard Burbage (1569–1619), who originally played Ferdinand, had been the leading actor of the King's Men for some years. It
is tempting to suppose that the list is authorial and that its ranking mirrors the play's
own scepticism about the pretensions of rank and inherited status. Though less celebrated than Burbage, John Lowin (1576–1653) was a prominent actor whose roles
included Falstaff, Hamlet, and Volpone. He became a joint manager of the King's Men
in 1623.
Taylor: The listing of a second set of names presumably reflects casting in a revival after
Burbage's death. Joseph Taylor (1586?–1652) was Burbage's successor as the leading actor of
the King's Men.

Cardinal,	1. H. Cundaile, 2. R. Robinson.
Antonio,	1. W. Ostler, 2. R. Benfield.
Delio,	J. Underwood.
Forobosco,	N. Towley.
Malateste.	
The Marquis of Pescara,	J. Rice.
Silvio,	T. Pollard.
The several mad-men,	N. Towley, J. Underwood etc.
The Dutchesse,	R. Sharpe.
The Cardinal's Mistress,	J. Tomson.
The Doctor,	
Cariola,	R. Pallant
Court Officers.	
Three young Children.	
Two Pilgrimes.	

List of Characters

THE DUCHESS OF MALFI (sister of Ferdinand and the Cardinal)

ECHO (from the Duchess's grave)

DANIEL DE BOSOLA (the Duchess's provisor of horse)

ANTONIO BOLOGNA (steward of the Duchess's household; later her husband)

DELIO (his friend)

Cundaile: Henry Condell (d. 1627) was a leading actor and shareholder in the King's Men, who served as one of the editors responsible for the publication of the First Folio of Shakespeare's works in 1623.

Robinson: Richard Robinson (d. 1648), an actor who had risen to prominence in his boyhood for his skill in female roles, graduated to adult parts from 1618 and became a prominent member of the company.

Ostler: William Ostler (d. 1614) was a former boy actor whose early death helps fix the date of Malfi's first performance.

Underwood: John Underwood was a contemporary of Ostler's in the Children of the Chapel Royal and subsequently in the King's Men, effectively replacing Ostler until his own death in 1624.

Forobosco: Although this character is mentioned at 2.2.30, he seemingly makes no actual appearance in the play. Perhaps, as Brown suggests (p. lvvii), his lines were removed as a result of cuts made in the course of production.

Towley: Nicholas Towley (1583–1623), another former boy actor, is known to have played a number of second rank parts for the King's Men. He may have played Malateste, for whom no actor is listed.

Rice: John Rice (dates unknown) was another boy actor who began playing adult roles with the King's Men from 1614.

Pollard: Thomas Pollard (dates unknown), usually specializing in comic roles, acted with the King's Men from 1613 to 1642, rising to become a shareholder in the company.

Sharpe: Richard Sharpe (1601–1632) was a boy actor who joined the company in 1616; he can have played the Duchess only in the later revival. He went on to become a shareholder and leading actor in the troupe.

Tomson: John Thompson (d. 1634) was a boy actor who played women's parts from 1619 until as late as 1631.

Pallant: Robert Pallant (b. 1605) was a boy player who joined the company in 1620; in the revival he doubled the part of Cariola with minor male roles.

CARIOLA (the Duchess's waiting-woman)
Three young CHILDREN (of the Duchess and Antonio)

FERDINAND (Duke of Calabria, brother of the Duchess and the
   Cardinal)
CARDINAL (brother of Ferdinand and the Duchess)
[FOROBOSCO (a minor court official)]
THE MARQUIS OF PESCARA (a soldier)
CASTRUCHIO (an old courtier, husband of Julia)
JULIA (a courtesan: the Cardinal's mistress and wife to Castruchio)
COUNT MALATESTE ⎱
SILVIO   ⎰ courtiers
RODERIGO
GRISOLAN
DOCTOR
OLD LADY
EIGHT MADMEN
TWO PILGRIMS
Executioners
Courtiers, Court officers, Attendants, Ladies, Servants, Church-
   men, Guards

THE SCENE: *Malfi (i.e. Amalfi), Rome, Loreto, the countryside near
Ancona, and Milan.*

The Duchess of Malfi

Act 1

1.1

[*Enter*] ANTONIO *and* DELIO.

DELIO   You are welcome to your country, dear Antonio!
  You have been long in France, and you return
  A very formal Frenchman in your habit,
  How do you like the French court?

ANTONIO   I admire it:
  In seeking to reduce both state and people   5
  To a fixed order, their judicious king
  Begins at home, quits first his royal palace
  Of flatt'ring sycophants, of dissolute
  And infamous persons—which he sweetly terms
  His master's masterpiece, the work of heaven,   10
  Consid'ring duly that a prince's court
  Is like a common fountain whence should flow
  Pure silver drops in general; but if't chance
  Some cursed example poison't near the head,

1.1. SD. Q1 follows the neoclassical practice of listing at the beginning of a scene all of the characters who appear in it, regardless of when they actually enter (see Collation). In this edition redundant names are silently omitted and reinserted at the point of their probable entry.

3. formal: (unduly) ceremonious. **habit:** dress, fashion; demeanor, behavior.

5–9. seeking . . . persons: Lucas suggests that this passage must have been added for a later revival because it apparently refers to Louis XIII's efforts to purge his court of Medici influence and to the associated murder of the Florentine soldier Concino Concini (April 1617).

11–15. prince's . . . spread: Echoing, as Brown points out, a figure from chapter 8 of Sir Thomas Elyot's *The Image of Governance* (1541): "the princis palaice is lyke a common fountayne or sprynge to his citie or country, wherby the people by the cleannes therof be longe preserued in honestie, or by the impurenes therof, are with sundry vyces corrupted. And untylle the fountain be purged, there can neuer be any sure hope of remedye" (D4v). Antonio's entire speech is loosely modeled on the passage from which this comes, while (as Dent shows) also borrowing (lines 16–22) from William Painter's *Palace of Pleasure* (1567); see pp. 127–60 in this volume. Webster's compositional practice, which often makes his writing seem like a mere mosaic of quotations from other writers, has been documented by successive editors, and most elaborately by R. W. Dent in *John Webster's Borrowing*; see p. xxiii in this volume. Only the more conspicuous examples will be noted here.

12. common fountain: public source of drinking water.

11

Death and diseases through the whole land spread.   15
And what is't makes this blessèd government
But a most provident council, who dare freely
Inform him the corruption of the times?
Though some o'th'court hold it presumption
To instruct princes what they ought to do,   20
It is a noble duty to inform them
What they ought to foresee.
          [*Enter*] BOSOLA.
                    Here comes Bosola,
The only court gall. Yet I observe his railing
Is not for simple love of piety;
Indeed, he rails at those things which he wants,   25
Would be as lecherous, covetous, or proud,
Bloody, or envious, as any man,
If he had means to be so.
          [*Enter*] CARDINAL.
                    Here's the Cardinal.
          [ANTONIO *and* DELIO *stand aside, observing.*]
BOSOLA [*To the* CARDINAL]   I do haunt you still.
CARDINAL   So.
BOSOLA   I have done you
Better service than to be slighted thus.   30
Miserable age, where only the reward
Of doing well is the doing of it!
CARDINAL   You enforce your merit too much.
BOSOLA   I fell into the galleys in your service, where, for two
     years together, I wore two towels instead of a shirt, with a   35
     knot on the shoulder, after the fashion of a Roman mantle.
     Slighted thus? I will thrive some way. Blackbirds fatten best in
     hard weather; why not I, in these dog-days?
CARDINAL   Would you could become honest!
BOSOLA   With all your divinity, do but direct me the way to it.   40
                              [*Exit* CARDINAL.]
     I have known many travel far for it, and yet return as arrant
     knaves as they went forth, because they carried themselves
     always along with them. —Are you gone? Some fellows, they

---

23. gall: sore, pustule; bitter bile; here a satirist.
25. wants: lacks.
31–32. only . . . of it: proverbial (Tilley, V81).
33. enforce: urge, emphasize (*OED* v. 4).
38. dog-days: the hottest and most unhealthy part of summer.
40. SD. Brown is surely correct to suggest that the Cardinal should make an early exit,
     rather than appearing to wait on Bosola's words.
41. arrant: downright, notorious.

say, are possessed with the devil, but this great fellow were
able to possess the greatest devil and make him worse.   45
ANTONIO [*Coming forward with* DELIO.]   He hath denied thee
   some suit?
BOSOLA   He and his brother are like plum trees that grow
   crooked over standing pools; they are rich and o'erladen, stagnant with fruit, but none but crows, pies, and caterpillars feed   50
   on them. Could I be one of their flattering panders, I would
   hang on their ears like a horse-leech till I were full, and then
   drop off. I pray leave me. Who would rely upon these miserable dependences in expectation to be advanced hopes of
   appointment tomorrow? What creature ever fed worse than   55
   hoping Tantalus? Nor ever died any man more fearfully than
   he that hoped for a pardon. There are rewards for hawks and
   dogs, when they have done us service; but for a soldier that
   hazards his limbs in a battle, nothing but a kind of geometry is
   his last supportation.   60
DELIO   Geometry?
BOSOLA   Ay, to hang in a fair pair of slings, take his latter swing
   in the world upon an honorable pair of crutches, from hospital
   to hospital. Fare ye well, sir. And yet do not you scorn us, for
   places in the court are but like beds in the hospital, where this   65
   man's head lies at that man's foot, and so lower and lower.
                                                        [*Exit.*]
DELIO   I knew this fellow seven years in the galleys
   For a notorious murder, and 'twas thought
   The Cardinal suborned it. He was released
   By the French general, Gaston de Foix,   70
   When he recovered Naples.
ANTONIO   'Tis great pity
   He should be thus neglected: I have heard
   He's very valiant. This foul melancholy
   Will poison all his goodness; for, I'll tell you,

---

49. **standing:** stagnant.
50. **pies:** magpies.
51. **panders:** pimps (i.e., courtiers).
52. **horse-leech:** a large and proverbially insatiable variety of leech.
56. **Tantalus:** in Greek mythology, condemned to perpetual thirst and hunger by being
   kept up to his neck in a lake overhung with fruit, but unable to drink from one or to reach
   the other. A proverbial figure of disappointment and frustration.
57–58. **hawks and dogs:** Q1's second "and" suggests that a word is missing here; Brown
   proposes "horses."
70. **Gaston de Foix:** a French general (1589–1512) who earned fame for his daring in the
   Italian wars but who was too young to have taken any part in the siege of Naples (1501).
   Marcus defends Q1's "Foux," suggesting a play on French *fou* (mad).
73. **foul:** loathsome, vile; dirty (and therefore, in some contexts, black). **melancholy:** In
   early modern psychophysiology the word described both a sullen, gloomy temperament
   and the material humor, otherwise known as "black bile," thought to cause such a
   disposition.

If too immoderate sleep be truly said   75
To be an inward rust unto the soul,
It then doth follow want of action
Breeds all black malcontents; and their close rearing,
Like moths in cloth, do hurt for want of wearing.
     [*Enter at one door*] CASTRUCHIO, SILVIO, RODERIGO, [*and*]
     GRISOLAN. ANTONIO *and* DELIO [*stand aside, observing.*]

DELIO   The presence 'gins to fill. You promised me   80
To make me the partaker of the natures
Of some of your great courtiers.

ANTONIO   The Lord Cardinal's
And other strangers' that are now in court?
I shall.
     [*Enter*] FERDINAND.
     Here comes the great Calabrian duke.

FERDINAND   Who took the ring oft'nest?

SILVIO   Antonio Bologna, my
  lord.   85

FERDINAND   Our sister Duchess' great master of her household?
Give him the jewel. When shall we leave
This sportive action and fall to action indeed?

CASTRUCHIO   Methinks, my lord, you should not desire to go
to war in person.   90

FERDINAND [*aside*]   Now, for some gravity. —Why, my lord?

CASTRUCHIO   It is fitting a soldier arise to be a prince, but not
necessary a prince descend to be a captain.

FERDINAND   No?

CASTRUCHIO   No, my lord. He were far better do it by a deputy. 95

FERDINAND   Why should he not as well sleep or eat by a deputy?
This might take idle, offensive, and base office from him,
whereas the other deprives him of honor.

---

78. **black malcontents:** The malcontent, a figure characterized by brooding, vindictive
melancholy, was a stock figure in Renaissance drama: well-known examples include
Shakespeare's Hamlet, Malevole in John Marston's *Malcontent,* and Vindice in Middleton's *Revenger's Tragedy.* As *Hamlet* reminds us, malcontents (like melancholics generally) favored black attire as the mark of their inward disposition, but "black" here also
connotes "evil."

79. **SD.** Modern editors usually remove Q1's scene division here, assuming the action to
be continuous; but Marcus (like David Gunby in his Penguin edition) retains the original division, arguing that a change of perspective is involved: where in 1.1 Antonio and
Delio have a detached choric role, guiding the audience's point of view, in 1.2 Antonio
is "plunged into the midst of the court" (pp. 73–74). The couplet at 1.1.78–79 suggests
that she may well be right, since Webster, more often than not, uses this form of dramatic punctuation to mark the end of a scene.

80. **presence:** the Duchess's official audience chamber.

85. **ring:** Riding at the ring, in which the horseman attempted to carry off a ring on the
tip of his lance, was a common form of chivalric competition; an unconscious irony is
involved because, later in the scene, Antonio's prowess will be rewarded with a very
different ring (1.1.394–403).

87. **jewel:** the victor's reward, but also anticipating the Duchess's description of herself at
lines 291–92.

CASTRUCHIO   Believe my experience: that realm is never long in
   quiet where the ruler is a soldier.   100
FERDINAND   Thou told'st me thy wife could not endure fighting.
CASTRUCHIO   True, my lord.
FERDINAND   And of a jest she broke of a captain she met full of
   wounds—I have forgot it.
CASTRUCHIO   She told him, my lord, he was a pitiful fellow, to   105
   lie, like the children of Ishmael, all in tents.
FERDINAND   Why, there's a wit were able to undo all the chirur-
   geons o'the city, for although gallants should quarrel and had
   drawn their weapons and were ready to go to it, yet her per-
   suasions would make them put up.   110
CASTRUCHIO   That she would, my lord. How do you like my
   Spanish jennet?
RODERIGO   He is all fire.
FERDINAND   I am of Pliny's opinion: I think he was begot by
   the wind. He runs as if he were ballasted with quicksilver.   115
SILVIO   True, my lord, he reels from the tilt often.
RODERIGO [and] GRISOLAN   Ha, ha, ha!
FERDINAND   Why do you laugh? Methinks you that are court-
   iers should be my touchwood: take fire when I give fire—that
   is, laugh when I laugh, were the subject never so witty.   120
CASTRUCHIO   True, my lord. I myself have heard a very good
   jest, and have scorned to seem to have so silly a wit as to
   understand it.
FERDINAND   But I can laugh at your fool, my lord.
CASTRUCHIO   He cannot speak, you know, but he makes faces.   125
   My lady cannot abide him.
FERDINAND   No?
CASTRUCHIO   Nor endure to be in merry company, for she says
   too much laughing and too much company fills her too full of
   the wrinkle.   130
FERDINAND   I would then have a mathematical instrument
   made for her face that she might not laugh out of compass. —I
   shall shortly visit you at Milan, Lord Silvio.

---

101. **fighting:** with a cruel glance at Castruchio's unhappy marriage (his wife being the
Cardinal's mistress).
106. **children of Ishmael:** Abraham's bastard son and his children were nomadic out-
casts. **tents:** punning on *tent* = dressing for a wound (OED n³. 2).
107. **chirurgeons:** surgeons.
109. **go to it:** fight. **put up:** sheathe their swords.
112. **jennet:** small Spanish sporting horse.
114-115. **Pliny's . . . wind:** In his *Natural History* (trans. 1601) Pliny speaks of mares in
Portugal that are reputedly impregnated by the wind (p. 222).
115. **ballasted with quicksilver:** Ferdinand's conceit is that *quick*silver (unlike other
ballast) would necessarily make a horse run quicker.
116. **reels . . . tilt:** sarcastic quibble: (1) the ballast rights his list (as with a boat); (2) he
swerves away when ridden at the tilt; (3) he staggers from the aftereffect of copulation.
119. **touchwood:** tinder.
132. **out of compass:** to excess (punning on *compass* as a mathematical instrument).

SILVIO   Your Grace shall arrive most welcome.

FERDINAND   You are a good horseman, Antonio. You have excel- 135
lent riders in France. What do you think of good horsemanship?

ANTONIO   Nobly, my lord. As out of the Grecian horse issued
many famous princes, so out of brave horsemanship arise the
first sparks of growing resolution that raise the mind to noble
action.   140

FERDINAND   You have bespoke it worthily.
        [*Enter*] CARDINAL, DUCHESS, CARIOLA, JULIA [*with
        attendants*].

SILVIO [*To* FERDINAND]   Your brother, the Lord Cardinal, and
sister Duchess.

CARDINAL   Are the galleys come about?

GRISOLAN   They are, my lord.

FERDINAND   Here's the Lord Silvio is come to take his leave.   145
        [FERDINAND, *the* CARDINAL, *and their followers confer
        among themselves.*]

DELIO [*To* ANTONIO]   Now, sir, your promise: what's that
Cardinal?
I mean his temper? They say he's a brave fellow,
Will play his five thousand crowns at tennis,
Dance, court ladies—and one that hath fought single
combats.

ANTONIO   Some such flashes superficially hang on him for 150
form. But observe his inward character: he is a melancholy
churchman. The spring in his face is nothing but the engen-
dering of toads. Where he is jealous of any man, he lays worse
plots for them than ever was imposed on Hercules, for he
strews in his way flatterers, panders, intelligencers, atheists, 155
and a thousand such political monsters. He should have been
pope, but instead of coming to it by the primitive decency of

---

137. **Grecian horse**: i.e., the Trojan horse. Given the bawdy wordplay above, the audience (though not the characters) may be expected to hear the familiar *whores* pun in the
repetitions of "horse" and "horsemanship" here.

151. **character**: the word had not yet developed its modern meaning. Related to alpha-
betical "character," it referred to sets of qualities imagined as engraved on a person
(especially the face) by experience or by the psychophysiological operation of the four
humors. It was popularized in the 17th century by collections of character types written
in imitation of the *Characters* of the Greek author Theophrastus (ca. 371–ca. 287
B.C.E.). Webster himself contributed several characters to the best known of these, *Sir
Thomas Ouerburie His Wife* (1616); see pp. 169–70 in this volume. **melancholy**: see
note to 1.1.73.

152. **spring**: i.e., youthfulness, but punning on *spring* as the water in which poisonous
creatures may breed.

155. **intelligencers**: spies.

157. **primitive decency**: pristine goodness and purity (i.e., before the early church was
supposedly corrupted by the practices of Roman Catholicism).

the church, he did bestow bribes so largely and so impudently
as if he would have carried it away without heaven's knowl-
edge. Some good he hath done.   160
DELIO   You have given too much of him. What's his brother?
ANTONIO   The Duke there? A most perverse and turbulent
    nature.
    What appears in him mirth is merely outside;
    If he laugh heartily, it is to laugh
    All honesty out of fashion.
DELIO   Twins?
ANTONIO   In quality.   165
    He speaks with others' tongues and hears men's suits
    With others' ears; will seem to sleep o'th'bench
    Only to entrap offenders in their answers;
    Dooms men to death by information,
    Rewards by hearsay.
DELIO   Then the law to him   170
    Is like a foul black cobweb to a spider:
    He makes it his dwelling and a prison
    To entangle those shall feed him.
ANTONIO   Most true.
    He ne'er pays debts unless they be shrewd turns,
    And those he will confess that he doth owe.   175
    Last, for his brother there, the Cardinal,
    They that do flatter him most say oracles
    Hang at his lips; and verily I believe them,
    For the devil speaks in them.
    But for their sister, the right noble Duchess,   180
    You never fixed your eye on three fair medals,
    Cast in one figure, of so different temper.
    For her discourse, it is so full of rapture
    You only will begin then to be sorry
    When she doth end her speech, and wish in wonder   185
    She held it less vainglory to talk much
    Than your penance to hear her. Whilst she speaks,
    She throws upon a man so sweet a look

---

158. **largely:** copiously, extensively. **impudently:** shamelessly.
166–69. **He . . . hearsay:** closely modeled on *Alexandrian Tragedy*, 2.1.570–78 (Dent).
167. **seem . . . bench:** pretend to sleep while sitting in judgment.
170–73. **law . . . feed him:** proverbial (Tilley, L116).
174. **shrewd:** bad.
182. **figure:** shape; here, by extension, a mold. **temper:** temperament (but also playing on
    the *temper* of the metal from which medals are cast).
183–98. closely modeled on a passage in G. Pettie's translation of a well-known conduct
    book, *The Civile Conversation of M. Steeven Guazzo* (1581), book 2, fol. 69v (Dent).

That it were able to raise one to a galliard.
That lay in a dead palsy, and to dote   190
On that sweet countenance. But in that look
There speaketh so divine a continence
As cuts off all lascivious and vain hope.
Her days are practiced in such noble virtue
That sure her nights—nay more, her very sleeps—   195
Are more in heaven than other ladies' shrifts.
Let all sweet ladies break their flatt'ring glasses
And dress themselves in her.
DELIO   Fie, Antonio,
You play the wire-drawer with her commendations.
ANTONIO   I'll case the picture up: only thus much—   200
All her particular worth grows to this sum:
She stains the time past, lights the time to come.
[CARIOLA *approaches* ANTONIO *confidentially.*]
CARIOLA   You must attend my lady in the gallery
Some half an hour hence.
ANTONIO   I shall.
                              [*Exeunt* ANTONIO *and* DELIO.]
FERDINAND   Sister, I have a suit to you.
DUCHESS   To me, sir?   205
FERDINAND   A gentleman here, Daniel de Bosola,
One that was in the galleys.
DUCHESS   Yes, I know him.
FERDINAND   A worthy fellow h' is. Pray let me entreat for
The Provisorship of your Horse.
DUCHESS   Your knowledge of him
Commends him and prefers him.
FERDINAND [*To an Attendant*]   Call him hither.   210
                              [*Exit Attendant.*]

---

189. **galliard:** lively dance in triple time.
190. **in . . . palsy:** paralyzed.
196. **shrifts:** acts of contrition.
199. **wire-drawer:** one who spins something out to extreme or overelaborate lengths.
200. **case:** close.
202. **She . . . come:** adapted from *Alexandrian Tragedy,* 3.3.1319 ("Staine of times past, and light of times to come"). Webster had used the same line a few months earlier in *A Monumental Columne,* his elegy for the protestant hero Prince Henry (line 278). See also 5.3.45–46. **stains:** obscures the luster of (*OED* n. 1c).
203. **gallery:** covered space for walking. As Marcus notes, the bare stage of the period allows the action of this scene to shift seamlessly from the present chamber to the gallery, where the Duchess's meeting with Antonio takes place (lines 351 ff.).
209. **Provisorship of your Horse:** an important court position, which Elizabeth I granted to her favorite, the Earl of Leicester.
210. **prefers:** promotes.

We are now upon parting. Good Lord Silvio,
Do us commend to all our noble friends
At the leaguer.
SILVIO   Sir, I shall.
DUCHESS   You are for Milan?
SILVIO   I am.
DUCHESS [*To Attendants*]   Bring the caroches. [*To* SILVIO] We'll   215
bring you down to the haven.
                    [*Exeunt all except the* CARDINAL *and* FERDINAND.]
CARDINAL   Be sure you entertain that Bosola
For your intelligence. I would not be seen in't,
And therefore many times I have slighted him
When he did court our furtherance, as this morning.
FERDINAND   Antonio, the great master of her household,   220
Had been far fitter.
CARDINAL   You are deceived in him:
His nature is too honest for such business.
          [*Enter*] BOSOLA.
He comes. I'll leave you.   [*Exit.*]
BOSOLA   I was lured to you.
FERDINAND   My brother here, the Cardinal, could never   225
Abide you.
BOSOLA   Never since he was in my debt.
FERDINAND   Maybe some oblique character in your face
Made him suspect you?
BOSOLA   Doth he study physiognomy?
There's no more credit to be given to th'face
Than to a sick man's urine, which some call   230
The physician's whore because she cozens him.
He did suspect me wrongfully.
FERDINAND   For that
You must give great men leave to take their times—
Distrust doth cause us seldom be deceived:
You see the oft shaking of the cedar tree   235

---

213. **leaguer:** siege. DUCHESS: Q1's speech attribution must be wrong, since Ferdinand has just made it clear that he is aware of Silvio's destination (cf. also line 133).
215. **caroches:** stately coaches.
217–18. **entertain . . . intelligence:** employ Bosola as your secret agent.
220. **furtherance:** advancement.
227. **oblique:** crooked (*OED* a. 4). **character:** mark, trait (*OED* n. 8a); reflecting the idea of individual nature as something inscribed or engraved on the countenance (see line 151).
228. **physiognomy:** the science of reading character in a person's physical features.
230. **sick man's urine:** a standard diagnostic tool (cf. Marlowe, *2 Tamburlaine*, 5.3.82).
231. **cozens:** cheats, deceives.
233. **take:** take the measure of, observe in a scientific fashion (*OED* v. 32b).
234. **Distrust . . . deceived:** proverbial (Tilley, T559).

Fastens it more at root.
BOSOLA   Yet take heed,
  For to suspect a friend unworthily
  Instructs him the next way to suspect you,
  And prompts him to deceive you.
FERDINAND [*Giving money.*]   There's gold.
BOSOLA   So:
  What follows? Never rained such showers as these at court   240
  Without thunderbolts i'th'tail of them:
  Whose throat must I cut?
FERDINAND   Your inclination to shed blood rides post
  Before my occasion to use you. I give you that
  To live i'th'court here and observe the Duchess,   245
  To note all the particulars of her 'havior—
  What suitors do solicit her for marriage,
  And whom she best affects: she's a young widow;
  I would not have her marry again.
BOSOLA   No, sir?
FERDINAND   Do not you ask the reason, but be satisfied   250
  I say I would not.
BOSOLA   It seems you would create me
  One of your familiars.
FERDINAND   Familiar? What's that?
BOSOLA   Why, a very quaint invisible devil—in flesh,
  An intelligencer.
FERDINAND   Such a kind of thriving thing
  I would wish thee; and ere long thou mayst arrive   255
  At a higher place by't.
BOSOLA [*Offering to return the money.*]
                        Take your devils,
  Which hell calls angels! These cursed gifts would make
  You a corrupter, me an impudent traitor;
  And should I take these, they'd take me to hell.
FERDINAND   Sir, I'll take nothing from you that I have given.   260
  There is a place that I procured for you
  This morning: the provisorship o'th'horse.

240–41. **Never . . . them:** alluding to Jupiter the Thunderer's rape of Danaë in a shower
  of gold.
243. **post:** hastily.
248. **best affects:** is most drawn to.
252. **familiars:** (1) intimates; (2) evil spirits (under the control of a necromancer or
  witch).
257. **angels:** gold coins.
258. **impudent:** shameless.

Have you heard on't?
BOSOLA   No.
FERDINAND   'Tis yours. Is't not worth thanks?
BOSOLA   I would have you curse yourself now, that your bounty,
    Which makes men truly noble, e'er should make   265
    Me a villain. Oh, that to avoid ingratitude
    For the good deed you have done me, I must do
    All the ill man can invent! Thus the devil
    Candies all sins o'er, and what heaven terms vile
    That names he complimental.
FERDINAND   Be yourself;   270
    Keep your old garb of melancholy; 'twill express
    You envy those that stand above your reach,
    Yet strive not to come near 'em. This will gain
    Access to private lodgings, where yourself
    May, like a politic dormouse—
BOSOLA   As I have seen some   275
    Feed in a lord's dish, half asleep, not seeming
    To listen to any talk, and yet these rogues
    Have cut his throat in a dream. What's my place?
    The provisorship o'th'horse? Say then my corruption
    Grew out of horse dung. I am your creature.
FERDINAND   Away!   280
BOSOLA   Let good men, for good deeds, covet good fame,
    Since place and riches oft are bribes of shame.
    Sometimes the devil doth preach.   *Exit* BOSOLA.
    [*Enter* CARDINAL, DUCHESS, *and* CARIOLA.]
CARDINAL [*To the* DUCHESS]   We are to part from you, and your
    own discretion
    Must now be your director.
FERDINAND   You are a widow: 285
    You know already what man is; and therefore
    Let not youth, high promotion, eloquence—
CARDINAL   No, nor anything without the addition, honor,
    Sway your high blood.
FERDINAND   Marry? They are most luxurious

---

270. **complimental:** courtly behavior, accomplishment.
271. **garb of melancholy:** Perhaps metaphorical, but Bosola is probably meant to be clad in black, like his fellow melancholic, Hamlet.
275. **politic:** cunning.
276. **Feed . . . dish:** dine at a great man's table.
280. **creature:** instrument, puppet (*OED* n. 8).
283. **Sometimes . . . preach:** proverbial (Tilley, D230, 266).
289. **high blood:** (1) aristocratic nature; (2) passionate desire. **luxurious:** lascivious.

Will wed twice.
CARDINAL   Oh, fie!
FERDINAND   Their livers are more spotted   290
Than Laban's sheep.
DUCHESS   Diamonds are of most value,
They say, that have passed through most jewelers' hands.
FERDINAND   Whores, by that rule, are precious.
DUCHESS   Will you hear me?
I'll never marry.
CARDINAL   So most widows say;
But commonly that motion lasts no longer   295
Than the turning of an hourglass—the funeral sermon
And it end both together.
FERDINAND   Now hear me:
You live in a rank pasture here, i'th'court.
There is a kind of honeydew that's deadly;
'Twill poison your fame. Look to't. Be not cunning,   300
For they whose faces do belie their hearts
Are witches ere they arrive at twenty years—
Ay, and give the devil suck.
DUCHESS   This is terrible good counsel.
FERDINAND   Hypocrisy is woven of a fine small thread,
Subtler than Vulcan's engine; yet, believe't   305
Your darkest actions—nay, your privat'st thoughts—
Will come to light.
CARDINAL   You may flatter yourself
And take your own choice, privately be married
Under the eaves of night.
FERDINAND   Think't the best voyage
That e'er you made, like the irregular crab,   310
Which, though't goes backward, thinks that it goes right
Because it goes its own way. But observe:
Such weddings may more properly be said
To be executed than celebrated.
CARDINAL   The marriage night

---

290. **livers:** the liver was supposed to be the seat of erotic desire.
291. **Laban's sheep:** Genesis 30.41–43.
295. **motion:** inclination (*OED* n. 9a).
299. **honeydew:** sweet, sticky substance found on certain plants, attractive to bees. Instances of naturally poisonous honey have been recorded since antiquity.
302–303. **witches . . . suck:** Witches were supposed to suckle the devil, usually through a third nipple, thought to be the hallmark of a witch.
304. **Hypocrisy . . . thread:** proverbial (Dent *Prov.*, H844.11).
305. **Vulcan's engine:** the finely woven net in which Vulcan trapped his adulterous wife Venus and her lover, Mars.
310. **irregular:** not conforming to the normal rules (of motion).
314. **executed:** (1) performed; (2) put to death.

Is the entrance into some prison.

FERDINAND   And those joys,   315
Those lustful pleasures, are like heavy sleeps
Which do forerun man's mischief.

CARDINAL   Fare you well.
Wisdom begins at the end—remember it.   [*Exit.*]

DUCHESS   I think this speech between you both was studied,
It came so roundly off.

FERDINAND   You are my sister.   320
[*Showing his dagger.*]   This was my father's poniard. Do you
    see?
I'd be loath to see't look rusty, 'cause 'twas his.
I would have you to give o'er these chargeable revels:
A visor and a mask are whispering-rooms
That were ne'er built for goodness. Fare ye well—   325
And women like that part which, like the lamprey,
Hath ne'er a bone in't.

DUCHESS   Fie, sir!

FERDINAND   Nay,
I mean the tongue—variety of courtship:
What cannot a neat knave with a smooth tale
Make a woman believe? Farewell, lusty widow.   [*Exit.*] 330

DUCHESS   Shall this move me? If all my royal kindred
Lay in my way unto this marriage,
I'd make them my low footsteps; and even now—
Even in this hate—as men in some great battles,
By apprehending danger, have achieved   335
Almost impossible actions—I have heard soldiers say so—
So I, through frights and threat'nings, will assay
This dangerous venture. Let old wives report
I winked and chose a husband. —Cariola,
To thy known secrecy I have given up   340

320. **roundly:** fluently, glibly (*OED* adv. 6).
321. **poniard:** dagger.
323. **chargeable revels:** costly festivities.
324. **visor:** mask. Here, presumably, a vizard mask, designed to cover the eyes alone. **mask:** denotes a more elaborate face mask. Both were common features of courtly entertainments, hence the designation "court masque." **whispering-rooms:** private chambers where secrets might be exchanged.
326–27. **part . . . in't:** Ferdinand's obscene jest necessarily points up the phallic significance of the dagger he flourishes. **lamprey:** a blood-sucking eel-like fish. The comparison to a penis gives his innuendo an even more sinister coloring.
329. **tale:** Punning on *tail* = penis (Williams, pp. 300–01).
330. **lusty:** (1) merry; (2) lustful (*OED*, a. 1, 4).
333. **make . . . footsteps:** make of their bodies steps to the altar.
334–38. **as men . . . venture:** The Duchess deliberately imitates the masculine language of chivalric adventure (see p. xxxi).
337. **assay:** attempt.
339. **winked:** closed my eyes. **winked and chose:** proverbial (Tilley, W501).

More than my life: my fame.

CARIOLA   Both shall be safe;
For I'll conceal this secret from the world
As warily as those that trade in poison
Keep poison from their children.

DUCHESS   Thy protestation
Is ingenious and hearty. I believe it.   345
Is Antonio come?

CARIOLA   He attends you.

DUCHESS   Good dear soul,
Leave me; but place thyself behind the arras,
Where thou mayst overhear us. Wish me good speed,
For I am going into a wilderness
Where I shall find nor path nor friendly clew   350
To be my guide. [CARIOLA *withdraws behind the arras.*]
　　　　[*Enter* ANTONIO.]
                              I sent for you. Sit down.
Take pen and ink, and write. Are you ready?

ANTONIO   Yes.

DUCHESS   What did I say?

ANTONIO   That I should write somewhat.

DUCHESS   Oh, I remember.   355
After these triumphs and this large expense,
It's fit, like thrifty husbands we enquire
What's laid up for tomorrow.

ANTONIO   So please your beauteous excellence.

DUCHESS   Beauteous?
Indeed, I thank you: I look young for your sake.   360
You have ta'en my cares upon you.

ANTONIO [*Rising.*]   I'll fetch your grace
The particulars of your revenue and expense.

DUCHESS   Oh, you are an upright treasurer; but you mistook,

---

341. **fame:** reputation, honor.
345. **ingenious:** sensible (*OED* a. 2). **hearty:** heartfelt.
347. **arras:** rich tapestry hanging. In theaters of the time an arras normally covered the "discovery space" at the rear of the stage in the center of the tiring-house facade.
350. **clew:** ball of thread used as a guide (as by Theseus to enable him to escape from the Cretan Labyrinth).
354. An amphibious line, which makes a complete pentameter with both 353 and (allowing for elision in "Oh, I") 355.
356. **triumphs:** a generic term for large displays of public pageantry (including coronations, weddings, funerals, and royal visits); here the Duchess presumably has in mind the joustings held to celebrate her brothers' visit.
357. **husbands:** stewards, managers (*OED*, n. 41, 5a), but with a glance at the future role she intends for Antonio.
360. **for your sake:** because of you (and the excellent service you offer); but hinting at "to please you."
363. **upright:** playing on the fact that Antonio has just risen to his feet.

For when I said I meant to make inquiry
What's laid up for tomorrow, I did mean   365
What's laid up yonder for me.
ANTONIO   Where?
DUCHESS   In heaven.
I am making my will, as 'tis fit princes should,
In perfect memory; and I pray, sir, tell me,
Were not one better make it smiling thus
Than in deep groans and terrible ghastly looks,   370
As if the gifts we parted with procured
That violent distraction?
ANTONIO   Oh, much better.
DUCHESS   If I had a husband now, this care were quit;
But I intend to make you overseer.
What good deed shall we first remember? Say.   375
ANTONIO   Begin with that first good deed began i'th'world
After man's creation—the sacrament of marriage.
I'd have you first provide for a good husband:
Give him all.
DUCHESS   All?
ANTONIO   Yes, your excellent self.
DUCHESS   In a winding-sheet?
ANTONIO   In a couple.   380
DUCHESS   Saint Winifred, that were a strange will!
ANTONIO   'Twere strange if there were no will in you
To marry again.
DUCHESS   What do you think of marriage?
ANTONIO   I take't as those that deny purgatory:
It locally contains or heaven or hell;   385
There's no third place in't.
DUCHESS   How do you affect it?
ANTONIO   My banishment, feeding my melancholy,
Would often reason thus—
DUCHESS   Pray let's hear it.

---

368. **In . . . memory:** i.e., when of sound mind.
373. **this . . . quit:** I should not need to worry (because my property would belong to him).
380. **In a . . . couple:** In this piece of wordplay the "winding-sheet" (shroud) is transformed into a pair of wedding sheets, reversing the sentimental fashion for women to be buried in their wedding sheets.
381. **Saint . . . will:** The 7th-century Welsh saint Winifred was beheaded by King Caradoc ap Alauc when she resisted his advances but was subsequently restored to life by Saint Beuno. The spring that welled from the ground after her martyrdom became known as Saint Winifred's Well, and was the oldest pilgrimage site in Britain. **will:** puns on *well* and allows for the double meaning (intention/sexual desire) on which Antonio plays in the following line.
384. **those . . . purgatory:** i.e., Protestants—a principal issue of dispute in the Reformation. Cf. also the proverbial "Marriage is a heaven or hell" (Dent *Prov.*, M680.11).
386. **affect:** like.

ANTONIO   Say a man never marry, nor have children—
   What takes that from him? Only the bare name   390
   Of being a father, or the weak delight
   To see the little wanton ride a-cockhorse
   Upon a painted stick, or hear him chatter
   Like a taught starling.
DUCHESS   Fie, fie, what's all this?
   One of your eyes is bloodshot—use my ring to't.   395
   [*Gives him a ring.*]
   They say 'tis very sovereign. 'Twas my wedding ring,
   And I did vow never to part with it,
   But to my second husband.
ANTONIO   You have parted with it now.
DUCHESS   Yes, to help your eyesight.
ANTONIO   You have made me
   stark blind.
DUCHESS   How?
ANTONIO   There is a saucy and ambitious devil   400
   Dancing in this circle.
DUCHESS   Remove him.
ANTONIO   How?
DUCHESS   There needs small conjuration when your finger
   May do it: thus.
   [*Puts her ring on his finger.*]
         Is it fit?
ANTONIO   What said you?   *He kneels.*
DUCHESS   Sir,
   This goodly roof of yours is too low built;
   I cannot stand upright in't, nor discourse,   405
   Without I raise it higher. Raise yourself,
   Or, if you please, my hand to help you: so.   [*Raises him.*]
ANTONIO   Ambition, madam, is a great man's madness,
   That is not kept in chains and close-pent rooms,

390–94. What . . . starling: Adapted from Thomas Elyot, *The Image of Governance* (1541), sig. Plv: "sterilitie can no more hurte me, but onely take from me the name of a father, or the dotynge pleasure to see my lytell sonne ryde on a cockhorse, or to here hymn chatter and speake lyke a wanton" (Dent).
396. sovereign: (1) potent, efficacious; (2) imbrued with the marital sovereignty attributed to a husband.
400–01. There . . . circle: Conjurors could protect themselves by confining in a circle the evil spirits they raised, but *raising the devil* was a slang term for stiffening the penis, while *ring* could stand for the vagina (Williams, pp. 97, 254, 260).
403. Is it fit?: (1) Does it fit? (2) Is this fitting?
404. roof . . . built: The Humble Man in Joseph Hall's *Characters* (1608) is "a true Temple of God built with a low roofe" (Lucas); cf. the Duchess's gesture at 4.2.218–20.
408. Ambition . . . madness: cf. Hall's description of *ambition* as "an aspiring, and a galant madnesse" (Dent).

But in fair, lightsome lodgings, and is girt   410
With the wild noise of prattling visitants,
Which makes it lunatic beyond all cure.
Conceive not I am so stupid but I aim
Whereto your favors tend; but he's a fool
That, being a-cold, would thrust his hands i'th'fire   415
To warm them.
DUCHESS   So, now the ground's broke,
You may discover what a wealthy mine
I make you lord of.
ANTONIO   Oh, my unworthiness!
DUCHESS   You were ill to sell yourself.   420
This dark'ning of your worth is not like that
Which tradesmen use i'th'city: their false lights
Are to rid bad wares off; and I must tell you,
If you will know where breathes a complete man—
I speak it without flattery—turn your eyes   425
And progress through yourself.
ANTONIO   Were there nor heaven
     nor hell,
I should be honest. I have long served virtue,
And ne'er ta'en wages of her.
DUCHESS   Now she pays it.
The misery of us that are born great!
We are forced to woo, because none dare woo us;   430
And as a tyrant doubles with his words,
And fearfully equivocates, so we
Are forced to express our violent passions
In riddles and in dreams, and leave the path
Of simple virtue, which was never made   435
To seem the thing it is not. Go, go brag
You have left me heartless! Mine is in your bosom:
I hope 'twill multiply love there—you do tremble:
Make not your heart so dead a piece of flesh
To fear more than to love me. Sir, be confident.   440
What is't distracts you? This is flesh and blood, sir;

---

413. aim: guess (*OED* v. 3).
419. amphibious line.
424. complete: perfect (*OED* n. 1).
426. Were there nor: even if there were neither.
426–27. Were . . . honest: adapted from Hall, *Characters*, "Honest man": "if there were no heauen, yet he would be vertuous" (Dent).
430. woo: The Q1 spelling, *woe*, highlights the fact that 17th-century pronunciation allowed for a pun here.
439–40. Make . . . love me: adapted from Hall, *Characters, Profane*: "To matter of Religion his heart is a piece of dead flesh, without feeling of loue, of feare" (Dent).

'Tis not the figure cut in alabaster
Kneels at my husband's tomb. Awake, awake, man!
I do here put off all vain ceremony,
And only do appear to you a young widow   445
That claims you for her husband, and, like a widow,
I use but half a blush in't.
ANTONIO   Truth speak for me!
I will remain the constant sanctuary
Of your good name.
DUCHESS   I thank you, gentle love;
And, 'cause you shall not come to me in debt,   450
Being now my steward, here upon your lips
I sign your *Quietus est*.   [*Kisses him.*]
                    This you should have begged now.
I have seen children oft eat sweetmeats thus,
As fearful to devour them too soon.
ANTONIO   But for your brothers?
DUCHESS   Do not think of them: 455
    [*Embraces him.*]
All discord, without this circumference,
Is only to be pitied and not feared;
Yet, should they know it, time will easily
Scatter the tempest.
ANTONIO   These words should be mine,
And all the parts you have spoke, if some part of it   460
Would not have savored flattery.
DUCHESS   Kneel.
    [CARIOLA *comes from behind the arras.*]
ANTONIO   Hah?
DUCHESS   Be not amazed—this woman's of my counsel.
I have heard lawyers say, a contract in a chamber
Per verba de presenti is absolute marriage.
    [DUCHESS *and* ANTONIO *kneel.*]
Bless, heaven, this sacred Gordian, which let violence   465
Never untwine!

442–43. the figure . . . tomb: In funerary sculpture of the period, a man's tomb fre-
    quently included the kneeling figure of his widow (see Figure 1 and cover illustration).
452. *Quietus est:* the phrase used to signal the formal discharge of a debt, but also to
    refer to death as a settlement of the debt to nature. See note to 3.2.185 and cf. 4.2.172
    ("*Here your perfect peace is signed*").
456. circumference: i.e., her encircling arms.
460. parts: (1) parts of speech; (2) matter, particulars (Brown).
464. Per . . . presenti: "By words as from the present": the phrase used to describe clan-
    destine marriage vows, which lacked the sanction of the church but were still consid-
    ered legally binding.
465. Gordian: the legendary Gordian knot, which could not be undone until Alexander
    the Great cut it with his sword.

ANTONIO   And may our sweet affections, like the spheres,
Be still in motion—
DUCHESS   Quickening, and make
The like soft music—
ANTONIO   That we may imitate the loving palms,
Best emblem of a peaceful marriage,   470
That ne'er bore fruit divided.
DUCHESS   What can the church force more?
ANTONIO   That Fortune may not know an accident,
Either of joy or sorrow, to divide
Our fixed wishes!
DUCHESS   How can the church build faster?
We now are man and wife, and 'tis the church   475
That must but echo this. [*They rise.*] —Maid, stand apart.—
I now am blind.
ANTONIO   What's your conceit in this?
DUCHESS   I would have you lead your fortune by the hand
Unto your marriage-bed—
You speak in me this, for we now are one.   480
We'll only lie, and talk together, and plot
T'appease my humorous kindred; and, if you please,
Like the old tale in *Alexander and Lodowick,*
Lay a naked sword between us, keep us chaste.
Oh, let me shroud my blushes in your bosom,   485
Since 'tis the treasury of all my secrets.
CARIOLA [*Aside*]   Whether the spirit of greatness or of woman
Reign most in her, I know not, but it shows
A fearful madness: I owe her much of pity.   *Exeunt.*

---

467. spheres: the concentric spheres of the old Ptolemaic universe, whose perpetual motion was believed to create a sublime music (line 469), inaudible to mortal ears.
468. Quickening: rousing (one another) (*OED* v. 2); perhaps with a play on the *quickening* of a child in the womb.
469–71. palms . . . divided: a common figure. According to Pliny, palm trees were fruitful only in pairs.
472. know: experience, undergo.
474. faster: more firmly (with a play on "hand*fast*ing," another term describing informal nuptials).
477–78. I now . . . fortune: Fortune (like Cupid, the god of love) was conventionally depicted as blind.
477. conceit: fanciful, witty notion (*OED* n. 8).
482. humorous: ill-humored; capricious (*OED* a. 3a–b).
483. *Alexander and Lodowick:* title of a contemporary ballad and of a (now lost) play performed by the Admiral's Men in 1597, telling of two friends so alike that Lodowick was able to marry the Princess of Hungary in Alexander's name; to avoid betraying his friend, Lodowick placed a naked sword in the marriage bed between himself and the princess.
485. shroud: hide; but with more sinister resonances (cf. 4.2.168).

Act 2

2.1

[*Enter*] BOSOLA [*and*] CASTRUCHIO.

BOSOLA You say you would fain be taken for an eminent courtier?

CASTRUCHIO 'Tis the very main of my ambition.

BOSOLA Let me see: you have a reasonable good face for't already, and your nightcap expresses your ears sufficient largely. I would have you learn to twirl the strings of your 5 band with a good grace, and in a set speech, at th'end of every sentence, to hum three or four times, or blow your nose till it smart again, to recover your memory. When you come to be a president in criminal causes, if you smile upon a prisoner, hang him, but if you frown upon him and threaten him, let 10 him be sure to 'scape the gallows.

CASTRUCHIO I would be a very merry president.

BOSOLA Do not sup a-nights; 'twill beget you an admirable wit.

CASTRUCHIO Rather it would make me have a good stomach to quarrel, for they say your roaring boys eat meat seldom, and 15 that makes them so valiant. But how shall I know whether the people take me for an eminent fellow?

BOSOLA I will teach a trick to know it. Give out you lie a-dying, and if you hear the common people curse you, be sure you are taken for one of the prime nightcaps. 20

[*Enter*] *an* OLD LADY.

You come from painting now?

OLD LADY From what?

BOSOLA Why, from your scurvy face-physic. To behold thee not painted inclines somewhat near a miracle. These in thy face

---

2.1. The first part of this scene, until the Duchess's entry, does little to advance the plot but serves to establish Bosola in his role of satyr-satirist, like Vindice in Thomas Middleton's *The Revenger's Tragedy*—a savage critic of courtly corruption who is nevertheless implicated in the wickedness he denounces.

1. courtier: Cambridge suggests "one who attends a law-court" (i.e., a lawyer), but a deliberate ambiguity may be involved, with Bosola pretending to misunderstand Castruchio's ambition.

2. main: principal object, purpose (*OED* n. 6, 7).

4. nightcap: apparently referring to the white skullcap worn by sergeants-at-law (Lucas). **expresses . . . sufficiently:** pushes out your ears enough (to make you look like the ass you are).

6. band: collar, ruff, but here perhaps referring to a lawyer's tabs. However, Brown compares the foppish courtier Amorphus in Ben Jonson's *Cynthia's Revels*, who deliberately plays with his "band-string" (*Cynthia's Revels*, 5.4.158).

6. set speech: formal, prepared oration.

9. president: presiding magistrate, judge. **causes:** cases.

13. wit: intelligence (as well as, probably, wittiness).

15. roaring boys: rowdy swaggerers.

20. prime nightcaps: most eminent lawyers (see also note to 2.1.4).

23. scurvy face-physic: contemptible beauty therapy.

here were deep ruts and foul sloughs the last progress. There 25
was a lady in France that, having had the smallpox, flayed the
skin off her face to make it more level; and whereas before she
looked like a nutmeg-grater, after she resembled an abortive
hedgehog.

OLD LADY   Do you call this painting?   30

BOSOLA   No, no—but careening of an old morphewed lady,
scabbed to make her disembogue again. There's roughcast
phrase to your plastic.

OLD LADY   It seems you are well acquainted with my closet?

BOSOLA   One would suspect it for a shop of witchcraft, to find 35
in it the fat of serpents, spawn of snakes, Jews' spittle, and
their young children's ordure—and all these for the face. I
would sooner eat a dead pigeon, taken from the soles of the
feet of one sick of the plague, than kiss one of you fasting.
Here are two of you, whose sin of your youth is the very patri- 40
mony of the physician, makes him renew his foot-cloth with
the spring and change his high-prized courtesan with the fall
of the leaf. I do wonder you do not loathe yourselves. Observe
my meditation now:

What thing is in this outward form of man   45
To be beloved? We account it ominous
If nature do produce a colt, or lamb,
A fawn, or goat, in any limb resembling
A man, and fly from't as a prodigy.
Man stands amazed to see his deformity   50
In any other creature but himself;
But in our own flesh, though we bear diseases
Which have their true names only ta'en from beasts,
As the most ulcerous wolf and swinish measle,

---

25. **sloughs:** muddy potholes (*OED* n. 1). **the last progress:** (at the time of) the last royal tour through the country.
31. **careening:** scouring, scraping clean (usually of a ship's bottom). **morphewed:** with a leprous or scurfy skin.
32. **disembogue:** sail out of a river or strait into open sea (*OED* v. 1). **plastic:** fine sculptural modeling (referring ironically to her cosmetic repairs).
34. **closet:** private chamber.
37. **ordure:** excrement.
38–39. **pigeon . . . feet:** a standard treatment for the plague.
40–41. **sin . . . physician:** i.e., physicians make their living from those who contracted venereal disease in their youth.
41. **foot-cloth:** a large, richly ornamented cloth hung over the back of a horse as a mark of its rider's status.
44. **meditation:** devotional exercise (*OED* n. 2). As Cambridge notes, Bosola's switch from prose to verse gives rhetorical emphasis to his move from particular satire to generalized moralization in the *contemptus mundi* tradition.
54. **wolf:** name for various erosive diseases, including what, using the Latin equivalent, is now called *lupus*, but also anticipating lycanthropia—the madness that persuades Ferdinand he has become a wolf (5.2.6–19). **measle:** i.e., measles—here conflated with a skin disease with the same name suffered by pigs. Both were confused with *mesel* (= leper, leprous).

Though we are eaten up of lice and worms,   55
And though continually we bear about us
A rotten and dead body, we delight
To hide it in rich tissue. All our fear—
Nay, all our terror—is lest our physician
Should put us in the ground, to be made sweet.   60
   [*To* CASTRUCHIO] Your wife's gone to Rome. You two couple,
   and get you to the wells at Lucca, to recover your aches.
                  [*Exeunt* CASTRUCHIO *and* OLD LADY.]
I have other work on foot. I observe our duchess
Is sick a-days: she pukes; her stomach seethes,
The fins of her eyelids look most teeming blue,   65
She wanes i'th'cheek, and waxes fat i'th'flank;
And—contrary to our Italian fashion—
Wears a loose-bodied gown. There's somewhat in't.
I have a trick may chance discover it,
A pretty one: I have bought some apricots,   70
The first our spring yields.
      [*Enter*] ANTONIO [*and*] DELIO.
DELIO [*To* ANTONIO]   And so long since married?
  You amaze me.
ANTONIO   Let me seal your lips forever;
  For, did I think that anything but th'air
  Could carry these words from you, I should wish
  You had no breath at all.   75
      [*To* BOSOLA]   Now, sir, in your contemplation?
  You are studying to become a great wise fellow?
BOSOLA Oh, sir, the opinion of wisdom is a foul tetter that rep-
  utation runs all over a man's body. If simplicity direct us to have
  no evil, it directs us to a happy being; for the subtlest folly
  proceeds from the subtlest wisdom. Let me be simply honest.   80
ANTONIO I do understand your inside.
BOSOLA   Do you so?
ANTONIO Because you would not seem to appear to th'world
  Puffed up with your preferment, you continue

---

58. **tissue:** rich cloth (often woven with silver or gold).
62. **aches:** i.e., venereal disease (often called Neapolitan bone-ache).
65. **fins:** edges. **teeming blue:** i.e., as if she were pregnant.
68. **loose-bodied:** as worn by older women in England, but perhaps also suggesting mor-
    ally loose (Gibbons).
77. **opinion . . . wisdom:** adapted from Montaigne, *Essays* II, xii, pp. 186–93.
77. **tetter:** pustular skin eruption.
81. **inside:** inward nature (*OED* n. 2c). This appears to be the earliest recorded use of the
    word in this sense, though it also appears in Middleton and Rowley's *The Old Law*
    (ca. 1618–19), which *OED* mistakenly attributes to 1599.

This out-of-fashion melancholy. Leave it, leave it.

BOSOLA   Give me leave to be honest in any phrase, in any com-   85
pliment whatsoever. Shall I confess myself to you? I look no
higher than I can reach. They are the gods that must ride on
winged horses; a lawyer's mule of a slow pace will both suit my
disposition and business. For mark me: when a man's mind
rides faster than his horse can gallop, they quickly both tire.   90

ANTONIO   You would look up to heaven, but I think
The devil that rules i'th'air stands in your light.

BOSOLA   Oh, sir, you are lord of the ascendant, chief man with
the Duchess; a duke was your cousin-german removed. Say
you were lineally descended from King Pippin—or he himself: 95
what of this? Search the heads of the greatest rivers in the
world, you shall find them but bubbles of water. Some would
think the souls of princes were brought forth by some more
weighty cause than those of meaner persons. They are
deceived: there's the same hand to them; the like passions   100
sway them. The same reason that makes a vicar go to law for a
tithe-pig and undo his neighbors makes them spoil a whole
province and batter down goodly cities with the cannon.

   [*Enter*] DUCHESS [*with Ladies and Attendants*], RODERIGO,
   [*and*] GRISOLAN.

DUCHESS   Your arm, Antonio. Do I not grow fat?
I am exceeding short-winded. —Bosola,   105
I would have you, sir, provide for me a litter,
Such a one as the Duchess of Florence rode in.

BOSOLA   The Duchess used one when she was great with child.

DUCHESS   I think she did. [*To a Lady*] Come hither; mend my
   ruff—

---

84. out-of-fashion: presumably because his public parade of melancholy (see 1.1.73
and 271) has been rendered inappropriate, given his recent promotion. But there may
also be a glance at the play in which the theater's best-known melancholic was celebrated
as the "glass of fashion" (*Hamlet*, 3.1.152)—in which case "fashion" will also refer to
the black garb expressive of a melancholy disposition. Pope recorded a theatrical tradition that John Lowin (who played Bosola) included Hamlet among his performances—
as did Joseph Taylor, who seems to have inherited the part (along with the role of
Ferdinand) from Richard Burbage.
87–88. gods . . . horses: from Montaigne, *Essays*, I, xlii, 304. Marcus notes the irony
that the mythic winged horse, Pegasus, was in fact mastered by a mortal, Bellerophon.
92. devil . . . air: See Ephesians 2.2 in the Bishops Bible, where the devil is called "the
governour that ruleth in the ayre" (Brown).
93. lord of the ascendant: a play on the astrological term for the planet supposed to rule
in the rising house of the zodiac.
94. cousin-german removed: first cousin, once removed.
95. King Pippin: i.e., Pepin, king of the Franks (d. 768), father of Charlemagne.
96–103. Search . . . cannon: modeled on two passages in Montaigne, II, xii, 301 and II,
xii, 170–71. Cf. also Webster's dedication to this play.

Here! When? Thou art such a tedious lady, and   110
Thy breath smells of lemon peels. Would thou hadst done!
Shall I swoon under thy fingers? I am
So troubled with the mother!
BOSOLA [*Aside*]   I fear too much.
DUCHESS [*To* ANTONIO]   I have heard you say that the French
      courtiers
Wear their hats on 'fore the King.   115
ANTONIO   I have seen it.
DUCHESS   In the presence?
ANTONIO   Yes.
DUCHESS   Why should not we bring up that fashion?
'Tis ceremony, more than duty, that consists
In the removing of a piece of felt.   120
Be you the example to the rest o'th'court;
Put on your hat first.
ANTONIO   You must pardon me:
I have seen, in colder countries than in France,
Nobles stand bare to th'prince, and the distinction
Methought showed reverently.   125
BOSOLA   I have a present for your grace.
DUCHESS   For me, sir?
BOSOLA   Apricots, madam.
DUCHESS   Oh, sir, where are they?
I have heard of none to-year.
BOSOLA [*Aside*]   Good. Her color rises.
DUCHESS [*Taking the fruit.*]   Indeed, I thank you. They are
      wondrous fair ones.
What an unskilful fellow is our gardener!   130
We shall have none this month. [*She eats.*]
BOSOLA   Will not your grace pare them?
DUCHESS   No.
They taste of musk, methinks; indeed they do.
BOSOLA   I know not. Yet I wish your grace had pared 'em.
DUCHESS   Why?
BOSOLA   I forget to tell you the knave gard'ner—   135
Only to raise his profit by them the sooner—
Did ripen them in horse dung.

---

113. **the mother:** hysteria (supposed, as its etymology would suggest, to emanate from
the womb)—with an ironic hint of pregnancy, as Bosola's sarcastic aside makes clear.
116. Probably amphibious, this completes line 114, while beginning another (incomplete,
but metrically regular) line. "I have" requires elision.
122. **put . . . first:** a way of publicly enacting his new status as her husband, while also
keeping it secret.
128. **to-year:** this year (cf. today).
135–37. **I . . . horse dung:** cf. 1.1.279–80.

DUCHESS   Oh, you jest!
  [*To* ANTONIO] You shall judge. Pray, taste one.
ANTONIO   Indeed, madam,
  I do not love the fruit.
DUCHESS   Sir, you are loath
  To rob us of our dainties. [*To* BOSOLA] 'Tis a delicate fruit;   140
  They say they are restorative?
BOSOLA   'Tis a pretty art,
  This grafting.
DUCHESS   'Tis so—a bett'ring of nature.
BOSOLA   To make a pippin grow upon a crab,
  A damson on a blackthorn. [*Aside*] How greedily she eats
     them!
  A whirlwind strike off these bawd farthingales,   145
  For, but for that and the loose-bodied gown,
  I should have discovered apparently
  The young springal cutting a caper in her belly!
DUCHESS   I thank you, Bosola: they were right good ones—
  If they do not make me sick.
ANTONIO   How now, madam?   150
DUCHESS   This green fruit and my stomach are not friends.
  How they swell me!
BOSOLA [*Aside*]   Nay, you are too much swelled already.
DUCHESS   Oh, I am in an extreme cold sweat.
BOSOLA   I am very sorry.
DUCHESS   Lights to my chamber! O good Antonio,
  I fear I am undone.
DELIO   Lights there, lights!   155
            Exit DUCHESS[, *Ladies, Attendants, and* BOSOLA].
ANTONIO   O my most trusty Delio, we are lost!
  I fear she's fall'n in labor, and there's left
  No time for her remove.
DELIO   Have you prepared
  Those ladies to attend her, and procured
  That politic safe conveyance for the midwife   160
  Your duchess plotted?
ANTONIO   I have.
DELIO   Make use then of this forced occasion:

---

140. **delicate:** pleasing to the palate, delicious (*OED* a. 1b).
143–44. **To make . . . blackthorn:** Bosola implies that the Duchess's womb is about to
   bear fruit and that her pregnancy results from a mixing of social kinds.
143. **pippin:** eating apple. **crab:** crab apple.
145. **bawd farthingales:** hooped petticoats that encourage sexual license.
148. **springal . . . caper:** stripling who frolics.
158. **remove:** departure (*OED* n. 5a).
160. **politic safe conveyance:** artfully contrived secret means of transport.

Give out that Bosola hath poisoned her
With these apricots; that will give some color
For her keeping close.
ANTONIO   Fie, fie! The physicians   165
Will then flock to her.
DELIO   For that you may pretend
She'll use some prepared antidote of her own,
Lest the physicians should re-poison her.
ANTONIO   I am lost in amazement. I know not what to think
on't.   *Exeunt.*

2.2

[*Enter*] BOSOLA.
BOSOLA   So, so: there's no question but her tetchiness and most
vulturous eating of the apricots are apparent signs of breeding.
          [*Enter*] OLD LADY.
Now?
OLD LADY   I am in haste, sir.
BOSOLA [*Preventing her leaving.*]   There was a young waiting-   5
woman had a monstrous desire to see the glass-house.
OLD LADY   Nay, pray let me go.
BOSOLA   And it was only to know what strange instrument it
was should swell up a glass to the fashion of a woman's belly.
OLD LADY   I will hear no more of the glass-house. You are still   10
abusing women?
BOSOLA   Who, I? No, only—by the way, now and then—mention
your frailties. The orange tree bears ripe and green fruit and
blossoms all together; and some of you give entertainment for
pure love—but more for more precious reward. The lusty   15
spring smells well, but drooping autumn tastes well. If we
have the same golden showers that rained in the time of Jupiter the Thunderer, you have the same Danaës still, to hold
up their laps to receive them. Didst thou never study the
mathematics?   20
OLD LADY   What's that, sir?
BOSOLA   Why, to know the trick how to make many lines meet
in one center. Go, go! Give your foster daughters good

---

164. **color:** pretext.
165. **close:** secluded, shut away (*OED* a. 4).
2. **breeding:** pregnancy.
6. **glass-house:** glass factory.
14. **give entertainment:** offer sexual favors (see Williams, p. 115).
15–16. **The lusty . . . tastes well:** the pleasures of youth may seem more attractive, but
older lovers gain richer rewards.
17–19. **golden . . . receive them:** cf. 1.1.240–41. Danaë's shower of gold was often used
as an allegory for commercial sex.
22. **lines:** bawdy pun on *loins* (see Williams, p. 189).
23. **center:** i.e., a whore's sexual organs.

counsel: tell them that the devil takes delight to hang at a
woman's girdle, like a false, rusty watch, that she cannot dis- 25
cern how the time passes.   [*Exit* OLD LADY.]
        [*Enter*] ANTONIO, DELIO, RODERIGO[, *and*] GRISOLAN
ANTONIO   Shut up the court gates!
RODERIGO   Why, sir? What's the danger?
ANTONIO   Shut up the posterns presently, and call
    All the officers o'th'court!
GRISOLAN   I shall, instantly.   [*Exit*]
ANTONIO   Who keeps the key o'th'park gate?
RODERIGO   Forobosco.   30
ANTONIO   Let him bring't presently.
                                [*Exit* RODERIGO.]
        [*Enter*] SERVANTS.
1 SERVANT   O gentlemen o'th'court, the foulest treason!
BOSOLA [*Aside*]   If that these apricots should be poisoned now,
    Without my knowledge!
1 SERVANT   There was taken even now
    A Switzer in the Duchess' bedchamber.
2 SERVANT   A Switzer!   35
1 SERVANT   With a pistol in his great codpiece.
BOSOLA   Ha, ha, ha!
1 SERVANT   The codpiece was the case for't.
2 SERVANT   There was
    A cunning traitor! Who would have searched his codpiece?
1 SERVANT   True, if he had kept out of the ladies' chambers.
    And all the molds of his buttons were leaden bullets.   40
2 SERVANT   Oh, wicked cannibal! A firelock in's cod-piece?
1 SERVANT   'Twas a French plot, upon my life.
2 SERVANT   To see what the devil can do!
        [*Re-enter* RODERIGO.]
ANTONIO   All the officers here?
SERVANTS   We are.
ANTONIO   Gentlemen,
    We have lost much plate, you know; and but this evening 45
    Jewels to the value of four thousand ducats
    Are missing in the Duchess' cabinet.

28. posterns: side entrances.
35. Switzer: Swiss mercenary.
36. pistol: punning on *pizzle*=penis (Marcus). codpiece: ornamental cover for male
    genitals.
41–42. firelock . . . French plot: "Firelock"=flintlock pistol, but playing on *fire* as a
    term for the pain of syphilis, otherwise known as the French disease (see Williams,
    pp. 125, 134).
45. plate: silver or gold utensils.

Are the gates shut?

1 SERVANT   Yes.

ANTONIO   'Tis the Duchess' pleasure
Each officer be locked into his chamber
Till the sunrising, and to send the keys   50
Of all their chests and of their outward doors
Into her bedchamber. She is very sick.

RODERIGO   At her pleasure.

ANTONIO   She entreats you take't not ill.
The innocent shall be the more approved by it.

BOSOLA   Gentleman o'th'woodyard, where's your Switzer now?   55

1 SERVANT   By this hand, 'twas credibly reported by one
o'th'black-guard.

                    [*Exeunt all except* ANTONIO *and* DELIO.]

DELIO   How fares it with the Duchess?

ANTONIO   She's exposed
Unto the worst of torture, pain, and fear.

DELIO   Speak to her all happy comfort.

ANTONIO   How I do play the fool with mine own danger!   60
You are this night, dear friend, to post to Rome.
My life lies in your service.

DELIO   Do not doubt me.

ANTONIO   Oh, 'tis far from me—and yet fear presents me
Somewhat that looks like danger.

DELIO   Believe it,
'Tis but the shadow of your fear, no more.   65
How superstitiously we mind our evils!
The throwing down salt, or crossing of a hare,
Bleeding at nose, the stumbling of a horse,
Or singing of a cricket, are of power
To daunt whole man in us. Sir, fare you well.   70
I wish you all the joys of a blessed father;
And, for my faith, lay this unto your breast:
Old friends, like old swords, still are trusted best.   [*Exit.*]
          [*Enter* CARIOLA.]

CARIOLA   Sir, you are the happy father of a son.
Your wife commends him to you.   75

---

54. **approved:** commended, esteemed (*OED* ppl.a. 3); earliest example of this usage.
55. **Gentleman o'th'woodyard:** i.e., low-ranking menial servants (cf. 2.5.43), parodying 1
    Servant's "gentlemen o'th'court" (2.2.32).
56. **black-guard:** lowest menials, kitchen knaves (*OED* n. 1).
62. **my life . . . service:** Delio is being sent to discover what the Cardinal may know of
    Antonio's affair with the Duchess, hence his overtures to the Cardinal's mistress in 2.4.
67–69. **throwing . . . cricket:** signs of ill-omen.
72. **lay . . . breast:** take this to heart.

ANTONIO   Blessèd comfort!
    For heaven sake, tend her well. I'll presently
    Go set a figure for 's nativity.   *Exeunt.*

2.3

    [*Enter*] BOSOLA [*with a dark lantern*].
BOSOLA   Sure I did hear a woman shriek. List! Hah?
    And the sound came, if I received it right,
    From the Duchess' lodgings. There's some stratagem
    In the confining all our courtiers
    To their several wards. I must have part of it;   5
    My intelligence will freeze else. List, again!
    It may be 'twas the melancholy bird,
    Best friend of silence and of solitariness,
    The owl, that screamed so.
        [*Enter*] ANTONIO [*with a horoscope*].
                                  Hah! Antonio?
ANTONIO   I heard some noise. Who's there? What art thou?   10
    Speak.
BOSOLA   Antonio? Put not your face nor body
    To such a forced expression of fear.
    I am Bosola, your friend.
ANTONIO   Bosola?
    [*Aside*] This mole does undermine me. [*Aloud*] Heard you not
    A noise even now?
BOSOLA   From whence?
ANTONIO   From the Duchess' lodging.   15
BOSOLA   Not I. Did you?
ANTONIO   I did, or else I dreamed.
BOSOLA   Let's walk towards it.
ANTONIO   No. It may be 'twas
    But the rising of the wind.
BOSOLA   Very likely.
    Methinks 'tis very cold, and yet you sweat.
    You look wildly.
ANTONIO   I have been setting a figure   20
    For the Duchess' jewels.

79. set . . . nativity: cast his horoscope.
2.3. SD. *dark lantern*: lantern with a device for concealing its light.
5. wards: posts, assigned rooms. part of it: be informed about it.
6. List: listen.
20–21. setting . . . jewels: using astrology to track down the Duchess's missing jewels.

BOSOLA   Ah—and how falls your question?
  Do you find it radical?
ANTONIO   What's that to you?
  'Tis rather to be questioned what design,
  When all men were commanded to their lodgings,
  Makes you a night-walker.
BOSOLA   In sooth, I'll tell you: 25
  Now all the court's asleep, I thought the devil
  Had least to do here; I came to say my prayers—
  And if it do offend you I do so,
  You are a fine courtier.
ANTONIO [*Aside*]   This fellow will undo me.
  [*To him*] You gave the Duchess apricots today: 30
  Pray heaven they were not poisoned.
BOSOLA   Poisoned? A Spanish fig
  For the imputation!
ANTONIO   Traitors are ever confident
  Till they are discovered. There were jewels stol'n too.
  In my conceit, none are to be suspected
  More than yourself.
BOSOLA   You are a false steward.   35
ANTONIO   Saucy slave! I'll pull thee up by the roots.
BOSOLA   Maybe the ruin will crush you to pieces.
ANTONIO   You are an impudent snake indeed, sir:
  Are you scarce warm, and do you show your sting?
[BOSOLA . . .]
ANTONIO   You libel well, sir.
BOSOLA   No, sir. Copy it out,   40
  And I will set my hand to't.
ANTONIO [*aside*]   My nose bleeds.
    [*Takes out handkerchief and drops horoscope.*]
  One that were superstitious would count
  This ominous, when it merely comes by chance.
  Two letters that are wrought here for my name
  Are drowned in blood!   45
  Mere accident. [*To* BOSOLA] For you, sir, I'll take order:
  I'th'morn you shall be safe. [*Aside*] 'Tis that must color

---

22. **radical:** fit to be judged, able to be decided (astrological term).
25. **night-walker:** one who walks at night with criminal intentions (*OED* n. 1)
29. **fine courtier:** i.e., someone scornful of pious practice.
31. **Spanish fig:** obscene gesture made by thrusting the thumb between two fingers (deriving originally from play on Italian *fico* = fig, and *fica* = vagina).
39. Q prints two successive speech-prefixes for Antonio at lines 38 and 40, suggesting (as Lucas first noted) that a short speech from Bosola has been dropped here.
44–45. **Two letters . . . blood:** i.e., the embroidered monogram on his blood-soaked handkerchief (Cambridge).
47. **safe:** safely shut away. **color:** disguise, conceal (*OED* v. 3).

Her lying-in. [*To* BOSOLA] Sir, this door you pass not:
I do not hold it fit that you come near
The Duchess' lodgings till you have quit yourself.   50
[*Aside*] *The great are like the base; nay, they are the same,*
When they seek shameful ways to avoid shame.   *Exit.*
BOSOLA   Antonio hereabout did drop a paper.
Some of your help, false friend. Oh, here it is.
What's here? A child's nativity calculated?   55
[*Reads:*] *The Duchess was delivered of a son 'tween the hours*
twelve and one in the night, Anno Dom. 1504—that's this
year—*decimo nono Decembris*—that's this night—*taken*
according to the meridian of Malfi—that's our duchess. Happy
discovery! *The Lord of the first house, being combust in the*   60
ascendant, signifies short life; and Mars being in a human sign,
joined to the tail of the Dragon, in the eighth house, doth
threaten a violent death. Caetera non scrutantur.
Why now, 'tis most apparent! This precise fellow
Is the Duchess' bawd. I have it to my wish: 65
This is a parcel of intelligency
Our courtiers were cased up for! It needs must follow
That I must be committed on pretence
Of poisoning her—which I'll endure, and laugh at.
If one could find the father now! But that   70
Time will discover. Old Castruchio
I'th'morning posts to Rome; by him I'll send
A letter that shall make her brothers' galls
O'erflow their livers. This was a thrifty way!
Though Lust do mask in ne'er so strange disguise,   75
She's oft found witty, but is never wise.   [*Exit.*]

---

50. quit: exonerated.
54. false friend: i.e., the dark lantern.
56. For a detailed exposition of the horoscope, see Cambridge. In fact, as editors have
   pointed out, Antonio's elder son proves to be his only surviving child at the end of the
   play.
58. *decimo nono Decembris:* December 19.
60. combust: If the ruling planet moved to close to the sun, its influence was burned up.
61. human sign: i.e., Aquarius, Gemini, Virgo, or Sagittarius.
63. *Caetera non scrutantur:* the remainder [of the horoscope] is not examined.
64. precise: strict, punctilious.
67. cased up: shut away.
68. committed: sent to prison.
72. posts: hurries off.
73–74. make . . . livers: fill them with bitter rage. The liver was the source of gall (otherwise known as black bile, or melancholy).

2.4

[*Enter*] CARDINAL and JULIA.

CARDINAL   Sit. Thou art my best of wishes: prithee tell me
  What trick didst thou invent to come to Rome
  Without thy husband.
JULIA   Why, my lord, I told him
  I came to visit an old anchorite
  Here, for devotion.
CARDINAL   Thou art a witty false one—   5
  I mean, to him.
JULIA   You have prevailed with me
  Beyond my strongest thoughts: I would not now
  Find you inconstant.
CARDINAL   Do not put thyself
  To such a voluntary torture, which proceeds
  Out of your own guilt.
JULIA   How, my lord?
CARDINAL   You fear   10
  My constancy because you have approved
  Those giddy and wild turnings in yourself.
JULIA   Did you e'er find them?
CARDINAL   Sooth, generally for women,
  A man might strive to make glass malleable
  Ere he should make them fixed.
JULIA   So, my lord.   15
CARDINAL   We had need go borrow that fantastic glass
  Invented by Galileo the Florentine,
  To view another spacious world i'th'moon,
  And look to find a constant woman there.
JULIA [*Weeping.*]   This is very well, my lord.
CARDINAL   Why do you weep?   20
  Are tears your justification? The selfsame tears
  Will fall into your husband's bosom, lady,
  With a loud protestation that you love him
  Above the world. Come, I'll love you wisely—

---

4. anchorite: hermit. Playing on the fact that the supposedly pious Cardinal is the real
object of her "devotion." Cf. 3.2.101–03.
11. approved: put to the test, tried out; sanctioned (*OED* v. 8; 5).
12. giddy: crazy; flighty, inconstant (*OED* v. 1a; 3a).
13. generally for: universally among.
16. fantastic glass: i.e., the telescope recently made famous by Galileo.
19. constant woman there: especially improbable because the changeable moon was a
symbol of inconstancy.
21. justification: vindication, defense (*OED* n. 3); but probably also playing on the theological sense: "the action whereby man is justified, or freed from the penalty of sin"
(*OED* n. 4).

That's jealously, since I am very certain   25
You cannot me make cuckold.
JULIA   I'll go home
To my husband.
CARDINAL   You may thank me, lady,
I have taken you off your melancholy perch,
Bore you upon my fist, and showed you game,
And let you fly at it. I pray thee, kiss me.   30
When thou wast with thy husband, thou wast watched
Like a tame elephant—still you are to thank me—
Thou hadst only kisses from him, and high feeding,
But what delight was that? 'Twas just like one
That hath a little fing'ring on the lute,   35
Yet cannot tune it. Still you are to thank me.
JULIA   You told me of a piteous wound i'th'heart,
And a sick liver, when you wooed me first,
And spake like one in physic.
CARDINAL   Who's that?
          [*Enter*] SERVANT.
[*To* JULIA] Rest firm—for my affection to thee,   40
Lightning moves slow to't.
SERVANT   Madam, a gentleman
That's come post from Malfi desires to see you.
CARDINAL   Let him enter. I'll withdraw.   *Exit.*
SERVANT   He says
Your husband, old Castruchio, is come to Rome,
Most pitifully tired with riding post.   [*Exit.*] 45
          [*Enter*] DELIO.
JULIA   Signor Delio! [*Aside*] 'Tis one of my old suitors.
DELIO   I was bold to come and see you.
JULIA   Sir, you are welcome.
DELIO   Do you lie here?
JULIA   Sure, your own experience
Will satisfy you, no: our Roman prelates
Do not keep lodging for ladies.
DELIO   Very well.   50
I have brought you no commendations from your husband,
For I know none by him.

---

29. **game:** (1) the falcon's quarry; (2) wantonness (Williams, p. 137).
31. **watched:** tended (*OED* v. 13a).
33. **high feeding:** rich diet.
35. **fing'ring:** For its phallic significance, see Williams p. 125. **lute:** a figure for female sexuality; cf. *viol* Williams pp. 325–26.
38. **sick liver:** i.e., one suffering from love melancholy (cf. 1.1.290, 2.3.73–74).
39. **in physic:** under medical treatment.

JULIA   I hear he's come to Rome?
DELIO   I never knew man and beast, of a horse and a knight,
   So weary of each other—if he had had a good back,
   He would have undertook to have borne his horse,   55
   His breech was so pitifully sore.
JULIA   Your laughter
   Is my pity.
DELIO   Lady, I know not whether
   You want money, but I have brought you some.
JULIA   From my husband?
DELIO   No, from mine own allowance.
JULIA   I must hear the condition, ere I be bound to take it.   60
DELIO   Look on't, 'tis gold. Hath it not a fine color?
JULIA   I have a bird more beautiful.
DELIO   Try the sound on't.
JULIA   A lute string far exceeds it.
   It hath no smell, like cassia, or civet,   65
   Nor is it physical, though some fond doctors
   Persuade us seeth't in cullises. I'll tell you,
   This is a creature bred by—
        [Enter] SERVANT.
SERVANT   Your husband's come,
   Hath delivered a letter to the Duke of Calabria
   That, to my thinking, hath put him out of his wits.   [Exit.] 70
JULIA   Sir, you hear?
   Pray let me know your business and your suit
   As briefly as can be.
DELIO   With good speed. I would wish you—
   At such time as you are non-resident
   With your husband—my mistress.   75
JULIA   Sir, I'll go ask my husband if I shall,
   And straight return your answer.   Exit.
DELIO   Very fine!
   Is this her wit or honesty that speaks thus?

---

54. **good back:** hinting at Castruchio's impotence.
56. **breech:** buttocks (*OED* n. 4).
63. Amphibious line.
64. **lute string:** glancing at the Cardinal's figure for his own erotic attentions to her (lines 34–36).
65. **cassia . . . civet:** perfumes derived from a cinnamon-like plant and from the civet cat.
66. **physical:** medicinal. **fond:** foolish.
67. **seeth't in cullisses:** boil it in a broth.
68. As the servant interrupts, Julia is presumably about to utter some truism about the viciousness of gold—"bred by the Devil," perhaps.
70. **out of his wits:** the first hint of the madness that will overcome Ferdinand in Act 3.
78. **honesty:** honor, chastity (*OED* n. 1a, 3b).

I heard one say the Duke was highly moved.
With a letter sent from Malfi. I do fear   80
Antonio is betrayed. How fearfully
Shows his ambition now! Unfortunate Fortune!
They pass through whirlpools, and deep woes do shun,
Who the event weigh, ere the action's done.   *Exit.*

2.5

[*Enter*] CARDINAL, *and* FERDINAND, *with a letter.*
FERDINAND   I have this night digged up a mandrake.
CARDINAL   Say you?
FERDINAND   And I am grown mad with't.
CARDINAL   What's the prodigy?
FERDINAND [*Showing him the letter.*]   Read there—a sister
    damned! She's loose i'th'hilts,
  Grown a notorious strumpet.
CARDINAL   Speak lower.
FERDINAND   Lower?
  Rogues do not whisper't now, but seek to publish't,   5
  As servants do the bounty of their lords,
  Aloud, and with a covetous, searching eye
  To mark who note them. Oh, confusion seize her!
  She hath had most cunning bawds to serve her turn,
  And more secure conveyances for lust   10
  Than towns of garrison for service.
CARDINAL   Is't possible?
  Can this be certain?
FERDINAND   Rhubarb, oh, for rhubarb
  To purge this choler! Here's the cursèd day
  To prompt my memory, and here't shall stick
  Till of her bleeding heart I make a sponge   15
  To wipe it out.
CARDINAL   Why do you make yourself
  So wild a tempest?
FERDINAND   Would I could be one,

---

1. **mandrake:** Seen as humanoid in its forked shape, this medicinal root, when pulled
from the ground, allegedly shrieked so hideously as to cause madness or even death.
3. **loose i'th'hilts:** unchaste—phallic sword metaphor (cf. 1.1.321–27).
8. **confusion:** ruin, perdition (*OED* n. 1).
11. **service:** (1) supplies; (2) sexual service (as of a mare by a stallion).
12. **rhubarb:** a well-known purgative.
13. **choler:** anger, but also one of the four bodily humors that (along with melancholy,
blood, and phlegm) made up the human constitution, so that the idea of purgation is to
be taken literally. **cursèd day:** i.e, that described in the child's horoscope, which Bosola
must have included with his letter.
14. **here't:** i.e., in his heart.

That I might toss her palace 'bout her ears,
Root up her goodly forests, blast her meads,
And lay her general territory as waste   20
As she hath done her honors!

CARDINAL   Shall our blood,
The royal blood of Aragon and Castile,
Be thus attainted?

FERDINAND   Apply desperate physic:
We must not now use balsamum, but fire,
The smarting cupping-glass, for that's the mean   25
To purge infected blood, such blood as hers.
There is a kind of pity in mine eye;
I'll give it to my handkercher; and, now 'tis here,
I'll bequeath this to her bastard.

CARDINAL   What to do?

FERDINAND   Why, to make soft lint for his mother's wounds,   30
When I have hewed her to pieces.

CARDINAL   Curs'd creature!
Unequal Nature, to place women's hearts
So far upon the left side!

FERDINAND   Foolish men,
That e'er will trust their honor in a bark
Made of so slight, weak bulrush as is woman,   35
Apt every minute to sink it!

CARDINAL   Thus
Ignorance, when it hath purchased honor,
It cannot wield it.

FERDINAND   Methinks I see her laughing—
Excellent hyena! Talk to me somewhat, quickly,
Or my imagination will carry me   40
To see her in the shameful act of sin.

CARDINAL   With whom?

FERDINAND   Happily with some strong-thighed
      bargeman,
Or one o'th'woodyard that can quoit the sledge,
Or toss the bar—or else some lovely squire

19–20. The equation between the body of the land and the body of its prince was a commonplace of political discourse and iconography.
19. **meads:** meadows.
23. **attainted:** tainted, sullied; infected, corrupted with disease or poison (*OED* n. 9–10).
24. **balsamum:** balm.
25. **cupping-glass:** hot glass used to extract blood by making a vacuum on the skin.
29. **this:** i.e., the handkerchief soaked in his tears of pity.
32. **Unequal:** unjust.
33. **left:** i.e, the sinister, ill-omened side.
34. **bark:** boat.
39. **hyena:** known for its cackling laugh; but also a type of female treachery (Cambridge).
43. **one o'th'woodyard:** cf. 2.2.56. **quoit the sledge:** throw the hammer: a traditional sport.
44. **toss the bar:** toss the caber (see note to line 43).

That carries coals up to her privy lodgings.   45
CARDINAL   You fly beyond your reason.
FERDINAND   Go to, mistress!
  'Tis not your whore's milk that shall quench my wildfire,
  But your whore's blood.
CARDINAL   How idly shows this rage, which carries you,
  As men conveyed by witches, through the air   50
  On violent whirlwinds! This intemperate noise
  Fitly resembles deaf men's shrill discourse,
  Who talk aloud, thinking all other men
  To have their imperfection.
FERDINAND   Have not you
  My palsy?
CARDINAL   Yes; I can be angry   55
  Without this rupture. There is not in nature
  A thing that makes man so deformed, so beastly,
  As doth intemperate anger. Chide yourself:
  You have divers men who never yet expressed
  Their strong desire of rest but by unrest,   60
  By vexing of themselves. Come, put yourself
  In tune.
FERDINAND   So. I will only study to seem
  The thing I am not. I could kill her now,
  In you, or in myself; for I do think
  It is some sin in us heaven doth revenge   65
  By her.
CARDINAL   Are you stark mad?
FERDINAND   I would have their bodies
  Burnt in a coal-pit with the ventage stopped
  That their cursed smoke might not ascend to heaven;
  Or dip the sheets they lie'n in pitch or sulfur,
  Wrap them in't, and then light them like a match;   70
  Or else to boil their bastard to a cullis,
  And give't his lecherous father to renew
  The sin of his back.
CARDINAL   I'll leave you.
FERDINAND   Nay, I have done.

---

55. palsy: here shaking-palsy (the uncontrollable trembling produced by his rage).
59. divers: many.
61–62. put . . . tune: In its ideal state, the human microcosm was supposed to be governed by a harmony matching the "music of the spheres" that governed the macrocosm
  (the universe).
67. coal-pit: charcoal pit. **ventage stopped:** vents blocked.
69–70. modeled on a passage in Painter (p. 35), where Otho, Prince of Urbino, inflicts
  this torture on one of his servants for sleeping late.
71. cullis: strong meat broth.
73. sin of his back: i.e., fornication.

I am confident, had I been damned in hell
And should have heard of this, it would have put me   75
Into a cold sweat. In, in. I'll go sleep—
Till I know who leaps my sister, I'll not stir;
That known, I'll find scorpions to string my whips,
And fix her in a general eclipse.   *Exeunt.*

Act 3

3.1

[*Enter*] ANTONIO *and* DELIO.

ANTONIO   Our noble friend, my most belovèd Delio,
    Oh, you have been a stranger long at court.
    Came you along with the Lord Ferdinand?
DELIO   I did, sir; and how fares your noble duchess?
ANTONIO   Right fortunately well. She's an excellent   5
    Feeder of pedigrees: since you last saw her,
    She hath had two children more, a son and daughter.
DELIO   Methinks 'twas yesterday. Let me but wink
    And not behold your face—which to mine eye
    Is somewhat leaner—verily I should dream   10
    It were within this half hour.
ANTONIO   You have not been in law, friend Delio,
    Nor in prison, nor a suitor at the court,
    Nor begged the reversion of some great man's place,
    Nor troubled with an old wife, which doth make   15
    Your time so insensibly hasten.
DELIO   Pray, sir, tell me,
    Hath not this news arrived yet to the ear
    Of the Lord Cardinal?
ANTONIO   I fear it hath.
    The Lord Ferdinand, that's newly come to court,
    Doth bear himself right dangerously.
DELIO   Pray, why?   20
ANTONIO   He is so quiet that he seems to sleep

---

77. **leaps:** fucks.
78. **scorpions:** perhaps meant literally, but scorpions were also rowel-like spikes attached
    to whips for particularly brutal scourging.
8. **wink:** see note to 1.1.339.
10–11. **verily . . . half hour:** A self-referential joke about the improbability of theatrical
    time. At the Blackfriars, for which the play was probably written, music played between
    the acts, making Delio's estimate approximately correct.
14. **reversion . . . place:** right of succession to some powerful courtier's office.
15–16. **which . . . hasten:** which accounts for the imperceptible slowness with which
    time moves for you.

The tempest out, as dormice do in winter.
Those houses that are haunted are most still,
Till the devil be up.
DELIO   What say the common people?
ANTONIO   The common rabble do directly say   25
She is a strumpet.
DELIO   And your graver heads,
Which would be politic, what censure they?
ANTONIO   They do observe I grow to infinite purchase.
The left-hand way; and all suppose the Duchess
Would amend it if she could—for, say they,   30
Great princes, though they grudge their officers
Should have such large and unconfinèd means
To get wealth under them, will not complain,
Lest thereby they should make them odious
Unto the people. For other obligation   35
Of love or marriage between her and me
They never dream of.
        [*Enter*] FERDINAND [*and*] DUCHESS.
DELIO [*Aside to* ANTONIO]   The Lord Ferdinand
Is going to bed.
FERDINAND [*To* DUCHESS]   I'll instantly to bed,
For I am weary. I am to bespeak
A husband for you.
DUCHESS   For me, sir? Pray, who is't?   40
FERDINAND   The great Count Malateste.
DUCHESS   Fie upon him!
A count? He's a mere stick of sugar candy:
You may look quite through him. When I choose
A husband, I will marry for your honor.
FERDINAND   You shall do well in't. [*To* ANTONIO] How is't,
worthy Antonio?   45
DUCHESS [*To* FERDINAND]   But, sir, I am to have private
    conference with you
About a scandalous report is spread
Touching mine honor.
FERDINAND [*To* DUCHESS]   Let me be ever deaf to't:

---

23. **still**: silent.
25. **directly**: plainly.
27. **politic**: diplomatic. **what censure they?**: what opinion do they express?
28. **purchase**: wealth.
29. **left-hand**: sinister, underhanded.
31–35. **Great . . . people**: close paraphrase of Donne, *Ignatius his Conclave*, p. 92 (Dent).
39. **bespeak**: arrange (*OED* v. 5).

One of Pasquil's paper bullets, court calumny,
A pestilent air which princes' palaces   50
Are seldom purged of. Yet, say that it were true—
I pour it in your bosom—my fixed love
Would strongly excuse, extenuate, nay, deny
Faults, were they apparent in you. Go, be safe
In your own innocency.
DUCHESS   Oh, blessed comfort!   55
This deadly air is purged.   *Exeunt [all but* FERDINAND].
FERDINAND   Her guilt treads on
Hot burning coulters.
          [*Enter*] BOSOLA.
                              Now, Bosola,
How thrives our intelligence?
BOSOLA   Sir, uncertainly.
'Tis rumored she hath had three bastards, but
By whom, we may go read i'th'stars.
FERDINAND   Why, some   60
Hold opinion all things are written there.
BOSOLA   Yes, if we could find spectacles to read them.
I do suspect there hath been some sorcery
Used on the Duchess.
FERDINAND   Sorcery? To what purpose?
BOSOLA   To make her dote on some desertless fellow   65
She shames to acknowledge.
FERDINAND   Can your faith give way
To think there's power in potions or in charms
To make us love, whether we will or no?
BOSOLA   Most certainly.
FERDINAND   Away! These are mere gulleries, horrid things   70
Invented by some cheating mountebanks
To abuse us. Do you think that herbs or charms
Can force the will? Some trials have been made
In this foolish practice, but the ingredients
Were lenitive poisons, such as are of force   75

---

49. **Pasquil:** a 15th-century cobbler notorious for his harsh tongue: satires and libels were customarily fixed to his statue in Rome.
57. **coulters:** plowshares. Walking on red-hot plowshares had been a form of trial-by-ordeal in medieval England (Brown).
65. **desertless:** undeserving. **fellow:** person of no esteem (*OED* n. 10c)
70. **gulleries:** impostures, tricks.
71. **mountebanks:** charlatans.
72. **abuse:** deceive (*OED* v. 4a).
73. **will:** with the secondary sense of sexual desire (Williams, pp. 337–38).
75. **lenitive:** with a soothing taste.

To make the patient mad; and straight the witch
Swears, by equivocation, they are in love.
The witchcraft lies in her rank blood. This night
I will force confession from her. You told me
You had got, within these two days, a false key   80
Into her bedchamber?
BOSOLA   I have.
FERDINAND   As I would wish.
BOSOLA   What do you intend to do?
FERDINAND   Can you guess?
BOSOLA   No.
FERDINAND   Do not ask, then.
He that can compass me and know my drifts
May say he hath put a girdle 'bout the world   85
And sounded all her quicksands.
BOSOLA   I do not
Think so.
FERDINAND   What do you think, then, pray?
BOSOLA   That you
Are your own chronicle too much, and grossly
Flatter yourself.
FERDINAND   Give me thy hand, I thank thee:
I never gave pension but to flatterers   90
Till I entertainèd thee. Farewell.
That friend a great man's ruin strongly checks
Who rails into his belief all his defects.   *Exeunt.*

3.2

[*Enter*] DUCHESS, ANTONIO, [*and*] CARIOLA.
DUCHESS [*To* CARIOLA]   Bring me the casket hither, and
     the glass.
[*To* ANTONIO] You get no lodging here, tonight, my lord.
ANTONIO   Indeed, I must persuade one.
DUCHESS   Very good.
I hope in time 'twill grow into a custom,
That noblemen shall come with cap and knee   5

---

78. rank: rebellious; lustful (*OED* a. 1; 13).
84. compass: hem in; fully understand (*OED* v. 6, 10). **drifts:** intentions, plots (*OED* n. 4a, 5).
93. *rails . . . defects*: forces him to recognize his own weaknesses by railing at them.
1. casket . . . glass: The Duchess calls for her jewelry box and mirror to prepare herself for bed.
5. cap and knee: A noblemen would doff his cap and kneel only to a prince; a wife, on the other hand, was expected to defer to her husband as ruler of the household.

To purchase a night's lodging of their wives.
ANTONIO   I must lie here.
DUCHESS   Must? You are a Lord of Misrule!
ANTONIO   Indeed, my rule is only in the night.
DUCHESS   To what use will you put me?
ANTONIO   We'll sleep together.
DUCHESS   Alas, what pleasure can two lovers find in sleep?   10
CARIOLA   My Lord, I lie with her often, and I know
   She'll much disquiet you.
ANTONIO [*To the* DUCHESS]   See, you are complained of.
CARIOLA   For she's the sprawling'st bedfellow.
ANTONIO   I shall like her
   The better for that.
CARIOLA   Sir, shall I ask you a question?   15
ANTONIO   I pray thee, Cariola.
CARIOLA   Wherefore still when you lie with my lady
   Do you rise so early?
ANTONIO   Laboring men
   Count the clock oftenest, Cariola,
   Are glad when their task's ended.
DUCHESS   I'll stop your mouth.   20
                                 [*Kisses him.*]
ANTONIO   Nay, that's but one: Venus had two soft doves
   To draw her chariot; I must have another. [*Kisses her.*]
   When wilt thou marry, Cariola?
CARIOLA   Never, my lord.
ANTONIO   Oh, fie upon this single life—forgo it!
   We read how Daphne, for her peevish flight,   25
   Became a fruitless bay tree, Syrinx turned
   To the pale empty reed, Anaxarete
   Was frozen into marble; whereas those
   Which married or proved kind unto their friends
   Were, by a gracious influence, transshaped   30

7. **Lord of Misrule:** a mock-prince chosen to preside over Christmas and carnival revels, during which the proper order of society was turned upside down.
15. Amphibious line, forming a loose hexameter with both line 14 and line 16.
17. **still:** always.
24–32. **Oh . . . stars:** Loosely paraphrased from Whetstone, C4r, this passage offers a witty reinterpretation of several stories in Ovid's *Metamorphoses*.
25. **Daphne:** saved from the erotic pursuit of Apollo by being turned into a laurel or bay.
26. **Syrinx:** turned into reeds to save her from Pan, who subsequently made his pipes from the syrinx reed.
27. **Anaxarete:** turned to stone by Venus as a punishment for her cruel indifference to the suicide of her spurned lover, Iphis.
29. **kind:** sexually accommodating. **friends:** lovers.
30. **gracious influence:** influx of divine grace (*OED* influence n. 3), imagined as a physical process effecting these miraculous transformations.

Into the olive, pomegranate, mulberry;
Became flowers, precious stones, or eminent stars.
CARIOLA   This is a vain poetry. But I pray you tell me:
    If there were proposed me wisdom, riches, and beauty
    In three several young men, which should I choose?   35
ANTONIO   'Tis a hard question. This was Paris' case,
    And he was blind in't, and there was great cause;
    For how was't possible he could judge right,
    Having three amorous goddesses in view,
    And they stark naked? 'Twas a motion   40
    Were able to benight the apprehension
    Of the severest counsellor of Europe.
    Now I look on both your faces so well formed,
    It puts me in mind of a question I would ask.
CARIOLA   What is't?
ANTONIO   I do wonder why hard-favored ladies,   45
    For the most part, keep worse-favored waiting-women
    To attend them, and cannot endure fair ones.
DUCHESS   Oh, that's soon answered.
    Did you ever in your life know an ill painter
    Desire to have his dwelling next door to the shop   50
    Of an excellent picture-maker? 'Twould disgrace
    His face-making, and undo him. I prithee,
    When were we so merry?—My hair tangles.
        [DUCHESS *tends to her toilette.*]
ANTONIO [*Aside to* CARIOLA]   Prithee, Cariola, let's steal forth
    the room
    And let her talk to herself—I have divers times   55
    Served her the like, when she hath chafed extremely:
    I love to see her angry. Softly, Cariola!
                        Exeunt [ANTONIO *and* CARIOLA].
DUCHESS   Doth not the color of my hair 'gin to change?
    When I wax gray, I shall have all the court
    Powder their hair with orris, to be like me.   60

---

36. Paris' case: In the so-called Judgment of Paris, the Trojan prince was asked to adjudicate the rival claims of Hera (riches), Athena (wisdom), and Aphrodite (love). His fateful choice of Aphrodite was rewarded by the goddess with the gift of Helen, wife of Menelaus, King of Sparta—thereby triggering the disastrous Trojan War.
36, 37. case, cause: In the context of Paris's judgment, both words quibble on their common legal sense, "lawsuit."
40. motion: (1) show, spectacle; (2) legal application made to a court; (3) emotion.
41. benight the apprehension: blind the understanding.
45. hard-favored: ugly.
55–56. divers . . . like: often treated her in such a fashion.
56. chafed: raged (*OED* v. 10).
59. wax: grow.
60. orris: a gray, violet-scented powder made from the root of the orris plant (a member of the iris family).

You have cause to love me: I entered you into my heart
Before you would vouchsafe to call for the keys.
    [*Enter* FERDINAND *unseen.*]
We shall one day have my brother take you napping:
Methinks his presence, being now in court,
Should make you keep your own bed. But you'll say   65
Love mixed with fear is sweetest. I'll assure you
You shall get no more children till my brothers
Consent to be your gossips. Have you lost your tongue?
    [*Turns and sees* FERDINAND.]
'Tis welcome:
For know, whether I am doomed to live or die,   70
I can do both like a prince.
                         FERDINAND *gives her a poniard.*
FERDINAND   Die then, quickly!
  Virtue, where art thou hid? What hideous thing
  Is it that doth eclipse thee?
DUCHESS   Pray, sir, hear me.
FERDINAND   Or is it true thou art but a bare name
  And no essential thing?
DUCHESS   Sir—
FERDINAND   Do not speak.
DUCHESS   No, sir.   75
  I will plant my soul in mine ears to hear you.
FERDINAND   O most imperfect light of human reason,
  That mak'st us so unhappy to foresee
  What we can least prevent, pursue thy wishes
  And glory in them! There's in shame no comfort,   80
  But to be past all bounds and sense of shame.
DUCHESS   I pray, sir, hear me: I am married—
FERDINAND   So.
DUCHESS   Haply not to your liking; but for that,
  Alas, your shears do come untimely now
  To clip the bird's wings that's already flown.   85
  Will you see my husband?
FERDINAND   Yes, if I could change

---

63. **brother:** Modern editors usually retain Q1's "brothers"; but the following lines indicate that the Duchess has Ferdinand in mind.
67. **get:** beget.
68. **gossips:** godparents; intimate confidants.
69. The short line here indicates a dramatic pause as the Duchess absorbs the shock of her brother's presence.
72–81. **Virtue . . . shame:** Ferdinand's lines are a close paraphrase of a passage in Sidney, *Arcadia*, 2, 1, *Works* I, p. 146.
83. **Haply:** perhaps.
84–85. **Alas . . . flown:** Again paraphrasing *Arcadia*, 2, 5, *Works* I, p. 177.

Eyes with a basilisk.
DUCHESS   Sure, you came hither
  By his confederacy.
FERDINAND   The howling of a wolf
  Is music to thee, screech owl—prithee, peace!
  [*Calling aloud.*] Whate'er thou art that hast enjoyed my   90
    sister
  (For I am sure thou hear'st me), for thine own sake
  Let me not know thee. I came hither prepared
  To work thy discovery, yet am now persuaded
  It would beget such violent effects
  As would damn us both. I would not for ten millions   95
  I had beheld thee; therefore use all means
  I never may have knowledge of thy name;
  Enjoy thy lust still, and a wretched life,
  On that condition. [*To the* DUCHESS] And for thee, vile
    woman,
  If thou do wish thy lecher may grow old   100
  In thy embracements, I would have thee build
  Such a room for him as our anchorites
  To holier use inhabit. Let not the sun
  Shine on him till he's dead; let dogs and monkeys
  Only converse with him, and such dumb things   105
  To whom Nature denies use to sound his name.
  Do not keep a paraquito, lest she learn it.
  If thou do love him, cut out thine own tongue
  Lest it bewray him.
DUCHESS   Why might not I marry?
  I have not gone about in this to create   110
  Any new world or custom.
FERDINAND   Thou art undone;
  And thou hast ta'en that massy sheet of lead
  That hid thy husband's bones, and folded it
  About my heart.
DUCHESS   Mine bleeds for't.
FERDINAND   Thine? Thy heart?

---

87. **basilisk:** mythical monster, king of the serpents, whose gaze could kill.
88. **wolf:** again anticipating Ferdinand's imaginary transformation in his final madness (cf. 2.1.54, 4.2.244, 292–94, 5.2.5–19).
89. **to thee:** compared to the sound of your voice. **screech owl:** ominous bird of death.
93. **work thy discovery:** discover your identity.
102–03. **Such . . . inhabit:** i.e., one of those cells in which especially pious hermits had themselves walled up.
107. **paraquito:** parrakeet.
109. **bewray:** betray.
112. **massy:** heavy.

What should I name't, unless a hollow bullet   115
Filled with unquenchable wildfire?
DUCHESS   You are, in this,
   Too strict, and—were you not my princely brother—
   I would say too wilful. My reputation
   Is safe.
FERDINAND   Dost thou know what reputation is?
   I'll tell thee—to small purpose, since th'instruction   120
   Comes now too late:
   Upon a time Reputation, Love, and Death
   Would travel o'er the world, and 'twas concluded
   That they should part and take three several ways.
   Death told them they should find him in great battles,   125
   Or cities plagued with plagues. Love gives them counsel
   To enquire for him 'mongst unambitious shepherds,
   Where dowries were not talked of, and sometimes
   'Mongst quiet kindred that had nothing left
   By their dead parents. "Stay," quoth Reputation,   130
   "Do not forsake me; for it is my nature
   If once I part from any man I meet
   I am never found again." And so, for you:
   You have shook hands with Reputation,
   And made him invisible. So, fare you well.   135
   I will never see you more.
DUCHESS   Why should only I,
   Of all the other princes of the world,
   Be cased up like a holy relic? I have youth,
   And a little beauty.
FERDINAND   So you have some virgins
   That are witches. I will never see thee more.   *Exit.* 140
            Enter ANTONIO *with a pistol* [*and* CARIOLA].
DUCHESS   You saw this apparition?
ANTONIO   Yes. We are
   Betrayed. How came he hither? [*To* CARIOLA] I should turn
   This to thee for that.   [*Points the pistol at* CARIOLA.]
CARIOLA   Pray, sir, do; and when
   That you have cleft my heart, you shall read there
   Mine innocence.
DUCHESS   That gallery gave him entrance.   145

115–16. hollow . . . wildfire: i.e., cannonball filled with gunpowder.
124. several: different.
140. never . . . more: Uncannily repeated in Antonio's exchange with the Echo from the
   Duchess's grave (5.3.43).
145. gallery: see note to 1.1.203.

ANTONIO   I would this terrible thing would come again,
   That, standing on my guard, I might relate
   My warrantable love. [[DUCHESS] *shows the poniard.*] Ha!
     What means this?
DUCHESS   He left this with me.
ANTONIO   And, it seems, did wish
   You would use it on yourself?
DUCHESS   His action   150
   Seemed to intend so much.
ANTONIO   This hath a handle to't
   As well as a point: turn it towards him,
   And so fasten the keen edge in his rank gall.
     [*Knocking within*]
   How now? Who knocks? More earthquakes?
DUCHESS   I stand
   As if a mine beneath my feet were ready   155
   To be blown up.
CARIOLA   'Tis Bosola.
DUCHESS   Away!
   Oh, misery! Methinks unjust actions
   Should wear these masks and curtains, and not we.
   You must instantly part hence: I have fashioned it already.
                       Ex[it] ANT[ONIO].
     [*Enter*] BOSOLA.
BOSOLA   The Duke your brother is ta'en up in a whirlwind,   160
   Hath took horse, and 's rid post to Rome.
DUCHESS   So late?
BOSOLA   He told me, as he mounted into th'saddle,
   You were undone.
DUCHESS   Indeed, I am very near it.
BOSOLA   What's the matter?
DUCHESS   Antonio, the master of our
     household,
   Hath dealt so falsely with me in's accounts: 165
   My brother stood engaged with me for money
   Ta'en up of certain Neapolitan Jews,
   And Antonio lets the bonds be forfeit.
BOSOLA   Strange! [*Aside*] This is cunning.

---

148. **warrantable:** authorized (i.e., by marriage).
153. **gall:** i.e., his liver, the source of gall (see note to 2.3.73–74).
155. **mine:** tunnel used to undermine enemy defences and destroy them with
   gunpowder.
158. **curtains:** veils (*OED* n. 1d).
159. **fashioned:** planned.
166. **stood engaged:** acted as guarantor.
167. **ta'en up:** borrowed.

DUCHESS   And hereupon
   My brother's bills at Naples are protested   170
   Against. Call up our officers.
BOSOLA   I shall.   *Exit.*
      [*Enter*] ANTONIO.
DUCHESS   The place that you must fly to is Ancona:
   Hire a house there. I'll send after you
   My treasure and my jewels. Our weak safety
   Runs upon enginous wheels: short syllables   175
   Must stand for periods. I must now accuse you
   Of such a feignèd crime as Tasso calls
   Magnanima mensogna, a noble lie,
   'Cause it must shield our honors.   [*Noises off*]
   Hark, they are coming!
      [*Enter*] BOSOLA [*and*] OFFICERS.
ANTONIO   Will your grace hear me?   180
DUCHESS   I have got well by you! You have yielded me
   A million of loss; I am like to inherit
   The people's curses for your stewardship.
   You had the trick in audit time to be sick
   Till I had signed your *Quietus*, and that cured you   185
   Without help of a doctor. Gentlemen,
   I would have this man be an example to you all—
   So shall you hold my favor—I pray, let him;
   For he's done that, alas, you would not think of;
   And, because I intend to be rid of him,   190
   I mean not to publish. [*To* ANTONIO] Use your fortune
      elsewhere.
ANTONIO   I am strongly armed to brook my overthrow,
   As commonly men bear with a hard year:
   I will not blame the cause on't, but do think
   The necessity of my malevolent star   195
   Procures this, not her humor. Oh, the inconstant

170–71. **My brother's . . . against:** i.e., the Jews have lodged a formal complaint about
   Ferdinand's failure to honor his promissory notes.
172. **Ancona:** an independent republic, beyond the political reach of the Duchess's brothers.
175. **enginous:** crafty, cunning.
176. **periods:** whole sentences.
178. *Magnanima mensogna*: From Torquato Tasso's crusader epic *Gerusalemme liberata*
   (1580), II.22. Translated in the following words, the phrase refers to a heroic deceit by
   which Sofronia seeks to save her fellow Christians from persecution.
181. **got well:** (1) profited financially; (2) proved fertile.
184. **audit time:** time set for formal examination of household accounts.
185. *Quietus*: (1) formal clearing of accounts; (2) release from life. See note to 1.1.452
   and cf. 4.2.172.
191. **publish:** make [his disgrace] publicly known (*OED* v. 1a).
192. **brook:** endure (*OED* v. 3).

And rotten ground of service! You may see:
'Tis e'en like him that in a winter night
Takes a long slumber o'er a dying fire
As loath to part from't, yet parts thence as cold   200
As when he first sat down.

DUCHESS   We do confiscate,
Towards the satisfying of your accounts,
All that you have.

ANTONIO   I am all yours; and 'tis very fit
All mine should be so.

DUCHESS   So, sir; you have your pass.

ANTONIO   You may see, gentlemen, what 'tis to serve   205
A prince with body and soul.   *Exit.*

BOSOLA   Here's an example for extortion: what moisture is drawn
out of the sea, when foul weather comes, pours down and runs
into the sea again.

DUCHESS   I would know what are your opinions of this Antonio.

SECOND OFFICER   He could not abide to see a pig's head gaping: 210
I thought your grace would find him a Jew.

THIRD OFFICER   I would you had been his officer, for your own
sake.

FOURTH OFFICER   You would have had more money.

FIRST OFFICER   He stopped his ears with black wool, and to   215
those came to him for money said he was thick of hearing.

SECOND OFFICER   Some said he was an hermaphrodite, for he
could not abide a woman.

FOURTH OFFICER   How scurvy proud he would look when the
treasury was full! Well, let him go.   220

FIRST OFFICER   Yes, and the chippings of the buttery fly after
him, to scour his gold chain!

DUCHESS   Leave us.   *Exeunt* [OFFICERS].
            What do you think of these?

BOSOLA   That these are rogues, that in's prosperity,
But to have waited on his fortune, could have wished   225
His dirty stirrup riveted through their noses,
And followed after's mule like a bear in a ring;

---

196. **humor:** mood, temper (*OED* n. 5).
203. **all yours:** With a double entendre playing on his roles as both servant and husband.
204. **pass:** permission to depart; passport (*OED* n. 8a).
205–06. **serve . . . body:** Antonio plays on the sexual sense of the verb (Williams, pp. 273–74); cf. 2.5.11.
215. **black wool:** Used as a remedy for deafness (Brown).
221. **chippings . . . buttery:** old crusts of bread (used to polish metal; cf. *Twelfth Night,* 2.3.107–108). **buttery:** store room for provisions; an insulting reminder that Antonio's gold chain of office is a badge of servile status.
227. **in a ring:** led by a ring (through his nose).

Would have prostituted their daughters to his lust;
Made their firstborn intelligencers; thought none happy
But such as were born under his blessed planet   230
And wore his livery. And do these lice drop off now?
Well, never look to have the like again:
He hath left a sort of flatt'ring rogues behind him;
Their doom must follow. Princes pay flatterers
In their own money: flatterers dissemble their vices,   235
And they dissemble their lies—that's justice.
Alas, poor gentleman!

DUCHESS   Poor? He hath amply filled his coffers.

BOSOLA   Sure, he was too honest. Pluto, the god of riches, when
he's sent by Jupiter to any man, he goes limping to signify that
wealth that comes on God's name comes slowly, but when he's   240
sent on the devil's errand, he rides post and comes in by scuttles.
Let me show you what a most unvalued jewel you have, in a wanton humor, thrown away to bless the man shall find him. He was
an excellent courtier and most faithful, a soldier that thought it
as beastly to know his own value too little as devilish to acknowl-   245
edge it too much. Both his virtue and form deserved a far better
fortune. His discourse rather delighted to judge itself than show
itself. His breast was filled with all perfection, and yet it seemed
a private whispering-room, it made so little noise of 't.

DUCHESS   But he was basely descended.   250

BOSOLA   Will you make yourself a mercenary herald, rather to
examine men's pedigrees than virtues? You shall want him: for

---

231. **his livery:** uniform identifying them as Antonio's servants. **lice drop off:** i.e., as lice
were supposed to abandon a dead body—a common figure for the greed and unfaithful-
ness of flatterers and parasites (Brown).
234. **doom:** judgment.
234–36. **Princes . . . lies:** close paraphrase of Mathieu, *Henry IV,* sig. Cc3r: "Princes
pay flattery with her owne money, Flatterers dissemble the vices of Princes, and Princes
dissemble the lyes of flatterers" (Dent).
238–60. Most editors follow Q1 in printing these lines as verse; but the metrical arrangements that result are often implausibly rough, even by Webster's elastic standards. Marcus's solution, in which lines 255–61 ("I would sooner . . . with virtue") are treated as prose
and the remainder as verse, only serves to highlight the problem. On balance it seems
best to regard Bosola's two speeches and the Duchess's interjection as rhythmic prose.
238–86. One of the peculiarities of this scene, as editors have remarked, is that it is
impossible to be certain of the degree of sincerity in Bosola's praise of Antonio; but
there is a painful irony in the fact that the same revelation that apparently confounds
his cynical view of the world (lines 264–67) supplies him with the very information he
has sought in his role as intelligencer.
238. **Pluto . . . riches:** properly Plutus, but this was a common confusion.
241. **by scuttles:** in basketfuls.
249. **whispering-room:** See note to 1.1.324.
251–52. **mercenary . . . virtues:** The Heralds' Office was responsible for investigating
the genealogies on which a man's claim to gentry or noble status depended. It was a
notoriously mercenary institution; thus, for example, Shakespeare—a provincial
tradesman's son—was able to buy a coat-of-arms for his family; see also line 285.
252. **want:** feel the lack of.

know, an honest statesman to a prince is like a cedar planted
by a spring: the spring bathes the tree's root; the grateful tree
rewards it with his shadow. You have not done so. I would 255
sooner swim to the Bermudas on two politicians' rotten blad-
ders, tied together with an intelligencer's heartstring, than
depend on so changeable a prince's favor. Fare thee well,
Antonio! Since the malice of the world would needs down
with thee, it cannot be said yet that any ill happened unto 260
thee, considering thy fall was accompanied with virtue.

DUCHESS   Oh, you render me excellent music!

BOSOLA   Say you?

DUCHESS   This good one that you speak of is my husband.

BOSOLA   Do I not dream? Can this ambitious age
Have so much goodness in't as to prefer   265
A man merely for worth, without these shadows
Of wealth and painted honors? Possible?

DUCHESS   I have had three children by him.

BOSOLA   Fortunate lady!
For you have made your private nuptial bed
The humble and fair seminary of peace.   270
No question but many an unbeneficed scholar
Shall pray for you for this deed, and rejoice
That some preferment in the world can yet
Arise from merit. The virgins of your land
That have no dowries shall hope your example   275
Will raise them to rich husbands. Should you want
Soldiers, 'twould make the very Turks and Moors
Turn Christians, and serve you for this act.
Last, the neglected poets of your time,
In honor of this trophy of a man,   280
Raised by that curious engine, your white hand,
Shall thank you in your grave for't, and make that
More reverend than all the cabinets

254–55. spring . . . shadow: Paraphrasing a passage from Sidney, *Arcadia* 1.15, *Works*
   I, p. 96.
259. down with thee: bring you down.
267. painted: pretended, false (*OED* ppl. a. 2b).
270. seminary: (1) seed bed (*OED* n. 1); (2) college, especially one devoted to the education of Roman Catholic priests (*OED* n. 4–5).
271. unbeneficed: without a church living; or perhaps, more generally, "without financial support" (Marcus).
281. Raised . . . hand: socially elevated by the hand you have given him in marriage, but
   the line inevitably recalls the Duchess's literal "raising" of Antonio at 1.1.404–07.
   curious engine: beautifully fashioned instrument.
283. reverend: revered. cabinets: council chambers (*OED* n. 7a).

Of living princes. For Antonio,
His fame shall likewise flow from many a pen,
When heralds shall want coats to sell to men.   285
DUCHESS   As I taste comfort in this friendly speech,
So would I find concealment.
BOSOLA   Oh, the secret of my prince,
Which I will wear on th'inside of my heart!
DUCHESS   You shall take charge of all my coin and jewels,
And follow him, for he retires himself   290
To Ancona.
BOSOLA   So.
DUCHESS   Whither, within few days,
I mean to follow thee.
BOSOLA   Let me think:
I would wish your grace to feign a pilgrimage
To Our Lady of Loreto, scarce seven leagues   295
From fair Ancona: so may you depart
Your country with more honor, and your flight
Will seem a princely progress, retaining
Your usual train about you.
DUCHESS   Sir, your direction
Shall lead me by the hand.
CARIOLA   In my opinion,   300
She were better progress to the baths
At Lucca, or go visit the Spa
In Germany; for, if you will believe me,
I do not like this jesting with religion,
This feigned pilgrimage.
DUCHESS   Thou art a superstitious fool—   305
Prepare us instantly for our departure.
Past sorrows, let us moderately lament them;
For those to come, seek wisely to prevent them.
                           Exit [*with* CARIOLA].
BOSOLA   A politician is the devil's quilted anvil,
He fashions all sins on him, and the blows   310
Are never heard; he may work in a lady's chamber—
As here for proof. What rests but I reveal
All to my lord? Oh, this base quality
Of intelligencer! Why, every quality i'th'world
Prefers but gain or commendation.   315

---

285. coats: i.e., coats-of-arms—the heraldic mark of gentle or noble birth. See also note
to 3.2.251–52.
295. Our . . . Loreto: famous pilgrimage shrine.
298. progress: See note to 2.1.25.
302. Lucca . . . Spa: mineral springs, well known for their curative properties. Spa is
actually in modern Belgium.
315. Prefers: promotes, helps to bring about (*OED* v. 2).

Now, for this act I am certain to be raised,
And men that paint weeds to the life are praised.   *Exit.*

3.3

[*Enter*] CARDINAL, FERDINAND, MALATESTE, PESCARA,
SILVIO, [*and*] DELIO.

CARDINAL   Must we turn soldier, then?
MALATESTE   The Emperor,
  Hearing your worth that way, ere you attained
  This reverend garment, joins you in commission
  With the right fortunate soldier, the Marquis of Pescara,
  And the famous Lannoy.
CARDINAL   He that had the honor   5
  Of taking the French king prisoner?
MALATESTE   The same.
                                    [*Showing a plan.*]
  Here's a plot drawn for a new fortification
  At Naples.   [*He and the* CARDINAL *confer privately.*]
FERDINAND   This great Count Malateste, I perceive,
  Hath got employment?
DELIO   No employment, my lord—
  A marginal note in the muster book that he is   10
  A voluntary lord.
FERDINAND   He's no soldier?
DELIO   He has worn gunpowder in's hollow tooth
  For the toothache.
SILVIO   He comes to the leaguer with a full intent
  To eat fresh beef and garlic, means to stay   15
  Till the scent be gone, and straight return to court.
DELIO   He hath read all the late service,
  As the city chronicle relates it,
  And keeps two painters going, only to express
  Battles in model.   20

---

1. **Emperor:** Charles V.
4. **Marquis of Pescara:** Historically Ferdinand's brother-in-law, Ferdinando Francesco d'Avolos (1489–1425), who defeated the French king Francis I at the battle of Pavia (1536).
5. **Lannoy:** The French-born Charles de Lannoy (ca. 1487–1527) commanded the victorious Spanish forces at Pavia.
10. **muster book:** record of troops in service.
11. **voluntary:** volunteer.
14. **leaguer:** see note to 1.1.213.
17. **late service:** most recent military operation(s) (*OED* n. 12b).
19. **painters:** Most editors prefer the Qc reading, supposing that the press correction is authorial. Marcus, however, argues that Delio refers to "workers in pewter who made toy soldiers for Malateste's military re-enactments."
20. **model:** drawing made to scale (*OED* n. 1).

SILVIO   Then he'll fight by the book.

DELIO   By the almanac, I think,
  To choose good days and shun the critical.
  That's his mistress' scarf.

SILVIO   Yes, he protests
  He would do much for that taffeta.   25

DELIO   I think he would run away from a battle
  To save it from taking prisoner.

SILVIO   He is horribly afraid
  Gunpowder will spoil the perfume on't.

DELIO   I saw a Dutchman break his pate once
  For calling him potgun: he made his head   30
  Have a bore in't, like a musket.

SILVIO   I would he had made a touchhole to't.

DELIO   He is indeed a guarded sumpter-cloth,
  Only for the remove of the court.

          [*Enter*] BOSOLA[; *confers privately with the* CARDINAL *and*
          MALATESTE.]

PESCARA   Bosola arrived? What should be the business?   35
  Some falling out amongst the cardinals?
  These factions amongst great men, they are like
  Foxes—when their heads are divided
  They carry fire in their tails, and all the country
  About them goes to wrack for't.

SILVIO   What's that Bosola?   40

DELIO   I knew him in Padua—a fantastical scholar, like such
  who study to know how many knots was in Hercules' club, of
  what color Achilles' beard was, or whether Hector were not
  troubled with the toothache. He hath studied himself half
  blear-eyed to know the true symmetry of Caesar's nose by a   45
  shoeing-horn; and this he did to gain the name of a speculative man.

21. Metrically amphibious line. **by the book:** like a mere theorist.
23. **critical:** days marked as dangerous in the astrological calendar or "almanac"
  (*OED* a. 4).
30. **potgun:** popgun and hence braggart (*OED* n. 2, 3), but the word could also refer to a
  mortar, in which case it might be a gibe at the Dutchman's stocky figure and (as Marcus
  suggests) include a reference to the notorious Dutch fondness for pots of ale.
32. **touchhole:** hole for igniting a musket; "probably also an obscene reference to the
  anus" (Cambridge).
33. **guarded:** ornamented (*OED* 3). **sumpter-cloth:** cloth covering for a pack animal.
34. **remove:** departure (*OED* n. 5a).
38–40. **Foxes . . . for't:** See Judges 15.4–5, where Samson sends foxes, with firebrands
  tied to their tails, to burn the Philistines' crops.
41. **Padua:** home to one of Europe's most celebrated universities.
41–44. **such who . . . toothache:** based on Mathieu's description of those who engage in
  studies so futile that they "spend whole nights to finde how many knots were in *Hercules*
  club, and of what colour *Achilles* beard was" (*Henry IV,* sig.Qq3v).
42. **Hercules' club:** used by the mythical hero to kill the Nemean lion.
43. **Achilles, Hector:** Greek and Trojan heroes from Homer's *Iliad.*
46–47. **speculative man:** theorist, one given to speculative reasoning.

PESCARA   Mark Prince Ferdinand:
A very salamander lives in's eye,
To mock the eager violence of fire.   50
SILVIO   That Cardinal hath made more bad faces with his
oppression than ever Michaelangelo made good ones. He lifts
up's nose like a foul porpoise before a storm.
PESCARA   The Lord Ferdinand laughs.
DELIO   Like a deadly cannon,
That lightens ere it smokes.   55
PESCARA   These are your true pangs of death—
The pangs of life, that struggle with great statesmen.
DELIO   In such a deformed silence, witches whisper
Their charms.
CARDINAL   Doth she make religion her riding hood   60
To keep her from the sun and tempest?
FERDINAND   That—
That damns her. Methinks her fault and beauty,
Blended together, show like leprosy,
The whiter the fouler. I make it a question
Whether her beggarly brats were ever christened.   65
CARDINAL   I will instantly solicit the state of Ancona
To have them banished.
FERDINAND   You are for Loreto?
I shall not be at your ceremony. Fare you well.
[*To* BOSOLA] Write to the Duke of Malfi, my young nephew
She had by her first husband, and acquaint him   70
With's mother's honesty.
BOSOLA   I will.
FERDINAND   Antonio!
A slave that only smelled of ink and counters,
And ne'er in's life looked like a gentleman
But in the audit time. —Go, go presently;
Draw me out an hundred and fifty of our horse,   75
And meet me at the fort bridge.   *Exeunt.*

---

49. **salamander:** lizard-like creature, supposed to be able to live in fire.
53. **like . . . storm:** cf. Tilley P483: "The porpoise plays before the storm."
55. **lightens:** flashes (*OED* v. 5–6).
69–70. **Duke . . . husband:** The play's only reference to this son, who seems to be forgotten in the final scene, where Delio calls on the assembled courtiers to help establish Antonio's son "In's mother's right" (5.5.110–11).
71. **honesty:** chastity (*OED* n. 3b)—ironic.
72. **counters:** disks used in accounting.
74. **audit time:** see 3.2.184.
75. **Draw . . . out:** lead out of camp or quarters (*OED* v. 87b).

3.4

[*Enter*] TWO PILGRIMS *to the shrine of Our Lady of Loreto.*
FIRST PILGRIM   I have not seen a goodlier shrine than this,
  Yet I have visited many.
SECOND PILGRIM   The Cardinal of Aragon
Is this day to resign his cardinal's hat.
His sister duchess likewise is arrived
To pay her vow of pilgrimage. I expect   5
A noble ceremony.
FIRST PILGRIM   No question. —They come.

> *Here the ceremony of the* CARDINAL'*s instalment in the habit
> of a soldier, performed in delivering up his cross, hat, robes,
> and ring at the shrine, and investing him with sword, hel-
> met, shield, and spurs. Then* ANTONIO, *the* DUCHESS, *and
> their [three] Children, having presented themselves at the
> shrine, are (by a form of banishment in dumb show expressed
> towards them by the* CARDINAL *and the state of Ancona)
> banished; during all which ceremony, this ditty is sung to
> very solemn music by divers churchmen, and then exeunt.*

Arms and honors deck thy story,
To thy fame's eternal glory;   The author disclaims
Adverse fortune ever fly thee;   this ditty to be his.
No disastrous fate come nigh thee!   10

I alone will sing thy praises
Whom to honor virtue raises,
And thy study, that divine is,
Bent to martial discipline is.
Lay aside all those robes lie by thee;   15
Crown thy arts with arms—they'll beautify thee.

O worthy of worthiest name, adorned in this manner,
Lead bravely thy forces on under war's warlike banner!
Oh, mayst thou prove fortunate in all martial courses;
Guide thou still, by skill, in arts and forces!   20
Victory attend thee nigh, whilst Fame sings loud thy powers;
*Triumphant conquest crown thy head, and blessings pour
      down showers!*

3.4. SD. *shrine . . . Loreto:* The image of the famous black virgin was well-known in
  England from pictorial representations; it will have been carefully represented in the
  theater's discovery space.
6. SD. *ditty:* The change from Q1a's "Hymne" to Q1b's "ditty," like the added disclaimer
  at lines 8–9, is almost certainly authorial, reflecting Webster's annoyance with an addition presumably made by the acting company.
19. **courses:** encounters (*OED* n. 5).

FIRST PILGRIM   Here's a strange turn of state! Who would
   have thought
  So great a lady would have matched herself
  Unto so mean a person? Yet the Cardinal   25
  Bears himself much too cruel.
SECOND PILGRIM   They are banished.
FIRST PILGRIM   But I would ask, what power hath this state
  Of Ancona to determine of a free prince?
SECOND PILGRIM   They are a free state, sir; and her brother
   showed
  How that the Pope, forehearing of her looseness,   30
  Hath seized into th'protection of the church
  The dukedom which she held as dowager.
FIRST PILGRIM   But by what justice?
SECOND PILGRIM   Sure I think by none,
  Only her brother's instigation.
FIRST PILGRIM   What was it with such violence he took   35
  Off from her finger?
SECOND PILGRIM   'Twas her wedding ring,
  Which he vowed shortly he would sacrifice
  To his revenge.
FIRST PILGRIM   Alas, Antonio!
  If that a man be thrust into a well,
  No matter who sets hand to't, his own weight   40
  Will bring him sooner to th'bottom. Come, let's hence.
  Fortune makes this conclusion general:
  All things do help th'unhappy man to fall.   *Exeunt.*

3.5

   [*Enter*] ANTONIO, DUCHESS, *Children,* CARIOLA[, *and*]
   Servants.
DUCHESS   Banished Ancona?
ANTONIO   Yes—you see what power
  Lightens in great men's breath.
DUCHESS   Is all our train
  Shrunk to this poor remainder?
ANTONIO   These poor men,
  Which have got little in your service, vow

---

25. **mean:** socially inferior.
28. **determine of:** pass judgment on.
40. **sets hand to't:** does it.
43. *unhappy:* unlucky.
2. **Lightens:** flashes.

   To take your fortune; but your wiser buntings,   5
   Now they are fledged, are gone.
DUCHESS   They have done wisely.
   This puts me in mind of death: physicians thus,
   With their hands full of money, use to give o'er
   Their patients.
ANTONIO   Right the fashion of the world!
   From decayed fortunes every flatterer shrinks;   10
   Men cease to build where the foundation sinks.
DUCHESS   I had a very strange dream tonight.
ANTONIO   What was't?
DUCHESS   Methought I wore my coronet of state,
   And on a sudden all the diamonds
   Were changed to pearls.
ANTONIO   My interpretation   15
   Is, you'll weep shortly; for to me the pearls
   Do signify your tears.
DUCHESS   The birds that live i'th'field
   On the wild benefit of nature live
   Happier than we; for they may choose their mates,
   And carol their sweet pleasures to the spring.   20
      [Enter] BOSOLA[, *with a letter*].
BOSOLA   You are happily o'erta'en.   *[Proffers her the letter.]*
DUCHESS   From my brother?
BOSOLA   Yes, from the Lord Ferdinand, your brother,
   All love and safety.
DUCHESS   Thou dost blanch mischief,
   Wouldst make it white. See, see! Like to calm weather
   At sea before a tempest, false hearts speak fair   25
   To those they intend most mischief.   *[Reads]* letter.
   "*Send Antonio to me; I want his head in a business.*"
   A politic equivocation!
   He doth not want your counsel, but your head—
   That is, he cannot sleep till you be dead.   30
   And here's another pitfall that's strewed o'er
   With roses—mark it, 'tis a cunning one:
   "*I stand engaged for your husband for several debts at Naples.*
   Let not that trouble him: I had rather have his heart than his
      money."

---

5. **buntings:** family of small birds, related to larks.
8. **give o'er:** abandon.
9. **Right:** exactly.
13–17. **Methought . . . tears:** based on Matthieu, *Henry IV*, H3r.
20. **carol:** sing.
21. **happily:** fortunately.

And I believe so too.

BOSOLA   What do you believe?   35

DUCHESS   That he so much distrusts my husband's love,
He will by no means believe his heart is with him
Until he see it. The devil is not cunning enough
To circumvent us in riddles.

BOSOLA   Will you reject that noble and free league   40
Of amity and love which I present you?

DUCHESS   Their league is like that of some politic kings,
Only to make themselves of strength and power
To be our after-ruin. Tell them so.

BOSOLA [*To* ANTONIO]   And what from you?

ANTONIO   Thus tell him: I will
    not come.   45

BOSOLA   And what of this?

ANTONIO   My brothers have dispersed
Bloodhounds abroad, which, till I hear are muzzled,
No truce—though hatched with ne'er such politic skill—
Is safe that hangs upon our enemies' will.
I'll not come at them.

BOSOLA   This proclaims your breeding.   50
Every small thing draws a base mind to fear
As the adamant draws iron. Fare you well, sir:
You shall shortly hear from 's.   *Exit.*

DUCHESS   I suspect some ambush.
Therefore, by all my love, I do conjure you
To take your eldest son and fly towards Milan—   55
Let us not venture all this poor remainder
In one unlucky bottom.

ANTONIO   You counsel safely.
Best of my life, farewell, since we must part—
Heaven hath a hand in't, but no otherwise
Than as some curious artist takes in sunder   60
A clock or watch, when it is out of frame,
To bring't in better order.

DUCHESS   I know not which is best,
To see you dead, or part with you. [*To their elder Son*]

---

46. this: i.e., the letter.
46–50. My brothers . . . them: a significant speech, as the only occasion on which Antonio speaks of Ferdinand and the Cardinal as brothers (i.e., brothers-in-law), thereby, as
Marcus notes, claiming "his place as one of the aristocratic family."
50. come at: approach. **breeding:** presumably the low breeding of a "base mind" (line
51). Later in the scene Bosola will sneer at Antonio as "this base, low fellow" (line 112).
52. adamant: magnet.
57. bottom: ship.
61. out of frame: out of order.

Farewell, boy;
Thou art happy that thou hast not understanding
To know thy misery; for all our wit   65
And reading brings us to a truer sense
Of sorrow. [*To* ANTONIO] In the eternal church, sir,
I do hope we shall not part thus.

ANTONIO   Oh, be of comfort!
Make patience a noble fortitude,
And think not how unkindly we are used: 70
Man, like to cassia, is proved best, being bruised.

DUCHESS   Must I, like to a slave-born Russian,
Account it praise to suffer tyranny?
And yet, O heaven, thy heavy hand is in't.
I have seen my little boy oft scourge his top,   75
And compared myself to't. Naught made me e'er
Go right but heaven's scourge-stick.

ANTONIO   Do not weep:
Heaven fashioned us of nothing, and we strive
To bring ourselves to nothing. —Farewell, Cariola,
And thy sweet armful!—If I do never see thee more,   80
Be a good mother to your little ones,
And save them from the tiger. Fare you well.

DUCHESS   Let me look upon you once more, for that speech
Came from a dying father. [*Kisses him.*] Your kiss is colder
Than that I have seen an holy anchorite   85
Give to a dead man's skull.

ANTONIO   My heart is turned to a heavy lump of lead,
With which I sound my danger. Fare you well.

                              Exit [with his elder Son].

DUCHESS   My laurel is all withered.

CARIOLA   Look, madam, what a troop of armèd men   90
Make toward us.

     Enter BOSOLA *with a guard,* [*wearing*] *vizards.*

DUCHESS   Oh, they are very welcome.

---

67. **eternal church:** the congregation of the faithful in heaven.
70. **unkindly:** cruelly; unnaturally.
71. **cassia:** thicker, coarser type of cinnamon bark. The idea is proverbial; see Tilley S746.
72–73. **like . . . tyranny:** from Sidney, *Astrophil and Stella*, Sonnet 2. Contemporary discourse contrasted the liberty of the free-born Englishman with the slavery endured by the lower orders in countries where serfdom and other forms of slavery prevailed.
77. **scourge-stick:** whip used to propel child's top.
78–79. **Heaven . . . to nothing:** cf. Donne, *First Anniversary,* lines 156–57: "of nothing he made us, and we strive too / To bring ourselves to nothing back." Theological explanations of creation tended to favor creation *ex nihilo* (out of nothing) as opposed to *ex chaos.* See note to 4.1.96.
87–88. **heavy . . . danger:** i.e., as a sailor uses a plummet to sound the depth of water.
89. **laurel:** A wreath of laurel was the usual victor's crown.

When Fortune's wheel is overcharged with princes,
The weight makes it move swift. I would have my ruin
Be sudden. —I am your adventure, am I not?
BOSOLA You are. You must see your husband no more.   95
DUCHESS What devil art thou, that counterfeits heaven's
        thunder?
BOSOLA Is that terrible? I would have you tell me
  Whether is that note worse that frights the silly birds
  Out of the corn, or that which doth allure them
  To the nets? You have hearkened to the last too much.   100
DUCHESS Oh, misery! Like to a rusty o'ercharged cannon,
  Shall I never fly in pieces? Come, to what prison?
BOSOLA To none.
DUCHESS   Whither then?
BOSOLA   To your palace.
DUCHESS   I have heard
  That Charon's boat serves to convey all o'er
  The dismal lake, but brings none back again.   105
BOSOLA Your brothers mean you safety and pity.
DUCHESS   Pity?
  With such a pity men preserve alive
  Pheasants and quails when they are not fat enough
  To be eaten.
BOSOLA   These are your children?
DUCHESS   Yes.
BOSOLA   Can they prattle?
DUCHESS   No.
  But I intend, since they were born accurst,   110
  Curses shall be their first language.
BOSOLA   Fie, madam,
  Forget this base, low fellow.
DUCHESS   Were I a man,
  I'd beat that counterfeit face into thy other.
BOSOLA One of no birth.
DUCHESS   Say that he was born mean:
  Man is most happy when's own actions   115
  Be arguments and examples of his virtue.
BOSOLA A barren, beggarly virtue.

92–93. Fortune's . . . swift: Building on the traditional emblem in which the figure of a
  king is seated at the top of Fortune's wheel and, as the blind goddess turns her handle,
  he plunges to the earth; here the wheel is accelerated by the weight of many princes.
94. adventure: object of your quest.
98. silly: simple, guileless; harmless (OED a. 1).
104. Charon: the ferryman whose boat, in classical myth, carried the souls of the dead
  across the river Styx.
113. counterfeit face: i.e., his vizard.

DUCHESS   I prithee, who is greatest, can you tell?
   Sad tales befit my woe: I'll tell you one.
   A salmon, as she swam unto the sea,   120
   Met with a dogfish, who encounters her
   With this rough language: "Why art thou so bold
   To mix thyself with our high state of floods,
   Being no eminent courtier, but one
   That for the calmest and fresh time o'th'year   125
   Dost live in shallow rivers, rank'st thyself
   With silly smelts and shrimps? And darest thou
   Pass by our dogship without reverence?"
   "Oh," quoth the salmon, "sister, be at peace:
   Thank Jupiter, we both have passed the net;   130
   Our value never can be truly known
   Till in the fisher's basket we be shown—
   I'th'market then my price may be the higher,
   Even when I am nearest to the cook and fire."
   So to great men the moral may be stretched: 135
   Men oft are valued high when they're most wretch'd.
   But come: whither you please. I am armed 'gainst misery,
   Bent to all sways of the oppressor's will.
   There's no deep valley but near some great hill.   *Exeunt.*

Act 4

4.1

   [*Enter*] FERDINAND, BOSOLA, [*and*] Servants [*with torches*].
FERDINAND   How doth our sister duchess bear herself
   In her imprisonment?
BOSOLA   Nobly—I'll describe her:
   She's sad, as one long used to't; and she seems
   Rather to welcome the end of misery
   Than shun it—a behavior so noble   5
   As gives a majesty to adversity.
   You may discern the shape of loveliness
   More perfect in her tears than in her smiles.
   She will muse four hours together, and her silence,

---

123. high . . . floods: the ocean.
127. silly: humble (*OED* a. 3b).
128. dogship: a parody of the usual honorific form (cf. *worship, lordship,* etc.), but given
   the marine context Q1's "dog-ship" may suggest a quibble.
139. *There's . . . hill:* proverbial (Tilley, H467).
3–6. She's . . . adversity: modeled on two passages in Sidney's *Arcadia,* 2, 29, and 1, 16,
   Works I, pp. 332, 16.
4. end of misery: i.e., death.

Methinks, expresseth more than if she spake.   10
FERDINAND   Her melancholy seems to be fortified
With a strange disdain.
BOSOLA   'Tis so, and this restraint,
Like English mastiffs that grow fierce with tying,
Makes her too passionately apprehend
Those pleasures she's kept from.
FERDINAND   Curse upon her!   15
I will no longer study in the book
Of another's heart. Inform her what I told you.   *Exit.*
          [*Enter*] DUCHESS [*and*] CARIOLA.
BOSOLA   All comfort to your grace!
DUCHESS   I will have none.
Pray thee, why dost thou wrap thy poisoned pills
In gold and sugar?   20
BOSOLA   Your elder brother, the Lord Ferdinand,
Is come to visit you, and sends you word,
'Cause once he rashly made a solemn vow
Never to see you more, he comes i'th'night,
And prays you, gently, neither torch nor taper   25
Shine in your chamber. He will kiss your hand
And reconcile himself; but, for his vow,
He dares not see you.
DUCHESS   At his pleasure.—
Take hence the lights.
          [*Exeunt* BOSOLA *and* Servants *with torches.*]
          [*Enter*] FERDINAND.
                    He's come.
FERDINAND   Where are you?
DUCHESS   Here, sir.
FERDINAND   This darkness suits you
well.   30
DUCHESS   I would ask you pardon.

---

14. apprehend: feel the force of, long for (*OED* v. 7).
17. SD. CARIOLA: The waiting lady's entrance is indicated by the group entry in Q1, but since she is given no lines in this scene, her function is unclear; presumably she should enter with the Duchess; and since the confrontation between Ferdinand and his sister will be most effective as a private encounter (as in 3.2), she may be intended to leave with Bosola and the servants at line 29.
19–20. wrap . . . sugar: proverbial (Tilley, P325).
21. elder brother: This has caused some confusion: the historical Ferdinand was older than his sister; but Webster's Duke later reveals that the Duchess was his elder twin (4.2.251–53). However, Bosola is surely referring to the fact that Ferdinand (as inheritor of the Dukedom of Calabria) must be the elder of the Aragonian brothers.
30. darkness: Despite its symbolic importance, the darkness (signaled here by the departure of the Servants with torches) had to be imagined by the audience—at least at the Globe, because such "public" outdoor theaters were fully illuminated throughout the performance; at "private" indoor theaters such as the Blackfriars, however, the use of window shutters and candles could enable more atmospheric effects.

FERDINAND   You have it;
  For I account it the honorablest revenge,
  Where I may kill, to pardon. Where are your cubs?
DUCHESS   Whom?
FERDINAND   Call them your children;
  For, though our national law distinguish bastards   35
  From true legitimate issue, compassionate nature
  Makes them all equal.
DUCHESS   Do you visit me for this?
  You violate a sacrament o'th'church
  Shall make you howl in hell for't.
FERDINAND   It had been well
  Could you have lived thus always, for indeed   40
  You were too much i'th'light. But no more;
  I come to seal my peace with you. Here's a hand
                              Gives her a dead man's hand.
  To which you have vowed much love; the ring upon't
  You gave.
DUCHESS   I affectionately kiss it.
FERDINAND   Pray do, and bury the print of it in your heart.   45
  I will leave this ring with you for a love token—
  And the hand, as sure as the ring; and do not doubt
  But you shall have the heart too. When you need a friend,
  Send it to him that owed it; you shall see
  Whether he can aid you.
DUCHESS [*Feeling the hand.*]   You are very cold.   50
  I fear you are not well after your travel.—
  Hah? Lights! Oh, horrible!
FERDINAND   Let her have lights enough.   *Exit.*
  [*Re-enter* BOSOLA *and* Servants *with torches.*]
DUCHESS   What witchcraft doth he practice, that he hath left
  A dead man's hand here?
          Here is discovered, behind a traverse, the artificial figures
          of ANTONIO *and his Children, appearing as if they were*
          dead.

---

36. **nature:** Bastards were in fact referred to as "natural children."
38. **You . . . church:** i.e., by calling into question the legitimacy of her marriage.
41. **i'th'light:** (1) in the public eye; (2) guilty of light or wanton behavior.
42. **SD. dead man's hand:** Ironically, as Bradbrook points out, although the hand of a dead person was considered a cure for madness, this hand (which the Duchess kisses, believing it to be Ferdinand's own) is designed to have the opposite effect. It will also have reminded the audience of the "hand of glory" used in necromantic witchcraft (Marcus).
43. **To . . . love:** Ferdinand now starts to hint that the hand is Antonio's.
48. **friend:** with a concealed play on *friend* = "lover."
49. **owed:** owned.
53–54. **witchcraft . . . hand:** see note to 4.1.42.SD.
54. **SD. traverse:** curtain closing off the discovery space at the rear of the stage.

BOSOLA   Look you, here's the piece from which 'twas ta'en.   55
   He doth present you this sad spectacle
   That, now you know directly they are dead,
   Hereafter you may wisely cease to grieve
   For that which cannot be recoverèd.
DUCHESS   There is not between heaven and earth one wish   60
   I stay for after this; it wastes me more
   Than were't my picture, fashioned out of wax,
   Stuck with a magical needle, and then buried
   In some foul dunghill; and yond's an excellent property.
   For a tyrant, which I would account mercy.
BOSOLA   What's that?   65
DUCHESS   If they would bind me to that lifeless trunk
   And let me freeze to death.
BOSOLA   Come, you must live.
DUCHESS   That's the greatest torture souls feel in hell:
   In hell that they must live and cannot die.
   Portia, I'll new-kindle thy coals again,   70
   And revive the rare and almost dead example
   Of a loving wife.
BOSOLA   Oh, fie! Despair? Remember
   You are a Christian.
DUCHESS   The church enjoins fasting:
   I'll starve myself to death.
BOSOLA   Leave this vain sorrow:
   Things being at the worst begin to mend;   75
   The bee, when he hath shot his sting into your hand,
   May then play with your eyelid.
DUCHESS   Good comfortable fellow,
   Persuade a wretch that's broke upon the wheel
   To have all his bones new set; entreat him live
   To be executed again. Who must dispatch me?   80
   I account this world a tedious theater,
   For I do play a part in't 'gainst my will.
BOSOLA   Come, be of comfort. I will save your life.
DUCHESS   Indeed I have not leisure to tend so small a business.

---

61. **stay:** wait.
62–64. **picture . . . dunghill:** magical practice attributed to witches, supposed to harm
   or kill the victim.
62. **picture:** effigy (*OED* n. 2d).
64. **property:** theatrical accessory.
70. **Portia:** Wife of the Roman tyrannicide Brutus, she committed suicide by swallowing
   hot coals after her husband's defeat and death at Philippi.
72. **Despair:** a mortal sin resulting from the conviction that one cannot be saved.
78. **wheel:** instrument of torture and execution.
82. **I do . . . my will:** adapted from Sidney, *Arcadia*, 2.29, *Works* 1, p. 333.

BOSOLA   Now, by my life, I pity you.
DUCHESS   Thou art a fool, then,   85
  To waste thy pity on a thing so wretched
  As cannot pity it. I am full of daggers.
  Puff! Let me blow these vipers from me.
  [*To a* SERVANT] What are you?
SERVANT   One that wishes you long life.
DUCHESS   I would thou wert hanged for the horrible curse   90
  Thou hast given me! I shall shortly grow one
  Of the miracles of pity. I'll go pray—no,
  I'll go curse.
BOSOLA   Oh, fie!
DUCHESS   I could curse the stars—
BOSOLA   Oh, fearful!
DUCHESS   And those three smiling seasons of the year
  Into a Russian winter—nay, the world   95
  To its first chaos.
BOSOLA   Look you, the stars shine still.
DUCHESS   Oh, but you must
  Remember, my curse hath a great way to go.
  Plagues, that make lanes through largest families,
  Consume them!
BOSOLA   Fie, lady!
DUCHESS   Let them, like tyrants,   100
  Never be remembered but for the ill they have done!
  Let all the zealous prayers of mortified
  Churchmen forget them!
BOSOLA   Oh, uncharitable!
DUCHESS   Let heaven, a little while, cease crowning martyrs,
  To punish them!   105
  Go, howl them this, and say I long to bleed:
  It is some mercy, when men kill with speed.   *Exit*

---

88. **vipers:** presumably by association with the pain of the imaginary daggers (line 87).
  But as Brown observes, "'*Puff:* let me *blow*' is . . . strange in relation to '*vipers*'"; so the
  Q word may represent a misreading of *vapors* (i.e., humoral exhalations from the organs
  of the body thought to cause psychological disorder; *OED* n. 3).
89. **SD.** SERVANT: Most editors include an entry for a servant at this point, but no motive is
  given for such an entry, nor is there any indication as to when this servant should exit; so
  it is easier to suppose that, among the servants who return at Ferdinand's call for light,
  there is one who responds to the Duchess's distress by stepping forward to offer comfort.
94. **three smiling seasons:** spring, summer, and autumn.
96. **first chaos:** Some accounts of the world's creation imagined it as emerging *ex chaos*
  rather than *ex nihilo* (see note to 3.5.78–79).
97. **Look . . . still:** capable of contradictory interpretations: (1) your curse is impotent;
  (2) the light from the stars still offers a promise of hope.
100. **Consume them:** i.e., her brothers.
102. **mortified:** dead to sin, ascetic (*OED* a. ppl. 1a).

[*Re-enter*] FERDINAND.

FERDINAND   Excellent—as I would wish! She's plagued in art:
These presentations are but framed in wax
By the curious master in that quality,   110
Vincentio Lauriola; and she takes them
For true substantial bodies.
BOSOLA   Why do you do this?
FERDINAND   To bring her to despair.
BOSOLA   Faith, end here,
And go no farther in your cruelty.
Send her a penitential garment to put on   115
Next to her delicate skin, and furnish her
With beads and prayer-books.
FERDINAND   Damn her! That body of hers,
While that my blood ran pure in't, was more worth
Than that which thou wouldst comfort, called a soul.
I will send her masques of common courtesans,   120
Have her meat served up by bawds and ruffians,
And, 'cause she'll needs be mad, I am resolved
To remove forth the common hospital
All the mad folk, and place them near her lodging;
There let them practice together, sing, and dance,   125
And act their gambols to the full o'th'moon.
If she can sleep the better for it, let her—
Your work is almost ended.
BOSOLA   Must I see her again?
FERDINAND   Yes.
BOSOLA   Never.
FERDINAND   You must.
BOSOLA   Never in mine own shape—
That's forfeited by my intelligence.   130
And this last cruel lie. When you send me next,
The business shall be comfort.
FERDINAND   Very likely!
Thy pity is nothing of kin to thee. Antonio
Lurks about Milan; thou shalt shortly thither

---

111. **Vincentio Lauriola:** unknown, perhaps invented by Webster.
120. **masques:** properly speaking, entertainments performed by courtiers, involving
    music, dance, and lavish spectacle; but Ferdinand's masques sound more like the wild
    antimasques of debased or monstrous characters, often performed by professional
    actors, that punctuated the stately action of masques proper.
126. **the full o'th'moon:** The full moon was believed to cause or exaggerate madness
    (hence *lunatic* from the Latin *luna* = "moon").
130. **by my intelligence:** by my role as your spy (of which the Duchess must now be fully
    aware).

To feed a fire as great as my revenge,   135
Which ne'er will slack till it have spent his fuel.
Intemperate agues make physicians cruel.   *Exeunt.*

4.2

[*Enter*] DUCHESS [*and*] CARIOLA. [*Noises of* MADMEN
offstage.]

DUCHESS   What hideous noise was that?

CARIOLA   'Tis the wild consort.
Of madmen, lady, which your tyrant brother
Hath placed about your lodging. This tyranny,
I think, was never practiced till this hour.

DUCHESS   Indeed, I thank him: nothing but noise and folly   5
Can keep me in my right wits, whereas reason
And silence make me stark mad. Sit down;
Discourse to me some dismal tragedy.

CARIOLA   Oh, 'twill increase your melancholy.

DUCHESS   Thou art deceived—
To hear of greater grief would lessen mine.   10
This is a prison?

CARIOLA   Yes, but you shall live
To shake this durance off.

DUCHESS   Thou art a fool—
The robin redbreast and the nightingale
Never live long in cages.

CARIOLA   Pray dry your eyes.
What think you of, madam?

DUCHESS   Of nothing. When I muse thus,   15
I sleep.

CARIOLA   Like a madman, with your eyes open?

DUCHESS   Dost thou think we shall know one another
In th'other world?

CARIOLA   Yes, out of question.

DUCHESS   Oh, that it were possible we might
But hold some two days' conference with the dead!   20
From them I should learn somewhat I am sure
I never shall know here. I'll tell thee a miracle:
I am not mad yet, to my cause of sorrow.

---

137. **Intemperate agues:** violent fevers.
1. **consort:** company, but also (given the wild noise of the madmen) ironically suggesting
a group of musicians.
12. **durance:** imprisonment (*OED* n. 5).

Th'heaven o'er my head seems made of molten brass,
The earth of flaming sulphur, yet I am not mad.   25
I am acquainted with sad misery
As the tanned galley-slave is with his oar—
Necessity makes me suffer constantly,
And custom makes it easy. Who do I look like now?
CARIOLA   Like to your picture in the gallery: 30
A deal of life in show, but none in practice;
Or rather, like some reverend monument
Whose ruins are even pitied.
DUCHESS   Very proper;
And Fortune seems only to have her eyesight
To behold my tragedy. [*Noise of* MADMEN *offstage*] How now,   35
What noise is that?
          [*Enter*] SERVANT.
SERVANT   I am come to tell you
Your brother hath intended you some sport:
A great physician, when the Pope was sick
Of a deep melancholy, presented him
With several sorts of madmen, which wild object,   40
Being full of change and sport, forced him to laugh,
And so th'impostume broke; the selfsame cure
The Duke intends on you.
DUCHESS   Let them come in.
SERVANT   There's a mad lawyer, and a secular priest;
A doctor that hath forfeited his wits   45
By jealousy; an astrologian,
That in his works said such a day o'th'month
Should be the day of doom, and, failing of't,
Ran mad; an English tailor, crazed i'th'brain
With the study of new fashion; a gentleman-usher   50
Quite beside himself with care to keep in mind
The number of his lady's salutations
Or "How do you" she employed him in each morning;

24–25. heaven . . . sulphur: cf. Deuteronomy 28.23: "And thy heaven that *is* over thy
head shall be brass, and the earth that *is* under thee *shall be* iron." But "molten" and
"flaming sulphur" suggest the fires of hell.
26–29. acquainted . . . easy: see p. xxiv, n. 7.
28. constantly: (1) with constancy; (2) continually (*OED* adv. 1; 3).
30. gallery: long narrow room, often used to display paintings (*OED* n. 5–6).
32–33. reverend . . . ruins: anticipating the carefully detailed setting of 5.3.
42. impostume: pustular cyst, abscess, boil (i.e., the pope's madness).
44. secular priest: one not belonging to a monastic or other religious order.
50. gentleman-usher: a gentleman attendant on a lady; chamberlain of the household
(*OED* n. 2).

A farmer, too, an excellent knave in grain,
Mad 'cause he was hindered transportation;   55
And let one broker that's mad loose to these,
You'd think the devil were among them.
DUCHESS   Sit, Cariola. —Let them loose when you please,
For I am chained to endure all your tyranny.
    [*Enter*] MADMEN.
    Here by a MADMAN *this song is sung, to a dismal kind of*
    music.

    Oh, let us howl some heavy note,   60
        Some deadly dogged howl,
    Sounding as from the threat'ning throat
        Of beasts and fatal fowl,
    As ravens, screech-owls, bulls, and bears!
    We'll bill and bawl our parts,   65
    Till irksome noise have cloyed your ears
        And corrosived your hearts.
    At last, whenas our choir wants breath,
        Our bodies being blest,
    We'll sing like swans, to welcome death,   70
        And die in love and rest.

FIRST MADMAN   Doomsday not come yet? I'll draw it nearer by a
    perspective, or make a glass that shall set all the world on fire
    upon an instant. I cannot sleep—my pillow is stuffed with a
    litter of porcupines.   75
SECOND MADMAN   Hell is a mere glasshouse, where the devils
    are continually blowing up women's souls on hollow irons, and
    the fire never goes out.

---

54. knave in grain: (1) ingrained rogue; (2) cheating dealer in grain.
55. hindered transportation: prevented from exporting (an act of 1613 forbade the
export of grain in times of shortage).
56. broker: retailer; middleman (*OED* n. 1; 3, 5).
59. SD. dismal . . . music: A contemporary setting for this song survives in three manu-
scripts, one of which attributes it to the composer Robert Johnson. It is reprinted in
Appendix 3 of Marcus (pp. 400–01). See also Cambridge, pp. 706–13.
61. dogged: dog-like; sullen, morose (*OED* a. 1a; 2c).
63. fatal fowl: birds of ill omen.
65. bill: presumably "make noises through the beak," though no other examples of this
usage exist. Q2's "bell" (bellow) makes ready sense, but (as Cambridge points out) mud-
dles the distinction between bird and beast.
66. cloyed: (1) pierced; (2) wearied (*OED* v. 3; 8a).
67. corrosived: eaten away.
70. sing like swans: Swans were believed to sing before dying (cf. *swan song*).
73. perspective: telescope, magnifying glass (*OED* n. 2).
76. glasshouse: glass factory.
77. hollow irons: glassblowers' pipes.

THIRD MADMAN   I will lie with every woman in my parish the
tenth night: I will tithe them over, like haycocks.   80
FOURTH MADMAN   Shall my 'pothecary outgo me because I am a
cuckold? I have found out his roguery: he makes alum of his
wife's urine and sells it to Puritans that have sore throats with
overstraining.
FIRST MADMAN   I have skill in heraldry.   85
SECOND MADMAN   Hast?
FIRST MADMAN   You do give for your crest a woodcock's head with
the brains picked out on't—you are a very ancient gentleman!
THIRD MADMAN   Greek is turned Turk; we are only to be saved
by the Helvetian translation.   90
FIRST MADMAN   Come on, sir, I will lay the law to you.
SECOND MADMAN   Oh, rather lay a corrosive: the law will eat to
the bone.
THIRD MADMAN   He that drinks but to satisfy nature is damned.
FOURTH MADMAN   If I had my glass here, I would show a sight   95
should make all the women here call me mad doctor.
FIRST MADMAN   What's he, a rope-maker?
                                        [*Points at another* MADMAN.]
SECOND MADMAN   No, no, no, a snuffling knave that, while he
shows the tombs, will have his hand in a wench's placket.
THIRD MADMAN   Woe to the caroche that brought home my wife   100
from the masque at three o'clock in the morning! It had a
large feather-bed in it.
FOURTH MADMAN   I have pared the devil's nails forty times,
roasted them in ravens' eggs, and cured agues with them.

---

80. **tenth . . . tithe:** parish priests were traditionally entitled to collect one-tenth (a
tithe) of their parishioners' annual income.
82–83. **alum . . . throats:** ammonia from urine was used to crystallize alum—a cure for
sore throats (Marcus).
83–84. **Puritans . . . overstraining:** i.e., from preaching their notoriously long
sermons.
87. **woodcock:** proverbially stupid.
88. **ancient gentleman:** sarcastic (the herald has sold this upstart a coat of arms).
89. **Greek . . . Turk:** i.e., original, pure Christianity (as represented by the Greek New
Testament) has been corrupted (by Rome) until it is now no better than Turkish (i.e.,
Mahometan) superstition.
90. **Helvetian translation:** i.e., the Geneva Bible, favored by Puritans.
91. **lay:** expound.
92. **lay a corrosive:** apply a caustic medicine (to the body).
95. **glass:** presumably another type of perspective, designed, like a small peepshow, to
present pornographic images (Cambridge).
97. **rope-maker:** This trade carried the stigma of being closely allied with that of the
hangman (Cambridge).
98. **snuffling knave:** perhaps, as Lucas suggests, an allusion to the nasal whine affected
by Puritans.
99. **placket:** petticoat; the slit at the top of a petticoat, hence the vagina (*OED* n. 2; 3a–b).
100. **caroche:** see note to 1.1.215.
104. **ravens:** Omens of death (see *Macbeth*, 1.5.36–8); in Welsh folklore the Devil could
transform himself into a raven. **agues:** see note to 4.1.137.

THIRD MADMAN   Get me three hundred milch-bats to make pos-   105
sets to procure sleep.
FOURTH MADMAN   All the college may throw their caps at me: I
have made a soap-boiler costive—it was my masterpiece.
>   *Here the dance, consisting of eight* MADMEN, *with music*
>   *answerable. Thereunto, after which* BOSOLA, *like an old*
>   *man, enters* [*and the* MADMEN *leave*].

DUCHESS   Is he mad too?
SERVANT   Pray question him. I'll leave you.
                                                                    [*Exit.*]
BOSOLA   I am come to make thy tomb.
DUCHESS   Hah, my tomb?   110
Thou speak'st as if I lay upon my deathbed,
Gasping for breath. Dost thou perceive me sick?
BOSOLA   Yes, and the more dangerously, since thy sickness is
insensible.
DUCHESS   Thou art not mad, sure. Dost know me?
BOSOLA   Yes.
DUCHESS   Who am I?
BOSOLA   Thou art a box of wormseed, at best but a salvatory of   115
green mummy. What's this flesh? A little crudded milk, fantastical puff paste. Our bodies are weaker than those paper
prisons boys use to keep flies in—more contemptible, since
ours is to preserve earthworms. Didst thou ever see a lark in a
cage? Such is the soul in the body: this world is like her little   120
turf of grass; and the heaven o'er our heads, like her looking
glass, only gives us a miserable knowledge of the small compass of our prison.

---

105. **milch-bats:** bats kept for milking—clearly a witchcraft fantasy. **possets:** hot milk
drinks, curdled with liquor and often used for medicinal purposes.
107. **throw their caps:** i.e., in recognition of triumph.
108. **costive:** constipated. Soap makers were notoriously prone to diarrhea. **SD.** *music*
answerable: i.e., wild and discordant (in contrast to the symbolic harmony in which a
masque was properly supposed to end).
113. **is insensible:** cannot be felt by the bodily senses.
115–50: Q1 prints this entire passage as though it were verse, but much of it, including
Bosola's long speeches, is plainly prose. Some editors attempt to distinguish episodes of
verse in the dialogue; but—apart from Bosola's self-consciously quoted couplet at lines
133–34—it seems better to follow Brown and to treat it as prose, albeit (as so often with
Webster) of a highly rhythmic kind.
115. **wormseed:** (1) a plant used to purge intestinal worms; (2) the seed from which
graveyard worms will grow. **salvatory:** ointment container.
116. **green mummy:** (1) fresh mummy (or, in the Duchess's case, still living flesh already
awaiting mummification); (2) *usnea,* the green lichen scraped from a skull, thought by
Paracelsians to have especially powerful curative properties; the most effective *usnea*
was supposedly to be found on the skull of one who had died a violent death. The extensive use of mummy (or *mumia*) in early modern medicine has been elaborately documented by Louise Noble, *Medicinal Cannibalism in Early Modern English Literature
and Culture* (London: Palgrave, 2011), and Richard Sugg, *Mummies, Cannibals, and
Vampires* (London: Routledge, 2011). **crudded:** curded.
117. **paste:** pastry. Elaborately shaped pastry creations were a feature of contemporary
banquets.

DUCHESS   Am not I thy duchess?

BOSOLA   Thou art some great woman, sure, for riot begins to sit 125
on thy forehead, clad in grey hairs, twenty years sooner than
on a merry milkmaid's. Thou sleep'st worse than if a mouse
should be forced to take up her lodging in a cat's ear. A little
infant that breeds its teeth, should it lie with thee, would cry
out as if thou wert the more unquiet bedfellow.   130

DUCHESS   I am Duchess of Malfi still.

BOSOLA   That makes thy sleeps so broken.
Glories, like glow-worms, afar off shine bright,
But looked to near have neither heat nor light.

DUCHESS   Thou art very plain.   135

BOSOLA   My trade is to flatter the dead, not the living. I am a
tomb-maker.

DUCHESS   And thou com'st to make my tomb?

BOSOLA   Yes.

DUCHESS   Let me be a little merry. Of what stuff wilt thou 140
make it?

BOSOLA   Nay, resolve me first, of what fashion?

DUCHESS   Why, do we grow fantastical in our deathbed? Do we
affect fashion in the grave?

BOSOLA   Most ambitiously. Princes' images on their tombs do 145
not lie as they were wont, seeming to pray up to heaven, but
with their hands under their cheeks as if they died of the
toothache. They are not carved with their eyes fixed upon the
stars, but as their minds were wholly bent upon the world, the
self-same way they seem to turn their faces.   150

DUCHESS   Let me know fully therefore the effect
Of this thy dismal preparation,
This talk fit for a charnel.

BOSOLA   Now I shall.
Here is a present from your princely brothers,
    [*Enter*] EXECUTIONERS [*with*] *a coffin, cords, and a bell.*
And may it arrive welcome, for it brings   155
Last benefit, last sorrow.

DUCHESS   Let me see it:
I have so much obedience in my blood,
I wish it in their veins to do them good.

---

125. **riot**: extravagance, excess, debauchery (*OED* n. 1a).
127–28. **mouse . . . cat's ear**: proverbial (Tilley, M1231).
142. **fashion**: pattern, design (*OED* n. 3a).
144. **fashion**: that which is fashionable (itself a relatively novel usage, dating from the
late 16th century).
145–50. **Princes' images . . . faces**: For this pronounced shift in funerary style, see Figures 1 and 2.
146. **as . . . wont**: as they used to.

BOSOLA   This is your last presence-chamber.
CARIOLA   Oh, my sweet lady!
DUCHESS   Peace, it affrights not me.
BOSOLA   I am the common bellman   160
    That usually is sent to condemned persons
    The night before they suffer.
DUCHESS   Even now thou said'st
    Thou wast a tomb-maker?
BOSOLA   'Twas to bring you
    By degrees to mortification. Listen: [*Rings his bell*]
        Hark! Now everything is still: 165
        The screech owl and the whistler shrill
        Call upon our dame aloud,
        And bid her quickly don her shroud.
        Much you had of land and rent;
        Your length in clay's now competent.   170
        A long war disturbed your mind;
        Here your perfect peace is signed.
        Of what is't fools make such vain keeping?
        Sin their conception, their birth weeping;
        Their life a general mist of error,   175
        Their death a hideous storm of terror.
        Strew your hair with powders sweet;
        Don clean linen; bathe your feet;
        And—the foul fiend more to check—
        A crucifix let bless your neck.   180
        'Tis now full tide 'tween night and day;
        End your groan, and come away.
CARIOLA   Hence, villains, tyrants, murderers! Alas,
    What will you do with my lady?—Call for help!
DUCHESS   To whom, to our next neighbors? They are mad folks. 185
BOSOLA   Remove that noise.
        [EXECUTIONERS *seize* CARIOLA.]
DUCHESS   Farewell, Cariola—

---

159. **presence-chamber:** the room in which monarchs and princes received visitors.
160. **common bellman:** In 1605 a John Webster (probably the dramatist's father) helped establish a charity to fund this office. The bellman was required to visit the condemned on the eve of their execution and to make a speech (accompanied by the tolling of a bell) designed "to put them in minde of their mortalitie" and thus "awake their sleepie senses from securitie, to saue their soules from perishing" (Brown).
164. **mortification:** (1) state of torpor preceding death; (2) process of mortifying the flesh as an instrument of spiritual purification.
166. **whistler:** "used of some nocturnal bird having a whistling note believed to be of ill omen" (OED n. 2a).
170. **competent:** sufficient; adequate for your rank (OED a. 3; 2).
172. **peace is signed:** see notes to 1.1.452 and 3.2.185.
177. **Strew . . . sweet:** i.e., as a bride might do.

In my last will I have not much to give:
A many hungry guests have fed upon me;
Thine will be a poor reversion.
CARIOLA   I will die with her.
DUCHESS   I pray thee, look thou giv'st my little boy   190
Some syrup for his cold, and let the girl
Say her prayers ere she sleep.
  [EXECUTIONERS *force* CARIOLA *off*.]
                                 Now, what you please. What death?
BOSOLA   Strangling. Here are your executioners.
DUCHESS   I forgive them.
The apoplexy, catarrh, or cough o'th'lungs
Would do as much as they do.   195
BOSOLA   Doth not death fright you?
DUCHESS   Who would be afraid on't,
Knowing to meet such excellent company
In th'other world?
BOSOLA   Yet methinks
The manner of your death should much afflict you,   200
This cord should terrify you?
DUCHESS   Not a whit.
What would it pleasure me to have my throat cut
With diamonds, or to be smothered
With cassia, or to be shot to death with pearls?
I know death hath ten thousand several doors   205
For men to take their exits, and 'tis found
They go on such strange geometrical hinges,
You may open them both ways—any way, for heaven sake,
So I were out of your whispering! Tell my brothers
That I perceive death, now I am well awake,   210
Best gift is they can give or I can take.
I would fain put off my last woman's fault:
I'd not be tedious to you.
EXECUTIONER   We are ready.

---

189. reversion: office obtained through the death of an incumbent.
190–92. I pray . . . sleep: The Duchess seems to have forgotten the waxwork figures that made her think her children dead.
194. apoplexy: stroke. **catarrh:** cerebral haemorrhage (*OED* n. 2). **cough o'th'lungs:** tuberculosis or pneumonia.
195–97. The scansion of these three partial lines is uncertain; but line 196 may be amphibious, forming a rough hexameter with 190, and a pentameter with line 197.
197–99. Who . . . world: adapted from Montaigne, I, xxv, p. 166.
204. cassia: see note to 3.5.71.
205–06. death . . . exits: proverbial (Tilley, D140).
212. last woman's fault: cf. Tilley, W676: "A woman's tongue is the last thing about her that dies."

DUCHESS   Dispose my breath how please you, but my body
   Bestow upon my women—will you?
EXECUTIONER   Yes.   215
DUCHESS   Pull, and pull strongly, for your able strength
   Must pull down heaven upon me.
   Yet stay—heaven gates are not so highly arched
   As princes' palaces: they that enter there
   Must go upon their knees. [*Kneels.*] Come, violent death,   220
   Serve for mandragora, to make me sleep!
   Go tell my brothers, when I am laid out,
   They then may feed in quiet.   *They strangle her.*
BOSOLA   Where's the waiting-woman?
   Fetch her. Some other strangle the children.
       [*Exeunt* EXECUTIONERS; *some return with* CARIOLA.]
   Look you, there sleeps your mistress.
CARIOLA   Oh, you are damned   225
   Perpetually for this! My turn is next;
   Is't not so ordered?
BOSOLA   Yes, and I am glad
   You are so well prepared for't.
CARIOLA   You are deceived, sir:
   I am not prepared for't; I will not die;
   I will first come to my answer, and know   230
   How I have offended.
BOSOLA   Come, dispatch her.
   [*To* CARIOLA.] You kept her counsel; now you shall
      keep ours.
CARIOLA   I will not die! I must not. I am contracted
   To a young gentleman.
EXECUTIONER [*Showing the noose.*]   Here's your wedding ring.
CARIOLA   Let me but speak with the Duke. I'll discover   235
   Treason to his person.
BOSOLA   Delays! Throttle her.
EXECUTIONER   She bites, and scratches!
CARIOLA   If you kill me now
   I am damned: I have not been at confession
   This two years.
BOSOLA [*To the* EXECUTIONER]   When?
CARIOLA   I am quick with child.
BOSOLA   Why then,

217–20. **heaven . . . knees:** a self-conscious reversal of the Duchess's gesture to Antonio
   in the wooing scene (1.1.403–07).
221. **mandragora:** mandrake root (see note to 2.5.1), commonly used as a sedative.
222. **laid out:** prepared for burial.
239. **quick with child:** a woman could not be executed so long as she was carrying a child.

Your credit's saved.
>   [EXECUTIONERS *strangle* CARIOLA.]
>   Bear her into th'next room;   240
>   [*Exeunt* EXECUTIONERS *with* CARIOLA's *body*]
> Let this lie still.
>   [*Enter*] FERDINAND.
> FERDINAND   Is she dead?
> BOSOLA   She is what
> You'd have her. But here begin your pity.
>   *Shows the* CHILDREN *strangled.*
> Alas, how have these offended?
> FERDINAND   The death
> Of young wolves is never to be pitied.
> BOSOLA   Fix your eye here.
> FERDINAND   Constantly.
> BOSOLA   Do you not weep?   245
> Other sins only speak; murder shrieks out.
> The element of water moistens the earth,
> But blood flies upwards and bedews the heavens.
> FERDINAND   Cover her face. Mine eyes dazzle; she died young.
> BOSOLA   I think not so; her infelicity   250
> Seemed to have years too many.
> FERDINAND   She and I were twins;
> And, should I die this instant, I had lived
> Her time to a minute.
> BOSOLA   It seems she was born first:
> You have bloodily approved the ancient truth
> That kindred commonly do worse agree   255
> Than remote strangers.
> FERDINAND   Let me see her face again—
> Why didst not thou pity her? What an excellent
> Honest man mightst thou have been
> If thou hadst borne her to some sanctuary,
> Or, bold in a good cause, opposed thyself,   260
> With thy advancèd sword above thy head,
> Between her innocence and my revenge!
> I bade thee, when I was distracted of my wits,
> Go kill my dearest friend, and thou hast done't.
> For let me but examine well the cause: 265

---

241. **let this lie still:** let the Duchess's body remain.
243–44. **death . . . pitied:** proverbial (Tilley, D145).
244. **wolves:** see notes to 2.1.54, 3.2.88, 4.2.293–95, and 5.2.5–19.
254. **approved:** proved.
264. **dearest friend:** The superlative underlines the potentially erotic significance of *friend* (see 3.2.29), thereby emphasizing the incestuous desire that seems to drive Ferdinand's behavior.

What was the meanness of her match to me?
Only, I must confess, I had a hope,
Had she continued widow, to have gained
An infinite mass of treasure by her death;
And that was the main cause—her marriage,   270
That drew a stream of gall quite through my heart.
For thee—as we observe in tragedies
That a good actor many times is cursed
For playing a villain's part—I hate thee for't,
And, for my sake, say thou hast done much ill well.   275
BOSOLA   Let me quicken your memory, for I perceive
You are falling into ingratitude: I challenge
The reward due to my service.
FERDINAND   I'll tell thee
What I'll give thee—
BOSOLA   Do.
FERDINAND   I'll give thee a pardon
For this murder.
BOSOLA   Hah?
FERDINAND   Yes; and 'tis   280
The largest bounty I can study to do thee.
By what authority didst thou execute
This bloody sentence?
BOSOLA   By yours.
FERDINAND   Mine? Was I her judge?
Did any ceremonial form of law
Doom her to not-being? Did a complete jury   285
Deliver her conviction up i'th'court?
Where shalt thou find this judgment registered
Unless in hell? See, like a bloody fool
Th'hast forfeited thy life, and thou shalt die for't.
BOSOLA   The office of justice is perverted quite   290
When one thief hangs another. Who shall dare
To reveal this?
FERDINAND   Oh, I'll tell thee:

267–69. I had . . . death: This is the first mention of any material motive, and it is ren-
    dered particularly implausible by the earlier reference to the Duchess's son by her first
    marriage (3.3.69–70), though Webster may simply have forgotten that detail as he seems
    to have done at the end of the play (see 5.5.108–11).
271. gall: black bile, melancholy—a reaction unlikely to be produced by the loss of mere
    "treasure."
275. ill: evil.
276. quicken: revive.

The wolf shall find her grave and scrape it up—
Not to devour the corpse, but to discover
The horrid murder.
BOSOLA   You, not I, shall quake for't.   295
FERDINAND Leave me.
BOSOLA   I will first receive my pension.
FERDINAND You are a villain!
BOSOLA   When your ingratitude
Is judge, I am so.
FERDINAND   Oh, horror,
That not the fear of him which binds the devils
Can prescribe man obedience!   300
Never look upon me more.
BOSOLA   Why, fare thee well.
Your brother and yourself are worthy men;
You have a pair of hearts are hollow graves,
Rotten, and rotting others; and your vengeance,
Like two chained bullets, still goes arm in arm.   305
You may be brothers: for treason, like the plague,
Doth take much in a blood. I stand like one
That long hath ta'en a sweet and golden dream:
I am angry with myself, now that I wake.
FERDINAND Get thee into some unknown part o'th'world   310
That I may never see thee.
BOSOLA   Let me know
Wherefore I should be thus neglected. Sir,
I served your tyranny, and rather strove
To satisfy yourself than all the world;
And, though I loathed the evil, yet I loved   315
You that did counsel it, and rather sought
To appear a true servant than an honest man.
FERDINAND I'll go hunt the badger by owl-light:
'Tis a deed of darkness.   *Exit.*
BOSOLA He's much distracted. Off, my painted honor!   320
While with vain hopes our faculties we tire,

292–95. wolf . . . murder: a folk superstition; cf. *White Devil*, 5.4.97–98. Ferdinand himself will become such a wolf in his lycanthropic fantasy at 5.2.5–19.
294. discover: uncover, reveal.
296. pension: fee, wages (*OED* n. 3a).
299. him . . . devils: God, or perhaps Satan.
305. chained bullets: chain shot, consisting of two cannon balls chained together (typically used in naval warfare).
307. take . . . blood: take root in families (*OED* v. 6a).
315–17. loved . . . true servant: The question of what constitutes true service—and how
the "love" which servants and masters were enjoined to have for one another is to be
manifested—is one to which the play repeatedly returns. See p. xxxiv in this volume.
320. painted: false, pretended.
321. tire (1) exhaust; (2) dress up.

We seem to sweat in ice and freeze in fire.
What would I do, were this to do again?
I would not change my peace of conscience
For all the wealth of Europe. —She stirs! Here's life!   325
Return, fair soul, from darkness, and lead mine
Out of this sensible hell! She's warm, she breathes!
Upon thy pale lips I will melt my heart
To store them with fresh color. —Who's there?
Some cordial drink!—Alas! I dare not call.   330
So pity would destroy pity. —Her eye opes,
And heaven in it seems to ope, that late was shut,
To take me up to mercy.
DUCHESS   Antonio!
BOSOLA   Yes, madam, he is living.   335
The dead bodies you saw were but feigned statues;
He's reconciled to your brothers: the Pope hath wrought
The atonement.
DUCHESS   Mercy!   *She dies.*
BOSOLA   Oh, she's gone again! There the cords of life broke.
Oh, sacred innocence, that sweetly sleeps   340
On turtles' feathers, whilst a guilty conscience
Is a black register wherein is writ
All our good deeds and bad—a perspective
That shows us hell: that we cannot be suffered
To do good when we have a mind to it!   345
This is manly sorrow:
These tears, I am very certain, never grew
In my mother's milk. My estate is sunk
Below the degree of fear. Where were
These penitent fountains while she was living?   350
Oh, they were frozen up. Here is a sight
As direful to my soul as is the sword
Unto a wretch hath slain his father. Come,
I'll bear thee hence   [*Lifts the* DUCHESS's *body*]

322. sweat . . . fire: figures oddly adapted from the oxymoronic language of Petrarchan love poetry.
327. sensible hell: living hell.
330. cordial: restorative (to the heart) (*OED* a. 2).
332. late: lately, until now.
334. Amphibious.
338. atonement: reconciliation (*OED* n. 2).
339. cords of life: heartstrings.
341. turtles: turtledoves—symbols of purity as well as marital fidelity.
348–49. estate . . . fear: degraded below the (shameful) status of fear itself.
348. mother's milk: standing for the condition of a child and also probably for effeminacy, as opposed to his "manly sorrow" (line 241). estate: condition (*OED* n. 1).

And execute thy last will—that's deliver   355
Thy body to the reverent dispose
Of some good women. That the cruel tyrant
Shall not deny me. Then I'll post to Milan,
Where somewhat I will speedily enact
Worth my dejection.   *Exit [with the body].* 360

Act 5

5.1

[*Enter*] ANTONIO [*and*] DELIO.
ANTONIO   What think you of my hope of reconcilement
To the Aragonian brethren?
DELIO   I misdoubt it,
For, though they have sent their letters of safe-conduct
For your repair to Milan, they appear
But nets to entrap you. The Marquis of Pescara,   5
Under whom you hold certain land in cheat,
Much 'gainst his noble nature hath been moved
To seize those lands, and some of his dependents
Are at this instant making it their suit
To be invested in your revenues.   10
I cannot think they mean well to your life
That do deprive you of your means of life,
Your living.
ANTONIO   You are still an heretic
To any safety I can shape myself.
DELIO   Here comes the Marquis:
        [*Enter*] PESCARA.
                                  I will make myself   15
Petitioner for some part of your land,
To know whither it is flying.
ANTONIO   I pray, do.   [*Stands aside.*]
DELIO   Sir, I have a suit to you.
PESCARA   To me?
DELIO   An easy one:

---

356. **reverent dispose:** respectful preparation for burial.
360. **Worth my dejection:** that will make my downfall worthwhile. The primary mean-
    ing of *dejection* must be "casting down . . . abasement" (*OED* n. 1–2), but it probably
    also includes "depression of spirits," i.e., despair (*OED* n. 3).
6. **in cheat:** subject to the feudal law of escheat (according to which lands would revert to
    their lord should a tenant die intestate. For legal purposes a man convicted of treason
    or felony was treated as being without heirs).
11–13. **I . . . living:** paraphrasing *Merchant of Venice*, 4.1.370–72.

There is the citadel of Saint Bennet,
With some demesnes of late in the possession   20
Of Antonio Bologna—please you bestow them on me?
PESCARA   You are my friend. But this is such a suit
Nor fit for me to give, nor you to take.
DELIO   No, sir?
PESCARA   I will give you ample reason for't
Soon in private. —Here's the Cardinal's mistress.   25
        [*Enter*] JULIA.
JULIA   My lord, I am grown your poor petitioner,
And should be an ill beggar, had I not
A great man's letter here, the Cardinal's,
To court you in my favor.   [*Gives* PESCARA *a letter.*]
PESCARA   He entreats for you
The citadel of Saint Bennet that belonged   30
To the banishèd Bologna.
JULIA   Yes.
PESCARA   I could not have thought of a friend I could
Rather pleasure with it—'tis yours.
JULIA   Sir, I thank you;
And he shall know how doubly I am engaged
Both in your gift and speediness of giving,   35
Which makes your grant the greater.   *Exit.*
ANTONIO [*Aside*]   How they fortify
Themselves with my ruin!
DELIO   Sir, I am
Little bound to you.
PESCARA   Why?
DELIO   Because you denied this suit to me, and gave't
To such a creature.
PESCARA   Do you know what it was?   40
It was Antonio's land, not forfeited
By course of law, but ravished from his throat
By the Cardinal's entreaty. It were not fit
I should bestow so main a piece of wrong.
Upon my friend; 'tis a gratification   45
Only due to a strumpet, for it is injustice.

---

19. **Bennet:** Benedict.
20. **demesnes:** estates.
27. **ill:** poor, incompetent.
32. **friend:** often used as a synonym for mistress and thus licensing the sexual suggestiveness of "pleasure" (line 33).
34–36. **how . . . greater:** cf. Tilley, G125, "He that gives quickly gives twice."
43–46. **It . . . injustice:** based on a story in Montaigne, I.xxix, p. 213.

Shall I sprinkle the pure blood of innocents
To make those followers I call my friends
Look ruddier upon me? I am glad
This land, ta'en from the owner by such wrong,   50
Returns again unto so foul an use
As salary for his lust. Learn, good Delio,
To ask noble things of me, and you shall find
I'll be a noble giver.
DELIO   You instruct me well.
ANTONIO [*Aside*]   Why, here's a man now would fright
    impudence   55
From sauciest beggars.
PESCARA   Prince Ferdinand's come to Milan,
Sick, as they give out, of an apoplexy;
But some say 'tis a frenzy. I am going
To visit him.   *Exit.*
ANTONIO [*Coming forward.*]   'Tis a noble old fellow.
DELIO   What course do you mean to take, Antonio?   60
ANTONIO   This night I mean to venture all my fortune—
Which is no more than a poor ling'ring life—
To the Cardinal's worst of malice. I have got
Private access to his chamber, and intend
To visit him about the mid of night,   65
As once his brother did our noble duchess.
It may be that the sudden apprehension
Of danger—for I'll go in mine own shape—
When he shall see it fraught with love and duty,
May draw the poison out of him and work   70
A friendly reconcilement. If it fail,
Yet it shall rid me of this infamous calling;
For better fall once than be ever falling.
DELIO   I'll second you in all danger; and, howe'er,
My life keeps rank with yours.   75
ANTONIO   You are still my loved and best friend.   *Exeunt.*

---

49. **ruddier:** According to the doctrine of the humors (see 2.5.13), a ruddy complexion
    was taken to be the mark of a sanguine (i.e., warm-hearted and sociable) disposition.
58. **frenzy:** manic behavior caused by inflammation of the brain.
72. **calling:** station in life (*OED* vbl. n. 10).
73. **better . . . falling:** adapted from Montaigne, I.xxxii, p. 233.
74. **howe'er:** however things turn out.
75. **keeps rank:** stays alongside (a military metaphor).

5.2

[*Enter*] PESCARA [*and*] *a* DOCTOR.

PESCARA   Now, doctor, may I visit your patient?
DOCTOR   If't please your lordship. But he's instantly
  To take the air here in the gallery
  By my direction.
PESCARA   Pray thee, what's his disease?
DOCTOR   A very pestilent disease, my lord,   5
  They call lycanthropia.
PESCARA   What's that?
  I need a dictionary to't.
DOCTOR   I'll tell you:
  In those that are possessed with't there o'erflows
  Such melancholy humor they imagine
  Themselves to be transformèd into wolves,   10
  Steal forth to churchyards in the dead of night
  And dig dead bodies up—as two nights since
  One met the Duke 'bout midnight in a lane
  Behind Saint Mark's Church, with the leg of a man
  Upon his shoulder; and he howled fearfully,   15
  Said he was a wolf—only the difference
  Was, a wolf's skin was hairy on the outside,
  His on the inside—bade them take their swords,
  Rip up his flesh, and try. Straight I was sent for,
  And, having ministered to him, found his grace   20
  Very well recovered.
PESCARA   I am glad on't.
DOCTOR   Yet not without some fear
  Of a relapse: if he grow to his fit again,
  I'll go a nearer way to work with him   25
  Than ever Paracelsus dreamed of. If
  They'll give me leave, I'll buffet his madness
  Out of him. Stand aside! He comes.
        [*Enter*] FERDINAND, MALATESTE, CARDINAL, [*and*] BOSOLA
        [*who stands apart, observing*].

---

3. **gallery:** covered space for walking. "Doctors recommended that melancholic patients should expose themselves only to warm, moist air, and take only moderate exercise" (Brown).
5–19. **A very . . . try:** adapted from Goulart; see pp. 161–66 in this volume. Ferdinand's fantasy echoes a recurrent set of images in the play. See 2.1.54, 3.2.88, 4.2.244, and 293–95.
6. **lycanthropia:** produced by an excess of melancholy, as Robert Burton explains in the *Anatomy of Melancholy* (1621), I.i.1.iv.
22. metrically amphibious line.
25. **nearer:** more direct (*OED* a. 5).
26. **Paracelsus:** Philippus von Hohenheim (1493–1541), celebrated Swiss-German physician and scientist-magician.

FERDINAND	Leave me.
MALATESTE	Why doth your lordship love this solitariness?

FERDINAND Eagles commonly fly alone: they are crows, daws, 30
jackdaws and starlings that flock together. —Look, what's that
follows me?

MALATESTE Nothing, my lord.

FERDINAND Yes!

MALATESTE 'Tis your shadow.   35

FERDINAND Stay it! Let it not haunt me!

MALATESTE Impossible, if you move and the sun shine—

FERDINAND I will throttle it. [*Throws himself upon the ground.*]

MALATESTE Oh, my lord, you are angry with nothing.

FERDINAND You are a fool. How is't possible I should catch my 40
shadow unless I fall upon't? When I go to hell, I mean to carry
a bribe; for, look you, good gifts evermore make way for the
worst persons.

PESCARA Rise, good my lord.

FERDINAND I am studying the art of patience.

PESCARA 'Tis a noble virtue.   45

FERDINAND To drive six snails before me from this town to
Moscow; neither use goad nor whip to them, but let them take
their own time—the patient'st man i'th'world match me for an
experiment!—and I'll crawl after, like a sheep-biter.

CARDINAL Force him up.   [*They raise him.*] 50

FERDINAND Use me well, you were best. What I have done, I
have done: I'll confess nothing.

DOCTOR Now let me come to him. —Are you mad, my lord? Are
you out of your princely wits?

FERDINAND What's he?   55

PESCARA Your doctor.

FERDINAND Let me have his beard sawed off and his eyebrows
filed more civil.

DOCTOR I must do mad tricks with him, for that's the only way
on't. —I have brought your grace a salamander's skin, to keep 60
you from sunburning.

29–81. Q1 prints these lines as verse and Marcus struggles gamely to make metrical sense
of them. Ferdinand's "Leave me" (line 28) seems to complete the Doctor's final verse line,
and there is a pronounced iambic rhythm to some sentences; however, in this period episodes representing madness were typically cast in prose (cf. 4.2.72–108), and the whole
passage is probably best treated as another example of Webster's rhythmic prose.

30–31. crows . . . starlings: i.e., inferior birds.

36. Stay: stop.

46. drive six snails: "To drive a snail" was a proverbial formula for futility (Tilley S582).

49. sheep-biter: dog that worries sheep.

58. more civil: in a more seemly fashion.

60. salamander's skin: This creature was supposed to live in fire, so its skin would be
proof against burning.

FERDINAND   I have cruel sore eyes.

DOCTOR   The white of a cockatrice's egg is present remedy.

FERDINAND   Let it be a new-laid one, you were best. —Hide me
    from him! Physicians are like kings: they brook no 65
    contradiction.

DOCTOR   Now he begins to fear me. Now let me alone with him.
        [FERDINAND *attempts to remove his gown.*]

CARDINAL   How now, put off your gown?

DOCTOR   Let me have some forty urinals filled with rosewater:
    he and I'll go pelt one another with them. Now he begins to
    fear me. —Can you fetch a frisk, sir? [*Some others seek to* 70
    restrain FERDINAND.] —Let him go, let him go, upon my peril.
    I find, by his eye, he stands in awe of me. I'll make him as
    tame as a dormouse.

FERDINAND   Can you fetch your frisks, sir?—I will stamp him
    into a cullis, flay off his skin to cover one of the anatomies this 75
    rogue hath set i'th'cold yonder in Barber-Surgeons' Hall. —
    Hence, hence! You are all of you like beasts for sacrifice [*Throws*
    the DOCTOR *down and beats him.*]; there's nothing left of you but
    tongue and belly, flattery and lechery.   [*Exit.*]

PESCARA   Doctor, he did not fear you throughly.   [*Exit.*] 80

DOCTOR   True, I was somewhat too forward.

BOSOLA [*Aside*]   Mercy upon me, what a fatal judgment
    Hath fall'n upon this Ferdinand!

PESCARA   Knows your grace
    What accident hath brought unto the prince
    This strange distraction?   85

CARDINAL [*Aside*]   I must feign somewhat. [*To them*] Thus they
        say it grew:
    You have heard it rumored for these many years,
    None of our family dies but there is seen
    The shape of an old woman, which is given
    By tradition to us to have been murdered   90
    By her nephews for her riches. Such a figure

---

62. **cruel sore eyes:** cf. 4.2.249.
63. **cockatrice's . . . remedy:** In fact the eggs of the cockatrice (or basilisk) were thought
    to be dangerously toxic.
70. **fetch a frisk:** cut a caper.
75. **cullis:** broth.
75–76. **anatomies . . . Hall:** In London the corpses of criminals were brought to Barber-
    Surgeon's Hall near Cripplegate for use in public dissections.
77–79. **You . . . belly:** adapted from Sir Thomas North's translation of Plutarch's Life of
    Phocion (*Lives*, 1572, p. 797).
80. **throughly:** thoroughly.
86. **I . . . somewhat:** The first half of the Cardinal's line appears to be amphibious, com-
    pleting Pescara's part line and thus suggesting quick cuing and a suitably hurried aside.
87–91. **You . . . riches:** adapted from Goulart, p. 620.

One night, as the prince sat up late at 's book,
Appeared to him; when, crying out for help,
The gentlemen of 's chamber found his grace
All on a cold sweat, altered much in face   95
And language. Since which apparition
He hath grown worse and worse, and I much fear
He cannot live.
BOSOLA [*To* CARDINAL]   Sir, I would speak with you.
PESCARA   We'll leave your grace,   100
Wishing to the sick prince, our noble lord,
All health of mind and body.
CARDINAL   You are most welcome.
                    [*Exeunt all but* CARDINAL *and* BOSOLA.]
[*Aside*] Are you come? So. This fellow must not know
By any means I had intelligence
In our duchess' death; for, though I counselled it,   105
The full of all th'engagement seemed to grow
From Ferdinand. [*To* BOSOLA] Now, sir, how fares our sister?
I do not think but sorrow makes her look
Like to an oft-dyed garment. She shall now
Taste comfort from me. Why do you look so wildly?   110
Oh, the fortune of your master here, the prince,
Dejects you; but be you of happy comfort:
If you'll do one thing for me, I'll entreat:
Though he had a cold tombstone o'er his bones,
I'd make you what you would be.
BOSOLA   Anything;   115
Give it me in a breath, and let me fly to't.
They that think long small expedition win,
For, musing much o'th'end, cannot begin.
                    [*Enter*] JULIA.
JULIA   Sir, will you come in to supper?
CARDINAL   I am busy. Leave me.
JULIA [*Aside*]   What an excellent shape hath that fellow!   *Exit.* 120
CARDINAL   'Tis thus: Antonio lurks here in Milan—
Enquire him out and kill him. While he lives,
Our sister cannot marry, and I have thought
Of an excellent match for her. Do this, and style me
Thy advancement.   125

---

99. Another amphibious line.
106. **The full . . . engagement:** the complete plan to use him in the plot.
117. **small expedition win:** never manage to act with any despatch.
124–25. **style . . . advancement:** count on me to bring about the advancement you seek.

BOSOLA   But by what means shall I find him out?
CARDINAL   There is a gentleman called Delio
Here in the camp that hath been long approved
His loyal friend: set eye upon that fellow,
Follow him to Mass; maybe Antonio—   130
Although he do account religion
But a school name—for fashion of the world
May accompany him; or else go enquire out
Delio's confessor, and see if you can bribe
Him to reveal it. There are a thousand ways   135
A man might find to trace him: as, to know
What fellows haunt the Jews for taking up
Great sums of money—for sure he's in want—
Or else to go to th'picture-makers and learn
Who bought her picture lately. Some of these   140
Happily may take—
BOSOLA   Well, I'll not freeze i'th'business:
I would see that wretched thing, Antonio,
Above all sights i'th'world.
CARDINAL   Do, and be happy.   *Exit.*
BOSOLA   This fellow doth breed basilisks in's eyes:
He's nothing else but murder; yet he seems   145
Not to have notice of the Duchess' death.
'Tis his cunning: I must follow his example:
There cannot be a surer way to trace
Than that of an old fox.
          [*Enter*] JULIA[, *pointing a pistol at* BOSOLA.]
JULIA   So, sir, you are well met.
BOSOLA   How now?
JULIA   Nay, the doors are fast enough.   150
Now, sir, I will make you confess your treachery.
BOSOLA   Treachery?
JULIA   Yes. Confess to me
Which of my women 'twas you hired to put
Love-powder into my drink?
BOSOLA   Love-powder?   155

---

126. This line forms a passable pentameter if "means" is scanned as disyllabic. Alterna-
    tively it may form a shared hexameter with the Cardinal's "Thy advancement," assum-
    ing that *thy* is elided into the first syllable of *advancement.*
128. **approved:** proved.
132. **school name:** empty word.
137. **haunt the Jews:** visit Jewish moneylenders (Christians were ostensibly forbidden to
    engage in usury). **taking up:** borrowing.
144. **basilisks:** see note to 3.2.87.
148–49. **There . . . fox:** proverbial (Tilley, W164).
154. **love-powder:** aphrodisiac.
155. Amphibious line.

JULIA   Yes, when I was at Malfi—
Why should I fall in love with such a face else?
I have already suffered for thee so much pain,
The only remedy to do me good
Is to kill my longing.   [*Threatens* BOSOLA *with her pistol.*]

BOSOLA   Sure your pistol holds   160
Nothing but perfumes or kissing-comfits.
Excellent lady,
You have a pretty way on't to discover
Your longing. Come, come, I'll disarm you,
And arm you thus.   [*Takes her pistol and embraces her.*]
             Yet this is wondrous strange.   165

JULIA   Compare thy form and my eyes together,
You'll find my love no such great miracle.
Now you'll say I am wanton. This nice modesty
In ladies is but a troublesome familiar
That haunts them.   170

BOSOLA   Know you me? I am a blunt soldier.

JULIA   The better.
Sure there wants fire where there are no lively sparks
Of roughness.

BOSOLA   And I want compliment.

JULIA   Why, ignorance
In courtship cannot make you do amiss,   175
If you have a heart to do well.

BOSOLA   You are very fair.

JULIA   Nay, if you lay beauty to my charge,
I must plead unguilty.

BOSOLA   Your bright eyes
Carry a quiver of darts in them sharper
Than sunbeams.

JULIA   You will mar me with commendation!   180
Put yourself to the charge of courting me,

---

160. kill my longing: kill the object of my desire (with a sexual innuendo).
161. kissing-comfits: confections to sweeten the breath.
163. discover: reveal.
168. nice: over-scrupulous; affected; foolish (*OED* a. 7, 5, 1).
169. familiar: familiar spirit (usually attending a witch).
171. Amphibious line.
173–74. Sure . . . roughness: you can't make a fire unless there's a rough, abrasive surface from which to strike incendiary sparks—perhaps playing on *spark* = a stylish young man (*OED* n² 2).
174. want compliment: lack the proper mastery of courtly manners.
176. do: Cambridge suggests a play on the obscene sense of the verb.
178–80. Your . . . sunbeams: Bosola's ignorance of courtly "compliment" (line 174) is immediately illustrated by his awkward mixing of two of the most clichéd tropes from contemporary love poetry.
181. charge: trouble.

Whereas now I woo you.   [*Kisses him.*]
BOSOLA [*Aside*]   I have it! I will work upon this creature. —
    [*To her*] Let us grow most amorously familiar.
                                          [*Embraces her again.*]
    If the great Cardinal now should see me thus,   185
    Would he not count me a villain?
JULIA   No, he might count me a wanton,
    Not lay a scruple of offense on you;
    For if I see and steal a diamond,
    The fault is not i'th'stone, but in me the thief   190
    That purloins it. I am sudden with you:
    We that are great women of pleasure use
    To cut off these uncertain wishes and unquiet longings,
    And in an instant join the sweet delight
    And the pretty excuse together. Had you been   195
    I'th'street, under my chamber window,
    Even there I should have courted you.
BOSOLA   Oh, you are an excellent lady!
JULIA   Bid me do somewhat for you presently
    To express I love you.   200
BOSOLA   I will, and if you love me,
    Fail not to effect it.
    The Cardinal is grown wondrous melancholy.
    Demand the cause. Let him not put you off
    With feigned excuse; discover the main ground on't.   205
JULIA   Why would you know this?
BOSOLA   I have depended on him,
    And I hear that he is fall'n in some disgrace
    With the Emperor—if he be, like the mice
    That forsake falling houses, I would shift
    To other dependence.
JULIA   You shall not need follow the wars: 210
    I'll be your maintenance.
BOSOLA   And I your loyal servant;
    But I cannot leave my calling.
JULIA   Not leave

189–91. **For . . . purloins it:** gender reversal of the usual courtly compliment, by which
    it is women who are compared to precious jewels (Marcus). Cf. 1.1.86, 291–92.
191. **sudden:** hasty, impetuous.
192–97. **We . . . you:** Julia here identifies herself as a courtesan; such "great women of
    pleasure," unlike mere prostitutes, could choose their own lovers.
201. Amphibious line.
206. **depended:** been employed in his service.
208–09. **mice . . . houses:** proverbial (Tilley, M 1243).
211. **maintenance . . . servant:** Julia and Bosola play with the conventional language of
    courtly love, according to which a lover presented himself as his mistress's "servant"; Julia
    gives this notion a literal twist by offering to make Bosola her kept man.

An ungrateful general for the love
Of a sweet lady? You are like some
Cannot sleep in featherbeds, but must   215
Have blocks for their pillows.

BOSOLA   Will you do this?

JULIA   Cunningly.

BOSOLA   Tomorrow I'll expect th'intelligence.

JULIA   Tomorrow? Get you into my cabinet,
You shall have it with you. Do not delay me,
No more than I do you. I am like one   220
That is condemned: I have my pardon promised,
But I would see it sealed. Go, get you in.
You shall see me wind my tongue about his heart
Like a skein of silk.   [BOSOLA *withdraws from view.*]
        [*Enter*] CARDINAL[, *followed by* SERVANTS.]

CARDINAL   Where are you?

SERVANT   Here.

CARDINAL   Let none, upon your lives,   225
Have conference with the Prince Ferdinand
Unless I know it.   [*Exeunt Servants.*]
[*Aside*]   In this distraction
He may reveal the murder.
Yond's my lingering consumption—
I am weary of her, and by any means   230
Would be quit off.

JULIA   How now, my lord?
What ails you?

CARDINAL   Nothing.

JULIA   Oh, you are much altered.
Come, I must be your secretary, and remove
This lead from off your bosom. What's the matter?

CARDINAL   I may not tell you.

JULIA   Are you so far in love with sorrow   235
You cannot part with part of it? Or think you
I cannot love your grace when you are sad,
As well as merry? Or do you suspect
I, that have been a secret to your heart
These many winters, cannot be the same   240
Unto your tongue?

---

218. **cabinet:** private chamber.
221–22. **pardon . . . sealed:** i.e., Julia expects prompt fulfilment of Bosola's promise of
    sexual satisfaction. "Sealed" may be a cue to kiss him (cf. 4.1.42–44).
229. **lingering consumption:** i.e., tuberculosis. Julia is like a lingering disease gradually
    wasting the Cardinal (and his fortune) away.
231. **quit off:** rid of her.
233. **your secretary:** the keeper of your secrets.
235–41. **Are . . . tongue:** adapted from *Arcadia*, 2, 5, *Works* I, p. 176.

CARDINAL   Satisfy thy longing—
The only way to make thee keep my counsel
Is not to tell thee.
JULIA   Tell your echo this—
Or flatterers, that like echoes still report
What they hear (though most imperfect)—and not me.   245
For, if that you be true unto yourself,
I'll know.
CARDINAL   Will you rack me?
JULIA   No, judgment shall
Draw it from you. It is an equal fault
To tell one's secrets unto all or none.
CARDINAL   The first argues folly.
JULIA   But the last, tyranny.   250
CARDINAL   Very well. Why, imagine I have committed
Some secret deed which I desire the world
May never hear of.
JULIA   Therefore may not I know it?
You have concealed for me as great a sin
As adultery. Sir, never was occasion   255
For perfect trial of my constancy
Till now. Sir, I beseech you.
CARDINAL   You'll repent it.
JULIA   Never.
CARDINAL   It hurries thee to ruin. I'll not tell thee.
Be well advised, and think what danger 'tis
To receive a prince's secrets: they that do   260
Had need have their breasts hooped with adamant
To contain them. I pray thee yet be satisfied:
Examine thine own frailty—'tis more easy
To tie knots than unloose them. 'Tis a secret
That, like a ling'ring poison, may chance lie   265
Spread in thy veins and kill thee seven year hence.
JULIA   Now you dally with me.
CARDINAL   No more—thou shalt know it:
By my appointment, the great Duchess of Malfi
And two of her young children four nights since
Were strangled.
JULIA   Oh, heaven! Sir, what have you done?   270

242–43. The only . . . thee: a proverbial sneer against women (Tilley, W649, S196).
247. rack me: put me on the rack.
250. argues: shows.
261. adamant: diamond—but often used (as here) to denote the strongest steel.

CARDINAL   How now! How settles this? Think you your bosom
 Will be a grave dark and obscure enough
 For such a secret?
JULIA   You have undone yourself, sir.
CARDINAL   Why?
JULIA   It lies not in me to conceal it.
CARDINAL   No?
 Come, I will swear you to't upon this book.   [*Holds out a bible*] 275
JULIA   Most religiously.
CARDINAL   Kiss it.   [*She kisses the bible.*]
 Now you shall never utter it: thy curiosity
 Hath undone thee; thou'rt poisoned with that book;
 Because I knew thou couldst not keep my counsel,
 I have bound thee to't by death.   280
   [BOSOLA *reveals himself and comes forward.*]
BOSOLA   For pity sake, hold!
CARDINAL   Ha! Bosola?
JULIA   I forgive you
 This equal piece of justice you have done;
 For I betrayed your counsel to that fellow:
 He overheard it—that was the cause I said   285
 It lay not in me to conceal it.
BOSOLA   O foolish woman,
 Couldst not thou have poisoned him?
JULIA   'Tis weakness
 Too much to think what should have been done.
 I go, I know not whither.   [*Dies.*]
CARDINAL   Wherefore com'st thou hither?
BOSOLA   That I might find a great man like yourself— 290
 Not out of his wits, as the Lord Ferdinand—
 To remember my service.
CARDINAL   I'll have thee hewed in pieces!
BOSOLA   Make not yourself such a promise of that life
 Which is not yours to dispose of.
CARDINAL   Who placed thee here?
BOSOLA   Her lust, as she intended.
CARDINAL   Very well: 295
 Now you know me for your fellow murderer.

---

271. **How settles this?**: How does that sink in? (*OED* v. 13b).
275. **book, SD.** *bible*: The ritual of swearing and kissing, together with Julia's "most religiously," make it plain "this book" must be a religious work, almost certainly the Bible.
281. Usually treated as forming a single hexameter line with line 282, but probably amphibious, also completing line 280.
283. **equal**: equitable.

BOSOLA   And wherefore should you lay fair marble colors
   Upon your rotten purposes to me,
   Unless you imitate some that do plot great treasons,
   And, when they have done, go hide themselves i'th'graves   300
   Of those were actors in't?
CARDINAL   No more.
   There is a fortune attends thee.
BOSOLA   Shall I go sue to Fortune any longer?
   'Tis the fool's pilgrimage.
CARDINAL   I have honors in store for thee.   305
BOSOLA   There are a many ways that conduct to seeming
   Honor, and some of them very dirty ones.
CARDINAL   Throw to the devil thy melancholy! The fire burns
   well:
   What need we keep a-stirring of 't, and make
   A greater smother? Thou wilt kill Antonio?   310
BOSOLA   Yes.
CARDINAL   Take up that body.
BOSOLA   I think I shall
   Shortly grow the common bier for churchyards!
CARDINAL   I will allow thee some dozen of attendants
   To aid thee in the murder.
BOSOLA   Oh, by no means.
   Physicians that apply horse leeches to any rank swelling use to   315
   cut off their tails, that the blood may run through them the
   faster. Let me have no train when I go to shed blood, lest it
   make me have a greater when I ride to the gallows.
CARDINAL   Come to me after midnight, to help to remove
   That body to her own lodging. I'll give out   320
   She died o'th'plague; 'twill breed the less inquiry
   After her death.
BOSOLA   Where's Castruchio, her husband?

297–98. **lay . . . me**: the comparison (as Brown explains) is with painting rotten wood to
   resemble marble; but the mention of graves (line 300) ensures a suggestive connection
   with the marble of tomb sculpture and the rot within. Cf. Middleton's commendatory
   verses (lines 7–11).
299–301. **Unless . . . in't**: adapted from George Chapman, *Penitential Psalms*, "A Great
   Man," line 62.
302. Amphibious line.
305. **'Tis . . . pilgrimage**: proverbial (Tilley, F600).
310. **smother**: suffocating smoke (*OED* n. 1).
312. **bier**: movable stand on which a corpse was conveyed to burial (*OED* n. 2).
315–18. another passage that, though printed as verse in Q1, is best regarded as rhythmic prose.
317–18. **train . . . gallows**: Condemned prisoners on their way to Tyburn were typically
   followed by a crowd of onlookers.
323. Amphibious line.

CARDINAL   He's rode to Naples
　　To take possession of Antonio's citadel.   325
BOSOLA   Believe me, you have done a very happy turn.
CARDINAL   Fail not to come. There is the master key
　　Of our lodgings [*Gives a key*]; and by that you may conceive
　　What trust I plant in you.
BOSOLA　　　　　　　　You shall find me ready.
　　　　　　　　　　　　　　　　　Exit [CARDINAL].

Oh, poor Antonio! Though nothing be so needful   330
To thy estate as pity, yet I find
Nothing so dangerous. I must look to my footing:
In such slippery ice pavements men had need
To be frost-nailed well—they may break their necks else.
The precedent's here afore me. How this man   335
Bears up in blood, seems fearless! Why, 'tis well:
Security some men call the suburbs of hell,
Only a dead wall between. Well, good Antonio,
I'll seek thee out, and all my care shall be
To put thee into safety from the reach   340
Of these most cruel biters that have got
Some of thy blood already. It may be
I'll join with thee in a most just revenge.
The weakest arm is strong enough that strikes
With the sword of justice. Still methinks the Duchess   345
Haunts me. There, there!—'Tis nothing but my melancholy.
O Penitence, let me truly taste thy cup,
That throws men down only to raise them up!   *Exit.*

331. **estate:** condition.
334. **be frost-nailed:** have hobnails on their boots.
336. **Bears up in blood:** "keeps up his courage" (Lucas); "persists in shedding blood" (Brown).
337. **Security . . . hell:** Security was the sin of over-confidence in one's own salvation; Bosola's aphorism is borrowed from Thomas Adams, *The Gallants Burden* (1612) C1ᵛ.
338. **dead:** continuous, but also playing on the usual meaning of the word to suggest the boundary between life and death.
341. **biters:** bloodsuckers.
342. **blood:** i.e., his wife and children.
344–45. **weakest . . . justice:** from Sidney, *Arcadia*, 3, 12, *Works*, I, p. 422.
345–46. **Still . . . there:** It may be (as Brown and others have suggested) that the Duchess's ghost was meant to appear at this point, and perhaps again in the following scene (see 5.3.45–46), but if no spirit were visible to the audience, they would be more likely to understand the haunting simply as a projection of the characters' melancholy.
347. **cup:** no doubt suggesting the cup of communion, tasted in the Protestant dispensation only after a formal act of contrition or penitence; but also perhaps echoing Christ's "Let this cup pass from me" (Matthew 26.39; see also Mark 14.36; Luke 22.42).

5.3

[*Enter*] ANTONIO [*and*] DELIO.

DELIO   Yond's the Cardinal's window. This fortification
Grew from the ruins of an ancient abbey;
And to yond side o'th'river lies a wall,
Piece of a cloister, which in my opinion
Gives the best echo that you ever heard—   5
So hollow and so dismal, and withal
So plain in the distinction of our words
That many have supposed it is a spirit
That answers.

ANTONIO   I do love these ancient ruins:
We never tread upon them but we set   10
Our foot upon some reverend history;
And questionless, here in this open court,
Which now lies naked to the injuries
Of stormy weather, some men lie interred
Loved the church so well, and gave so largely to't,   15
They thought it should have canopied their bones
Till doomsday; but all things have their end:
Churches and cities, which have diseases like to men,
Must have like death that we have.

ECHO [*from the* DUCHESS's *grave.*]   *Like death that we have.*

DELIO   Now the echo hath caught you.

ANTONIO   It groaned, methought,
and gave   20
A very deadly accent.

ECHO   *Deadly accent.*

DELIO   I told you 'twas a pretty one: you may make it
A huntsman, or a falconer, a musician,
Or a thing of sorrow.

ECHO   *A thing of sorrow.*

ANTONIO   Ay, sure, that suits it best.

ECHO   *That suits it best.*   25

5.3. This scene seems designed as a response to the graveyard scene in *Hamlet* with its
stress on the ephemerality of worldly greatness. Though entirely of Webster's invention,
it was clearly inspired by George Wither's *Prince Henry's Obsequies* (1612); see pp. xxii
and 171 in this volume.

1–2. fortification . . . abbey: a detail that belongs more to the landscape of post-Reformation
England, with its many ruined abbeys (Figure 3) than to Renaissance Italy. As Marcus
points out, the architecture of the Cardinal's residence mirrors his transformation
from cleric to soldier at 3.4.6 SD.

10–11. we . . . history: from Montaigne (translating Cicero), *Essays*, III.ix, p. 247.

14–17. some . . . doomsday: The wealthy and powerful typically sought to have themselves interred inside the church because of the superstition that burial near the altar
(*ad sanctos*) improved their prospect of salvation.

17. all . . . end: proverbial (Tilley, E120).

ANTONIO   'Tis very like my wife's voice.
ECHO   *Ay, wife's voice.*
DELIO   Come, let's walk farther from't.
I would not have you go to th'Cardinal's tonight—
Do not.
ECHO   *Do not.*   30
DELIO   Wisdom doth not more moderate wasting sorrow
Than time: take time for't—be mindful of thy safety.
ECHO   *Be mindful of thy safety.*
ANTONIO   Necessity compels me.
Make scrutiny throughout the passages
Of your own life; you'll find it impossible   35
To fly your fate.
[ECHO]   *Oh, fly your fate!*
DELIO   Hark! The dead stones seem to have pity on you
And give you good counsel.
ANTONIO   Echo, I will not talk with thee,
For thou art a dead thing.
ECHO   *Thou art a dead thing.*   40
ANTONIO   My duchess is asleep now,
And her little ones, I hope sweetly. Oh, heaven,
Shall I never see her more?
ECHO   *Never see her more.*
ANTONIO   I marked not one repetition of the echo
But that; and on the sudden, a clear light   45
Presented me a face folded in sorrow.
DELIO   Your fancy, merely.
ANTONIO   Come, I'll be out of this ague;
For to live thus is not indeed to live—
It is a mockery and abuse of life.
I will not henceforth save myself by halves;   50
Lose all, or nothing.
DELIO   Your own virtue save you!
I'll fetch your eldest son, and second you.

---

28. Amphibious line.
35–36. impossible . . . fate: proverbial (Tilley, F83).
40. Amphibious line.
45–46. on . . . sorrow: cf. *A Monumental Column*, p. 173 in this volume, and 1.1.202. See also p. xxii in this volume. It is not clear whether this vision is simply Antonio's fantasy, or whether the audience is meant to share his glimpse of the sorrowful face; however, the wording suggests that Webster envisaged a staging of this scene that would make use of a spectacular property that the King's Men had recently employed in Thomas Middleton's (?) *The Lady's Tragedy* (*The Second Maiden's Tragedy*) (1611).
46. folded: enveloped (OED, v. 8a).
47. ague: fit of shaking, fever.

It may be that the sight of his own blood,
Spread in so sweet a figure, may beget
The more compassion. However, fare you well.   55
Though in our miseries Fortune have a part,
Yet in our noble suff'rings she hath none;
Contempt of pain, that we may call our own.   *Exeunt.*

5.4

[*Enter*] CARDINAL, PESCARA, MALATESTE, RODERIGO, [*and*]
GRISOLAN [*with torches*].

CARDINAL   You shall not watch tonight by the sick prince:
    His grace is very well recoverèd.
MALATESTE   Good my lord, suffer us.
CARDINAL   Oh, by no means;
    The noise and change of object in his eye
    Doth more distract him. I pray, all to bed;   5
    And though you hear him in his violent fit,
    Do not rise, I entreat you.
PESCARA   So, sir, we shall not.
CARDINAL   Nay, I must have you promise
    Upon your honors, for I was enjoined to't
    By himself; and he seemed to urge it sensibly.   10
PESCARA   Let our honors bind this trifle.
CARDINAL   Nor any of your followers.
MALATESTE   Neither.
CARDINAL   It may be, to make trial of your promise
    When he's asleep, myself will rise and feign
    Some of his mad tricks, and cry out for help,   15
    And feign myself in danger.
MALATESTE   If your throat were cutting,
    I'd not come at you, now I have protested against it.
CARDINAL   Why, I thank you.   [*Walks apart.*]
GRISOLAN   'Twas a foul storm tonight.
RODERIGO   The Lord Ferdinand's chamber shook like an osier.
MALATESTE   'Twas nothing but pure kindness in the devil   20

---

54. **Spread:** displayed (*OED*, ppl. a. 1a).
55–58. Most editors follow Sampson's conjecture and give these lines to Antonio. How-
    ever, as Marcus points out, the text offers no warrant for this since, although there is a
    page break after "compassion," the catchword is "However," and there is no sign of a
    speech's prefix having been omitted.
5.4. SD. *with torches*: The conventional way of indicating a nighttime scene; the torches
    must depart with the group of courtiers at line 21, leaving the stage in darkness, because
    Bosola is at first able to hear, but not see, the Cardinal (lines 31–32). Cf. note at 4.1.30.
5. **distract him:** drive him mad (*OED*, v. 6).
10. **sensibly:** with strong feeling (*OED*, adv. 2b).
11. **bind:** commit us to.
19. **osier:** slender species of willow.

To rock his own child.   *Exeunt [all except* CARDINAL].
CARDINAL   The reason why I would not suffer these
  About my brother is because at midnight
  I may with better privacy convey
  Julia's body to her own lodging. Oh, my conscience!   25
  I would pray now, but the devil takes away my heart
  For having any confidence in prayer.
      [*Enter* BOSOLA *unnoticed.*]
  About this hour I appointed Bosola
  To fetch the body. When he hath served my turn,
  He dies.   *Exit.*
BOSOLA   Ha?   30
  'Twas the Cardinal's voice. I heard him name
  Bosola, and my death. —Listen! I hear one's footing.
      [*Enter*] FERDINAND.
FERDINAND   Strangling is a very quiet death.
BOSOLA [*Aside*]   Nay, then, I see I must stand upon my guard.
FERDINAND   What say to that? Whisper softly: Do you   35
    agree to't?
  So it must be done i'th'dark: the Cardinal
  Would not for a thousand pounds the doctor should see it.
                                          Exit.
BOSOLA   My death is plotted; here's the consequence of murder.
  We value not desert, nor Christian breath,
  When we know black deeds must be cured with death.   40
      [*Enter*] ANTONIO [*and*] SERVANT.
SERVANT   Here stay, sir, and be confident, I pray.
  I'll fetch you a dark lantern.   *Exit.*
ANTONIO   Could I take him at his prayers,
  There were hope of pardon.
BOSOLA   Fall right my sword!
      [*Stabs* ANTONIO.]
  I'll not give thee so much leisure as to pray.
ANTONIO   Oh, I am gone! Thou hast ended a long suit   45
  In a minute.
BOSOLA   What art thou?
ANTONIO   A most wretched thing,
  That only have thy benefit in death
  To appear myself.
      [*Re-enter*] SERVANT [*with lantern.*]

---

32. **footing:** footsteps.
42. **dark lantern:** see note to 2.3.0 SD.
45. **suit:** quest; "i.e. punning on 'pray' of the previous line" (Brown).
47–48. **That . . . myself:** who, thanks to the fact that you have killed me, can now dare
  to reveal myself.

SERVANT	Where are you, sir?

ANTONIO   Very near my home. —Bosola?

SERVANT   Oh, misfortune!

BOSOLA   Smother thy pity; thou art dead else. —Antonio?   50
  The man I would have saved 'bove mine own life!
  We are merely the star's tennis balls, struck and banded
  Which way please them. O good Antonio,
  I'll whisper one thing in thy dying ear
  Shall make thy heart break quickly: thy fair duchess   55
  And two sweet children—

ANTONIO   Their very names
  Kindle a little life in me.

BOSOLA   —Are murdered!

ANTONIO   Some men have wished to die
  At the hearing of sad tidings; I am glad
  That I shall do't in sadness. I would not now   60
  Wish my wounds balmed nor healed, for I have no use
  To put my life to. In all our quest of greatness,
  Like wanton boys, whose pastime is their care,
  We follow after bubbles blown in th'air.
  Pleasure of life, what is't? Only the good hours   65
  Of an ague, merely a preparative to rest,
  To endure vexation. I do not ask
  The process of my death; only commend me
  To Delio—

BOSOLA   Break, heart!

ANTONIO   —And let my son fly the courts of princes.   [*Dies.*]

BOSOLA   Thou seem'st to have loved Antonio?

SERVANT   I brought him
    hither   70
  To have reconciled him to the Cardinal.

BOSOLA   I do not ask thee that.
  Take him up, if thou tender thine own life,
  And bear him where the Lady Julia
  Was wont to lodge. —Oh, my fate moves swift!   75
  I have this cardinal in the forge already;

---

49. **home:** death, the grave.
52–53. **We . . . them:** a commonplace; see, e.g., Montaigne, *Essays* III.ix, p. 201: "*The gods perdie doe reckon and racket us men as their tennis-balles.*"
60. **in sadness:** in earnest.
63. **whose . . . care:** who care only for the games they play.
68. **process . . . death:** how my death came about.
69. **Break, heart!:** extra-metrical interjection.
73. **tender:** value.
76. **forge:** blacksmith's fire, where iron is heated (before being struck with the "hammer," line 77).

Now I'll bring him to th'hammer. Oh, direful misprision!
I will not imitate things glorious,
No more than base; I'll be mine own example. —
On, on; and look thou represent, for silence,   80
The thing thou bear'st.   *Exeunt [with* ANTONIO's *body].*

5.5

[*Enter*] CARDINAL, *with a book.*

CARDINAL   I am puzzled in a question about hell:
He says, in hell there's one material fire,
And yet it shall not burn all men alike.
Lay him by. How tedious is a guilty conscience!
When I look into the fishponds in my garden,   5
Methinks I see a thing armed with a rake
That seems to strike at me.
        [*Enter*] BOSOLA, *and* SERVANT *with* ANTONIO's *body.*
                                Now, art thou come?
Thou look'st ghastly:
There sits in thy face some great determination,
Mixed with some fear.
BOSOLA   Thus it lightens into action: 10
I am come to kill thee.
CARDINAL   Ha? Help! Our guard!
BOSOLA   Thou art deceived. They are out of thy howling.
CARDINAL   Hold! And I will faithfully divide
Revenues with thee.
BOSOLA   Thy prayers and proffers
Are both unseasonable.
CARDINAL   Raise the watch!   15
We are betrayed!
BOSOLA   I have confined your flight.
I'll suffer your retreat to Julia's chamber,
But no further.

---

77. **direful misprision:** dreadful error.
80. **represent:** imitate.
2–3. **in hell . . . alike:** The Cardinal appears to be reading Luis de Granada, *Spiritual and Heavenly Exercises* (trans. 1598); his lines closely paraphrase a passage from sig. I10 (Dent).
5–7. **When . . . me.** Webster's source here is an anecdote in Ludwig Lavater, *Of Ghosts and Spirits* (1572), where, however, the phantasm in the fishpond is armed with a sword. Citing William Bullein's *A Dialogue against the Fever Pestilence* (1564), Brennan suggests that the implement is "the Devils golden rake," which "raketh . . . in the conscience of the coveitous," symbolizing the Cardinal's worldly avarice. But it may simply be a detail invented to enhance the grotesque quality of the scene (as in the visions of hell created by Hieronymus Bosch, Pieter Breughel, and others).
7. **Now . . . come:** Editors are divided as to whether this should be seen as completing line 7, or as beginning line 8 (which would remain one syllable short). It should perhaps be treated as amphibious.
8. **ghastly:** terrifying; like a ghost; full of fear (*OED* a. 1–3).
10. **lightens:** illuminates (his obscure "determination"); flashes like a lightning bolt.

CARDINAL   Help! We are betrayed!
    [*Enter above*] PESCARA, MALATESTE, RODERIGO[, *and*
    GRISOLAN].
MALATESTE   Listen!
CARDINAL   My dukedom for rescue!
RODERIGO   Fie upon his counterfeiting!
MALATESTE   Why, 'tis not the Cardinal?
RODERIGO   Yes, yes, 'tis he;   20
    But I'll see him hanged ere I'll go down to him.
CARDINAL   Here's a plot upon me! I am assaulted! I am lost,
    Unless some rescue!
GRISOLAN   He doth this pretty well,
    But it will not serve to laugh me out of mine honor.
CARDINAL   The sword's at my throat!
RODERIGO   You would not bawl so
    loud then.   25
MALATESTE   Come, come,
    Let's go to bed—he told us thus much aforehand.
PESCARA   He wished you should not come at him; but believe't,
    The accent of the voice sounds not in jest.
    I'll down to him, howsoever, and with engines   30
    Force ope the doors.   [*Exit* PESCARA *above.*]
RODERIGO   Let's follow him aloof,
    And note how the Cardinal will laugh at him.
               [*Exeunt others above.*]
    [*Enter*] SERVANT *with* ANTONIO's *body.*
BOSOLA   There's for you first—   *He kills the* SERVANT.
    'Cause you shall not unbarricade the door
    To let in rescue.   35
CARDINAL   What cause hast thou to pursue my life?
BOSOLA [*Showing* ANTONIO's *body.*]   Look there.
CARDINAL   Antonio?
BOSOLA   Slain by my hand unwittingly.
    Pray, and be sudden: when thou killed'st thy sister,
    Thou took'st from Justice her most equal balance,
    And left her naught but her sword.
CARDINAL   Oh, mercy!   40
BOSOLA   Now it seems thy greatness was only outward;
    For thou fall'st faster of thyself than calamity

---

19. **My . . . rescue:** perhaps echoing *Richard III*, 5.7.6 (Gibbons); see note to 5.5.46.
30. **engines:** tools.
31. **aloof:** at a distance (*OED* adv. 3).
38. **thou:** Marcus notes how from this point Bosola shifts from the polite *you* to the
    familiar (and therefore disrespectful) *thou.*
39–40. **equal . . . sword:** Justice was allegorically represented as a blindfolded figure with
    a set of scales in one hand and a sword in the other.

Can drive thee. I'll not waste longer time. There!
[*Stabs the* CARDINAL.]

CARDINAL   Thou hast hurt me!

BOSOLA   Again!   [*Stabs him again.*]

CARDINAL   Shall I die like a leveret
Without any resistance? Help, help, help!   45
I am slain!
    [*Enter*] FERDINAND.

FERDINAND   Th'alarum! Give me a fresh horse!
Rally the vaunt-guard, or the day is lost!
[*Attacks the* CARDINAL].

Yield, yield! I give you the honor of arms,
Shake my sword over you: will you yield?

CARDINAL   Help me! I am your brother.

FERDINAND   The devil!   50
My brother fight upon the adverse party?
There flies your ransom.
He wounds the CARDINAL *and in the scuffle gives* BOSOLA *his death wound.*

CARDINAL   Oh, justice!
I suffer now for what hath former been;
Sorrow is held the eldest child of sin.

FERDINAND   Now you're brave fellows! Caesar's fortune was   55
harder than Pompey's: Caesar died in the arms of prosperity,
Pompey at the feet of disgrace; you both died in the field. The
pain's nothing; pain many times is taken away with the apprehension of greater, as the toothache with the sight of a barber
that comes to pull it out. There's philosophy for you!   60

BOSOLA   Now my revenge is perfect: sink, thou main cause
Of my undoing!   *He kills* FERDINAND.
            The last part of my life
Hath done me best service.

FERDINAND   Give me some wet hay—I am broken-winded.

---

44. **leveret**: young hare.
46. **Give . . . horse**: Ferdinand imagines himself on the battlefield. Gibbons, citing further echoes of *Richard III* (5.5.132; 5.7.7, 13), suggests that "for those spectators who
recognise the quotation the absurdity will be doubled—Ferdinand believing himself to
be a king in a famous Shakespeare play and speaking lines from it. In the original production the effect would have been further enhanced [by the fact that] the actor playing Ferdinand (Burbage), had played . . . Richard III." See note to 5.5.19.
47. **vaunt-guard**: vanguard.
48. **give . . . arms**: offer you the honorable terms of surrender due to a prisoner of rank.
52. **There . . . ransom**: there goes any chance of earning ransom from you.
53–57. **Caesar's . . . disgrace**: Paraphrase of George Whetstone, *Heptameron* (1582),
sig. H2.
59. **barber**: Dental operations were performed by barber-surgeons in Webster's day.
64. **wet hay**: regarded as a remedy for broken-winded horses.

I do account this world but a dog kennel.   65
I will vault credit and affect high pleasures
Beyond death.
BOSOLA   He seems to come to himself,
  Now he's so near bottom.
FERDINAND   My sister, oh, my sister! There's the cause on't.
  Whether we fall by ambition, blood, or lust,   70
  Like diamonds, we are cut with our own dust.   [*Dies.*]
CARDINAL   Thou hast thy payment too.
BOSOLA   Yes, I hold my weary soul in my teeth—
  'Tis ready to part from me. I do glory
  That thou, which stood'st like a huge pyramid   75
  Begun upon a large and ample base,
  Shalt end in a little point, a kind of nothing.
       [*Enter below*] PESCARA, MALATESTE, RODERIGO[, *and*]
       GRISOLAN.
PESCARA   How now, my lord?
MALATESTE   Oh, sad disaster!
RODERIGO   How comes this?
BOSOLA   Revenge—for the Duchess of Malfi, murdered
  By th'Aragonian brethren; for Antonio,   80
  Slain by this hand; for lustful Julia,
  Poisoned by this man; and lastly for myself,
  That was an actor in the main of all,
  Much 'gainst mine own good nature, yet i'th'end
  Neglected.
PESCARA   How now, my lord?
CARDINAL   Look to my brother.   85
  He gave us these large wounds, as we were struggling
  Here i'th'rushes. And now, I pray, let me
  Be laid by and never thought of.   [*Dies.*]
PESCARA   How fatally, it seems, he did withstand
  His own rescue!
MALATESTE [*To* BOSOLA]   Thou wretched thing of blood,   90
  How came Antonio by his death?
BOSOLA   In a mist; I know not how—
  Such a mistake as I have often seen
  In a play. Oh, I am gone!
  We are only like dead walls or vaulted graves   95

66. **vault credit:** outdo belief.
71. **Like . . . dust:** cf. Tilley, D323, "Diamonds cut diamonds."
87. **rushes:** strewn on the floor in houses and on stages.
92. **In a mist:** cf. 4.2.175.
95. **dead walls:** see note to 5.2.338.

That, ruined, yields no echo. Fare you well:
It may be pain, but no harm to me to die
In so good a quarrel. Oh, this gloomy world!
In what a shadow, or deep pit of darkness,
Doth womanish and fearful mankind live!   100
Let worthy minds ne'er stagger in distrust
To suffer death or shame for what is just—
Mine is another voyage.   [*Dies.*]

PESCARA   The noble Delio, as I came to th'palace,
Told me of Antonio's being here, and showed me   105
A pretty gentleman, his son and heir.

    [*Enter*] DELIO [*with* ANTONIO's *son*].

MALATESTE   Oh, sir, you come too late.

DELIO   I heard so, and
Was armed for't ere I came. Let us make noble use
Of this great ruin, and join all our force
To establish this young hopeful gentleman   110
In's mother's right. These wretched eminent things
Leave no more fame behind 'em than should one
Fall in a frost and leave his print in snow—
As soon as the sun shines, it ever melts
Both form and matter. I have ever thought   115
Nature doth nothing so great for great men
As when she's pleased to make them lords of truth:
Integrity of life is fame's best friend,
Which nobly, beyond death, shall crown the end.   *Exeunt.*

FINIS.

96.   **no echo:** Contrast the Echo in 5.3.
99–100.   adapted from Sidney, *Arcadia* 5 (*Works*, II, 177).
110–11.   **establish . . . right:** As various editors note, Webster here seems to forget the
    existence of the Duchess's son by her first marriage, who would presumably have been
    the true heir to the Dukedom of Malfi (see note to 4.2.267–69).
116–17.   paraphrase of *Arcadia* II.vii (*Works*, I.190).
118.   **Integrity of life:** translating *integer vitae*, a famous phrase from Horace, *Odes* I, xxii.
119.   cf. Tilley, E116, "The end crowns all."

Malfi: Collation

The Actors' Names] *before Dedication, Q1*
The Doctor . . . Officers] *Lucas 2; bracket opposite* Cariola *and*
Court Officers *Q1*
1.1. SD] *Q4;* Antonio, and Delio, Bosola, Cardinall. *Q1*
22 SD] *Brown;* BOSOLA 0 SD *Q1*
28 SD] *Brown;* CARDINALL 0 SD *Q1*
33–66] *as verse Q1*
40 SD] *Brown; after* them, *line 43 Dyce 1*
46 SD] *Cambridge*
58 dogs,] *Q2;* dogges, and *Q;* dogs and horses, *conj Lucas.*
66 SD] *Q4*
70 Foix] *Q2 (*Foyx*);* Foux *Q*
79 SD] *after Bevington;* SCENA II / Antonio, Delio, Ferdinand,
Cardinall, Dutchesse, Castruchio, Siluio, Rodocico, Grisolan, Bosola,
Iulia, Cariola. *Q*
83 SD] *Brown; at line 79. Q1*
89–140] *as verse Q1*
141 SD] *Dyce 1; at line 78. 1–2 Q1*
145 SD] *this ed. (after Bevington)*
150–60] *as verse Q1*
174 shrewd] *Q2;* shewed *Q1*
202 SD] *Bevington*
204 SD] *Marcus (after Q4)*
210 SD 1] *Bevington*
210 SD 2] *Dyce 1*
213 leaguer] *Q2;* leagues *Q1*
213 DUCHESS] *Sampson;* Ferd. *Q1*
215 SDD 1,2] *Bevington*
215 SD 3] *Dyce 1*
222 SD] *Bevington*
223 SD] *Dyce 1*
239 SD] *Bevington*
241–42] *one line Q1*
256 SD] *after Bevington*
283 SD 2] *Dyce 1*

318 SD] *Q4*
321 SD] *Bevington*
330 SD] *Q4*
351 SDD] *after Dyce 1*
356 these] *Dyce 1*; this *Q1*
361 SD] *Cambridge*
372 distraction] *Q3*; distruction *Q1*
374 you] *Q2*; yon *Q1*
395 SD] *after Cambridge*
403 SD 1] *after Dyce 1*
407 SD] *Dyce 2*
452 SD] *Brown*
455 SD] *Cambridge*
461 SD] *Dyce*
464 de] *Sampson; not in Q*
464 SD] *after Dyce 2*
476 SD] *Cambridge*
487 SD] *this ed. (after Marcus)*
2.1 SD] *Q4; Bosola, Castruchio, an Old Lady, Antonio, Delio, Duch-esse, Rodorico, Grisolan. Q1*
1–44] *as verse Q1*
21 SD] *after Dyce 1; 0 Q1*
61 SD] *Cambridge*
61–62] *as verse Q1*
62 SD] *Dyce 1*
72 SD 1] *after Q4*
72 SD 2] *this ed.*
75 SD] *Lucas*
77–80] *as verse Q1*
85–90] *as verse Q1*
93–103] *as verse Q1*
103 SD Enter . . . Attendants] *after Q4; 0 Q1*
103 SD RODERIGO . . . GRISOLAN] *0 Q1*
109 SD] *Cambridge*
112 swoon] *Dyce 1 (after Q2 swound); sound Q1*
113 SD] *Dyce 2*
114 SD] *Cambridge*
118 DUCHESS] *Q4 (and annotated copies of Q1)*
125 Methought] *Q4;* My thought *Q1*
128 SD] *Dyce 2*
129 SD] *Bevington*
131 SD] *Bevington*
138 SD] *Cambridge*
140 SD] *Bevington*
141–42 pretty art, / This] *Cambridge;* pretty / Art this *Q*

152 SD] *Cambridge*
155 SD] *as Q4; Exit Duchesse Q1*

2.2 SD] *Dyce 1; Bosola, old Lady, Antonio, Rodorigo, Grisolan:*
seruants, Delio, Cariola Q1
1–26] *as verse Q1*
2 SD] *Dyce1*
5 SD] *this ed.*
13 bears] *Q4; beare Q1*
26 SD 1] *Dyce 1*
26 SD 2] *Dyce 1; at* line 0 *Q*
29 SD] *Dyce 1*
31 SD 1] *this ed.*
31 SD 2] *Dyce 1;* line 0 *Q1*
33 SD] *Q4*
43 SD] *this ed.*
54] *this ed; Q1 lines* The Innocent / Shall
56 SD] *Dyce 1*
73 SD 1] *Dyce 1*
73 SD 2] *Dyce 1;* line 0 *Q; Enter Cariola with a Child Q4*

2.3 SD] *Q4; Bosola, Antonio Q1*
9 SD] *Cambridge; Enter Antonio, with a Candle his Sword drawn Q4*
14 SDD] *Dyce 1;* (This . . . me) *Q1*
29–30 SDD] *after Q4*
39 BOSOLA] *after Lucas*
41 SD 1] *Dyce 2*
41 SD 2] *Cambridge*
46–51 SDD] *after Dyce 2*
56 SD] *Dyce 2*
67 cased] *Q2* (cas'd); caside *Q1*

2.4 SD] *Q4; Cardinall, and Iulia, Seruant, and Delio Q1*
12 turnings] *Q3;* turning *Q1*
39 SD] *Dyce 1; at* line 0 *Q1*
40 SD] *Cambridge*
45 SD 1] *Dyce 1*
45 SD 2] *Q4; at* line 0 *Q1*
46 SD] *Brennan*
68, 70 SDD] *Q4*

2.5.30 mother's] *Q2* (mothers); mother *Q1*
43 o'th'] *Q3;* th' *Q1*

3.1 SD] *Q4; Antonio, and Delio, Duchesse, Ferdinand, Bosola Q1*
37 SD 1] *after Q4* (Duchess, Ferdinand, Bosola)

37 SD 2] *this ed.*
38 SD] *this ed.*
45 SD] *this ed.*
46 SD] *this ed.*
48 SD] *this ed.*
56 SD] *Dyce 2; 0 Q; 37 Q4*
87–88 you / Are] *Sampson;* are / Your *Q1*

3.2. SD] *Q4 (subs); Dutchesse, Antonio, Cariola, Ferdinand, Bosola, Officers Q1*
1–2 SDD] *this ed.*
13–16] *this ed.; Q lines* For . . . bedfellow. / I . . . that. / Sir . . . question. / I . . . Cariola.
20 SD] *Lucas (subs)*
22 SD] *Lucas (subs)*
53 SDD] *this ed.*
57 SD] *Dyce 1; Exeunt Q1*
60 orris] *this ed.;* arras *Q1*
62 SD] *Q4 (after line 62)*
63 brother] *this ed.;* brothers *Q1*
68 SD] *Lucas*
68–69] *as Q4; one line Q1*
78 us] *Q4; not in Q1*
86–87] *Sampson; Q1 lines* Yes . . . I / Could . . . Basilisque
90 SD] *this ed.*
99 SD] *this ed.*
140 SD 2] *Dyce 1; Enter . . . Pistoll after* apparition *line 139 Q1*
142 SD] *this ed.*
143 SD] *Lucas*
148 SD] *Q1* ("she shewes the poniard," opp. line 150)
153 SD] *Lucas*
169 SD] *Dyce 2*
171 SD 2] *Q4*
179 SD] *this ed.*
191 SD] *this ed.*
223 SD] *Dyce 1; after line 216 (Exeunt) Q1*
238–61] *as verse Q1* (. . . riches, / When . . . man / He . . . wealth / That . . . sent / One . . . scuttles.: / Let . . . iewell, / You . . . away, / To . . . excellent / Courtier . . . it / As beastly . . . little, / As devilish . . . much, / Both . . . fortune: / His . . . perfection, / And . . . roome. / It . . . of't. / But . . . descended. / Will . . . herald, / Rather . . . vertues // You . . . him, / For . . . prince, / Is . . . Spring, / The . . . tree, / Rewards . . . so, / I . . . Polititians / Rotten . . . hartstring / Then . . . fauour. / Fare-thee-well . . . world / Would . . . yest / That . . . fall, / Was . . . virtue.)
308 SD] *Q4 (subs); Exit Q1*

3.3 SILVIO, [*and*] DELIO] *Q4 (subs); Siluio, Delio, Bosola Q1*
6 SD] *Gibbons (subs.)*
8 SD] *this ed.*
12–13] *Lucas; one line Q1*
19 painters] *Q1c; pewterers Q1a–b*
33 DELIO] *Q1 (but only as catchword on sig. I2v, not at beginning of speech on H1)*
34 SD] *this ed. (after Gibbons)*
41–47] *as verse Q1* (I . . . scholler, / Like . . . in / Hercules . . . was, / Or . . . tooth-ach, / He hath . . . know the / True . . . and this / He . . . man)
51–53] *as verse Q1* (That . . . oppression / Then . . . ones, / He . . . storme)
73 life] *Q2; like Q1*
75 hundred] *Q2; hundredth Q1*

3.4.6 SD *habit*] *Q1b; order Q1a*
6 SD *of*] *Q2*
6 SD [*three*]] *this ed.*
6 SD *in dumb show*] *Q1b; not in Q1a*
6 SD *ditty*] *Q1b; Hymne Q1a*
7 *Arms*] *Q1b; The Hymne / Armes Q1a*
8–9 The . . . his] *Q1b; not in Q1a*
29 sir] *Q1b; not in Q1a*
31 Hath] *Q1b; had Q1a*

3.5 SD] *Q4 (subs); Antonio, Duchesse, Children, Cariola, Seruants. Bosola, Souldiers, with Vizards Q1*
26 SD] *Q4 (subs); A Letter Q1*
27–28] *Dyce 1; one line Q1*
63 SD] *this ed.*
67 SD] *this ed.*
76–78] *Dyce 1; And . . . right, / But Q1*
84 SD] *this ed.*
88 SD *with* . . . *Son*] *Dyce 1 (subs.)*
91 SD *Enter* . . . *guard*] *Q1b; not in Q1a*
93 SD [*wearing*] *vizards*] *after Q Souldiers with Vizards (at 0)*
91 move] *Q1a (moue); more Q1b*
97 BOSOLA] *Q1b; not in Q1a*
101 DUCHESS] *Q1b; Ant. Q1a*
101 o'ercharged] *Q2; ore-char'd Q1*
103–05] *Dyce 1; Q1 lines* "I . . . conuay / All . . . againe"
106–07] *Dyce 1; Q1 lines* pitie. / Pitie . . . alive
107 a] *Q1b; not in Q1a*
128 dogship] *Marcus; dog-ship Q1*

4.1 SD] *Gibbons; Ferdinand, Bosola, Dutchesse, Cariola, Seruants Q1*
29 SD 1] *this ed.*
50 SD] *this ed.*
52 SD 2] *this ed., after Lucas*
88 vipers] *Q1;* vapors *conj. Brown*
89 SD] *this ed.*
97–98 Oh . . . go] *Dyce 1; one line Q1*
105–06] *Dyce 1; one line Q1*

4.2 SD] *this ed.; Dutchesse, Cariola, Seruant, Mad-men, Bosola,*
Executioners, Ferdinand. Q1
15–16] *Marcus; Q1 lines . . . nothing: / When . . . sleepe. / Like*
35 SD] *this ed.*
36 SD] *Q4*
59 SD 1] *Dyce 2*
65 bill] *Q1; bell Q2*
97 SD] *this ed.*
108 SD and . . . leave] *Brown*
109 SD] *Brown*
154 SD Enter EXECUTIONERS] *Q4; A Coffin, Cords, and a Bell Q1*
164 SD] *Q4*
186 SD] *Brennan*
192 SD] *Q4 subs.*
220 SD] *Dyce 2*
224 SD] *this ed. (after Brennan)*
232 SD] *this ed.*
234 SD] *Brennan*
239 SD] *this ed.*
240 SD 1] *Dyce 2*
240 SD 2] *Q4 (subs)*
241 SD] *Q4; at 0 Q1*
353–54] *Dyce 1; one line Q1*
354 SD] *this ed.*
360 SD [with the body] *Q4 (subs.)*

5.1 SD] *Q4; Antonio, Delio, Pescara, Iulia Q1*
15 SD] *this ed; at 0 Q1*
17 SD] *after Sampson*
25 SD] *Q4; at 0 Q1*
29 SD] *after Dyce 2*
36 SD 2] *Sampson*
55 SD] *Sampson*
59 SD] *Cambridge*

5.2 SD] *Q4 (subs.); Pescara, a Doctor, Ferdinand, Cardinall, Malat-*
este, Bosola, Iulia

27–28] *this ed.; Q1 lines* They'll . . . him / Stand
38 SD] *Q4 (subs.)*
50 SD] *Dyce 2*
67 SD] *after Lucas*
70–71 SD] *this ed.*
77–78 SD] *Q4*
79 SD] *Q4*
80 SD] *Brown*
86 SDD] *Dyce 2 (subs.)*
99 SD] *this ed.*
102 SD] *Q4 (subs.)*
103 SD] *Brown*
107 SD] *Dyce 2 (subs.)*
118 SD] *Q4*
120 SD] *Dyce 2*
140 bought] *Dyce 1;* brought *Q1*
149 SD] *Lucas 1 (subs.)*
159 SD] *this ed.*
161–62] *Brown; one line Q1*
165 SD] *this ed. (after Lucas "Embraces her")*
167–70] *Marcus; Q1 lines* You'll . . . say, / I . . . Ladies / Is . . . them
174–5 Why . . . amiss] *Thorndike; one line Q1*
182 SD] *this ed.*
183 SD] *Dyce 2*
184 SD 1] *Dyce 2*
184 SD 2] *this ed.*
195–97] *this ed.; Q1 lines* And the . . . streete, / Vnder . . . there / I . . . you
202–03] *Dyce 1; as one line Q1*
212–16] *this ed.; Q1 lines* Not . . . an / Vngratefull . . . Lady? / You . . . feather-beds, / But . . . pillows.
224 SD 1] *this ed. (after Q4 Exit* BOSOLA*)*
224 SD 2] *Dyce 1 (subs.)*
227 SD 1] *Hazlitt*
227 SD 2] *Dyce 2*
274–75] *Dyce 1; Q1 lines* it. / No . . . booke.
275 SD] *Weis (subs.)*
276 SD] *Brennan (subs.)*
280 SD] *this ed.; Enter* BOSOLA *Q4*
289 SD] *Q4*
295–96] *Dyce 1; Q1 lines* intended. / Very . . . murderer
319–22] *this ed.; Q1 lines* (Come . . . body / To . . . Plague; / Twill . . . death
328 SD] *this ed.*

5.3 SD] *Gibbons; Antonio, Delio, Eccho (from the Dutchesse Graue.)*
Q1
19 SD] *this ed.;* 0 *Q1*
28 let's] *Q4;* let's us *Q1*
34 passages] *Q4;* passes *Q1*
36 [ECHO]] *Q4*

5.4 SD] *Dyce 1 (subs.); Cardinall, Pescara, Malateste, Rodorigo,
Grisolan, Bosola, Ferdinand, Antonio, Seruant. Q1*
5.4 SD with torches] *this ed.*
18 SD] *Gibbons*
27 SD] *Gibbons (subs.)*
32 SD] *Dyce 1;* 0 *Q1*
33 quiet] *Q2;* quiein *Q1*
34 SD] *Dyce 2*
48 SD] *Q4 (subs.)*
69 SD] *Dyce 1*

5.5 SD] *Q4; Cardinall (with a Booke), Bosola, Pescara, Malateste,
Rodorigo, Ferdinand, Delio, Seruant with Antonio's body*
7 SD] *Q4;* 0 *Q1*
7–8 That . . . ghastly] *Dyce 2; one line Q1*
15–16 Raise . . . betrayed] *Lucas 1; one line Q1*
18 SD] *Dyce 2*
26–27] *McIlwraith; one line Q1*
31 SD] *Dyce 1 (subs.)*
32 SD] *Marcus (subs.)*
33–34] *Lucas; one line Q1*
43 SD] *Q4*
44 SD] *Dyce 2*
55–60] *as prose Dyce 1; Q lines* Now . . . fellowes / Cæsars . . . Pompeys: / Cæsar . . . prosperity, / Pompey . . . field, / The paine's . . . away, with / The apprehension . . . fight / Of . . .
71 SD] *Dyce 1*
77 SD] *Q4 (subs.);* 0 *Q1*
81 this] *Q4;* his *Q1*
88 SD] *Q4*
103 SD] *Q4*
106 SD] *Q4;* 0 *Q1*

CONTEXTS

Sources and Analogues

WILLIAM PAINTER

The Infortunate Marriage of a Gentleman Called Antonio Bologna with the Duchess of Malfi, and the Pitiful Death of Them Both†

The xxiii Novel

The greater honor and authority men have in this world, and the greater their estimation is, the more sensible and notorious are the faults by them committed, and the greater is their slander. In like manner more difficult it is for that man to tolerate and sustain fortune, which all the days of his life hath lived at his ease, if by chance he fall into any great necessity, than for him which never felt but woe, mishap, and adversity. Dionysius the Tyrant of Sicilia, felt greater pain when he was expelled his kingdom than Milo did, being banished from Rome. For so much as the one was a sovereign lord, the son of a king, a justiciary on earth, and the other but a simple citizen of a city, wherein the people had laws, and the laws of magistrates had in reverence. So likewise the fall of a high and lofty tree, maketh a greater noise, than that which is low and little. High towers and stately palaces of princes be seen further off than the poor cabins and homely shepherds' sheepcotes. The walls of lofty cities salute the viewers of the same farther off than the simple caves, which the poor do dig below the mountain rocks. Wherefore it behoveth the noble, and such as have charge of common wealth, to live an honest life, and bear their port upright, that none have cause to take ill example upon discourse of their deeds and naughty life. And above all that modesty ought to be kept by women, whom as their race, noble birth, authority, and name maketh them more famous, even so their virtue, honesty, chastity, and continency more praiseworthy. And behoveful it is that, like as they wish to be

---

† From William Painter, *The Second Tome of the Palace of Pleasure, Containing Store of Goodly Histories, Tragical Matters, and other Moral Argument, Very Requisite for Delight and Profit* (London, 1567).

honored above all other, so their life do make them worthy of that honor, without disgracing their name by deed or word, or blemishing their brightness which may commend the same. I greatly fear that all the princely facts, the exploits and conquests done by the Babylonian Queen Semiramis never was recommended with such praise as her vice had shame, in records by those which left remembrance of ancient acts. Thus I say, because a woman being as it were the image of sweetness, courtesy and shamefastness, so soon as she steppeth out of the right tract and leaveth the smell of her duty and modesty, besides the denigration of her honor, thrusteth herself into infinite troubles and causeth the ruin of such which should be honored and praised, if women's allurement solicited them not to folly. I will not here endeavour myself to seek for examples of Samson, Solomon, or other which suffered themselves fondly to be abused by women; and who by mean of them be tumbled into great faults, and have incurred greater perils. Contenting myself to recite a right pitiful history done almost in our time, when the French under the leading of that notable captain, Gaston de Foix, vanquished the force of Spain and Naples at the journey of Ravenna in the time of the French king called Lewis XII, who married the lady Mary, daughter to King Henry VII, and sister to the victorious prince of worthy memory, King Henry VIII, wife (after the death of the said Lewis) to the puissant gentleman, Charles, late Duke of Suffolk.

In that very time then lived a gentleman of Naples, called Antonio Bologna who, having been Master of Household to Frederick of Aragon, sometime King of Naples, after the French had expelled those of Aragon out of that city, the said Bologna retired into France, and thereby recovered the goods which he possessed in his country. The gentleman, besides that he was valiant of his person, a good man of war, and well esteemed amongst the best, had a passing number of good graces, which made him to be beloved and cherished for every wight; and for riding and managing of great horse, he had not his fellow in Italy. He could also play exceeding well and trim upon the lute, whose faining voice so well agreed thereunto that the most melancholic persons would forget their heaviness upon hearing of his heavenly noise. And besides these qualities, he was of personage comely, and of good proportion. To be short, Nature having travailed and displayed her treasure house for enriching of him, he had by art gotten that which made him most happy and worthy of praise, which was the knowledge of good letters, wherein he was so well trained as by talk and dispute thereof, he made those to blush that were of that state and profession. Antonio Bologna, having left Frederick of Aragon in France, who, expulsed out of Naples, was retired to King Lewis, went home to his house to live at rest and to avoid trouble, forgetting the delicates of courts and houses of great men, to be the only husband of his own revenue. But what? It is impossible to eschew that which the heavens have determined upon us; and less the unhap which seemeth to follow us as it were naturally proceeding from our mother's womb, in such a wise as many times, he which seemeth the wisest man, guided by misfortune, hasteth himself with stooping head to fall headlong into his death and ruin. Even so it chanced to this Neapolitan gentleman; for in the very same place where he attained his advancement, he received his diminution and decay; and by that house which preferred him to what he had, he was deprived both of his estate and life, the discourse whereof you shall understand. I have told you already, that this gentleman was master of the King of Naples' household, and—being a gentle person, a good courtier, well trained up, and wise for government of himself in the court and in the service of princes—the Duchess of Malfi thought to entreat him that he would serve her in that office which he served the king. This Duchess was of the house of Aragon and sister to the Cardinal of Aragon, which then was a rich and puissant personage. Being thus resolved, [she] was well assured that she was not deceived, for so much as she was persuaded that Bologna was devoutly affected to the house of Aragon, as one brought up there from a child. Wherefore sending for him home to his house, she used unto him these, or like words: 'Master Bologna, sith¹ your ill fortune—nay, rather the unhap of our whole house—is such as your good lord and master hath forgone his state and dignity, and that you therewithal have lost a good master, without other recompense but the praise which every man giveth you for your good service, I have thought good to entreat you to do me the honor as to take charge of the government of my house, and to use the same as you did that of the king your master. I know well that the office is too unworthy for your calling, notwithstanding you be not ignorant what I am, and how near to him in blood to whom you be so faithful and loving a servant; and albeit that I am no queen, endued with great revenue, yet with that little I have I bear a princely heart; and such as you by experience do know what I have done, and daily do, to those which depart my service, recompensing them according to their pain and travail: magnificence is observed as well in the courts of poor princes, as in the stately palaces of great kings and monarchs. I do remember that I have read of a certain noble gentleman, a Persian borne, called Ariobarzanes, who used great examples of courtesy and stoutness towards king Artaxerxes, wherewith the king wondered at his magnificence and confessed himself to be vanquished. You shall take advice of this request, and I in the meantime do think you will not refuse the same, as well for that my

1. Since.

demand is just, as also being assured that our house and race is so well imprinted in your heart, as it is impossible that the memory thereof can be defaced.' The gentleman, hearing the courteous demand of the Duchess, knowing himself how deeply bound he was to the name of Aragon, and led by some unknown provocation to his great ill luck, answered her in this wise: 'I would to God, madam, that with so good reason and equity I were able to make denial of your commandment, as justly you require the same: wherefore for the bounden duty which I owe to the name and memory of the house of Aragon, I make promise that I shall not only sustain the travail, but also the danger of my life, daily ready to be offered for your service; but I feel in mind I know not what, which commandeth me to withdraw myself to live alone at home at my house, and to be content with the little I have, forgoing the sumptuous charge of princes' houses—which life would be well liked of myself, were it not for the fear that you, madam, should be discontented with my refusal, and that you should conceive, that I disdained your offered charge, or contemn your court for respect of the great office I bare in the court of the king, my lord and master; for I cannot receive more honor than to serve her, which is of that stock and royal race. Therefore at all adventures I am resolved to obey your will, and humbly to satisfy the duty of the charge wherein it pleaseth you to employ me, more to pleasure you for avoiding of displeasure than for desire I have to live an honorable life in the greatest prince's house of the world, sith I am discharged from him in whose name resteth my comfort and only stay, thinking to have lived a solitary life, and to pass my years in rest, except it were in the poor ability of my service to that house, whereunto I am bound continually to be a faithful servant. Thus, madam, you see me to be the readiest man of the world to fulfil the request, and accomplish such other service wherein it shall please you to employ me.' The Duchess thanked him very heartily, and gave him charge of all her household train, commanding each person to do him such reverence as to herself, and to obey him as the chief of all her family. This lady was a widow, but a passing fair gentlewoman, fine and very young, having a young son under her guard and keeping, left by the deceased Duke her husband, together with the duchy, the inheritance of her child. Now consider her personage being such, her easy life and delicate bringing up, and daily seeing the youthly trade and manner of courtiers' life, whether she felt herself pricked with any desire, which burned her heart the more incessantly as the flames were hidden and covert—from the outward show whereof she stayed herself so well as she could. But she, following best advice, rather esteemed the proof of marriage, than to burn with so little fire, or to incur the exchange of lovers, as many unshamefast strumpets do, which be rather given over than satisfied with pleasure of love; and, to say the truth, they be not guided by wisdom's lore, which suffer a maiden ripe for marriage to be long unwedded, or young wife long to live in widow's state, what assurance soever they made of their chaste and staid life. For books be so full of such enterprises, and houses stored with examples of such stolen and secret practises, as there need no further proof for assurance of our cause, the same of itself being so plain and manifest. And a great folly it is to build the fantasies of chastity, amid the follies of worldly pleasures. I will not go about to make those matters impossible, ne[2] yet will judge at large, but there be some maidens and wives which wisely can contain themselves amongst the troop of amorous suitors. But what? The experience is very hard, and the proof no less dangerous, and perchance in a moment the mind of some perverted, which all their living days have closed their ears from the words of those that have made offer of loving service. We need not run to foreign histories, ne yet to seek records that be ancient, sith we may see the daily effects of the like practised in noble houses and courts of kings and princes. That this is true, example of this fair duchess, who was moved with that desire which pricketh others that be of flesh and bone. This lady waxed very weary of lying alone, and grieved her heart to be without a match, specially in the night, when the secret silence and darkness of the same presented before the eyes of her mind the image of the pleasure which she felt in the lifetime of her deceased lord and husband, whereof now feeling herself despoiled, she felt a continual combat, and durst not attempt that which she desired most, but eschewed the thing whereof her mind liked best. 'Alas,' she said, 'is it possible after the taste of the value of honest obedience, which the wife oweth unto her husband, that I should desire to suffer the heat which burneth and altereth the martyred minds of those that subdue themselves to love? Can such attempt pierce the heart of me to become amorous by forgetting and straying from the limits of honest life? But what desire is this? I have a certain unacquainted lust, and yet very well know not what it is that moveth me, and to whom I shall vow the spoil thereof. I am truly more fond and foolish than ever Narcissus was, for there is neither shadow nor voice upon which I can well stay my sight, nor yet simple imagination of any worldly man whereupon I can arrest the conceit of my unstaid heart and the desires which provoke my mind. Pygmalion loved once a marble pillar, and I have but one desire, the colour whereof is more pale than death. There is nothing which can give the same so much as one spot of vermillion rud.[3] If I do discover these appetites to any wight,[4] perhaps they will move me for

2. Nor.
3. Red.
4. Person.

my labor, and for all the beauty and noble birth that is in me, they will make no conscience to deem me for their jesting stock, and to solace themselves with rehearsal of my fond conceits. But sith there is no enemy in the field, and that but simple suspicion doth assail us, we must break off the same, and deface the entire remembrance of the lightness of my brain. It appertaineth unto me to show myself as issued forth of the noble house of Aragon. To me it doth belong to take heed how to err or degenerate from the royal blood whereof I came.' In this sort that fair widow and young princess fantasied in the night upon the discourse of her appetites. But when the day was come, seeing the great multitude of Neapolitan lords and gentlemen which marched up and down the city, eyeing and beholding their best beloved, or using talk of mirth with them whose servants they were, all that which she thought upon in the night vanished so soon as the flame of burned straw or the powder of the cannon shot, and [she] purposed for any respect to live no longer in that sort, but promised the conquest of some friend that was lusty and discreet. But the difficulty rested in that she knew not upon whom to fix her love, fearing to be slandered and also that the light disposition and manner of most part of youth were to be suspected, in such wise as giving over all them which vaunted upon their jennets, Turkey pal-freys, and other coursers[5] along the city of Naples, she purposed to take repast of other venison, than of that fond and wonton troop. So her mishap began already to spin the thread which choked the air and breath of her unhappy life. Ye have heard before that Master Bologna was one of the wisest and most perfect gentlemen that the land of Naples that time brought forth, and for his beautiful pro-portion, gallantness, valiance, and good grace, without comparison. His favor was so sweet and pleasant as they which kept him company had somewhat to do to abstain their affection. Who then could blame this fair princess, if (pressed with desire of match to remove the ticklish instigations of her wanton flesh, and having in her pres-ence a man so wise) she did set her mind on him, or fantasy to marry him? Would not that party, for calming of his thirst and hunger, being set at the table before sundry sorts of delicate viands, ease his hunger? Methink[s] the person doth greatly forget himself which, having handfast upon occasion,[6] suffereth the same to vanish and fly away, sith it is well known that she, being bald behind, hath no place to seize upon, when desire moveth us to lay hold upon her—which was the cause that the Duchess became extremely in love with the Master of her House, in such wise as before all men she spared not to praise the great perfections wherewith he was enriched, whom

5. Chargers. "Jennets": small Spanish horses. "Palfreys": saddle horses (especially smaller ones for women).
6. "Handfast upon occasion": grip on opportunity.

she desired to be altogether hers. And so she was enamoured that it was as possible to see the night to be void of darkness as the Duchess without the presence of her Bologna, or else by talk of words to set forth his praise, the continual remembrance of whom (for that she loved him as herself) was her only mind's repast. The gentleman that was full wise, and had at other times felt the great force of the passion which proceedeth from extreme love, immediately did mark the countenance of the Duchess, and perceived the same so near as unfeignedly he knew that very ardently the lady was in love with him; and albeit he saw the inequality and difference between them both, she being sorted out of the royal blood, yet knowing love to have no respect to state or dignity, determined to follow his fortune and to serve her which so lovingly showed herself to him. Then, suddenly reproving his fond conceit, he said unto himself: 'What folly is that enterprise, to the great prejudice and peril of mine honor and life? Ought the wisdom of a gentleman to stray and wander through the assaults of an appetite rising of sensuality, and that reason give place to that which doth participate with brute beasts deprived of all reason by subduing the mind to the affections of the body? No, no! A virtuous man ought to let shine in himself the force of the generosity of his mind. This is not to live according to the spirit, when pleasure shall make us forget our duty and safeguard our conscience. The reputation of a wise gentleman resteth not only to be valiant and skilful in feats of arms, or in service of the noble; but needful it is for him by discretion to make himself glorious to all posterity. Love pricketh and provoketh the spirit to do well, I do confess, but that affection ought to be addressed to some virtuous end tending to marriage, for otherwise that virtuous image shall be soiled with the villainy of beastly pleasure. Alas!' said he, 'how easy it is to dispute, when the thing is absent which can both force and violently assail the bulwarks of most constant hearts. I full well do see the truth, and do feel the thing that is good, and know what behoveth me to follow; but when I view that divine beauty of my lady, her grace's wisdom, behavior and courtesy, when I see her to cast so loving an eye upon me, that she useth so great familiarity, that she forgetteth the greatness of her house to abase herself for my respect, how is it possible that I should be so foolish to despise a duty so rare and precious, and to set light by that which the noblest would pursue with all reverence and endeavour? Shall I be so much void of wisdom to suffer the young princess, to see herself contemned of me, to convert her love to tears, by setting her mind upon another, to seek mine overthrow? Who knoweth not the fury of a woman— specially of the noble dame, by seeing herself despised? No, no, she loveth me, and I will be her servant, and use the fortune proffered. Shall I be the first simple gentleman that hath married or loved a princess? Is it not more honorable for me to settle my mind upon a place so high, than upon some simple wench by whom I shall neither attain profit or advancement? Baldwin of Flanders, did not he a noble enterprise when he carried away Judith the daughter of the French king, as she was passing upon the seas into England, to be married to the king of that country? I am neither pirate nor adventurer, for that the lady loveth me. What wrong do I then to any person by yielding love again? Is not she at liberty? To whom ought she to make accompt[7] of her deeds and doings, but to God alone and to her own conscience? I will love her, and carry like affection for the love which I know and see that she beareth unto me, being assured that the same is directed to good end, and that a woman so wise as she is will not commit a fault so filthy as to blemish and spot her honor.' Thus Bologna framed the plot to entertain the Duchess (albeit her love already was fully bent upon him) and fortified himself again all mishap and perilous chance that might succeed, as ordinarily you see that lovers conceive all things for their advantage, and fantasy dreams agreeable to that which they most desire, resembling the mad and Bedlam persons, which have before their eyes the figured fancies which cause the conceit of their fury, and stay themselves upon the vision of that which most troubleth their offended brain. On the other side, the Duchess was in no less care of her lover, the will of whom was hid and secret, which more did vex and torment her than the first of love that burned her so fervently. She could not tell what way to hold, to do him understand her heart and affection. She feared to discover the same unto him, doubting either of some fond and rigorous answer, or of revealing of her mind to him, whose presence pleasured her more than all the men of the world. 'Alas,' said she, 'am I happed into so strange misery that with mine own mouth I must make request to him which with all humility ought to offer me his service? Shall a lady of such blood as I am be constrained to sue, where all other be required by importunate instance of their suitors? Ah, love, love! whatsoever he was that clothed thee with such puissance,[8] I dare say he was the cruel enemy of man's freedom. It is impossible that thou hadst thy being in heaven, sith the clemency and courteous influence of the same investeth man with better benefits than to suffer her nursechildren to be entreated with such rigor. He lieth which saith that Venus is thy mother, for the sweetness and good grace that resteth in that pitiful goddess, who taketh no pleasure to see lovers pierced with so eager travails as that which afflicteth my heart. It was some fierce cogitation of Saturn that brought thee forth, and sent thee into the world to break the ease of them which live at rest without any

7. Account.
8. Power.

passion or grief. Pardon me, Love, if I blaspheme thy majesty, for the stress and endless grief wherein I am plunged, maketh me thus to rove at large, and the doubts which I conceive do take away the health and soundness of my mind. The little experience in thy school causeth this amaze in me, to be solicited with desire that countersaith the duty, honor and reputation of my state: the party whom I love, is a gentleman, virtuous, valiant, safe, and of good grace. In this there is no cause to blame Love of blindness, for all the inequality of our houses, apparent upon the first sight and show of the same. But from whence issue the monarchs, princes, and greater lords, but from the natural and common moss of earth, whereof other men do come? What maketh these differences between those that love each other, if not the sottish opinion which we conceive of greatness and pre-eminence, as though natural affections be like to that ordained by the fantasy of men in their laws extreme. And what greater right have princes to join with a simple gentlewoman, than the princess to marry a gentleman—and such Antonio Bologna is, in whom heaven and nature have forgotten nothing to make him equal with them which march amongst the greatest. I think we be the daily slaves of the fond and cruel fantasy of those tyrants which say they have puissance over us; and that, straining our will to their tyranny, we be still bound to the chain like the galley slave. No, no! Bologna shall be my husband, for of a friend I purpose to make him my loyal and lawful husband, meaning thereby not to offend God and men together, and pretend to live without offense of conscience, whereby my soul shall not be hindered for anything I do, by marrying him whom I so strangely love. I am sure not to be deceived in love. He loveth me so much or more as I do him, but he dareth not disclose the same, fearing to be refused and cast off with shame. Thus two united wills, and two hearts tied together with equal knot cannot choose but bring forth fruits worthy of such society. Let men say what they list, I will do none otherwise than my head and mind have already framed semblably. I need to make accompt to any person for my face, my body, and reputation being in full liberty and freedom. The bond of marriage made shall cover the fault which men would deem; and, leaving mine estate, I shall do no wrong but to the greatness of my house, which maketh me amongst men right honourable. But these honors be nothing worth where the mind is void of contention, and where the heart, pricked forward by desire, leaveth the body and mind restless without quiet.' Thus the Duchess founded her enterprise, determining to marry her Household Master, seeking for occasion and time, meet for disclosing of the same; and albeit that a certain natural shamefastness, which of custom accompanieth ladies, did close her mouth, and made her to defer for a certain time the effect of her resolved mind, yet in the end, vanquished with love and impatience, she was forced to break off silence, and to assure herself in him—rejecting fear conceived of shame, to make her way to pleasure, which she lusted more than marriage, the same serving her but for a mask and coverture to hide her follies and shameless lusts, for which she did the penance that her folly deserved. For no colorable deed or deceitful trumpery can serve the excuse of any notable wickedness. She, then, thoroughly persuaded in her intent, dreaming and thinking of nought else but upon the embracement of her Bologna, ended and determined her conceits and pretended follies, and upon a time sent for him up into her chamber—as commonly she did for the affaires and matters of her house—and, taking him a side unto a window, having prospect into a garden, she knew not how to begin her talk (for the heart being seized, the mind troubled, and the wits out of course, the tongue failed to do his office), in such wise, as of long time she was unable to speak one only word. He, surprised with like affection, was more astoned[9] by seeing the alteration of his lady. So the two lovers stood still like images beholding one another, without any moving at all, until the lady, the hardiest of them both, as feeling the most vehement and greatest grief, took Bologna by the hand and, dissembling what she thought, used this or such like language: 'If any other besides yourself, gentleman, should understand the secrets which now I purpose to disclose, I doubt what speech were necessary to colour my words; but, being assured of your discretion and wisdom, and with what perfection nature hath endued you, and art, having accomplished that in you which nature did begin to work, as one bred and brought up in the royal court of the second Alphonse, of Ferdinando and Frederick of Aragon, my cousins, I will make no doubt at all to manifest to you the hidden secrets of my heart, being well persuaded that when you shall both hear and savor my reasons, and taste the light which I bring forth for me, easily you may judge that mine advice cannot be other than just and reasonable. But if your conceits shall stray from that which I shall speak, and deem not good of that which I determine, I shall be forced to think and say that they which esteem you wise and sage and to be a man of good and ready wit be marvellously deceived. Notwithstanding my heart foretelleth that it is impossible for Master Bologna to wander so far from equity, but that by and by he will enter the lists, and discern the white from black, and the wrong from that which is just right. For, so much as hitherto I never saw thing done by you which preposterated or perverted the good judgement that all the world esteemeth to shine in you, the same [is] well manifested and declared by your tongue, the right judge of the mind: you know and see how

9. Stunned, astonished.

I am a widow through the death of that noble gentleman of good remembrance, the Duke, my lord and husband; you be not ignorant also that I have lived and governed myself in such a wise in my widow state as there is no man so hard and severe of judgement that can blazon reproach of me in that which appertaineth to the honesty and reputation of such a lady as I am, bearing my port so right as my conscience yieldeth no remorse, supposing that no man hath wherewith to bite and accuse me. Touching the order of the goods of the Duke, my son, I have used them with such diligence and discretion as, besides the debts which I have discharged sithens[1] the death of my lord, I have purchased a goodly manor in Calabria, and I have annexed the same to the dukedom of his heir; and at this day do not owe one penny to any creditor that lent money to the Duke, which he took up to furnish the charges in the wars which he sustained in the service of the kings, our sovereign lords, in the late wars for the kingdom of Naples. I have, as I suppose, by this means stopped the slanderous mouth, and given cause unto my son during his life to accompt himself bound unto his mother. Now, having till this time lived for other, and made myself subject to more than nature could bear, I am intended to change both my life and condition. I have till this time run, travelled, and removed to the castles and lordships of the dukedom, to Naples and other places, being in mind to tarry as I am, a widow. But what? New affairs and new counsel hath possessed my mind. I have travailed and pained myself enough, I have too long abidden[2] a widow's life; I am determined therefore to provide a husband, who by loving me, shall honor and cherish me according to the love which I shall bear to him, and my desert. For to love a man without marriage, God defend my heart should ever think; and [I] shall rather die a hundred thousand deaths, than a desire so wicked shall soil my conscience, knowing well that a woman which setteth her honor to sale is less than nothing, and deserveth not that the common air should breathe upon her, for all the reverence that men do bear or make them. I accuse no person, albeit that many noble women have their foreheads marked with the blame of dishonest life, and, being honored of some, be nevertheless the common fable of the people. To the intent, then, that such mishap happen not to me, and perceiving myself unable still thus to live, being young as I am, and (God be thanked) neither deformed nor yet painted, I had rather be the loving wife of a simple fere[3] than the concubine of a king or great prince. And what? Is the mighty Monarch able to wash away the fault of his wife which hath abandoned him, contrary to the duty and honesty which the undefiled

1. Since.
2. Abided in.
3. Mate.

bed requireth? No less, then, princesses that whilom[4] trespassed
with those which be of baser stuff than themselves. Messalina with
her imperial robe could not so well cover her faults, but that the his-
torians do defame her with name and title of a common woman.
Faustina, the wife of the sage monarch Marcus Aurelius, gained like
report by rendering herself to others' pleasures, besides her lawful
spouse. To marry myself to one that is mine equal, it is impossible,
for so much as there is no lord in all this country meet[5] for my degree
but is too old of age, the rest being dead in these later wars. To marry
a husband that yet is but a child is folly extreme, for the inconve-
niences which daily chance thereby, and the evil entreaty that ladies
do receive when they come to age and their nature wax cold, by reason whereof, embracements be not so favourable, and their husbands, glutted with ordinary meat, use to run in exchange. Wherefore
I am resolved without respite or delay, to choose some well quali-
tied and renowned gentleman, that hath more virtue than riches, of
good fame and bruit,[6] to the intent I may make him my lord, espouse,
and husband. For I cannot employ my love upon treasure, which may
be taken away, where riches of the mind do fail, and shall be better
content to see an honest gentleman with little revenue to be praised
and commended of every man for his good deeds, than a rich carl[7]
cursed and detested of all the world. Thus much I say, and it is the
sum of all my secrets, wherein I pray your counsel and advice. I know
that some will be offended with my choice, and the lords my brothers—specially the Cardinal—will think it strange, and receive the
same with ill digesture,[8] that much ado shall I have to be agreed with
them and to remove the grief which they shall conceive against me
for this mine enterprise; wherefore I would the same should secretly
be kept, until without peril and danger either of myself or of him
whom I pretend to marry, I may publish and manifest, not my love
but the marriage which I hope in God shall soon be consummate
and accomplished with one whom I do love better than myself, and
who (as I full well do know) doth love me better than his own proper
life.' Master Bologna, which till then harkened to the oration of the
Duchess without moving, feeling himself touched so near, and hearing that his lady had made her approach for marriage, stood still
astoned, his tongue not able to frame one word, only fantasied a
thousand chimeras in the air, and formed like number of imaginations in his mind, not able to conjecture what he was to whom the
Duchess had vowed her love and the possession of her beauty. He

4. Once, at some past time.
5. Suitable.
6. Reputation.
7. Churl; miser.
8. Digestion.

could not think that this joy was prepared for himself for that his lady spake no word of him, and he less durst open his mouth, and yet was well assured that she loved him beyond measure. Notwithstanding, knowing the fickleness and unstable heart of women, he said unto himself that she would change her mind for seeing him to be so great a coward as not to offer his service to a lady by whom he saw himself so many times both wantonly looked upon and entertained with some secrecy more than familiar. The Duchess which was a fine and subtle dame, seeing her friend rapt with the passion and standing still unmoveable through fear, pale and amazed, as if he had been accused and condemned to die, knew by that countenance and astonishment of Bologna, that she was perfectly beloved of him; and so, meaning not to suffer him any longer to continue that amaze, ne yet to further fear[9] him with her dissembled and feigned marriage of any other but with him, she took him by the hand; and beholding him with a wanton and luring eye (in such sort as the curious philosophers themselves would awake, if such a lamp and torch did shine within their studies) she said thus unto him 'Signor Antonio, I pray you be of good cheer, and torment not yourself for anything I have said; I know well and of long time have perceived what good and faithful love you bear me, and with what affection you have served me sithens first you used my company. Think me not to be so ignorant but that I know full well by outward signs what secrets be hid in the inner heart, and that conjectures many times do give me true and certain knowledge of concealed things; and am not so foolish to think you to be so undiscreet, but that you have marked my countenance and manner, and thereby have known that I have been more affectioned to you, than to any other. For that cause,' said she, straining him by the hand very lovingly, and with cheerful colour in her face, 'I swear unto you and do promise that if you think meet, it shall be none other but yourself whom I will have, and desire to take to husband and lawful spouse, assuring myself so much of you, as the love which so long time hath been hidden and covered in our hearts shall appear by so evident proof as only death shall end and undo the same.' The gentleman, hearing such sudden talk and the assurance of that which he most wished for—albeit he saw the danger extreme whereunto he launched himself by espousing his great lady, and the enemies he should get by entering such alliance—notwithstanding, building upon vain hope, and thinking at length that the choler of the Aragon brother would pass away if they understood the marriage, determined to pursue with purpose, and not to refuse the great preferment, being so prodigally offered; for which cause he answered his lady in this

9. Frighten.

manner: 'If it were in my power, madam, to bring to pass that which I desire for your service by acknowledging of the benefits and favors which depart unto me, as my mind presenteth thanks for the same, I would think myself the happiest gentleman that liveth, and you the best served princess of the world. For one better beloved (I dare presume to say, and so long as I live will affirm) is not to be found. If till this time I delayed to open that which now I discover unto you, I beseech you, madam, to impute it to the greatness of your estate, and to the duty of my calling and office in your house, being not seemly for a servant to talk of such secrets with his lady and mistress. And truly the pain which I have endured to hold my peace and to hide my grief hath been more noisome to me than one hundred thousand like sorrows together, although it had been lawful to have revealed them to some trusty friend. I do not deny madam but of long time you did perceive my folly and presumption, by addressing my mind so high as to the Aragon blood, and to such a princess as you be. And who can beguile the eye of a lover, specially of her, whose paragon for good mind, wisdom, and gentleness is not? And I confess to you, besides, that I have most evidently perceived how certain love hath lodged in your gracious heart, wherewith you bare me greater affection than you did to any other within the compass of your family. But what? Great ladies' hearts be fraught with secrets and conceits of other effects, than the minds of simple women, which caused me to hope for none other guerdon of my loyal and faithful affection than death—and the same very short, sith[1] that little hope, accompanied with great, nay rather extreme passion, is not able to give sufficient force both to suffer and to stablish my heart with constancy. Now, for so much as of your motion,[2] grace, courtesy, and liberality the same is offered, and that it pleaseth you to accept me for yours, I humbly beseech you to dispose of me not as husband, but of one which is, and shall be your servant for ever, and such as is more ready to obey than you to command. It resteth now madam, to consider how, and in what wise our affairs are to be directed, that things being in assurance, you may so live without peril and brute of slanderous tongues, as your good fame and honest port may continue without spot or blemish.'

Behold the first act of the tragedy, and the provision of the fare which afterwards sent them both to their grave, who immediately gave their mutual faith; and the hour was assigned the next day that the fair princess should be in her chamber alone, attended upon with one only gentlewoman, which had been brought up with the Duchess from her cradle, and was made privy to the heavy marriage of

1. Since. "Guerdon": reward.
2. Desire.

these lovers which was consummate in her presence. And for the present time they passed the same in words, for ratification whereof they went to bed together. But the pain in the end was greater than the pleasure, and had been better for them both—yea, and also for the third—that they had showed themselves so wise in the deed as discreet in keeping silence of that which was done. For albeit their marriage was secret, and thereby politicly governed themselves in their stealths and robberies of love, and that Bologna more oft held the state of the steward of the house by day, than of lord of the same, and by night supplied that place, yet in the end, the thing was perceived which they desired to be closely kept. And, as it is impossible to till and culture a fertile ground but that the same must yield some fruit, even so the Duchess after many pleasures (being ripe and plentiful) became with child, which at the first astoned the married couple; nevertheless the same so well was provided for as the first childbed was kept secret, and none did know thereof. The child was nursed in the town, and the father desired to have him named Frederick, for remembrance of the parents of his wife. Now fortune, which lieth in daily wait and ambushment, and liketh not that men should long loiter in pleasure and pastime, being envious of such prosperity, cramped so the legs of our two lovers as they must needs change their game, and learn some other practise; for so much as the Duchess, being great with child again and delivered of a girl, the business of the same was not so secretly done, but that it was discovered. And it sufficed not that the bruit was noised through Naples, but that the sound flew further off. As each man doth know that Rumor hath many mouths, and with the multitude of his tongues and trumps[3] proclaimeth in divers and sundry places the things which chance in all the regions of the earth. Even so that babbling fool, carried the news of that second childbed to the ears of the Cardinal of Aragon the Duchess' brother, being then at Rome. Think what joy and pleasure the Aragon brothers had, by hearing the report of their sister's fact![4] I dare presume to say, that albeit they were extremely wroth with this happened slander, and with the dishonest fame which the Duchess had gotten throughout Italy, yet far greater was their sorrow and grief, for that they did not know what he was that so courteously was allied to their house, and in their love had increased their lineage. And therefore swelling with despite, and rapt with fury to see themselves so defamed by one of their blood, they purposed by all means, whatsoever it cost them, to know the lucky lover that had so well tilled the Duchess their sister's field. Thus, desirous to remove that shame from their eyes, and

3. Trumpets.
4. Action, deed.

to be revenged of a wrong so notable, they sent espial[5] round about, and scouts to Naples, to view and spy the behaviour and talk of the Duchess, to settle some certain judgement of him, which stealingly was become their brother-in-law. The Duchess' court being in this trouble, she did continually perceive in her house her brothers' men to mark her countenance, and to note those that came thither to visit her, and to whom she used greatest familiarity, because it is impossible but that the fire, although it be raked under the ashes, must give some heat. And albeit the two lovers used each other's company without showing any sign of their affection, yet they purposed to change their estate for a time, by yielding truce to their pleasures. Yea, and although Bologna was a wise and provident personage, fearing to be surprised upon the fact, or that the Gentlewoman of the Chamber, corrupted with money or forced by fear, should pronounce any matter to his hindrance or disadvantage, [he] determined to absent himself from Naples—yet not so suddenly but that he made the Duchess his faithful lady and companion privy of his intent. And as they were secretly in their chamber together, he used these or suchlike words: 'Madam, albeit the right good intent and unstained conscience is free from fault, yet the judgement of men hath further relation to the exterior appearance than to virtue's force and innocency itself, as ignorant of the secrets of the thought; and so, in things that be well done, we must of necessity fall into the sentence of those, whom beastly affection ravisheth more than ruled reason. You see the solemn watch and guard which the servants of the lords your brothers do within your house, and the suspicion which they have conceived by reason of your second childbed, and by what means they labor truly to know how your affairs proceed and things do pass. I fear not death where your service may be advanced, but if herein the maiden of your chamber be not secret, if she be corrupted, and if she keep not close that which she ought to do, it is not ignorant[6] to you that it is the loss of my life, and [I] shall die suspected to be a whoremonger and varlet—even I (I say) shall incur that peril, which am your true and lawful husband. This separation chanceth not by justice or desert, sith the cause is too righteous for us; but rather your brethren will procure my death, when I shall think the same in greatest assurance. If I had to do but with one or two, I would not change the place, ne march one step from Naples; but be assured that a great band, and the same well-armed, will set upon me. I pray you, madam, suffer me to retire for a time, for I am assured that when I am absent, they will never soil their

5. Spies.
6. Unknown.

hands or imbrue their swords in your blood. If I doubted anything
at all of peril touching your own person, I had rather a hundred
hundred times die in your company than live to see you no more.
But out of doubt I am that if the things were discovered, and they
knew you to be begotten with child by me, you should be safe,
where I should sustain the penance of the fact, committed without
fault or sin. And therefore I am determined to go from Naples to
order mine affaires, and to cause my revenue to be brought to the
place of mine abode, and from thence to Ancona, until it pleaseth
God to mitigate the rage of your brethren, and recover their good
wills to consent to our marriage. But I mean not to do or conclude
anything without your advice. And if this intent do not like you, give
me counsel, madam, what I were best to do, that both in life and
death you may know your faithful servant and loving husband is
ready to obey and please you.' This good lady hearing her husband's
discourse, uncertain what to do, wept bitterly, as well for grief to
lose his presence, as for that she felt herself with child the third time.
The sighs and tears, the sobs and heavy looks which she threw forth
upon her sorrowful husband gave sufficient witness of her pain and
grief. And if none had heard her, I think her plaints would have well
expressed her inward smart of mind. But, like a wise lady, seeing
the alleged reasons of her husband, licensed him, although against
her mind, not without utterance of these few words, before he went
out of her Chamber: 'Dear husband, if I were so well assured of the
affection of my brethren as I am of my maid's fidelity, I would entreat
you not to leave me alone, specially in the case I am, being with
child. But, knowing that to be just and true which you have said,
I am content to force my will for a certain time that hereafter we
may live at rest together, joining ourselves in the company of our
children and family, void of those troubles which great courts ordinarily bear within the compass of their palaces. Of one thing I must
entreat you, that so often as you can by trusty messenger, you send
me word and intelligence of your health and state, because the same
shall bring unto me greater pleasure and contentation than the welfare of mine own; and because also, upon such occurrents as shall
chance, I may provide for mine own affairs the surety of myself and
of our children.' In saying so, she embraced him very amorously, and
he kissed her with so great sorrow and grief of heart as the soul
thought in that ecstasy out of his body to take her flight, sorrowful
beyond measure to leave her whom he loved for the great courtesies
and honor which he had received at her hands. In the end, fearing
that the Aragon espials would come and perceive them in those
privities, Bologna took his leave, and bad his lady and spouse
farewell.

And thus was the second act of this tragical history: to see a fugitive husband secretly to marry, especially her, upon whom he ought not so much as to look but with fear and reverence. Behold here (O ye foolish lovers) a glass of your lightness, and ye women, the course of your fond behaviour. It behoveth not the wise suddenly to execute their first motions and desires of their heart, for so much as they may be assured that pleasure is pursued so near with a repentance so sharp to be suffered, and hard to be digested, as their voluptuousness shall utterly discontent them. True it is, that marriages be done in heaven, and performed in earth; but that saying may not be applied to fools, which govern themselves by carnal desires, whose scope is but pleasure, and the reward many times equal to their folly. Shall I be of opinion that a household servant ought to solicit, nay rather suborn, the daughter of his lord without punishment, or that a vile and abject person dare to mount upon a prince's bed? No, no! Policy requireth order in all, and each wight ought to be matched according to their quality, without making a pastime of it to cover our follies, and know not of what force love and destiny be, except the same resisted. A goodly thing it is to love, but where reason loseth his place, love is without his effect, and the sequel rage and madness. Leave we the discourse of those which believe that they be constrained to follow the force of their mind, and may easily subdue themselves to the laws of virtue and honesty, like one that thrusteth his head into a sack, and thinks he cannot get out: such people do please themselves in their loss, and think all well that is noisome to their health, daily following their contrary. Come we again, then, to Sir Bologna, who, after he had left his wife in her castle, went to Naples, and having [a]sessed a rent upon his lands, and levied a good sum of money, he repaired to Ancona, a city of the patrimony of the Roman Church, whither he carried his two children which he had of the Duchess, causing the same to be brought up with such diligence and care, as is to be thought a father well affectioned to his wife would do, and who delighted to see a branch of the tree that to him was the best beloved fruit of the world. There he hired a house for his train, and for those that waited upon his wife, who in the meantime was in great care and could not tell of what wood to make her arrows, perceiving that her belly began to swell and grow to the time of her delivery, seeing that from day to day her brothers' servants were at her back, void of counsel and advice, if one evening she had not spoken to the gentlewoman of her chamber, touching the doubts and peril wherein she was, not knowing how she might be delivered from the same. That maiden was gentle and of a good mind and stomach and loved her mistress very dearly, and, seeing her so amazed and tormenting herself to death, minding to fray her no further, ne to reprove her of her fault, which could not be amended, but rather to provide for the danger whereunto she had headlong cast herself, gave her this advice: 'How now, madam,' said she, 'is that wisdom which from your childhood hath been so familiar in you, dislodged from your breast in time, when it ought chiefly to rest for encountering from those mishaps that are coming upon us? Think you to avoid the dangers, by thus tormenting yourself, except you set your hands to the work, thereby to give the repulse to adverse fortune? I have heard you many times speak of the constancy and force of mind which ought to shine in the deeds of princesses, more clearly than amongst those dames of baser house, and which ought to make them appear like the sun amid the little stars. And yet I see you now astoned, as though you had never foreseen, that adversity chanceth so well to catch the great within his clutches, as the base and simple sort. Is it but now that you have called to remembrance that which might ensue your marriage with Sir Bologna? Did his only presence assure you against the weights of fortune, and was it the thought of pains, fears and frights which now turmoileth your dolorous mind? Ought you thus vex yourself, when need it is to think how to save both your honor and the fruit within your entrails? If your sorrow be so great over Sir Bologna, and if you fear your childbed will be descried,[7] why seek you not means to attempt some voyage for covering of the fact, to beguile the eyes of them which so diligently do watch you? Doth your heart fail you in that matter? Whereof do you deem? Why sweat and fret you before you make me answer?' 'Ah, sweet heart,' answered the Duchess, 'if thou feltest the pain I do suffer, thy tongue would not be so much at will as thou showest it now to be for reproof of my small constancy. I do sorrow specially for the causes which thou allegest, and above all for that I know well that if my brethren had never so little intelligence of my being with child, I were undone and my life at an end; and peradventure, poor wench, thou shouldest bear the penance of my sin. But what way can I take that still these candles may not give light, and I may be voided of the train which ought to wait upon my brethren? I think if I should descend into hell, they would know whether any shadow there were in love with me. Now guess, if I should travel the realm or retire to any other place, whether they would leave me at peace? Nothing less, sith they would suddenly suspect that the cause of my departure proceeded of desire to live at liberty, to dally with him whom they suspect to be other than my lawful husband. And it may be as they be wicked and suspicious, and will doubt of my greatness, so shall I be far more infortunate by travelling, than here in misery amid mine anguish; and you, the rest that be keepers of my Counsel, shall fall into greater

7. Discovered.

danger, upon whom no doubt they will be revenged and flesh themselves for your unhappy[8] waiting and attendance upon us.' 'Madam,' said the bold maiden, 'be not afraid, and follow mine advice; for I hope that it shall be the means both to see your spouse, and to rid those troublesome varlets out of your house, and in like manner safely to deliver you into good assurance.' 'Say your mind,' said the lady, 'for it may be that I will govern myself according to the same.' 'Mine advice is,' then said the gentlewoman, 'to let your household understand that you have made a vow to visit the holy temple of our lady of Loretto (a famous place of pilgrimage in Italy), and that you command your train to make themselves ready to wait upon you for the accomplishment of your devotion, and from thence you shall take your journey to sojourn in Ancona, whither, before you depart, you shall send your movables and plate, with such money as you shall think necessary. And afterwards God will perform the rest, and through his holy mercy will guide and direct all your affairs.' The Duchess hearing the maiden speak those words, and amazed of her sudden invention, could not forebear but to embrace and kiss her, blessing the hour wherein she was borne, and that ever she chanced into her company, to whom afterwards she said: 'My wench, I had well determined to give over mine estate and noble port,[9] joyfully to live like a simple gentlewoman with my dear and well-beloved husband, but I could not devise how I should conveniently depart this country without suspicion of some folly; and sith that thou hast so well instructed me for bringing the same to pass, I promise thee that so diligently thy counsel shall be performed, as I see the same to be right good and necessary. For rather had I see my husband, being alone without title of Duchess or great lady, than to live without him, beautified with the graces and foolish names of honor and preeminence.' This devised plot was no sooner grounded, but she gave such order for execution of the same, and brought it to pass with such dexterity as the lady in less than eight days had conveyed and sent the most part of her movables, and specially the chiefest and best, to Ancona, taking in the meantime her way towards Loretto after she had bruited her solemn vow made for that pilgrimage. It was not sufficient for this foolish woman to take a husband more to glut her libidinous appetite than for other occasion, except she added to her sin another execrable impiety, making holy places and duties of devotion to be, as it were, the ministers of her folly. But let us consider the force of lovers' rage, which so soon as it hath seized upon the minds of men, we see how marvellous be the effects thereof, and with what straint[1] and puissance that madness subdueth the

8. Unfortunate. "Flesh themselves": gratify their destructive rage.
9. Grand style of living.
1. Application of force.

wise and strongest worldlings. Who would think that a great lady would have abandoned her estate, her goods, and child, would have misprized her honor and reputation, to follow like a vagabond, a poor and simple gentleman, and him besides that was the household servant of her court? And yet you see this great and mighty duchess trot and run after the male like a female wolf or lioness when they go to salt,[2] and forget the noble blood of Aragon whereof she was descended, to couple herself almost with the simplest person of all the trimmest gentlemen of Naples. But turn we not the example of follies to be a matter of consequence: for if one or two become bankrupt of their honor, it followeth not, good ladies, that their fact[3] should serve for a match to your deserts, and much less a patron for you to follow. These histories be not written to train and trap you to pursue the thousand thousand slippery sleights of love's gallantise, but rather carefully to warn you to behold the semblable[4] faults, and to serve for a drug to discharge the poison which gnaweth and fretteth the integrity and soundness of the soul. The wise and skilful apothecary or compositor of drugs, dresseth viper's flesh to purge the patient from hot corrupted blood, which conceiveth and engendereth leprosy within his body. In like manner, the fond love and wicked ribaldry of Semiramis, Pasiphae, Messalina, Faustina, and Romida is showed in writ that every one of you should fear to be numbered and recorded amongst such common and dishonorable women. You princes and great lords, read the follies of Paris, the adulteries of Hercules, the dainty and effeminate life of Sardanapalus, the tyranny of Phalarus Busiris or Dionysius of Sicily, and see the history of Tiberius, Nero Caligula, Domitian and Heliogabalus, and spare not to number them amongst our wanton youths which soil themselves with such villainies more filthily than the swine do in the dirt. All this intendeth it an instruction for your youth to follow the infection and whoredom of those monsters. Better it were all those books were drenched in some bottomless depth of seas than Christian life by their means should be corrupted; but the example of the wicked is induced for to eschew and avoid them, as the life of the good and honest is remembered to frame and address our behaviour in this world to be praiseworthy and commended. Otherwise the holiness of sacred writ should serve for an argument to the unthrifty and luxurious to confirm and approve their beastly and licentious wickedness. Come we again, then, to our purpose: the good pilgrim of Loretto went forth her voyage to achieve her devotions, and visit the saint for whose relics she was departed the country of the Duke her son. When had done her suffrages at Loretto,

2. Sexual excitement.
3. Crime.
4. Similar. "Gallantise": gallantry.

her people thought that the voyage was at an end, and that she would have returned again into her country. But she said unto them that sith she was so near Ancona, being but fifteen miles off, she would not return before she had seen that ancient and goodly city, which divers histories do greatly recommend, as well for the antiquity, as for the pleasant seat thereof. All were of her advice, and went to see the antiquities of Ancona, and she to renew the pleasures which she had before begun with her Bologna, who was advertised of all her determination, resting now like a god, possessed of all the jewels and riches of the Duchess, and had taken a fair palace in the great street of the city, by the gate whereof the train of his lady must pass. The harbinger of the duchess posted before to take up lodging for the train, but Bologna offered unto him his palace for the lady. So Bologna, which was already well-beloved in Ancona, and entered new amity and great acquaintance with the Gentlemen of the city, with a goodly troop of them went forth to meet his wife, to whom he presented his house, and besought her that she and her train would vouchsafe to lodge with him. She received the same very thankfully, and withdrew herself unto his house, who conducted her thither not as a husband, but like him that was her humble and affectionate servant. But what needeth much discourse of words? The Duchess, knowing that it was impossible but each man must be privy to her fact, and know what secrets hath passed between her and her husband, to the end that no other opinion of her childbed should be conceived but that which was good and honest, and done since the accomplishment of the marriage, the morrow after her arrival to Ancona, assembled all her train in the hall, of purpose no longer to keep secret that Sir Bologna was her husband, and that already she had had two children by him, and again was great with child and when they were come together after dinner, in the presence of her husband, she spake unto them these words: 'Gentlemen, and all ye my trusty and loving servants, high time it is to manifest to every of you, the thing which hath been done before the face, and in the presence of Him who knoweth the most obscure and hidden secrets of our thought. And needful it is not to keep silent that which is neither evil done ne hurtful to any person. If things could be kept secret and still remain unknown, except they were declared by the doers of them, yet would not I commit the wrong in concealing that which to discover unto you doth greatly delight me, and delivereth my mind from exceeding grief, in such wise as if the flames of my desire could break out with such violence as the fire hath taken heat within my mind, ye should see the smoke mount up with greater smoulder than that which the Mount Gibel[5] doth vomit forth at certain seasons of

5. I.e., Etna.

the year. And to the intent I may not keep you long in this suspect, this secret fire within my heart, and that which I will cause to flame in open air, is a certain opinion which I conceive for a marriage by me made certain years past, at what time I chose and wedded a husband to my fantasy and liking, desirous no longer to live in widow state, and unwilling to do the thing that should prejudice and hurt my conscience. The same is done, and yet in one thing I have offended, which is by long keeping secret the performed marriage; for the wicked bruit dispersed through the realm by reason of my childbed, one year past, hath displeased some, howbeit my conscience receiveth comfort, for that the same is free from fault or blot. Now know ye therefore what he is, whom I acknowledge for my lord and spouse, and who it is that lawfully hath me espoused in the presence of this gentlewoman whom you see, which is the witness of our nuptials and accord of marriage. This gentleman here present, Antonio Bologna, is he to whom I have sworn and given my faith, and he again to me hath engaged his own. He it is whom I accompt for my spouse and husband, and with whom henceforth I mean to rest and continue. In consideration whereof, if there be any here amongst you all that shall mislike of my choice, and is willing to wait upon my son the Duke, I mean not to let[6] them of their intent, praying them faithfully to serve him and to be careful of his person, and to be unto him so honest and loyal as they have been to me, so long as I was their mistress. But if any of you desire to still make your abode with me, and to be partakers of my wealth and woe, I will so entertain him, as he shall have good cause to be contented— if not, depart ye hence to Malfi, and the steward shall provide for either of you according to your degree; for, touching myself, I do mind no more to be termed an infamous Duchess; rather had I be honoured with the title of a simple gentlewoman, or with that estate which she can have that hath an honest husband, and with whom she holdeth faithful and loyal company, than reverenced with the glory of a princess, a subject to the despite of slanderous tongues. Ye know,' she said to Bologna, 'what hath passed between us; and God is the witness of the integrity of my conscience, wherefore I pray you bring forth our children, that each man may behold the fruits raised of our alliance.' Having spoken those words, and the children brought forth into the hall, all the company stood still so astoned with that new success and tale as though horns suddenly had started forth their heads, and rested unmoveable and amazed, like the great marble pillar of Rome called Pasquile, for so much as they never thought ne conjectured that Bologna was the successor of the Duke of Malfi in his marriage bed.

6. Hinder.

This was the preparative of the catastrophe and bloody end of this tragedy. For of all the Duchess servants, there was not one that was willing to continue with their ancient mistress, who with the faithful maiden of her chamber remained in Ancona, enjoying the joyful embracements of her husband, in all such pleasure and delights as they do which, having lived in fear, be set at liberty and out of all suspicion, plunged in a sea of joy, and fleeting[7] in the quiet calm of all pastime, where Bologna had none other care, but how to please his best beloved, and she studied nothing else but how to love and obey him, as the wife ought to do her husband. But this fair weather lasted not long, for although the joys of men do not long endure, and waste in little time, yet delights of lovers be less firm and steadfast, and pass away almost in one moment of an hour. Now the servants of the Duchess which were retired, and durst tarry no longer with her, fearing the fury of the Cardinal of Aragon, brother to the lady, the very day they departed from Ancona, devised amongst themselves that one of them should ride in post to Rome to advertise the Cardinal of the lady's marriage, to the intent that the Aragon brethren should conceive no cause to accuse them of felony and treason. That determination speedily was accomplished, one posting towards Rome, and the rest galloping to the country and castles of the Duke. These news reported to the Cardinal and his brother, it may be considered how grievously they took the same, and for that they were not able to digest them with modesty, the youngest of the brethren, yelled forth a thousand curses and despites, against the simple sex of womankind. 'Ha!' said the Prince, transported with choler, and driven in to deadly fury, 'what law is able to punish or restrain the foolish indiscretion of a woman that yieldeth herself to her own desires? What shame is able to bridle and withdraw her from her mind and madness? Or with what fear is it possible to snaffle them from execution of their filthiness? There is no beast be he never so wild, but man sometime may tame, and bring to his lure and order. The force and diligence of man is able to make mild and strong and proud, and to overtake the swiftest beast and fowl, or otherwise to attain the highest and deepest thing of the world: but this incarnate devilish beast the woman, no force can surmount her, no swiftness can approach her mobility, no good mind can prevent her sleights and deceits, they seem to be procreated and born against all order of nature, and to live without law, which governeth all other things endued with some reason and understanding. But what a great abomination is this, that a gentlewoman of such a house as ours is hath forgotten her estate and the greatness of her alliance, besides

---

7. Swimming.

the nobility of her deceased husband, with the hope of the toward[8] youth of the Duke, her son and our nephew. Ah, false and vile bitch, I swear by the almighty God and by his blessed wounds, that if I can catch thee, and that wicked knave thy chosen mate, I will pipe ye both such a galliard, as ye never felt the like joy and mirth. I will make ye dance such a bloody bargenet, as your whorish heat for ever shall be cooled. What abuse have they committed under title of marriage, which was so secretly done as their children do witness their filthy embracements, but their promise of faith was made in open air, and serveth for a cloak and vizard for their most filthy whoredom? And what if marriage was concluded? Be we of so little respect, as the carrion beast would not vouchsafe to advertise us of her intent? Or is Bologna a man worthy to be allied or mingled with the royal blood of Aragon and Castile? No, no! Be he never so good a gentleman, his race agreeth not with kingly state, but I make to God a vow, that never will I take one sound and restful sleep until I have dispatched that infamous fact from our blood, and that the caitiff[9] whoremonger be used according to his desert.' The Cardinal also was out of quiet, grinding his teeth together, chattering from the jackanapes' paternoster,[1] promising no better usage of their Bologna than his younger brother did. And the better to entrap them both (without further stir for that time) they sent to the lord Gismondo Gonzago, the Cardinal of Mantua, then legate for Pope Julius II at Ancona, at whose hands they enjoyed such friendship as Bologna and all his family were commanded speedily to avoid the city. But for all that the legate was able to do, of long time he could not prevail, Bologna had so great intelligence within Ancona. Nevertheless whiles he deferred his departure, he caused the most part of his train, his children, and goods to be conveyed to Siena, an ancient city of Toscana, which, for the state and liberties, had long time been at wars with the Florentines, in such wise as the very same day that the news came to Bologna that he should depart the city within fifteen days, he was ready, and mounted on horseback to take his flight to Siena, which brake for sorrow the hearts of the Aragon brethren, seeing that they were deceived and frustrate of their intent, because they purposed by the way to apprehend Bologna, and to cut him in pieces. But what? The time of his hard luck was not yet expired, and so the march from Ancona served not for the theatre of those two infortunate lovers' overthrow, who certain months lived in peace in Toscana. The Cardinal night nor day did sleep, and his brother still did wait to perform his oath of revenge. And seeing their enemy out of fear, they dispatched a post to Alfonso Castruccio, the

8. Promising, hopeful.
9. Base.
1. Apes' "our father"—i.e., gibberish.

Cardinal of Siena, that he might entreat the Lord Borghese, chief
of the signory there, that their sister and Bologna should be banished the country and limits of the city, which with small suit was
brought to pass. These two infortunate husband and wife were
chased from all places, and so unlucky as whilom Jocasta was, or
Oedipus, after his father's death and incestuous marriage with his
mother, uncertain to what Saint to vow themselves, and to what
place to take their flight. In the end they determined to go to Venice, and to take their flight to Romagna, there to embark themselves
for to retire to the safeguard of the city, environed with the sea Adri-
aticum, the richest in Europa. But the poor souls made their reck-
oning there without their host, failing half the price of their banquet.
For being upon the territory of Forli, one of the train afar off did
see a troop of horsemen galloping towards their company, which by
their countenance showed no sign of peace or amity at all, which
made them consider that it was some ambush of their enemies. The
Neapolitan gentleman seeing the onset bending upon them, began
to fear death, not for that he cared at all for his mishap and ruin,
but his heart began to cleave for heaviness to see his wife and little
children ready to be murdered, and serve for the pastime of the
Aragon brethren's eyes, for whose sakes he knew himself already
predestinate to die, and that for despite of him, and to accelerate his
death by the overthrow of his, he was assured that they would kill
his children before his face and presence. But what is there to be
done, where counsel and means to escape do fail? Full of tears,
therefore, astonishment and fear, he expected death so cruel as man
could devise, and was already determined to suffer the same with
good courage, for anything that the Duchess could say unto him.
He might well have saved himself and his eldest son by flight, being
both well mounted upon good Turkey horses, which ran so fast as
the quarrel[2] discharged forth of a crossbow. But he loved too much
his wife and children, and would keep them company both in life
and death. In the end the good lady said unto him: 'Sir, for all the
joys and pleasures which you can do me, for God's sake save yourself and the little infant next you, who can well endure the galloping of the horse. For sure I am that, you being out of our company,
we shall not need to fear any hurt. But if you do tarry, you will be
the cause of the ruin and overthrow of us all, and receive thereby
no profit or advantage: take this purse therefore and save yourself,
attending better Fortune in time to come.' The poor gentleman,
Bologna, knowing that his wife had pronounced reason, and perceiving that it was impossible from that time forth that she or her train
could escape their hands, taking leave of her, and kissing his

2. Bolt.

children, not forgetting the money which she offered unto him, willed his servants to save themselves by such means as they thought best. So giving spurs unto his horse, he began to flee amain,[3] and his eldest son, seeing his father gone, began to follow in like sort. And so for that time they two were saved by breaking of the intended ill luck like to light upon them. And in a place to rescue himself at Venice, he turned another way, and in great journeys arrived at Milan. In the meantime the horsemen were approached near the Duchess, who seeing that Bologna had saved himself, very courteously began to speak unto the lady—were it that the Aragon brethren had given them that charge, or feared that the lady would trouble them with her importunate cries and lamentation. One therefore amongst them said unto her: 'Madam, we be commanded by the lords your brethren to conduct you home to your house, that you may receive again the government of the duchy and the order of the Duke your son, and do marvel very much at your folly for giving yourself thus to wander the country after a man of so small reputation as Bologna is, who, when he hath glutted his lusting, lecherous mind with the comeliness of your noble personage, will despoil you of your goods and honour, and then take his legs into some strange country.' The simple lady, albeit grievous it was unto her to hear such speech of her husband, yet held her peace and dissembled what she thought, glad and well contented with the courtesy done unto her, fearing before that they came to kill her, and thought herself already discharged, hoping upon their courteous dealings that she and her children from that time forth should live in good assurance. But she was greatly deceived, and knew within short space after the good will her brethren bare unto her. For so soon as these gallants had conducted her into the Kingdom of Naples, to one of the castles of her son, she was committed to prison with her children, and she also that was the secretary of her infortunate marriage. Till this time Fortune was contented to proceed with indifferent quiet against those lovers, but henceforth ye shall hear the issue of their little-prosperous love, and how, pleasure having blinded them, never forsook them until it had given them the overthrow. It booteth not here to recite[4] fables or histories, contenting myself that ladies do read, without too many weeping tears, the pitiful end of that miserable princess, who, seeing herself a prisoner in the company of her little children and well-beloved maiden, patiently lived in hope to see her brethren appeased, comforting herself for the escape of her husband out of the hands of his mortal foes. But her assurance was changed into an horrible fear, and her hope to no

3. Without delay; at full speed.
4. There is no point in here reciting.

expectation of surety, when, certain days after her imprisonment, her jailer came in, and said unto her: 'Madam, I do advise you henceforth to consider upon your conscience, for so much as I suppose that even this very day your life shall be taken from you.' I leave for you to think what horror and trance assailed the feeble heart of this poor lady, and with what ears she received those cruel news; but her cries and moans, together with her sighs and lamentations, declared with what cheer she received that advertisement. 'Alas!' said she, 'is it possible that my brethren should so far forget themselves as, for a fact nothing prejudicial unto them, cruelly to put to death their innocent sister, and to imbrue the memory of their fact in the blood of one which never did offend them? Must I, against all right and equity, be put to death before the judge or magistrate have made trial of my life, and known the unrighteousness of my cause? Ah, God most righteous and bountiful Father, behold the malice of my brethren, and the tyrannous cruelty of those which wrongfully do seek my blood. Is it a sin to marry? Is it a fault to fly and avoid the sin of whoredom? What laws be these, where marriage bed and joined matrimony is pursued with like severity, as murder, theft, and adultery? And what Christianity in a Cardinal, to shed the blood which he ought to defend? What profession is this, to assail the innocent by the highway side, in place to punish thieves and murderers? O Lord God, thou art just and dost all things righteously: I see well that I have trespassed against thy majesty in some other notorious crime than by marriage; I most humbly therefore beseech thee to have compassion upon me, and to pardon mine offences, accepting the confession and repentance of me thine humble servant for satisfaction of my sins, which it pleased thee to wash away in the precious blood of thy son, our Saviour, that, being so purified, I might appear to the holy banquet in thy glorious kingdom.' When she had thus finished her prayer, two or three of the ministers which had taken her besides Forli, came in, and said unto her: 'Now, madam, make ready yourself to go to God, for behold your hour is come.' 'Praised be that God,' said she, 'for the wealth and woe which it pleaseth him to send us. But I beseech you, my friends, to have pity upon these little children and innocent creatures. Let them not feel the smart which I am assured my brethren bear against their poor unhappy father.' 'Well, well, madam,' said they, 'we will convey them to such a place as they shall not want.' 'I also recommend unto you', quoth she, 'this poor maiden; and entreat[5] her well, in consideration of her good service done to the infortunate Duchess of Malfi.' As she had ended those words, the two ruffians did put a cord about her neck, and strangled her. The maiden,

---

5. Treat.

seeing the piteous tragedy commenced upon her mistress, cried out amain, and cursed the cruel malice of those tormentors, and besought God to be witness of the same; and crying out upon his Divine Majesty, she besought him to bend his judgement against them which causeless (being no Magistrates) had killed such innocent creatures. 'Reason it is,' said one of the tyrants, 'that thou be partaker of the joy of thy mistress's innocency, sith thou hast been so faithful minister and messenger of her follies.' And suddenly caught her by her hair of the head, and instead of a carcanet placed a rope about her neck. 'How now!' quoth she, 'Is this the promised faith which you made unto my lady?' But those words flew into the air with her soul, in company of the miserable Duchess.

But hearken now the most sorrowful scene of all the tragedy. The little children, which had seen all the furious game done upon their mother and her maid, as nature provoked them—or as some presage of their mishap led them thereunto—kneeled upon their knees before those tyrants, and embracing their legs, wailed in such wise, as I think that any other, except a pitiless heart spoiled of all humanity, would have had compassion. And impossible it was for them to unfold the embracements of those innocent creatures, which seemed to forethink their death by the wild looks and countenance of those roisters.[6] Whereby I think that needs it must be confessed that nature hath in herself, and upon us, imprinted some sign of divination, and specially at the hour and time of death, in such wise as the very beasts feel some conceits, although they see neither sword nor staff, and endeavour to avoid the cruel passage of a thing so fearful as the separation of two things so nearly united, even the body and soul—which, for the motion[7] that chanceth at the very instant, showeth how nature is constrained in that monstrous separation and more than horrible overthrow. But who can appease a heart determined to do evil and hath sworn the death of another, forced thereunto some special commandment? The Aragon brethren meant hereby nothing else but to root out the whole name and race of Bologna. And therefore the two ministers of iniquity did like murder and slaughter upon those two tender babes as they committed upon their mother, not without some motion of horror for doing of an act so detestable. Behold here how far the cruelty of man extendeth, when it coveteth nothing else but vengeance, and mark what excessive choler the mind of them produceth, which suffer themselves to be forced and overwhelmed with fury. Leave we apart the cruelty of Euchrates, the son of the king of Bactria, and of Phraates, the son of the Persian Prince, of Timon of Athens, and of an infinite number

6. Swaggering bullies.
7. Emotion, passion.

of those which were rulers and governors of the Empire of Rome; and let us match with these Aragon brethren one Vitoldus, Duke of Lithuania, the cruelty of whom constrained his own subjects to hang themselves, for fear least they should fall into his furious and bloody hands. We may confess also these brutal brethren to be more butcherly than ever Otho, Earl of Monferrato and Prince of Urbino, was, who caused a yeoman of his chamber to be wrapped in a sheet powdered with sulphur and brimstone, and afterwards kindled with a candle, [who] was scalded and consumed to death, because only he waked not at an hour by him appointed. Let us not excuse them also from some affinity with Maufredus, the son of Henry, the second emperor, who smoldered[8] his own father, being an old man, between two coverlets. These former furies might have some excuse to cover their cruelty, but these had no other cause but a certain beastly madness which moved them to kill those little children, their nephews, who by no means could prejudice or annoy the duke of Malfi or his title in the succession of his Duchy, the mother having withdrawn her goods, and was assigned her dowry; but a wicked hart must needs bring forth semblable works according to his malice. In the time of these murders, the infortunate lover kept himself at Milan with his son Frederick, and vowed himself to the Lord Silvio Savello, who that time besieged the castle of Milan, in the behalf of Maximilian Sforza, which in the end he conquered and recovered by composition with the French within. But that charge being achieved, the general Savello marched from thence to Cremona with his camp, whither Bologna durst not follow, but repaired to the Marquis of Bitonte, in which time the Aragon brethren so wrought as his goods were confiscate at Naples, and he driven to his shifts to use the golden ducats which the Duchess gave him to relieve himself at Milan, whose death although it was advertised by many, yet he could not be persuaded to believe the same, for that divers[9] which went about to betray him, and feared he should fly from Milan, kept his beak in the water (as the proverb is) and assured him both of the life and welfare of his spouse, and that shortly his brethren-in-law would be reconciled, because that many noble men favoured him well, and desired his return home to his country. Fed and filled with that vain hope, he remained more than a year at Milan, frequenting the company and well entertained of the richest merchants and gentleman of the city; and above all other, he had familiar access to the house of the lady Hippolita Bentivoglia, where, upon a day after dinner, taking his lute in hand, whereon he could exceedingly well

8. Smothered.
9. Various people.

play, he began to sing a certain sonnet, which he had composed upon the discourse of his misfortune, the tenor whereof is this:

THE SONG OF *ANTONIO BOLOGNA,* THE HUSBAND
OF THE DUCHESS OF MALFI.

If love, the death, or tract of time, have measured my distress,
    Or if my beating sorrows may my languor well express,
Then love come soon to visit me, which most my heart desires,
    And so my dolor finds some ease, through flames of fancy's
        fires.
The time runs out his rolling course for to prolong mine ease,
    To th'end I shall enjoy my love, and heart himself appease.
A cruel dart brings happy death, my soul then rest shall find;
    And sleeping body under tomb shall dream time out of mind.
And yet the love, the time, nor death, looks not how I decrease,
    Nor giveth ear to anything of this my woeful peace.
Full far I am from my good hap, or half the joy I crave,
    Whereby I change my state with tears, and draw full near my
        grave.
The courteous gods that gives me life, now moves the Planets all
    For to arrest my groaning ghost, and hence my sprite to call.
Yet from them still I am separed by things unequal[1] here;
    Not meant the Gods may be unjust, that breeds my changing
        cheer:
For they provide by their foresight that none shall do me harm,
    But she whose blazing beauty bright hath brought me in a
        charm.
My mistress hath the power alone to rid me from this woe,
    Whose thrall I am, for whom I die, to whom my sprite shall go.
Away my soul, go from the griefs that thee oppresseth still,
    And let thy dolor witness bear, how much I want my will.
For since that love, and death himself, delights in guiltless blood,
    Let time transport my troubled sprite, where destiny seemeth
        good.

His song ended, the poor gentleman could not forbear from pouring forth his lukewarm tears, which abundantly ran down his heavy face; and his panting sighs truly discovered the alteration of his mind, which moved each wight of that assembly to pity his mournful state; and one specially of small acquaintance, and yet knew the devises which the Aragon brethren had trained and conspired against him: that unacquainted gentleman his name was Delio, one very well learned and of trim invention, and very excellently hath indited

---

1. Unjust. "Separed": separated.

in the Italian vulgar tongue. Who, knowing the gentleman to be husband to the deceased Duchess of Malfi came unto him, and taking him aside, said: 'Sir, albeit I have no great acquaintance with you—this being the first time that ever I saw you, to my remembrance—so it is that virtue hath such force, and maketh gentle minds so amorous of their like as when they do behold each other they feel themselves coupled, as it were, in a band of minds, that impossible it is to divide the same. Now knowing what you be, and the good and commendable qualities in you, I compt[2] it to my duty to reveal that which may chance to breed you damage: know you, then, that I of late was in company with a nobleman of Naples, which is in this city banded with certain company of horsemen, who told me that he had a special charge to kill you, and therefore prayed me (as he seemed) to require you not to come in his sight, to the intent he might not be constrained to do that which should offend his conscience, and grieve the same all the days of his life. Moreover, I have worse tidings to tell you, which are, that the Duchess, your wife, is dead by violent hand in prison, and the most part of them that were in her company. Besides this, assure yourself that if you do not take heed to that which this Neapolitan captain hath deferred,[3] other will do and execute the same. This much I have thought good to tell you, because it would very much grieve me that a gentleman so excellent as you be should be murdered in that miserable wise, and would deem myself unworthy of life, if, knowing these practices, I should dissemble the same.' Whereunto Bologna answered: 'Sir Delio, I am greatly bound unto you, and give you hearty thanks for the good will you bear me. But of the conspiracy of the brethren of Aragon, and the death of my lady, you be deceived, and some have given you wrong intelligence. For within these two days I received letters from Naples, wherein I am advertised that the right honorable reverend Cardinal and his brother be almost appeased, and that my goods shall be rendered again, and my dear wife restored.' 'Ah, sir,' said Delio, 'how you be beguiled and fed with follies, and nourished with sleights of court. Assure yourself that they which write these trifles make such shameful sale of you as the butcher doth of his flesh in the shambles, and so wickedly betray you as impossible it is to invent a treason more detestable. But bethink you well thereof.' When he had said so, he took his leave, and joined himself in company of fine and pregnant wits, there assembled together. In the meantime, the cruel spirit[s] of the Aragon brethren were not yet appeased with the former murders, but needs must finish the last act of Bologna his tragedy by loss of his

2. Count.
3. Offered.

life, to keep his wife and children company so well in another world, as he was united with them in love in this frail and transitory passage. The Neapolitan gentleman before spoken of by Delio, which had taken an enterprise to satisfy the barbarous Cardinal, to bereave[4] his countryman of life, having changed his mind, and differing from day to day to sort the same to effect, which he had taken in hand, it chanced that a Lombard of larger conscience than the other, inveigled with covetousness and hired for ready money, practised the death of the Duchess' poor husband. This bloody beast was called Daniel de Bozola, that had charge of a certain band of footmen in Milan. This new Judas and assured man-queller, within certain days after, knowing that Bologna oftentimes repaired to hear service at the church and convent of St Francis, secretly conveyed himself in ambush, hard besides the Church of Saint James, whether he came (being accompanied with a certain troop of soldiers) to assail the infortunate Bologna, who was sooner slain that he was able to think upon defence, and whose mishap was such that he which killed him had good leisure to save himself, by reason of the little pursuit made after him. Behold here the noble fact[5] of the Cardinal, and what savour it hath of Christian purity to commit a slaughter for a fact done many years past upon a poor gentleman which never thought him hurt. Is this the sweet observation of the Apostles, of whom they vaunt themselves to be the successors and follower? And yet we cannot find nor read that the Apostles, or those that stepped in their trace, hired ruffians and murderers to cut the throats of them which did them hurt. But what? It was in the time of Julius II, who was more martial than Christian, and loved better to shed blood than give blessing to the people. Such end had the infortunate marriage of him which ought to have contented himself with that degree and honor that he had acquired by his deeds and glory of his virtues, so much by each wight recommended. We ought never to climb higher than our force permitteth, ne yet surmount the bounds of duty, and less suffer ourselves to be haled[6] fondly forth with desire of brutal sensuality. The sin being of such nature that he never giveth over the party whom he mastereth until he hath brought him to the shame of some notable folly. You see the miserable discourse of a princess' love, that was not very wise, and of a gentleman that had forgotten his estate, which ought to serve for a looking glass to them which be over hardy in making enterprises, and do not measure their ability with the greatness of their attempts, where they ought to maintain themselves in reputation, and bear the title of well advised,

4. Deprive, rob.
5. Deed.
6. Hauled.

foreseeing their ruin to be example to all posterity, as may be
seen
by the death of Bologna, and of all them which sprang of him,
and of his infortunate spouse his lady
and mistress.
But we have discoursed enough hereof, sith
diversity of other histories do call us
to bring the same in place, which
were not much more happy
than those whose history
ye have already
tasted.

GEORGE WHETSTONE

From The Fourth Day's Exercise[†]

* * * [B]y the example of other men's advancements * * * the meanest
may be raised by the yielding fancy of the mighty. I promise that
such an upstart had more need of ten eyes toward the malice of his
wife's kindred than of one tongue to move her to kindness. A woman
cannot mislike affectionated proffers, because they proceed of love;
but her kindred disdaineth his attempt, for that the conclusion ten-
deth both to their and her dishonour. A woman, seeing her servant's
passions, cannot but sustain him with pity; her kindred, seeing him
in a good way to be beloved, will lie in wait for his life. For, though
she may dispose of her affection, her kindred hath an interest in her
honor, which, if she consent to stain, or diminish, she doth injury
to her whole house.

The Cardinal of Aragon avenged the base choice of his sister, the
Duchess of Malfi, with the death of herself, her children, and her
husband; and alleged in defence that he had done no injury to nature,
but purged his house of dishonour. 'For nature,' quoth he, 'is perfect, and who blemisheth her is a monster in nature, whose head,
without wrong to nature, may be cut off.'

'Yea,' quoth Soranzo, 'but this Cardinal, for all his habit and gloss
of justice, is for this act so often registered as a tyrant, as I fear me
he will never come among the number of saints. But the example of
these marriages are usual, and such ensuing vengeance is but rare;
and, besides her especial contentment, a woman loseth none of her
general titles of dignity by matching with her inferior.'

---

† From George Whetstone, *An Heptameron of Civill Discourses* (London, 1582).

'Indeed,' quoth Dondolo, 'in common courtesy she enjoyeth them, but in the strict construction of the law she is degraded; and by this mean is bound to entertain the meaner with familiarity, lest they (being proud or reputing her scornfully) do cross her over the thumbs with the follies of her fancy. But admit the mean servant marry with his mistress, and escapeth the malice of her friends—which success, one among ten such suitors hardly attaineth—let him yield to pay this rent for his good fortune: to suffer his wife to rule, to direct, and to command his own determinations.'

SIMON GOULART

From Admirable and Memorable Histories Containing the Wonders of Our Time[†]

A while after the battle of Ravenna, given in the year 1512, a Nea-politan gentleman called Anthony Bologna, having been steward to Frederick of Aragon, King of Naples, who (being despoiled of his estate) retired into France, was called by the Duchess of Malfi—a great lady issued from the house of Aragon, sister to a cardinal, one of the greatest in his time, widow to a great nobleman, and mother to one only son—to be her steward. The which he having accepted, a while after, this widow being young and fair, having regarded him with a lascivious eye, she desired him but to cover her fault, she sought the colour of marriage; and, after many vain discourses in her thoughts, instead of flying to the counsel and good advice of her bretheren and honorable kinsfolks, (whereof she had many) and to accept a party fit for her quality—the which might easily have been found near or far off—transported with her desire, she discovers her thoughts unto this gentleman, who, drunk with his own conceit, and forgetting the respect which he owed unto his lady and to her house, neither yet remembering his own mean estate, would not excuse himself nor give her such counsel as he ought in this occurrent; but, being presumptuous and lustful, he yielded to join (under the veil of a secret marriage) with her, who had long before cast unchaste looks at him, and with whom he had rashly and against all duty fallen in love. These two unadvised creatures then lying together, in the presence of a chamber-maid only, under the colour of mar-riage so behaved themselves as after some months the Duchess was with child, and brought in bed of a son, the which was conveyed secretly into the country. This first delivery remained secret; but,

† From Simon Goulart, *Admirable and Memorable Histories*, trans. Edward Grimeston (London, 1607).

being again with child and delivered of a daughter, the news were presently spread over all, and came to the ears of the Cardinal and of another brother at Rome. Being about to enquire who it might be that had been so familiar with their sister, Bologna, seeing that it was generally noted, took his leave of her, she being with child, meaning to retire to Naples, and then to Ancona, there to attend some other event of their affairs. Having carried his two children with him, and hired a convenient house, the Duchess sent her richest stuff thither, and soon after, under color of a pilgrimage to Loretto, at her return she goes to Ancona with all her train, where, the next day after her arrival, having called all her gentlemen and household servants, she gave them to understand that Bologna was her husband, and that she was resolved to continue with him, suffering them that would go and serve the young Duke, her son, to depart, and promising good recompenses to them that should remain with her, showing them their two children. Her servants, amazed at this discourse, left the Duchess and Bologna; and, being parted from her presence, they sent one among them to Rome to advertise the Cardinal and the Prince of all their sister's fact.[1] The first attempt of these two brethren against Bologna and his pretended wife was to have them chased out of Ancona by the credit which they had with Sir Gismond of Gonzago, the pope's legate in that place. They retired speedily then to Siena; but they must needs depart from thence, being expelled by Alfonso Castruccio, Cardinal of Siena, and by the justice of Siena. After divers consultations, they resolved to retire to Venice, and to that end to take the way of Romagna; but, being upon the territory of Forli, they discover afar off a troop of horses galloping towards them. The Duchess was presently of an opinion that Bologna should save himself with his son, who was now grown big—the which they did, being both well mounted, and retired to Milan. These horsemen, having failed of part of their prey, spake graciously unto the Duchess, and conducted her, with her other two children, into the realm of Naples, into one of the castles of the young Duke her son, where she was presently imprisoned with the two children she had by Bologna and her chambermaid. Some few days after, three of them which had taken her in the plain of Forli came into her chamber and denounced her death unto her, suffering her to recommend herself unto God; then they tied a cord about her neck and strangled her; which done, they lay hold on the chambermaid, who cried out with open throat, and strangled her also; and in the end they seize upon the two young children, and send them after the mother and the maid.

1. Conduct.

The two brethren continuing their course caused Bologna's goods at Naples to be confisked;[2] and, having discovered that he was at Milan, they suborn certain men to feed him with hope that in time they will make his peace, making him believe that his wife and children were yet alive; who, although he were advertised by a gentleman of Milan of the Duchess' death, and of an ambush that was laid for him, yet would he not believe anything, nor retire himself out of Milan, where there were murderers suborned to kill him—of which number there was a certain Lombard, a captain of a company of foot. So, as soon after, Bologna, going out of the friars where he had been to hear mass, he was compassed about by a troop of soldiers and their captain, who slew him presently, being about two years after the Duchess' death. As for his son, who was not then with him, he was forced to fly out of Milan, to change his name, and to retire himself far off, where he died unknown.

* * *

To the former histories we will join some touching the lycanthropes and madmen, the which we will consider of two sorts. For there be lycanthropes in whom the melancholic humor doth so rule, as they imagine themselves to be transformed into wolves. This disease * * * is a kind of melancholy, but very black and vehement; for such as are touched therewith go out of their houses in February, counterfeit wolves in a manner in all things, and all night do nothing but run into churchyards and about graves, so as you shall presently discover in them a wonderful alteration of the brain, especially in the imagination and thought, which is miserably corrupte, in such a sort as the memory hath some force—as I have observed in one of these melancholic lycanthropes, whom we call wolves: for he that knew me well, being one day troubled with his disease, and meeting me, I retired myself apart, fearing that he should hurt me; having eyed me a little, he passed on, being followed by a troop of people; he carried then upon his shoulders the whole thigh and the leg of a dead man. Being carefully looked unto, he was cured of this disease. Meeting me another time, he asked me if I had not been a-feared whenas he encountered me in such a place—which makes me think that his memory was not hurt nor impaired, in the vehemency of his disease, although his imagination were much. * * *

William of Brabant writes in his history, that a man of a settled judgement was sometimes so tormented with an evil spirit that, at a certain season of the year, he imagined himself to be a ravening wolf, running up and down the woods, caves and deserts, especially after young children. Moreover, he saith that this man was often found

2. Confiscated.

running in the deserts, like a man out of his wits, and that in the end by the grace of God, he came to himself again and was cured.

There was also, as Job Fincel reports, in his *Second Book of Miracles,* a countryman near unto Pavia, in the year 1541, who thought himself to be a wolf, setting upon divers men in the fields, and slew some. In the end, being with great difficulty taken, he did constantly affirm that he was a wolf, and that there was no other difference, but that wolves were commonly hairy without, and he was betwixt the skin and the flesh. Some (too barbarous and cruel wolves in effect) desiring to try the truth thereof, gave him many wounds upon the arms and legs: but, knowing their own error and the innocency of the poor melancholy man, they committed him to the surgeons, in whose hands he died within few days after. Such as are the afflicted with that disease are pale, their eyes are hollow, and they see ill, their tongue is dry, they are much altered, and are without much spittle in the mouth. Pliny and others write that the brain of a bear provokes brutish imaginations. And he saith that in our time some made a Spanish gentleman eat thereof, whose phantasy was so troubled, as he imagined that he was transformed into a bear, flying into the mountains and desert. * * *

As for those lycanthropes, which have the imagination so impaired and hurt that, besides by some particular power of Satan they seem wolves and not men, to them that see them run, doing great spoil, Bodin * * * maintains that the Devil may change the figure of one body into another, considering the great power which God hath given him in this elementary world; he maintains that there be lycanthropes transformed really from men into wolves, alleging divers examples and histories to that purpose. In the end, after many arguments, he maintains the one and the other sort of lycanthropia. And, as for this represented in the end of this chapter, the conclusion of his discourse was that men are sometimes changed into beasts, the human reason remaining, whether it be done by the power of God immediately, or that this power is given to Satan, the executioner of his will, or rather of his fearful judgements. And if we confesses (saith he) the truth of the holy writ in Daniel, touching the transformation of Nebuchdnezzar, and of the history of Lot's wife, changed into an immovable pillar, it is certain that the change of a man into an ox, or into a stone is possible, and by consequence possible into all other creatures. * * * In the rank and number of ecstatics, are put those which they call lycaons and lycanthropes, which imagine themselves to be changed into wolves, and in their form run up and down the field, falling upon troops of great and small cattle, tear in pieces what they encounter, and go roaring up and down churchyards and sepulchres. In the fourth book of Herodotus, there is a passage touching the Neurians, a people of Scythia, who transformed themselves into wolves, the which he faith he could not believe, notwithstanding any report that was made unto him. For my part, I have felt it fabulous and ridiculous, that which hath been often reported of this transformation of men into wolves. But I have learned by certain and tried signs, and by witnesses worthy of credit, that they be not things altogether invented and incredible which are spoken of such transformations, which happen every year, twelve days after Christmas, in Livonia and the countries thereabout, as they have learned by their confessions which have been imprisoned and tormented for such crimes. Behold how they report it to be done: presently after that Christmas day is past, a lame boy goes through the country and calls the Devil's slaves together, being in great numbers, and enjoins them to follow him; if they stay anything,[3] then presently comes a great man, holding a whip made of little chains of iron, where-with he makes them to advance; and sometimes he handles these wretches so roughly, as the marks of his whip stick long by them, and he puts them that have been beaten to great pain. Being upon the way, behold they are all (as it seems to them) changed and transformed into wolves. They are thousands of them together, having for their conductor and guide this whip-carrier, after whom they march, imagining that they are become wolves. Being in the open champian countries,[4] they fall upon such troops of cattle as they find, tear them in pieces, and carry away what they can, committing many other spoils; but they are not suffered to touch nor to hurt any reasonable creature. When they approach near unto any river, their guide (say they) divides the water with his whip, so as they seem to open, and to leave a dry path betwixt both to pass through. At the end of twelve days, all the troop is dispersed, and everyone returns unto his house, having laid away his wolf's form, and taken that of man again. This transformation (say they) is done after this manner: those which are transformed fall suddenly to the ground, like unto them that have the falling-sickness, and remain like dead men, void of all feeling; they stir not from thence, neither go into any other place, neither are they transformed into wolves, but are like unto dead carcasses—for although you shake them and roll them up and down, yet they make no show of life. From thence is sprung an opinion that the souls taken out the bodies enter into these phantoms or visions, running with the shapes of wolves; then, when the work enterprised by the Devil is finished, they return into their bodies, which then recover life. The lycanthropes themselves confirm this opinion, confessing that the bodies do not leave their human form, neither yet receive that of a wolf, but

3. If they hold back at all.
4. Level, open country; unenclosed land.

only that the souls are thrust out of their prisons, and fly into
wolves' bodies, by whom they are carried for a time. Others have
maintained, that lying in irons in a dungeon, they have taken the
form of a wolf, and have gone to find out their companions many
days' journey off. Being examined how they could get out of a strong
and close prison, why they have returned, and how they could pass
over rivers that were large and deep, they answered that no irons,
walls, nor doors could hinder their getting out, that they returned
by constraint, and that they did fly over rivers, and run by land.

THOMAS BEARD

Of Whoredoms Committed under Color
of Marriage[†]

Seeing that oftentimes it falleth out that those which in show seem
most honest think it a thing lawful to converse together as man and
wife by some secret and private contract—without making account
of the public celebration of marriage as necessary, but for some
worldly respects, according as their foolish and disordinate[1] affections mispersuadeth them, to dispense therewith—it shall not be
impertinent, as we go, to give warning how unlawful all such conversation is, and how contrary to good manners, and to the laud-
able customs of all civil and well-governed people. For it is so far
from deserving the name of marriage, that on the other side it can
be nothing but plain whoredom and fornication—the which name
and title Tertullian giveth to all secret and privy meetings which
have not been allowed of, received, and blessed by the Church of
God. Again, besides the evil example which is exhibited, there is this
mischief, moreover, that the children of such a bed cannot be
esteemed legitimate; yea God himself accurseth such lawless familiarity, as the mischiefs that arise therefrom do declare, whereof this
one example which we allege shall serve for sufficient proof.

In the reign of Louis IX, King of France, and Julius II, Pope of
Rome, there was a gentleman of Naples called Antonio Bologna that
had been governor of Frederick of Aragon's house, when he was King
of Naples, and had the same office under the Duchess of Malfi after
she was widow; with whom in protract of time he grew to have such
secret and privy acquaintance (albeit she was a princess and he her
servant) that he enjoyed her as his own wife. And thus they conversed

---

† Thomas Beard, "Of Whoredomes Committed under Colour of Marriage," in *The The-*
atre of Gods Judgments (London, 1597).
1. Inordinate, immoderate. "Converse": engage in sexual intercourse.

secretly together, under the color of marriage accorded betwixt them, the space of certain years, until she bore unto him three children; by which means their private dealings, which they so much desired to smother and keep close, burst out and bewrayed[2] itself. The matter being come to her brothers' ears, they took it so to the heart that they could not rest until they had revenged the vile injury and dishonour which they pretended to have been done to them and their whole house equally by them both. Therefore when they chased them first from Ancona, whither in hope of quietness they had fled out of Naples, they drave them also out of Tuscany; who, seeing themselves so hotly pursued on every side, resolved to make towards Venice, thinking there to find some safety. But in the midway she was overtaken and brought back to Naples, where in short space she miserably ended her life; for her brothers' guard strangled her to death, together with her chambermaid (who had served instead of a bawd to them) and her poor infants which she had by the said Bologna. But he, by the goodness of his horse escaping, took his flight to Milan, where he sojourned quietly a long while, until, at the instant pursuit of one of her brothers, the Cardinal of Aragon, he was slain in the open streets when he least mistrusted any present danger. And this was a true cardinal-like exploit indeed, representing that mildness, mercifulness, and good name which is so required of every Christian, in traitorously murdering a man so many years after the first rancour was conceived (that might well in half that space have been digested[3]), in fostering hatred so long in his cruel heart, and waging ruffians and murderers to commit so monstrous an act—wherein, albeit the Cardinal's cruelty was most famous, as also in putting to death the poor infants, yet God's justice bare the sway, that used him as an instrument to punish those who, under the veil of secret marriage, thought it lawful for them to commit any villainy. And thus God busieth sometime the most wicked about his will, and maketh the rage and fury of the devil himself serve for means to bring to pass his fearful judgements.

2. Betrayed.
3. Got over.

Widows

JOHN WEBSTER

From Sir Thomas Overbury His Wife[†]

A *Virtuous Widow*

[She] is the palm-tree that thrives not after the supplanting of her husband. For her children's sake she first marries, for she married that she might have children, and for their sakes she marries no more. She is like the purest gold, only employed for princes' medals: she never receives but one man's impression; the large jointure moves her not, titles of honor cannot sway her. To change her name were (she thinks) to commit a sin should make her ashamed of her husband's calling; she thinks she hath travelled all the world in one man; the rest of her time therefore she directs to heaven. Her main superstition is she thinks her husband's ghost would walk should she not perform his will: she would do it, were there no prerogative court. She gives much to pious uses, without any hope to merit by them; and, as one diamond fashions another, so is she wrought into works of charity with the dust or ashes of her husband. She lives to see herself full of time; being so necessary for earth, God calls her not to heaven till she bee very aged; and even then, though her natural strength fail her, she stands like an ancient pyramid, which, the less it grows to man's eye, the nearer it reaches to heaven. This latter chastity of hers, is more grave and reverend than that ere she was married. For in it is neither hope, nor longing, nor fear, nor jealousy. She ought to be a mirror for our youngest dames to dress themselves by when she is fullest of wrinkles. No calamity can now come near her, for, in suffering the loss of her husband, she accounts all the rest trifles: she hath laid his dead body in the worthiest monument that can be—she hath buried it in her own heart. To conclude, she is a relic that, without any superstition in the world, though she will not be kissed, yet may be reverenced.

---

† From John Webster, *Sir Thomas Overburie His Wife* (London, 1616).

An Ordinary Widow

[She] is like the herald's hearse-cloth; she serves to many funerals, with a very little altering the colour. The end of her husband begins in tears; and the end of her tears begins in a husband. She uses to [go to] cunning women to know how many husbands she shall have, and never marries without the consent of six midwives. Her chiefest pride is in the multitude of her suitors; and by them she gains, for one serves to draw on another, and with one at last she shoots out another, as boys do pellets in elder guns. She commends to them a single life, as horse-coursers do their jades, to put them away. Her fancy is to one of the biggest of the guard, but knighthood makes her draw in a weaker bow. Her servants or kinsfolk are the trumpeters that summon any to this combat; by them she gains much credit, but loseth it again in the old proverb: *fama est mendax*.[1] If she live to be thrice married, she seldom fails to cozen[2] her second husband's creditors. A churchman she dare not venture upon, for she hath heard widows complain of dilapidations; nor a soldier, though he have candle-rents in the city, for his estate may be subject to fire; very seldom a lawyer, without he show his exceeding great practice, and can make her case the better; but a knight with the old rent may do much, for a great coming in,[3] is all-in-all with a widow—ever provided, that most part of her plate and jewels (before the wedding) lie concealed with her scrivener. Thus, like a too ripe apple, she falls of herself; but he that hath her is lord but of a filthy purchase, for the title is cracked. Lastly, while she is a widow, observe ever, she is no morning woman: the evening, a good fire, and sack may make her listen to a husband; and if ever she be made sure, 'tis upon full stomach to bed-ward.

---

1. Fame is deceitful (Latin).
2. Cheat.
3. Grand entrance. "Dilapidations": sums charged against incumbents for allowing church property to fall into disrepair. "Candle-rents": rents from (deteriorating) house properties.

Remembering the Dead

GEORGE WITHER

From Prince Henry's Obsequies†

* * * Rome's locusts do begin to swarm;
Their courage now with stronger hopes they arm,
And, taking hold of this thy transmutation,
They plot again to sue for toleration.
Yea, Hell, to double this our sorrow's weight,
Is new contriving of old eighty-eight.[1]
Come then, and stand against it to defend us,
Or else her guiles, her plots, or force will end us.
This last-last time, sweet Prince, I bid thee rise:
My Britons droop already, each man flies;
And if thou save us not from our great foes,
They quickly will effect our overthrows.
Oh, yet he moves not up his living head,
And now I fear indeed he's dead.
                         Spirit. He's dead.
Britain.   What voice was that, which from the vaulted roof
Of my last words did make so plain a proof?
What was it seemed to speak above me so,
And says he's dead? Was't Echo, yea or no?
                              Spirit. No.
Britain.   What, is it some disposed to flout my moan?
Appear! Hast thou a body, or hast none?
                            Spirit. None.
Britain.   Sure, some illusion! Oh, what art? Come hither!
My prince's ghost, or fiend, or neither?
                         Spirit. Neither.
Britain.   Indeed his ghost in heaven rests, I know.
Art thou some angel for him, is it so?
                           Spirit. So.

† From George Wither, *Prince Henries Obsequies* (London, 1612).
1. I.e., the attempted invasion of England by the Spanish Armada in 1588.

Britain.   Do not my real griefs with visions feed.
In earnest speak: art so indeed?
                            Spirit.   Indeed.
Britain.   What power sent thee now into my coast?
Was it my darling Henry's ghost?
                            Spirit.   's ghost.
Britain.   Th'art welcome, then; thy presence grateful is.
But tell me, lives he happily in bliss?
                            Spirit.   Y's.
Britain.   Say, hath he there the fame that here he had,
Or doth the place unto his glory add?
                            Spirit.   Add.
Britain.   May I demand what thy good errands be?
To whom is that he told to thee?
                            Spirit.   To thee.
Britain.   Oh, doth he mind me yet, sweet spirit, say?
What is thy message? I'll obey.
                            Spirit.   Obey.
Britain. I will not to my power one tittle[2] miss.
Do but command, and say 'do this'.
                            Spirit.   Do this.
Britain.   But stay, it seems that thou hast made thy choice
To speak with Echo's most unperfect voice:
In plainer wise declare why thou art sent,
That I may hear with more content.
                            Spirit.   Content.

*   *   *

Britain.   O stay, and do not leave me yet alone.
Spirit.   My errand's at an end, I must be gone.
Britain.   Go then, but let me ask one word before.
Spirit.   My speech now fails, I may discourse no more.
Britain.   Yet let me crave thus much, if so I may,
By Echo thou reply to what I say.
                            Spirit.   Say.
Britain.   First tell me, for his sake thou count'st most dear,
Is Babel's fall and Jacob's rising near?
                            Spirit.   Near.
Britain.   Canst thou declare what day that work shall end,
Or rather must we yet attend?
                            Spirit.   Attend.

---

2. The slightest thing.

Britain.   Some land must yield a prince that blow to strike:
May I be that same land or no, is't like?
                              Spirit.   Like.
Britain.   Then therefore 'tis that Rome bear us such spite.
Is she not plotting now to wrong our right?
                              Spirit.   Right.
Britain.   But from her mischiefs and her hands impure,
Canst thou our safe deliverance assure?
                              Spirit.   Sure.
Britain.   Then, notwithstanding this late loss befell
And we feared much, I trust 'tis well.
                              Spirit.   'Tis well.
Britain.   Then fly thou to thy place! If this be true,
Thou, God, be praised; and griefs, adieu!
                              Spirit.   Adieu!

JOHN WEBSTER

A Monumental Column[†]

*Erected to the Living Memory of the Ever-Glorious Henry,
Late Prince of Wales*

A FUNERAL ELEGY

The greatest of the kingly Race is gone,
Yet with so great a reputation
Laid in the earth, we cannot say he's dead;
But, as a perfect diamond set in lead
(Scorning our foil), his glories do break forth,
Worn by his maker, who best knew his worth.
Yet to our fleshly eyes, here does belong
That which we think helps grief, a passionate tongue.
Methinks I see men's hearts pant in their lips:
*We should not grieve at the bright sun's eclipse
But that we love his light.* So travellers stray,
Wanting both guide and conduct of the day;
Nor let us strive to make this sorrow old—
For wounds smart most, when that the blood grows cold.
If princes think that ceremony meet
To have their corpse embalmed to keep them sweet,
Much more they ought to have their fame expressed

† John Webster, *A Monumental Columne* (London, 1613).

In Homer, though it want Darius' chest,[1]
To adorn which, in her deserved throne,
I bring those colors, which Truth calls her own.
Nor gain, nor praise by my weak lines are sought—
Love that's born free, cannot be hired nor bought.
Some great inquisitors in nature say
Royal and generous forms sweetly display
Much of the heavenly virtue, as proceeding
From a pure essence, and elected breeding.
Howe'er, truth for him thus much doth importune:
His form, and virtue, both deserved his fortune;
For 'tis a question not decided yet
Whether his mind or fortune were more great.
Methought I saw him in his right hand wield
A Caduceus; in the other Pallas'[2] shield.
His mind quite void of ostentation,
His high erected thoughts looked down upon
The smiling valley of his fruitful heart.
Honour and Courtesy in every part
Proclaimed him and grew lovely in each limb;
He well became those virtues which graced him.
He spread his bounty with a provident hand,
And not like those who sow the ungrateful sand.
His rewards followed reason, ne'er were placed
For ostentation, and to make them last,
He was not like the mad and thriftless vine,
That spendeth all her blushes at one time;
But, like the orange tree, his fruits he bore—
Some gathered, he had green and blossoms' store.
We hoped much of him, till death made hope err:
We stood as in some spacious theatre,
Musing what would become of him, his flight
Reached such a noble pitch above our sight;
Whilst he, discreetly wise, this rule had won:
Not to let fame know his intents, till done.
Men came to his court as to bright academies
Of virtue and of valour; all the eyes
That feasted at his princely exercise
Thought that by day Mars held his lance, by night
Minerva[3] bore a torch to give him light.

---

1. Presumably Webster is imagining the elaborately carved tomb chest of the Persian emperor Darius the Great.
2. Pallas Athene, Greek goddess of wisdom, frequently represented as a martial figure. "Caduceus": staff borne by Hermes/Mercury, messenger of the gods.
3. Roman goddess of wisdom, identified with Pallas Athene.

As once on Rhodes, Pindar reports of old,
Soldiers expected it would rain down gold,[4]
Old husbandmen in the country began to plant
Laurel[5] instead of elm, and made their vaunt
Their sons and daughters should such trophies wear
Whenas the prince returned a conqueror
From foreign nations; for men thought his star
Had marked him for a just and glorious war.
And sure his thoughts were ours: he could not read
Edward the Black Prince's life, but it must breed
A virtuous emulation to have his name
So lag behind him both in time and fame—
He that like lightning did his force advance,
And shook to the centre the whole realm of France,
That of warm blood opened so many sluices,
To gather and bring thence six flower-de-luces;[6]
Who ne'er saw fear but in his enemies' flight;
Who found weak numbers conquer, armed with right;
Who knew his humble shadow spread no more
After a victory than it did before;
Who had his breast instated with the choice
Of virtues, though they made no ambitious noise;
Whose resolution was so fiery still,
It seemed he knew better to die than kill:
And yet drew Fortune, as the adamant steel,
Seeming to have fixed a stay upon her wheel;
Who jestingly would say it was his trade
To fashion death-beds, and hath often made
Horror look lovely, when in the fields there lay
Arms and legs so distracted one would say
That the dead bodies had no bodies left;
He that of working pulse sick France bereft,
Who knew that battles, not the gaudy show
Of ceremonies, do on Kings bestow
Best theatres, t'whom naught so tedious as sport,
That thought all fans and ventoys[7] of the court
Ridiculous and loathsome to[8] the shade
Which, in a march, his waving ensign made.
Him did he strive to imitate, and was sorry

---

4. According to the Greek poet Pindar, snowflakes of gold rained on the island of Rhodes at the moment of Athene's birth.
5. As a symbol of military triumph.
6. I.e., fleurs-de-lys, the French royal badge subsequently incorporated in the English royal arms.
7. Fans.
8. Compared to.

He did not live before him, that his glory
Might have been his example; to these ends,
Those men that followed him were not by friends
Or letters preferred to him: he made choice
In action, not in complimental voice;
And as Marcellus did two temples rear
To Honour and to Virtue,[9] placed so near
They kissed, yet none to Honour's got access,
But they that passed through Virtue's, so to express
His worthiness, none got his countenance[1]
But those whom actual merit did advance.
Yet, alas! All his goodness lies full low.
Oh greatness! What shall we compare thee to?
To giants, beasts, or towers framed out of snow,
Or like wax-gilded tapers, more for show
Than durance? Thy foundation doth betray
Thy frailty, being built on such clay.
This shows the all-controlling power of fate,
That all our scepters and our chairs of state
Are but glass-metal, that we are full of spots,
And that, like new writ copies, to avoid blots
Dust must be thrown upon us; for in him
Our comfort sunk and drowned learning to swim.
And though he died so late, he's no more near
To us than they that died three thousand year
Before him; only memory doth keep
Their fame as fresh as his from death or sleep.
Why should the stag or raven live so long,
And that their age rather should not belong
Unto a righteous prince whose lengthened years,
Might assist men's necessities and fears?
Let beasts live long, and wild, and still in fear,
The turtle-dove never out-lives nine year.
Both life and death have equally expressed,
Of all, the shortest madness is the best.
We ought not think that his great triumphs need,
Our withered taunts: can our weak praise feed
His memory, which worthily contemns[2]
Marble and gold and oriental gems?
His merits pass our dull invention,
And now methinks I see him smile upon

9. Temples of Apollo and Diana adjacent to the Theatre of Marcellus and wrongly cred-
ited to Marcellus, nephew of Augustus.
1. Favor.
2. Treats as of small value.

Our fruitless tears, bids us disperse these showers,
And says his thoughts are far refined from ours.
As Rome of her beloved Titus[3] said,
That from the body, the bright soul was fled
For his own good and their affliction,
On such a broken column we lean on;
And for our souls, not him, let us lament
Whose happiness is grown our punishment.
But surely God gave this as an allay,[4]
To the blessed union of that nuptial day
We hoped—for fear of surfeit, thought it meet
To mitigate, since we swell with what is sweet.
And for sad tales suit grief, 'tis not amiss
To keep us waking. I remember this:
Jupiter on some business once sent down
Pleasure unto the world that she might crown
Mortals with her bright beams; but (her long stay
Exceeding far the limits of her day)
Such feasts and gifts were numbered to present her
That she forgot Heaven and the God that sent her.
He calls her thence in thunder, at whose lure,
She spreads her wings and, to return more pure,
Leaves her eye-seeded[5] robe wherein she's suited,
Fearing that mortal breath had it polluted.
Sorrow that long had lived in banishment,
Tugged at the oar in galleys, and had spent
Both money and herself in court delays,
And sadly numbered many of her days
By a prison calendar, though once she bragged
She had been in great men's bosoms, now all ragged
Crawled with a tortoise pace or somewhat slower;
Nor found she any that desired to know her,
Till by good chance (ill hap for us) she found,
Where Pleasure laid her garment from the ground:
She takes it, dons it; and to add a grace
To the deformity of her wrinkled face,
An old court lady, out of mere compassion,
Now paints it o'er or puts it into fashion;
When, straight from country, city, or from court,
Both without wit or number there resort
Many to this imposter. All adore

3. Emperor of Rome, 79–81 C.E.
4. Alloy.
5. Pleasure presumably wears a gown decorated with eyes, as Fame's was embroidered with
   ears and tongues.

Her haggish falsehood; usurers from their store
Supply her and are cozened; citizens buy
Her forged titles; riot and ruin fly,
Spreading their poison universally.
Nor are the bosoms of great statesmen free
From her intelligence,[6] who lets them see
Themselves and fortunes in false perspectives.
Some landed heirs consort her with their wives,
Who, being a bawd, corrupts their all-spent oaths:
They have entertained the devil in Pleasure's clothes;
And since this cursed masque, which to our cost
Lasts day and night, we have entirely lost
Pleasure, who from heaven wills us be advised
That our false Pleasure is but Care disguised.
Thus is our hope made frustrate, oh sad ruth!
Death lay in ambush for his glorious youth;
And, finding him prepared, was sternly bent
To change his love into fell ravishment.
O cruel tyrant, how canst thou repair
This ruin? Though hereafter thou should'st spare
All mankind, break thy dart and ebon[7] spade:
Thou canst not cure this wound, which thou hast made.
Now view his death-bed; and from thence let's meet
In his example our own winding sheet.
There his humility, setting apart
All titles, did retire into his heart.
O blessed solitariness that brings,
The best content, to mean men and to kings.
Manna their fates; from heaven the dove there flies
With olive to the Ark (a sacrifice
Of God's appeasement); ravens in their beaks
Bring food from heaven; God's preservation speaks
Comfort to Daniel in the lion's den,
Where contemplation leads us happy men
To see God face to face. And such sweet peace
Did he enjoy; amongst the various press
Of weeping visitors it seemed he lay
As kings at revels sit—wished the crowd away,
The tedious sport done, and himself asleep;
And in such joy, did all his senses steep,
As great accountants (troubled much in mind),
When they hear news of their *Quietus* signed.

6. Surveillance.
7. Ebony; hence black.

Never found prayers, since they conversed with death,
A sweeter air to fly in than his breath.
They left in's eyes nothing but glory shining;
And, though that sickness with her over-pining
Look ghastly, yet in him it did not so:
He knew the place to which he was to go
Had larger titles, more triumphant wreaths
To instate him with; and forth his soul he breathes
Without a sigh, fixing his constant eye,
Upon his triumph—immortality.
He was rained down to us out of heaven, and drew
Life to the spring, yet like a little dew
Quickly drawn thence; so, many times miscarries
A crystal glass whilst that the workmen varies
The shape in the furnace (fixed too much upon
The curiousness of the proportion),
Yet breaks it ere't be finished, and yet then
Moulds it anew, and blows it up again,
Exceeds his workmanship, and sends it thence
To kiss the hand and lip of some great prince;
Or, like a dial broke in wheel or screw
That's ta'en in pieces to be made go true,
So to eternity he now shall stand,
New formed and gloried by the all-working hand.
Slander, which hath a large and spacious tongue
Far bigger than her mouth, to publish wrong,
And yet doth utter't with so ill a grace
Whilst she's a-speaking no man sees her face
That like dogs lick foul ulcers, not to draw
Infection from them, but to keep them raw.
Though she oft scrape up earth from good men's graves
And waste it in the standishes[8] of slaves,
To throw upon their ink, shall never dare
To approach his tomb, be she confined as far
From his sweet relics as is heaven from hell.
No witchcraft shall instruct her how to spell
That barbarous language which shall sound him ill;
Fame's lips shall bleed, yet ne'er her trumpet fill
With breath enough; but not in such sick air
As make waste elegies to his tomb repair,
With scraps of commendation more base
Than are the rags they are writ on—oh, disgrace
To nobler poesy! This brings to light,

8. Ink stands.

Not that they can, but that they cannot write;
Better they had ne'er troubled his sweet trance,
So silence should have hid their ignorance:
For he's a reverend subject to be penned
Only by his sweet *Homer* and my friend.
Most savage nations should his death deplore,
Wishing he had set his foot upon their shore
Only to have made them civil. This black night
Hath fallen upon's by Nature's oversight;
Or, while the fatal sister[9] sought to twine
His thread and keep it even, she drew it so fine
It burst. O all composed of excellent parts,
Young, grave Maecenas of the noble arts,
Whose beams shall break forth from thy hollow tomb,
Stain the time past and light the time to come.
O thou that in thy own praise still wert mute,
Resembling trees—the more they are ta'en with fruit,
The more they strive to bow and kiss the ground;
Thou—that in quest of man hast truly found
That while men rotten vapours do pursue,
They could not be thy friends, and flatterers too—
That, despite all injustice, would have proved
So just a steward for this land, and loved
Right for its own sake—now (oh, woe the while!)
Fleetest[1] dead in tears, like to a moving isle.
Time was when churches in the land were thought
Rich jewel-houses; and this age hath b[r]ought
That time again—think not I feign, go view
Henry the Seventh's Chapel, and you'll find it true:
The dust of a rich diamond's there enshrined,
To buy which thence, would beggar the West Inde.[2]
What a dark night piece of tempestuous weather,
Have the enragèd clouds summoned together,
As if our loftiest palaces should grow
To ruin, since such highness fell so low.
And angry Neptune makes his palace groan
That the deaf rocks may echo the land's moan.
Even senseless things seem to have lost their pride,
And look like that dead month in which he died—
To clear which, soon arise that glorious day,
Which in her sacred union shall display

9. Clotho, the first of the three Fates, who spins the thread of each person's life.
1. Floats, swims.
2. West Indies.

Infinite blessings, that we all may see
The like to that of Virgil's golden tree,[3]
A branch of which being split, there freshly grew
Another that did boast like form and hue.
And for these worthless lines, let it be said
I hasted till I had this tribute paid
Unto his grave, so let the speed excuse,
The zealous errors of my passionate muse.
Yet, though his praise here bear so short a wing,
Thames has more swans[4] that will his praises sing
In sweeter tunes, be-pluming his sad hearse
And his three feathers,[5] while men live, or verse.
And by these signs of love let great men know
That sweet and generous favour they bestow
Upon the Muses never can be lost;
For they shall live by them, when all the cost
Of gilded monuments shall fall to dust;
They grave in metal that sustains no rust;
Their wood yields honey and industrious bees,
Kills spiders and their webs like Irish trees.
A poet's pen like a bright scepter sways,
And keeps in awe dead men's dispraise or praise.
Thus took he acquaintance of all worldly strife:
The evening shows the day, and death crowns life.

My impresa[6] *to your lordship: a swan flying*
to a laurel for shelter; the mot[7]
           Amor est mihi causa.[8]

FINIS

The Speech of Amade le Grand[†]

Of all the triumphs which your eye has viewed,
This the fair monument of gratitude,
This chiefly should your eye and ear employ
That was of all your brotherhood the joy:

---

3. I.e., the tree from which Aeneas broke the golden bough that enabled him to enter the underworld.
4. I.e., poets.
5. Henry's badge as Prince of Wales.
6. Emblem.
7. Motto.
8. Love is my motive (Ovid, *Metamorphoses*, I, 507).
† From John Webster, *Monuments of Honour* (London, 1624), sig. C2–C2v.

Worthy Prince Henry, fame's best president,
Called to a higher court of parliament
In his full strength of youth and height of blood—
And, which crowned all, when he was truly good—
On virtue and on worth he still was throwing
Most bounteous showers, where'er he found them growing.
He never did disguise his ways by art
But shooted his intents unto his heart,
And loved to do good, more for goodness sake
Than any retribution man could make.
Such was this prince, such are the noble hearts,
Who when they die, yet die not in all parts,
But from the integrity of a brave mind,
Leave a most clear and eminent fame behind.
Thus hath this jewel not quite lost his ray,
Only cased up 'gainst a more glorious day.
And be't remembered that our company
Have not forgot him who ought ne'er to die.
Yet, wherefore should our sorrow give him dead,
When a new phoenix springs up in his stead
That, as he seconds him in every grace,
May second him in brotherhood and place.
Good rest, my Lord; integrity, that keeps
The safest watch and breeds the soundest sleeps,
Make the last day of this your holding seat
Joyful as this, or rather more complete.

JOHN WEEVER

From Ancient Funeral Monuments[†]

Chapter 1. Of Monuments in General

A monument is a thing erected, made, or written for a memorial of
some remarkable action, fit to be transferred to future posterities;
and thus generally taken, all religious foundations, all sumptuous
and magnificent structures, cities, towns, towers, castles, pillars,
pyramids, crosses, obelisks, amphitheaters, statues and the like, as
well as tombs and sepulchres, are called monuments. Now above all
remembrances by which men have endeavoured, even in despite of
death, to give unto their fames eternity, for worthiness and continuance, books or writing have ever had the pre-eminence. * * *

---

† From John Weever, *Ancient Funeral Monuments* (London, 1631), sig. B1–B3, B5v.

Horace thus concludes the third book of his lyric poesy:

> *Exegi monimentum aere perennius,*
> *Regalisque situ, etc.*[1]
> A monument than brass more lasting, I,
> Than princely pyramids in site more high,
> Have finished, which neither fretting showers,
> Nor blustering winds, nor flight of years and hours,
> Though numberless, can raze. I shall not die
> Wholly; nor shall my best part buried lie
> Within my grave.

And Martial (*Lib. 10, Ep. 2*) thus speaks of books and writings:

> * * * Writings no age can wrong, nor thieving hand,
> Deathless alone those monuments will stand.
> My books are read in every place;
> And when Licinius' and Messala's high
> Rich marble towers in ruined dust shall lie,
> I shall be read, and strangers everywhere
> Shall to their farthest homes my verses bear.

> * * * In like manner Ovid gives an endless date to himself and to his *Metamorphoses* in these words:

> *Iamque opus exegi etc.*[2]
> And now the work is ended, which Jove's rage,
> Nor fire, nor sword shall raze, nor eating age.
> Come when it will, my death's uncertain hour,
> Which only of my body hath a power,
> Yet shall my better part transcend the sky,
> And my immortal name shall never die:
> For wheresoe'er the Roman eagles spread
> Their conquering wings, I shall of all be read;
> And if we prophets truly can divine,
> I in my living fame shall ever shine.

Saint Jerome in like manner, in one of his epistles, writeth of the perpetuity of a funeral elegy which he made himself to the dear memory of his beloved Fabiola, who was buried in the city of Bethlehem—not because the said elegy was cut or engraven upon her sepulchre, but for that he had written it down in one of his volumes. * * * Books, then, and the Muses' works are of all monuments the most permanent; for of all things else there is a vicissitude, a change both of cities and nations. * * *

---

1. Horace, Odes 3.80.1–2, translated in the following two lines.
2. *Metamorphoses* 15.871, translated in the following line.

It is vanity for a man to think to perpetuate his name and memory by strange and costly great edifices, for

> Not sumptuous pyramids to skies up-reared,
> Nor Elean Jove's proud fane, which heaven compeered,[3]
> Nor the rich fortune of Mausoleus' tomb,
> Are privileged from death's extremest doom;
> Or fire, or storms their glories do abate,
> Or, by age shaken, fall with their own weight.[4]

We have many examples here in England of the small continuance (as I may so call it) of magnificent strong buildings, by the sudden fall of our religious houses, of which a late nameless versifier hath thus written:

> What sacred structures did our elders build,
> Wherein Religion gorgeously sat decked?
> Now all thrown down, religion exiled,
> Made brothel-houses, had in base respect,
> Or ruined so that, to the viewer's eye,
> In their own ruins they entombèd lie;
> The marble urns of their so zealous founders
> Are diggèd up, and turned to sordid uses;
> Their bodies are quite cast out of their bounders,
> Lie uninterred. Oh, greater what abuse is?
>   Yet in this later age we now live in,
>   This barbarous act is neither shame nor sin.

*　*　*

Likewise upon this forgotten city a nameless late writer hath made this epitaph:

> Stay thy foot that passest by,
> Here is wonder to descry,
> Churches that interred the dead,
> Here themselves are sepulchrèd;
> Houses, where men slept and waked,
> Here in ashes under-raked.
> In a word to allude,
> Here is corn where once Troy stood;
> Or more fully home to have,
> Here's a city in a grave.
> Reader, wonder think it then,
> Cities thus would die like men;
> And yet wonder think it none,
> Many cities thus are gone.

3. Rivaled. "Fane": temple.
4. Translated from Propertius, 3.2.17–24.

But I will conclude this chapter with these two stanzas following, taken out of Spenser's poem * * * speaking of the vanity of such princes who * * * think to gain a perpetuity after death by erecting of pillars and such like monuments to keep their names in remembrance, whenas it is only the Muses' works which give unto man immortality:

> In vain do earthly princes then, in vain,
> Seek with pyramides to heaven aspired,
> Or huge colosses, built with costly pain,
> Or brazen pillars, never to be fired,
> Or shrines, made of the metal most desired,
>   To make their memories for ever live—
>   For how can mortal immortality give?
> For deeds do die, however nobly done,
> And thoughts of men do in themselves decay;
> But wise words taught in numbers for to run,
> Recorded by the Muses, live for aye,
> Ne[5] may with storming showers be washed away,
>   Ne bitter breathing winds with harmful blast,
>   Nor age, nor envy shall them ever waste.

*   *   *

Chapter 3. Of Sepulchres answerable to the degree of the person deceased * * *

Sepulchres should be made according to the quality and degree of the person deceased, that by the tomb everyone might be discerned of what rank he was living; for monuments answerable to men's worth, states, and places have always been allowed, and stately sepulchres for base fellows have always lien open to bitter jests; therefore it was the use and custom of reverend antiquity to inter persons of the rustic or plebeian sort in Christian burial, without any further remembrance of them, either by tomb, gravestone, or epitaph. Persons of the meaner sort of gentry were interred with a flat gravestone, comprehending the name of the defunct, the year and day of his decease, with other particulars, which was engraven on the said stone or upon some plate. And gentlemen which were of more eminency had their effigies or representation cut or carved upon a term or pedestal, as it were of a pillar, raised somewhat above the ground, *umbelico tenus;* and this image had no arms, but was formed from the waist upwards upon a term,[6] which did bear a true resemblance of the favour of the party defunct. Upon the said term (commonly)

5. Nor.
6. Pedestal. *"Umbelio tenus"*: as far as the navel (Latin).

were inserted the name, progeny, match, issue, vocation, and employment of the defunct, with the day, year, and place of his death.

Noblemen, princes, and kings had (as it befitteth them, and as
some of them have at this day) their tombs or sepulchres raised aloft
above ground, to note the excellency of their state and dignity; and
withal their personages delineated, carved, and embossed at the full
length and bigness, truly proportioned throughout, as near to the
life and with as much state and magnificence as the skill of the arti-
ficer could possibly carve and form the same; the materials of which
were alabaster, rich marble, touch, rauce, porphyry, polished brass
or copper, like unto that made to the memory of King Henry VII in
Westminster, who dwelleth more richly dead (saith Viscount Saint
Alban[7] in his history of that king's reign) in the monument of his
tomb than he did alive in Richmond or any of his palaces, it being
the stateliest, the most curious dainty monument of Europe, both
for the chapel and for the sepulchre.

And as stately monuments were not due nor allowed to every man
that was of ability to erect the same, so swelling titles, lofty inscrip-
tions or epitaphs were prohibited to be inscribed, insculpt, or
engraven upon the sepulchres of men of mean desert, but only upon
the monuments of such as were of virtue, wisdom and valour—as
martial men, or persons of eminent place of government in the weal
public. Which is not observed altogether in these times; for by some
of our epitaphs more honor is attributed to a rich quondam tradesman or griping usurer than is given to the greatest potentate
entombed in Westminster; and their tombs are made so huge great
that they take up the church and hinder the people from divine service. Besides, if one shall seriously survey the tombs erected in these
our days, and examine the particulars of the personages wrought
upon their tombs, he may easily discern the vanity of our minds,
veiled under our fantastic habits and attires, which in time to come
will be rather provocations to vice than incitations to virtue; and so
the temple of God shall become a schoolhouse of the monstrous habits and attires of our present age, wherein tailors may find out new
fashions. And, which is worse, they garnish their tombs nowadays
with the pictures of naked men and women, raising out of the dust
and bringing into the Church the memories of the heathen gods and
goddesses, with all their whirligigs; and this (as I take it) is more
the fault of the tomb-makers, than theirs who set them a-work.

7. I.e., Francis Bacon.

Contemporary Responses

HENRY FITZGEFFREY

From Satires and Satirical Epigrams[†]

But hsst! with him crabbed Websterio,
The playwright-cartwright—whether?[1] either!
No further! Look as ye'd be looked into;
Sit as ye would be read; Lord! Who would know him?
Was ever man so mangled with a poem?
See how he draws his mouth awry of late,
How he scrubs, wrings his wrists, scratches his pate!
A midwife! Help! By his brain's coitus,
Some centaur strange, some huge Bucephalus,[2]
Or Pallas—sure engendered in his brain!
Strike, Vulcan, with thy hammer once again![3]

HORATIO BUSINO

Horatio Busino, Chaplain to the Venetian Ambassador, Describes a Performance of *The Duchess of Malfi* [‡]

7th *February, 1618*

The religion of this kingdom is at least that of Jesus Christ, but disastrously modified: as is well known, after Henry VIII, by unbridled lust for a woman named Anna Boleyn, had repudiated his lawful wife, he separated himself from the ancient Roman church, from which he had before his apostasy received the title of Defender of

---

† From Henry Fitzgeffrey, *Satyres and Satyricall Epigrams* (London, 1617).
1. Which of the two?
2. Stallion belonging to Alexander the Great.
3. Vulcan, god of fire, would strike his anvil every time his wife, Venus, was unfaithful—thereby causing eruptions from Mt. Etna.
‡ From Horatio Busino, Journal (February 7, 1618).

the Faith for a book against Luther. This title has been retained by
his successors and is borne by his present majesty. The entire popu-
lation abominates the popedom most utterly, having for it the same
detestation which is commonly entertained for the Devil or Antichrist
himself. * * *

The English deride our religion as detestable and superstitious,
and never represent any theatrical piece, not even a satirical tragicomedy, without larding it with the vices and iniquity of some
Catholic churchman, which move them to laughter and much
mockery, to their own satisfaction and to the regret of the good. On
one occasion, my colleagues of the embassy saw a comedy performed in which a Franciscan friar was introduced, cunning and
replete with impiety of various shades, including avarice and lust.
The whole was made to end in tragedy, the friar being beheaded
on the stage. Another time they represented the pomp of the Cardinal in his identical robes of state, very handsome and costly, and
accompanied by his attendants, with an altar raised on the stage,
where he pretended to perform service, ordering a procession. He
then re-appeared familiarly with a concubine in public. He played
the part of administering poison to his sister upon a point of honour; and, moreover, of going into battle, having first gravely depos-
ited his Cardinal's robes on the altar through the agency of his
chaplains. Last of all, he had himself girded with a sword and put
on his scarf with the best imaginable grace, all this they do in deri-
sion of ecclesiastical pomp which in this kingdom is scorned and
hated mortally.

CRITICISM

Sociopolitical Background

MARK H. CURTIS

From The Alienated Intellectuals
of Early Stuart England[†]

Three hundred years ago Thomas Hobbes, the inveterate critic of
Oxford his Alma Mater and her sister Cambridge, laid a heavy
charge against the two ancient English universities. He found them
guilty of breeding sedition. "The core of rebellion . . . ," he wrote in
passion, "are the universities".[1] As he developed his specifications
against them, he likened them to the wooden horse of Troy. Out of
them had poured in the years preceding the English Civil War, just
as earlier in the centuries of popish superstition, the chief corrupt-
ers of the king's loyal subjects. They produced and let loose upon
Stuart England both Puritan ministers and disobedient ambitious
gentlemen. He put his point in these words:

> As the Presbyterians brought with them into their churches
> their divinity from the universities, so did many of the gentle-
> men bring their politics from thence into the parliament. . . .
> And though it be not likely that all of them did it out of malice,
> but many of them out of error, yet certainly the chief leaders
> were ambitious ministers and ambitious gentlemen; the minis-
> ters envying the authority of bishops, whom they thought less
> learned; and the gentlemen envying the privy council, whom
> they thought less wise than themselves. For it is a hard matter
> for men, who do all think highly of their own wits, when they
> have also acquired the learning of the university, to be per-
> suaded that they want any ability requisite for the government
> of a commonwealth. . . . [2]

---

† Mark H. Curtis, "The Alienated Intellectuals of Early Stuart England," *Past and Present* 23 (1962), pp. 25–43. Reprinted by permission of Oxford University Press. Notes
have been renumbered.
1. *Behemoth* in *The English Works of Thomas Hobbes of Malmesbury*, ed. Sir William Moles-
worth, (London, 1840), vi. p. 236.
2. *Ibid.*, pp. 192–3.

As this passage suggests, Hobbes traced back the streams of rebellion to a source in the courses of study at Oxford and Cambridge. The divinity imbibed at the two universities enabled the Presbyterian clergy to appear to the people as men more righteous than others—true ministers of Christ and ambassadors of God. It gave to their preaching the power to bring men into great dependence upon them and provided the doctrines that taught their fellow countrymen to look upon the king and the bishops as their oppressors. The politics that the universities instilled came from the study of Greek and Roman history and philosophy. In reading about the deeds and thoughts of the famous men of antiquity, young gentlemen learned to extol popular government "by the glorious name of liberty" and disgrace monarchy "by the name of tyranny".[3] Thus, by the education that they provided, Oxford and Cambridge bred the seducers of the people and brought the kingdom to disobedience and rebellion.

* * * The universities were dangerous to English society in the early seventeenth century. I also agree that their success in educating and training divines and young gentlemen was the source of this danger. I part company with the crusty philosopher and observer of his own times at two points: in making the universities the principal cause of rebellion and in specifying that the courses of study pursued at Oxford and Cambridge necessarily and almost inexorably inspired disloyalty and disobedience.

* * *

The effect of university education on Stuart politics operated in more subtle but nonetheless significant ways than those that Hobbes condemned. The universities were dangerous—though not the "core of rebellion"—because they were, paradoxical as it may seem, too successful in carrying out their primary task of training men for service to Church and State. As vigorous effective institutions of higher education they unwittingly worked against the peace and tranquillity of the realm not because they instilled subversive doctrines but because they prepared too many men for too few places. Having been geared to the extraordinary demands for trained men which the Elizabethan Church and State made upon them, they poured out into early Stuart society more educated talent than that society in its unreformed condition could put to work in ways that would contribute either to its own health or to the satisfaction of the individuals concerned. As Lord Chancellor Ellesmere so succinctly put the matter in a conference between the bishops and the judges as early as 1611:

3. *Ibid.*, pp. 168, 193–6.

It is somewhat hard . . . that £8 per annum should be thought a sufficient maintenance for him who hath *curam animarum* when many in this company doth make better allowance to their grooms who have but *curam equorum* and I think that we have more need of better livings for learned men than of more learned men for these livings, for learning without living doth but breed traitors as common experience too well sheweth.[4]

The success of the universities thus became a double-acting acid within early Stuart society: in the first place it exposed the depths of abuse in the old corruption and hence made it less tolerable than ever, and at the same time it precipitated an insoluble group of alienated intellectuals who individually and collectively became troublemakers in a period of growing discontent with the Stuart regime.

The men to whom the term "alienated intellectuals" is herein applied are not to be understood as being primarily an economically oppressed and exploited class. As I shall show below, some undoubtedly had reason to think of themselves in some such ways, yet most of them probably received adequate livings in one form or another. Nor were they wholly unattached or isolated within English society. Frustration rather than exploitation or absolute isolation was the common experience of these men. They suffered frustration in the pursuit of their professions or careers, for opportunities to use their training and talents to the full were not available to them. As a consequence they frequently had to accept posts or roles which, no matter how remunerative, could not entirely satisfy them. These positions gave them employment and livelihood but left them restless and critical because they did not offer sufficient challenge to their sense of duty or did not appease their self-esteem and desire for recognition and honour. If in time some satisfactions did accrue to them, they frequently came in ways that were perverse. In other words these men, both clergymen and laymen, while they were within Stuart society, did not share all the opportunities, privileges, and responsibilities that were the perquisites of full unequivocal membership of that community. Being thus to some degree alienated from it, especially from its inner circles, they simultaneously viewed certain aspects of it with greater realism and objectivity than many of their contemporaries and yet on critical occasions acted and spoke irresponsibly. They were, to use a modern phrase, "angry young men", but "angry young men" whose bitterness grew to be far more intense than that of their twentieth-century counterparts.

To appreciate the growth of an alienated class among the clergy, one must recall the conditions of the Elizabethan Church that provided extra stimulus to university development in the late sixteenth

---

4. Conference between the bishops and the judges before the privy council on the jurisdiction of the Court of High Commission, 23 May 1611, Folger Libr., MS. V.a. 121, fol. 124.

century. It is well known, for instance, that immediately after Elizabeth's accession, the Church had an extraordinary need for large numbers of educated clergymen. By 1558 England had in the short space of twenty-five years passed through a succession of religious changes, going from medieval Catholicism to Henrician Catholicism, to moderate Protestantism, to radical Protestantism, and finally back to communion with Rome. Aside from leaving the ordinary Englishman uncertain about what he should believe and how he should worship, these changes had decimated the clergy: many suffered deprivation; some resigned. At the accession of Elizabeth not only were ten bishoprics vacant but at least 10 to 15 per cent of the parish churches were without incumbents. In the dioceses of London and Canterbury some populous archdeaconries had vacancies in one-third of their parishes. Pluralists and unordained readers could not and did not make up for these deficiencies. Furthermore only a small fraction of the clergy holding livings were qualified and licensed to preach. In many places such a condition had existed for at least five years; in some for a decade or more. At any time and place in the life of the Church such a condition would have been serious. In a Protestant country still in the throes of the Reformation it was perilous.[5] The only remedy lay in training sufficient clergymen to preach and to minister to the spiritual needs of the nation.

*　*　*

The usual source of supply for vacancies in the Church was the pool of men educated in the universities. In the course of the Elizabethan period Oxford and Cambridge had geared themselves to meet an unusual demand for trained talents in both Church and State. By the close of Elizabeth's reign, they were drawing abreast of the needs of the Church and in the first decade of the Stuart period they had, I believe, surpassed them. *　*　*

The condition in which the supply of clergymen was greater than the need for them gave the authorities in the Church a great advantage in dealing with Puritans who refused to conform to ecclesiastical laws and regulations. But of even greater importance was the part it played in creating a class of dissatisfied and alienated intellectuals within the clergy. As the shortage of ministers was transformed into an oversupply, this change brought the abuses within the Church into even more prominence than ever. Now they began to affect in direct, immediate, and painful ways the prospects and fortunes of a small but growing number of articulate people. Abuses such as pluralities and non-residence, which even James I and

5. W. H. Frere, *The English Church in the Reigns of Elizabeth and James I,* (London, 1924), pp. 104–9.

Bancroft acknowledged as undesirable, became in the eyes of these men and their sympathizers intolerable evils. Impatience with them could be heard in the way that critics refuted arguments used to justify them. To the claim that pluralities were necessary in order to provide large enough clerical incomes to encourage learning, the House of Commons, invoking experience as their authority, answered that "pluralists heaping up many livings into one hand do by that means keep divers learned men from maintenance, to the discouragement of students and the hindrance of learning".[6]

Discouraged some students of divinity may have been, but few of them suffered the despair that would have made them give up their studies. Hence the universities continued to provide them the usual rewards for their academic achievements and they departed to find such posts as they could. * * *

* * *

A vivid phrase from a speech in the Parliament of 1621 provides a link between the clerical and lay side of this story. In attacking the evil of the sale of offices, a member of the House of Commons said: "That in the cheapness of all things offices grow dearer and are indeed of a greater price than benefices".[7] Although this particular person opposed the sale of offices because buyers needed to resort to acceptance of bribes and extortion of excessive fees to recover their costs, and not because it prevented well qualified men from serving the monarch, his words give an indication that in the State as well as in the Church offices were hard to come by. G. E. Aylmer has recently shown that such sentiments rose from actual conditions and not merely from the bitterness of disappointed office seekers.[8] In his analysis of the system of office holding in the early seventeenth century, he shows that rigidity had set in. Opportunities to win honour and profit for oneself and to advance the good of one's prince and commonwealth were not growing in the financially hard-pressed court of James I and were probably declining in Charles I's reign after 1629. Furthermore under James I galloping venality and creeping monopoly had combined to poison the sources of patronage. They not only discouraged but frequently revolted some well-intentioned, prospective servants of the State. Complaints about the court and the indignities of waiting on patrons and winning influence—complaints that are levelled against every system of

6. "Petition concerning Religion, 1610", J. R. Tanner, ed., *Constitutional Documents of the Reign of James I*, (Cambridge, 1930), p. 79.
7. William Noy's speech, 3 May 1621, as reported by John Pym, *Commons Debates, 1621*, ed. Wallace Notestein, F. H. Relf, and H. Simpson, 7 vols., (New Haven, 1935), iv. p. 295.
8. G. E. Aylmer, "Office Holding as a Factor in English History, 1625–42", *History*, xliv (1959), pp. 229–232; see also Aylmer, *The King's Servants* (London, 1961), Ch. iii, Chap. iv, section iv.

patronage—took on in these years overtones of disillusionment and even disgust that had formerly been less obvious. Although merit, as Aylmer notes, might still recommend a candidate for office to a patron, patrimony operating through a system of purchases and reversions usually determined who held places under the Stuarts. The disregard of merit became especially flagrant in the days of Buckingham's ascendancy, for he virtually monopolized the distribution of patronage.

All of these points are relevant to this discussion of the role of the universities in the growing discontent with the Stuart regime. Through most of the sixteenth century when the Tudors were increasing the power and responsibilities of the central government, and therefore the chances for men to serve their prince, matters had been different. To be sure patronage and influence greased the wheels of the State then as later, but it seems to have been a less sticky and less contaminating kind of lubricant than that used in the seventeenth century. Moreover the changes that were both limiting and causing distaste for places in the service of the prince were occurring just at the time that the universities were reaching the peak of their Renaissance development. As a result of what has been called a "cultural revolution", young gentlemen and noblemen had since Elizabeth's accession been coming to Oxford and Cambridge in rising numbers. In the period between 1603 and 1640 this movement reached flood tide.[9]

The growing enrolment of young gentlemen in the universities is, however, only part of the problem. Another is related to what the sons of the gentry and nobility learned there. This is not to say that Hobbes was correct in denouncing the study of classical history. He was not, but one aspect of university education did generate discontent. The humanists of the sixteenth century, whose criticism of the university curriculum had wrought significant changes in the arts course, had taught Englishmen a lesson that they retained for at least a couple of generations. Not only did they effect a change in social ideals so that learning was accepted as one of the attributes of a gentleman but they instilled the idea that learning in the *literae humaniores* imparted that peculiar wisdom and judgement needed in the conduct of public affairs. Hence university men among the gentry had reason to pride themselves on being especially qualified to serve the State. The new scholars who appeared in Oxford and Cambridge may not indeed have all come to read for degrees but most of them were there to equip themselves for the life that hopefully lay before them. Gabriel Harvey sensed this fact as early as the

9. J. H. Hexter, "The Education of the Aristocracy in the Renaissance", *Journal of Modern History*, xxii (1950), pp. 1–20; Mark H. Curtis, *Oxford and Cambridge in Transition* (Oxford, 1959), Ch. iii.

1580s. Forty years later Henry Peacham showed that this attitude toward university education had become a commonplace. In his book *The Compleat Gentleman* he warned his younger readers that in going to the university they were leaving childish things and entering on adult life and that the industry and conduct shown there would be telling factors in determining their success or failure in later careers.[1] The practical consequences of such attitudes can be found in the letters of application written to patrons of the period. Wherever the applicant could honestly do so, he set forth the educational qualifications he had gained at the universities. One typical suitor, who was not blind to his own faults, asked the Earl of Salisbury to consider him for the post of clerk of the council in a letter that reads in part: "I was brought up 18 years past in the University of Cambridge, having been master of arts and fellow of Jesus College, where though I played the truant yet I think I did not altogether lose my time".[2]

Thus again the success of the universities—and in this connection perhaps someone ought also to give attention to the Inns of Court—was breeding trouble for the Stuarts. Oxford and Cambridge were striving to give young gentlemen the knowledge that would make them skilled and wise in the service of the monarch and to indoctrinate them with a sense of the high calling for which they were supposedly destined. Instead they seem to have prepared a goodly number of them for frustration. When one contrasts, for instance, the mediocrity that Professor David H. Willson found generally characteristic of the privy council under the first two Stuarts with the abilities of men like Sir Edwin Sandys, Sir John Eliot, John Pym, and John Selden, to name but a few university men who were actively interested in politics but failed to find satisfying positions in the king's service, the consequences of this conjunction of circumstances can begin to be fully appreciated.[3] Here again the outpouring of university men into a world unable to put their trained talents to constructive use generated impatience with the old corruption and helped create the body of men who would be among its most formidable opponents. Even as early as 1625 the feelings expressed by some of these men were becoming ominous in tone. One member of parliament, in sharply criticizing the sale of honours and offices, spoke in these terms:

1. Henry Peacham, *The Compleat Gentleman*, ed. G. S. Gordon, (Oxford, 1906), p. 38.
2. Robert Kayle to Sir Michael Hicks, 13 May 1605, Brit. Mus., MS. Lansd. 89, fol. 105. Kayle wanted Salisbury's help in securing the place and asked Hicks to intercede with Salisbury for him. There are many other examples of letters like this one among Hicks's papers.
3. David H. Willson, *The Privy Councillors in the House of Commons, 1604–1629*, (Minneapolis, 1940), pp. 82–98.

> If worthy persons have been advanced freely to places of great-
> est trust, I shall be glad. [But] Spencer was condemned in . . .
> 15 Edward II for displacing good servants about the king and
> putting in his friends and followers. . . . The like in part was laid
> by parliament on de la Pole.[4]

To understand that Oxford and Cambridge as effective institutions of higher education had been instrumental in creating a
group of alienated intellectuals does not, of course, account for the
principles and policies that suggested alternatives to the unreformed
society of Stuart England. It merely explains how maladjustments
within English society produced discontented individuals who provided some of the leadership to the opposition. On the other hand
it was not merely historical accident that these men more often than
not voiced Puritan religious doctrines and liberal constitutional ideals in expressing their criticism of what was and in delineating their
vision of what could be. The changes in Oxford and Cambridge that
had made them successful institutions took place under the aegis
of social, intellectual, and religious movements to which these opposition doctrines and ideals also owed some of their origins and nur-
ture. It was therefore natural for the alienated intellectuals to find
the means of remedying the abuses from which they suffered in ide-
alisms so closely woven into the fabric of their existence. Hobbes, it
can thus be seen, overstates his case against the universities by making the courses of study the source of rebellion. Although experiences at Oxford and Cambridge may have heightened awareness of
opposition principles and may have increased capacities to understand and apply them, no such drastic indictment of the universities is needed to explain the espousal of Puritan and republican ideas
by university men. In this matter Ellesmere was both more obser-
vant and more profound than Hobbes when he said that "learning
without living doth but breed traitors as common experience too
well sheweth".

Perhaps the proper conclusion to this paper is a word of caution,
not to weaken what has been set forth but to keep it in perspective.
At no time in the early Stuart period was this group of clergymen
and laymen whom I have designated alienated intellectuals large in
numbers. In the whole period from 1603 to 1640 the universities had
probably enrolled less than 25,000 students. The proportion of
those who became frustrated and alienated because their society had
no satisfying callings for them would probably be no more than
15 to 20 per cent of that total. Furthermore, as far as the clergy was
concerned, the graduates who could not find regular livings in the

---

4. Speech in the parliament held in Oxford, 25 August 1625, Brit. Mus., MS. Harl. 6846,
   fol. 166v.

Church were only a part of the group of discontented critics. As Christopher Hill has shown the economic privation suffered by many parsons also engendered restlessness and protest. Nor must it be forgotten that some men who held good livings were critics because of their principles. The importance of the group described did not, however, arise from its numerical strength, but rather from the character and training of its members. They were a significant segment of the educated, talented, sensitive, conscientious men in Stuart society—men who would be capable of giving leadership and direction to the causes that they shared in common with others. For that reason understanding of the social conditions that produced them—especially the unwitting role of the universities and other institutions of education—helps to explain the rising storm that shattered the Stuart system of government and swept England into the agonies of Civil War.

Webster's Reputation, Seventeenth through Nineteenth Centuries

DON D. MOORE

From Webster: The Critical Heritage[†]

In his address to the reader in the 1612 quarto of 'The White Devil', John Webster, responding to charges of his slowness as a writer, seems confident of his own critical heritage. * * *

Indeed, as in his Preface to 'The Devil's Law Case', Webster never seemed to doubt that his works would be found worthy. And if 'The White Devil' failed at the Red Bull Theatre, it was due to the absence of 'a full and understanding auditory',[1] not to the absence of the writer's art.

More than three ages have now passed, and Webster's self-evaluation has proven, in many ways, accurate. His major tragedies, 'The White Devil' and 'The Duchess of Malfi', are the focus of attention in the study, the school, and, increasingly, on the stage. Dissertations are written; symposia are held; editions are plentiful. At the same time, however, Webster's prophetic comments are not wholly accurate. For almost two ages Webster was available, having not fully disappeared with his fellows; but few seemed to care. And with his revival in the early nineteenth century, heralded by Lamb's appreciation, Webster began to generate one of the most peculiar critical histories of any author of any time: by some he is praised unstintingly as being second only to Shakespeare in tragic art, and he is damned to the lowest circles by others. Since 1850 his tragedies have been staged more often than those of any of Shakespeare's contemporaries except Jonson; the results have brought delight and dole in equal scale. Webster endures, but not quite in the fashion he may have imagined: in 1949, for example, we learned that Webster

† Don D. Moore, Introduction to *Webster: The Critical Heritage* (London: Routledge & Kegan Paul, 1981), pp. 1–25. Notes have been renumbered. Reprinted by permission of Taylor & Francis Books UK.

1. 'The White Devil', ed. J.R. Brown (1958), p. 2. Cf. Dekker's similar phrasing in 'If it be not Good, the Devil is in It' (1612).

rose above his fellows through his 'intellectual and spiritual insight',[2] but elsewhere that there is, finally, 'something a trifle ridiculous about Webster'.[3]

Contemporary Reputation

As has often been noted, what we know about Shakespeare seems voluminous when compared with what we know of Webster in his own time. * * *

We remain in a mist, to use a Websterian image, regarding his general reputation in his own time. Certain things are sure: from Webster himself we learn the fate of 'The White Devil', which was not surprising. The theatre audience at the Red Bull in Clerkenwell was 'a plain man's playhouse, where clownery, clamor, and spectacle vied with subject matter flattering to the vanity of tradesmen'.[4] Such a house might well have been confused by a drama of old conventions but troublingly new ideas, with characters who did not fit the older stereotypes. Webster did not lack confidence, however, and perhaps never did, as evidenced by his dedications to 'The Duchess of Malfi' and 'The Devil's Law Case'. We have in the Preface to 'The White Devil' his well-known references to his colleagues; we note that he begins the list with the two serious and classical writers, Chapman and Jonson, and ends with the master writers of the popular theatre, Shakespeare, Dekker, and Heywood. There is little doubt that Webster would prefer to be read by the 'light' of the first two learned playwrights, and with Jonson's defensive Preface to 'Sejanus' before him, no doubt saw himself as above the popular theatre. Still, his 'good opinion of other men's labors' is not particularly effusive, and Webster here, as in the other dedicatory epistles, seems at this time an independent, confident man. That near the end of his career he would return in a collaborative role to the Red Bull was an unanticipated and probably an unpleasant irony: 'Keep the Widow Waking', written with Ford, Dekker, and Rowley, was performed there in 1624.

The commendatory verses for the 1623 edition of 'The Duchess of Malfi' are from three playwrights not praised in 'The White Devil' preface, and we may wonder at Webster's reputation in 1623 because of the absence of certain of those mentioned. Instead, we have Middleton, Ford, and Rowley, all collaborators with Webster but of different levels of learning and interests. Yet though Rowley's verse befits his usual hack level, Middleton's and Ford's do indicate a genuine awareness of the merit of the play; and we may note also

---

2. David Cecil, 'Poets and Storytellers' (1949), p. 29.
3. Ian Jack, The Case of John Webster, 'Scrutiny', XVI (March 1949), p. 43.
4. L.B. Wright, 'Middle Class Culture in Elizabethan England' (1935), p. 609.

that Middleton and Rowley wrote no other prefatory verse. The famous description by Henry Fitzjeffrey remains our only personal glimpse of Webster, and the unflattering portrait therein is the first of many intermittent but vivid assaults on Webster and his art which continue well into the twentieth century. Objecting to 'The Duchess' for religious reasons is Orazio Busino, Venetian envoy in England in 1618. That the play was thus available in 1618 indicates, along with the cast-lists, its theatrical success, as does the printing of 'The Duchess' in 1623 when presumably it was off the stage. Nevertheless, after rising briefly to great heights, Webster's power in the field of tragedy declined: 'The Devil's Law Case' is a less than challenging play of episodic structure belonging to 1616–20; there were dull collaborations; 'Appius and Virginia', in the 1620s (?), does manifest a unity of tone, but that tone is unexciting and simplistic. In his end was his beginning.

Webster in the Later Seventeenth Century

For a period of time afterwards we find Webster in the commonplace books (Edmund Pudsey had earlier garbled eight quotations from 'The White Devil', c. 1616) and as a ghostly influence on such writers as James Shirley, Nathaniel Richards, and Robert Baron. In 1648, an unlicensed royalist newsbook, 'Mercurius Pragmaticus', referred to 'famous Webster' in a roll-call of poets including Seneca, Sophocles, Shakespeare, and Jonson[5] (Webster being singled out for the lone adjective); but it is Samuel Sheppard who provides us with the one mid-century appreciation with his epigram on 'The White Devil' in 1651 and his inclusion of Webster in a literary hall of fame in his laboured epic 'The Fairy King'. The latter effort includes Webster in a House of Eloquence, ranking behind More, Sidney, Spenser, Chapman, and Wotton. The work was never published, a blessing for the public. His epigram on 'The White Devil', however, marks the beginning of a rudimentary character criticism: Vittoria is a 'fam'd whore', Flamineo is 'The Devil's darling', and the like. Given the absence of any kind of real criticism, we have to settle for Sheppard. Webster shortly made his first of many appearances in poetic anthologies in John Cotgrave's 'The English Treasury of Wit and Language' (1655), and is represented by 104 quotations from his plays. * * * Webster ranks sixth behind Shakespeare (154 quotations), Beaumont and Fletcher (112), Jonson (111), Chapman (111), and Greville (110).[6]

---

5. Quoted in G.E. Bentley, 'Shakespeare and Jonson' (1945), p. 288.
6. See G.E. Bentley's John Cotgrave's 'English Treasury of Wit and Language' and the Elizabethan Drama, 'Studies in Philology', XL (April 1943), p. 192.

The early 1660s found Webster on the stage once more: 'The White Devil' was performed twice in October of 1661 and again the following December; there would be another recorded performance in late summer of 1671. The quarto of 1671 tells us that it had been 'divers times Acted by the Queenes Maiestes seruants in Drury Lane'; the third and fourth quartos (1665 and 1672) note performances at the Theatre Royal by the King's Company. More successful seems 'The Duchess of Malfi': it was performed on 30 September 1662, with London's finest talent. Betterton played Bosola, Mary Saunderson was the Duchess, with Henry Harris as Ferdinand. John Downes records that it was 'so exceedingly excellently acted in all parts, chiefly Duke Ferdinand and Bosola, it filled the house eight days successively, proving one of the best stock tragedies'.[7] Samuel Pepys, however, had some opinions of Webster which sound similar to those of some modern reviewers. Taking advantage of this brief revival of Webster was Francis Kirkman, who published 'A Cure for a Cuckold' in 1661 with a Preface which is of interest: 'As for this play, I need not speak anything in its commendation, and the author's names, Webster and Rowley, are (to knowing men) sufficient to declare its worth.'[8] Again, Rowley was in good company.

Thus Webster was kept tenuously alive through sporadic performances and new editions of his plays. 'Appius and Virginia' was reprinted in 1654 (reissued in 1659) and again in 1679, due to Betterton's adaptation called 'The Roman Virgin'. (The actor's revision never saw print, which may tell us something of its merit.) Webster's appearance in play lists such as Edward Archer's (1656) and Kirkman's (1661 and 1671) indicates that the reading of old plays did not stop for a Civil War and a Restoration.[9] Edward Phillips made Webster the subject of a brief but error-filled account in his effort at theatre history in 'Theatrum Poetarum' (1675); William Winstanley did little better in his 'Lives of the Most Famous English Poets' (1687), usually copying indiscriminately from Phillips. It remained for Gerard Langbaine to bring together the play lists and the attempt at biographies in his 'Account of the English Dramatic Poets' in 1691, a revision of his 'New Catalogue of English Plays' of 1688. His account is [cited] here chiefly for the historical record; but for a century it was the standard source for Webster documentation. In

7. John Downes, 'Roscius Anglicanus', ed. Montague Summers (1928), p. 29. It would be staged again on 25 November 1668, 31 January 1672, and at court on 13 January 1686. ('The London Stage', ed. William Van Lennep (1965), I, p. 40).
8. Noted by F.L. Lucas, 'The Complete Works of John Webster' (1927), III, p. 29.
9. Tso-Liang Wang's 'The Literary Reputation of John Webster to 1830' (1975) studies the playlists effectively, pp. 1–38. Wang's book in the Salzburg monograph series has been a welcome aid for this entire period; I have also drawn freely upon my own 'John Webster and His Critics, 1617–1964' (1966) and referred to G.K. and S.K. Hunter's 'John Webster: A Critical Anthology' (1969).

1698 Charles Gildon republished the material in his 'Lives of the Poets', adding almost as an afterthought that Webster was at one time clerk of St Andrew's parish, thus confusing the dramatist's biography for over a century. Dyce in his 1830 edition firmly challenged the accuracy of the remark, C.W. Dilke having been dubious in his 'Old English Plays' (1814–15) which included 'Appius and Virginia'.

James Wright in 'Country Conversations' (1694) helps bring the sparse Webster references to a placid and perhaps symbolic close at the end of the century. A country gentleman, Trueman, chats with his visiting city friends on a variety of topics, from the merits of the older drama and the new to proper garden arrangement. We eventually hear one Julio, upon seeing some picturesque ruins preserved by a neighbouring squire, quoting Antonio's 'ruins' speech from 'The Duchess' (V, iii, 9–19). Indeed, we learn that Julio was one 'who omitted no occasion to magnify the wit of the dramatic poets of the last age'.[1] The passage, soon to be the Webster favourite in eighteenth-century anthologies, is ascribed to Webster, the play, and the speaker, and is the only quotation in the book apart from translated passages. Wright, son of Abraham Wright, produced in 1699 the 'Historica Histrionica', in which he briefly refers to 'The Duchess' as the first of a group of plays that had the names of the actors set against their parts.

Between the publications of Wright, there had been a touch of Webster in another play: Joseph Harris's 'The City Bride' (1696) was a reworking of 'A Cure for a Cuckold' with poetry turned to prose amid music, song, and the latest in Restoration repartee. The plot at least remained essentially Webster's. However, Webster was briefly taken to task in 1698 for one aspect of his plotting in 'The Duchess'.

Thus if the years immediately following the Restoration were briefly propitious for Webster, the next twenty-five years were not. He had not completely disappeared, but we have fewer and fewer straws to grasp. Shakespeare, Jonson, Beaumont and Fletcher remain visible, sometimes on stage and in books of poetic miscellany, dedications of Restoration plays, and in critical works of Dryden, Cowley, and others.[2] Nevertheless, Webster, if less acknowledged, still had an influence in the melodramas of Southerne, Otway, and others who dealt with the themes of lust and betrayal. * * *

The Eighteenth Century

Generally speaking, there is no critical heritage of John Webster between 1700 and 1800. The dramatic bibliographers were acquainted

1. James Wright, 'Country Conversations', ed. Charles Whibley (1927), p. 57.
2. Cf. Herbert Weisinger, The Seventeenth Century Reputation of the Elizabethans, 'Modern Language Quarterly', VI (March 1945), pp. 13–21.

with him; poetry anthologies sometimes included him; and scholars, turning increasing attention to the age of Shakespeare, knew his plays.[3] But even for Malone, Steevens, and Capell, Webster was for an age, not for all time. Pope's one allusion in 1728 sums up most of the commentary: 'Webster, Marston, Goff, Kyd, and Massinger were the persons instanced as tolerable writers of tragedy in Ben Jonson's time.'[4] And Webster's stage history for over a century can be told as quickly: three performances of a revised 'Duchess of Malfi', and two adaptations, one not staged, the other lasting two performances.

On 22 July 1707, 'The Unfortunate Duchess, or, The Unnatural Brothers' was performed at the lavish Queen's Haymarket, the first playhouse to be constructed in the century. Two more performances followed on 29 July and 8 August. The reviser is unknown, but the cast was excellent, including John Verbruggen, Mary Porter, John Mills, Barton Booth, and others. The text, in the form of the fourth quarto, was published in 1708 and indicates cuts and stage directions. Missing was the pilgrim scene (III, iv), the fables, and the lines in Act III, scene iii indicating a son of the first marriage. Some of the language is, of course, purged: 'lecher' becomes 'lover', for instance, amid other laundering. Compared to what awaited Webster, however, the 1708 text seems pure.

In 1707, Nahum Tate, plagiarist and poet laureate, favoured his public with a newly published play called 'Injur'd Love, or, The Cruel Husband'. Nowhere does Tate admit his theft (who would know?); he does admit in an epilogue that he 'chose a Vessel that would bear the shock / Of Censure; Yes, old built but Heart of Oak'. The vessel, however, cannot bear the shock of Tate. Though 'The White Devil' fares better than did 'King Lear' in Tate's hands—some scenes follow in their regular Websterian order with little rewriting, and the villains meet their deaths as in the original—conformity and convention are observed. Vittoria, no longer the blazing Jacobean femme fatale, is truly innocent of adultery with Brachiano (making the trial scene ridiculous), and, indeed, in her own praise of Isabella's purity we realize we have reached the age of sentimental drama, an age wherein, on stage at least, the earth groans at the thought of a broken marriage. It is salutary to know that 'Injur'd Love' never injured an audience: no record of a performance exists.[5]

3. Cf. R.D. Williams, Antiquarian Interest in the Elizabethan Drama Before Lamb, 'PMLA', LIII (June 1938), pp. 434–44.
4. Quoted by Joseph Spence, 'Anecdotes, Observations, and Characters of Books and Men', ed. S.W. Singer, newly introduced by Barnaby Dobree (1964), p. 44.
5. Wang, op.cit., studies Tate's burglary as does Hazleton Spencer, Nahum Tate and 'The White Devil', 'Journal of English Literary History', I (1934), pp. 235–49.

On 18 December 1731, Lewis Theobald writes to William Warburton:

> I have apply'd my uneasie Summer Months upon the Attempt of a Tragedy. *Sit verbo venia*! I have a Design upon the Ladies Eyes, as the Passage to their Pockets. . . . I'll indulge myself, in submitting a Pair of soliloquies to you, as a taste of my poor Workmanship. I lay my scene in Italy. My heroine is a young Widow Dutchess, who has two haughty Spanish Brothers, yet enjoin her not to marry again. She, however, marries the Master of her Household on the morning I open my scene. . . . [6]

There follow two soliloquies from his 'tragedy' with lines from Webster sometimes recognizable, but not apparently to the scholar Warburton. Such was the state of Webster scholarship.

The play, now called 'The Fatal Secret', was staged twice at Covent Garden on 4 and 6 April 1733, with James Quin as Bosola, Lacy Ryan as Ferdinand, and Mrs Hallam as the Duchess; and it is worse than 'Injur'd Love'. Theobald in his Preface, which affords us our one piece of neo-classic comment on Webster, blames politics and the weather for the brief run of the play; we can blame Theobald. Admitting his larceny in the Preface (one hopes he'd been caught), he writes of Webster's violation of the unities and his 'wild and undigested Genius'. In the process of taming and digesting this genius, however, Theobald regularizes the play into an unintentional farce. If the plot consequently moves more quickly, it is at the expense of everything else. No children are born, obvious morals are drawn, horrors are softened, Webster's lines disappear, but in this brave new world the Duchess herself does not: at the end of the play, having been safely stowed away by Bosola, she emerges alive, well, and tedious. An anonymous letter writer to the 'Grubstreet Journal' on 25 April, protesting the refusal of his own work by the theatre manager who has instead staged lesser plays, reports triumphantly that 'The Fatal Secret' 'met with the Fate it deserved'.[7] On this note, Webster's plays left the English stages for over a century.

* * *

The Earlier Nineteenth Century

In a modestly brief autobiography written in 1827 at the request of William Upcott, Charles Lamb added at the end of an incomplete

---

6. Quoted in R.F. Jones, 'Lewis Theobald' (1919), p. 291.
7. Reprinted in the 'Gentleman's Magazine' (1733), p. 194. Wang, op.cit., also considers Theobald's version, as does R.K. Kaul in What Theobald Did to Webster, 'Indian Journal of English Studies', II (1961), pp. 138–44.

list of his works one comment: 'He was also the first to draw the Public attention to the old English Dramatists in a work called "Specimens of the English Dramatic Writers who lived about the time of
Shakespeare" * * *.[8]

Lamb brought for the first time a genuinely critical acumen to the
works of the writers as opposed to the antiquarian appreciation of
the anthologists and the historical dictionaries. It was an impressionistic approach to the plays as literature, not as antique curiosities,
and owes its method partly to the Longinian influence on Romantic criticism, an emphasis on appreciative ecstasy in the reader,
rather than on an Augustan inquiry through analytic, judicial
investigation. Bishop Hurd had earlier written of the 'pure, strong,
and perspicacious' language of the age of Elizabeth; and Wordsworth only recently had defined poetry as the 'spontaneous over-
flow of powerful feelings' in his Preface (1802) to the 'Lyrical
Ballads'. As Wordsworth concentrated on 'fitting to metrical arrange-
ment a selection of the real language used by men', so Lamb, in
printing large extracts from the dramatists, chose scenes (rather
than the anthologists' quotations) of the 'deepest quality':

> The kind of extracts which I have sought after have been, not
> so much passages of wit and humour, though the old plays are
> rich in such, as scenes of passion, sometimes of the deepest
> quality, interesting situations, serious descriptions, that which
> is more nearly allied to poetry than to wit, and to tragic rather
> than to comic poetry. The plays which I have made choice of
> have been, with few exceptions, those which treat of human life
> and manners, rather than masques, and Arcadian pastorals,
> with their train of abstractions, unimpassioned deities, passion-
> ate mortals * * *. My leading design has been, to illustrate what
> may be called the moral sense of our ancestors. To show in what
> manner they felt, when they placed themselves, by the power
> of imagination in trying situations, in the conflicts of duty and
> passion, or the strife of contending duties; what sort of loves
> and enmities theirs were; how their griefs were tempered, and
> their full-swoln joys abated: how much of Shakspeare shines in
> the great men his contemporaries, and how far in his divine
> mind and manners he surpassed them and all mankind.[9]

* * * T.S. Eliot would later criticize Lamb's poetic emphasis, and
hold him responsible for beginning a near-fatal dichotomy between

---

8. Quoted by E.V. Lucas in 'The Works of Charles and Mary Lamb' (1904), IV, p. 597.
9. Ibid., p. 1. Lamb's selections were later often cited by others in the journals. Stendhal,
   in a chapter of 'Armance' (1827), quotes part of Cornelia's dirge as an epigraph.

drama and poetry.[1] Indeed, all too often during the remainder of the century Webster is called a poet, not a playwright. Nevertheless, Lamb's generous selections and his marginalia led to renewed awareness of Webster and his fellows, and to critical arguments over Lamb's observations well into our own time. * * *

Something of a minor Elizabethan revival took place in the journals in the years following the 'Specimens'. 'Blackwood's' in 1818 began a series on the early English drama wherein Webster is found by John Wilson to be a master of scenes rather than structure, although Wilson accentuates the positive. Nevertheless, Wilson seems to have been the first critic to consider the problem of losing the main character in the fourth act of a five-act play. Other unsigned appreciations appeared in the 'European Magazine' in October and November of 1820 and in the 'Retrospective Review' for 1823, neither of which bears reprinting. The 'European Magazine' defends the early English dramatists against Voltaire and neo-classic strictures: 'The spirit of English tragedy is of too severe and mighty a character to bend down to any rules but its own' (p. 302), although the writer notes without real comment a great irregularity in Websterian structure. The enthusiasm of the author in the 'Retrospective Review' leads to the statement that Webster is entitled 'to the gratitude of every lover of the histrionic art; we say of the histrionic art because they [his plays] are much better calculated for representation than most of our early dramas' (p. 88). We are not told why this is so. Both writers quote appreciatively.

More important in reinstating the dramatist in the public mind were the lectures by William Hazlitt in 1819. Combining Lamb's evocative impressionism with more specific historical and comparative criticism, Hazlitt is the first to tell us that 'The White Devil' and 'The Duchess of Malfi' 'come the nearest to Shakespear of any thing we have upon record', a comparison both accepted and challenged by critics of the future. Not surprisingly, Hazlitt avoids real comment on Webster's structure, as Hazlitt himself rarely attains a stylistic symmetry of plan. Of interest is his preference for 'The White Devil', since for Hazlitt the final horrors of 'The Duchess' 'exceed the just bounds' of tragedy. He notes that he writes 'under correction', a deferential bow, perhaps, to his friend Lamb whose

---

1. Cf. T.S. Eliot, The Possibility of a Poetic Drama in 'The Sacred Wood' (1928) and Four Elizabethan Dramatists in 'Elizabethan Essays' (1934). Eliot himself would review 'The Duchess of Malfi' in 'Arts and Letters', III (Winter 1920), pp. 36–9. The production was a disaster, and Eliot's commentary is little better, with its several surprisingly untenable remarks on the staging of poetic drama. Eliot also did a radio critique of Webster, reprinted in the 'Listener', 18 December 1941, pp. 825–6. See my discussion of Eliot's influential role in Webster criticism in 'Webster and His Critics', pp. 97–108.

evocative tributes to the fifth act were to become a standard point of argument.

In 1830 came the text of Webster which would serve readers for almost a century. Alexander Dyce, clergyman editor, included in 'The Works of John Webster' the two major tragedies, 'The Devil's Law Case', 'Appius and Virginia', 'Northward Ho', 'The Thracian Wonder', 'The Famous History of Thomas Wyatt', and 'The Malcontent'. * * * He is among the first to celebrate the wooing scene in 'The Duchess of Malfi', 'a subject most difficult to treat'; elsewhere his criticism is generally impressionistic appreciation. Dyce's work received favourable notice: the London 'Literary Gazette' commended 'Mr. Dyce's labours to the favour of all literary persons' (17 April 1830, p. 255); Sir Walter Scott, having included the two major tragedies in 'The Ancient British Drama' (edited anonymously in 1810), writes in 1831 to Dyce and notes Webster as 'one of the best of our ancient dramatists'.[2]

* * *

1850–1900

On 20 November 1850, audiences at the Sadler's Wells Theatre saw 'The Duchess of Malfi', the first staging in over a century. With the production begins a new phase of Webster's critical heritage, the responses to the plays as acted. And this response is a divided one, to say the least. Critics would disagree throughout the remainder of the century, one side celebrating the poetic power of Webster's tragic vision, while others, especially the stage critics, would vigorously attack what they characterized as episodic structure, absurd improbabilities, and gross excesses. And within the anti-Webster group would come another complaint, that of decadence and immorality. Nor surprisingly, the Victorian popular novelist and reformer Charles Kingsley first makes the charge not long after the 1850 production. And while we may dismiss the moral charges of the Victorians, the reviews of Webster on the stage in the nineteenth century sound, on occasion, sadly similar to those in our own time.[3]

To be sure, what the Sadler's Wells audience saw was not wholly Webster's 'Duchess of Malfi' but, as the printed text informs us, one

---

2. 'Letters of Sir Walter Scott', ed. H.J.C. Grierson (1937), XII, 1. Making Webster further available for the Victorians would be W.C. Hazlitt's four-volume edition of Webster in 1857, reprinted in 1897. Generally an inferior copy of Dyce.
3. From reviews of 'The Duchess of Malfi' in November 1892 and July 1971: 'At moments when the audience should have wept, it tittered' ('Nation'); 'Bosola confesses to having some conscience and kills his fellow villains. And the audience titters and goes home' ('Spectator'). I do not mean to imply that all Webster productions meet with titters and failure, but the record is not a happy one.

'Re-Constructed for Stage Performance by R.H. Horne'.[4] Richard Hengist (Henry) Horne, author of the 'farthing epic' 'Orion' and well-known journalist, editor, and critic, took Webster's play and turned it into a stage piece that afforded certain actresses their most famous role for the next twenty-five years in England and the USA. However, in his adaptation, we lose a considerable portion of Webster. As Horne tells us in his introduction (No. 28),

> All the terrors (shorn and abated of the excesses in the original) are still left here in all their genuine tragic force. But it must also be borne in mind that nothing like a shocking *reality* must be presented;—the whole being softened by stage arrangements—in short, by *Art*—so as to be seen through a poetical and refining medium.

This artistic softening results in a play of tight construction, fluent and unmemorable Fletcherian verse, and a tone not of moral ambiguity but of melodrama, sentimental and black and white. Minor characters disappear, and major characters constantly inform us as to their intentions. Thus the Cardinal (now Cardinal Graziani) confides in the audience often, manipulates Ferdinand, and uses Julia, now sexually rehabilitated by Horne, as an unwitting instrument in his melodramatic villainy. The madmen are heard offstage in the tidying up of the plot: those who hear them will assume the noise to be the ravings of the mad Duchess, whose estate will then come into the management of her brothers. (And, of course, 'shocking reality' must be avoided.) The Duchess (now called Marina and re-entering after her strangling to cry 'Mercy' and die on stage) is not the occasionally sensual young woman of Webster but one who shares this kind of business in the torture scene with Bosola:

> *Bos.* Thou art an over-ripe fruit, that not being duly gathered, art fallen to rot on the soil. There's not a hand shall take thee up.
> *Duch.* (*Looking upwards.*) A hand *will* take me up!—A fallen fruit? No; I am a seed, whose mortal shell must lie and rot i' the earth before the flower can rise again to the light. (*Looking round as on her prison.*) Didst thou ever see a lark in a cage?—such is the soul in the body. The world is like its little turf of grass; and the heaven o'er our heads, like its looking-glass, only gives us a miserable knowledge of the small compass of our prison.

---

4. Published by John Tallis in 1850. Two other texts exist, the Lord Chamberlain's licensing copy (BM Add. MS 43031, vol. CLXVII) and Samuel Phelps's prompt-book in the Folger Library (Cat. No. D. b. 5–9). A careful study of Horne's revision is in Frank Wadsworth's Shorn and Abated: British Performances of 'The Duchess of Malfi', 'Theatre Survey', X (1969), pp. 89–104.

We realize that something is dreadfully awry here: the author has horned in and given to the Duchess Bosola's original lines, thus completely reversing Webster's meaning. Yet George Henry Lewes, not an admirer of Webster, felt that 'unless you have the two books side by side, you cannot tell whether you are reading Webster or Horne'. However, the 'Athenaeum' critic, having read Webster better than Lewes but still objecting to having Webster exhumed, nevertheless realized that 'we have here not even Webster'.

But with sophisticated lighting (the stage slowly darkened for moments of tension), scenic splendour (Horne's text opens on 'A Bridge in Malfi with Gardens Beyond'), and various sound effects (bells counterpointed the madmen's cries), the Webster-Horne 'Duchess' played for twenty-five years, though often to mixed reviews. There was even a revision of the revision, published around 1860 in 'Cumberland's Acting Plays' by George Daniel (1789–1864), the miscellaneous writer, satiric poet and friend of Lamb. While not exactly on the level of Macready's stage restoration of the Fool to 'King Lear', Daniel at least restored the dead man's hand to 'The Duchess of Malfi'. And in the USA, there were some remarkable last scenes, courtesy of 'Uncle Tom's Cabin'.

While Isabella Glyn, Alice Marriot, and Emma Waller often received favourable personal notices (Glyn built a career as the Duchess), the play did not always receive the same. As noted earlier, a dichotomy came to exist among Webster's critics. There would be those from Swinburne through Eliot and into the later twentieth century who would attest to the power of Webster's tragic vision, his revelation of man's inhumanity to man, his stoicism in the face of horror and, throughout all, his poetry. But the theatrical critics, particularly in the new age of the 'well-made play', would decry the looseness of Webster when seen on the stage, and in 'The Duchess' the collection of corpses in the fifth act. Webster read and Webster seen often generate different responses, even with changes of taste and attitudes. In reviews from 1850 into the 1970s we realize that tears in the study sometimes change to titters in the audience in many productions of 'The Duchess of Malfi', and the fault does not always seem to be eccentric direction or acting. (To be sure, a 1919 production in which Ferdinand died standing on his head did little to enhance Webster's poetic vision.)

Thus William Poel's production of 'The Duchess' in 1892 which brought forth much of Webster's original text (though amid cuts, rearrangement, and stylized horrors) also brought forth William Archer, translator of Ibsen, friend of Shaw, champion of a new, believable drama 'of rational construction', and Webster's most vociferous enemy. And though we may smile indulgently at Archer, uninformed as he was about the Elizabethans, certain of his objections seem to be borne out by audience reactions to productions in our own time.[5]

Attacking on the moral front were Canon Charles Kingsley and, later, the traditionalist William Watson, both of whom indirectly relate to Archer and his call for real people acting rationally upon the stage, particularly if 'rationally' can be defined as 'morally'. Kingsley, writing 'Plays and Puritans' not long after Horne's adaptation, protested the lack of moral purpose in the Elizabethans, scoffing at the idea of improvement by negative illustration:

> As the staple interest of the comedies is dirt, so the staple interest in the tragedies is crime. Revenge, hatred, villainy, incest, and murder upon murder, are their constant themes and (with the exception of Shakespeare, Ben Jonson in his earlier plays, and perhaps Massinger) they handle these horrors with little or no moral purpose, save that of exciting or amusing the audience, and of displaying their own power of delineation in a way which makes one but too ready to believe the accusations of the Puritans.

Watson, over thirty years later, would complain in much the same fashion:

> Cynicism, disgust, and despair were brief and casual refuges of Shakespeare's spirit. These moods are the permanent and congenial dwelling places of minds like Webster's. . . . The ethical infertility of such a presentation of the world is manifest enough, but how shortsighted and shallow seems the criticism which professes to see any kinship between Shakespeare and a type of mind so defective in sanity of vision, so poor in humour, so remote from healthful nature, so out of touch with genial reality.

'Genial reality', however, is of course in the eye of the beholder. For Swinburne in his long appreciation, far more enthusiastic than Lamb-like, for Symonds and for other late Victorians, Webster's world may have represented an escape from the reality Kingsley and Watson represented. G.K. Hunter has suggested that

> The revival of interest in the early dramatists noticeable in the last quarter of the nineteenth century must be associated with

---

5. Eliot in Four Elizabethan Dramatists, op. cit., commented on a paradoxical similarity between Archer and Swinburne in that both are discussing the distinction between poetry and drama: 'Swinburne as well as Mr. Archer allows us to entertain the belief that the difference between modern drama and Elizabethan drama is represented by a gain of dramatic technique and the loss of poetry.' In this essay, however, originally written in 1924, we end with an inverted similarity between Archer and Eliot: the weakness of the Elizabethans is not their lack of realism 'but it is the same weakness of modern drama, it is the lack of a convention'.

the anti-Victorian or decadent strain in the library life of the time . . . the exploration of past decadence is a liberation from the present and a means of justifying their own tastes.[6]

William Poel would defend Webster against Archer's arrows by an appeal to the historical accuracy on Webster's part, and his picture of the 'manners and morals of the Italian Renaissance as they appeared to the imagination of Englishmen'. * * * Although Poel meant Jacobean Englishmen, certain late Victorians found in Webster a corresponding attitude of mind, an attitude quite dissimilar to Tennyson's seeming assurance of meeting his Pilot after crossing the bar or Browning's cheery greeting to the unseen. * * * This fin de siècle attitude would be true for the young Rupert Brooke in his vigorously written 'John Webster and the Elizabethan Drama', published posthumously in 1916. Brooke, more than any critic before him, could see in Webster a unity of tone:

> The end of the matter is that Webster was a great writer; and the way in which one uses great writers is two-fold. There is the exhilarating way of reading their writing; and there is the essence of the whole man, or of the man's whole work, which you carry away and permanently keep with you. This essence generally presents itself more or less in the form of a view of the universe, recognisable by its emotional rather than logical content.[7]

Yet some later Victorians could not go quite that far. Gosse, Ward, Saintsbury, even Symonds, and others find Webster the master of mosaics, the creator of the powerful dramatic moment. From Symonds's introduction to Webster comes a remark which would, if sometimes obliquely, be considered in many twentieth-century studies:

> in 'Vittoria Corombona' and 'The Duchess of Malfi', each part is etched with equal effort after luminous effect upon a murky background; and the whole play is a mosaic of these parts. It lacks the breadth which comes from concentration on a master-motive.

And Swinburne's observation that 'no poet is morally nobler' indicates Webster's occupation in their minds: for the Victorian lover of poetry, Webster's characters exist not on a stage, but on a page.

In 1899 came Sidney Lee's end-of-the-century estimate of Webster for the 'Dictionary of National Biography' and it is unsatisfactory if unsurprising. Even though the playwright is 'rarely coarse'

6. G.K. Hunter, op.cit., p. 53.
7. Rupert Brooke, 'John Webster and the Elizabethan Drama' (1916), p. 161.

and worked with a 'true artistic sense', Webster 'with a persistence that seems unjustifiable in a great artist . . . concentrated his chief energies on repulsive themes and characters'. But before the entry is over, we hear of the miraculous touches that only Shakespeare could rival and the 'essential greatness of his conceptions'.

Chronicling varying responses in the critical heritage of John Webster is somewhat reminiscent of the Duchess's 'going into a wilderness' / Where I shall find no path or friendly clue / To be my guide'. We can nevertheless summarize generally that those who proclaim Webster's greatness emphasize throughout the century his power in creating a dark and terrible poetic vision, a vision which for many is a moral one. Less wholehearted critics fall into three broad categories. First, there are those in the earlier part of the century who emphasize the passion and Gothic horror of Webster. For many, Webster surpasses most in the ability to create the terrible and the terrifying; yet he flows with too great a facility and should be stopped sooner. Fanciers of Webster's Gothic power exist, of course, into the later nineteenth century. Second, there are the critics among the later Victorians who see Webster as the creator of the great poetic moment, yet without a totality of meaning. The third group is dominated by Archer, with support from the moralists, who care little for personification but greatly for probability. Yet even in this latter group of Webster's most implacable critics, there is reluctant testimony to Webster's troublesome power.

Looking ahead to the twentieth century, further generalizations seem possible. The years would bring global wars which would tragically attest to the credibility of Webster's horrific vision of man's inhumanity. Writing on the dead man's hand in 'The Duchess of Malfi', F.L. Lucas in his great 1927 edition of Webster could note, 'Too many of the present generation have stumbled about in the darkness among month-old corpses on the battlefields of France to be much impressed by the falsetto uproar which this piece of "business" occasioned in nineteenth century minds.'[8] And in 1945 a rare stage success of 'The Duchess of Malfi' occurred in London shortly after commanders at Buchenwald and Dachau had proven the truth of creations like Ferdinand and the Cardinal. In an accidental but telling stroke, the London 'Times' placed its review of the play underneath five newly released pictures of German concentration camps.[9]

Webster's world is, alas, closer. Twentieth-century critics have dealt with Webster with more sympathy and with more enlightenment than were found in the nineteenth, though in many ways they

8. F.L. Lucas, op. cit., I, pp. 33–4.
9. As I first noted in 'John Webster and His Critics', p. 155. See also Edmund Wilson's observations in Notes at the End of a War, published originally in the 'New Yorker', 2 June 1945, p. 47.

have built on what is recorded here. And as in the previous century, there remains disagreement still. Approaches have been made to a concept of moral vision, with Irving Ribner and Robert Ornstein, naming two of many, disagreeing over the degree attempted or achieved.[1] Eliot's comment in 'Four Elizabethan Dramatists' that Webster was a 'genius directed toward chaos' (his view itself owing something to the later Victorians) generated differing responses from several Cambridge critics, among them Muriel Bradbrook and L.G. Salingar. Though they conclude that Webster mixes convention with naturalism, Salingar is far more distressed than Bradbrook.[2] Later critics such as Travis Bogard, I.S. Ekeblad, and J.L. Calderwood turn to counterpoint and ritual to explain Webster, finding a shaping vision based on generic fusion of tragedy and satire (Bogard) or ritualistic images which bring a subtle order out of seeming chaos.[3] J.R. Brown's excellent Revels introductions to the tragedies draw on occasion from these approaches. Most recently critics have moved away from questions of moral vision and attempts to account for a unity of tone and instead have considered the 'absurdist' element in the plays, in which a 'conventional form' does not lead to a 'conventional conclusion'.[4] Indeed, in a collection of essays on Webster in 1970[5] comparison is made more frequently with the works of Beckett, Pinter, and Ionesco than with any Jacobean dramatist, and for many Webster has increasingly become our contemporary rather than Shakespeare's.

But in the theatres Webster's fortunes continue to be limited in spite of several major productions. After efforts in the study in praise

1. Cf. Irving Ribner's 'Jacobean Tragedy: The Quest for Moral Order' (1962) and Robert Ornstein's 'The Moral Vision of Jacobean Tragedy' (1960).
2. Cf. Muriel Bradbrook's 'Themes and Conventions of Elizabethan Tragedy' (1935) and L.G. Salingar's Tourneur and the Tragedy of Revenge in 'The Age of Shakespeare', ed. Boris Ford (1956). Salingar's is an updating of a 'Scrutiny' article in 1938. In her 'John Webster: Citizen and Dramatist' (1980), M.C. Bradbrook relates Webster's effort to embody incompatibles to his 'difficult position between the gentry and the citizens. Webster constantly recalls, delicately and indirectly, the struggle of such a divided self.' She suggests that Webster was also influenced by the baroque art of Inigo Jones, 'the movement and perspective of his masques', thus disagreeing in effect with Ralph Berry (see n. 4 below).
3. Cf. Travis Bogard's 'The Tragic Satire of John Webster' (1955), I.S. Ekeblad's The 'Impure Art' of John Webster, 'Review of English Studies', IX (August 1958), pp. 253–67, and J.L. Calderwood's The Duchess of Malfi: Styles of Ceremony, 'Essays in Criticism', XII (1962), pp. 133–47.
4. Norman Rabkin (ed.), 'Twentieth Century Interpretations of "The Duchess of Malfi"', p. 8. Ralph Berry, in 'The Art of John Webster' (1972), sees in the dramatist's technique the principles of early baroque artistry, and further claims for many of Webster's characters an existential outlook of which Camus would approve. And we may hope that Maurice Charney has helped terminate Webster-Shakespeare comparisons with his Webster vs. Middleton, or the Shakespearean Yardstick in Jacobean Tragedy in 'English Renaissance Drama', ed. Standish Henning, Robert Kimbrough, and Richard Knowles (1976). Charney sensibly suggests that we centre on what is distinctive and un-Shakespearean in the Jacobean dramatists.
5. 'John Webster', ed. Brian Morris (1970), Mermaid Critical Commentaries.

of Webster, critics in the theatre have all too often continued to hear titters replacing terror and to see comedy replacing catharsis. * * * Una Ellis-Fermor wrote many years ago that although 'The Duchess of Malfi' was 'susceptible of a more or less naturalistic presentation', its musical and poetic values were 'utterly alien to any plausible stage representation'.[6] In 1971 we had 'The Duchess' staged in two ways: at the Royal Court in an avant-garde approach, and later at Stratford in 'realistic' fashion. Reviews for both were poor, with some critics rising to heights of humorous invective. In a recent BBC television production, presented naturalistically, Bosola seemed lost in a structural mist and took longer to die than Bottom's Pyramus.

Sometimes it is obviously the director's fault; yet sometimes it is Webster's. For all the appeal to myth, ritual, symbol, and absurdist canons, Webster's plays on stage admit to at least two confusing perspectives: the court of Malfi, for instance, is seen in naturalistic terms while Ferdinand and the Cardinal inhabit the nightmare world of the grotesque.[7] That a director can successfully fuse these perspectives in a truly satisfying stage performance has yet to be fully demonstrated. It is not surprising that we learn from the 1623 title-page that the play was cut even from the time of its first performance. In the study the job of synthesis seems easier, especially when we forget Ezra Pound's cogent remark that 'the medium of drama is not words, but people moving about on a stage using words'. Nor was William Empson invoking the shade of William Archer by claiming that it is 'clearly wrong to talk as if coherence of character is not needed in poetic drama, only coherence of metaphor and so on'.[8]

A parallel which I drew some years ago still seems valid: Webster remains the Tennessee Williams of the Jacobeans. With women at the centre of his plays, Webster is, like Williams, darkly theatrical and poetically effective at his best, yet extravagantly rhetorical and implausible in his excesses. Like Williams, his outlook is intense but narrow, and inconsistent in tone even within that narrowness. And he, like Williams, has consequently generated a most divided critical heritage.

6. Una Ellis-Fermor, 'The Jacobean Drama' (1936), pp. 43–4.
7. Cf. Lois Potter's Realism versus Nightmare: Problems of Staging 'The Duchess of Malfi', 'The Triple Bond', ed. Joseph Price (1975), pp. 170–89. It is reassuring to note some positive reviews for a staging of 'The Duchess' at the Round House, London, in April 1981. For the 'Guardian', Adrian Noble's production preserved 'the Websterian balance between decadence and tenderness' (12 April 1981, p. 25).
8. William Empson, 'The Structure of Complex Words' (1951), p. 231.

The Play in Its Own Time

D. C. GUNBY

The Duchess of Malfi: A Theological Approach[†]

Until comparatively recently the standard view of *The Duchess of Malfi* was of a melodrama distinguished by its poetry. Today the tendency is to see the play in more or less existentialist terms. To John Russell Brown, for instance, the play is 'a unity of empirical, responsible, sceptical, unsurprised, and deeply perceptive concern for the characters and society portrayed'.[1] Similarly J. R. Mulryne speaks of the dramatist's 'restless, mocking intelligence',[2] while Robert Ornstein believes that Webster

> presents in art the skeptical, pragmatic nominalism of the late Renaissance; the weariness with meaningless abstraction and endless debates over words.[3]

To my mind the more recent view is as far from the truth as the older one. Although they contain characters like Flamineo, Bosola, and Romelio, Webster's plays reveal, I would argue, an outlook not pragmatic but dogmatic, not wearily nominalist but vigorously didactic, not sceptical but fideistic. And the faith upon which Webster's world-view rests is, it seems to me, that of Jacobean Anglicanism. By discussing *The Duchess of Malfi* in the light of the views of the Jacobean Church of England, particularly on providence and free will, grace, security, and despair, the limitations of evil and the sovereignty of God, I hope to demonstrate what seems to me basic to an understanding of the play—that it is essentially a work of theodicy.

† D. C. Gunby, "*The Duchess of Malfi:* A Theological Approach," from Brian Morris (ed.), *John Webster* (London: Ernest Benn, 1970), pp. 181–204. Notes have been renumbered. Reprinted by permission.
1. John Russell Brown, ed., *The Duchess of Malfi*, The Revels Plays (1964), p. xlix.
2. '*The White Devil* and *The Duchess of Malfi*', in *Stratford-upon-Avon Studies 1: Jacobean Theatre*, ed. John Russell Brown and Bernard Harris (1960), pp. 200–25.
3. *The Moral Vision of Jacobean Tragedy* (Madison, Wisc., 1960), p. 134.

An examination of the character and motives of Ferdinand might seem an unpromising first step towards justifying this assertion. The Duke's behaviour is so irrational, his reaction, to his sister's marriage so disproportionately violent, that it seems inexplicable except as insanity. The problem is aggravated by Ferdinand's reluctance to explain his actions (see, for instance, I.i.275–6 and III.ii.127 ff.), and by his one muddled and unconvincing attempt to 'examine well the cause' of his behaviour. His admission of avarice, of hopes—'(Had she continu'd widow) to have gain'd / An infinite masse of Treasure by her death,' (IV.ii.303–4),[4] reads like evasion, or an attempt to rationalise motives too terrible to face.

What these motives are Webster reveals obliquely, through images of fire, storm, darkness, hell, and animal savagery.[5] Closely patterning these images, Webster establishes, within the framework of theme and character, three interrelated levels of motivation, all of them contributing to an understanding of the suffering and death of the Duchess, and of the remorse and retribution attending her murderers.

At the simplest level, it is clear that with Ferdinand Webster started from the traditional concept of the choleric man, just as he based the Cardinal on the phlegmatic, the Duchess on the sanguine, and Bosola on the melancholic. The images of fire which characterise the Duke's speech thus aptly mirror his fierce energy and ungovernable temper. From the touchy rebuke of I.i.124–6 to his final admission that he is consumed by 'a fire, as great as my revenge, / Which nev'r will slacke, till it have spent his fuell' (IV.i.168–9), we see the accuracy of Pescara's comment:

> Marke Prince *Ferdinand*,
> A very *Salamander* lives in's eye,
> To mocke the eager violence of fire.   (III.iii.58–60)

In revealing what Antonio rightly calls a 'perverse, and turbulent Nature', the storm imagery is equally appropriate. The Duchess is optimistic that 'time will easily / Scatter the tempest' (I.i.539–40), but in II.v Ferdinand loses control of himself so completely that his brother has to rebuke him for making himself 'So wild a Tempest' (II.v.24). The Duke himself seizes on the metaphor:

> Would I could be one,
> That I might tosse her pallace 'bout her eares,
> Roote up her goodly forrests, blast her meades,

---

4. My quotations are from Lucas's edition of *The Duchess of Malfi* (1927).
5. The importance of some, at least, of these groups of images is discussed by Moody E. Prior in *The Language of Tragedy* (New York, 1947), pp. 121–32. Prior concentrates, however, more on their atmospheric than their architectonic value.

> And lay her generall territory as wast,
> As she hath done her honors.   (II.v.25–9)

The fire and storm images symbolise more than choler, however. In II.v a second level of motive emerges with Ferdinand's obsessive linking of fire with his sister, the Duchess. When the Cardinal says, 'Shall our blood / (The royall blood of *Arragon,* and *Castile*) / Be thus attaincted?' (II.v.30–2), Ferdinand cries,

> Apply desperate physicke—
> We must not now use Balsamum, but fire,
> The smarting cupping-glasse, for that's the meane
> To purge infected blood, (such blood as hers:)
>   (II.v.33–6)

A little later he implies that the fire is burning within himself:

> Goe to (Mistris.)
> 'Tis not your whores milke, that shall quench my wild-fire,
> But your whores blood.   (II.v.62–4)

It is not only the link between fire and blood which is significant, but also the different meanings which blood has for the brothers. To the Cardinal it is synonymous with rank or lineage; but to Ferdinand it is, as Inga-Stina Ekeblad first pointed out, literally his sister's blood.[6] This distinction is part of the evidence adduced by critics in favour of incestuous jealousy as Ferdinand's motive for persecuting his sister. Since the play has been thoroughly combed for signs of this unnatural (and perhaps unconscious) passion, the matter need not be gone over in detail.[7] All that needs saying here is that the fires and storms which rage inside Ferdinand are those of lust as well as of choler.

   Alongside this complex pattern of motives and emotions, resting on the twin connotations of storm and fire as metaphors for anger and lust, Webster develops a third level, more important than either:

> I would have their bodies
> Burn't in a coale-pit, with the ventage stop'd,
> That their curs'd smoake might not ascend to Heaven:
> Or dippe the sheetes they lie in, in pitch or sulphure,
> Wrap them in't, and then light them like a match: (II.v.87–91)

Webster draws on the traditional association of fire and wind with hell to reinforce the frequent images of devils and witchcraft,

---

6. 'A Webster Villain', *Orpheus,* III (1956), 131.
7. For reliable summaries, see McD. Emslie, 'Motives in Malfi', *Essays in Criticism,* IX (1959), 391–405; and J. R. Brown's introduction to the Revels Plays *Duchess,* pp. lii–liv.

and to establish them in the pattern of meaning and motive. The relationship is brought out explicitly in V.iv, when the courtiers comment on the storm which had raged earlier:

> *Grisolan:* 'Twas a foule storme to-night.
> *Roderigo:* The Lord *Ferdinand's* chamber shooke like an Ozier.
> *Malateste:* 'Twas nothing but pure kindnesse in the Divell,
>   To rocke his owne child.   (V.iv.23–6)

One might not, perhaps, take seriously this hint at a direct relationship between Ferdinand's violence and that of the elements, and of demonic origins for both, were it not part of an elaborate and carefully articulated pattern. Through this pattern is revealed the fundamental reason for the brothers' persecution of their sister.

A second storm image involves witchcraft in the pattern. When Ferdinand loses control of himself in II.v, his brother reproves him in these terms:

> How idlely shewes this rage!—which carries you,
> As men convai'd by witches, through the ayre,
> On violent whirle-windes—   (II.v.65–7)

The remark is apt, for Ferdinand early reveals his obsession with witchcraft, particularly in relation to his sister. In I.i he warns her that

> . . . they whose faces doe belye their hearts,
> Are Witches, ere they arrive at twenty yeeres,
> I: and give the divell sucke.   (I.i.343–5)

This tells us more about Ferdinand than about the Duchess. So too does his involuntary cry, 'The witch-craft lies in her rancke b[l]ood' (III.i.94), which follows a casual reference to witches in another context. The principal significance of the repeated references to witchcraft, however, lies in the Jacobean belief that witches were demonically possessed. It is no coincidence that the offering of the severed hand and the use of the wax effigies are related to the rites of witchcraft (see IV.i.65–6 and 73–6), for as will become clear, Ferdinand is himself possessed by the Devil, and his torment of his sister is explicitly antireligious.

Moving from the storm images to those of fire, we find the same relationship with the idea of hell and devils. The comment of the Second Madman tells us that

> Hell is a meere glasse-house, where the divells are continually blowing up womens soules, on hollow yrons, and the fire never goes out.   (IV.ii.81–3)

Behind this, as behind the ravings of the other madmen, lies an important statement. For along with a topical reference to the glass factory and a stock comment on feminine vanity, we are offered a mirror to Ferdinand's actions. In seeking to destroy his sister's soul, Ferdinand is creating a hell on earth, a hell whose fires burn within himself. In this connection it is important to note Webster's borrowing from Deuteronomy to describe the Duchess's plight:[8]

> Th'heaven ore my head, seems made of molten brasse, the earth of flaming sulphure, yet I am not mad: (IV.ii.27–8)

Here, then, is the deepest motive underlying the actions of Ferdinand and his brother. For even if incestuous feelings are admitted as implicit in the Duke's conduct, and if the choleric element in his nature is acknowledged; and, equally, if pride of lineage and a cold selfishness born of his phlegmatic temperament are put forward to explain the Cardinal's behaviour it is nonetheless clear that Webster's fundamental concern is with a conflict between good and evil, in which the brothers are demonically impelled to destroy good, in the person of the Duchess, through an unwilling Bosola. The metaphoric and dramatic means by which Webster makes this clear must now be considered.

First Webster constantly and directly associates both Ferdinand and the Cardinal with the Devil. Bosola says of the Cardinal:

> Some fellowes (they say) are possessed with the divell, but this great fellow, were able to possesse the greatest Divell, and make him worse.   (I.i.45–8)

The malcontent's bitter jibe is quickly reinforced by Antonio's estimate:

> Last: for his brother, there, (the Cardinall)
> They that doe flatter him most, say Oracles
> Hang at his lippes: and verely I beleeve them:
> For the Divell speakes in them.   (I.i.187–90)

During Bosola's interview with Ferdinand later in the scene, frequent reference is made to hell and devils. Bosola accuses the Duke of making him 'a very quaint invisible Divell, in flesh: / An intelligencer', and at first refuses payment, saying

> Take your Divels
> Which Hell calls Angels: these curs'd gifts would make
> You a corrupter, me an impudent traitor,
> And should I take these, they'll'd take me [to] Hell.   (I.i.285–8)

8. See M. C. Bradbrook, 'Two Notes Upon Webster', MLR, XLII (1947), 281–94.

But driven to accepting a post which will enable him to spy on the Duchess, and make him in his own eyes 'the divells quilted anvell', he comments bitterly:

> . . . Thus the Divell
> Candies all sinnes [o'er]: and what Heaven termes vild,
> That names he complementall.   (I.i.299–301)

However, the most illuminating comment in the earlier part of the play, because of the light it sheds on the relationship of Ferdinand to Bosola, is made by Antonio:

> You would looke up to Heaven, but I thinke
> The Divell, that rules i'th'aire, stands in your light.   (II.i.97–8)

Having thus established Ferdinand and the Cardinal on the side of hell in this conflict, Webster sets up in opposition to them the positive goodness of the Duchess and Antonio. Virtue and serenity are keynotes in Antonio's praise of his mistress in I.i:

> Her dayes are practis'd in such noble vertue,
> That sure her nights (nay more her very Sleepes)
> Are more in Heaven, then other Ladies Shrifts.   (I.i.205–7)

This impression is strengthened by subsequent images, by Antonio's vow that he 'will remaine the constant Sanctuary' of the Duchess's good name, and the Duchess's plea that Ferdinand explain

> Why should onely I,
> Of all the other Princes of the World
> Be cas'de-up, like a holy Relique?   (III.ii.160–62)

Later, when the Duchess confesses to Bosola her secret marriage, she receives even from him an apparently sincere tribute:

> Fortunate Lady,
> For you have made your private nuptiall bed
> The humble, and faire Seminary of peace,   (III.ii.323–5)

The irony is bitter, since this peace is already threatened.

Webster develops this contrast between the order of the Duchess's life and the disorder of her persecutors', between peace and conflict, religion and anti-religion, by employing in imagery and action the archetypal symbols of good and evil—light and darkness. It is significant how much of the action of The Duchess of Malfi takes place either at night (five scenes: II.iii, II.v, III.ii, V.iv, and V.v) or in the gloom of prison (two scenes: IV.i and IV.ii). It is significant, too, that in at least two of these scenes (II.iii and V.iv) there are storms in progress. It is against this background that the gentle and luminous figure of the Duchess, who in Antonio's loving words, 'staines the

time past: lights the time to come' (I.i.214), faces the persecution of
the brothers who threaten to 'fix her in a generall ecclipse' (II.v.102).

In IV.i this threat comes closer when Ferdinand visits his sister
under cover of darkness. His ostensible reason for doing this is
announced by Bosola:

> Your elder brother the Lord *Ferdinand*
> Is come to visite you: and sends you word,
> 'Cause once he rashly made a solemne vowe
> Never to see you more; he comes i'th' night:
> And prayes you (gently) neither Torch, nor Taper
> Shine in your Chamber: he will kisse your hand:
> And reconcile himselfe: but, for his vowe,
> He dares not see you: (IV.i.25–32)

The Duchess agrees, the lights are removed, and Ferdinand enters.
His first words, 'This darkenes suites you well', reveal his perverted
values: it is he whom the darkness suits; it was he who requested it,
unable to face his sister without its protection. He is closer to the
truth when he says:

> It had bin well,
> Could you have liv'd thus alwayes: for indeed
> You were too much i'th' light: (IV.i.48–50)

For behind the pun lies the irony of an attitude akin to that of Iago's
resentment of Cassio: 'He hath a daily beauty in his life / That makes
me ugly.' It is significant, too, that Ferdinand needs darkness for his
diabolical trick of giving his sister the dead hand. As she calls dis-
tractedly for lights and he rushes from the room, we feel the dev-
ilishness of behaviour which seems surely inspired by more than
mere anger or unnatural lust.

I have suggested that 'Th' Arragonian brethren' are diabolically
driven in persecuting their sister. The time has now come to elaborate on this motivation. Ferdinand, it has been said, is usually
reluctant to explain his actions. But on one occasion, in IV.i, he
makes an explicit, if gnomic, confession:

> *Bosola:* Why doe you doe this?
> *Ferdinand:* To bring her to despaire.   (IV.i.139–40)

That this statement is to be interpreted in a specifically religious
sense can be inferred from Bosola's earlier reproof of the hysterical
Duchess:

> O fye: despaire? remember
> You are a Christian.   (IV.i.87–8)

The importance of Ferdinand's admission lies in the fact that bringing man to despair was considered one of the Devil's chief aims,

since in despairing of God's mercy, his love, or even his very existence, man lost all hope of salvation.[9] * * *

To find the positive values which the play offers, we must first consider the character of the Duchess and then her relationship with
Bosola. I do not intend to discuss the already exhaustively treated—
and it seems to me, peripheral—questions of the Duchess's guilt, or
the propriety of the remarriage of widows.[1] It is obvious, after all,
where our sympathies are meant to lie: the moral issues are never
in doubt. For present purposes the Duchess's remarriage is important only in that it highlights three important traits of character: her
courage, pride, and wilfulness. We see these traits equally displayed
in her refusal to be swayed by her brothers' threats, her determination that 'if all my royall kindred / Lay in my way unto this marriage:
/ I'll'd make them my low foote-steps' (I.i.382–4). There is evidence
of her pride in her wooing, too. For although she claims to 'put of[f]
all vaine ceremony, / And onely . . . appeare . . . a yong widow', she
nonetheless raises the kneeling Antonio with

> Sir,
> This goodly roofe of yours, is too low built,
> I cannot stand upright in't, nor discourse,
> Without I raise it higher: raise your selfe,
> Or if you please, my hand to helpe you: so.   (I.i.478–82)

It is no accident that we are never told the Duchess's name, for here
she is very much the great lady, acutely conscious of her status, even
in love, while later, isolated and facing death, she reaches a state of
humility such that she wants nothing more than anonymity, and,
reversing her earlier gesture, kneels to enter heaven. We can chart
the full distance of the spiritual pilgrimage revealed by these two
acts, by considering her relationship with Bosola, particularly in
III.v, IV.i, and IV.ii.

Bosola is generally recognised as a man divided against himself.
Forced by penury to serve a cause he knows to be wrong, he miti-
gates when he can the effects of the evil he is doing. Webster uses
this conflict to demonstrate that a man can be at once an agent of
God and of the Devil. Bosola torments the Duchess yet comforts her,
destroys yet saves her. In a conflict like this the Jacobeans firmly
believed that God could always nullify the intrigues of the Devil.
As Calvin put it:

> Now when we say that Satan resisteth God, that the works of
> Satan disagree with the works of God, we doe therewithall

---

9. For a valuable discussion of the significance of despair, see Arieh Sachs, 'The Religious
   Despair of Doctor Faustus', *JEGP*, LXIII (1964), 625–47.
1. On these issues, see Emslie, op. cit.; Clifford Leech, *Webster: The Duchess of Malfi*
   (1963), pp. 51–7; F. W. Wadsworth, 'Webster's *Duchess of Malfi* in the Light of Some
   Contemporary Ideas on Marriage and Remarriage', *PQ*, XXXV (1956), 394–407.

affirme that this disagreement and strife hangeth vpon the sufferance of God.[2]

Through Bosola this is demonstrated, not crudely, as in the homilectic tales of Thomas Beard or in a play like Massinger and Dekker's *The Virgin Martyr,* but subtly, presenting divine providence in its continuity rather than as random miraculous intervention.

We find clear indications of this continuity in III.v. First Antonio and the Duchess acknowledge the existence of divine order in their lives. Antonio says:

> Best of my life, farewell: Since we must part,
> Heaven hath a hand in't: but no otherwise,
> Then as some curious Artist takes in sunder
> A Clocke, or Watch, when it is out of frame
> To bring't in better order.   (III.v.74–8)

The Duchess is similarly convinced that her suffering is not without purpose:

> Must I like to a slave-borne Russian,
> Account it praise to suffer tyranny?
> And yet (O Heaven) thy heavy hand is in't.
> I have seene my litle boy oft scourge his top,
> And compar'd my selfe to't: naught made me ere
> Go right, but Heavens scourge-sticke.   (III.v.90–95)

Here too we see Bosola for the first time as agent of providence. For when the Duchess breaks down he arrests her hysteria through her pride:

> *Bosola:* Fye (Madam)
>   Forget this base, low-fellow.
> *Duchess:* Were I a man:
>   I'll'd beat that counterfeit face, into thy other—
>   (III.v.139–42)

The crisis passes, and the scene ends with one of the tales to which so many critics have taken exception. As a recent editor of the play has noted, however, this is more than the 'apparently simple fable':

> the Fisher is God; the gathering in of the fishes is a harvest at which not wheat and tares, but good and bad fish are to be judged; the Market is the Judgement; the Cook is another symbol for God; the fire represents hell-fire: at the Judgement one is as close to hell as to the joys of heaven.[3]

---

2. John Calvin, *The Institution of Christian Religion,* tr. Thomas Norton (1611), p. 70.
3. Elizabeth M. Brennan, ed., *The Duchess of Malfi,* The New Mermaids (1964), p. xxi.

In the remaining acts this separation and judgement of the good and
the bad is demonstrated. But before the Duchess can enter heaven
she must pass through severe trial; since

> when God will send his own servants to heaven, he sends them
> a contrary way, even by the gates of hell.[4]

In IV.i the gates of hell gape wide, for through his elaborate torments Ferdinand almost succeeds in breaking the Duchess's spirit.
She wishes only for death:

> That's the greatest torture soules feele in hell,
> In hell: that they must live, and cannot die:
> *Portia*, I'll new kindle thy Coales againe,
> And revive the rare, and almost dead example
> Of a loving wife.   (IV.i.82–6)

At this point Bosola steps in, reproving her for giving way to despair,
and offering what comfort he can to divert her from thoughts of suicide. The Duchess, however, lapses into hysteria and self-pity, wishing on the world the chaos which seems to fill her own life:

> *Duchess:* I could curse the Starres.
> *Bosola:* Oh fearefull!
> *Duchess:* And those three smyling seasons of the yeere
>   Into a Russian winter: nay the world
>   To its first Chaos.   (IV.i.115–19)

Bosola's reply, 'Looke you, the Starres shine still', has often been
taken, as by F. L. Lucas, to express 'the insignificance of human
agony before the impassive universe'.[5] But it is also a further
attempt to strengthen the Duchess in her suffering; an affirmation
of faith in the divine order which still exists, undisturbed by the
chaos around her. In this one great line Bosola's double role is
epitomised.

Towards the end of the scene we are given a clear indication that
in future Bosola's help to the Duchess will be more direct. Revolted
by what is happening, he protests to Ferdinand, and when his protests are dismissed, bluntly declares the terms on which he will continue to carry out the Duke's orders:

> *Bosola:* Must I see her againe?
> *Ferdinand:* Yes.
> *Bosola:* Never.
> *Ferdinand:* You must.

---

4. William Perkins, *Works*, 3 vols. (1616–18), i, 492.
5. *The Complete Works of John Webster*, 4 vols. (1927), ii, 179.

> *Bosola:* Never in mine owne shape,
>   That's forfeited, by my intelligence,
>   And this last cruell lie: when you send me next,
>   The businesse shalbe comfort.   (IV.i.158–64)

Thus, in a manner wholly characteristic, Webster provides a naturalistic explanation of the disguises which Bosola will adopt—disguises whose purpose is not only to make him unrecognisable, but also to symbolise his role in the Duchess's purification and preparation for death.

For the Duchess, IV.i is a spiritual nadir; thereafter, as Bosola predicted, 'Things being at the worst, begin to mend' (IV.i.92). Hence when IV.ii opens we find her in a more composed state of mind, self-pity and hysteria replaced by quiet resignation:

> I am acquainted with sad misery,
>   As the tan'd galley-slave is with his Oare,
>   Necessity makes me suffer constantly,
>   And custome makes it easie—   (IV.ii.29–32)

Not even the madmen, symbols of a world disordered and depraved, can shake her composure. In one sense, therefore, she is prepared for death. In another she is not. Bosola still has to free her from pride. In III.v consciousness of rank had helped to keep her from despair and suicide. Now it is a hindrance, an impediment to be set aside if she is to enter heaven. Now, therefore, Bosola directs all his efforts towards instilling in the Duchess an awareness of the insignificance of rank by comparison with the lasting reality of death. First he must convince her that she is 'sick':

> *Bosola:* I am come to make thy tombe.
> *Duchess:* Hah, my tombe?
>   Thou speak'st, as if I lay upon my death bed,
>   Gasping for breath: do'st thou perceive me sicke?
> *Bosola:* Yes, and the more dangerously, since thy
>   sicknesse is insensible.   (IV.ii.115–20)

As yet the Duchess is unwilling—and unable—to understand. It is important, however, that we should appreciate his diagnosis. We can do so by glossing his statement with this passage from an anonymous devotional work, *The House of Mourning*:

> Consider the evil of this security you are in, of this disposition of heart, when you cry, peace, peace, to your selves in the midst of God's displeasure. It is an evil disease, a spiritual Lethargy. That disease we know in the body, it takes a man with sleep, and so he dieth. . . . It is more dangerous, because it is a senseless disease, a disease that takes away the senses from the soul: and diseases (we know) that take away the senses, are

dangerous: for it is not only a sign that nature is overcome by
the disease, but besides, it draweth men from seeking for cure.
Thus it is with the spiritual Lethargy; it shews not only that sin
hath prevailed in the heart . . . , but it hindreth you from seeking the means to escape out of it.[6]

Clearly the Duchess's sickness is security or spiritual lethargy,
scarcely less dangerous to the soul than despair. As Lancelot
Andrewes remarks in one of his sermons:

Now perseverance we shall attain, if we can possess our souls
with the due care, and rid them of security. . . . And, to avoid
security, and to breed in us due care, St. Bernard saith, 'Fear
will do it.' Vis in timore securus esse? securitatem time; 'the
only way to be secure in fear, is to fear security.'[7]

Bosola's task is to make the Duchess recognise her peril. So when
she asks the question, 'Who am I?' he replies:

Thou art a box of worme-seede, at best, but a salvatory of greene
mummey: what's this flesh? a little cruded milke, phantasticall
puffe-paste: our bodies are weaker then those paper prisons
boyes use to keepe flies in: more contemptible: since ours is to
preserve earth-wormes: (IV.ii.123–7)

This stark vision is, however, offset by what follows:

didst thou ever see a Larke in a cage? such is the soule in the
body: this world is like her little turfe of grasse, and the Heaven
ore our heades, like her looking glasse, onely gives us a miserable knowledge of the small compasse of our prison.

(IV.ii.127–31)

Here Bosola is speaking wholly in the *contemptu mundi* tradition,
placing, as Donne often does in his sermons, human existence in
an eternal perspective.

The Duchess, however, still seeks to assert herself: 'Am not I, thy
Duchesse?' Bosola again refutes her claim:

Thou art some great woman sure, for riot begins to sit on thy
fore-head (clad in gray haires) twenty yeares sooner, then on a
merry milkmaydes. Thou sleep'st worse, then if a mouse should
be forc'd to take up her lodging in a cats eare: a little infant,
that breedes it's teeth, should it lie with thee, would crie out,
as if thou wert the more unquiet bed-fellow.   (IV.ii.133–8)

6. ΘΡΗΝΟΙΚΟΣ, *The House of Mourning* (1672), p. 155.
7. *Ninety Six Sermons*, ed. J. P. Wilson and James Bliss, 5 vols. (Oxford, 1841–3), ii, 72.

Once more the Duchess tries, crying 'I am Duchesse of *Malfy* still', and once more Bosola replies, more bluntly than before:

That makes thy sleepes so broken:
'Glories (like glowe-wormes) afarre off, shine bright,
But look'd to neere, have neither heate, nor light.'   (IV.ii.139–42)

This time he is successful, and the Duchess answers quietly, 'Thou art very plain. Bosola drives home his point by introducing what might seem gratuitous satire:

Duchess: Do we affect fashion in the grave?
Bosola: Most ambitiously: Princes images on their tombes
        Do not lie, as they were wont, seeming to pray
        Up to heaven: but with their hands under their cheekes,
        (As if they died of the tooth-ache)—they are not carved
        With their eies fix'd upon the starres; but as
        Their mindes were wholy bent upon the world,
        The selfe-same way they seeme to turne their faces.
                                           (IV.ii.152–9)

The Duchess recognises a little, at least, of the deeper significance of this passage, for she says quietly:

        Let me know fully therefore the effect
        Of this thy dismall preparation,
        This talke, fit for a charnell?   (IV.ii.160–62)

This long exchange has indeed been a preparation. Its success we may judge from the Duchess's reception of the 'present' her brothers have sent: the coffin, cords, and bell:

        Let me see it—
        I have so much obedience, in my blood,
        I wish it in ther veines, to do them good.   (IV.ii.167–9)

The Duchess has attained humility. Consequently Bosola can drop the role of tomb-maker, and take up his second disguise:

        Bosola: I am the common Bell-man,
                That usually is sent to condemn'd persons
                The night before they suffer:
        Duchess: Even now thou said'st,
                Thou wast a tombe-maker?
        Bosola: 'Twas to bring you
                By degrees to mortification: (IV.ii.173–9)

Having been brought 'by degrees to mortification', the Duchess must now have her thoughts directed towards eternity—the purpose of the bellman in Jacobean England. In the famous dirge, intoned to the tolling of the bell, Bosola calls on the Duchess to 'don her shrowd', contrasting the turmoil of this life with the serenity to come:

> A long war disturb'd your minde,
> Here your perfect peace is sign'd— (IV.ii.186–7)

Then he re-emphasises the vanity of earthly concerns:

> Of what is't fooles make suck vaine keeping?
> Sin their conception, their birth, weeping:
> Their life, a generall mist of error,
> Their death, a hideous storme of terror— (IV.ii.188–91)

and ends with a renewed call to purification before the journey to eternity.

Bosola's preparation of the Duchess is complete. Although Webster never explicitly states that she has attained a state of grace, we can infer this from her composure in the face of death, composure which enables her to counter Bosola's question, 'Doth not death fright you?' with the calm assurance of

> Who would be afraid on't?
> Knowing to meete such excellent company
> In th'other world.   (IV.ii.216–28)

A more specific indication, however, is the degree to which she is now free from earthly concerns, and able to focus her thoughts upon heaven. For as Richard Baxter says in his treatise upon 'that Excellent unknown Duty of *Heavenly Meditation*', *The Saints Everlasting Rest*:

> Consider, A heart set upon heaven, will be one of the most unquestionable evidences of thy sincerity, and a clear discovery of a true work of saving grace upon thy soul.[8]

Or again:

> How shall I know that I am truly sanctified? Why, here is a mark that will not deceive you, if you can truly say that you are possessed of it; Even, a heart set upon Heaven.[9]

Unlike Cariola, therefore, who clings to life, lying, begging, and fighting for a moment's respite, the Duchess faces her executioners with no more than a momentary tremor, revealed in a longing to be 'out of your whispering', and kneels to accept the gift of death:

> Pull, and pull strongly, for your able strength,
> Must pull downe heaven upon me:

---

8. 4th ed. (1653), pt. 3, p. 207.
9. Pt. 3, p. 207.

> Yet stay, heaven gates are not so highly arch'd
> As Princes pallaces—they that enter there
> Must go upon their knees: (IV.ii.237–41)

The Duchess's pilgrimage is over. What is left of the lives of Bosola
and his masters illustrates that in the Duchess's death evil did not
vanquish good, but was itself defeated.

Had I time, I would now seek to demonstrate this view, showing
how justice is done—and seen to be done—according to a pattern
of retribution as apt as it is all-embracing. I would try to show that
in every respect the fate which befalls Ferdinand and the Cardinal
can be related to what has happened earlier. I would show (as critics have in part done)[1] that Ferdinand's 'cruell sore eyes' and fear of
the light were directly related to his need for darkness in IV.i, and
to the famous 'Cover her face: Mine Eyes Dazell'. I would emphasise the significance of the Duke's Lycanthropia—its connection
with wolves and witchcraft, with his incestuous passion for his sister, and through the traditional beliefs that wolves disclose murders
by digging up the victims and that those suffering from Lycanthropia have wolf's hair under the skin like the hair shirts of penitents,
with the twin emotions of guilt and remorse. I would emphasise, too,
that the diabolic impulses underlying the actions of Ferdinand and
the Cardinal lead them, as the two men clearly see, into the mouth
of hell. I would dwell particularly, in this connection, on the fact
that the brothers suffer finally from the despair which they had tried
to induce in their sister, and that the Cardinal finds himself, like
Marlowe's Faustus or Shakespeare's Claudius, unable to pray for
mercy:

> . . . O, my Conscience!
> I would pray now: but the Divell takes away my heart
> For having any confidence in Praier.   (V.iv.30–32)

Since, however, I have space to develop none of these points, I
will conclude my commentary with a discussion of one aspect of the
last act: the roles of Antonio and Bosola. In doing so, I will try to
refute the view, persuasively argued by Gunnar Boklund, that
Bosola's sense that 'We are meerely the Starres tennys-balls (strooke,
and banded Which way please them)', represents the play's final
message. Boklund writes:

> The theme of retribution that occupies Webster throughout the
> act is simple only if superficially considered. No religious sig-
> nificance can be extracted from it, for the perversity of

---

1. See, for instance, Prior, op. cit., pp. 124–6.

superhuman intervention is demonstrated as thoroughly as is
the bankruptcy of human intelligence. The Aragonian brothers are killed, but so is Antonio. Not only does providence lack
a tool in *The Duchess of Malfi*, it does not even operate, even in
the form of nemesis. What governs the events is nothing but
chance.[2]

On the contrary it is perfectly possible to reconcile the confusion
and futility of the last act with a providential order.

I described Bosola earlier as a man divided against himself. He
has 'loath'd the evill' he has had to commit, yet carried out his
orders, partly in hopes of reward, and partly, as he tells Ferdinand,
because he 'rather sought / To appeare a true servant, then an honest man' (IV.ii.358–9). When the Duke proves ungrateful, Bosola no
longer has an anodyne for his conscience, and is stricken with
remorse:

> What would I doe, we[r]e this to doe againe?
> I would not change my peace of conscience
> For all the wealth of Europe: (IV.ii.365–7)

Since he is obviously penitent, and since, too, his role has been that
of an agent of God as well as of the Devil, we may wonder whether
he will escape damnation. When the Duchess stirs, it seems briefly
as though he will, and all his long-frozen humanity breaks forth in
joy and hope:

> . . . She stirres; here's life:
> Returne (faire soule) from darkenes, and lead mine
> Out of this sencible Hell: She's warme, she breathes:
> Upon thy pale lips I will melt my heart
> To store them with fresh colour: who's there?
> Some cordiall drinke! Alas! I dare not call:
> So, pitty would destroy pitty: her Eye opes,
> And heaven in it seemes to ope, (that late was shut)
> To take me up to mercy.   (IV.ii.367–75)

Yet heaven only 'seemes to ope.' The Duchess's recovery is only
momentary, and her death confirms Bosola in despair and remorse:

> Oh, she's gone againe: there the cords of life broake:
> Oh sacred Innocence, that sweetely sleepes
> On Turtles feathers: whil'st a guilty conscience
> Is a blacke Register, wherein is writ
> All our good deedes, and bad: a Perspective

---

2. *The Duchess of Malfi: Sources, Themes, Characters* (Cambridge, Mass., 1962), pp.
   129–30.

That showes us hell; that we cannot be suffer'd
To doe good when we have a mind to it!   (IV.ii.382–8)

His chance of salvation has gone, his change of heart comes too late.
He is damned.

Yet even with his 'estate. . . . suncke below / The degree of feare',
Bosola tries to warn Antonio of the plot against him, and to join him
in 'a most just revenge'. His motives are mixed: he wishes to destroy
the brothers, but he also wants to atone for what he has done, and
hopes, however faintly, that atonement will bring the fruits of
penitence:

The weakest Arme is strong enough, that strikes
With the sword of Justice: Still me thinkes the Dutchesse
Haunts me: there, there! . . .'tis nothing but my mellancholy.
O Penitence, let me truely tast thy Cup,
That throwes men downe, only to raise them up.   (V.ii.379–83)

Only when his plans miscarry, and by a stroke of bitter irony he slays
'the man I would have sav'de 'bove mine owne life!' (V.iv.62), does
he recognise the futility of his efforts, and abandon hope.

Bosola's part in the death of Antonio, an 'accident' if one may call
it that, proves conclusively both to him and to us, that the time is
past when atonement is possible. To understand why Antonio should
be the victim we must consider his character.

The Duchess's husband is an honest man, a loving husband and
father, and a faithful friend, but he is also hesitant and ineffectual
in a crisis, and unimpressive beside his more vigorous wife. As
Boklund's study of the source-material shows, the original Antonio
was a glowingly cavalier figure; at Webster's hands he is transformed
into a character of thoroughgoing ordinariness.[3] In part, no doubt,
Webster's motives for this are dramatic. The Duchess must stand
alone. Yet one may also suspect didactic considerations, since there
are hints that Antonio is intended to illustrate the limitations of neo-
stoic philosophy. The more oblique of these, the stress placed on
Antonio's lack of ambition, and his bloodless and hesitant approach
to life, both of which might be related to the neo-stoic belief in the
contentment that retirement brings, and to the ideal of the golden
mean, or *mediocritas,* can be quickly passed over, since to linger
would be to exaggerate the strength of the argument. Rather more
attention is due, however, to what Antonio says on matters religious
and philosophical. At one point the Cardinal remarks that Antonio
accounts 'religion / But a Schoole-name' (V.ii.136–7). This is patently
untrue, yet it may not be oversubtlety to detect in Antonio's

3. Op. cit., pp. 92–6.

utterances on religion a generality which makes them as likely to be the product of a stoic as of a Christian outlook. There may be nothing more than orthodox piety in his view of the enforced parting as a move by heaven to bring himself and the Duchess 'in better order', or in his conviction that 'Heaven fashion'd us of nothing: and we strive, / To bring ourselves to nothing:' (III.v.97–8). But alongside these remarks stands another with a distinctly stoic air:

> Make Patience a noble fortitude:
> And thinke not how unkindly we are us'de:
> Man (like to *Cassia*) is prov'd best, being bruiz'd.   (III.v.87–9)

Later in the play the stoic element becomes more explicit, with Antonio talking in terms of 'Necessitie' (V.iii.41–4), and seeing his predicament less in terms of submission to heaven than in relation to the stoic doctrine of will:

> Though in our miseries, Fortune have a part,
> Yet, in our noble suffrings, she hath none—
> Contempt of paine, that we may call our owne.   (V.iii.70–72)

Pain, Antonio seems to assert, is pain only if the sufferer chooses to acknowledge it. The distinction is the traditional stoic one between external circumstances and the individual's response to them.

For all his philosophising, however, Antonio cuts an increasingly sorry figure as the play progresses, and by the last act he is drifting aimlessly in the vague hope of reconciliation with his persecutors. Nor do his dying moments raise his stature, particularly when they are compared with those of his wife. For where in her last minutes we can discover a deep sense of the value of death in relation to the life to come, Antonio's last speech is essentially negative:

> . . . I would not now
> Wish my wounds balm'de, nor heal'd: for I have no use
> To put my life to: In all our Quest of Greatnes . . .
> (Like wanton Boyes, whose pastime is their care)
> We follow after bubbles, blowne in th'ayre.
> Pleasure of life, what is't? onely the good houres
> Of an Ague: meerely a preparative to rest,
> To endure vexation: I doe not aske
> The processe of my death: onely commend me
> To *Delio*.   (V.iv.73–82)

To him death seems not a prelude to something highly prized, but an end to what he no longer cares about. Like the Cardinal, he wishes to 'be layd by, and never thought of' (V.v.113). Here, I suggest, is the core of Webster's criticism of the amalgam of Christian and stoic beliefs upon which Antonio seems to base his attitudes. The Jacobeans believed, traditionally, that the chief end of philosophy was to teach men how to die. Measured by this yardstick, Antonio's beliefs are unimpressive.

It is now clear why Antonio dies as he does. Without the Duchess he is aimless and apathetic, only half-alive. Yet his death needs to be a fitting one, and in the apparently casual irony of an 'accident' we can find a reflection of the aimlessness which has preceded it.

With this in mind, we see the fifth act not as Gunnar Boklund's game of blind chance, but as a carefully organised sequence of events demonstrating at all points the guiding hand of providence. To say this, of course, is to raise a crucial issue, that of responsibility. As the agent of providence, Bosola has acted (like Hamlet and Vindice) as both a minister and scourge, one through whom God works both to save and to destroy.[4] Like Vindice (if not like Hamlet), he ends his life in the jaws of hell. Is this just? Logic says that it is not, if Bosola has not been a free agent, but acting under divine compulsion. Theologically, however, this view of Bosola's role is untenable. It is true that the Church of England believed quite literally that there was 'a special providence in the fall of a sparrow,' and that it exhorted the faithful to eschew belief in chance and see God's hand in all things:

> Thus must we in all things that be done, whether they be good or evil (except sin, which God hates and causes not,) not only look at the second causes, which be but God's means and instruments whereby he works, but have a further eye, and look up to God.[5]

It is also true, however, that Anglicans believed in man's freedom of will. As Thomas Rogers puts it in *The Catholic Doctrine of the Church of England*:

> We deny not, that man, not regenerate, hath free will to do the works of nature, for the preservation of the body, and bodily estate; which things had and have the brute beast, and profane gentile.[6]

How these two beliefs were reconciled is explained by Peter Baro, Lady Margaret Professor of Divinity at Cambridge from 1574 to 1596, in the course of a disputation on the theme 'God's purpose and decree taketh not away the liberty of man's corrupt will':

> God the creator and governor of all things is not the destroyer of the order by him appointed, but the preserver. For he would that in the nature of things that there should be divers and

---

4. For an excellent discussion of this subject, see F. T. Bowers, 'Hamlet as Minister and Scourge', *PMLA*, LXX (1955), 740–49.
5. James Pilkington, *Works*, ed. J. Scholefield (Cambridge, 1853), p. 227.
6. Ed. J. J. S. Perowne (Cambridge, 1854), p. 104.

sundry causes, namely some necessary and othersome also
free and contingent: which according to their several natures,
might work freely and contingently, or not work. Whereupon
we conclude, that secondary causes are not enforced by God's
purpose and decree, but carried willingly and after their own
nature.[7]

Bosola, it is clear, is one of these 'secondary causes'. God has worked
through him, taking advantage of his divided nature, his desire to
serve Ferdinand yet comfort the Duchess. Yet Bosola has never been
under compulsion: he has not been 'enforced by God's purpose and
decree, but carried willingly and after his own nature'. His free
moral choices have come first, and God's use of them second. He
must therefore bear the responsibility for what he has done.

Were this not so, of course, we would find Bosola far less interesting than we do. As it is we can respond simultaneously to his agony
of soul and to the reassurances that our understanding of the action
gives us, and in our recognition of the latter discover an added poignancy in his ignorance of the extent to which he has really served
the cause of good. There is a similar complexity in our response to
his final attempt to make sense of his life, with all its confusion, horror, and lost chances:

> *Malateste:* Thou wretched thing of blood,
>   How came *Antonio* by his death?
> *Bosola:* In a mist: I know not how,
>   Such a mistake, as I have often seene
>   In a play: Oh, I am gone—
>   We are only like dead wals, or vaulted graves,
>   That ruin'd, yeildes no eccho: Fare you well—
>   It may be paine: but no harme to me to die,
>   In so good a quarrell: Oh this gloomy world,
>   In what a shadow, or deepe pit of darknesse,
>   Doth (womanish, and fearefull) mankind live!
>   Let worthy mindes nere stagger in distrust
>   To suffer death, or shame, for what is just—
>   Mine is another voyage.   (V.v.116–29)

For we know, as Bosola does not, that Antonio's death was meaningful, just as we also know that he has been the unwitting instrument in assuring the triumph of that cause which part of him always
longed to serve. His may be 'another voyage' from that of 'worthy
mindes', but it has not been made entirely in vain.

---

7. Quoted by H. C. Porter in *Reformation and Reaction in Tudor Cambridge* (Cambridge,
   1958), p. 377.

Bosola dies confused and lost. But we are able to respond fully to the note of optimism upon which *The Duchess of Malfi* ends. Firstly there is the presentation of the surviving child of the Duchess and Antonio; a symbol, like Giovanni in *The White Devil,* of hope, innocence, and renewal. Then follows what can be read simply as moral comment:

> . . . These wretched eminent things
> Leave no more fame behind 'em, then should one
> Fall in a frost, and leaves his print in snow—
> As soone as the sun shines, it ever melts,
> Both forme, and matter: I have ever thought
> Nature doth nothing so great, for great men,
> As when she's pleas'd to make them Lords of truth:
> *'Integrity of life, is fames best friend,*
> *Which noblely (beyond Death) shall crowne the end.*
> (V.v.138–46)

There is also, however, a deeper and more specifically religious level of meaning in this last, choric utterance. Through what is, significantly, the only sun image in a dark play, Webster offers a confident assertion of the power of God to counter and destroy evil. That this confidence is not wrongly or lightly placed, the play as a whole has testified.

Theatrically Oriented Readings

ROWLAND WYMER

From *The Duchess of Malfi*†

Webster's second tragedy repeats and reworks many of the situations, themes, characters, images and even individual lines from *The White Devil*. Once more we find ourselves in a sixteenth-century Italian court where the ruthlessness of great men and the corrupt authority of the Catholic church—a linkage vividly dramatised by the Cardinal's exchange of his ecclesiastical robes for armour—combine to crush any possibilities of healthy or honest existence. Once more there is the close scrutiny of how men and women meet their deaths, as if only in their final extremity can their value be truly known. The similarities between the two plays are such that many critical generalisations about Webster fail to make any real distinction between his two masterpieces. Yet any analysis should begin by acknowledging the much greater emotional range of *The Duchess of Malfi*, a difference largely brought about by the introduction of a protagonist with whom the audience can more easily sympathise. The explosive cynicism and violence of *The White Devil* is still present but is now counterpointed with scenes of romantic and domestic intimacy, whose impact is deepened by their elegiac tone. The character of the Duchess brings the play much closer to commonly perceived norms of tragedy, whether Shakespearean or Aristotelian. Terror is now conjoined with pity (a word used much more frequently than in *The White Devil*).

The difference between the two plays emerges clearly in the different strategy of characterisation adopted. Whilst there is an equivalent complexity of treatment in *The Duchess of Malfi*, it is not grounded, except perhaps in the case of Bosola, in a general premise of radical moral paradox. It is not easy to 'read' people in this play (Antonio's boast to Bosola, 'I do understand your inside', is

† Rowland Wymer, *"The Duchess of Malfi,"* from *English Dramatists: Webster and Ford.* (London: St Martin's Press, 1995), 52–72, 156–157. Notes have been renumbered. Reproduced with permission of Palgrave Macmillan.

greeted with a contemptuous 'Do you so?') but there is a much stronger impression of a core of moral and psychological identity beneath the surface 'contradictions'. Rather than make each of his characters a 'white devil', Webster seems to have started with a groundplan based on the four personality types of Elizabethan humour psychology, a procedure also followed by Shakespeare in *Julius Caesar*.[1] To say that Webster initially saw the Duchess as corresponding to the sanguine type, Ferdinand to the choleric, the Cardinal to the phlegmatic, and Bosola to the melancholic, tells us little about the final effects achieved but does suggest a desire for strong dramatic contrasts based on clearly distinct personalities. The imposition of a homogenous overall design by a director, as was done by Philip Prowse for the National Theatre in 1985, can flatten these differences, robbing the play of a good deal of its real life and leaving the audience with 'the sensation of watching a lot of interchangeable black figures scurrying about inside a beautifully-lit glass jar'.[2] The Duchess and her brothers may be 'cast in one figure' but they are of entirely 'different temper' and the staging should enforce this. Likewise, Bosola's status as a malcontent is better registered if he alone, rather than the whole cast, is dressed in black. After his 'promotion' to the provisorship of the horse he is told by Ferdinand 'Keep your old garb of melancholy', and it seems likely that he remains dressed in black throughout, a costuming equally appropriate to his later roles of tomb-maker and revenger.

The Duchess of Malfi is not a play which radically challenges the supposition of a coherent and continuous personal identity, but it does suggest emotional complexities and depths of a kind unusual in the theatre outside the works of Shakespeare. The dominant impression is not of unresolvable psychological discontinuities but of secret inner lives which can only be excavated at great cost to all concerned. Ferdinand threatens the Duchess:

> Your darkest actions: nay, your privat'st thoughts,
> Will come to light.
>
> (I. ii. 238–9)

but he recoils from what he finds in both her and himself:

> Curse upon her!
> I will no longer study in the book
> Of another's heart:
>
> (IV. i. 15–17)

1. In Shakespeare's play, Caesar corresponds to the phlegmatic type, Brutus to the melancholic, Cassius to the choleric, and Antony to the sanguine. For a detailed argument relating this characterisation to an overall symbolic design, see T. McAlindon, *Shakespeare's Tragic Cosmos* (Cambridge: Cambridge University Press, 1991) ch. 4.
2. Michael Billington, *Guardian*, 6 July 1985.

and the knowledge destroys them both. Bosola's strenuous efforts to uncover the Duchess's secrets mirror the endeavours of the audience to penetrate the façades of characters whose mysterious inner selves are constantly being hinted at. The Cardinal seems to have the energetic worldliness which Webster's contemporaries saw as typical of Italian Renaissance Catholicism:

> They say he's a brave fellow, will play his five thousand crowns
> at tennis, dance, court ladies, and one that hath fought single
> combats.   (I. ii. 76–9)

But these are only 'flashes' which 'superficially hang on him, for form'. His 'inward character' has a cold and joyless emptiness which seems closer to the monkish vice of accidie than to the sensuality and ruthlessness of the Borgia popes. The particular challenge of this role for an actor is to allow this despairing blankness to show through enough to modify an otherwise potentially two-dimensional picture of Machiavellian villainy. Similarly, what appears mirth in Ferdinand 'is merely outside'. When he first enters, surrounded by his courtiers, he seems a typical enough Renaissance prince, suavely conversing of horsemanship and war. Then some laughter at a sexual innuendo provokes him into an outburst which shatters the flow of aristocratic banter:

> Why do you laugh? Methinks you that are my courtiers should
> be my touchwood, take fire when I give fire; that is, laugh when
> I laugh, were the subject never so witty—
>
> (I. ii. 43–6)

In the theatre these lines are usually succeeded by a strained silence (Webster's concluding dash may be a way of marking this pause), a silence broken sometimes by a sinister chuckle from Ferdinand himself as the cue for the resumption of merriment. With great dramatic economy, Webster has suggested turbulences and instabilities, perhaps of a sexual nature, beneath the surface courtliness and hinted at how terrifying such hidden disturbances might become when combined with despotic power.

In a play of many secrets, Ferdinand's dark and twisted sexuality is the most secret thing of all, unremarked upon by any character in the play, including Ferdinand himself. The reluctance of some critics to accept that his relationship with the Duchess is contaminated by unconscious incestuous attraction is understandable given the absurd excesses which have often accompanied psychoanalytic criticism and the general rarity of unacknowledged motives in Elizabethan and Jacobean drama. Even at its most sophisticated, it was a drama of expressive plenitude rather than one of implication and subtext, and it is hard to think of many comparably compelling examples of unexplained feelings. One, perhaps, would be the mysterious melancholy voiced by Antonio at the beginning of *The Merchant of Venice* ('In sooth I know not why I am so sad'). This creates an immediate puzzle for the audience which is never resolved explicitly but whose solution, as in the case of Ferdinand, requires the inference of a 'love that dare not speak its name'. Webster may have had this example in mind since he repeats Shakespeare's unusual tactic of deliberately foregrounding a psychological problem which he does not intend to clear up:

> FERDINAND: . . . she's a young widow,
>   I would not have her marry again.
> BOSOLA: No, sir?
> FERDINAND: Do not you ask the reason: but be satisfied,
>   I say I would not.
>
>   (I. ii. 179–82)

The point of this exchange is surely to leave the audience very much *un*satisfied and to stimulate the kind of search for small behavioural clues frequently expected of modern audiences but less usual in the Jacobean theatre. Such clues are found in the inappropriate erotic tone which colours Ferdinand's interchanges with his sister ('Farewell, lusty widow'), the hysterical fury with which he imagines her in 'the very act of sin' with a succession of imaginary lovers, and the emotional violence which dissolves his unconvincing attempts at rationalisation into syntactical chaos:

> For let me but examine well the cause;
> What was the meaning of her match to me?
> Only I must confess, I had a hope,
> Had she continu'd widow to have gain'd
> An infinite mass of treasure by her death:
> And that was the main cause; her marriage,
> That drew a stream of gall quite through my heart;
>   (IV. ii. 279–85)

The textual evidence, although subtle, is collectively overwhelming and, despite the long critical tradition of arguing that Webster's characterisation is casual and incoherent, the danger for a modern director lies less in ignoring this subtext than in giving it vulgar overemphasis of the kind common in Freudian treatments of the Hamlet-Gertrude relationship. In a recent French adaptation of *The Duchess of Malfi*, Ferdinand planted a fish impaled on a knife between his sister's thighs.[3] With stage business like this it is difficult to

---

3. *La Duchesse de Malfi*, adapted by Claude Duneton and directed by Matthias Langhoff, at the Theatre de la Ville, Paris. Reviewed in *The Times Literary Supplement*, 24 May 1991, p. 19.

sustain the peculiar atmosphere of this play, an atmosphere heavy with the secrecy of thoughts and feelings not known fully even to their possessors.

The always difficult and technically demanding process of exposition whereby we are introduced to the major characters and their relationships is handled with particular brilliance in *The Duchess of Malfi*. The first act takes the form of one continuous flowing scene, mixing formal commentary with naturalistic interchanges, and constantly shuffling and recombining the main figures into different groupings. We see Bosola with the Cardinal, the Cardinal with Ferdinand, the Duchess with both her brothers, the Duchess alone with Ferdinand; the Duchess alone with Antonio. The stage is never cleared of actors (so the introduction of a scene division by D. C. Gunby in the Penguin edition has no authority) but seems to shift from a crowded open court to the intimacy of the Duchess's private chamber. This kind of fluid, though strictly 'illogical' transition is always possible in a theatre where locations are established by the words of the actors rather than scenery. The effect of this kaleidoscopic pattern of interactions, mixed in with commentary from Delio, Antonio and Bosola, is extremely complex, much more so than, for instance, the opening of *The Revenger's Tragedy,* where the court are straightforwardly paraded as objects of disgust before the satirical gaze of Vindice. In Webster's play, too, we are continually prompted to make judgements but these are of a very provisional nature and subject to constant modification, as we match one comment against another and both against an unfolding sequence of actions, a process which goes on through the play.

Nowhere is this process of adjustment more evident than in the case of Bosola. As ex-convict, spy, gaoler, comforter, executioner and penitent avenger, he presents special difficulties for audience and actor alike. His subsequent moral gyrations are carefully prepared for by two early pieces of commentary from Antonio (already given some interpretive authority by his opening speech on the French court). In the first few minutes of a play the audience is particularly anxious to get its bearings and is gratefully attentive to speeches such as the following:

> Here comes Bosola
> The only court-gall: yet I observe his railing
> Is not for simple love of piety:
> Indeed he rails at those things which he wants,
> Would be as lecherous, covetous, or proud,
> Bloody, or envious, as any man,
> If he had means to be so.
>
> (I. i. 22–8)

Bosola's cynicism is given the most cynical gloss possible and his character is comfortably assimilated to a type familiar from previous satirical drama and literature. Hence it is unsettling***when only fifty lines later Antonio himself provides a very different perspective:

> 'Tis great pity
> He should be thus neglected, I have heard
> He's very valiant. This foul melancholy
> Will poison all his goodness . . .
>
> (I. i. 73–6)

Since Webster constructed Bosola's part by combining several different figures from his sources and since disguise is used (as in many Renaissance plays) to extend his dramatic functions beyond the limits of what is humanly plausible, it may seem irrelevant to probe the question of his 'character' too deeply. Yet theatre history indicates that in the most highly praised productions of *The Duchess of Malfi* (the Haymarket in 1945 and the Manchester Royal Exchange in 1980) Cecil Trouncer and Bob Hoskins succeeded in making sense of the part and projecting an all-too-human suffering and anguish. Some forms of drama can indeed dispense with the concept of character but not plays which hope to move pity as well as terror in an audience.

In fact Bosola seems less puzzling as soon as one realises that he is an inhabitant of what Primo Levi, writing of Auschwitz, called 'The Grey Zone', that space in which the distinction between guard and prisoner, oppressor and victim, starts to break down. Levi quotes a survivor of the 'Special Squad' of prisoners who helped the Germans operate the crematoria at Auschwitz as saying: 'You mustn't think that we are monsters; we are the same as you, only much more unhappy.'[4] Bosola, driven by his poverty, does not have the moral or material strength to resist the murderous orders of his masters, but he can never wholly extinguish his conscience and so is filled with a corrosive self-hatred. His continued capacity to feel pity, which so surprises Ferdinand ('Thy pity is nothing of kin to thee'), would not have surprised Primo Levi. Recording an incident in which members of the 'Special Squad' tried to save a young woman who had miraculously revived after the gassing, he wrote: 'Compassion and brutality can coexist in the same individual and in the same moment, despite all logic; and for all that compassion itself eludes logic.'[5] This seems a more appropriate way of approaching the problem of Bosola,

---

4. Primo Levi, *The Drowned and the Saved*, trans. Raymond Rosenthal (London: Abacus [Sphere Books], 1989) ch. 3, 'The Grey Zone', p. 36.
5. Ibid., p. 39.

as it presents itself in the theatre, than that of treating him semioti-
cally as a mobile signifier, without depth or human truth.

The constant modification of provisional judgements takes place
in relation to the Duchess as well as Bosola. It quickly becomes
apparent that she is both more and less than the plaster saint of
Antonio's initial encomium, a speech which, in the Manchester
Royal Exchange production, was delivered with the actors 'frozen'
and a spotlight on the Duchess, increasing the iconic effect:

> in that look
> There speaketh so divine a continence,
> As cuts off all lascivious, and vain hope.
> Her days are practis'd in such noble virtue,
> That, sure her nights, nay more, her very sleeps,
> Are more in heaven, than other ladies' shrifts.
>   (I. ii. 123–8)

Within minutes she shows herself to be no 'figure cut in alabaster'
but a passionate and spirited woman whose desire to love and be
loved is stronger than any fear of her menacing brothers. Her defiance of them may be rash ('it shows / A fearful madness') but it
springs from an essential innocence, 'the innocence of abundant life
in a sick and melancholy society, where the fact that she has "youth
and a little beauty" is precisely why she is hated'.[6] No twentieth-
century production has succeeded in making her unsympathetic,
though crude forms of historical criticism continue to attempt this
feat. Well-documented Renaissance social prejudices against widows
remarrying (seen in the bitter line from *Hamlet*, 'None wed the second but who killed the first') and against alliances that cross class
barriers are cited to 'prove' that Jacobean audiences must have seen
the Duchess as seriously blameworthy in marrying her steward. Such
arguments ignore the way major literature works against as well as
within prevailing ideologies, especially when these are not wholly
determinant of social practice (it was normal for young widows to
remarry and not unknown for great ladies to marry beneath themselves), and are no more convincing when given a modern feminist
twist than they were as part of older versions of historical criticism.
According to Lisa Jardine, Ferdinand's ravings about his sister's
'looseness' take on special authority because 'only men surround the
Duchess; the audience can do little more than accept their version
of her behaviour and motives'.[7] On this reading, the moment she
marries Antonio she is transformed into a 'lascivious whore. It is not

---

6. Northrop Frye, *Anatomy of Criticism: Four Essays* (Princeton, NJ: Princeton University
   Press, 1957), p. 219.
7. Lisa Jardine, *Still Harping on Daughters: Women and Drama in the Age of Shakespeare*
   (Brighton: Harvester, 1983), p. 72.

merely that her brothers see her as such; the dominant strain in the subsequent representation is such.'[8] This account seems to posit an intellectually inert audience who are unable to perceive a meaningful contrast between what is said about a character and how she or he actually behaves (a distinction central to any complex dramaturgy) and who are unable to feel a moral and emotional preference for love and tenderness when these are set against violent perversity.

Contrary to what Jardine says, the 'dominant strain' in the representation of the Duchess, prior to the roles of prisoner and martyr thrust upon her in Act IV, is that of lover, wife and mother. Much of the emotional effect of the play derives from its intimation of how precarious personal and domestic happiness are, how vulnerable to tyrannical violence and to the exigencies of life in general. When Delio asks, 'How fares it with the Duchess?' and is told by Antonio, 'She's expos'd / Unto the worst of torture, pain, and fear' (II. iii. 65–6), the lines anticipate her sufferings in prison but their immediate reference is to the labour of childbirth. Quietly embedded beneath the play's surface conflicts are the successive stages of a woman's life-journey through courtship, marriage and childbirth, to ageing, parting and death. Within this sequence there are many moments of gaiety, love and laughter but the underlying pressure of time and mortality is always felt, constantly suggesting an inescapable sadness at the heart of existence. The wooing of Antonio takes place whilst the Duchess draws up her will and the language of love is inflected with imagery of death. The laughter of the bedchamber scene ('I prithee / When were we so merry?') is quickly followed by the first fears of ageing ('Doth not the colour of my hair 'gin to change?'). Different interpretations of a play as complex as *The Duchess of Malfi* will always tend to bring different scenes into prominence but evidence drawn from actual performances should carry a particular weight. After the prison scenes of Act IV (seen as crucial in virtually every account of the play), it is remarkable how often theatre critics have singled out the wooing scene and the bedchamber scene for special praise, often commending as well the scene of parting near Ancona and the echo scene. These are episodes of extraordinary emotional delicacy whose impact in the theatre is out of all proportion to their length, and which make it impossible to classify the play as a 'tragical satire' that takes its dominant tone from Bosola's cynicism. Even in Peter Gill's Brechtian production for the Royal Court in 1971, the scenes between Antonio and the Duchess carried a special charge as the actors responded to the

---

8. Ibid., p. 77.

nuances of Webster's language, at once naturalistic and poetic, to rise above the uniform and distancing bleakness of the chosen production style.

It has become commonplace in Marxist and feminist analyses of society and literature to see personal relations and family life as reproducing and enforcing oppressive political structures rather than opposing them or creating a free emotional space. For Althusser, the celebrated French Marxist philosopher and wife murderer, the family was 'the most terrible, unbearable, and frightening of all Ideological Apparatuses of the State'. Yet those tyrannies with genuinely totalitarian ambitions (such as the regimes of Hitler, Stalin and Mao) have consistently viewed domestic loves and loyalties as threateningly independent of state power and a source of potential resistance. The extensive theorisation of the family as a source of oppression dwindles into insignificance when confronted with the actuality of state violence against the family. The scene on the road near Ancona—the little family group clutching a few possessions and confronted by armed men—awakens memories of a hundred newsreels and no doubt had a similar emotional impact on seventeenth-century audiences who were not ignorant of the effects of war and tyranny on domestic happiness. With some naïvety, given the nature of her brothers, the Duchess had hoped to create a secure circle of personal happiness for herself and Antonio:

> All discord, without this circumference,
> Is only to be pitied, and not fear'd.
> (I. ii. 387–8)

She fails tragically but her struggle is not thereby stripped of its emotional and moral value nor does her secret family life cease to suggest a powerful alternative to the diseased world of the court.

The moment when this dimension of the play, together with much else, comes most sharply into dramatic focus is probably the bedchamber scene. The atmosphere of domestic cosiness, often increased by the presence of children's toys onstage (a concretisation of such allusions as 'I have seen my little boy oft scourge his top'), coexists from the beginning with a sense of menace which becomes horribly palpable when Ferdinand approaches his sister unseen. The stage picture of the Duchess brushing her hair before a mirror whilst her brother advances from behind with a dagger has a raw melodramatic force, but it also carries a wealth of iconographic significance, some of it possibly self-contradictory. For Keith Sturgess, 'a Renaissance moral emblem of shattering power is achieved: the vain woman, her vanity symbolised by the mirror, visited by Death as a retribution for a moral laxity of which the play never acquits her'.[9] However, it is always possible to interpret such a tableau less moralistically and more lyrically and wistfully, seeing the woman's long hair as a potently sensuous image of the preciousness of life, youth and beauty in the face of death, time and barely guessed at horrors. Some such archetypal opposition is involved in the famous lines from *The Waste Land*:

> A woman drew her long black hair out tight
> And fiddled whisper music on those strings
> And bats with baby faces in the violet light
> Whistled, and beat their wings
> And crawled head downward down a blackened wall . . .[1]

An equally potent modern rendering of the primal opposition which shapes Webster's scene is Gustav Klimt's painting *Death and Life,* in which a lovingly interlocked family group (stylised to resemble a patterned quilt) is menaced by a sinister skull-figure wielding a club. Conjunctions of death and life in Renaissance art and literature frequently manage to combine, as in Webster's tableau, a 'medieval' sense of life's vanity with a more 'modern' sense of life's irreplaceable value. Moreover, any allegorical reading of this scene would have to acknowledge that Ferdinand suggests the Devil as much as he does Death. When he hands the Duchess a dagger, the implication is that he is tempting her to suicide rather than simply threatening her with murder:

> DUCHESS: He left this with me.
> *She shows the poniard.*
> ANTONIO: And it seems, did wish
> You would use it on yourself?
> DUCHESS: His action seem'd
> To intend so much.
>
>   (III. ii. 150–2)

With this gesture Ferdinand aligns himself with the diabolical agents of the morality plays whose attempts to damn the Mankind figure frequently culminated in a temptation to that final despair of God's mercy which suicide was thought to indicate (a convention followed also in *Doctor Faustus* when Mephostophilis hands Faustus a dagger

9. Keith Sturgess, *Jacobean Private Theatre* (London: Routledge, 1986) p. 114. Although I disagree with Sturgess's emphasis here, I think his chapter on *The Duchess of Malfi* is generally excellent.
1. T. S. Eliot, *The Waste Land*, ll. 377–81 in *Collected Poems 1909–1962* (London: Faber, 1974). Webster's hold on Eliot's imagination was such that the bedchamber scene may actually be a source for these lines. In Act IV, the numerous suggestions of a marriage ritual make it almost certain that Webster intended the Duchess to go to her death with her hair loose and flowing like a bride's.

near the climax of the play).[2] In his obsessive and destructive opposition to the Duchess's marriage, Ferdinand does indeed sometimes
resemble Shakespeare's demi-devil Iago, whilst anticipating the
lonely, jealous agony of Milton's Satan when confronted with the
married bliss of Adam and Eve:

> Sight hateful, sight tormenting! thus these two
> Imparadised in one another's arms,
> The happier Eden, shall enjoy their fill
> Of bliss on bliss, while I to hell am thrust.[3]

The devilish aspect of Ferdinand is not something which appears
momentarily and casually in the bedchamber scene. It is a consistent motif in the play, sustained by patterns of verbal imagery and
pieces of stage business. The interpretation of his actions put forward above by Antonio and the Duchess should cause us to rethink
the significance of that earlier moment when Ferdinand presented
his sister with a dagger:

> You are my sister,
> This was my father's poniard: do you see,
> I'ld be loath to see't look rusty, 'cause 'twas his.
> (I. ii. 252–3)

As well as the more obvious implications of murderous threat,
offended family honour and disturbed sexuality (the latter heightened by the intimacy of the moment since it is the first time Ferdinand and the Duchess are seen alone together), we should probably
be aware of an emblematic aspect, derived from morality play representations of the temptation to despair. A modern director, by such
devices as getting Ferdinand to finger his weapon suggestively, is
more likely to emphasise the sexual dimension to the exclusion of
all else and, indeed, Webster often seems to aim for more significance than any particular performance is capable of encompassing.
However, the diabolic persecution of Act IV ('Why do you do this?',
'To bring her to despair') is most dramatically effective when viewed
as part of a larger pattern of meaning which has been built into the
play from the very beginning and which can be glimpsed in the
smallest of gestures.

Carefully prepared for in the three previous acts, the scenes of
suffering and death in the prison (once the Duchess's palace) are
unmatched in English drama for their relentless intensity. Their

---

2. I have discussed this topic, and its relevance to *The Duchess of Malfi,* more fully in *Suicide and Despair in the Jacobean Drama* (Brighton: Harvester, 1986).
3. Milton, *Paradise Lost,* IV. 505–8, in Milton, *Poetical Works,* ed. D. Bush (London: Oxford
University Press, 1966).

non-naturalistic 'excesses' (the dead man's hand, the waxwork figures and the masque of madmen) have provoked some of the most
hostile criticism ever directed at a major dramatist (including Shaw's
famous gibe at Webster as the 'Tussaud laureate') but I have yet to
see a production in which these scenes were ever less than wholly
compelling. If there are problems with Webster's play, they are to be
found in the fifth act rather than the fourth. The triangle of relationships between Bosola, Ferdinand and the Duchess is developed with
such moral and emotional intensity that Webster is able to move
from full-blown symbolic and poetic effects to touches of intimate
naturalism without ever losing his grip on the essential psychology of
his situations. The grotesque trick with the dead man's hand (with its
hints of diabolism and witchcraft) is accompanied by the simple,
misplaced compassion of 'You are very cold. / I fear you are not well
after your travel' (IV. i. 51–2). The surreal, dreamlike poetry with
which the Duchess expresses her indifference to the means of execution can modulate suddenly into a burst of all-too-human irritation
at the whispered preparations going on around her:

> What would it pleasure me, to have my throat cut
> With diamonds? or to be smothered
> With cassia? or to be shot to death, with pearls?
> I know death hath ten thousand several doors
> For men to take their exits: and 'tis found
> They go on such strange geometrical hinges,
> You may open them both ways: any way, for Heaven
>   sake,
> So I were out of your whispering.
>   (IV. ii. 216–23)

The diamonds, cassia and pearls form part of an elaborate and justly
admired network of recurrent verbal images, but the suddenly con-
textualised immediacy of the final phrase is what shows Webster to
be a great *dramatic* poet.

   Much of Act IV is indeed highly ritualistic rather than naturalistic
in form and where there are traceable sources for the details of the
Duchess's ordeal, these tend to be literary rather than historical. But
it is easy to exaggerate the distance between poetic art and life. Jacobean audiences might well have been reminded of the actual plight
of Lady Arabella Stuart, cousin to James I, whose secret marriage to
William Seymour aroused the anger of the king. The lovers attempted
to flee to Europe but only Seymour succeeded in reaching Ostend.
Arabella was captured at sea and brought back to be imprisoned in
the Tower, where she went mad from grief. Modern audiences,
lacking such an immediate political context, are nevertheless read-
ily drawn into intense participation in the human conflict between

tormented persecutor, suffering victim and self-divided go-between. Some of Webster's theatrical symbolism (such as the parodic evocation of a wedding masque) requires elucidation by modern scholarship, but much of it, revolving as it does around the immutable reality of death, remains immediately intelligible. When Bosola, disguised as an old man, speaks of grey hairs and the frailty of the flesh, he speaks to all audiences, past and present. The impersonal, choric quality of some of his speeches does not rob them of their contextual edge since they form a crucial part of the moral and spiritual 'testing' of the Duchess, a testing whose outcome is made to seem more important than anything else in the play.

These prison scenes represent Webster's most eloquent and extended exploration of the notion, common in both Christian and classical teaching, that in suffering and death we find the touchstones of human value.* * * Up to a point his basic strategy resembles that of Shakespeare in *Titus Andronicus* and *King Lear*, or Kyd in *The Spanish Tragedy*—that of heaping a series of disasters upon the protagonist until grief cracks the foundations of personality producing a disintegration into madness. The masque of madmen, whatever else it might accomplish, powerfully projects this possibility but, of course, the crucial point is that the Duchess, though brought to the very brink, does not disintegrate. The pressures upon her identity ('Who am I?', 'Am I not thy Duchess?') are resisted initially by an aristocratic and Stoic assertion of self, described by Ferdinand as 'a strange disdain', which crystallises in the famous 'I am Duchess of Malfi still' (IV. ii. 141). The full resonance of this line requires a recognition of how precarious as well as forceful an assertion it is. The dominant meaning of 'still' may be that of 'constantly' or 'always' (Elizabeth I's motto was 'Semper eadem'—'Always the same') but the weaker sense of 'yet', 'for the moment', creates an undercurrent of provisionality which is increased by the fact that a title is being used to signify personal identity, a title which can easily come to seem 'but a bare name, / And no essential thing'. Aristocratic pride helps save the Duchess from despair but, in the face of Bosola's relentless emphasis on mortality, it gives way to something less assertive though equally heroic—the stance of the martyr.

The Duchess indirectly confirms her assimilation to this archetype when she hopes vainly that heaven will 'a little while, cease crowning martyrs' to punish her brothers. After the Bible, no book exerted more influence on the Protestant imagination of this period, shaping its structures of feeling, than Foxe's *Acts and Monuments*, with its massively detailed accounts (with accompanying woodcuts) of the thousands of noble deaths endured by Christians (and, latterly, Protestants) for their faith. Webster and Dekker, when writing *Sir Thomas Wyatt*, had turned to Foxe for some of the details of

Lady Jane Grey's death, and would have found there some classic articulations of the difficult middle path between pride and despair which a Christian faced with death is required to tread. In her affliction, Lady Jane had prayed 'that I may neyther be too much puffed up with prosperitie, neither too much pressed down wyth adversitie: least I beeyng too full, should denie thee my GOD, or beeyng too lowe brought, should despayre and blaspheme thee my Lord and Saviour'.[4] The Duchess swings between nihilistic despair ('I could curse the stars') and the aristocratic confidence of 'I am Duchess of Malfi still', before attaining, with help from Bosola which may be partly unconscious, the calm humility of a martyr's death.

> Pull, and pull strongly, for your able strength
> Must pull down heaven upon me:
> Yet stay, heaven gates are not so highly arch'd
> As princes' palaces: they that enter there
> Must go upon their knees.
>   (IV. ii. 230–4)

As she drops to her knees we are probably meant to recall the moment when she lifted Antonio up from his knees to bring him level with her 'greatness'. If such a visual echo seems too harshly didactic in its implications we should also recall how the Duchess and Antonio knelt together to perform their secret marriage and remember her words at Ancona: 'In the eternal Church, sir, / I do hope we shall not part thus' (III. v. 68–9).

The moral and emotional impact of the Duchess's death depends a great deal on the special value attached to martyrdom in Christian teaching but, within the context of Webster's play, its full significance is less easy to describe. As in *King Lear,* we are forced to recognise the possibility that the value we see in certain ways of living and dying has no metaphysical sanction. The Duchess dies nobly but there is no evidence that her fate disturbs the universe in any way ('Look you, the stars shine still'). Moreover, faced with the mass slaughter of innocents in the twentieth century, it has become more difficult, even perhaps offensive, to continue to look for and assert a moral or religious value in suffering. From one point of view, Auschwitz marked the end of all such theodicy. Yet, as Emmanuel Levinas has argued, the perception of suffering as something useless and devoid of meaning, unrationalisable, may be the step to realising its full moral significance in the compassion and sense of injustice it arouses in others.[5]

4. John Foxe, *Acts and Monuments,* 4th edn (London: John Day, 1583) p. 1422.
5. Emmanuel Levinas, 'Useless Suffering', trans. Richard Cohen, in *The Provocation of Levinas: Rethinking the Other,* ed. R. Bernasconi and D. Wood (London: Routledge, 1988) pp. 158–67.

Webster, of course, dramatises this process explicitly in the growing emotional involvement of Bosola with his prisoner. His refusal
to appear before her undisguised after the 'cruel lie' of the waxwork
bodies is at one level a 'device' to extend the symbolic possibilities
of his role, but it also has an emotional truth rooted in his increased
pity for the Duchess and growing self-hatred. The bond between the
two characters is quietly implied by the Duchess's choice of simile
to describe her suffering:

> I am acquainted with sad misery,
> As the tann'd galley-slave is with his oar.
> (IV. ii. 27–8)

Although these lines are spoken out of Bosola's hearing, they help
to explain the painful sense of kinship felt by the ex-prisoner in the
galleys for the woman he is guarding. This compassion reaches a
focal point at the moment of her brief 'revival', a moment of great
dramatic intensity which arguably surpasses its model in *Othello*:

> She stirs; here's life.
> Return, fair soul, from darkness, and lead mine
> Out of this sensible hell. She's warm, she breathes:
> Upon thy pale lips I will melt my heart
> To store them with fresh colour. Who's there?
> Some cordial drink!
> (IV. ii. 339–44)

It is in the nature of Webster's art, however, that uncomplicated primary emotions are not sustained beyond a certain point, being
quickly overlaid with ironies and qualifications. The existential trap
closes again round Bosola, preventing his feelings being translated
into saving actions ('Alas! I dare not call: / So pity would destroy
pity'). Moreover, it was only after being refused his reward by Ferdinand that his change of heart became fully articulate. His sense
of injustice is a strange compound of compassion and self-interest,
which means that, while he becomes a channel for the powerful feelings of moral outrage engendered by the Duchess's death, we never
cease to judge him.

The undeniable sense of value and significance emerging from the
events of Act IV is subjected to severe challenges in Act V. A recog-
nisably Shakespearean tragic affirmation is succeeded by scenes of
violent confusion which at times seem closer to the black comedy
of modern 'absurd' theatre than to conventional notions of the tragic.
Figures cross a darkened stage, muttering mad and murderous
thoughts. Men are struck down by accident in 'Such a mistake as I
have often seen / In a play'. Every director has to take firm decisions
about where audience laughter is desirable and where it must be

avoided at all costs. The 1989 RSC production at the Swan was crit-
icised, like many of its predecessors, for giving 'insufficient guid-
ance about where laughter is legitimate'[6] and some reviewers were
inclined to blame the play rather than its direction: 'Nothing can
prevent its final scene from appearing highly risible to a modern
audience'.[7] The simple empirical refutation of this last claim is that
major productions this century (such as Adrian Noble's at Manchester in 1980) have managed to stage the last scene in such a way as
to leave the audience stunned rather than tittering. The most difficult moment is always when the mad Ferdinand enters to join the
struggle between Bosola and the Cardinal. It was partly the excellence of Mike Gwilym's acting which made this scuffle seem terrifying rather than merely ludicrous (he had succeeded in establishing
a real continuity between Ferdinand's mad behaviour and his earlier signs of instability), but another important factor was Noble's
decision to put Gwilym in modern hospital clothes. This authoritative and sobering sign of 'real' insanity made it more difficult to
maintain an amused distance from his wild behaviour, as the clini-
cal whiteness of his garments was flecked with blood.

Laughter or terror in the face of meaningless violence are by no
means the only responses prompted by the last act of Webster's play.
There is also a counter-movement in the fragile but persistent and
poignant sense of the Duchess's continued presence. In early 1625,
Webster contributed some verses to an engraving of James I and his
family. In this picture James is shown flanked by his dead wife,
Queen Anne, and his dead son, Prince Henry, each bearing a skull,
as well as by all his important living relatives.[8] The picture does not
simply act as a *memento mori* reminding us that in the midst of life
we are in death; it also asserts the importance and life of the dead,
their continuing place in the world of the living. Bosola remains
haunted by the Duchess, the dying Ferdinand's thoughts return
obsessively to his sister, and Antonio hears the melancholy echo that
issues from his wife's grave. The location of this immensely effective scene, a fort built on the ruins of an ancient abbey, simultaneously and paradoxically insists both on the mutability of life and
the persistence of the past, reminding a Jacobean audience of the
'bare ruined choirs' to be found all over post-Reformation England.
It is only when Antonio refuses to converse with the echo on the

6. Paul Taylor, *Independent*, 9 December 1989.
7. Charles Osborne, *Daily Telegraph*, 11 December 1989.
8. The single surviving copy of this engraving is not the original but a reworked version
   dating from after 1633. Births and deaths subsequent to the first printing have resulted
   in a number of changes and James himself now holds a skull. For more detailed descriptions, see Bernard M. Wagner, 'New Verses by John Webster', *Modern Language Notes*,
   vol. XLVI (1931) pp. 403–5, and Charles Forker, *Skull Beneath the Skin: The Achievement of John Webster* (Carbondale and Edwardsville: Southern Illinois University Press,
   1986) pp. 169–70.

grounds that it is 'a dead thing' that his own fate seems to be sealed. The vision of his wife which follows ('on the sudden, a clear light / Presented me a face folded in sorrow') may well have involved the kind of primitive lighting effect which became possible in the indoor Blackfriars but remains very moving even when staged as only his 'fancy'. These moments have a considerable cumulative impact and they were taken further by Philip Prowse in 1985 when he caused the Duchess's ghost to remain onstage throughout the last act. Reviewers were divided about the effects of this but the objection that it was inconsistent with Webster's view of death as 'a black void'[9] seems misplaced. The sense of communion between the living and the dead is very strong in his plays, even if the precise nature of any 'other world' is left in doubt. The power of the echo scene is itself enough to challenge and ironise Bosola's despairing conclusion:

> We are only like dead walls, or vaulted graves
> That, ruin'd, yields no echo.
>
> (V. v. 97–8)

The felt presence of the Duchess in Act V does much to vindicate Webster's closing couplet, the most memorable of the many *sententiae* which adorn his plays:

> *Integrity of life is fame's best friend,*
> *Which nobly, beyond death, shall crown the end.*
>
> (V. v. 120–1)

However, whether visibly onstage or not, the Duchess was powerless to save her husband or avert the final bloodbath. In immediate and practical terms all hope for social and moral renewal comes to rest on Antonio's young son, brought on by Delio at the end of the play. Delio speaks confidently of 'this young hopeful gentleman' but we may remember with unease that there is another claimant to the dukedom, a son by the Duchess's first husband, and that the horoscope for Antonio's firstborn predicted a 'short life' and 'a violent death'. In thus undercutting his ending Webster may have been thinking of the recent death of Prince Henry, which had robbed critics of James's rule of their best hope for the future. The uncertainties awaiting Antonio's son were dramatised with great economy in the last few moments of Adrian Noble's production. Standing centrestage and surrounded by courtiers, the young boy had every man kneel to him in turn before suddenly casting his gaze upward towards the inscrutable stars, the stars which had looked down calmly on his mother's death. It was a fitting conclusion to a play which, no less than *King Lear,* provokes anguished questioning rather than simply a feeling of blank hopelessness.

9. Michael Billington, *Guardian,* 6 July 1985.

Dramaturgical Approaches

INGA-STINA EWBANK

Webster's Realism, or, "A Cunning Piece Wrought Perspective"†

What I want to talk about in this paper is not how Webster copies life, but how he makes us accept as 'real' the life he creates. 'Realism' is a notoriously vague critical term, and Webster's art has often proved to be refractory to conventional critical vocabulary. More than that of any other Jacobean dramatist, his art seems to build on a continual shifting of perspective—a method that makes both the moral attitude and the artistic unity of his plays difficult to define. Sometimes he seems to regard his action and characters as pegs to hang language on; sometimes he seems to regard language as a tool for communicating the felt life of a character or a situation. The vicissitudes of Webster criticism are a measure of how difficult it is to find a way to describe the sense in which Webster's people and their context are alive, or 'real'. We have had the Tussaud Webster, the Elizabethan Webster whose dramatic world was 'intensely contemporary', the Jacobean Webster of the 'downward (realist) estimate' of humanity, and recently Webster Our Contemporary, to whom reality is absurd.[1] Each of these Websters has his own validity, and all I hope to do here is to discuss a notion which I have found helpful in trying to see Webster's peculiar virtues, and faults, for what they are. I should also say that, in approaching

---

† Inga-Stina Ewbank, "Webster's Realism, or, 'A Cunning Piece Wrought Perspective,'" in Brian Morris (ed.), *John Webster* (London: Ernest Benn, 1970), pp. 159–78. Notes have been renumbered. Reprinted by permission of the Ewbank estate.
1. Travis Bogard, *The Tragic Satire of John Webster* (Berkeley and Los Angeles, 1955), p. 16 and *passim*, speaks of the kinship between Webster's dramatic world and the contemporary political and social English scene; and so, in various ways, do F. L. Lucas, *The Complete Works of John Webster*, 4 vols (1927), and John Russell Brown, from whose Revels editions of *The White Devil* (1960) and *The Duchess of Malfi* (1964) my quotations in the text of this paper are taken. G. K. Hunter has an interesting discussion of the Jacobean 'realism' of Webster's attitude in 'English Folly and Italian Vice', in *Stratford-upon-Avon Studies I: Jacobean Theatre* (1960), esp. p. 87. For Webster Our Contemporary, see Norman Rabkin's introduction to *Twentieth Century Interpretations of 'The Duchess of Malfi'* (Englewood Cliffs, N.J., 1968), esp. p. 8.

Webster, I make the assumption that, in his two tragedies at least, he is a serious dramatist: which means, first, that the subject of his plays is human beings and their relationships and, second, that he is not playing tricks on us with a rag-bag of devices and a notebook of quotations but is dramatising a genuine vision of life—that is, that his dramatic method is identical with his way of seeing his subject.

One of the most effective instances I know of one critic spiking the guns of all the others is in Ben Jonson's sonnet 'In Authorem' prefixed to Nicholas Breton's *Melancholike Humours* (1600):

> Looke here on *Bretons* worke, the master print:
>   Where, such perfections to the life doe rise.
> If they seeme wry, to such as looke asquint,
>   The fault's not in the object, but their eyes.
>
> For, as one comming with a laterall viewe,
>   Unto a cunning piece wrought perspective,
> Wants facultie to make a censure true:
>   So with this Authors Readers will it thrive:
>
> Which being eyed directly, I divine,
>   His proofe their praise, will meete, as in this line.[2]

In the comfortable finality of Jonson's verdict, 'a laterall viewe' will produce an incoherent jumble, whereas, if the work is viewed from the appropriate angle, there is 'perfection to the life'—which I take to be the Elizabethan-Jacobean version of that unsatisfactory nineteenth-century term 'realism'.[3] Readers of the *Melancholike Humours* may not be so sure that 'the fault's not in the object, but their eyes'; but readers of Webster (and producers and audiences) may find some illumination in the image that underlies Jonson's critical vocabulary here.

The connotations of Jonson's adjective 'perspective' are best explained by the *O.E.D.* definition of the related noun ('perspective', sb. 4b):

> A picture or figure constructed so as to produce some fantastic effect; e.g. appearing distorted or confused except from one particular point of view, or presenting totally different aspects from different points.

---

2. Ed. G. B. Harrison (1929), p. 7.
3. The earliest *O.E.D.* entry for 'realism' in its modern literary sense is 1856.—Cf. Webster's discussion of 'the true imitation of life' in the postscript to *The White Devil* and 'An Excellent Actor', ed. Lucas, iv, 42–3.

We know that such pictures or figures were popular in the Elizabethan-Jacobean age.[4] Although they are more of a freak than a phenomenon to be taken seriously in the history of art, the ideas behind them seem to have appealed to writers. The young William Drummond of Hawthornden, visiting the Fair of St Germains in 1607, was particularly impressed by the display of perspectives, which he calls 'double Pictures', for their image of the moral doubleness of life, such as

> A Lady weeping over her dead Husband, accompanied with many Mourners, the First View; the second representing her Second Nuptials, Nymphs and Gallants revelling naked, and going to Bed.[5]

Shakespeare, too, was interested in the properties of perspectives and in their application to human experience: he seems to have found in them a metaphor for the unreality of reality.[6] Thus Richard II's Queen is told that

> Each substance of a grief has twenty shadows,
> Which shows like grief itself, but is not so;
> For sorrow's eye, glazed with blinding tears,
> Divides one thing entire to many objects,
> Like perspectives which, rightly gaz'd upon,
> Show nothing but confusion—ey'd awry,
> Distinguish form. (R.II, II.ii. 14–20)

4. The best known examples of perspectives in this country are Holbein's painting 'The Ambassadors' in the National Gallery and the puzzle-portrait of Edward VI in the National Portrait Gallery. Both are early (1533 and 1546, respectively), but the taste for this kind of art seems to have lingered on well through the seventeenth century. On this, see Rosemary Freeman, *English Emblem Books* (1948), who also draws attention to Drummond's account. A brief but clear account of the technique, as well as popularity, of the perspective is in James Byam Shaw, 'The Perspective Picture: A Freak of German Sixteenth-Century Art', in *Apollo*, VI (1927), 208–14 (reprinted in *J.B.S. Selected Writings*, 1968). See also Jurgis Baltrusaitis, *Anamorphoses ou Perspectives curieuses* (Paris, 1955) and review article on this book in *Sele Arte*, IV.20 (September–October 1955), 7–17; and Arpad Weixlgärtner, 'Perspektivische Spielereien bei Renaissance Künstlern', in *Festschrift der Nationalbibliothek in Wien* (Vienna, 1926), pp. 849–60.—I am much indebted to Mr J. B. Trapp of the Warburg Institute for help in the matter of perspectives.
5. *The Works of William Drummond of Hawthornden* (Edinburgh, 1711), p. 141.
6. It is not always easy to see just how Shakespeare envisaged the perspective. Only in Sonnet XXIV could he possibly be using the word 'perspective' in the modern, technical sense, and even this instance is ambiguous. Cf. Dover Wilson's edition of *The Sonnets* (Cambridge, 1966), pp. 123–4; J. W. Lever, *The Elizabethan Love Sonnet* (1956), p. 203; and the extended discussion of Shakespeare and perspectives in A. H. R. Fairchild, 'Shakespeare and the Arts of Design', *University of Missouri Studies*, XII, 1 (1937), 125–30. In the instance which I quote from *Richard II*, as well as in *H.V.*, V. ii.315, *All's Well*, V.iii.48–52, and *Twelfth Night*, V.i.208–9, he has in mind various forms of distortions of vision. Shakespeare's interest in 'cozening pictures' was shared by, e.g., Drayton: see *Mortimeriados*, 2332–8, and Kathleen Tillotson's helpful note on these lines (*The Works of Michael Drayton*, V, 1941, 43). More important it was shared by other dramatists whom Webster admired: see *The Alchemist*, III.iv.88–100; and many instances in Chapman (*Hero and Leander*, III.125–6; *Ovids Banquet of Sence*, st.3; *Eugenia*, 173–80; *All Fools*, I.i.47–8; *Chabot*, I.i.68–72).

The idea behind the perspective must have been an attempt to overcome the static quality of pictorial art. Perspectives (in the ordinary sense) are distorted in the whole or part of the picture; several images are superimposed one upon another; and the very point is that, for the viewer, there should be a confusion of impressions until he finds the right viewpoint, when one image clicks into focus. This asks for a peculiar kind of collaboration from the viewer, and his experience of the work will have a kind of dynamism: through confusion to clarity. Furthermore, the aim of the perspective must have been to fix in images the transient quality of reality: the way one impression will, with a change of viewpoint, change into its opposite.[7]

It is my contention that the method of Webster's art in his tragedies is much akin to that of the perspective, and that in *The Duchess of Malfi* in particular he uses the perspective method to achieve a unique kind of 'realism'—a realism at the heart of which lies, not a certainty, but a question about what is the real nature, the real estimate, of man. But before we look at what this means, we should, I think, look at what it does *not* mean.

Drummond was also much excited by another kind of picture at the Fair of St Germains, one in which the artist had turned Venus into a *memento mori* by representing her

> lying on a Bed with stretched out Arms, in her Hand she presented to a young Man (who was adoring her, and at whom little Love was directing a Dart) a fair Face, which with much Ceremony he was receiving, but on the other side, which should have been the hinder part of that Head, was the Image of Death; by which *Mortality* [the painter] surpassed the others [who had also depicted Venus], more than they did him by *Art*.[8]

Obviously this kind of picture is like a paradigm of the art—the vision and technique—of, say, Tourneur: the skull under the milk-bathed

---

7. This, at least, is the aim which struck the poets who used the perspective analogy. Thus Chapman describes 'Religion': 'Her lookes were like the pictures that are made, / To th'optike reason; one way like a shade, / Another monster like, and euery way / To passers by, and such as made no stay, / To view her in a right line, face to face, / She seem'd a serious trifle; all her grace, / Show'd in her fixt inspection; and then / She was the onely grace of dames and men' (*Eugenia*, 173–80; cf. Phyllis Brooks Bartlett's note on these lines in her edition of *The Poems of George Chapman*, N.Y., 1962, p. 456).—Though I do not wish to embark on a rigid *ut pictura poesis* analysis of Webster, it is worth noting how often his characters see themselves, each other, and even their own deeds (cf. Lodovico's 'night-piece') in terms of a painting, and also that to Webster 'an excellent actor' is 'an exquisite painter' (Lucas, op. cit., 43). Wylie Sypher's comment on mannerist art as an 'experiment with many techniques of disproportion and disturbed balance' (*Four Stages of Renaissance Style*, Garden City, N.Y., 1956, p. 116) is also relevant. It is also noteworthy that the new appreciation of Webster in recent decades coincides with an interest in *trompe l'oeil* phenomena, and paintings requiring visual readjustment, such as the Ferdinand-like mental landscape of Salvador Dali's 'The Great Paranoiac'.

8. Op. cit., p. 140. * * *

skin and the yellow labours of the silk-worm. The *raison d'être* of the picture, its structure and its meaning, is in the static visual (and implicitly moral) contrast between Venus and Death. Similar is the local effect of the 'pot of lily-flowers with a skull in it' which the ghost of Brachiano carries,[9] and of many other verbal and physical emblems scattered throughout Webster's tragedies—not least the famous 'apricocks' ripened in horse-dung. But this doubleness is not the art of the perspective, for the perspective cannot be simply allegorised: it is, rather, an image of the flux of the human mind, of the relativity of truth depending on viewpoint, and of the confusion and uncertainty when we grope for what is real. Something of this is contained in that complex moment of discovery in *Twelfth Night* when Orsino sees

> One face, one voice, one habit, and two persons!
> A natural perspective, that is and is not.   (*T.N.*, V.i.208–9)

Similarly, moving from *The White Devil* to *The Duchess of Malfi* is often a question of moving from a world of emblems to one of natural perspectives, that are and are not. To take just one example, Flamineo's analysis of 'the maze of conscience' in his breast produces Brachiano's ghost, so conveniently equipped with his flowerpot. The situation is tangible enough: this ghost is clearly meant to be more objective than the ghost of Isabella which Francisco almost at will conjures up from his 'melancholic thought'; and Flamineo is made to tell us that it represents a mode of reality which is 'beyond melancholy'. It is a static and self-explanatory comment—it is noteworthy that Flamineo, who is otherwise only too keen to turn situations into verbal emblems, does not expound on it—and represents the ultimate in direct experience:

> I do dare my fate
> To do its worst.   (*W.D.*, V.iv.144–5)

Now, when the Cardinal in *The Duchess of Malfi* looks into his 'tedious' conscience, the effect is not an emblem. Instead, as in a perspective from a certain viewpoint, his view of ordinary reality is jolted into a fearsome image:

> When I look into the fish-ponds, in my garden,
> Methinks I see a thing, arm'd with a rake
> That seems to strike at me:—   (*D.M.*, V.v.5–7)

And when Bosola, over the dead body of the Duchess, speaks of 'a guilty conscience' as

9. See J. R. Brown's note at *The White Devil*, V.iv.123, and R. W. Dent, *John Webster's Borrowing* (Berkeley and Los Angeles, 1960), pp. 161–2.

> a black register, wherein is writ
> All our good deeds and bad, a perspective
> That shows us hell!   (*D.M.*, IV.ii.357–9)

then his conscience has, as it were, become an optical instrument
for producing a 'perspective' picture (*O.E.D.*, sb. 2). In effect Bosola
is describing the 'perspective' nature of a human consciousness:
good and bad deeds superimposed upon each other in a confusion
which at this particular moment, under this angle of vision, crystallises into a vision of hell. (One might compare this to Vittoria's out-
cry, upon the death of Brachiano, 'O me! this place is hell.') In each
of these last two cases it is a character within the play who is transcribing his experience of a world where things are and are not, but
both seem to me to be performing within a small compass what
Webster was doing in the play as a whole.

   This, of course, is not the same as transcribing a world where
things simply are not what they seem. That is the doubleness of the
Venus-Death picture which Drummond saw. Needless to say, there
is that direction in Webster's art, too: the satiric impulse to strip
appearances down to reality. Assuming that Webster saw eye to eye
with Dekker in the *Ho!* plays, he must have started his dramatic
career from a vision of life as a comic panorama with satirical poten-
tialities. The 'realism' of these city-comedies is a matter of looking
so closely at the surface of ordinary life that the stuff hidden under
the surface also becomes apparent. Again a speech by a single character may epitomise the view of the plays as wholes; thus Bellamont, in *Northward Ho!*, describes Sturbridge Fair:

> I tel you Gentlemen I haue obseru'd very much with being at
> *Sturbridge*; it hath afforded me mirth beyond the length of fiue
> lattin Comedies; here should you meete a *Nor-folk* yeoman ful-
> but; with his head able to ouer-turne you; and his pretty wife
> that followed him, ready to excuse the ignorant hardnesse of
> her husbands forhead; in the goose market number of freshmen,
> stuck here and there, with a graduate: like cloues with great
> heads in a gammon of bacon: here two gentlemen making a
> mariage betweene their heires ouer a wool-pack; there a Min-
> isters wife that could speake false lattine very lispingly; here two
> in one corner of a shop: Londoners selling their wares, and other
> Gentlemen courting their wiues; where they take vp petticoates
> you should finde schollers and towns-mens wiues crouding tog-
> ither while their husbands weare in another market busie
> amongst the Oxen; twas like a campe for in other Countries so
> many Punks do not follow an army. I could make an excellent
> discription of it in a Comedy. . . .   (*N.H.*, I.i.39–54)[1]

---

1. *The Dramatic Works of Thomas Dekker*, ed. Fredson Bowers, ii, 412.

In the comedies, as in this example (though one cannot help feeling that Bellamont's 'excellent description' might have made a better play than either of the two), the verbal pleasure lies as much in the transcription of the surface as in the analysis of what is found underneath it. In the tragedies, the satirist characters find their pleasure, and expend their verbal energy, in elaborating on the falseness of appearances, as in Bosola's

> There's no more credit to be given to th' face
> Than to a sick man's urine, which some call
> The physician's whore, because she cozens him:—
> (D.M., I.i.236–8)

Flamineo and Bosola are, or course, the great 'strippers'; they think of themselves as (in Bosola's phrase) 'Men that paint weeds to the life'; whether those 'weeds' are Vittoria in her love, or her grief; or the Old Lady with her revolting cosmetics cupboard; or the Duchess herself as 'a box of worm-seed'. In *The Duchess of Malfi* such stripping sometimes pushes the play towards psychological drama where the characters have what we like to think of as a 'modern' insight into each other's motives; thus the Cardinal's reply to Julia's 'I would not now / Find you inconstant':

> Do not put thyself
> To such a voluntary torture, which proceeds
> Out of your own guilt.   (D.M., II.iv.7–10)[2]

Both plays, then, are full of 'realists' with a clear view of life as corruption under a splendid surface. But in *The Duchess of Malfi* at least, this is not the ultimate viewpoint, or stance, of the play. In *The White Devil* the final stance does not seem to get us much beyond the simply double picture, not even in Flamineo's

> While we look up to heaven we confound
> Knowledge with knowledge. O I am in a mist;
> (W.D., V.vi.259–60)

*   *   *

* * * Often, in *The White Devil*, viewpoints are moved around so schematically that there is no chance to focus on, or feel about, any one of them. The love scene between Vittoria and Brachiano in I.ii, commented on realistically or cynically by Flamineo, from one

---

2. Norman Rabkin, op cit., p. 6, thinks that this insight of the Cardinal's 'would do credit to any psychoanalyst'. Related to this interest in the play is, no doubt, the tendency of its characters to deal with each other in terms of shock-therapy: Ferdinand's masque of madmen being, of course, the most notable example; but cf., e.g., Antonio's intention to surprise the Cardinal, as 'the sudden apprehension / Of danger . . . May draw the poison out of him' (V.i.68–71).

direction, and moralistically by Cornelia, from another, seems to
me one such example; we can admire the visual grouping, the symmetry of the scheme, but it is difficult to perceive any 'perfection to
the life'. And this, of course, is the great danger of the perspective
method: that there will be nothing but 'laterall views' presented to
us, that nothing will emerge from the confusion, leaving us all in
a mist. Here, I think, lies the main reason for the precariousness of
Webster's art.[3]

In *The Duchess of Malfi*, however, by a more assured use of the
same method, Webster manages to render a world which is not just
confused but unfathomable. The plot jerks are here truly productive of adjustments in the angle of vision. The Duchess, in the bed
chamber scene, turns around, expecting to see Antonio and Cariola, and instead sees Ferdinand; Bosola thinks he has killed the Cardinal and finds it is Antonio—at each point a whole world-view is
suddenly changed. The wooing scene, where structure and language
insistently remind us that the Duchess woos herself and Antonio to
death as well as to marriage, and the Duchess's death scene, with
its parody of the marriage masque, are only the most sustained
examples of 'cunning pieces wrought perspective'. But within other
scenes this method of organising reality—cutting across spatial and
temporal determinations and superimposing two images in a new
kind of present[4]—is even clearer. In defiance of all logic of verisimilitude, and in a superb twist of the conventional echo-device, the
Duchess becomes, as it were, psychologically present when Antonio
sees her:

> . . . on the sudden, a clear light
> Presented me a face folded in sorrow.   (V.iii.44–5)[5]

The antithesis to this 'real' presence is that other superimposition
of her image, in Ferdinand's rage in II.v:

> Methinks I see her laughing—
> Excellent hyena!—talk to me somewhat, quickly,

---

3. * * * One condition of 'perspective' art seems to be that one image never *quite* incorpo-
rates or excludes another. One is always conscious of elements waiting to become part
of an image other than that on which one is focusing—thus concentration is undermined
and confusion is always around the corner. In this connection, it is worth remembering
that—with the single exception of Holbein's 'Ambassadors'—none of the great Renaissance artists made serious use of the 'perspective' technique, any more than Shakespeare relied on the method of varied but unresolved perspectives.
4. I am borrowing my descriptive vocabulary here from Dorothy van Ghent, whose analysis of the way Estella's image and Miss Havisham's merge in the mind of Pip in *Great
Expectations* has helped me to come to terms with Webster's technique. See 'The Dickens World: A View from Todgers's', *The Sewanee Review*, LVIII (1950), 419–38,
esp. 430–31.
5. Cf. J. R. Brown, ed., *The Duchess of Malfi*, p. xx, on the probable stage-effect here.

> Or my imagination will carry me
> To see her, in the shameful act of sin. (II.v.38–41)

The intensity of Ferdinand's involvement is suggested by the very confusion of sense impressions here: 'I *see* her laughing— / Excellent hyena!' Instead of being stopped, Ferdinand is egged on by the Cardinal's 'With whom?' to imagine the over-sexed objects of the Duchess's desire, until, as James L. Calderwood puts it, Ferdinand 'directly addresses his sister from his imaginative station as voyeur':[6]

> Go to, mistress!
> 'Tis not your whore's milk that shall quench my wild-fire,
> But your whore's blood. (II.v.46–8)

And so the actual scene on stage is overlaid with one, in Ferdinand's mind, beyond any censor's imagination. We know that the Duchess is not a 'whore', just as we know that she is not really there in the Echo scene, but the vigour of Ferdinand's evocation provides a viewpoint from which, albeit momentarily and with a near-certainty that it is with 'a laterall view', we see the goings-on at Malfi. When we move from the romantic-idealistic wooing at the end of Act I—

> *Antonio:* And may our sweet affections, like the spheres,
>   Be still in motion.
> *Duchess:*   Quickening, and make
>   The like soft music— (I.i.482–4)

to the physical realities of the Duchess's pregnancy at the beginning of Act II, then we are particularly conscious of one image of the Duchess being overlaid by another.[7]

It is, of course, in the hallucinations of madness that the human mind behaves most like a perspective picture—despite Francisco's somewhat self-conscious comment that

> Statesmen think often they see stranger sights
> Than madmen. (*W.D.*, IV.i.117–18)

And the character of Ferdinand, in which image and actuality fuse, so that he *becomes* the tempest, the wild-fire, even the devil, and finally the wolf, of his own verbal imagery, is, of course, the most notable projection of Webster's perspective vision. Here we are no longer in the emblematic world of satire where, for example, animal imagery is used to show people as they 'really' are. But Ferdinand's madness is only a concentration of the relationship which, largely

---

6. *The Duchess of Malfi*: 'Styles of Ceremony', *Essays in Criticism*, XII (1962), 141.
7. Bosola's scene with the Old Lady forms, as it were, the landscape out of which this image of the Duchess emerges. Cf. Erhard Schön's perspective woodcut representing lovers.

through the imagery,[8] is established between people and animals,
people and devils, people and things, in this play. Bosola starts out
comparing the two brothers to 'plum-trees, that grow crooked over
standing pools' in an elaborate simile, of a set-piece nature, but
before he reaches the end of it, the 'they' and the 'their' of his discourse refer indiscriminately and interchangeably to the trees and
the brothers; and before the act is over, their corruption has been
demonstrated in word and deed. The persecutors of the Duchess,
in the course of the action, *become* beasts of prey, so that, only once
she is dead, 'they then may feed in quiet'. We may feel, in the antagonists of the Duchess, a lack not only of logical motivation but also
of an inner life; but this is substituted for by the overall creation of
a demonic world in which people and animals have exchanged attributes, and in which—as Dorothy van Ghent says about Dickens's
imaginative world[9]—'living creatures [are manipulated] as if they
were not human but things'. Part of that gruesome confusion against
which the humanity of the Duchess is defined is a grotesque dismemberment of the human body itself. The 'leg of a man' which Ferdinand carries over his shoulder in his madness, and his vision of
the other characters as reduced to nothing but 'tongue and belly',
may come straight out of Webster's commonplace book,[1] but they
are integral with the vision of a world in which a doctor may have
his skin flayed off to cover one of his 'anatomies' and in which 'a
lady in France, . . . having had the smallpox, flayed the skin off her
face to make it more level' (II.i.26–8). We accept as 'real', in terms
of this vision, the dead hand that the Duchess is given, much as we
accept as real the way Mr Vholes in *Bleak House* 'takes off his close
black gloves as if he were skinning his hands, lifts off his tight hat,
as if he were scalping himself, and sits down at his desk', or the way
the Coketown capitalists wish that Providence had seen fit to make
the factory hands 'only hands, or, like the lower creatures of the sea-
shore, only hands and stomachs'. In each case the grotesquery of
the image is not an end in itself but a viewpoint from which we can
feel about the inhumanity of man. The reason why this kind of dismemberment is so 'real' in *The Duchess of Malfi*—whereas we hardly
remember Francisco's intention of playing football with the head of
Brachiano, except as a piece of gratuitous horror—is, at least partly,
that in the later play there is also so much assertion of the opposite
possibility and the opposite viewpoint: of ordinary, wholesome,
and fruitful humanity. There is not only a thematic contrast
between the sterile and perverted sexuality of the brothers and the

8. See Hereward T. Price, 'The Function of Imagery in Webster', *PMLA* LXX, (1955), 717–
   39; and, on Ferdinand in particular, my article in *Orpheus,* III (1956), 126–33.
9. Op. cit., 422.
1. See Dent, op. cit., pp. 246–8.

philoprogenitiveness of the Duchess and Antonio, but also, in the handling of the latter couple, a genuine evocation of normal, domestic, love—so that the Duchess's dying words,

> I pray thee, look thou giv'st my little boy
> Some syrup for his cold, and let the girl
> Say her prayers, ere she sleep,   (*D.M.*, IV.ii.203–5)

are part of a *felt* context and not just an incidental piece of sentimentality.

Both Webster's Italianate tragedies contain elements of domestic drama. The quarrel between Brachiano, on the one hand, and Monticelso and Francisco, on the other, in II.i, begins in the triple-pillar idiom of *Antony and Cleopatra*. * * * As the quarrel develops, the tone becomes definitely bourgeois:

> *Francisco:* You shift your shirt there
>   When you retire from tennis.
> *Brachiano:* Happily.
> *Francisco:* Her husband is lord of a poor fortune,
>   Yet she wears cloth of tissue.   (II.i.52–5)

But in *The White Devil* this tone is not sustained in any important fashion; it remains part of the sociological documentation of the play. * * * In *The Duchess of Malfi,* the relationship of Antonio and the Duchess (whatever we think of the remarriage of widows) comes to form a strain of simplicity, of almost bourgeois sentiment, which establishes a viewpoint and a value.

When the Duchess woos Antonio, his initial vision of marriage is altogether domestic (I.i.398–403); and so is his response, in III.i, to Delio's inquiry about 'your noble duchess':

> Right fortunately well: she's an excellent
> Feeder of pedigrees; since you last saw her,
> She hath had two children more, a son and daughter.
>   (III.i.5–7)

This attitude is reflected in the couple's understanding of larger issues, too: to the persecuted Duchess, God's dealings with her make sense in terms of her little boy and his 'scourge-stick' (III.v.78–81), and the dying Antonio uses the conventional, but here strangely apt, image of boys chasing soap-bubbles to express his sense of the vanity of human wishes (V.iv.64–6). The greater wholeness of *The Duchess* compared with *The White Devil* means, among other things, that, where in the earlier play we are made to explore single and separate attitudes, in the later we are made to focus on man as an integral being. Instead of a single abortive flash of 'compassion' in Flamineo, we have the whole of Act V devoted to the effect of the

Duchess's death on her brothers and their tool; instead of a couple of speeches, the Duchess has two whole long scenes in which to face death and define who she is. Thus the viewpoint of innocence and simple love, which in *The White Devil* is represented by some rather mawkish set-pieces from Giovanni and a glimpse of Isabella, is brought into full action in *The Duchess of Malfi* through the Duchess and her children (who fortunately do not speak). Family relationships are very important in *The White Devil*, but they are, it seems to me, mainly used as pointers to the theme of social disintegration rather than being explored *as* relationships—so that, for example, the brother-brother killing moves away from human reality towards symbolism. Cornelia's motherly grief goes some way towards being an exception from this rule, and no doubt Webster is here feeling his way to a realised situation; but it is significant that he has to do it through such particularly wholesale borrowings from Shakespeare. In *The Duchess of Malfi*, on the other hand, family relationships are the very stuff on which the play is made. Robert Ornstein, in his sensitive treatment of the play, points out that

> The Duchess' strength is not a lonely existential awareness of self but a remembrance of love, expressed in her parting words to Cariola and in her answers to Bosola.[2]

As a sister, the Duchess is defeated by a confused and demonic world; but as a wife and mother she gains a kind of victory. The peculiar effect of her death scene is, at least partly, achieved by the superimposition upon each other of these two images of her; and this perspective effect is concentrated in the famous moment when Ferdinand, looking at her dead body, suddenly sees her from a human viewpoint—that is, sees what he has done to his twin sister. Truly may his eyes 'dazzle' when he sees her face. That moment is perhaps the clearest indicator of where the peculiar 'realism' of *The Duchess of Malfi* lies: in doing what E. M. Forster calls 'bouncing' us into accepting as real a world where verisimilitude and fantasy, actuality and metaphor, have merged. They have merged into a 'perspective' which, 'eyed directly', gives an insight into human suffering: into what man may do to man.

It goes without saying, and is in any case implicit in what I have said already, that Webster's language is very largely instrumental in this 'bouncing' process. Yet I shall have to say something about the language in particular, for I believe that in Webster's linguistic patterns we see the same kind of 'perspective' technique: through confusion (here expressed as verbal profusion, intricate analogies, and extended similes) to a kind of simple literalness—yet one which is

---

2. *The Moral Vision of Jacobean Tragedy* (paperback ed., Madison and Milwaukee, 1965), p. 148.

meaningful only in relation to the confusion from which it has emerged. Here again we have to make a distinction between the two tragedies. Needless to say, there are many similarities: both plays have the same tendency towards generalising experience into axioms or *sententiae,* the same ability to embody emotion in a flash of striking imagery or a plain statement, the same tortuous and often apparently contrived looking for analogies, and the same emergence of a kind of clarity, often literalness, in characters' speeches as they face death. But there is also a different kind of concern about language in the two plays, respectively.

In *The White Devil* the importance of language as a self-conscious device is constantly kept before us. Language in the *realpolitik* world of the court is part of the power-struggle. * * *

* * *

[But] J. R. Mulryne, in his illuminating essay on Webster's style, has spoken, particularly in reference to *The Duchess of Malfi,* of 'a self-critical intelligence behind the words on the page, checking any tendency to false rhetoric, deflating over-emphatic statement or posturing'.[3] I would agree with this but go still further and say that, in many of these instances of deflation, Webster is concerned with the ultimate inability of language, even when metaphorical, to reach and convey some kinds of experience. One remembers Bosola's description of the suffering Duchess: 'her silence, / Methinks expresseth, more than if she spake' (IV.i.9–10). At key-points in *The Duchess of Malfi* the characters, like Edgar at the end of *King Lear,* speak what they feel, not what they ought to say; and the reality of what they feel is as much in what they do *not* speak as in their spoken words. Not only that, but the moments of rejecting elaborate language tend also to be moments at which we are made to view the perspective from a new viewpoint—notably, of course, in the dialogue between the Duchess and Bosola in IV.ii.

The language of *The Duchess of Malfi* as a whole tends to serve less of a social-political function than that in *The White Devil.* Webster is less concerned with defining the nature of the court as such and more with defining the nature of the whole world in which the Duchess in particular and man in general live. The language, as has often been pointed out, is subservient to the vision of the play as a whole. So, when the Duchess asks Bosola 'Who am I?', his answer,

> Thou art a box of worm-seed, at best, but a salvatory of green mummy:—what's this flesh? a little crudded milk, fantastical puff-paste; our bodies are weaker than those paper prisons boys

3. 'The White Devil and The Duchess of Malfi', in Stratford-upon-Avon Studie 1: Jacobean Theatre (1960), p. 216.

> use to keep flies in; more contemptible, since ours is to preserve
> earth-worms. Didst thou ever see a lark in a cage? such is the
> soul in the body: this world is like her little turf of grass, and
> the heaven o'er our heads, like her looking-glass, only gives us
> a miserable knowledge of the small compass of our prison,
>
> (IV.ii.124–33)

is an epitome of one of the ways in which the play's language tries
to define man: through the realistic, 'stripping', imagery of moral satire, and through a series of associatively linked metaphors which
turn the question over and over, worrying away at it, like a dog with
a bone. The Duchess's plain retort, 'Am not I thy duchess?', turns
Bosola towards another kind of realism, and he tries to look at her
from the outside, as she really is, but again his vision is distracted
into metaphors, and again the Duchess punctures his flow:

> I am Duchess of Malfi still.

And when Bosola counters this assertion with a *sententia* which, like
so many of the Webster characters' *sententiae*, appears to try to get
away from the human situation at issue,

> *Glories, like glow-worms, afar off shine bright,*
> *But look'd to near, have neither heat, nor light,*

then it is met by her calmly deflating irony: 'Thou art very plain'.
But the effect of this is not simply to discredit Bosola's language (as
was the case with Lodovico's rejection of 'painted comforts'). The
simplicity of the Duchess's replies must be understood in terms of
Bosola's contortions, not as simple contrast, but rather as end-
product. In the structure of this dialogue we are, I think, witness-
ing a movement rather like that of Herbert's 'Prayer':

> Prayer; the Churches banquet, Angels age,
> Gods breath in man returning to his birth,
> The soul in paraphrase, heart in pilgrimage,
> The Christian plummet sounding heav'n and earth;
> Engine against th'Almightie, sinners towre,
> Reversed thunder, Christ-side-piercing spear,
> The six-daies world transposing in an houre,
> A kinde of tune, which all things heare and fear;
> Softnesse, and peace, and joy, and love, and blisse,
> Exalted Manna, gladnesse of the best,
> Heaven in ordinarie, man well drest,
> The milkie way, the bird of Paradise,
> Church-bels beyond the starres heard, the souls bloud,
> The land of spices; something understood.

The poem works through an *accelerando* of elaborate attempts at
analogy to rest in a resolution which, in pointed contrast, is plain

and literal: 'something understood'. Yet the simplicity is meaningful only in relation to the complexity of what has gone before: both are necessary stages in the process, enacted by the poem, of finding a truth, defining an experience which, we feel, in the end exists beyond words altogether. Similarly, it is Bosola's speeches which fill the Duchess's plain replies with meaning: she is both 'a box of worm-seed' and 'thy duchess', both a grey-haired woman who cannot sleep and 'Duchess of Malfi still'. Each of them may see only, or mainly, one side of the dialectic, but we see the whole dramatic image. And that image, in which Bosola's view of the Duchess and her own view are superimposed upon one another, is very much 'a cunning piece wrought perspective'. Nor is it cunningness for its own sake, but a view into a particular human situation as well as an intuition of a whole human condition. In so far as this is 'perfection to the life', Webster is a realist.

LEE BLISS

From *The Duchess of Malfi* †

* * *

For three hundred lines Webster has withheld his heroine. She moves forward at last, simultaneously to complete the first act's pan-oramic view and to plunge us into the play's action. Webster's dra-matic skill is evident not only in her suggested complexity,[1] but in the wooing scene's structural effectiveness. [Here he] introduces a potentially comic dilemma: young lovers frustrated by tyrannic family opposition.[2] He encourages our sympathetic rejection of the

---

† Lee Bliss, "The Duchess of Malfi," in *The World's Perspective: John Webster and the Jaco-bean Drama* (New Brunswick, NJ: Rutgers University Press, 1983), pp. 137–70, 232–35. Copyright © 1983 by Lee Bliss. Reprinted by permission of Rutgers UP. Notes have been renumbered.

1. As with the circuitous and often contradictory evaluations of Bosola, Webster offers us apparently irreconcilable views of both the Duchess's actions and her character. Clif-ford Leech usefully discusses Webster's divergent perspectives and suggests that this technique "brings her close to us" and involves our sympathies; see *Webster: "The Duch-ess of Malfi,"* Barron's Studies in English Literature No. 8 (Great Neck, N.Y.: Barron's Educational Series, 1963), p. 49.

2. Jane Marie Luecke is right to see the heroine as "rather a woman than a duchess; she seeks rather to lose herself in the social act of sex-marriage-childbearing, and she places herself in an 'abnormal but usual' social situation by committing the social error of marrying below her class—all of which is the specific matter of comedy rather than of tragedy"; see "*The Duchess of Malfi:* Comic and Satiric Confusion in a Trag-edy," *Studies in English Literature, 1500–1900,* 4 (1964), p. 277. Although Luecke overstates the case for romantic "comedy," certainly part of the fourth act's power derives from our feeling, at some deep level, that "for her transgression of a social convention, this woman is forced to pay not comic consequences but the tragic extreme" (pp. 277–278).

brothers' peremptory and gratuitously nasty demands. Equally clearly, however, her soliloquy reveals that the Duchess shares her brothers' indifference to the claims of either "simple honesty" or public duty. Ferdinand's demeaning image of the self-confident "irregular crab" who thinks its own way "right" is not inaccurate. Her sudden resolve to make her "royal kindred" into "low footsteps" to her will suggests she shares their stubborn egotism and even accepts their rebuke as a challenge to her sovereign freedom. The battle imagery in which she couches her decision hints a recognition of danger but also recalls the Arragonian family penchant for self-aggrandizement. The Duchess may reject future critics as "old wives," but Cariola's ambivalence encourages our own: free of Ferdinand's personal animus, Cariola sees her mistress's action in ominous domestic terms, as dangerous poison. She is not at all sure whether the proclaimed heroic endeavor is urged by "the spirit of greatness" or merely a private woman's foolish will (I.i.504–506).

Certainly in the wooing itself the Duchess demonstrates both sides of her character. She seeks the domestic satisfactions of love and marriage, but in her reckless willfulness seems possessed by a quality as perilous as what Antonio calls the "great man's madness," ambition. Surrounded by fawning suitors and flatterers, ambition becomes dangerously convinced of its power (made "lunatic, beyond all cure"); to obtain its desires it feels justified in leaving "the path / Of simple virtue, which was never made / To seem the thing it is not" (I.i.446–448). She dismisses as insignificant Antonio's realistic fears about her brothers' reaction; she refuses to be bothered by nebulous consequences and shrugs off a tempest that "time will easily / Scatter" (I.i.471–472). Paradoxically, in trying to set aside her nobility she exercises the very dignity, courage, and stubborn willfulness natural to her royal position. Yet the Duchess is foolish as well as charming, and an ominous undertone in the courtship's imagery combines with Cariola's assessment to make us uneasy about the choice itself as well as its prospects for worldly happiness.[3] The wooing both initiates the plot's action and prepares us for its course. However variously our uncertain response to this marriage may be explained away by critical appeals to contemporary opinion,

---

3. On the imagery's suggestions of death as well as love, see especially Hereward T. Price, "The Function of Imagery in Webster," in *Elizabethan Drama: Modern Essays in Criticism*, ed. R. J. Kaufmann (New York: Oxford University Press, 1961), p. 241; but also Inga-Stina Ekeblad [Ewbank], "The 'Impure Art' of John Webster," in *"The Duchess of Malfi,"* ed. Norman Rabkin, Twentieth Century Interpretations (Engle- wood Cliffs, N.J.: Prentice-Hall, 1968), p. 63; and Gunnar Boklund, *"The Duchess of Malfi": Sources, Themes, Characters* (Cambridge, Mass.: Harvard University Press, 1962), p. 92.

Webster himself creates the internal contradictions that ensure ambivalence.[4]

Structurally, the wooing brilliantly focuses the first act's seemingly aimless social maneuvering while it also balances Antonio's opening speech. In playing off Antonio's recipe against a leisurely exploration of princes' courts, Webster has suggested Malfi's urgent need for attention to public matters. In this context, the audience's own feelings about second marriages violating degree are irrelevant: unconcerned with her duchy's political health, the Duchess seeks private happiness at the expense of public stability. As a ruler, she can no more be lauded for the example she sets than her brothers. Each sibling pursues an essentially private will, and Clifford Leech rightly notes that she "only refers to her people when she is concerned with how her reputation fares at their hands."[5] Yet everything in the wooing scene militates against the terms set up by Antonio's prologue, and the initial public context comes to seem less and less relevant or helpful in explaining our response. Webster supports the Duchess's verbal attempts at divestiture by briefly eradicating all but that personal "circumference" she seeks to establish. Dubious but sympathetic, even Cariola is relegated to the scene's borders; no interposed commentators degrade the lovers' vows or, for the moment, interrupt our sympathetic involvement in domestic romance.

Webster allows us to experience the Duchess's goal, a haven beyond the aggressive, treacherous world of political maneuvering, and we come to value her for precisely the nonpolitical desires she here represents.[6] She may be a "bad" ruler, certainly a poor

4. Accounts of "contemporary opinion" differ from critic to critic. Frank W. Wadsworth, searching Renaissance literature for "a more modern and democratic voice," manages to find several and presents them in "Webster's *Duchess of Malfi* in the Light of Some Contemporary Ideas on Marriage and Remarriage," *Philological Quarterly*, 35 (1956), esp. p. 402; William Empson's bluff approach wittily dismisses detractors of the Duchess in "Mine Eyes Dazzle," *Essays in Criticism*, 14 (1964), pp. 80–86. James L. Calderwood, on the other hand, believes that any audience would strongly condemn the Duchess's violation of degree, for in marrying Antonio she threatens the cosmological as well as the social order; see "*The Duchess of Malfi*: Styles of Ceremony," *Essays in Criticism*, 12 (1962), pp. 133–147. In *Curs'd Example: "The Duchess of Malfi" and Commonweal Tragedy* (Columbia: University of Missouri Press, 1978), Joyce E. Peterson agrees. In his Revels edition, Brown comes closest to the effect of Webster's ambiguous treatment: "There is no clear judgement in the play, only that Bosola and Ferdinand at last declare her to be innocent" See John Webster, *The Duchess of Malfi*, ed. John Russell Brown (London: Methuen, 1964), p. liv.
5. Clifford Leech, "An Addendum on Webster's Duchess," *Philological Quarterly*, 37 (1958), p. 255.
6. With the wooing scene, Webster has introduced a new element, one that cannot be fully accounted for by the play's preceding discussions but which challenges the court's idea of love, marriage, and human relatedness. No colossus "past the size of dreaming," the Duchess displays a different, wholly domestic and apolitical heroism. In her fine Mermaid Critical Commentaries essay, "Webster's Realism, or, 'A Cunning Piece Wrought Perspective,'" Inga-Stina Ewbank notes that "the relationship of Antonio and the Duchess . . . comes to form a strain of simplicity, of almost bourgeois sentiment, which establishes a viewpoint and a value" (p. 173) in Brian Morris (ed.), *John Webster* [London: Ernest Benn, 1970] pp. 159–98 (p. 173).

example of Antonio's ideal; yet any political consequences of her decision are to her accidental. She should not be—and does not strive to be—a ruler at all. The Duchess does not so much misuse or evade public responsibility as seem unaware of its claims. The political world that reappears throughout the play—in satiric "court" scenes, in the Cardinal's military investiture, in conversations about war and horsemanship and impatience with inaction—is in her eyes "irrelevant." The Duchess continually closes out the great world to which she inextricably belongs and instead attempts to establish a private sphere, a world of intimate relationships and family concerns to which she can devote herself as private individual. Royally cavalier about deception, about her general responsibilities, about her marriage's social or political ramifications, the Duchess denies the world act 1 portrays; yet that rejection paradoxically takes the form of an affirmation we can only applaud. Her private, domestic, and comic drama is one of courtship and marriage. By creating two of the most powerfully affecting scenes of domestic happiness in theater history, Webster lets us, too, withdraw momentarily from the public arena where time is history and individual happiness irrelevant.

In this play the two worlds, like the scenes that represent them, are in opposition. We do not see the Duchess, or Antonio, try to bridge this gap; indeed, their attempt to divorce public and private, day and night, ensures their helpless vulnerability in a world inimical to romantic comedy's assumptions or goals. By endowing these lovers with the sympathetic wit, charm, and harmonious accord appropriate to their purpose (and denied Bracciano and Vittoria), Webster can use his generic contrasts to dramatize the desirability of the Duchess's choice as well as the impossibility of its attainment, both her culpability in political and social terms and the unimportance of any terms that inhibit reestablishing fundamentally valuable human relationships.

In sexual and maternal love the Duchess alone is fruitful; society is preserved in her, though its order may be questioned. Paradoxically, the political world seems to support, even necessitate, the cynical watchfulness of Bosola's self-protective "realism." The Duchess's chamber, the lovers' new world, is circumscribed, penetrated, and destroyed by the great world it cannot exclude. Yet enclosing comedy within tragedy allows Webster more than the sentimental poignance of blasted happiness. Through the Duchess's choice, and her refusal to repudiate comedy's goals when called to tragedy's accounting, Webster suggests what is perhaps a blind, but certainly ineradicable human drive toward relatedness, union, and love's self-effacement. Although Bosola and Antonio are in many ways elaborately paralleled throughout *The Duchess of Malfi*, in generic terms it is Bosola and the Duchess who prove to be the play's real antagonists, the poles of its dialectic.

In acts 2 and 3 Webster pulls us back from the wooing scene's narrow and sympathetic concentration on the lovers; we see their intimate harmony only once more, in the hair-brushing scene whose domestic security and easy banter collapse when Ferdinand usurps both Antonio's place and the first husband's right to vengeance. * * * Webster * * * holds us back from the lovers and unsettles his romantic focus. The lovers' discovery and flight is crosscut with scenes of satiric comedy, abrupt shifts from Malfi to Rome, and in general a return to the panoramic view that places all characters at the critical distance enforced by Bosola's reductionist observations. Seen from outside their affection's "circumference," the lovers themselves shrink to the surrounding court's common humanity. Preoccupied with ugly physical details, Bosola's jaundiced eye sees an unattractively pregnant woman: the Duchess "is sick o' days, she pukes . . . she wanes i' th' cheek, and waxes fat i' th' flank" (II.i. 64–66). Bosola's coarse devaluation is answered by no Petrarchan hyperbole; irritable, short-winded, greedily hungry, the Duchess herself contributes to his reductive picture. Bosola's conclusion—that such "tetchiness" and "vulturous eating" are "apparent signs of breeding"—is accurate in point of fact, and the Duchess's behavior corroborates his bold assertion that the "souls of princes" are not "brought forth by some more weighty cause than those of meaner persons," since the "like passions sway them" (II.i.101–104).

As secret lovers, Antonio and the Duchess often seem comically inept, and their plight is distanced by comic interludes as well as by demeaning commentary. Dramatic tension encouraged by the Duchess's dangerously sudden labor dissipates in comic repartee with the Old Lady and uproarious laughter over the Switzer's lethal codpiece. So too later, the dramatic confrontation in Ancona is deferred for a reprise of I.i, with its pithy "characters" and "irrelevant" witty banter about Malatesta's Parolles-like soldiery and the coming war. The potentially melodramatic banishment is distanced by dumbshow and superseded by the Cardinal's spectacular investiture and the pilgrims' judiciously "objective" commentary.

Under pressure, Antonio is "lost in amazement" and bumbling. The "politic safe conveyance" for the midwife proves ineffectual; he rashly insults Bosola, then drops the nativity figure at the intelligencer's feet. Despite Ferdinand's presence in Malfi and her people's rumored censure, the Duchess eagerly believes that asserting her submission ("When I choose / A husband, I will marry for your honour") and hypocritically appealing to Ferdinand's trust and "fix'd love" have "purg'd" all "deadly air" (III.i.42–43, 52, 56). Naïvely self-confident, she insists on having her man and her position too;

even after Ferdinand's nighttime visitation she seems to think preserving her "weak safety" depends on only one more "enginous" ruse, the *magnanima menzogna* that will "shield our honours" (III. ii.176–181). During Antonio's "trial," as J. R. Brown notes, both lovers delight in playing publicly the game of ambiguous meanings.[7] Like comedy's self-deluding fools, the Duchess follows Bosola's advice because he tells her what she wants to hear.

That the lovers should lack Bosola's finesse in courtly intrigue is neither surprising nor blameworthy, but lack of skill in deception does not guarantee the deceivers' innocence. Antonio's self-accusation carries weight: "The great are like the base—nay, they are the same— / When they seek shameful ways, to avoid shame" (II.iii.51–52). In pursuing all her desires the Duchess is like her brothers: she wants both Antonio and her duchy, while the Cardinal maintains his public position and secretly enjoys Julia on the side. In wanting the game's prizes, the Duchess has accepted its rules; the easy lies, the "shifts" and paltering, demean the lovers even while naïve ineptitude makes them comic dupes of Bosola's more skillful maneuvering.

Yet though the lovers suffer personal as well as social exposure in acts 2 and 3, they do not, like Bussy or Antony, claim a superhuman stature in the face of demeaning reality. Indeed, the lovers see themselves in no more heroic terms than Bosola's. Antonio remarks to Delio that his wife is "an excellent / Feeder of pedigrees" (III.i.5–6); content with being a nighttime lord of misrule, Antonio's first concern, both before the marriage and after its discovery, is for safety.[8] The Duchess asserts to Ferdinand her ability to live or die like a prince, yet hers is no heroic passion. Her true context is the private and domestic sphere of wifely devotion. Bosola's scathing analysis of court loyalty and hyperbolic praise of her steward give the Duchess her chance to acknowledge Antonio with honor, and she cannot resist a display of connubial pride: "This good one that you speak of, is my husband" (III.ii.275). In proving her claim to Antonio's virtues she reveals the true locus of her concern; the boast to "have had three children by him" suggests the standards by which she

---

7. Brown, Revels introduction, p. xlvi. Ferdinand shares his sister's sense of humor: he mocks her *magnanima menzogna* in the "politic equivocations" of his letter requesting Antonio's return, and again later when he offers her the dead-man's hand (IV.i).

8. Critical views of Antonio run the full spectrum. In "Some Contemporary Ideas" Wadsworth tries at length to prove that, barring his social standing, Antonio was fashioned as both the ideal Renaissance husband and an exemplar of "patience and fortitude" (p. 405); Ornstein, however, finds Antonio completely overshadowed by the woman who wooed him, an almost faceless man whose "contemptible death is appropriate," as he says in *The Moral Vision of Jacobean Tragedy* (Madison: University of Wisconsin Press, 1960), p. 144. Analyzing the play's relation to its sources in *Sources, Thomas, Characters*, Boklund perhaps wisely splits the difference: he sees Antonio as a carefully presented average man, sympathetic though a "hesitant falterer" far less heroic or ambitious than the sources' major-domo (p. 93).

defines her own value. She naïvely expects Bosola to honor the trust she asks for; she allows her new friend's "direction" to lead her "by the hand" (III.ii.313).

Bosola's sarcastic descant on the idea of marriage as a suitable reward for service makes the proud wife before him rather ridiculous, in her role as duchess. Yet Bosola's ridicule also demonstrates how much her acts exceed his understanding, how inadequate the context in which he places them. Her gullibility, too, sets her apart. She did not marry Antonio to reward his long service to virtue; that is merely one of the wooing scene's private jokes. Rather, his virtues helped win her love, and love is outside the world of service and payment which Bosola's speech portrays. In this sense, it is Bosola who does not understand. To him the central meaning of her life, which she has just revealed in wifely pride, is marketable information for which he is "certain to be rais'd" (III.ii.330).

Both here and after the banishment Bosola speaks for as well as serves the antagonistic outer world that denies the Duchess not only her life but the values by which she has lived. A world of covert, variously illicit amours—from Castruccio and the Old Lady to Julia's several relations with the Cardinal, Delio, and Bosola—it can never rise above the level of brief, embittered, and commercialized sexual encounters. Sexually as well as politically, from the Arragonian brethren to the petty courtiers whose youthful sins are "the very patrimony of the physician," self-seeking egoists exploit each other's needs. The inconstancy attributed to women is shared by their lovers: when the Cardinal swears to "love . . . wisely" he means "jealously," self-protectively; Julia has become his "ling'ring consumption" before she seeks sexual excitement elsewhere (II.iv.24–25; V.ii.228). Bosola's complete detachment is only an extreme version of the cynical defensiveness that distinguishes other relationships: if we are essentially coterminous with our animal bodies, we can seek momentary physical pleasures or, like Bosola in his "meditation," strip human beings of their material masks to discover nothing "in this outward form . . . to be belov'd" (II.i.45–46).

The only extreme, "heroic" passion is Ferdinand's, but it is merely the distorted complement of his brother's cool rationalism. In both brothers, self-interest dominates their personalities' narrow concentration: they seem the unintegrated halves of one solipsistic being. The Cardinal exhibits in perverse, Machiavellian form his sister's intelligence—the wit and judgment with which she prizes Antonio's virtue and directs the wooing scene, the calm self-acceptance with which she faces adversity. While the Cardinal remains cool and noncommittal until scene 5 of the fifth act, Ferdinand shares and debases his sister's passionate physicality and tenacious emotional commitments; impetuous, unreflective egoism loves and fears the blood they share. Identifying himself with his sister as well as with the husband's role he cannot quite usurp, Ferdinand can in her punish himself, and by fixing her in "a general eclipse," quench his own "wild-fire."[9]

Ferdinand's prurient sexual fantasies have as little to do with the Duchess's private world—those tender but prosaic scenes of companionable raillery between husband, wife, and friend—as the Cardinal's cold generalities about women and marriage or Bosola's certainty that ugly (albeit "natural") sexuality drives her to employ her steward as pander. The Duchess's self-appointed judges neither pity nor understand her. They cannot conceive of a love which also prompts rational choice, an affection embracing but also exceeding sexual desire. Her particular violations of their code lie beyond their categories. Explaining Malfi's response to Delio, Antonio finds the same misinterpretations there: the common people think her a strumpet while "graver heads" believe Antonio an unscrupulous opportunist, but "for other obligation / Of love, or marriage . . . they never dream of" (III.i.35–37).

The demeaning acts, the foolish choices that deny the lovers' heroic stature and demonstrate their practical naïveté, also set them apart from the world they inhabit. The hair-brushing scene gains power from its precariousness, suspended as it is on the thread of Ferdinand's anticipated entrance, but also from its apparent impossibility when so many deny even the emotions that created it. Challenged by her brother, the Duchess cannot explain, let alone persuade. She places her case in a generalized human context, urging the marriage's naturalness. Disingenuously, she suppresses the obvious fact that, for a woman in her position, this particular marriage has indeed "gone about" to create new "custom"; she equivocates about her reputation's safety. Yet Ferdinand's hysterical revulsion overshadows her evasiveness. Like Bosola and the Cardinal, Ferdinand sees only one meaning in "love" and "marriage": his passion focuses on a sexual union which must be punished. As Ferdinand's fable makes clear, his notion of love has nothing to do with the court; love exists, if at all, only in a make-believe pastoral world ("'mongst unambitious shepherds, / Where dowries were not talk'd

---

9. The violent sexuality and disproportion of Ferdinand's outrage, combined with the voyeuristic description of her probable sexual partners and confused desire to prolong his horror, all suggest that incestuous love motivates his hysteria. Such possibilities are discussed at some length by Clifford Leech in *Webster: "The Duchess of Malfi"* (London: Edward Arnold, 1963) and in *John Webster: A Critical Study* (London: Hogarth Press, 1951). McD. Emslie also explores the suggestion of incest in "Motives of Malfi," *Essays in Criticism,* 9 (1959), pp. 391–405; see especially p. 395 for Emslie's discussion of the line hinting at Ferdinand's perverse desire for the continuation of his sister's affair. Then, too, as Brown notes in his edition, "a hidden motivation for Ferdinand is in keeping with the general mode of characterization" (p. lii).

of") or between impoverished, equally unambitious cousins "that had nothing left / By their dead parents" (III.ii.127–130). Ferdinand cannot see her truth, for the Duchess has found love in the courts of princes. Yet in pursuing desire beyond society's prescribed bounds she has ignored his truth, for Ferdinand's instances suggest the only genres in which such love may be safe.[1]

Ferdinand flees, refusing to meet again his sister's eyes; the Cardinal directs from Rome the revenge to which he vowed to sacrifice his sister's wedding ring. Bosola is their perfect agent and representative. Personally bound to Ferdinand yet sharing the Cardinal's cool detachment, Antonio's social equal and philosophical opposite, Bosola usurps brothers' and husband's place alike. That he does not share Ferdinand's punitive obsession, the goal of despair or madness, is clear, though he paradoxically carries out his master's orders with both gusto and reluctance. In his perverse way, Bosola woos the Duchess while tormenting her. She alone challenges the carefully constructed philosophy by which Bosola has accommodated his bothersome conscience to the world's demands. As a man who has intentionally, though not wholly successfully, chosen to "look no higher than I can reach" (II.i.89), Bosola's bitter humor attempts to reduce all others to his own level of self-disgust. He pushes, prods, taunts the Duchess, trying to force the acquiescence that would justify his life. Yet the compulsive honesty evident in Bosola's earlier self-laceration forces him to accept whatever she can, under pressure, become. Having seen through the trappings of metaphoric as well as real cosmetics and found nothing worthy of love, he grasps an opportunity to search the inward man. Unlike Ferdinand, Bosola is not impelled to destroy whatever resists his definitions; he carries on Ferdinand's "persecution" in the impersonal, detached mode of his earlier meditation.

From the Duchess's arrest in act 3 until her death at Bosola's hands, Webster focuses his play on their confrontation. Bosola's discussions with Ferdinand, the waxwork display, and the dance of the madmen serve not as misguided fragmentation but rather as punctuation to that central dialogue toward which Webster has moved us. The Duchess's "play" is over. Her romantic comedy is shattered by the violent egotism that, unleashed, issues both in Ferdinand's insane aspiration to godhead (for he wishes not merely to usurp divine punishment but to create in the limited world of her prison

---

1. Ferdinand's examples suggest, indeed, the kind of play to which the Duchess is temperamentally suited. In one sense at least she is, as Ornstein says in *The Moral Vision of Jacobean Tragedy*, "a heroine of Shakespearean romantic comedy, graceful, witty, wanton and innocent at the same time, who woos and wins her husband in spite of himself": this characterization, he maintains, also suggests Webster's boldness as a tragedian (p. 147).

his fantasy's mad sister and dead family) and, ultimately, in the mad-men's complete solipsistic alienation.[2] Stripped not only of her title but also of her drama and its sustaining props, she is forced to dis-cover how the values she lived by may sustain her in another drama, defined by Ferdinand's "properties," in which she must "play a part . . . 'gainst my will" (IV.i.85). To Antonio she admits both guilt and doubt, but she does not fully join his retreat to conventional, aphoristic acceptance of the world's injustice as God's inscrutable wisdom. Although Bosola presses her admission of pragmatic folly, she cannot be forced to admit worthlessness in Antonio or error in marrying him; she refuses Bosola's or her brothers' right to judge or punish her.[3]

The Duchess does not simply defy Bosola. She challenges the assumptions on which he bases his taunts, forces on him the dilemma of knowledge confounding knowledge. To Bosola's certainty she returns a question: "I prithee, who is greatest? can you tell?" (III.v.123). As her parable of the dogfish and salmon points out, our humanity binds us to frailty, yet man's imperfection implies for her no cynic's assurance. Nor does she maintain that Antonio's merit raised him in any worldly, social sense, only that "man is most happy when's own actions / Be arguments and examples of his virtue" (III.v.120–121). In the pragmatic terms by which Bosola has lived, a "barren, beggarly virtue" is meaningless, but he is to learn that there is fulfillment in "so good a quarrel," even if the price of that satis-faction is death.

Majestic in adversity, the Duchess demonstrates that disdain of the world which Bosola affects; by incarnating one side of his per-sonality, she offers him a different model from Ferdinand and the greatness he represents. To some extent, she has shared Bosola's ambivalent attitude toward the world's prizes: she wanted her duchy, yet also denied its claim to define or constrict her identity. Waxwork tortures and the threat of death bring her to see that the two posi-tions she valued—duchess and wife—are incompatible and that to only one of them is she ultimately, mortally, committed. The pilgrims

2. Many critics find the madmen an apt symbol of Webster's fragmented world and a pro-leptic introduction to the chaos of act 5. For an interpretation of the madmen's masque as Ferdinand's delayed and demonic celebration of his sister's marriage, see Inga-Stina Ekeblad's "The 'Impure Art' of John Webster."
3. There is some doubt about the guilt for which the Duchess feels she needs "heaven's scorge-stick" (III.v.81). She may refer to that life of constant deception to which efforts at preserving position and honor led her; she certainly knows that Bosola and her bro-thers merely "counterfeit heaven's thunder" (III.v.100). M. C. Bradbrook suggests that it "is through the awakening of responsibility that the Duchess develops into a tragic fig-ure." This acceptance of her fate as a necessary "scorge-stick" marks an important change in her response, a coming to terms with her deeds: "She never acknowledges that her brothers have the right to judge her; but she does acknowledge that she is in need of a corrected judgment." See *Themes and Conventions of Elizabethan Tragedy* (1935; rpt. Cambridge: Cambridge University Press, 1960), pp. 203–204.

acknowledged the injustice of her persecution, yet accepted it as the way of the world. The Duchess will not, cannot accept; her greatest achievement lies in discovering the strength to find life unworthy of such a price. With her husband and children "dead," life has no significance, and she begs death's mercy. Bosola cannot yet either understand or believe such a discovery, for he has made life itself, at any price, his highest value. Torn between pity and mockery, he suggests that Ferdinand has appeased his wrath: in Bosola's eyes her mourning is "vain sorrow," and she should be happy if her family's deaths can purchase her own life.

* * * Bosola provides the mocking antiphonal response to the Duchess's cosmic imprecations. If "the stars shine still" upon human misery as well as happiness, then the curses' invocation of heavenly absolutes is a comical and futile self-delusion. Yet Bosola's mocking ironies fail to protect him. The woman he cannot understand begins to mine the bases of his self-definition; she moves him to inexplicable pity. The man he thought he understood moves beyond explicable motivation's reasonable bounds; Ferdinand refuses "comfort" because he demands despair as well as death. Bosola's world as well as the Duchess's is shaken. Perhaps for Bosola, too, the madmen's "noise and folly" represent the real, while silence or logical discussion would be false rationalization, ultimately so out of touch with mad reality as to induce true insanity.

Like his master unable to bear the Duchess's direct gaze, Bosola doffs "mine own shape" for the old man's disguise.[4] The only "comfort" he can now bring is the persuasiveness of his own contempt for humanity. As the choric voice of the *contemptus mundi* tradition, Bosola extends the satiric reductionism of his earlier "meditation": the body's grossness now hedges and infects the soul, and a heaven that reflects merely the "small compass of our prison" renders meaningless both earthly acts and religious certainty. The pressure of such nihilism forces the Duchess beyond resignation to necessity's "sad misery"; against its terms she must define herself and her life. Bosola insists on her common humanity as well as her mortality; he has never granted rank any automatic moral stature. The Duchess's famous reaffirmation of her social identity—"I am

---

4. Bosola's shape-changing may lack the trickster's gusto and playfully self-conscious theatricality, but it is just as necessary to his sense of identity. Bosola's various roles—from Paduan scholar and later intelligencer to the fourth act's formal disguise as old man/tombmaker/bellman—are all self-protective attempts to live with his divided nature. In *The Art of John Webster* (Oxford: Clarendon Press, 1972), Ralph Berry calls "the most important characteristic of Bosola . . . his behaviour [as] a series of role-playing changes," for it is the result of having chosen "a course of action that is ultimately opposed to his inner values" (p. 139). See also C. G. Thayer, "The Ambiguity of Bosola," *Studies in Philology*, 54 (1957), pp. 162–171, and Irving Ribner, *Jacobean Tragedy: The Quest for Moral Order* (London: Methuen, 1962), esp. pp. 110–115.

Duchess of Malfi still"—is met with the impassivity of the death Bosola represents. He reiterates her title's significance: examined closely, such worldly glory signifies broken sleeps and offers "neither heat, nor light" (IV.ii.145).[5] * * * In Bosola's role as bellman the maxim is straightforward moral counsel; in his ambivalent position as follower and servant of greatness, even while he criticizes it, the advice calls attention to his own self-delusions as well as those of the Duchess. Ironically, by violating her title to assume that maternal identity so strongly emphasized throughout the play, the Duchess has created life, both "heat" and "light." Her self-discovery holds a proleptic significance for Bosola; it will shatter the compromises by which he now straddles two roles.

The Duchess's acceptance of Bosola's new "comfort" is swift, complete, and far greater than Bosola himself can grasp. Adjusting to the waxwork "dead" had already loosened her hold on life; incarceration and torture both challenged and clarified the significance of her worldly identity as duchess. Bosola's "plainness" shows her the emptiness of titles when men no longer choose to recognize them, or when confronted with death. With extraordinary poise she jokes with Bosola about the time's fashion in tombmaking, even about the manner of her own death. Instead of Vittoria's and Flamineo's sarcastic defiance, we are returned to the light banter of earlier domestic scenes.

The Duchess both accepts Bosola into her "last presence-chamber" and marks the gulf that separates them. Bosola has prostituted himself to a world that disdains the ideals by which he judges both it and himself. His death remains "a hideous storm of terror," just as his life was "a general mist of error." To his surprise, the Duchess not only receives death "now I am well awake, / Best gift is they can give, or I can take" (IV.ii.224–225), but seems even eager for it. She holds to a reality beyond man's arbitrary redefinition, one in which significance does not lie at the mercy of the powerful. At times her defense is couched in terms of traditional absolutes, as when she reminds Ferdinand that he and (by implication) the Cardinal violate sacraments they cannot in fact abrogate. Yet the Duchess lacks Cornelia's unshakable faith: at least momentarily unsure of posthumous union or the "eternal Church," she, like Flamineo, wishes for "some two days' conference with the dead" to settle all doubts about

---

5. Discussing Webster's use of language, in "Webster's Realism," Ewbank notes that the Duchess's plain answers do not merely discredit Bosola's words. Both simplicity and complexity are necessary to the process of defining a truth or experience that exists, finally, beyond words: "She is both 'a box of worm-seed' and 'thy duchess,' both a grey-haired woman who cannot sleep and 'Duchess of Malfi still.' Each of them may see only, or mainly, one side of the dialectic, but we see the whole dramatic image" and the views become superimposed upon one another (p. 178).

this world's conduct (IV.ii.21–23). Mystery does not confound the Duchess, however. She chose to believe and act in a "knowledge" Flamineo rejected for lack of guarantees; her assertions are the more powerful for her only intermittent participation in Cornelia's certainties. Though without either "path" or "friendly clew," she has entered that uncharted land of the values men make for themselves, and the unknown world of love has given her life a meaning sufficient to withstand her torturers' jerry-built reign of terror. Having known that good, she can brush aside the fear of death which "should," according to Bosola, afflict her. Hers has not been the weeping from birth or mist of error of his dirge. She draws strength from what her persecutors cannot understand; in her final composure she transforms former curses into forgiveness of her executioners, her wish for general chaos into concern for Cariola and for her children.[6] In the face of death she transcends self-absorption and despair.

Regal poise gives way to impatience with their amazed procrastination: "any way, for heaven-sake, / So I were out of your whispering" (IV.ii.222–223). She remains Duchess of Malfi "still"; while suffering and loss have brought some clarification of her world, her relation to it, and a sense of her own hierarchy of values, she remains that curious and confusing mixture of womanliness and nobility, self-sacrificing dedication and willfulness. Webster seems self-consciously to play his Duchess's death against Cleopatra's. The loves for which they die differ markedly, but the Duchess's purely domestic and maternal concern is quite clearly, however unusually, its own value and not merely a watered-down, misunderstood version of Cleopatra's heroic aspiration. Still, with perhaps Shakespearean inspiration, Webster has managed in terms of his own play's values to fuse in one final paradoxical heroism the "spirit of greatness" with the apparently incompatible, willful, and earthbound "spirit of woman." In the end, the very behavior that had in earlier acts diminished the heroine's stature both fuels and lends additional power to her final self-transcendence. The Duchess commands her own executioners, even summons "violent death" as if it should do her bidding; yet she assumes in the same moment a posture of true humility that denies the arrogance of "princes' palaces." As she goes toward heaven upon her knees she has yet a moment to spare for one last unholy message to her brothers.

6. Ornstein rightly questions the prevalent idea of the Duchess as a symbol of solitary integrity whose famous cry defeats the chaos that surrounds and threatens her. In *The Moral Vision of Jacobean Tragedy* he maintains that the "Duchess' strength is not a lonely existential awareness of self but a remembrance of love, expressed in her parting words to Cariola and in her answers to Bosola. . . . Webster's other heroes and heroines die obsessed with their sins and follies, projecting their individual experiences as the pattern of man's fate. The Duchess is the only one to move out of self" (p. 148).

Webster has taken some care to avoid the univocal pathos of martyred innocence. While the spectacular trappings of this ritualized murder encourage a stereotypical response, the Duchess herself prevents such simplification. She retains her complex, earthy individuality to the end, and the comedy of Cariola's futile evasions returns us promptly to the world of scrambling vitality to which the Duchess too belonged. The play does not turn elegiac, nor does it affect domestic tragedy's pat conversions or the saintly exaltation of *Sophonisba* or *The Second Maiden's Tragedy*.

Ferdinand may be struck by guilt, but Bosola quickly drops his appeal to "pity" when he sees his master falling into "ingratitude." An element of bizarre comedy hedges the dispute waged over the dead woman's body, as master and servant try futilely to transfer their own responsibility and self-hatred. At base, it is a serious struggle to establish the terms in which Bosola's "service" should be interpreted, a test of the Duchess's effect on the worldly ethic she finally transcended. Although Ferdinand turns moralist, condemning Bosola's failure to be the "honest man" who, "bold in a good cause," would oppose his sword "between her innocence and my revenge" (IV.ii.274–278), the high moral tone is both hypocritical and laughably inappropriate. The two of them have helped create a world in which this ideal cannot exist, or exists only to be spurned in the way Ferdinand and the Cardinal rejected Antonio as "too honest for such business" as theirs (I.i.230). Bosola maintains that the issue is not one of right or wrong, by which both men stand condemned, but of payment for services loyally rendered. The wheel has come full circle, and Bosola is again asking reward for murder; but he now seeks more than physical self-preservation. Bosola's and Ferdinand's opposed voices spring from the same desperate solipsism. Seeking moral justification, each refuses to be defined as this deed's creature; each uses his general argument to dissociate himself from the body they both deny.

The "play" has broken down again. The "villain's part" with which Bosola protected himself explodes when Ferdinand repudiates his "service" and identifies actor and man. * * * Instead of the playwright's delight, the intriguer's pride in his ingenious "night-piece," Ferdinand's "revenge" dissolves in guilt and madness. Webster's generic juggling, even fragmentation, reflects not loss of control but increased mastery of his drama's components; the more flexible use of revenge conventions aptly serves this play's development. In *The Duchess of Malfi* the repeated collapse of individual dramas seems to suggest the futility of human hopes and plans more emphatically than *The White Devil*'s untroubled villains and wholly successful revenge play. Yet in the *Duchess* failure depends only partly on chance, though that demigod presides over a good deal of the fifth act's comedy of errors. While the clash of powerful wills threatens any individual's external ordering, the intriguer's plans now founder equally on his own unacknowledged complexity. Even those who reject, ignore, or exploit conventional religious sanctions exhibit an innate moral sense that conflicts with, even undermines, their proclaimed self-sufficiency.

The Duchess's death forces upon her tormentors what her living, misunderstood presence could never accomplish. Each finally confronts his own nature's contradictory impulses. Ferdinand escapes his deeds in madness, but even insanity cannot free him from his suppressed conscience, the self who was his sister's twin and his "dearest friend"; he tries in comic earnest to kill the shadow-self that dazzled him in the dead woman's eyes. The Cardinal is briefly troubled by his pond's reflection, a "thing arm'd with a rake" that mirrors his inner wasteland, yet in his nearly complete emotional ennui he can lay by as "tedious" his conscience's awkward promptings. It is in Bosola, where strong contradictions have run close to the surface throughout, that the Duchess's murder creates as well as destroys. Yet even here her effect is not immediate; it comes only after Ferdinand has demolished the bases for Bosola's service to him and bondage to the world. The would-be Machiavel's credo—that by seeing into society's dark heart he can use its evil for his own worldly gain—is finally exposed as the foolish obverse of idealism, for he has naïvely believed that if goodness is scorned then loyal service to evil will be rewarded. Arguments from both personal loyalty and economic necessity have earned him nothing. Clearly distraught at losing his devious and delicate adjustment to what he had thought were life's realities, Bosola faces an appalling freedom. Without a justifying patron, Bosola is left with Ferdinand's demand that he accept the very moral responsibility he has carefully argued he does not possess.

Violent disillusionment cannot itself take even the conscience-ridden Bosola much farther than Flamineo's despair, and the ex post facto resolution that "were this to do again" he would not sell his "peace of conscience" cannot solve his present predicament. The Duchess's momentary return exacerbates his sense of spiritual as well as physical loss, but also offers him a way to redefine his empty life. Needing both moral support and personal commitment, Bosola fastens upon the reviving Duchess as his key to atonement and salvation. In shockingly Petrarchan terms he woos the woman he murdered. Belatedly, he grasps her significance and seeks his own "heaven" in love and dedication. He tries to transfer the "love" he bore Ferdinand to one who might help him realize his "better nature." His own *magnanima menzogna,* assuring her that Antonio is not only alive but reconciled to her brothers, seems part unconscious tribute to the love that absorbs even her last flicker of life, part pity and the "comfort" Ferdinand had refused, and part a selfish desire to revive her as his new guide by giving her reasons to live. * * * Bosola explicitly admits that he needs a Beatrice to "take me up to mercy" (IV.ii.349), and this admission also frees him to acknowledge the naturalness of humane feelings, the "penitent fountains" that bind people. The Duchess dies, but Bosola has found in her a significance around which his despair of advancement, frustrated good intentions, pity, and guilty conscience can organize the ambiguous "somewhat" worthy his "dejection."

As many commentators have noted, act 5 pursues the consequences of the Duchess's murder. It could also with some justice be called Bosola's Revenge, for this murderer has assumed the part usually reserved for relative or lover. Yet the act is hardly distinguished by tight construction * * * we are returned to an "objective," panoramic view, crowded with characters pursuing separate goals. Webster only gradually directs his characters, and our attention, towards the denouement's final "presence-chamber" in the Cardinal's palace. The irony now lies not in the revengers' ultimate control but in Webster's, and in the cool detachment with which he reveals their inability to command even their wills, much less events. The characters, like the scenes, seem to move aimlessly, paradoxically determined to shape what safety they can yet also hesitating, waiting for others' direction or chance's resolution.

Charges of poor dramatic construction, of anticlimactic thinness, fall wide of the mark if based solely on the Duchess's "premature" death. Webster's theatrical sense may have faltered; certainly the act lacks a focus, a hero. Yet this choice is purposeful, not inherent in the material. Webster denies Bosola and Antonio the prominence or development by which either might dominate act 5 as a male Cleopatra or determined revenger. Moreover, although the Duchess in some sense stands behind the events of the act and the assemblage of corpses with which it closes, hers is not the revenging spirit of Shakespeare's Julius Caesar, omnipotent even in death. Act 5 demonstrates all too clearly how little she has affected the quality of life in this play's world, for the lesson of her wilderness voyage was a private one, and her final affirmation was quite literally incarcerated in act 4. Those who presided at her death were fundamentally affected, yet one finds refuge in madness and the other is more confused than transformed by what he has learned. The rest of their world was insulted against the impact of her imprisonment. The Duchess dies, as she had tried to live, in private.

* * *

Part of the fifth act's impression of unfocused triviality comes, of course, from its juxtaposition with the unmediated complexity and power of the Duchess's death and Bosola's personal crisis. Comic, even farcical intrusions further block our sympathies;[7] they also help characterize the individuals who remain. Into a world ignorant of the Duchess's murder comes mad Ferdinand, himself now one of the obsessed caricatures of humanity with which he tortured his sister. Ferdinand's confused babble and the comic exchange with the buffoon doctor which breaks down in fisticuffs form an interlude of low comedy. Our response is double: from our distanced, privileged position Ferdinand's ravings are also powerful, grotesque reminders of what he has done. We know the deed he cannot name and refuses to confess; we see the grisly connections between a dead man's leg and the Duchess's final message that her brothers might now "feed in quiet"; we feel the utter inappropriateness of using salamander skin to cure the "cruel sore eyes" that dazzled at the sight of a murdered sister.

Our knowledge keeps us critically distant from the stage maneuverings, and Webster continues to enforce this rapid oscillation between comic and grotesque. Ferdinand's humorous violence with the pompous doctor is succeeded briefly by the Cardinal's evasions and his order for Antonio's murder, then by Julia's misguided travesty of romantic comedy. It is, of course, her unconscious imitation of the Duchess's wooing, and Webster can use its superficial resemblances to define more firmly the Duchess's real singularity. More important, the comic associations of love-at-first-sight, coupled with a woman's bold and witty wooing, become shockingly misplaced both in the context of death and madness and when the principals are not young lovers but murderers and adulterers. Light banter plays effectively against the situation's realities and lends power to the "romance's" concluding triple betrayal.

Julia here functions as more than the Duchess's foil. Like the comic doctor, she represents a self-deluded, pleasure-seeking world that knows nothing of the Duchess's life or death and remains unconcerned with the nature of the power which provides its sustenance. Frivolously pursuing their own immediate goals, these people are insulated against the horror that surrounds and directs them. Misfortune may be accepted "philosophically," as it was by the pilgrims at Loretto, but most escape knowledge of their world's real inhumanity or learn it only when they suddenly become caught in the struggle, like the Duchess, Julia, and the nameless servant dispatched by Bosola. Julia dies a pawn in a game she did not even know

---

7. In "*The Duchess of Malfi*: Act V and Genre," *Genre*, 3 (1970), pp. 351–363, Normand Berlin usefully discusses Webster's comic distancing. See also Brown's introduction to his Revels Plays edition, and Lois Potter, "Realism Versus Nightmare: Problems of Staging *The Duchess of Malfi*," in *The Triple Bond: Plays, Mainly Shakespearean, in Performance*, ed. Joseph G. Price (University Park: Pennsylvania State University Press, 1975), pp. 170–189.

existed; she is both pathetically innocent and also part of the commonplace world that seeks, in public and private realms, its own petty desires. Dying, she finds her life meaningless, yet like her betters she cannot escape the void within. * * *

In this lethal but trivial world the Cardinal plays a chief role. His cool, unemotional detachment is more terrifying than Ferdinand's impassioned raving. Almost inhuman, he requires neither the emotional satisfactions of affection nor the intellectual consolation of rationalizing his deeds. If Ferdinand claims too many motives, the Cardinal offers nothing beyond his agreement that the Duchess taints their noble Arragonian blood. Yet the shedding of his "blood" seems not to touch him. * * * Indeed, the narrow self-absorption marking his lost humanity now also ensures his comic downfall. Unable to see beyond the prison of his own nature, he becomes the inflexible victim of his own craft. Himself indifferent to the Duchess's murder, he assumes he can still employ the usual politic lies, the usual rearrangement of others to further his own dark ends. Offering the same old methods and expecting the same results, he promises Bosola that for one more "thing" in service he will "make you what you would be" (v.ii.115–117). When Bosola discovers him to be a "fellow murderer," the Cardinal still expects proffered fortune and honors to ensure his tool's loyalty. The smug certainty of psychological penetration and control no longer adequately corresponds to reality. Others now resist their place in the Cardinal's drama. Bosola has learned the practical lesson that suing to fortune is "the fool's pilgrimage." He can withstand the fearless image of the man who "bears up in blood" both because he guesses the Cardinal's real intentions—to hide his murderer's identity "i' th' graves / Of those were actors in 't" (v.ii.300–301)—and because the Duchess's very different image still haunts him.

The Cardinal's misprision is given comic scope: the arch-Machiavel churchman becomes the ridiculous and ineffectual plotter of farce, hoist with his own petard. The carefully, even comically elaborated instructions to his courtiers set up a practical joke on the world which kills him; we watch as his almost compulsive plotting weaves the web of destruction intended for others ever more closely about his own person. If earlier commentary portrayed him as a center of evil and corruption, act 5 defines him as a fool. In this new perspective we see him deceived by his own cynical reductionism, confident that his "tedious" conscience is his only worry since men will always act according to a few basic, manipulable emotions. Though the Cardinal begs for life, he dies under the merciless doctrine by which he ruled. The courtiers' mocking comments, highlighted by the good Pescara's single dissenting voice, only emphasize how completely the Cardinal's ethics guide his court.

* * * In *The Duchess of Malfi* the villains are not merely unsuccessful in practical terms, they are dismissed by Webster's dramatic treatment. As powerful princes they can wield destruction, but in act 5 Webster's comic reduction undercuts their initial dark persuasiveness. In other ways, too, the later play suggests that the Machiavels' worldly ethic inadequately encompasses their world. Although the courtiers who laugh at the Cardinal's pleas remind us of the false friends who spurned Antonio's "decay'd fortunes," they do not fully represent either Malfi or Milan. Malatesta and other courtiers whom one can look quite through are balanced by Delio and Pescara. In *The Duchess of Malfi* goodness is neither relegated to peripheral commentators nor qualified by its own trite and formulaic generalities. Fallible worldlings perhaps, though for that reason the more persuasive, good men exist at all social levels and even, like Pescara, function successfully in positions of power. Though Bosola may betray the Duchess's trust, Delio and Cariola remain faithful, and (departing from his source) Webster has some of the Duchess's servants follow her in adversity. If loyal service without reward is known to this world, so is unfeigned friendship. Delio offers Antonio support in all danger, for friends' lives "keep rank" together. Pescara refuses to bestow upon his friend "so main a piece of wrong" as Antonio's "ravish'd" lands; he chides Delio to ask only "noble things of me, and you shall find / I'll be a noble giver" (v.i.44–54). Some courtiers, or a Julia, seek to "fortify themselves" with others' ruin, but Pescara displays an innate sense of justice that the play suggests men may either ignore or follow.

Such departures from the prevailing opportunism, together with a surprising persistence of conscience in even the most hardened Machiavels, should produce a world of comparative sweetness and light, one in which exterminating this particular nest of vipers might indeed leave man free to pursue his "better nature." Optimism is not, however, the play's dominant impression, and over Delio's last hopeful words hangs the shadow of the fifth act's uncertain, self-perpetuating world. * * * One of the fifth act's most striking features is the very lack of inevitability in its deaths. Moreover, while some characters accept their fates as just retribution for sin, others can find no meaning beyond chance in the final events of their lives. It is just this bumbling quality of purposes mistook and accidental judgments that keeps us aloof from assertions of supernatural direction, whether benevolent or malign.

Here, where either Bosola or Antonio might offer to penetrate the play's mist, Webster enhances rather than resolves perplexity. The Duchess found—created—self-giving love, trust, and even humility in a world where nothing, even language, is what it seems and all absorb themselves in self-assertion and preferment. Yet the two men she most vitally and creatively affected can draw no positive significance from her life or death. Both are as burdened by their past actions and habits of mind as they are liberated from their attempts to satisfy the world's demands. Far from being the just revenger Bosola contemplates joining, Antonio desires only an end to indecision and his nebulous, fugitive state. If, as Delio says, the Echo can be shaped to the speaker's wishes, Antonio makes it reflect his own desire for release.[8] Once a virtuous follower of stronger wills, he now presumes on "necessity" to compel him toward some resolution; in seeking a "fate" he cannot fly, he refuses the good counsel of Delio and the Duchess-echo. Though he says he wants reconciliation with the Cardinal, we watch an unarmed man walk meekly to his death.

Disillusionment saps Antonio's life even before he offers it to the Cardinal's "worst of malice"; more concerned with maintaining his own slippery footing, Bosola can find no positive direction for his devotion, only uncertain gropings toward an ethic of revenge. Individually they move in and out of the last act's loosely structured scenes, contributing their own uncertainty to the final grisly comedy. Bosola, man of action and professional murderer, rashly kills Antonio instead of the Cardinal and thus ironically fulfills the Cardinal's orders to the letter, though Antonio is the man he would most have spared. This last "direful misprision" caps a life spent misprizing value, and Bosola's habitual inclination to deny responsibility for failure finds immediate rationalization: "We are merely the stars' tennis-balls, struck and banded / Which way please them" (v.iv.54–55). The virtuous Antonio, others' passive instrument throughout, even more strongly feels himself the victim of a malevolent universe. Two such apparently different lives have brought these courtiers to the same blank despair.[9] For Antonio, too, "in all our quest of greatness . . . we follow after bubbles, blown in th' air" (v.iv.64–66). Despite his share in the domestic felicity from which the Duchess drew such strength, Antonio finds in that relationship neither positive countervalues nor even an intuition of real possibilities for meaning. Knowledge of her death for him merely confirms life's essentially penitential nature; its pleasures seem only the "good hours / Of an ague" that humanity is well out of (v.iv.67–69).

8. Although the echo scene focuses on Antonio's melancholy, Cecil W. Davies may be correct in seeing that the "true marriage of Antonio and the Duchess is surely symbolized in the way in which his own words become her warning to him." See "The Structure of *The Duchess of Malfi*: An Approach," *English*, 12 (1958), p. 90.

9. In *The Moral Vision of Jacobean Tragedy* Ornstein forges rather too tight a negative similarity between Antonio and Bosola; they do, however, both seek "security" above all and, ironically, "neither Antonio's honesty nor Bosola's policy secure them against their fates." As he points out, "it is hardly an accident that they cause each other's death, for in life they were brothers under the skin, men who committed spiritual suicide before a sword-thrust ended their miserable lives" (p. 142).

Each character dies bound to the life he has lived. The Cardinal prevaricates to the courtiers with his last breath; then, perhaps with a glance toward that family honor he has at least nominally been protecting, he asks to "be laid by, and never thought of" (v.v.90). Bosola, too, is the deeds' creature. His intuition of another philosophy, another way of life, has altered but also confused him, and the Cardinal perceptively notes that his murderer's "great determination" is "mix'd with some fear" (v.v.9–10). Though he can "glory" at the Cardinal's cowardice and in killing Ferdinand claim his "revenge is perfect," Bosola remains self-concerned and discontented. He dies rationalizing his own part ("much 'gainst mine own good nature"), complaining still of having been "neglected" (v.v.86–87).[1] Reckless fear and hatred of the Cardinal cause him to murder Antonio, but that death is unintelligible to him—"in a mist: I know not how" (v.v.94). New and old knowledges shape an impossible conclusion: the world's "deep pit of darkness" daunts fearful men, who are "only like dead walls, or vaulted graves, / That ruin'd, yields no echo"; yet men should also live moral lives, not fearing to "suffer death, or shame for what is just" (v.v.97–104). He knows, really, only that he has failed to respond to such a complex challenge, that the "good quarrel" has come too late and that his "is another voyage" (v.v.105).

Bosola's double vision of both depravity and possibilities for hope, the tempering of his earlier fatalism with a final affirmation of free and responsible choice, confirms our own ambiguous response to act 5 and its reflection back upon the play. The whole of the final act, and especially the echo scene, attests to the fact that men are not merely "dead walls." The echo of the Duchess affects all the principal characters, though only of Bosola might it be said that the effect was beneficial and illuminating.

Yet even here Webster clearly demonstrates a tragic sense both of man's personal limitations and of his world's distortion of individual attempts to coerce it into humanly satisfying shape. The larger world's resistance qualifies both Bosola's exhortation to virtue and Delio's sanguine expectations for "this young, hopeful gentleman." Delio's concluding assertions are as wide of the play's mark as Antonio's opening disquisition on the ideal commonwealth. In both public and private spheres, the just or humane life proves elusive. Bosola must be denied any prospect of worldly advancement or reward and forced, like Vittoria and Flamineo, to abandon his strong covenant

---

1. In *Webster: "The Duchess of Malfi,"* Leech's analysis of the Bosola who pursues revenge in act 5 is acute: though sympathizing with Antonio and dedicated to a woman he hoped would save his soul, Bosola is seen "slaying an innocent servant without compunction, mistakenly killing Antonio, complaining always of being neglected. As an instrument of justice he is pitifully imperfect, while he had shown address as tormentor and executioner" (p. 27).

with the world before he will face himself and his life's meaning. Then, bitter and needing a new source of moral direction, he identifies himself with the avenging sword of justice—with the spirit, that is, of the Duchess's curses. But the Duchess's last word was "mercy," and the Cardinal echoes her just before Bosola stabs him. The Cardinal, of course, is selfishly begging for the life he has so thoroughly forfeited, but his cry reminds us of those larger questions of value which the play has raised. Is there a place for mercy or love in this world? Delio introduces Antonio's son and heir in the hope that there is, yet both Ferdinand's fable of Reputation and Antonio's dying injunction that his "son fly the courts of princes" must give us pause. The "young, hopeful gentleman" may inherit only sorrow.

Our perplexed response to both the young ruler and Delio's final speech, our suspicion that perhaps nature seldom if ever fashions men "lords of truth," is heightened by our inability to comprehend the workings of the nature that presides over the play's world. Each character lives according to his own understanding of the natural and cosmic order and, taken together, they interpret their experiences in as contradictory ways as the play's critics. Webster's ironic structure, especially in the last act, only increases our uncertainty. If a cosmic order exists, allowing us to seek our lives' direction in the stars, then men have not found the proper means of communication: the son and heir whose horoscope predicted most horrible and early death is one of the few characters to remain alive at the play's end. If there is justice above—and *The Duchess of Malfi* offers this claim more support than the earlier play—then it operates as enigmatically and inefficiently as Albany's heavenly "justicers" in *King Lear*. In this world, too, "one thief hangs another" and the widow who violated social codes, the innocent servant, and their murderers all receive the same sentence. Yet set against such suggestions of chance or, worse yet, an indefinable "mist," we feel Bosola's assumption of the revenger's role to be significant. His execution of punishment, however distorted, not only illustrates his belief in an order of justice but also, by realizing that belief in action, in a sense demonstrates its existence.

The play itself seems to indicate neither an optimistic nor a totally pessimistic author, only one acutely aware both of life's possibilities, given man's potential for exaltation as well as self-delusion, and its ultimate mystery. * * *

If man does, partly, fashion his world, then the Duchess is more important for the new, unprecedented world she sought to create than for her proud refusal to recant when threatened with death. Looking for romantic comedy she finds instead a tragic world, one in which discovering possibilities for true creation arouses the opposition that will destroy it. Her stubborn courage both creates and jeopardizes her unorthodox relationship; the venture's success is affected by her personal human frailties and also undermined by external limitations of social position and her more powerful brothers' opposition. For the latter barriers she bears no responsibility, but over them she has little control; her attempt merely to deny them is both naïve and dangerous. Romantic naïveté characterizes tragic heroes as well as comic lovers, of course, and she continues to haunt us, and her survivors, because she eludes the meanings imposed upon her. She is not simply Ferdinand's lustful widow; she belongs neither to Bosola's revenge play nor to Delio's tidy melodrama.

The Duchess exemplifies the limits and triumphs of the tragic hero's paradoxical freedom; she also marks Webster's final alteration of heroic tragedy. As the titular, if not the only, protagonist, she is an unambitious woman, defined by basically bourgeois goals and committed to pettily hypocritical, irresponsible as well as foolish, means. Despite her soliloquy's proud defiance, she does not initially have a hero's stature. The aristocratic pride that leads her to assert that she can live or die like a prince is finally substantiated in her death; yet royal strength and willfulness coexist with the common physicality and domestic yearnings that lead her to choose her steward as husband and become "an excellent / Feeder of pedigrees." The world does not offer her an Antony or a Bussy, but neither does she seek heroic passion. Without the suffering that exposes illusions and ends in death she would have remained the reckless, happily self-indulgent woman who defied public responsibilities as well as her brothers' commands. Nobility appears only under pressure; then, unexpectedly, from her only partially realized and always threatened domestic ideal she draws the strength to withstand grisly and bizarre attempts to force submission or madness.

However unheroic her stature or the private and individual alternative she tries to forge, she shares with other tragic heroes the ability to discover value for which her world—and her own life—offers neither precedent nor example. Like them she seems initially other, and less worthy, than she finally proves herself to be. In the intimate domesticity of her longings she sounds the note not of Cleopatra but of newly wise Lear, discovering sufficiency in a walled prison with Cordelia, or the prematurely aged Macbeth who laments his destruction of the friendship and trust that make life meaningful. Yet neither her briefly glimpsed life nor her death in themselves suggest the scope or deep significance of Lear or Macbeth. The values for which the Duchess so nobly dies are not hard-won discoveries. She chooses them instinctively, and though desiring her rank and social position, she easily turns her back on the delusive attractions of power. Indeed, despite the effective immediacy of her three major scenes, the Duchess is kept as remote and distanced as

Shakespeare's later tragic heroes. Her "story" gains full significance only in Webster's context, in conjunction with that opposite and "lover" who both qualifies and extends her private meanings.

In discarding Antonio in favor of Bosola, indeed fashioning him out of even skimpier source material than went into Flamineo's christening, Webster shows as much daring as in the portrayal of his resolutely unambitious heroine. He throws away Antony to accept an Enobarbus substitute and so redirects the possible triumph of romantic passion into a less exalted but also less exclusive sphere. Bosola's mocking voice bars our fully sympathetic involvement with the Duchess. As interposed commentator his cynical observations undermine her stature; as trickster intriguer he finds her comically easy prey. * * * To a large extent Webster allows this "presenter's" stance to control our response, and he thus builds our identification with this surrogate audience. Witty, cynically realistic, detached, Bosola * * * brings himself close to us, for he represents the rationalizing spirit of accommodation in us all. He offers us the distance he tries to establish in his own life, that protective gap between the coolly observing self and the dangers of belief or commitment. He gains prominence as Ferdinand and Antonio fall away; he becomes the play's second protagonist and through him we participate in the Duchess's death. In his revaluation and transferred allegiance Bosola carries us with him and alters our sympathetic delight in the two lovers' witty poise and warmth. His gritty resistance to the Duchess's charms, his stubborn reluctance to admit her effect or renegotiate his life, set off but also blunt the melodramatic thrill of stoic majesty in adversity. Bosola survives, and his plight ensures our concentration not on the Duchess's brave death but on the meaning of the life that gave her such strength, on precisely what significance it can bear for us beyond its obvious private and individual value. Her courage becomes important less in its own right than in its effect on Bosola, for in refusing to accept or justify his materialist challenges she undermines his assumptions about man's nature and value. In both subjective and practical senses, Bosola's apparent mastery breaks down.

Through Bosola we discover in the Duchess a term, a humanity, between the play's melodramatic villainy and its foolish heroine's infuriating refusal to pursue heroic stature. As observer and actor Bosola both distances us and yet draws us into the play, even involves us in her torture and death. He discovers and in part exemplifies her larger significance, yet he also marks its limits. Finding no action worthy his dejection, Bosola moves away from us into his own mist. Indeed, to the extent that we have shared Bosola's viewpoint, we are relieved when Webster severs our dramatic intimacy. Yet as Bosola recedes into the shifting groups of act 5, Webster's structure forces

us to share his sense of disorientation and emptiness: though separate from him now, we are in a strange and impersonal way more
discomfitingly identified. Webster has locked us within the particular "game" into which Bosola had sought to turn his life, the practical struggle for subsistence drained of all moral meaning. The last
act's farcical treatment of tragic motifs is grotesquely compelling,
unsatisfying, and beyond easy dismissal. Webster has thrown away
the glorious intensity of act 4, as well as a possible romantic double
climax, to gain other ends.

* * *

CHRISTINA LUCKYJ

"Great Women of Pleasure": Main Plot and Subplot in *The Duchess of Malfi*[†]

It is a commonplace to say that Webster cannot construct plays—to
agree with George Rylands, who directed the 1945 revival of *The
Duchess of Malfi*, that "Webster could handle a scene but he could
not compass a plot."[1] Even though our notion of "plot" with regard
to the Elizabethan and Jacobean dramatists has changed after the
important work of Maynard Mack and Bernard Beckerman, who,
among others, have illuminated the multiple, analogical nature of
Shakespeare's dramatic construction, it remains acceptable to speak
of the "unplotted undulations" of Webster's drama.[2] As John Russell Brown points out in his edition of *The Duchess of Malfi*, "the
structure of the play is yet to be vindicated."[3] Compounding the
problem of dramatic construction is one of moral interpretation.
Some critics like to see the play as a cautionary tale against marrying an inferior; other critics and directors invariably treat it as
melodrama with a heroic martyr at its center. Webster himself
included a subplot in *The Duchess of Malfi* which, though it has
received little serious critical attention, may have been intended as

---

[†] Christina Luckyj, "'Great Women of Pleasure': Main Plot and Subplot in *The Duchess
    of Malfi*." *Studies in English Literature* 27.2 (1987), 267–83. Reprinted with permission
    from SEL *Studies in English Literature 1500–1900*. Notes have been renumbered.
[1]. George Rylands, "On the Production of *The Duchess of Malfi*," *The Duchess of Malfi*,
    ed. G. H. W. Rylands and C. Williams (London: Sylvan, 1945), p. vi.
[2]. Maynard Mack, "The Jacobean Shakespeare," *Jacobean Theatre*, ed. J. R. Brown and
    Bernard Harris, Stratford-upon-Avon Studies 1 (London: Edward Arnold, 1960); Ber-
    nard Beckerman, *Shakespeare at the Globe 1599–1609* (New York: Macmillan, 1962).
    The phrase comes from Herbert Whittaker's review of the 1971 Stratford, Ontario pro-
    duction in *The Globe and Mail*, 9 June 1971, p. 15.
[3]. John Russell Brown, ed., *The Duchess of Malfi*, by John Webster (London: Methuen,
    1964), p. 62. All citations to the play refer to this edition.

an interpretive key to certain aspects of the main plot. An examination of the function of the subplot in *The Duchess of Malfi* illuminates both Webster's dramatic construction and his moral emphasis in the play.

The adventures of the Cardinal's mistress that form the Julia subplot were pure invention on Webster's part. Gunnar Boklund tells us that Webster did not borrow the subplot from any source, used as he was to borrowing.[4] Nor is the subplot strictly "necessary" to the main plot, a fact which has led some critics to dismiss it as "a mere excrescence on the play."[5] Yet the structural significance of the Julia subplot need not be limited to its contribution to the linear narrative. Since Webster evidently labored to invent a rough analogy to the Duchess's situation, he presumably intended it to serve a useful dramaturgical function in the play.

William Poel's contention that Julia is "designed as a set-off to the Duchess; as an instance of unholy love in contrast to the chaste love of the Duchess,"[6] has become virtually a tradition in Webster criticism, shared by a large number of modern critics.[7] In describing the Duchess in contrast to Julia, many of these critics use language which tends to misrepresent her. The Duchess's wooing of Antonio is profound and convincing precisely because it is not "chaste," as she herself points out.

> This is flesh and blood, sir;
> 'Tis not the figure cut in alabaster
> Kneels at my husband's tomb.
>   (I.i.453–55)

The Duchess is a woman of sexual energy and vulnerability; she appears pregnant on the stage in the following act. Theatrical critics

---

4. Gunnar Boklund, *"The Duchess of Malfi": Sources, Themes, Characters* (Cambridge: Cambridge Univ. Press, 1962), p. 42.

5. William Archer, "Webster, Lamb and Swinburne," *New Review* 8,44 (1893); rpt. in G. K. and S. K. Hunter, eds., *John Webster: A Critical Anthology* (Harmondsworth: Penguin, 1969), p. 85.

6. William Poel, "A New Criticism of Webster's *Duchess of Malfi*," *Library Review* 2 (1893); rpt. in Hunter, p. 87. Poel's 1892 production of *The Duchess of Malfi* at the Opera Comique restored the Julia subplot for the first time since the seventeenth century. His interpretation of the subplot did not convince the critics, however. A review in the *Nation* complained that "the intrigue of the Cardinal with Julia apparently had no other use in the tragedy save to add one more corpse to the many strewing the stage in that indescribable fifth act" (10 November 1892; rpt. in *Webster: The Critical Heritage,* ed. Don D. Moore [London: Routledge, 1981], p. 128).

7. See Normand Berlin, "*The Duchess of Malfi:* Act V and Genre," *Genre* 3 (1970): 356; Lee Bliss, *The World's Perspective: John Webster and the Jacobean Drama* (New Brunswick, N.J.: Rutgers Univ. Press, 1983), p. 160; M. C. Bradbrook, *John Webster: Citizen and Dramatist* (London: Weidenfeld, 1980), p. 155; Travis Bogard, *The Tragic Satire of John Webster* (Berkeley and Los Angeles: Univ. of California Press, 1955), p. 138; Clifford Leech, *Webster: "The Duchess of Malfi"* (London: Edward Arnold, 1963), p. 32; Richard Levin, *New Readings vs. Old Plays: Recent Trends in the Reinterpretation of English Renaissance Drama* (Chicago: Univ. of Chicago Press, 1979), p. 98; Jacqueline Pearson, *Tragedy and Tragicomedy in the Plays of John Webster* (Manchester: Manchester Univ. Press, 1980), p. 61.

have been quick to emphasize these important qualities. The reviewer of the 1971 Royal Shakespeare Company production for *The Listener* felt that the death scene failed because "Miss Dench retained stoic dignity but, never having shared her passion with us, now kept us at a distance."[8] Michael Billington of the *Guardian* pointed to the same essential qualities when he complained, in a review of the 1985 National Theatre production, "Even when Ms. Bron's Duchess divests herself of her wrappings, she never finds the virtuous, mettlesome, sexually-charged woman underneath."[9] By way of contrast, several critics praised Helen Mirren's portrayal of the Duchess in the 1980 Royal Exchange production—one called her "playful, lascivious and vain";[1] another alluded to "her capacity for affection and her deep sexual awareness."[2] The Duchess's intense sexuality, so vital in performance, has been downplayed by critics who wish to emphasize the differences between the Duchess and Julia. Clifford Leech claims that "the general attitudes [in the play] to Julia and the Duchess are polar opposites" (p. 32), citing the Cardinal's contempt for Julia and Pescara's reference to her as a strumpet (V.i.46), in contrast to Antonio's first idealized view of the Duchess's "divine . . . continence" (I.i.199). Leech's moral distinctions appear doubtful, however, when one remembers the epithets applied to the Duchess by her brothers, for whom she is a "notorious strumpet" (II.v.4). Moreover, the structural justification for this interpretation of the subplot is dubious. If Julia were intended as a foil to the Duchess, she appears utterly redundant. As Boklund comments, by the final act of the play, "reader and spectator . . . have formed definite opinions about the Duchess' conduct, and neither praise nor blame, be it open or implied, will now affect their judgment" (p. 158).

Other critics have proposed Julia as a parody of the Duchess, designed to undercut and qualify her values. Boklund suggests that "since the main action of the play is based on the consequences of a deliberate flouting of the laws guarding social decorum, the by-plot may serve to provide a commentary in word and action on the heroine's behavior."[3] Such attempts to find a "tragic flaw" in the Duchess, reflected and confirmed in Julia, are difficult to support

8. Charles Lewson, "Sick Stallion," *The Listener,* 22 July 1971, p. 125.
9. Michael Billington, "Well-Dressed Decadence Without Relief," *The Guardian,* 6 July 1985, p. 8.
1. Lucy Hughes-Hallett, "'The Duchess of Malfi'," *Now,* 26 September 1980.
2. Jacqueline Pearson, "Man Bites Man," *TLS,* 26 September 1980, p. 1064.
3. Boklund, p. 78. See also Ralph Berry, *The Art of John Webster* (Oxford: Clarendon Press, 1972), pp. 38–41; Fernand Lagarde, *John Webster,* 2 vols. (Toulouse: Association des Publications des Lettres et Sciences Humaines de Toulouse, 1968), 2:851; Clifford Leech, *John Webster: A Critical Study* (London: Hogarth Press, 1951), p. 75; J. R. Mulryne, "Webster and the Uses of Tragicomedy," in *John Webster,* ed. Brian Morris (London: Ernest Benn, 1970), p. 153; Joyce E. Peterson, *Curs'd Example: "The Duchess of Malfi" and Commonweal Tragedy* (Columbia and London: Univ. of Missouri Press, 1978), pp. 88–104.

with the text. Webster's sources, Painter and Belleforest, condemn
the Duchess's actions, and Webster's deliberate deviation from them
in this regard brings him closer to the spirit of the Italian original,
a novella by Bandello which treats the Duchess with "tolerant understanding" and sexual pragmatism. As Boklund himself admits, in
Webster "there is no case for the prosecution" (p. 102). If Julia were
intended as a parody or ironic reflection of the Duchess, Webster's
careful construction designed to emphasize the Duchess's virtue
throughout the play would seem pointless. Some critics sound alarm-
ingly like the hysterical Ferdinand when they claim that, "Lower in
her sexual drive than 'a beast that wants discourse of reason,' the
Duchess of Malfi, like Hamlet's mother, steps out of the path of duty
and marries for lust."[4] As William Empson puts it, "A play intended
as a warning against marrying a social inferior would have to be constructed quite differently."[5] If the Julia subplot can be explained as
an integral part of the play's construction, its function must transcend that of foil or parody.

Clearly, interpretation of the Julia subplot involves moral judgment of the Duchess. Yet often that moral judgment not only fails
to allow for the warm humanity of the Duchess on the stage, but
also reduces the status of the play as "tragedy." Those critics who
emphasize the analogies between the Duchess and Julia come per-
ilously close to reading the play as a cautionary tale. Those who con-
centrate on the differences tend to exaggerate the "saintliness" of
the Duchess and to read the play as melodrama. Underlying both
these perspectives is another implicit moral judgment—that Julia is
meant to be condemned as a wanton, promiscuous, morally reprehensible woman.

Directors of the play have also tended to impose this interpretation on the character of Julia, sometimes deliberately using stage
effects to undercut the immediate import of the language to the confusion of critics and theater audiences alike. For example, in the
1960 Royal Shakespeare Company production, the scene in which
Julia rejects first the Cardinal, then Delio, was reinterpreted by Don-
ald McWhinnie's staging. What began as rejection ended in mute
consent, as she knelt to kiss the Cardinal's ring (II.iv.37), and later
stalked off with Delio's proffered bribe (II.iv.76).[6] Visual effects con-
tradicted the scene's language and made Delio's bewilderment at
her "wit or honesty" (II.iv.77) incomprehensible. In the final act of

---

4. Lisa Jardine, *Still Harping on Daughters: Women and Drama in the Age of Shakespeare*
   (Sussex: Harvester Press, 1983), p. 71.
5. William Empson, "Mine Eyes Dazzle," *EIC* 14 (1964); rpt. in Hunter, p. 298.
6. Details about this production were provided by the promptbook held by the Shakespeare
   Birthplace Trust, Stratford-upon-Avon.

the same production, Julia's open lasciviousness with Bosola made her a caricature of lust that so jarred with her tragic death that one critic commented in utter confusion, "Sian Phillips did not shirk the part of the Cardinal's mistress Julia, but what can any actress today make of the last scenes?"[7] In the 1985 National Theatre production, director Philip Prowse's conception of Julia was clear from the beginning when she made a dramatic entrance in the first act on the Duchess's cue, only to turn and kneel finally before a much more modest Duchess. The invented stage moment established her clearly as the Duchess's foil as well as her servant.

Critics and directors may have ceased their moral condemnation of the Duchess and instead tended to beatify her, but their moral prejudices continue to vent themselves on Julia. Her contribution to the dramatic texture and design of the play has been largely ignored in favor of the accepted view of her as a stock Jacobean whore. It is Clifford Leech's sensitivity to the text that allows him, however briefly, to entertain a third possibility in the analogical relation between the two plots. He points out "how erroneous it would be to regard the Duchess as outside the normal sphere of sexual passion," and declares that, despite the differences between them, "there is enough resemblance between the two actions of the play to keep strongly in our minds the force of the passion that urges the Duchess to speak."[8] Leech's tentative suggestion moves toward a realistic, human view of the Duchess essential to performance, but remains a suggestion, which he does not support with close examination of the text.

In fact, few critics provide a detailed reading of the three scenes of the play in which Julia figures. Only close attention to these scenes in their dramatic context can determine their relation to the rest of the play. And such close attention makes some critical claims about Julia's character seem surprising. For Boklund, she is "guided by the two forces of lust and avarice" (p. 157); for Clifford Leech she is a "rank whore";[9] for Richard Levin she is a "flagrant adulteress" (p. 98). However, actresses who attempt to play Julia this way must find themselves working directly against the text at several points.

Before Julia appears for the first time in II.iv, the audience is prepared by Bosola for her appearance. After Bosola has picked up the horoscope and discovered that the Duchess has given birth to a son, he gleefully closes the scene (II.iii) with a couplet which carries over into the following scene.

7. Philip Hope-Wallace, "The Stratford Company Goes to Town," *Guardian*, 17 December 1960.
8. Leech, *Webster: "The Duchess of Malfi,"* p. 33.
9. Leech, *John Webster*, p. 75.

> Though lust do mask in ne'er so strange disguise,
> She's oft found witty, but is never wise.
>
> (II.iii.76–77)

At the opening of the next scene, the Cardinal echoes Bosola's couplet when he describes Julia as a "witty false one" (II.iv.5). At first Julia appears to be a fulfillment of Bosola's and the Arragonian brothers' degraded vision of the Duchess, which has dominated the stage since the beginning of the second act.[1] The device is similar to that used by Shakespeare in *Othello*, where, as Mack points out, "Bianca . . . may be thought to supply in living form on the stage the prostitute figure that Desdemona has become in Othello's mind" (p. 30). Yet just as, in *Othello*, Iago's vision of Bianca as a "notable strumpet" (V.i.78) is cast into doubt by her loyalty to Cassio, very early in the scene Julia's words and stage actions begin to contradict the Cardinal's version of her. Her first speech, with its anxious, halting rhythm, betrays the deep inner struggle of a woman who has compromised herself for uncertain gain and finds herself the victim of a cynical and abusive man.

> You have prevail'd with me
> Beyond my strongest thoughts: I would not now
> Find you inconstant.
>
> (IV.ii.6–8)

These are hardly words that convey the "lust and avarice" of a "flagrant adulteress." On the contrary, they imply that her decision to commit adultery was a painful one, the result of an ongoing struggle between the demands of sexuality and morality. As the interview progresses, Julia defends her own constancy and integrity as the Cardinal attacks them. In the face of his cruel misogyny, she finally bursts into tears when her objections can no longer be heard. If the scene begins as a confirmation of Bosola's degraded perspective on the Duchess, it moves away from that perspective as it continues. The scene is clearly written to overturn an audience's initial impression of Julia. The "whore" and "adulteress" cannot be quite so easily dismissed.

The Cardinal's assault on the "giddy and wild turnings" (II.iv.12) of women both echoes the satiric perspective of Bosola that dominated the previous three scenes and anticipates the crazed misogyny of Ferdinand in the following scene (II.v).[2] The scene suspends and extends the previous action—its precise form is unexpected, and

---

1. Hereward T. Price also makes this point in "The Function of Imagery in Webster," *PMLA* 70 (September 1955); rpt. in Hunter, p. 195.
2. There are some precise verbal echoes of Bosola in the Cardinal's speeches: both use images of glass manufacture for female sexuality (II.ii.6–10; II.iv.13–14), as well as animal imagery (II.i.47–55; II.iv.27–34).

it carries the audience away from the world of the Duchess. At the same time, however, it exploits the tension and energy that have been built up over the previous three scenes regarding the Duchess's escalating danger. The scene is an analogical replay of the situation between Bosola and the Duchess throughout the second act, since Julia is another woman victimized by the cruel cynicism of men. Again, the satiric vision is pitted against the vulnerability of human love and sexuality with their inherent compromises. In both cases, two voices are heard in opposition to each other[3]—the tough against the vulnerable, the deeply cynical against the merely human. As Bosola's meditation on death and decay (II.i.45–60) is set against the stage image of the pregnant Duchess, swollen with life, the Cardinal's diatribe on the inconstancy of women is contrasted with Julia's long-suffering silence. Like Bosola (and like Iago in *Othello*), the Cardinal attempts to degrade women by generalizing them and by reducing them to the level of mere animals. The Duchess and Julia both contradict this version of themselves with their stage presences.

Following the interview between the Cardinal and Julia is an exchange between Julia and Delio that has puzzled most critics. Archer simply admits that "the relevance of the passage in which Delio makes love to the Cardinal's mistress utterly escapes me."[4] Lois Potter claims that the exchange "must inevitably be confusing in performance,"[5] though she suggests that it recalls Ferdinand's bribery of Bosola in Act I and reiterates the play's "service and reward" motif. If the echo is there, it is designed to enforce a contrast; Bosola finally accepts the gold while Julia rejects it. In his edition of the play, Brown suggests that the incident is designed "to aggravate the audience's sense of a growing web of intrigue and an increasing complexity of character" (p. 62). That the exchange is designed deliberately to confuse appears a weak explanation at best. Neither critic accounts for the particular nature of the incident—another kind of exchange would presumably serve just as well to reinforce a theme or to suggest intricacy of plot. Nor does either critic examine the dramatic rhythm of the exchange. Its dramatic impact is, however, unmistakable.

The first part of the interchange between Julia and Delio centers on Julia's old husband, Castruchio, who has already appeared twice in the play. As Ferdinand's poker-faced advisor in Act I, and as an

---

3. For the notion of "two voices," I am of course indebted to Mack's "The Jacobean Shakespeare," pp. 19–20.
4. Archer, in Hunter, p. 85.
5. Lois Potter, "Realism vs. Nightmare; Problems of Staging *The Duchess of Malfi*," in *The Triple Bond*, ed. Joseph G. Price (Univ. Park and London: Pennsylvania State Univ. Press, 1975), p. 180.

aspiring courtier and the object of Bosola's mockery in Act II, Castruchio quickly impresses an audience as a foolish old man. His marital relationship to Julia, to which Webster suddenly draws attention in this scene, appears to be the culmination of his function in the play, since he disappears completely after his mention here. A foolish, impotent old man married to an obviously desirable young woman—whom Bosola later describes as "very fair" (V.ii.177)—recalls the marriage of Camillo and Vittoria in *The White Devil*. There, the husband's inadequacy helped to exonerate the wife's adultery. Here, the first explicit identification of Julia's deceived husband with foolish old Castruchio (whose name suggests castration) shifts the scene even further in the direction of Julia's redemption in the eyes of the audience. The terse reply Julia makes to Delio's mockery of her husband—"Your laughter is my pity" (II.iv.56–57)—with its brevity betrays her suffering.

Delio then offers her his gold, drawing attention to its physical properties by mockingly treating it as an aesthetic object. Julia rejects not only the gold itself, but also the crude materialism it represents.[6] In reply, she evokes a world of positive aesthetic values and refined sensual beauty—of beautiful birds, music, and fragrance. It is a world in which the Duchess also lives, and which she conjures up most eloquently just before her death in lines like these:

> What would it pleasure me to have my throat cut
> With diamonds? Or to be smothered
> With cassia? or to be shot to death with pearls?
>   (IV.ii.215–18)

The struggle between two polarized views of life, between the crudely sexual and the delicately sensual, is articulated throughout the play's main action in the characters of Ferdinand and the Duchess.[7] Here, its mere suggestion is enough to associate Julia with the Duchess's refined sensuality. Finally, Julia's categorical rejection of Delio's sexual offer, combined with the disclosure of her unhappy marriage to Castruchio, is clearly designed to capture audience sympathy for Julia. Together, they confirm the impression of abused integrity suggested in her relationship with the Cardinal at the beginning of the scene. As Julia remains in the foreground, the background shifts around her so that the vulnerable victim of the Cardinal's misogyny can exhibit self-assured integrity. The question of Delio's motives is less important than the dramatic impact of Julia's

---

6. I find it difficult to accept Peterson's view that Julia's refusal indicates that Delio "simply has not offered enough" (p. 93).
7. See Roger Warren, "'The Duchess of Malfi' on the Stage," in *John Webster*, ed. Brian Morris, p. 65.

reassertion of her integrity. And that integrity is not undercut by Julia's witty reply to Delio:

> Sir, I'll go ask my husband if I shall,
> And straight return your answer.
> (II.iv.75–76)

On the contrary, Julia's need to rely on the outward form of conventional morality by calling on her husband illuminates its inadequacy as a standard of human behavior. The courage she displays appears more significant since the audience knows that it is unsupported by the facts of her marital relationship. Delio may wonder, "Is this her wit or honesty that speaks thus?" (II.iv.77), but an audience is left in little doubt. Because Julia, like the Duchess, is forced to exceed the bounds of respectability, her "virtue" must be judged according to another standard. One might say, in the spirit of Empson, that a scene intended to portray a "flagrant adulteress" and a clear contrast to the Duchess would have to be constructed quite differently.

Just before Julia's final dismissal of Delio's offer, a servant enters to report,

> Your husband's come,
> Hath deliver'd a letter to the Duke of Calabria,
> That, to my thinking, hath put him out of his wits.
> (II.iv.67–69)

The audience is suddenly reminded of what has been going on in the play's main action. Bosola's report of the birth of the Duchess's "illegitimate" child has been delivered by Castruchio to the Arragonian brothers. The servant's report briefly anticipates the following scene, with Ferdinand's reassertion of his crazed view of the Duchess as a "notorious strumpet" (II.v.4). As we are reminded of Ferdinand's distorted vision of the Duchess, Delio imposes his degraded perspective on Julia, making her a sexual offer. Julia's rejection of that offer thus has the effect of salvaging the Duchess's values by association. At this point, Julia's function in the play transcends mere analogy to anticipate the reassertion of the Duchess's integrity after Bosola's and Ferdinand's assault upon it throughout the second act.

The second act, with its opening parody of the Duchess and Antonio in the figures of the Old Lady and Castruchio, tends to modify, if not to obliterate, the delicate power of the tender wooing scene that closes the first act. While an audience may have little difficulty rejecting the Arragonian brothers' tyrannical moralism in favor of the Duchess's individualism in the first act, it finds few alternatives to Bosola's relentless cynicism in the second. Bosola takes over from Antonio as the Duchess's observer in the second act, and audience response is to some extent conditioned by his vision of life and sexuality as purely physical and subject to decay. Moreover, at both times that Julia appears, the Duchess has been absent from the stage for a prolonged period. Bosola's gift of "apricocks" to the Duchess sends her into labor in the first scene of Act II; she quickly leaves the stage and does not reappear until the following act. The only momentary reanimation of her presence is an offstage "shriek" Bosola hears at the beginning of II.iii, realistically suggesting her offstage labor, but also conveying the deeper suffering that shapes her character in preparation for the death scene. Her absence from the stage throughout most of the second act may represent this implied process of necessary psychic change, what Mack (p. 35) calls the "second phase" in the development of the tragic hero or heroine. When Julia comes onto the stage, the audience is set up to judge her as the Duchess's enemies have judged the Duchess. With this scene, however, Webster overturns the simplified prejudices of conventional morality that are inevitably part of an audience's response, a response we share with the Duchess's enemies. Webster's presentation of Julia is consistent with his portrait of Vittoria in *The White Devil* and, ultimately, with his interest in the figure of the Duchess. It allows him to draw attention to something he evidently considered very important—that "whore," a word applied by social convention to someone unchaste, does not fully exhaust the psychological reality of the woman. This is true of Vittoria, of Julia, and most of all, of the Duchess.[8] The first of Julia's scenes functions as analogical probability at a point in the play when the Duchess is most vulnerable to the attacks of her enemies because she is not present on the stage.

Bosola's cynical, satiric vision presents a challenge to the Duchess's values that intensifies them by contrast when they are reasserted. But Bosola's vision also serves another purpose in the play's dramatic construction by further humanizing and illuminating the Duchess. The Duchess is above all, as she herself makes clear, an intensely sexual woman. The "apricocks" scene (II.i) becomes, in performance, not an indictment of the Duchess, but a further

8. Although she does not discuss the Julia subplot, Linda Woodbridge's view of Webster's manipulation of antifeminist stereotypes in his plays is similar to my own when she remarks that, in *The Duchess of Malfi*, "The question of female sexuality is precisely what Webster seems interested in exploring," and, in *The White Devil*, "The moral ambiguity readers experience in the play stems partly from Webster's attempt to achieve sympathy for a fallen woman, to turn a whore into a hero" (*Women and the English Renaissance: Literature and the Nature of Womankind 1540–1620* [Urbana and Chicago: Univ. of Illinois Press, 1984], pp. 259–62). Furthermore, according to Woodbridge, Webster's treatment of both his minor and his major female characters reflects a general trend in plays of the second decade of the seventeenth century. As she notes, "Even the image of prostitutes underwent a face-lifting in the drama during the *hic mulier* years" (p. 261).

confirmation of the directness and sensual delight she exhibited in the wooing scene. It is precisely this sensual Duchess that Webster wanted to capture in Julia.

When Julia appears again in the first scene of Act V to request Antonio's property from Pescara, she immediately represents those who crudely profit from the ruin of the couple. Yet the focus of the scene shifts quickly from Julia's appropriation of Antonio's land to Pescara's hypocrisy. The scene centers, not on Julia's immoral action, but on the moral turpitude of those who condemn her as a "strumpet" in order to excuse their own actions. Pescara's guilt is thinly disguised by his abuse of Julia; his own fault is greater than hers. He grants Antonio's land to the Cardinal's mistress as "salary for his [the Cardinal's] lust" (V.i.52), defending his sycophantic action with perverse self-righteousness.[9] The moral status of Julia is again made relative, since her moralizing accusers are unreliable. Her appearance here is intended to drain off possible moral condemnation from the audience in the following scene.

Julia's appearance in the following scene (V.ii), as in the second act, restages for emphasis an aspect of the Duchess's experience that threatens to disappear with her. Whereas Julia's first appearance reflects the Duchess's position as a victim of the cruel cynicism of men and anticipates the Duchess's restoration, her final appearance recalls the Duchess's fate in miniature and anticipates the futile revenge of Bosola.

Julia's wooing of Bosola in the second scene of Act V seems deliberately designed to recall the Duchess's wooing of Antonio in Act I. Webster goes to considerable lengths to establish visual and verbal parallels between the two incidents. In both cases, the woman is the wooer (I.i.442; V.ii.183) and uses roughly similar phrases to express her admiration for her man with striking directness (I.i.453–59; V.ii.167–72). In both cases, the woman puts herself at great risk for her lover. While Webster clearly did not intend the crude seduction of Bosola to be a direct echo of the tender wooing of Antonio, the parallels between the two scenes appear to be as significant as the differences, which have frequently been emphasized by critics. During performances of the play, the later scene is clearly linked to the earlier one, not by its reiterated images, but by its similar effect on an audience. The two wooing scenes are virtually the only extended actions in the play to evoke laughter and delight in an audience predisposed to expect danger. As in Act I, in the last act the play's relentless machinery of crime and revenge is suspended while we watch the digressive banter of lovers.

9. I cannot agree with the reading of this scene proposed by Bliss, who claims: "Some courtiers, or a Julia, seek to 'fortify themselves' with others' ruin, but Pescara displays an innate sense of justice" (p. 163).

Noting the differences between the two wooing scenes, critics have proposed interpretations of the later scene as a foil to, or parody of, the earlier one. Yet, as has been argued earlier, the dramaturgical advantages of either at this late stage in the action are limited. A foil appears superfluous, since the stature of the Duchess is by this point fixed. She is clearly exalted beyond all the characters of the fifth act. A parody seems groundless, since it would undercut the tragic intensity of her loss. There is, however, a third possibility, consistent with Webster's treatment of Julia in the second act. Here, as there, she may be intended as a mirror for the main action, reflecting its broad outlines in simplified analogical fashion from a different moral perspective. Shakespeare uses a similar dramatic strategy in the final act of *Othello;* Bianca, falsely accused by Iago of Cassio's murder, recalls Desdemona's plight as she has also been presented as a "whore" responsible for her man's destruction.

When Julia enters, pointing a pistol at Bosola and accusing him of treachery (V.ii.151), she continues the language of violence, intrigue, and deception used by the Cardinal and Bosola in their preceding interview. Similarly, when the Duchess offers her wedding ring to Antonio, visual and verbal echoes recall Ferdinand's bribery of Bosola in the same scene, and the interview is fraught with overtones of danger. In both scenes, however, the context of love and sexuality defuses the play's threatening language. The oppressive intrigue of the court is mockingly parodied and transformed by Julia. Her wit takes Bosola and the audience by surprise, as she abruptly turns apparent aggression into playful love-making. Webster sustains a tone throughout the scene that carefully avoids both romantic and sexual cliché. When Bosola attempts to seduce Julia with a conventional line, saying

> Your bright eyes
> Carry a quiver of darts in them, sharper
> Than sunbeams
>   (V.ii.179–81)

Julia abruptly cuts him off and asserts her own status as the wooer. When he takes the opposite tack and decides to "grow most amorously familiar" (V.ii.185) with her, Julia responds with pragmatic intelligence, again drawing the focus away from Bosola and onto her own power.

> For if I see and steal a diamond,
> The fault is not i'th' stone, but in me the thief
> That purloins it:—I am sudden with you;
> We that are great women of pleasure use to cut off

These uncertain wishes, and unquiet longings,
And in an instant join the sweet delight
And the pretty excuse together.

(V.ii.190–96)

While the scene verges on caricature, it develops a sustained contrast between Bosola's limited conventional attitude and Julia's
strong unconventional one. The echoes of the wooing scene of Act
I, however distorted or exaggerated, are nonetheless startling in performance. The entire scene is structured to highlight the energy,
wit, and exuberance of Julia, glimpsed only briefly in her earlier
interchange with Delio. In both wooing scenes, Webster challenges
the popular antifeminist stereotype that "a harlot is full of words,"[1]
and links the Duchess and Julia in their common deviation from the
conventional "good" woman. In the earlier scene (II.iv), the assertion of Julia's sexual integrity was necessary to suggest by analogy
the Duchess's dramatic recovery at a point when it seemed threatened. In the later scene, the "splendidly sensual" and "voluptuous"[2]
Julia re-evokes by association quite a different quality in the Duchess. Again, the recollection is a timely one in the play's dramatic
rhythm, since Bosola's perspective on the Duchess as "sacred
innocence" (IV.ii.355) threatens to distort her by exalting her.
With Julia in the final act as an analogical reassertion of the Duchess's strong sexuality, a balance is restored.

In the final act, Julia reanimates by association, not the Duchess
of the recent death scene, but the Duchess of the wooing scenes—
playful, confident, sensual, and direct. If, as I have argued, Webster
attempts to recall such qualities in the Duchess by exaggerating
them in Julia, he does so at considerable risk. The success of his
strategy rests finally on performance—on an actress who can play
Julia in this scene as a strong, vital woman rather than as a vulgar
strumpet. Such risks, however, are unavoidable for the dramatist.
In this instance, Webster takes the risk of falling into crude bur-
lesque, for the greater advantage of clarifying his tragic construction. The recollection at this point of the young, carefree, and
childless Duchess of the beginning of the play leads an audience to
appreciate precisely what has been lost and gained in the course of
the play's tragic action. The changes that are forced upon the Duchess enrich and develop her as a character who can finally face her
death with courage. Yet at the same time those changes rob her of
her innocent confidence that "time will easily / Scatter the tempest"

1. Woodbridge, p. 77.
2. D. H., "Magnificent Make-Believe," review of *The Duchess of Malfi*, Royal Shakespeare
   Company, Aldwych, London. *Bristol Evening Post*, 16 December 1960; Milton Shulman,
   "Horror Unlimited Hits the Aldwych," *Evening Standard*, 16 December 1960.

(I.i.471–72). With the appearance of Julia in the final act, the audience can measure the distance it has travelled since the wooing scene. Loss of the Duchess's youthful insouciance is balanced against the recollection of the richness of her spirit in adversity. The evocation of this simple tragic paradox is the main dramaturgical function of Julia at this stage in the play.

If the wooing of Bosola is intended as an echo of the Duchess's lighthearted wooing of Antonio, then the subsequent interview with the Cardinal plunges the audience directly into the death scene. The opposed perspectives of the play's main action—the Duchess's youthful vitality and the irrational menace of her enemies—are recalled in the confrontation between Julia and the Cardinal. Julia is still witty and playful, but the Cardinal is dangerously bitter. Comic and tragic perspectives illuminate each other in their dialogue, remaining at cross purposes until the Cardinal confesses his crime:

> By my appointment, the great Duchess of Malfi,
> And two of her young children, four nights since,
> Were strangled.
>
> (V.ii.268–70)

The Cardinal's syntax imitates the dramatic suspense of the interview, delaying the final shock until the end of the sentence, thus heightening its impact. The witty innocence of Julia's playful persuasions acts as a foil to the Cardinal's bald and horrifying declaration. His admission of guilt is directly followed by a restaging of the crime, for Julia immediately pays for her indiscretion with her death. The death of the Duchess in the fourth act is painstakingly prepared for from the play's very beginning, so that its dramatic shock is greatly mitigated. For Julia, "love" is more irresponsible, knowledge of evil more sudden, and death more abrupt than for the Duchess, yet the compressed juxtaposition of these extremes of love and death recalls the Duchess's tragic fate with new force. This simplified—almost caricatured—recollection of the Duchess's life and death clarifies the essential tragic meaning of the play's action. As T. C. Worsley summarized it in a review of the 1960 Royal Shakespeare Company production, "As we see her first the Duchess is a woman of high natural spirits and vitality, and it is that buoyancy of heart that it is so terrible to see being desolated."[3] Julia's part in the final act is a microcosm of the main action, her cruel death a striking contrast to her strength and vitality. And, unlike Cariola—the Duchess's foil in death—Julia accepts her death with dignity, though it is undeserved.

3. "'The Duchess of Malfi,'" *Financial Times,* 16 December 1960.

During the final act, Bosola's role as an onlooker and accomplice during the Duchess's death is restaged. After Julia's death, he argues with the Cardinal about "reward," vows vengeance for the Duchess's murder, and drags the body off the stage, exactly as he had done at the end of Act IV. His complaint as he picks up Julia's body—"I think I shall / Shortly grow the common bier for churchyards" (V.ii.311–12)—reinforces the analogue. In the staging of the scene, Bosola's vengeful soliloquy is invariably delivered as he kneels over Julia's body, precisely as he had knelt over the Duchess's body earlier. While it keeps the memory of the Duchess alive, the repetition of the sequence of crime and revenge also suggests the futility of Bosola's attempt at vengeance, futility that is later confirmed in his botched murder of Antonio.

It would, of course, be dangerous to overstate the case for the parallels between the two plots. Certainly the two women belong to sharply contrasting worlds throughout the play, and such contrasts give the play its richly varied texture. Julia is involved in the petty, broken world of the Duchess's enemies as the Duchess herself never is, and the parallels between the two women heighten their differences. Conversely, however, Webster exploits the obvious differences between them in order to reveal surprising similarities, which serve his dramatic ends. The differences between the Duchess and Julia may emphasize the Duchess's calm self-sufficiency, but the similarities between them suggest the vulnerability of women in a hostile masculine world. The play's final emphasis falls on Julia and, by analogy, on the Duchess—not as a single, heroic individual destroyed by crazed villains, but as an ordinary, vital young woman stifled by misogyny. Rather than undercutting or further exalting the Duchess's stature in the final act, Julia restores the Duchess by analogy to the world of common humanity, to which she firmly belonged throughout the play.

In conclusion, the Julia subplot has an important dramatic function in *The Duchess of Malfi*. The presentation of Julia as a character is clearly consistent with the interest Webster displays in challenging conventional morality with his other heroines, the Duchess and Vittoria. Close examination of the scenes in which Julia figures reveals not a "flagrant adulteress" but a woman of some integrity; not a fickle temptress, but a sexually vital woman. That integrity and sexual vitality are not incompatible is a major concern of *The Duchess of Malfi*. The Julia subplot clarifies and restates Webster's primary concerns in the play's main action. As a "glass" for events in the Duchess's life, Julia reflects their essence in compressed, sometimes caricatured, form. In a review of the 1971 Royal Shakespeare Company production of the play, one reviewer described Julia as "the most genteel whore, cooing like a dove in a cage of hawks,"[4] a description which could apply equally well to the Duchess. Like the Duchess, Julia is caged and finally killed by the predatory Arragonian brothers. And like the Duchess, Julia remains fully sexually alive to the last moment.

4. P. W., "A Tidy Murder," *Sunday Mercury,* 18 July 1971.

Feminist Accounts

THEODORA A. JANKOWSKI

Defining/Confining the Duchess:
Negotiating the Female Body in John Webster's
The Duchess of Malfi†

The relatively rapid appearance in mid-sixteenth-century Britain of three reigning female monarchs severely taxed existing early modern political theory. The rich discourse that explored the various ramifications of the nature of authority and male rulership had been remarkably silent about both the potential for and the nature of possible female rule. Thus, the presence of Mary Tudor and Mary Stuart on British thrones served to point out—to political theorists especially—that no language existed for describing the nature of female rule. That a large discourse did exist for describing married women—one that showed them to be subservient to their husbands— did not make the task of creating a political discourse for women any easier. In fact, the existence of such a powerful mode of describing married women as subject to their husbands prompted John Knox to argue in 1558 that the nature of female rule was "unnatural."[1] Whether this pronouncement was universally accepted or not is not important. What is important is that various "disastrous" events in the reigns of the two Marys served to cast severe doubt upon the nature of female rule itself, especially given the fact that monarchs *had* to marry to produce heirs. So strong was the traditional belief in women as subservient beings that John Aylmer had some difficulty in supporting the concept of a female monarch. His not very

---

† Theodora Jankowski, "Defining/Confining the Duchess: Negotiating the Female Body in John Webster's *The Duchess of Malfi*," in Dympna Callaghan (ed.), *The Duchess of Malfi: Contemporary Critical Essays*, New Casebooks (Basingstoke: Macmillan, 2000), pp. 80–103. Previously in *Studies in Philology* 87 (1990), 221–45. Copyright © 1990 by the University of North Carolina Press. Used by permission of the publisher. Notes have been renumbered.
1. [John Knox], *The First Blast of the Trumpet Against the Monstruous regiment of women* ([Geneva], 1558; rptd., Amsterdam: Theatrum Orbis Terrarum and New York: Da Capo, 1972) (S.T.C. No. 15070).

convincing argument was that a woman ruler could be "subject to" her husband as he was her husband and yet "rule over" him as she was his magistrate. While Aylmer's solution was, at best, "tricky," his basic aversion to female rule on principle did not help his argument carry the day.[2] Elizabeth I clearly did not find his solution helpful, since she avoided the problem altogether by remaining "virgin." But despite Elizabeth's avoidance of matrimony, the vexed question of a female sovereign's marriage does surface in a number of early modern plays, notably John Webster's *The Duchess of Malfi* where it becomes a central issue.

The Duchess of Malfi is an unusual play not only because it explores questions of rulership as they relate to a female sovereign, but also because it explores these questions as regards the sovereign's marriage. The play thus participates in the discursive construction of women in the early modern period and helps to reveal the contradictions in the notion of a female ruler. These contradictions are explored in the ways in which the Duchess is represented as using her body natural and her body politic.[3] Webster's Duchess of Malfi establishes a system of rule in which she fails to consider her body's potential, either as a means to power or as a means by which she can lose power. This widow attempts to secure herself politically by divorcing her natural body from her political one by creating a private second marriage that exists simultaneously with—but hidden from—her orbis life as a ruler. In this double position of wife and ruler, then, the Duchess becomes an uneasy and threatening figure. I will argue, therefore, that, despite the character's failure to create a successful means by which she can rule as a woman sovereign, she challenges Jacobean society's views regarding the representation of the female body and woman's sexuality.

Critics have rarely considered the Duchess of Malfi as a political character despite the fact that she rules Malfi as Regent for her son, the minor heir to the Duke of Malfi, her dead husband. Given her role as sovereign ruler, the Duchess needs also to be viewed as a political figure. Yet Kathleen McLuskie observes that the critical history of *The Duchess of Malfi* reflects an "unease with a woman character who so impertinently pursues self-determination."[4] This

2. [John Aylmer], *An Harborouue for Faithfull and Treuue Subiectes, agaynst the late blowne Blaste, concerninge the Government of VVemen* (Strasborowe, 1559; rptd., Amsterdam: Theatrum Orbis Terrarum and New York: Da Capo, 1972) (S.T.C. No. 1005).
3. Marie Axton (*The Queen's Two Bodies: Drama and the Elizabethan Succession* [London: Royal Historical Society, 1977]) explains that by 1561 Queen Elizabeth I had been legally endowed with a body natural and a body politic. Axton discusses the legal implications of this "fiction" of the two bodies and bases her work on Edmund Plowden's 1561 reference to the monarch's two bodies as reported by F. W. Maitland in "The Crown as Corporation" in *Collected Papers*, ed. H. A. L. Fisher (Cambridge, 1911). Her work is also influenced by that of Ernst Kantorowicz (*The King's Two Bodies* [Princeton: Princeton Univ. Press, 1957]) which, she feels, "did not explore the Elizabethan setting in any depth" (15).
4. Kathleen McLuskie, "Drama and Sexual Politics: The Case of Webster's Duchess," in *Drama, Sex, and Politics*, ed. James Redmond (Cambridge: Cambridge Univ. Press, 1985), 88.

"unease" has led to a criticism that focuses primarily on the Duchess's private roles of wife, mother, unruly widow, or victimized woman and slights consideration of her public role as ruler.[5] The only sustained political reading of the play is presented by Joyce E. Peterson who argues that the Duchess improperly sets the private claims of her body natural above the public claims of her body politic.[6] As a result of her "anarchic will," Webster's character places her private desire to marry Antonio above her public responsibility as a ruler, an action that identifies her with her corrupt brothers. Peterson also suggests that the "generic expectations . . . insist inexorably on her culpability as a ruler, on her responsibility for her own fate, and, worse, for the disruption of her duchy" (p. 78).

While I agree that much of the tension of *The Duchess of Malfi* derives from the conflicting claims of the Duchess's bodies natural and politic, I do feel that Peterson's judgment of the Duchess as a "bad" ruler fails to take account of how Renaissance gender ideologies are made. Her harsh reading of the Duchess may be based upon what she rightly perceives to be an action directly subversive of prevailing ideologies, but which she does not examine as such. It seems to me, then, that Peterson's failure to consider the overall implications of early modern sexual, social, and political attitudes toward women leads to her reading of this play as a simple lesson in bad rulership. By not discussing why the Duchess's marriage is so threatening and by reproducing oppressive gender ideologies in an unqualified way, Peterson blunts her argument and simplifies the very complex nature of the representation of "woman"—especially "woman as ruler"—displayed in this play.

The Duchess of Malfi is a play that is clearly concerned with questions of gender ideology, but its employment of various, often

5. While a great number of works can be mentioned in this context, I call particular attention to the following, which have been most influential in overall criticism of this play: Travis Bogard, *The Tragic Satire of John Webster* (Berkeley and Los Angeles: Univ. of California Press, 1955); Clifford Leech, *Webster: The Duchess of Malfi* (London: Edward Arnold, 1963; rptd. 1968); Robert Ornstein, *The Moral Vision of Jacobean Tragedy* (Madison and Milwaukee: Univ. of Wisconsin Press, 1965); Muriel Bradbrook, *John Webster: Citizen and Dramatist* (New York: Columbia Univ. Press, 1980); Jacqueline Pearson, *Tragedy and Tragicomedy in the Plays of John Webster* (Totowa, NJ: Barnes and Noble, 1980); and Charles R. Forker, *Skull Beneath the Skin: The Achievement of John Webster* (Carbondale and Edwardsville: Southern Illinois Univ. Press, 1986).

6. Joyce E. Peterson, *Curs'd Example: The Duchess of Malfi and Commonweal Tragedy* (Columbia and London: Univ. of Missouri Press, 1978). The following critics are not primarily concerned with a "political" reading of the play or the Duchess's character, though they do comment negatively upon several of her "political" actions; Eloise K. Goreau, *Integrity of Life: Allegorical Imagery in the Plays of John Webster* (Salzburg: Institut für Englische Sprache und Literatur, 1974); Anthony E. Courtade, *The Structure of John Webster's Plays* (Salzburg: Institut für Anglistik und Amerikanistik, 1980); Lee Bliss, *The World's Perspective: John Webster and the Jacobean Drama* (New Brunswick: Rutgers Univ. Press, 1983); Lisa Jardine, *Still Harping on Daughters: Women and Drama in the Age of Shakespeare* (Brighton and Sussex: Harvester and Totowa, NJ: Barnes and Noble, 1983); Robert P. Griffin, *John Webster: Politics and Tragedy* (Salzburg: Institut für Englische Sprache und Literatur, 1972); and Robert Ornstein.

contradictory, literary and social discourses regarding gender relations makes it difficult to analyze. However, the contradictions between these conventions serve both to foreground the tensions implicit within socially-constructed ideas of "woman," or the female protagonist, and present interpretive problems for deciding which is the privileged discourse. This ideological juxtaposition can be observed as early as I.1, where three major questions are introduced: first, the political context of the play as a whole, specifically the first presentation of the Duchess as a reigning sovereign and public figure; second, the presentation of the brothers and their political and familial relationship to the Duchess; and third, the presentation of the Duchess as a private figure and the character's development of her unusual "new world and custom" in her secret marriage to Antonio. The display of contesting ideologies characteristic of this scene may make the play difficult to analyze, but simplification of the work through unified readings deprives it of its ideological complexity.

In order to understand the ways in which the Duchess is figured as a political character, it is necessary to examine the political context in which this character is presented. Antonio's description of the ideal French court and its "judicious king" does just this.[7] The description acts as a touchstone for the accepted Renaissance ideal of court life that is contrasted to Malfi and Rome,[8] places the play within a political framework, and indicates that the entire first act is an examination of the political natures of the four "princes"—three actual and one "spiritual"—who appear in this play: the Duchess herself; Ferdinand, the "perverse" Duke of Calabria; the corrupt Cardinal; and the "spirit" of the King of France, the emblem of the "judicious king."

It is against this dual background of corruption and idealism that Webster places the political persona of the Duchess of Malfi. Her presentation as a sovereign in a courtly setting both reinforces Antonio's description of her as an ideal ruler who differs in some essential way from her brothers (I.1.187–205) and insists upon the necessity of her occupying a political space. The fact that his speech can, on one level, be seen as the idealized portrait of a "woman,"

---

7. John Webster, *The Duchess of Malfi*, ed. John Russell Brown. The Revels Plays (Manchester: Manchester Univ. Press and Baltimore: Johns Hopkins Univ. Press, 1981), 8–9. (I.1.5–22). All further references to this play will be to this edition.
8. The juxtaposition of the "ideal" or "moral" French court and the Machiavellian Italian view of politics is noted by: Richard Bodtke, *Tragedy and the Jacobean Temper: The Major Plays of John Webster* (Salzburg, Institute für Englische Sprache und Literatur, 1972); Arthur C. Kirsch, *Jacobean Dramatic Perspectives* (Charlottesville: Univ. Press of Virginia, 1972); Sanford Sternlicht, *John Webster's Imagery and the Webster Canon* (Salzburg: Institut für Englische Sprache und Literatur, 1972); William Mahaney, *Deception in the John Webster Plays: An Analytical Study* (Salzburg: Institut für Englische Sprache und Literatur, 1973); and Eloise K. Goreau and Robert P. Griffin.

does not alter the fact that the opening line—"the right noble duchess" (187)—serves to indicate that the speech must be seen as relating to the idealized public figure that Antonio feels the Duchess, in contrast to her Machiavellian brothers, is.

That the major discussion between the Duchess and her brothers concerns their exercise of familial authority to forbid her to remarry makes this scene seem more private than public. Citing traditional early modern objections to a second marriage for widows—"they are most luxurious / Will wed twice" (297–298)[9]—the brothers appear to forbid her remarriage because she is their sister, not because of her political position as Duchess. Yet such overtly political references to the court as "a rank pasture" (306) whose deadly "honey-dew" (307) might tempt the Duchess to act against her brothers' interests reinforce the political sense of the scene. However, this is not to deny that the reference to the Duchess as a "sister" seems to involve consideration of her natural rather than her political body. Thus, in less than 100 lines we appear to move from contemplation of the body politic of the Duchess—as exemplar of Antonio's ideal of courtly virtue—to a picture of her widow's body natural at the mercy of her brothers' fears of her remarriage and early modern notions of the hypersexuality of widows.

And yet this encounter can be seen as being as political as the description of the French court and involving exclusively the Duchess's body politic. Catherine Belsey and Susan Wells[1] speak of the problems involved in trying to separate public from private space in the early modern period, especially as these spaces relate to the family. Belsey indicates that

9. Inga-Stina Ekeblad, "The 'Impure Art' of John Webster," in *Twentieth-Century Interpretations of The Duchess of Malfi*, ed. Norman Rabkin (Englewood Cliffs: Prentice-Hall, 1968), Ian Scott-Kilvert, *John Webster* (London: Longmans Green, 1964; rev. and rptd. 1970), and Joseph Henry Stodder, *Moral Perspective in Webster's Major Tragedies* (Salzburg: Institut für Englische Sprache und Literatur, 1974) feel that there was a strong Renaissance attitude against the second marriage of widows. But there were, in fact, no legal or ecclesiastical prohibitions against such remarriage. Frank W. Wadsworth ("Webster's *Duchess of Malfi* in the Light of Some Contemporary Ideas on Marriage and Remarriage," *PQ* 35 [1956]: 394–407) has compiled a long list of works that reflected positively upon the question. Paradoxically, though, the strong opinion against a widow's remarrying was coupled with the desire to marry her as soon as possible so that she was again under a man's control. As Lisa Jardine indicates, "widows of wealthy men were married off again with quite undignified haste where those responsible for them considered it financially advantageous to the line to do so" (83).

1. Catherine Belsey, "Disrupting Sexual Difference: Meaning and Gender in the Comedies," in *Alternative Shakespeares*, ed. John Drakakis (London and New York: Methuen, 1985) and Susan Wells, *The Dialectics of Representation* (Baltimore and London: Johns Hopkins Univ. Press, 1985). The following critics also discuss the juxtaposition of the Duchess's public and private selves, though not as they relate to the political implications of gender roles or relations: Jane Marie Luecke, "*The Duchess of Malfi*: Comic and Satiric Confusion in Tragedy," *SEL* 4(1964):275–290; Susan H. McLeod, *Dramatic Imagery in the Plays of John Webster* (Salzburg: Institut für Englische Sprache und Literatur, 1977); Ralph Berry, *The Art of John Webster* (Oxford: Clarendon Press, 1972); and Muriel Bradbrook, Anthony Courtade, Robert P. Griffin, and William Mahaney.

> in the sixteenth and early seventeenth centuries these two
> meanings of the family—as dynasty and as private realm of
> warmth and virtue—are both in play and indeed in contrast.
> In 1527 and for many years to come it was the dynastic mean-
> ing which was dominant. (p. 169)[2]

But although the sense of "family" as "dynasty" was the paramount
"reading" of the concept, Belsey points out that an "alternative"
notion of the family as "a little world of retreat" from the public space
"where the wife enters into partnership with the husband" was also
beginning to emerge (p. 173). We are tempted, I feel, with our
twentieth-century eyes to view things like early modern family relationships as though they were more like our own than less. Thus, the
temptation throughout this play is to feel that Ferdinand and the
Cardinal take an inordinate amount of interest in the potential
marital (e.g., private) affairs of their sister. This is perhaps an appropriate twentieth-century reading, but not necessarily an appropriate early modern one. While I do not wish to minimize the "private"
complexity of the Aragon family's relationships, I do think it is important to acknowledge the "political" or dynastic nature of the early
modern aristocratic marriage.

The Duchess is a sovereign ruler, a fact her brothers never forget.
Silvio announces the entrance of Ferdinand's family to him as "your
brother, the Lord Cardinal, and sister Duchess" (I.1.148) and the
Cardinal recalls the "high blood" (297)—noble birth—that the
Duchess possesses. The choral urgings of the two brothers to prevent the sister's marriage seem somewhat odd, especially when
Ferdinand calls upon his "father's poniard" (331) to help with the
argument, unless the objections of the brothers are viewed on dynastic grounds. Once we read the family as a Renaissance dynastic
unit, it becomes easier to understand the brothers'—and their
father's spirit's—earnest arguments. It also becomes easier to understand Ferdinand's obsession with the Duchess's blood and her reference to "all [her] royal kindred" (341) who might lie in the path of
her proposed marriage to a steward of lower rank, which would
pollute this blood.[3] Thus, the argument over the marriage can be
seen as a dynastic argument concerned with the Duchess's body
politic. This highly political scene, then, initially focusing on the
ideal court of the French king, also serves to present the Duchess
as a political figure both in her own right and as a member of a

---

2. Susan Wells feels that during the Jacobean period, the family was not only beginning
   to have a history, but was establishing its own identity as an entity distinct from church
   and state (69).
3. Leonard Tennenhouse (*Power on Display: The Politics of Shakespeare's Genres* [New York
   and London: Methuen, 1986]) discusses the mutilation of the female body in Jacobean
   drama especially in terms of the "metaphysics of blood" (Chapter 3, esp. 118–122).

political dynasty—whether of Malfi or Aragon. The focus on the Duchess, until her brothers' departure, is completely on her body politic.

However, viewing the early modern family as a dynastic unit does not fully account for the explicit sexual tension in this encounter of the Aragonian siblings. The brothers may be justified in taking an interest in their sister's marital affairs, but it is rather difficult to see how they can be justified in their inordinate interest in her sexual being as well. The nature of Renaissance dynastic marriage served almost totally to objectify the woman. She became an object of commerce who—passed from father to husband—sealed a bargain of greater or lesser economic significance.[4] As her body was seen as an object of trade to be owned by either father or husband, the products of her body—her children—were also seen as objects of commerce to be used to solidify further trade agreements between her (husband's) and other families. Thus, the woman's biological life—her ability or inability to produce viable offspring—becomes as much a possession of her male owners as her physical body itself. Thus, as Ferdinand and the Cardinal feel justified in controlling their sister's "use" as a wife, they also feel justified in controlling the biological uses of her body—its ability to produce offspring. In this sense, their inquiry into the chastity of their sister's body is understandable, though grotesque, for her production of children the patriarchy considers illegitimate would decrease her value as a trade article for her family.

And yet the brothers'—especially Ferdinand's—questions regarding her own use of her body go beyond questioning her chastity to expressing both fear of and desire for her sexual being. The very nature of woman's objectification within dynastic marriage leads to Ferdinand's obsessive sexual questioning. That a wife's body became, in essence, a vessel for reproducing her husband's or her father's bloodlines made it necessary for that vessel to remain unpolluted by sexual contact with unapproved males. This situation necessitated confining a woman and preserving her chastity at all costs. Yet the mere fact that the woman existed within the world and was a living being capable of disposing of her own body, of polluting her dynastic vessel through unauthorized sexual contact, led to extreme anxiety on the part of her male owners.

Ferdinand's obsessive desire to confine his sister and preserve her chastity—coupled with his equally obsessive fear that she will dispose of her body as she chooses—leads directly to his fearful imaginings of her as an excessively sexual creature. Thus she becomes,

---

4. Eve Kosofsky Sedgwick, *Between Men: English Literature and Male Homosocial Desire* (New York: Columbia Univ. Press, 1985), 38.

for him, one of those diseased women whose "livers are more spotted / Than Laban's sheep" (298–299), or a whore, or witch who "give[s] the devil suck" (311).[5] The reference to their father's poniard—in addition to recalling his patriarchal spirit—is, of course, phallic, as is the reference to the lamprey. While the references to whores and witches may be viewed as traditional early modern labels for a widow's sexual excesses,[6] Ferdinand's reference to the poniard (and his implicit threat to use it) and to the lamprey/tongue/(penis) imply the demand (and desire) for more intimate sexual knowledge. These references also serve to point out Ferdinand's technique of asserting his power over his sister by symbolically dismembering her body, a technique discussed by Nancy J. Vickers and Francis Barker.[7] Ferdinand's implication that all a woman can enjoy of a man is his tongue/penis suggests that all *she* is is a mouth/vagina, a container for these objects. Confusion results, however, in trying to discover whether the brothers try to control their sister's behavior as "private" widow or as "public" Duchess. In fact, once they have left, it is difficult to say whether Webster is presenting the Duchess as either political or private woman, as embodiment of either body politic or body natural. The boundaries of the Duchess's two bodies are indistinct and perpetually slipping. In the speech denying her "royal kindred" power to stop her marriage (I.1.341–349), she is represented as acting like a sovereign, willing to make her family into "low footsteps" if they try to control her. But her assertion that she will choose a "husband"—rather than a consort—seems to indicate that she is acting as a private woman. However, once Antonio appears,

5. In fact, as Lisa Jardine indicates, "active sexuality codes for female breach of decorum" in the play (76–77).
6. The traditional stereotype of the oversexed widow is also discussed in: Simon Shepherd, *Amazons and Warrior Women: Varieties of Feminism in Seventeenth-Century Drama* (New York: St. Martins, 1981); Katherine Usher Henderson and Barbara F. McManus, *Half Humankind: Contexts and Texts of the Controversy about Women in England, 1540–1640* (Urbana and Chicago: Univ. of Illinois Press, 1985); and Lisa Jardine. This attitude led, in the drama, as Barbara J. Todd ("The Remarrying Widow: A Stereotype Reconsidered," in *Women in English Society 1500–1800*, ed. Mary Prior [London and New York: Methuen, 1985]) explains, to the creation of "an enduring stereotype of the early modern widow as a woman who anxiously sought a husband at any cost" (55).
   Todd has also indicated that the widow's legal identity—an identity denied single and married women—has further led to her being considered an anomalous—and, therefore, fearful—creature. This identity gave her a "voice" and often allowed her to "speak out," a situation also denied single and married women. The threatening nature of the verbal, or "shrewish," woman, and her identification with whores and harlots, has been documented by Catherine Belsey (*The Subject of Tragedy* [London and New York: Methuen, 1985]), Peter Stallybrass ("Patriarchal Territories: The Body Enclosed" in *Rewriting the Renaissance: The Discourses of Sexual Difference in Early Modern Europe*, eds. Margaret W. Ferguson, Maureen Quilligan, and Nancy J. Vickers [Chicago and London: Univ. of Chicago Press, 1986], 123–142), and Lisa Jardine.
7. Nancy J. Vickers ("Diana Described: Scattered Woman and Scattered Rhyme," *Critical Inquiry* 8[1981]: 265–79) and Francis Barker ("Into the Vault," in Barker, *The Tremulous Private Body: Essays on Subjection* [London and New York: Methuen, 1984]) discuss the prevailing Renaissance image of the female body as silent, dismembered and, therefore, powerless.

she again is represented in her political persona. Antonio is shown to respond to her as his Duchess, and she is shown to be in total control of both the scene and her secretary. It is as sovereign ruler that she shows Antonio what she "make[s him] lord of" (430) and it is as ruler that she laments "the misery" of being born great, "forc'd to woo, because none dare woo us" (442). But later in the same speech, she is represented as shifting into a private mode:

> I do here put off all vain ceremony,
> And only do appear to you a young widow
> That claims you for her husband, and like a widow,
> I use but half a blush in't.
>
> (I.1.456–459)

And she appears to continue in this mode for the remainder of the scene.

Even though the Duchess may not have acted precisely in her body politic at the end of the scene, she has acted in a political way. With the power of her body politic, the power of a sovereign prince, she has violated existing patriarchal conventions of marriage to create her own concept of the state. To do so, this character has drawn upon an ideology of marriage quite different from the dynastic union her brothers speak of. The Protestant notion of the "companionate marriage" began, as John C. Bean indicates, as a rationalist humanist reaction to the emotionalism of courtly love and consisted, as John Halkett explains, of "a relatively modern concept of marriage as a partnership of love and mutual helpfulness."[8] Thus the Duchess chooses a man below her in estate to be, not her consort, but her husband: not a man to support her as a ruler, but a man to support her as a woman. She has eliminated the problems of the consort trying to wrest power from the woman ruler—who was thought

---

8. John C. Bean, "Passion Versus Friendship in the Tudor Matrimonial Handbooks and Some Shakespearean Implications," *Wascana Review*, 9(1974): 231–240 and John Halkett, *Milton and the Idea of Matrimony* (New Haven and London: Yale Univ. Press, 1970), 16. The following critics also agree that the Protestant focus on "friendship" as a basis for marriage and the view of marriage as equal to celibacy led to a more positive attitude toward women and more autonomy for them within marriage: Carroll Camden, *The Elizabethan Woman: A Panorama of English Womanhood, 1540 to 1640* (London: Cleaver-Hume and New York and Houston: Elsevier, 1952, 56; Juliet Dusinberre, *Shakespeare and the Nature of Women* (New York: Barnes and Noble, 1975), 53, 83; Catherine M. Dunn, "The Changing Image of Women in Renaissance Society and Literature," in *What Manner of Woman: Essays in English and American Life and Literature*, ed. Marlene Springer (New York: New York Univ. Press, 1977), 22; Velma Bourgeois Richmond, "Shakespeare's Women," *Midwest Quarterly* 19(1977–78): 330–342, p. 333; Betty Travitsky, ed., *The Paradise of Women* (Westport, CT and London: Greenwood Press, 1981), 7. While the notion of marriage Webster's Duchess conceives of with Antonio is closer to the philosophical concept of the Protestant "companionate marriage" than to the "dynastic marriage" her brothers have in mind, it is important to remember that neither marriage concept granted the woman a right to choose her own husband.

to be subject to her male husband—by not naming Antonio as her consort.

The Duchess's marriage has occasioned much critical concern because it is to a person below her in degree and because she enters into it "irregularly" or without her brothers' consent. Antonio is clearly represented as a worthy person whose "nobility of character" validates the Duchess's free choice of him as a husband. Yet the nature of Antonio's character is a direct result of Webster's juxtaposition of contrasting discourses in the play. In direct contrast to the custom that placed women under the control of their male family members is a long humanist tradition that both recognized the great importance of nobility of character in a man and validated a woman's right to the free choice of a husband, a tradition reinforced in Henry Medwall's *Fulgens and Lucres* (c. 1497).[9] In this play, a wealthy man from an ancient family and a poor man of personal integrity court Fulgens' daughter. Yet Fulgens refuses to choose Lucres's husband, stressing not only that the choice must be hers, but that she must also accept the obligation such freedom of choice entails.[1] This tradition of a woman's free choice even appears in Painter's story of the Duchess of Malfi, the source of Webster's play.[2] Fifteenth- and sixteenth-century women may have been coerced into propertied, political, or dynastic marriages, but they, theoretically, should have entered into them purely as a result of free choice. Thus, the Duchess's actively choosing Antonio can be seen as an action that recalls Lucres's acceptance of duty in choosing a husband.[3] Various men may be proposed to Lucres, but it is her moral duty to exercise her freedom of choice and choose the one who is best for her, whom she feels to be most honorable.

9. Henry Medwall, *Fulgens and Lucrece,* in *Five Pre-Shakespearean Comedies,* ed. Frederick S. Boas (London, Oxford, New York: Oxford Univ. Press, 1934; rptd., 1970), ix. This play is a retelling of Buonaccorso da Montemagno, "Controuersia de Nobilitate," trans. John Tiptoft as "The Declamacion of Noblesse" in R. J. Mitchell, *John Tiptoft* (London, New York, Toronto: Longmans, Green and Co., 1938).

1. Catherine Belsey indicates that, while Lucres asks her father's advice, she clearly makes the unconstrained choice her freedom allows her in favor of virtue (*Tragedy,* 194–200). "The play thus affirms marriage as the location of liberal and affective values rather than as a guarantee of dynastic continuity" (194). Belsey also indicates that *The Duchess of Malfi* "claims for its heroine the right to choose a husband" (200).

2. William Painter, "The Palace of Pleasure, Vol. II, xxiii Novel" (1567) in *The Palace of Pleasure,* Vol. III, ed. Joseph Jacobs (1580; rptd., London: David Nutt: 1890). Spelling modernized as regards long "s."

   let men say what they list, I will doe none otherwyse than my heade and mynd have already framed. Semblably I neede not make accompt to any persone for my fact, my body, and reputation beynge in full libertie and freedome (13).

3. Richard Bodtke points out that the Duchess is "true to earlier Renaissance humanistic values of true nobility" in seeing "the man not his rank" (171). While Catherine Belsey indicates that in wooing Antonio the Duchess opts for personal virtue over nobility of birth (*Tragedy,* 197–198), Frank Whigham ("Sexual and Social Mobility in *The Duchess of Malfi,*" PMLA 100 [1985]: 167–186) argues that the Duchess violates her class rank by choosing a "base lover" (170) who could potentially contaminate the ruling elite (168).

By having the Duchess choose a husband beneath her in rank, but virtuous, Webster calls on a tradition that is in direct contrast to the one he earlier presented as influencing the Aragonian brothers. The reflection of these two discourses within the play—one that validates male family members' rights over the bodies of their female "property" and one that mandates a woman's free choice as a moral necessity—is an example of the ideologically contradictory nature of *The Duchess of Malfi*. The extreme difference of these two conflicting discourses as regards the position of women serves to foreground the character of the Duchess and her dilemma as woman and sovereign ruler. While the brothers are shown to support that tradition which validates the power of the patriarchal family over women, the Duchess can be seen as challenging that discourse either by creating a new one or by consciously harking back to a tradition which, at least philosophically, granted women a certain measure of autonomy. It is not surprising that the character should be aligned to this humanistic tradition since the power it grants a woman provides a space whereby the Duchess can use her political autonomy to create a marriage situation in which she, as ruler, is not subsumed by the power the dynastic marriage paradigm would grant to any husband over any wife.

The Duchess is further represented as manifesting her political authority by engaging in an "irregular" marriage—one that is not sanctified by any representative of the church. The Duchess's exchange of vows with Antonio constitutes a *sponsalia per verba de praesenti*. Such a marriage, as Margaret Loftus Ranald indicates, "created the status of virtual matrimony at that moment, without future action on the part of the persons concerned. It could even be upheld in courts against a later, consummated contract."[4] Thus, when the Duchess and Antonio exchange their *de praesenti* vows in I.1, they are, in fact, legally marrying themselves, although in an unusual way. However, their promises are followed by a physical consummation which was not allowed partners in a *de praesenti* spousal. Such a union that resulted in physical consummation was still valid, though irregular, and the action was deplored. Ecclesiastical penalties were generally imposed which usually involved public penance and, in rare cases, excommunication. The latter sentence could be circumvented by payment of a fine. The couple was then required to ratify their marriage by recelebrating it in church.

It is clear, then, that although the Duchess's marriage to Antonio *itself* is legal, the *consummation* of it is irregular and would open the couple to ecclesiastical penalties. However, it also seems clear

4. Margaret Loftus Ranald, "'As Marriage Binds, and Blood Breaks': English Marriage and Shakespeare," *SQ* 30(1979): 68–81.

that the Duchess is aware of the Church's traditional role in a *sponsalia per verba de praesenti* for, after she and Antonio pledge their love, she questions:

> What can the church force more? . . .
> How can the church bind faster?
> We now are man and wife, and 'tis the church
> That must but echo this.
>
> (I.1.488; 491–493)

Although the Duchess recognizes the church's traditional role in legitimizing a marriage contract, she is also depicted as scorning the church's ability to have power over her as a secular ruler. Her employing a marriage *per verba de praesenti* rather than a fully ecclesiastical wedding accomplishes more, it seems to me, than simply secrecy. In marrying Antonio the Duchess is shown to challenge her brothers first, by exercising her woman's "freedom of choice"—as Lucres did—and second, by recognizing and validating Antonio's personal worth over his social position. She is also shown to challenge them by exercising her power as a ruler both by denying the church its rights in the legitimizing of her marriage as well as in courting a husband, rather than a consort.

In her marriage and its ramifications, the Duchess can be viewed as a subversive character. Marriage was the major means of controlling female sexuality and legitimizing the means of inheritance between patriarchal families and governments. In challenging marriage in any way, therefore, the Duchess challenges the very essence of gender relations within patriarchal early modern society. I see the character's reaction to marriage as subversive on two levels: first, in her decision to keep her marriage "private" and separate from her "public" identity as ruler; second, in her unconventional concept of what a marriage between a man and a woman might be like. This marriage—both the choosing of a virtuous husband and the ceremony itself—represents the major conflict between the Duchess's natural and political bodies in the play. In actively choosing her own husband and in marrying him in a way that scorns accepted legal practices, the Duchess reinforces her sense of self as a political person. She is represented as demonstrating her own right to choose a husband and her right to determine how she—as ruler of Malfi—will legitimize her choice. However, despite her attempt to take political control over the marriage ceremony, the Duchess does not make the marriage part of her strategy for rule. That she is presented as opting to keep her marriage secret indicates that she has not determined an effective way to integrate marriage into her public life as ruler.

In I.1, the Duchess moves back and forth between acting as a prince and as a woman. Her political self exerts itself as she, being "born great," proposes to Antonio despite her brothers' prohibitions against remarriage (468). Yet her refusal to make Antonio her consort argues that her union is to be considered a "private" marriage. Her political self also asserts its power to legitimize the marriage through a *sponsalia per verba de praesenti*. But it is the character's private self that urges her husband to lead her to their marriage bed. The confusion in this scene as to whether the woman or the prince prevails is part of the major problem of just how to read the Duchess throughout the play. We are invited to see her marriage to Antonio as a marriage for love between two attractive people, one of whom is a woman ruler. The problem with this view is that we are asked to accept the fact that this reigning woman—the living exemplar of a respected theory of rule—would make not only a non-political marriage, but a politically disastrous one as well. And yet this same woman has directed her talents to creating a new discourse of rule, one which does not simply replicate the patriarchal conventions determined by her society and its male rulers, but which attempts to fuse a traditional female role—wife and mother—with a non-traditional one—ruler. The ultimate effect of I.1., therefore, is to present us with a very political character. The Duchess may opt to keep her marriage "private," but her doing so must be acknowledged a political decision. Keeping her natural and political bodies separate may not be the most effective political strategy. However, there is no doubt that this strategy must be recognized as a political one made by a sovereign who is conscious of the political implications of all activities she engages in.

Although the Duchess may have made an unfortunate political choice regarding separating her natural and political bodies, she makes a rather unique decision concerning the fundamental nature of her marriage with Antonio. Webster has represented the implications of such a marriage over time in III.2, which depicts the first private view we have had of Antonio and the Duchess since I.1. This scene presents the Duchess as wife in the new "private" family life she has created, and it reads as an inversion of the traditional Renaissance marriage where the husband has total control over the wife.[5] Yet it is also clear that while the Duchess may be shown to take the "lead" in the bantering in the scene, Antonio is not exactly "subject" to his wife in the same way that Renaissance women were expected

---

5. Muriel C. Bradbrook sees the marriage as a reversal of order, and condemns the Duchess for acting contrary to accepted Renaissance patterns of behavior for women (146, 150). But as critics like Kathleen McLuskie indicate, the point of the play is that it is *about* "the possibility of so unconventional a marriage" (86). In fact, by separating her private life from her public life, the Duchess is shown to adhere to a notion of family and marriage that is more similar to the "private" notion of marriage outlined by Catherine Belsey than to the "public" notion of dynastic marriage her brothers have been discussing.

to be subject to their husbands. His joking reference to his "rule" being "only in the night" (III.2.8) indicates both that the marriage is sexually fulfilling and that Antonio is meant to accept the parameters of the marriage the Duchess has created and not to envy her position as ruler.

The Duchess is represented as being radically different from the traditional picture of the Renaissance wife in this scene. Not only is she a woman who is capable of commanding her husband specifically as regards his sexual desires (III.2.4–6), and refusing him— "you get no lodging here tonight, my lord" (2). But she is also a woman who thoroughly enjoys her sexuality[6]—"Alas, what pleasure can two lovers find in sleep?" (10)—and the products of it, her children (66–68). Antonio's behavior is similarly radical for he is represented as not challenging his wife regarding his "rights" to her body or bed, and chafes her with the observation that

> Labouring men
> Count the clock oft'nest . . . [and]
> Are glad when their tasks' ended,
> (III.2.18–20)

which forces her to "stop" his mouth with a kiss (20). The bantering continues with Antonio's begging another kiss and his sneaking off with Cariola so that the Duchess will be left speaking to herself. Antonio is depicted as teasing his wife in this way because he loves "to see her angry" (57).

Webster's extraordinary picture of marriage contrasts sharply with the prevailing early modern notion that women were marginalized or objectified creatures that required domination by men. Yet however much we may applaud this idealistic, egalitarian, and companionate marriage, we still must realize that it exists in almost direct conflict with the Duchess's position as sovereign ruler of Malfi. By keeping her body natural divorced from her body politic and secreting her husband, the Duchess opens herself to accusation as a whore and a witch—women who do not follow accepted patterns of behavior. Her pregnancies convince her brothers and her subjects that she is sexually involved with a man—a situation that allows her to be viewed as an oversexed widow and play directly into Ferdinand's hands. That she has, in fact, married, but married in secret to a man some feel is inferior presents her as violating still more accepted patriarchal codes of female behavior. By not actively challenging the

---

6. In analyzing *Arden of Feversham*, Catherine Belsey states that in making a sexual choice of Mosby over Arden, Alice Arden "may be committing herself to a form of power more deadly still, and less visible" (*Tragedy*, 144). To me, it is clear that the Duchess of Malfi, in her choice of Antonio as lover and husband commits herself to power in just the same way that Belsey sees Alice Arden as doing.

Renaissance discourse of "woman," the Duchess, effectually, allows herself to be read as "whore."

One way to contain women who acted in ways contrary to accepted patterns of female behavior was to label them "whores" or "witches." This technique of containment through stereotypic "naming" has been used several times on the Duchess, as I have indicated above. Another way to contain women characters is to control representations of their bodies. As labeling marginalizes women by giving them the "names" of those who live on the margins of acceptable society— whores or witches—the focus on only certain parts of a woman's body "dismembers" her by negatively contrasting her amputated/ lacking condition to the completeness of the socially-acceptable male body. Ferdinand's depiction of his sister as a mouth/vagina (I.1) is just such an example of dismemberment. But the female body does not need to be "dismembered" to be marginalized. Sometimes the mere focus on a woman's biology or her use of cosmetics serves negatively to contrast her body to the fixed image of maleness all men, by definition, possess. Bosola's discovery of the Duchess's pregnancy in II.1 continues consideration of how the female body is represented in the play. Bosola is depicted, in this scene, as first condemning the Old Lady for her face-painting, or "face-physic" (23). In a series of particularly loathsome images, Bosola is shown to accuse the Old Lady—and, by association, all women—of engaging in thoroughly disgusting practices in order to present to the world a facial image that differs from reality. He tells of the French woman who flayed the skin off her face to make it more level (27–28), a process which made her resemble "an abortive hedgehog" (29). He then lists the cosmetic contents of a woman's closet and indicates that they are more suitable "for a shop of witchcraft" (35). The ultimate effect of this listing of disgusting objects and disagreeable practices is to stress Bosola's anti-feminism, which causes the character to aver that he "would sooner eat a dead pigeon, taken from the soles of the feet of one sick of the plague, than kiss one of you [e.g., women] fasting" (II.1.38–40). From this woman-hating stance, the character proceeds to describe the Duchess in her pregnancy:

> I observe our duchess
> Is sick o' days, she pukes, her stomach seethes,
> The fins of her eyelids look most teeming blue,
> She wanes i'th' cheek, and waxes fat i'th' flank;
> And (contrary to our Italian fashion)
> Wears a loose-body'd gown—there's somewhat in't!
> (II.1.63–68)

Although there is clearly as much revulsion in Bosola's description of the pregnant woman as in his earlier descriptions of cosmetics, revulsion regarding female nature is not the only thing these two descriptions have in common. Make-up and face-painting, no matter what the cosmetics contain, serve the purpose of "disguising" a woman and hiding some part of her from the male gaze. The essential fear of men as regards cosmetics is that they will create a mask of beauty and gull a man into accepting a "naturally" ugly woman as "artificially" beautiful. In the same way, a loose-bodied gown—or "bawd farthingales" (148)—disguises a swelling body and "the young springal cutting a caper in [the Duchess's] belly" (151). Thus, from what we are shown to be the point of view of the intelligencer, women are adept as deceivers of men because they use cosmetics and costume to disguise/hide the defects of their bodies to present themselves as something they are not—beautiful or chaste.

But the image of the pregnant Duchess can be seen as something more than simply an emblem of disguise or trickery. The body of a pregnant woman is very different from the body of a non-pregnant woman, as Bosola's description of II.1.63–68 attests. However, to go one step farther, a woman's body is radically different from a man's body because it *can* become pregnant. Thus, while for a man constancy of bodily image may be desirable, constancy of bodily image for a woman may not necessarily be desirable. Given the female body's ability to become pregnant, the necessity of that pregnancy for the production of heirs to the patriarchal line, and the lack of reliable birth control methods in the early modern period, the pregnant body must be seen as an alternative image of the female body with as much power as the traditional non-pregnant image. And since, despite the innate fallaciousness of the phrases, a woman may be "slightly pregnant" or "very pregnant," there cannot be *one* acceptable image of the "pregnant" woman. Women in the sixteenth and seventeenth centuries—if they were not virgins—drifted into and out of pregnancy with alarming regularity. Thus, the female body—in direct contrast to the male body—is a body in a state of constant flux. And, as such, it is capable of producing a certain uneasiness. The nature of woman's biology necessitates a flexible image of her body which is in direct contrast to the fixed image of the male body. This fact accounts for both the Duchess's refusal to be concerned about the inevitability of the greying of her hair (III.2.58–60), and Bosola's uneasiness at his inability to find the constant within the Duchess's vastly (and continuously) changing bodily shape. Women's bodies are threatening because they are ever-changing and cannot be confined to a single shape.[7] Bosola's wish to confine/define the

7. Susan Wells contrasts the Duchess's "static, remote, dedicated to matrimony" royal body—which she sees imaged in the alabaster tomb figure—to her "eroticized, individual body." She feels that the play most often places us in "a world of fragile and fertile bodies" in which the social distinctions—class, status, etc.—that normally determine our experience of the body are subverted (66). The fixed, alabaster royal body of the Duchess can also be seen as more like the fixed male body that Bosola finds easier to accept than the changeable pregnant body he is confronted with.

Duchess's body by her clothes, to remove it from the loose-bodied gowns that hide it, is played out in II.2 when the Duchess is both literally and figuratively "confined" during the birth of her child.

The Duchess's figurative confinement results from her failure to consider the implications her changing shape will have upon her subjects. In separating her body natural from her body politic, the Duchess has not provided a means for dealing with the fact that her married body natural is expected to become pregnant while her "widowed" body politic is expected to remain "unpregnant," constant of shape. When her pregnancy impinges upon her political body and its shape changes, she does nothing beyond wearing a loose gown to disguise it. Far from being successful at concealing her pregnancy, this stratagem simply serves to call attention to both her stereotyped changing female shape and her stereotyped sexuality. In allowing these stereotypes room for consideration, the Duchess forces consideration of herself as *woman* rather than *ruler* and foregrounds her body natural at the expense of her body politic.

Bosola is not the only male character to espouse negative attitudes towards women. We can contrast this character's views on cosmetics, pregnancy, and old age with Ferdinand's views on the sexual nature of women's bodies, especially his sister's. I have already mentioned the lamprey/tongue/(penis) pun in 1.1.336–38 and the implication that the Duchess's interest in men is purely sexual, her body nothing more than a mouth/vagina to contain the tongue/penis of a man. In II.5, Ferdinand tells the Cardinal that the Duchess is "loose i'th' hilts" (3), another sexual reference, since the blade of a sword or dagger was inserted into its hilt. Finally, Ferdinand's anger and fury at his sister is represented as carrying him out of the realm of metaphor and into that of specific images where he "sees" her

> in the shameful act of sin. . . .
>   Happily with some strong thigh'd bargeman;
> Or one o'th' wood-yard, that can quoit the sledge,
> Or toss the bar, or else some lovely squire
> That carries coals up to her privy lodgings.
>
>   (II.5.41–5)

Thus his fury is directly the result of the Duchess's desire to keep her marriage secret. While Ferdinand does not learn of the marriage, he does learn of the children. The sexual activity necessary to engender them prompts his misogynistic outburst and is the direct result of the Duchess's failure to control the effects of her private life on her public one. Instead of defusing the threats to her political persona caused by her first pregnancy, she fuels them by having subsequent pregnancies. That this last image of his sister is less objectified than some of Ferdinand's earlier images does not discount the fact that it still represents the Duchess as an exclusively sexual creature who will couple with any man who is available.

Although in many respects Ferdinand's preoccupations with the Duchess's sexuality can be seen as simply obsessive or paranoid, on another level his fears are well-grounded, for Webster has represented the Duchess as being very different in regard to her sexuality from accepted images of early modern women. She is neither chaste virgin nor unregenerate whore (except, perhaps, in what Webster has depicted of Ferdinand's mind), yet she is something that normally does not appear in the early modern drama—a loving wife who is also a sexually mature and active woman. The Duchess is presented as marrying in order to fulfill her physical love for Antonio as well as her emotional attachment to him. Further, and as the play progresses, the Duchess and Antonio are shown to be loving parents to the children who are the products of their marriage. Thus, we can view the Duchess as a figure who values and takes control of her own sexuality by marrying against custom and her family. Further, by not making Antonio her consort, by not granting him a place in her political life, the Duchess is depicted as not granting her children by Antonio a place in her political life as well. Removed from the political realm, these children are never thought of as the heirs or commodities in a dynastic marriage, but as offspring who need a mother's care:

> I pray thee, look thou giv'st my little boy
> Some syrup for his cold, and let the girl
> Say her prayers, ere she sleep.
> (IV.2.202–204)

Since the Duchess's children are kept so secret, their existence so shadowy, they become completely invisible as regards the court of Malfi. But by removing the children from the public gaze, the Duchess is represented as controlling her biology through the products of it as completely as she is represented as controlling her sexuality.

Ultimately, the Duchess's marriage and sexual politics are represented as so revolutionary that she must be punished for her actions. After Ferdinand appears in her chamber in III.2, the Duchess tries to avoid discovery by concocting a plot whereby Antonio and her children leave Malfi for a place of safety. Although the Duchess is represented as not having tried to integrate her private life into her public life, her decisive actions in her public persona are used to try to preserve her husband and allow the couple to live, eventually, as private individuals. But her plot does not work and she is punished, first by having her duchy taken from her and second by imprisonment in her own palace.

Since the Duchess has been stripped of her political power in III.4, it is essentially as a private woman that she is punished in Act IV. As Bosola was shown to have chafed at the fact that it was impossible sufficiently to confine women or their bodies, in this act the Duchess is represented as finally being completely confined and the victim of various tortures. Her body is still depicted as being a subject both Ferdinand and Bosola focus on. And Ferdinand, perhaps for the first time, is depicted as viewing his sister's body as complete (IV.1.121–123), rather than as simply a vagina. This change of focus is interesting and perhaps refers to the fact that, for the first time, Ferdinand can be absolutely sure of his sister's chastity. Totally confined physically, the Duchess is denied the possibility of any and all sexual activity. She is now, finally, a vessel that may be trusted with the Aragon family's pure dynastic blood. Yet, despite this, Ferdinand is shown to see his sister as mad, for women who act in a way contrary to accepted social norms are often considered mad. Bosola's focus on the Duchess's body has also changed. Where earlier he was represented as seeing the Duchess's female body as swollen with pregnancy or concealed by clothing or disgusting cosmetics, he now describes it as being no more than "a box of worm-seed" (124) or a preserve of earthworms. Although the images are not positive, they are not particularly sexist either. They are emblems of mortality, images common to both men and women, rather than socially-sanctioned images of anti-feminism.

Finally, the scenes of the Duchess's imprisonment give a mixed message regarding the Duchess herself. She is shown to indicate her position as victim both by the reference to her body as food—"Go tell my brothers, when I am laid out, / They then may feed in quiet" (IV.2.236–37)—and when she says "I am chain'd to endure all your tyranny" (IV.2.60). The character is also shown to be a martyr[8] and is represented as comparing herself to Portia "the rare and almost dead example / Of a loving wife" (IV.1.73–74). In addition to these images of martyrs, Webster reminds us that the woman in prison had a political identity which she still claims: "I am Duchess of Malfi still" (IV.2.142). Yet despite her claims to a political self, the Duchess is totally powerless in prison and totally without her sovereign power. But in a very real way we are made to witness the punishment of the Duchess of Malfi as well as the wife of Antonio. The Duchess's line identifying herself as still Duchess of Malfi recalls

8. T. F. Wharton, "'Fame's Best Friend': Survival in *The Duchess of Malfi*," in *Jacobean Miscellany I*, ed. James Hogg (Salzburg: Institut für Englische Sprache und Literatur, 1980), 21. Wharton feels that it is "little short of astounding that Webster should be able to make a religious martyr so natural an ending for his Duchess," given her various anti-religious remarks throughout the play. Further, he states that "she assumes her own salvation with such massive assurances that she makes death seem, not a defect, but an award" (22).

her political identity and the nobility of her death reinforces it (IV.2.230–234). There is a certain cosmic sense about the Duchess's death as though she both realizes her position in the universe and accepts responsibility for both her life and her death. That she is shown not to cry out or beg for mercy places her at a moral advantage over Cariola, who is represented as begging for mercy, and Ferdinand, who is represented as denying the murder he is implicated in. Her death manages, for a moment, to cause Ferdinand to reconsider his part in it—"I bade thee, when I was distracted of my wits, / Go kill my dearest friend, and thou hast done't" (IV.2.279–280)— and Bosola to view her as a saint—"Return, fair soul, from darkness, and lead mine / Out of this sensible hell" (IV.2.342–43). In fact, Bosola's conviction that the Duchess has the power to lead his soul out of hell recalls Antonio's earlier boast to Delio that the Duchess's looks "were able to raise one to a galliard / That lay in a dead palsy" (I.1.196–97). Yet there is something profoundly ironic in this scene.

This final representation of the Duchess as martyr, as woman idealized through suffering comes actually from a much more traditional discourse of womanhood than previous representations of the Duchess as ruler. This "martyred" view of woman comes both from the patient Griselda stories, which validate the wife who is faithful, forgiving, silent, and patient, and the images of the Virgin Mary and Hecuba as mothers prostrate with grief.[9] In a society that limits women's options to those of wife or mother, creatures whose identities can easily be subsumed by their husbands or children, a talent for suffering nobly (and quietly) becomes the only means by which a woman can be viewed as "heroic." Thus the final representation of Webster's protagonist is not as ruler, but as idealized suffering wife/mother/woman. Her cry, "I am Duchess of Malfi still," becomes ironic, for this seeming validation of her political self occurs within a context that more completely validates her private self as wife and mother.

The "mixed messages" present in this scene are characteristic of the "mixed messages" regarding the Duchess's character that are presented throughout the play and are what contribute to the play's ideologically contradictory nature. In Act IV, our final view of the Duchess is of a character punished primarily for her violation of social custom as a woman, yet also for her violation of political custom as a sovereign. Thus *The Duchess of Malfi* can be viewed as a subversive play because it challenges the basic concept of the early

---

9. Belsey, *Tragedy*, 164–71. Lisa Jardine, 181–195 and "*The Duchess of Malfi*: A Case Study of the Literary Representation of Women," in *Teaching the Text*, eds. Susanne Kappeler and Norman Bryson (London and Boston: Routledge and Kegan Paul, 1983), 207–208. Marilyn L. Williamson, *The Patriarchy of Shakespeare's Comedies* (Detroit: Wayne State Univ. Press, 1986), 64–74.

modern marriage, a marriage in which the woman was completely objectified, used only to serve the business or physical needs of her father, her husband, or their joint families. The Duchess is represented as reacting against this social construct of marriage by creating an entirely new concept of the estate, one in which men and women are companions, equal partners, friends, and lovers. She is shown to control her own sexuality, not simply by refusing her body to her husband, but by demanding a relationship with him in which her sexuality is acknowledged, validated, and fulfilled. Further, in spite of dynastic practices, she removes her children from consideration as heirs, seeing them as belonging to herself, rather than her family, thus allowing her effectively to control her biology as well as her sexuality. Even though her refusal to unite her body natural and her body politic—or to consider an alternative way to integrate her private married life into her life as a ruler—leads to her unsuccessful reign as a sovereign, the very nature of her marriage is so revolutionary and challenges social custom to such a degree that the Duchess must be punished for her audacity in creating it. Despite this attempt to contain the subversive nature of the Duchess, the overall impetus of Acts I–IV remains subversive, especially since allowing the Duchess to die as a tragic figure in Act IV presents her as taking over even the powers of a male tragic protagonist, foregrounds her further, and invests her character and its subversive ideology with great power.

But if Act IV leaves us with a fairly strong picture of the Duchess as a character who would subvert her society's political and social ideologies by re-creating patriarchal discourses regarding marriage, what are we to make of Act V? This curious act appears to be an afterthought that abruptly changes the focus and mood of the play. By foregrounding the male characters, it attempts to contain all of the subversive aspects of the Duchess's rule and restore patriarchal order. And yet the containment is far from complete because the restored order is so dubious. Civil authority is represented by a lycanthropic Duke who robs graveyards and ecclesiastical authority by a Machiavellian Cardinal who murders his mistress. The naively innocent Antonio accepts the brothers at face value and is killed, accidentally, as Bosola murders them to avenge their sister. The Duchess's reign may have been threatening to accepted patriarchal notions of rule, but the final picture of Ferdinand, Antonio, Bosola, and the Cardinal hardly reassures an audience of any of the male characters' abilities to control the state or their moral right to do so. Even the honorable Delio's final entrance casts doubt upon this picture of restored patriarchal order. Antonio's friend appears with the child who will inherit "in's mother's right" (V.5.113). To reinforce the patriarchal order this act ostensibly supports, this child should be the son of the Duchess's first marriage, the son of the dead Duke of Malfi. And he *should* inherit "in his *father's* right." But this son is curiously the child of the Duchess and Antonio, the son of the Duke of Malfi having somehow disappeared during the course of the play. Thus the inheritance pattern that should reflect primogeniture and support patriarchal order does neither. True it restores a male ruler to the duchy, but one who has no legal right to the title which he acquires through a matriarchal rather than a patriarchal inheritance pattern.

Act V, then, is a curious construct. In an attempt to erase or contain the power revealed by the Duchess in Acts I–IV, it focuses on "traditionally" male questions of government and inheritance. Yet the rulers it presents—Ferdinand, the Cardinal, and the Duchess's son—are either totally reprehensible morally or come to the title illegally through the female line. Thus, while ostensibly attempting to reinforce the patriarchy and erase the subversive elements of Acts I–IV, Act V, in fact, questions the nature of the social constructs it reinforces and the men who represent them. While not actually arguing in favor of the marital/political paradigm the Duchess has created, this Act's insistence upon establishment of the son of the Duchess's irregular marriage in "her" right does seem to reinforce her political power while simultaneously attempting to deny it. Finally, the discontinuous nature of Act V makes it as difficult to "read" as earlier acts. While it must be acknowledged that an attempt is made to "cover over" the subversive elements of Acts I–IV, the fabric of that covering certainly is dubious at best. It contains holes through which a newly-created, though contradictory, ruling practice can be viewed. Thus while presenting the "official" patriarchal picture of rule, Act V allows simultaneous consideration of the Duchess's subversive attempts at rulership as a corrective to an existing system that is imaged as morally corrupt.

Monuments and Ruins

BRIAN CHALK

From Webster's "Worthyest Monument": The Problem of Posterity in *The Duchess of Malfi*[†]

For John Webster, death was not merely an artistic preoccupation; it was a fundamental part of the family business. Webster's father ran a successful coach transport firm and was a prominent member of the Guild of Merchant Taylors. Coach makers had no guild of their own but were admitted to the Taylor's Guild on the grounds that there was "a close and obvious connection between tailors, who made trappings for funerals, plays and pageants, and the men who provided hearses for coffins."[1] While Webster's father did not participate directly in the royal funerals that his more celebrated son occasionally commemorated poetically, he likely provided hearses to transport plague victims to burial pits. Webster inherited this enterprise, and his contemporaries in the theatrical community were clearly well aware of this and even amused by the overlaps between the two professions. Henry Fitzgeffrey's nickname for Webster—"Crabbed (*Websterio*)/The *Play-wright, Cart-wright*"—alludes directly to the family business and strongly suggests that Webster himself took more than a passing interest in running it.[2] * * *

* * *

This essay argues that Webster's paradoxical desire for his works to endure for posterity and his disbelief in this possibility generates the pathos that drives his tragedies. Webster's skepticism that plays can provide a stable vehicle for literary posterity, moreover, intersects provocatively with Jacobean attitudes toward the purpose and efficacy of monuments and provides evidence of his feelings on both.

† Brian Chalk, "Webster's 'Worthyest Monument': The Problem of Posterity in *The Duchess of Malfi*." *Studies in Philology* 108 (2011), 379–402. Copyright © 2011 by the University of North Carolina Press. Used by permission of the publisher.

1. *Oxford Dictionary of National Biography* (2004), s.v. "Webster, John (1578–1638?)" by David Gunby, http://www.oxforddnb.com/view/article/28943.
2. Ibid.

In *The White Devil* and *The Duchess of Malfi*, Webster is deeply pre-occupied with death and its relationship to monuments—how people die, how they are represented in death, and how they may or may not be memorialized. This interest in monumentality and its relationship to commemoration, which features repeatedly in Webster's prefaces, resurfaces as a crucial framing device in his plays. In much the same way that Webster characterizes himself and his fellow playwrights, the characters in his two great tragedies fixate on thoughts of an afterlife to which they are denied any certainty of access. In *The Duchess of Malfi*, the characters that surround the Duchess attempt to dramatize prematurely her commemoration in order to dispel their own fears of death and its effects. Denied control over their lives and the manner of their deaths, Webster's characters appear suspended in a liminal zone between these two realms. In *The Duchess of Malfi*, I will suggest, the characters in various ways rely on the symbolic value of the Duchess herself: they see her as a monumental emblem that provides the elusive stability that they seek. Ultimately, however, in the play's final act, this drive toward futurity collapses the present with the future and evacuates both of meaning.

I. Flattering the Dead

In his *Devotions Upon Emergent Occasions*, assuming a decidedly Protestant perspective, John Donne dismisses the importance of postmortem rituals to the individuals whom they honor, claiming that "in our funerals we ourselves have no interest; there we cannot advise, we cannot direct."[3] The lavish funeral processions and monuments of the Jacobean era, however, suggest that the living took a much greater interest in their posthumous accommodations than Donne allows. For a Protestant culture that had severed its commemorative connections to the dead, monuments, both statuary and poetic, had become charged symbols that represented the precarious enterprise of attempting to secure a posthumous existence. The early seventeenth century saw a striking increase in the building of funeral monuments, over one-third of which were commissioned and built while the subjects they depicted were still alive.[4] Whereas the impulse to build monuments is traditionally thought to derive from the desire to mold and stabilize history, those built during the Jacobean era were just as often meant to mold the present as a means of manipulating the future.

---

3. Donne, *Devotions Upon Emergent Occasions Together With Death's Duel*, ed. Andrew Motion (New York: Cosmo Classics, 2007), 44.
4. See Nigel Llewellyn, *The Art of Death: Visual Culture in the English Death Ritual, 1500–1800* (London: Reaktion Books, 1991), 17.

Rather than seek to commemorate a life well lived, post-Reformation statuary representations seemed designed to allow their subjects to straddle the border between this world and the next. As John Weever explains in *Ancient Funerall Monuments*, this practice was not without historical precedent:

> It was vsuall in ancient times, and so it is in these our dayes, for persons of especiall ranke and qualities to make their own Tombes and Monuments in their life-time, partly for that they might haue a certain house to put their head in (as the old saying is) whensoever they should bee taken away by death, out of this their Tenement, the world; and partly to please themselves, in the beholding of their dead countenance in marble. But most especially because thereby they thought to preserve their memoryes from oblivion.[5]

Weever describes both the practical considerations and the odd psychological dynamics that motivate the living to construct their own monuments. Persons of "especiall ranke and qualities," according to Weever, take pleasure in the "beholding of their dead countenance in marble." Weever's wording here is striking; the people that he describes wish to be represented not only in marble, but also as "dead," as if seeing themselves in this state somehow granted them the vicarious experience of mourning their deaths in advance. The deepest fear that these structures address, however, is that without them the memories of the individuals they depict will be lost in "oblivion," and therefore they seek to concretize a posthumous place in present reality.

In utilizing the monument as a symbol of poetic immortality, then, Renaissance writers were not only participating in an age-old competition between poets and sculptors, which pitted the memorializing powers of one against the other, but they were also responding to a society that was deeply invested in the idea that commemorative monuments had the potential to stabilize their subjects' claims on the afterlife. Jonson, for his part, participated fully in this practice. Self-consciously mimicking Horace with his 1616 folio, Jonson meant to construct a monument to himself in his own lifetime.[6] In addition to poets, prose stylists such as Thomas Browne were openly critical of this approach. In *Hydriotaphia, or Urne-Buriall*, Browne pointedly emphasizes the superficial and even blasphemous nature of such devices. The desire of the living to commemorate themselves in advance of their death, he claims, may stem from an innate urge to confirm the immortality of the soul, but this impulse inevitably

5. Weever, *Ancient Funerall Monuments* (London, 1631), 18.
6. See *Ben Jonson's 1616 Folio*, ed. Jennifer Brady and W. H. Herendeen (Newark: University of Delaware Press, 1991).

gets confused with and caught up in worldly vanities and results in a tendency to imagine the afterlife as some sort of perpetuation of life as lived on earth. Building monuments to commemorate the dead, Browne contends, does not honor or reinforce Protestant beliefs; instead it grossly contradicts them:

> To extend our memories by Monuments . . . whose duration we cannot hope, without injury to our expectations, in the advent of the last day, were a contradiction to our beliefs. We whose generations are ordained in this setting part of time, are providentially taken off from such imaginations. And being necessitated to eye the remaining particle of futurity, are naturally constituted unto thoughts of the next world, and cannot excusably decline the consideration of that duration which maketh Pyramids pillars of snow, and all that's past a moment.[7]

Browne's lines, which seem to echo subtly Shakespeare's "Sonnet 55," call attention to the fact that statuary representations themselves deteriorate and cannot sustain memory in the way that their subjects hope they will. More to the point, lavish funerary monuments, no matter how splendid, do nothing to ameliorate the judgment that we all must face "in the advent of the last day." Hence, Browne continues, they have no substantive value, for they represent nothing more than a "fruitless continuation" that will "only arise unto late posterity as Emblems of mortall vanities."[8]

Despite these criticisms, however, we can detect that Browne believes that the drive that produces these monuments is deeply human, for as mortals we "are naturally constituted unto thoughts of the next world." To deny a man the hope that he will continue to exist in some form after he has died is to deal him the most devastating blow:

> It is the heaviest stone that melancholy can throw at a man, to tell him he is at the end of his nature; or that there is no further state to come, unto which this seemes progressionall, and otherwise made in vaine . . . But the superiour ingredient and obscured part of ourselves, whereto all present felicities afford no resting contentment, will be able at last to tell us we are more then our present selves: and evacuate such hopes in the fruition of their own accomplishments.[9]

Here Browne powerfully captures the pathos inherent in these bids for self-perpetuation, a pathos that, I hope to show, brings us into

7. Browne, *Sir Thomas Browne: The Major Works*, ed. C. A. Patrides (London: Penguin Books, 1977), 309.
8. Ibid., 308.
9. Ibid., 305–6.

contact with the dramatic effect that Webster aimed to produce in his tragedies. Monuments do produce emotion in those who view them, but not for the reason that their subjects intend. Because it is painful to imagine a future in which they are absent from the ongoing life of the world, the monumental subjects that Browne describes commission their effigies in the hope of preemptively mourning their own imagined absence. There is pathos in the monument because it symbolizes an impossible and yet shared wish to prevent that absence. Monuments to the dead, in this way, paradoxically become collective rather than individual expressions of the human condition. We not only need to believe that death does not represent the "end" of our "nature" and that there is a "further state to come," but we also cling desperately to the notion that this future condition, this "obscured part of ourselves," is somehow both continuous with and superior to our present form. We want to believe, in Browne's words, that we are "*more* then our present selves" (my emphasis).

Webster, invested in both the business of death and its theatrical representation, was in a unique position to appreciate Browne's perspective. The ambivalent attitude that we saw in the preface to *The White Devil* surfaces in *A Monumental Column,* his elegy to Prince Henry, where he comments on the expenses devoted to commemorative monuments in a vein similar to Browne's. The poem, like most of its type, suggests that poetry has the potential to memorialize its subjects in a more lasting manner than can statuary representations. In the dedicatory letter, however, Webster warns that his poem falls short of fully embracing these immortalizing powers: "Onely here (though I dare not say you shall find him live: for that assurance were worth many kingdomes,) yet you shall perceive him draw a little breath, such as gives us comfort His Critticall day is past and the Glory of a new life risen."[1] The reassurance that we derive from poetic commemorations of the dead, Webster stresses even in this fairly conventional dedication, is designed to give *us* comfort. The dead are gone irrevocably; the best poetry can achieve is to serve as a diversionary tactic that temporarily obscures this fact.

Nevertheless, the death of Prince Henry seems to have made a lasting impression on Webster, who commemorated him a second time twelve years later in a script for a civic pageant written to celebrate Sir John Gore's inauguration as mayor entitled *Monuments of Honor.* Hence, despite his skeptical attitude toward poetry's immortalizing abilities, Webster attempts to create a poetic response to the young prince's untimely demise and in so doing yields valuable

---

1. Webster, *A Monumental Column*, in *The Complete Works of John Webster,* ed. F. L. Lucas, 4 vols. (London: Chatto & Windus, 1927), 3: lines 16–17. All subsequent quotations from this and other non-dramatic works by Webster are from this edition and will be cited parenthetically within the text by volume, work, and page or line.

insight into his views on how to respond to such tragedies in a dignified manner. Although "Death lay in ambush" for this "glorious youth," he found the "sternely bent" prince immune to fear. Not surprisingly, Webster uses the prince's death as an occasion to remind readers that a similar fate awaits them. He describes the appearance of the prince's deathbed with theatrical immediacy:

> Now view his death-bed; and from thence let's meet
> In his example our own winding-sheete
> There his humility, setting apart
> All titles, did retire into his heart.
> The best content, to meane men and to Kings!
>
> (201–5)

The image of the "winding-sheete," which frequently recurs in Webster's tragedies, serves here to connect rather than separate the reader from the deceased prince. However grand, the prince's death shroud provides an example of what is to come; what can be gained from seeing it, however, is the example that the prince sets by meeting death with a dignity that exposes ornamental ceremonies as unnecessary. Webster further stresses this point by criticizing the present age in a manner that, once again, anticipates Browne's:

> Time was when Churches in the land were thought
> Rich Jewel-houses, and this Age hath bought
> That time againe—thinke not I faine—go view
> *Henry* the sevenths Chappell, and you'le find it true,
> The dust of a rich Diamond's there inshrin'd
> To buy which thence, would begger the *West-Inde*.
>
> (289–94)

Alluding to renovations to Westminster Abbey initiated by King James, Webster interprets monuments as expressing worldly rather than spiritual concerns. Far from sacred sites intended to inspire profound meditation, funeral chapels have now become "Rich Jewel-houses" that advertise the wealth of the deceased. Those who visit "*Henry* the sevenths Chappell" are more interested in viewing the diamond "there inshrin'd" than the resting place of the late king. To honor Prince Henry, Webster sought to combat this tendency by constructing a poetic monument that paradoxically calls attention to its own superfluity, a monument that commemorates the deceased by refuting the notion that grand commemorative processes are sufficient replacements for them.

If Webster allows his readers a glimpse of divine transcendence in his poems, he provides no such comfort to his theatrical audience. * * *

* * *

II. Learning to Die

In *The Duchess of Malfi*, Webster engages in a more sustained analysis of memorialization: * * * [he] explores the consequences of attempting to manipulate and control the fame of others in the hope of deflecting attention from one's own inevitable demise. This process provides a sinister spin on the monument-making strategies of Jacobean England's elite. Rather than build representations of themselves, the characters imagine the Duchess herself as a monumental emblem that provides the elusive stability that they seek. Instead of providing comfort, the attempt to control the conditions that surround death decays characters prematurely while they are still alive.

As a new widow, the Duchess is a particularly dangerous figure to her brothers. An early exchange makes clear that their desire to control both her present and posthumous reputation is at the center of their concerns:

Duchess: I'll never marry.
Cardinal: So most widows say,
          But commonly that motion lasts no longer
          Than the turning of an hour-glass; the funeral sermon
          And it, end both together.
Ferdinand: Now hear me:
          You live in a rank pasture, here i'th' court;
          There is a kind of honey dew that's deadly:
          'Twill poison your fame.

                                        (1.1.293–99)

Speaking as if the funeral rites that her husband received should also apply to the Duchess's love life, the Cardinal has little faith that the desires of a widow can be controlled—"commonly" they will out. More to the point, Ferdinand specifically introduces her "fame" as a cause of anxiety. Soon after, Ferdinand warns Bosola not to probe too deeply beneath the surface of his commands:

Ferdinand: she's a young widow,
          I would not have her marry again.
Bosola: No sir?
Ferdinand: Do not you ask the reason, but be satisfied
          I say I would not.

                                        (1.1.246–49)

Ferdinand's initial explanation would seem satisfactory to a subordinate, but by quickly denying Bosola further information, he creates the sense that mysterious desires lurk beneath his requests. The incestuous undertones to these desires are often thought to be at the root of Ferdinand's anxieties concerning his sister. While Webster clearly keeps the possibility of repressed incest operable in the play, this does not account sufficiently for Ferdinand's obsessive need to sculpt metaphorically the Duchess into an exemplary widow figure.[2] As Garrett A. Sullivan observes, both Ferdinand and the Cardinal consistently speak of the Duchess in a manner that aims to evacuate "her of subjectivity in the name of lifeless monumentality."[3] Ferdinand, though, even more so than his brother, desires that his sister serve as a *living* monument, a subject that possesses the reassuring permanence of the dead.

Although she quickly rebels against their wishes by marrying Antonio, the Duchess initially seems oddly willing to understand herself in the terms that her brothers dictate. Before the fated marriage takes place, she insists on constructing her will, as if to collapse the rites of marriage with the rituals surrounding death. This rebellion against her brothers shows the remarkable vitality of her character, but the cool resignation with which she accepts her fate is suggestive of the *ars moriendi* tradition. The importance that Protestant culture placed on dying with dignity exerted considerable pressure on individuals not only to acknowledge that death was imminent * * * but also to exploit the experience's didactic potential for the sake of others.[4] The sick were expected to "die well" amidst a room of spectators anxiously scrutinizing their every move. In *The Duchess of Malfi*, however, the danger that the Duchess faces stems directly from those who claim to be guided by their interest in preserving her fame. As he hurriedly exits the stage, the Cardinal reminds us that "Wisdom begins at the end: Remember it," rushed advice that takes on a threatening resonance (1.1.319).[5] Anticipating her demise, the Duchess prepares her will because "tis fit" that princes should perform such tasks "in perfect memory," in the hope that doing so will prevent the "deep groans, and terrible ghastly looks" that normally accompany death (1.1.367–70). In attempting to prepare to die well in order to impose a pleasing representation

---

2. The more compelling critical treatments of this issue, I would argue, link the suggestion of incest to more prominent thematic strands within Webster's structure. Frank Whigham's well known account, for example, interprets Ferdinand's "incestuous inclination" as a "social posture." More specifically, Whigham argues that Ferdinand is a "threatened aristocrat, frightened by the contamination of his ascriptive social rank and obsessively preoccupied with its defense" ("Sexual and Social Mobility in *The Duchess of Malfi,*" PMLA 100 [1985]: 169).

3. Sullivan, *Memory and Forgetting in English Renaissance Drama: Shakespeare, Marlowe, Webster* (Cambridge: Cambridge University Press, 2005), 130.

4. See Eamon Duffy, *The Stripping of the Altars: Traditional Religion in England, c. 1400–c. 1580* (New Haven: Yale University Press, 1993), 313–27.

5. Christopher Sutton's immensely popular *ars moriendi* manual, for example, insists that recognition of mortality is an essential step toward self-knowledge: "Well the perfection of our knowledge is to know God & our selves: our selves wee best know, when we acknowledge our mortall being" (*Disce Mori* [London, 1601], 8).

of herself on the future, the Duchess seeks, in a sense, to liberate herself from her brothers' commands by leading a posthumous existence.

In doing so, however, she paradoxically renders herself complicit with their wishes. When Antonio initially resists her advances, she strikingly describes herself in the way that Ferdinand seeks to understand her: "What is't distracts you?" she asks Antonio, "This is flesh and blood, sir; / 'Tis not the figure cut in alabaster / Kneels at my husband's tomb" (1.1.443–45). Even as she affirms her corporeality, by articulating and denying Ferdinand's wishes the Duchess gives voice to their presence in the play and activates them in Antonio's mind. His witty response—"I will remain the constant / Sanctuary of your good name" (1.1.450–51)—shows that he has missed the point of the Duchess's message and that, like her brothers, he positions her from the perspective of the dead. His initial description of them as "three fair medals, / Cast in one figure" (my emphasis) moreover, evokes the fixed, statuary figure from which she wishes to distinguish herself (1.1.179–80). Antonio's reverence for the Duchess is suggestive not only of his love for her and of his humble social status but also of the uncanny effect that she has on all of the characters who surround her. Even at her most lively, the Duchess seems to possess the aura and powers of the spectral echo that she will become.

The Duchess's complex relationship to the afterlife does not only rest upon her impending death. When she claims that by remarrying she has not sought to "create any new world, or custom" (3.2.112), the Duchess paints an accurate picture of Jacobean England. During the time that Webster was writing, roughly a third of marriages were remarriages.[6] Widows were thus common figures who needed to be acknowledged and accounted for in everyday life. In his *Rule and Exercises of Holy Dying,* Jeremy Taylor articulates a view toward widows disturbingly similar to Ferdinand's, insisting that "a widow must be a mourner; and she that is not, cannot so well secure the chastity of her proper state."[7] Funeral monuments of the time, moreover, often depict widows in precisely this manner. The widow * * * is seen kneeling in prayer beside the figure of her husband. The portrayal, depicted with a lifelikeness that was an innovation of the early seventeenth century, conveys the intensity of the widow's despair; * * * when a man who had been married twice predeceased his second wife, both the dead first wife and the living widow would be depicted kneeling behind him in effigy. Rather than figures devoted to keeping their husbands' memories alive, widows

---

6. Arthur Kinney, ed., *Renaissance Drama: An Anthology of Plays and Entertainments* (Maiden: Blackwell Publishers, 2002), 560.
7. Taylor, *The Rule and Exercises of Holy Dying,* quoted in *Renaissance Drama,* ed. Kinney, 560.

seemed meant to represent a sort of death *in* life, a state that, in the Duchess's case, intensifies her availability as a vehicle for premature memorialization.

Webster himself writes of widows in a pair of character sketches that he contributed to a volume of literary portraits compiled by Sir Thomas Overbury—sketches that appear to have been written at roughly the same time that he produced *The Duchess of Malfi*. A "Virtuous Widow," according to Webster, has nothing to fear, for

> No calamity can now come neere her, for in suffering the Losse of her husband, shee accounts all the rest trifles: she hath laid his dead body in the worthyest monument that can be: Shee hath buried it in her own heart. (4.39)

A truly virtuous widow, in these terms, is essentially a living monument to her deceased husband. She is "a relic that without any superstition in the world, though she might not be kissed, yet may be reverenced" (ibid.). An "Ordinarie Widow," on the other hand, "is like the heralds' hearse-cloth, She serves to many funerals, with a very little altering the color. The end of her husband begins in tears; and the end of her tears begins in a husband" (ibid., 39). Webster's sketches suggest the inherent memorialization embodied by women simply as a result of outliving their husbands, a trope clearly echoed in the confusing representational roles inhabited by the Duchess. Though she is clearly more "ordinary" than "virtuous" by this criterion, the Duchess does not fit comfortably into either of the categories that Webster describes. She will not conform to the "worthiest" monumental shape demanded of the virtuous, and yet Webster imbues her character with a *gravitas* unsuitable to the vulgar figure that the "ordinary" widow suggests.

The Duchess's refusal to assume the role of the virtuous widow that Webster describes sets the play's tragic results in motion. Ferdinand's discovery of her marriage to Antonio shatters the illusion of fixity that his sister provides for him, and proves to be a discovery that permanently destabilizes his own identity. Ferdinand's expressions of anger and trepidation stem from the realization that the Duchess has the capacity to alter herself from the monumental figure that he desires or, worse yet, that some unknown agent has produced this change. The clearest alteration that takes place, her rapid succession of pregnancies, ultimately allows Bosola to expose the marriage. When Ferdinand hears of the marriage, he punishes himself by picturing his sister with some "strong thighed bargeman" or "lovely squire" who carries "coals up to her privy lodgings" (2.5.42 and 44–45). The focus of Ferdinand's anger, as he himself makes clear, is the Duchess's body: "Damn her! That body of hers, / While that my blood ran pure in't, was more worth / Than that which thou wouldst comfort, called a soul" (4.1.121–23). The Duchess's body, from this perspective, derives its value solely from its capacity to serve as a vessel for the Aragonian royal blood. When the Duchess intermixes this blood with the lower-ranking Antonio's to produce offspring, she corrupts both. In this way, the presence of the Duchess's children severs not only Ferdinand's current relationship with his identity but also his notion of how it will sustain itself for posterity.

In the scenes leading up to the Duchess's death, Ferdinand attempts to reconcile his conflicting drives by forcing her to assume the monumental shape that she resists. His strategy, as he puts it, is to "plague her in art" (4.1.111). Strikingly, Ferdinand's "art" consists primarily of a series of set pieces meant to transform theatrically her prison into a funeral chamber. Bosola, who assumes a bewildering number of roles throughout the course of the fourth act, becomes the lead actor in this dramatic enterprise. His central role, as he tells the Duchess, is that of a "tomb maker," whose job is to "flatter the dead, not the living" (4.2.139–40). Ferdinand's plan initially seems successful. Bosola's description of her after she is imprisoned suggests that the Duchess has taken on the qualities of the monument that Ferdinand longs for her to become:

> She's sad, as one long used to't, and she seems
> Rather to welcome the end of misery
> Than shun it; A behaviour so noble
> As gives majesty to adversity.
> You may discern the shape of loveliness
> More perfect in her tears than in her smiles;
> She will muse four hours together, and her silence,
> Methinks, expresseth more than if she spake.
>
> (4.1.3–10)

Like a mourning funerary statue, the Duchess has been reduced to the "shape" of a person whose expressive capacities are limited to silent gestures. This differentiates her from the shape-shifting Ferdinand as well as from Bosola, who agrees to see the Duchess but "never in mine own shape" (4.1.134). Cariola reinforces this comparison when she tells the Duchess that she appears "A deal of life in show, but none in practice" or, more specifically, "like some reverend monument / Whose ruins are even pitied" (4.2.32–34).

Ferdinand's crudest device—presenting Antonio and the Duchess's children to her as wax figures—seems to allude directly to innovations in funeral monuments made in the seventeenth century. Statuary representations had become more realistic in an attempt to represent accurately the individual qualities of the deceased and deflect thoughts away from the corrupting mortal body. During royal funeral processions, a lifelike effigy was often displayed in order to assure the public that the monarch had made a seamless transition toward immortal dignity. Prince Henry's procession, for example, featured an apparently jarringly convincing wooden effigy "wth several joints both in the arms and legges and bodie to be moved to sundrie accions first for the carriage in the Chariot and then for the standing and for setting uppe the same in the Abbye."[8] In the play, Ferdinand puts this new technology to horrifying use. In a grotesque literalization of the *memento mori* tradition, he first offers the Duchess a severed hand and then wax figures made to resemble the corpses of Antonio and her children. In a reversal of royal processional practices, Ferdinand produces figures that "appear to be dead" rather than alive. As he hurriedly leaves the stage, a curtain opens to reveal "*the figures of Antonio and his children, appearing as if they were dead*" (direction following 4.1.55). As editors of the play have noted, Webster's stage direction seems to ignore the fact that Antonio fled with only their eldest son. Although this apparent oversight may represent carelessness on Webster's part, the editor of the Oxford edition seems correct to suggest that the primary objective of the wax show is to trick the Duchess into believing that everyone that she loves is dead.[9] As the rest of the scene makes clear, verisimilitude is clearly not among Ferdinand's priorities. While the "wax figures," likely played by the actors themselves, may have been meant to fool the audience, it is not clear that the Duchess herself is taken in by Ferdinand's device.[1] Although she is terrified by the sight, the Duchess reacts as though she is not fooled:

> There is not between heaven and earth one wish
> I stay for after this: it wastes me more
> Than were't my picture, fashion'd out of wax,
> Stuck with a magical needle then buried
> In some foul dunghill.
>
> (4.1.61–65)

Even when shocked, the Duchess seems perfectly capable of distinguishing between the dead and "pictures fashion'd out of wax." She provides further evidence of her awareness of her brother's design

8. Quoted in Nigel Llewellyn, *Funeral Monuments in Post-Reformation England* (Cambridge: Cambridge University Press, 2000), 37.
9. Weis, ed., *The Duchess of Malfi*, 398n. In her introduction to the new Arden edition of the play, Leah Marcus points out that "the actors playing Antonio and her children could easily have stood in the discovery space to be revealed when the traverse was drawn" (*The Duchess of Malfi*, ed. Leah S. Marcus, Arden Early Modern Drama [London: A & C Black, 2009], 262).
1. David Bergeron explores the possibility that, with Ferdinand's wax figures, Webster specifically intends to allude not only to Prince Henry's funeral procession but also to Hermione's statue in *The Winter's Tale* ("The Wax Figures in *The Duchess of Malfi*," *Studies in English Literature* 18 [1978]: 332–33).

when she describes her cell as a "tedious theatre," in which she must "play a part in't 'gainst my will" (4.1.84–85). Rather than driving her to despair, Ferdinand's antics seem to stir her out of her lassitude. His confidence that theatrical representations can fool his sister, I would argue, relates thematically to his conception that he can freeze her into a mourning funerary statue. The Duchess's consistent defiance of the roles that Ferdinand sets out for her as well as her allusions to the artificial appearance of what she has seen suggests that he is wrong in both cases.

Despite his frequent role changes, Bosola offers the play's most clearsighted commentary on the function that memorial representations fulfill. Bosola's critique, which could apply directly to Jacobean burial customs, inadvertently converts the Duchess to his way of thinking. Directly before her murder, the Duchess cheerfully engages her self-proclaimed "tomb maker" in a dialogue that questions the value of elaborate tombs and epitaphs:

> *Duchess:*   Why do we grow fantastical in our death-bed?
>   Do we affect fashion in the grave?
> *Bosola:*   Most ambitiously. Princes' images on their tombs do
>   not lie as they were wont, seeming to pray up to
>   heaven, but with their hands under their cheeks, as if
>   they died of the tooth-ache. They are not carved with
>   their eyes fixed upon the stars, but as their minds
>   were wholly bent upon the world, the selfsame way
>   they seem to turn their faces.
>
> (4.2.146–53)

In an analysis that recalls Webster's criticisms in *A Monumental Column*, Bosola confirms that funeral monuments reflect worldly rather than spiritual concerns. The manner in which they are portrayed aestheticizes death in order to obscure its effects but does nothing to ameliorate them. "Prince's images on their tombs," Bosola argues, are designed to look "as if they died of the tooth-ache," but they do not fool anyone.[2] Elaborate funeral rites and expensive monumental likenesses do not aim to represent a relationship between the mortal world and the afterlife; instead they merely aspire to suspend the monumental subject in a relationship to the world suggestive of their positions in life.

---

2. Webster criticizes royal funeral monuments on similar grounds in his tragicomedy *The Devil's Law Case*:

> *Romelio:*   Vain the ambition of kings,
>   Who seek by trophies and dead things
>   To leave a living name behind,
>   And weave but nets to catch the wind.
>
> (5.4.126–29)

Dismissing the relevance of her manner of death, the Duchess defeats by literalizing the image of the "figure cut in alabaster" that she had earlier assured Antonio she was not. When her executioners approach, the Duchess kneels before them, but she does not become the effigy that her brothers envision. Before the Duchess is executed, her killers enter with not only the cord with which they will strangle her but also a "coffin" and a "bell" (4.4.165). Startled by her composure, Bosola asks, "Doth not death fright you?" (4.2.202). The Duchess responds with childlike assurance: "Who would be afraid on't / Knowing to meet such excellent company / In th'other world?" (4.2.202–4). Her response to the question of whether she is frightened by the manner in which she will die transcends this innocent perspective and is even more surprising:

> Not a whit
> What would it pleasure me to have my throat cut
> With diamonds? or to be smothered
> With cassia? or to be shot to death with pearls?
> I know death hath ten thousand several doors
> For men to take their exits.
>   (4.2.207–12)

Unlike the monarchs that Bosola criticizes, the Duchess has no interest in appearing as if she died of a "tooth-ache." The luxurious implements that she mentions—"diamonds," "cassia," "pearls"—do nothing to obscure or assuage the effects of a cut throat or suffocation. Instead of seeking comfort in a contrived dying phrase, she requests that Bosola tell her brothers that she "perceives" death and that she is "well awake" (4.2.215–16). As she prepares to be executed by strangulation, the Duchess thinks movingly on the living rather than on how she will be memorialized: "I pray thee look thou giv'st my little boy / Some syrup for his cold, and let the girl / Say her prayers ere she sleeps" (4.2.195–97). The Duchess escapes their manipulations and refuses to signify anything beyond the brave acceptance of death.

After the Duchess is strangled, the characters that surround her ironically fall victim to the very devices that they employed to drive her to despair. Although she lacks the "art" that normally adorns the bodies of deceased royalty, the Duchess becomes a sight that afflicts Ferdinand's eyes as if she were encased in diamonds: "Cover her face: mine eyes dazzle: she died young" (4.2.256).[3] Bosola, oddly moved by the sight of the yet living body that he has just ordered strangled, reacts like a version of King Lear whose Cordelia momentarily

---

3. Ferdinand's phrasing ironically reframes his earlier characterization of the Duchess as a "young" widow.

returns from the grave: "She stirs; here's life. / Return, fair soul, from darkness, and lead mine / Out of this sensible hell. She's warm, she breathes" (4.2.333–35). This Cordelia, however, quickly transforms into Desdemona. When she breathes the word "Antonio," Bosola reassures her that he is alive, defying his earlier stance by sending her to death with a pleasing fiction: "The dead bodies you saw were feigned statues: / He's reconciled to your brothers; the Pope hath wrought / The atonement" (4.2.342–44). Despite his earlier skepticism, Bosola tearfully recognizes the tragic consequences of the Duchess's death: "Where were / These penitent fountains while she was living? / O, they were frozen up" (4.2.356–58). In seeking to comply with Ferdinand's orders to convert the Duchess into a monument, Bosola recognizes that, in his "frozen" rigidity, he himself came to resemble one. Bosola's former satirical lens allowed him to approach his role in the Duchess's death with ironic detachment, but the sight of her corpse bridges this divide and forces him to acknowledge that he too is guilty of the attempt to theatricalize death to advance his own designs.

In a discussion of *Othello*, Kenneth Burke claims that the fourth act of a Shakespearean tragedy normally prepares the audience to "relinquish those figures who are about to die for our edification." If the playwright allows his characters to "die well," Burke suggests, then the final act serves as a "requiem in which we participate at the ceremonious death of a portion of ourselves."[4] Webster, as we have seen, deviates from the formula that Burke describes by taking the Duchess before either the characters or the audience is ready to lose her, and her absence haunts the play's final act. Bosola identifies the nature of their crimes against their sister when he tells Ferdinand and the Cardinal that their hearts are a pair of "hollow graves, / Rotten and rotting others" (4.2.311–12). The phrase "*hollow* graves" (my emphasis) emphasizes their desire to construct an immortal monument that ignores the corporeal evidence of mortality that inevitably resides within it.

The loss of the Duchess at the play's center, moreover, places the onus on Bosola and Ferdinand to retain the play's dramatic intensity. While Bosola's actions push the plot forward, it is Ferdinand whose stage presence becomes more dynamic. When forced to look inward rather than at his idealized, fixed image of the Duchess for an organizing principle, Ferdinand finds that he can conceive of himself and his future only in terms of a *lycanthropos* or wolf man, a figure who functions to desecrate and destroy emblems of transcendence. According to Robert Burton, "Lycanthropia, or wolf-madness," refers to the condition "when men run howling about

---

4. Burke, "*Othello:* An Essay to Illustrate a Method," *Hudson Review* 4 (1951): 178.

graves and fields in the night, and will not be persuaded but that
they are wolves."[5] Ferdinand's psychological transformation, which
Webster foregrounds in numerous ways earlier in the play, provides
a fitting outcome to his obsessions. As if to prove that her tomb is
not the "hollow grave" that Bosola claims his heart is, Ferdinand
insists that "the wolf shall find her grave, and scrape it up; / Not to
devour the corpse, but to discover / The horrid murder" (4.2.301–3).
While Ferdinand's lycanthropy reflects a typical Protestant association of wolves with the Catholic Church and its spiritual depreda-
tions, the emphasis once again is on exposing the impotence of
commemorative rituals in the face of mortality.[6] Ferdinand's particular form of madness manifests itself as an impulse to uncover
corpses and thus undo burial rites; he continues the attempt to control his sister's legacy, therefore, by verifying the inert materiality
of her murdered body.

The events that follow solidify the play's paradoxical relationship
with memorialization. The funereal setting that Ferdinand created
to trap the Duchess theatrically expands and envelops the entire
play. As Antonio unknowingly strolls through the graveyard where
his wife is buried, he ponders the relevance of the ruins that surround him:

Antonio: I do love these ancient ruins:
We never tread upon them but we set
Our foot upon some reverend history
And questionless, here in this open court,
Which now lies naked to the injuries
Of stormy weather, some men lie interred
Loved the church so well, and gave so largely to't,
They thought it should have canopied their bones
Till doomsday. But all things have their end:
Churches and cities, which have diseases like to men,
Must have like death that we have.

Echo: Like death that we have.
                                                      (5.3.9–19)

Unlike *The White Devil*, in which characters return from the grave
to illustrate what a "mockery" death makes of its victims, after the
death of its eponymous heroine, *The Duchess of Malfi* presents her
only in the form of an echo that serves to deny rather than confirm

---

5. Burton, *The Anatomy of Melancholy*, ed. Holbrook Jackson (New York: New York Review
of Books, 2001), 141.
6. For a succinct and informative summary of the Protestant association of Catholics and
wolves, see Marcus, ed., *The Duchess of Malfi*, 27–32. Although the connection between
Ferdinand's lycanthropy and Protestant invective seems clear, I do not mean to suggest
that the play endorses a staunchly Protestant *or* Catholic position. On the contrary, as
I indicated above, Webster's perspective on Protestant compensations for the eradica-
tion of Catholic commemorative rituals was highly critical.

her transcendence. Similar to the Duchess, the dead who "Loved the church so well" have entered a theatrical context, in which they must "play a part" against their wills. The voice of the echo sounds uncannily like the Duchess, but the sight of the tombs reminds Antonio that all that connects us to their inhabitants is that they too are subject to decay. Far from providing assurance of a posthumous reunion, the "dead stones" of the Duchess's tomb caution Antonio that he is also a "dead thing." When he questions whether they shall meet again, the echo gloomily predicts that he "shall never see her more" (5.4.43).

The significance of the echo—and the face that Antonio believes appears to him "folded in sorrow" when it speaks—reframes the crimes that Ferdinand and the Cardinal committed against the Duchess. Similar to the Duchess's brothers, Antonio positions her as the "figure cut in alabaster" that kneels before her prior husband's grave. His reflections on the dead that surround him place Antonio at a remove from the experiences that he describes and mirror the peripheral role that he serves in the play. I would therefore suggest that the echo functions in the play much in the same way that monuments do: just as monuments are meant to compensate for the loss of the dead that they represent, the echo creates the impression that some form of posthumous communication is possible. But what Antonio hears is the reverberation of his own voice returning back to him in distorted form.

The view that the Duchess is a monument that refuses rather than confirms transcendence diverges from most critical accounts of the play. Michael Neill, for example, agrees with most critics when he concludes that "A monument properly speaks for those whom the grave has silenced; but in this play the dramatist allows the murdered heroine herself to speak. . . . [*The Duchess of Malfi*] places at the centre of its symbolic system a monument of fame which stands . . . for the eternizing artifice of the play itself."[7] The idea that the echo restores the Duchess to Antonio ignores the fact that at this point Antonio does not realize that she is dead and therefore cannot be in a position to commemorate her loss genuinely. More broadly, Neill and others neglect to consider that Webster constantly calls our attention to the fact that although monuments purport to speak for the dead, they are much more likely to reflect the needs of the living. If the Duchess herself is a monument, then she retains

7. Neill, *Issues of Death: Mortality and Identity in English Renaissance Tragedy* (New York: Oxford University Press, 1997), 331. Other notable readings that either implicitly or explicitly support this conclusion include M. C. Bradbrook, *John Webster, Citizen and Dramatist* (New York: Columbia University Press, 1980), 142–65; and, more recently, Huston Diehl, *Staging Reform, Reforming the Stage* (Ithaca: Cornell University Press, 1997), 209.

her dignity by refusing to conform to the shape that these eternizing tropes idealistically and, to Webster, naively, describe. In both
his plays and his poems, Webster gives us every reason *not* to interpret commemorative symbolism straightforwardly.

The play's concluding scenes reinforce the danger that Webster
affixes to projecting one's own voice onto the dead; the remaining
living characters are all too willing to sink into the oblivion that the
echo describes. The succession of deaths that occur invite unflattering comparisons with that of the Duchess and are shaped by mis-
conceptions on the part of the characters responsible for her murder
as to what her posthumous wishes would be. Although the Duchess's
only request was that her body be returned to her women, Bosola
makes a belated, disastrous attempt to become her avenger that
results in his accidental murder of Antonio. Suddenly afflicted by
conscience, the formerly calculating Cardinal sees visions "armed
with a rake / That seem to strike at him" when he looks in his "fishponds" (5.5.5–7). His dying words are to pray that he "Be laid by,
and never thought of" (5.5.89). Ferdinand is only partly right when
he dies with the words "My sister! O my sister! There's the cause
on't: / Whether we fall by ambition, blood or lust, / Like diamonds,
we are cut with our own dust" (5.5.70–72). As he prepares to join
them, Bosola describes the dead that surround him as "dead walls,
or vaulted graves, / That, ruined, yield no echo" (5.5.96–97).

With the words that end the play, Delio contradicts these messages, instructing the audience to "make noble use / of this great
ruin" (5.5.109–10). His method, however, as Sullivan points out, is
to participate in the act of "commemorating some while consigning
others to oblivion," which continues the play's critique of "bending
historical events to one's desires and in the service of the future."[8]
The "ruined," lifeless bodies that cover the stage provide the clearest sense of the function that monuments fulfill. Rather than provide evidence of a transcendent ordering system, funerary
monuments are exposed as compensatory mechanisms that supply
reality with only fictional coherence. The corpses on the stage, in
Delio's words, are "wretched eminent things," which will "leave no
more fame behind'em than should one / Fall in a frost, and leave
his print in snow" (5.5.113–14). Delio's description of a quickly fad-
ing impression also serves to characterize aptly the ephemeral realm
of theatrics to which the play itself belongs. The future that Delio
describes for these characters, I suggest, is not unlike the predic-
tion that Webster offers for Jacobean drama in general in the preface to *The White Devil*. Rather than living monuments, Webster

---

8. Sullivan, *Memory and Forgetting*, 130.

aims to produce works that subsist because they do not know how to die.

In the commendatory poems prefacing the *The Duchess of Malfi,* Webster's contemporary dramatists and sometime collaborators Thomas Middleton, William Rowley, and John Ford make a bid for the author's relevance to literary posterity by stressing the enduring qualities of the play in general and of the Duchess in particular. All three, moreover, employ the monument as their metaphorical vehicle to convey their message. In preserving the memory of the Duchess with his play, Middleton claims, Webster has cemented his posthumous reputation: "Thy monument is raised in thy life-time; / And 'tis most just; for every worthy man / Is his own marble" (7–9). Referring to the echo scene, Rowley's encomium follows the same train of thought: "Yet my opinion is, she might speak more, / But never, in her life, so well before" (29–30). Claiming, somewhat hyperbolically, that the play "transcends" the masterpieces of Rome and Greece, Ford asserts that all future playwrights will take "life" from Webster's "clear pen," from which "memory hath lent / A lasting fame, to raise his monument" (37–38). Despite the enthusiasm of these tributes, the logic that underwrites them contradicts rather than highlights the most memorable qualities of Webster's heroine, who does not seek to concretize her status through the tears of her observers. For a more accurate appraisal of the Duchess's legacy, we might consider the manner in which Webster commemorates Prince Henry in *Monuments of Honor:*

> Such was this Prince, such are the noble hearts,
> Who when they dye, yet dye not in all parts:
> But from the Integrety of a Brave mind,
> Leave a most Cleere and Eminent Fame behind.
>   (359–62)

The prince, like the Duchess, distinguishes his death by facing it with the integrity and clarity of a "brave mind." Throughout his works, Webster takes issue with the idea that a monument, poetic or otherwise, can dictate the terms of our legacy or, more specifically, designate on whom posterity will confer remembrance. The question of what comes after this life, as well as of whether that which we leave behind has enduring value for succeeding generations, I have tried to show, is a problem that both haunts and humanizes his characters. In his poetry, plays, and prefaces, Webster stubbornly refuses to provide his readers the comfort that he denies his poetic and theatrical subjects.

The Bonds of Service

BARBARA CORRELL

From Malvolio at Malfi: Managing Desire in Shakespeare and Webster[†]

> They are the lords and owners of their faces,
> Others but stewards of their excellence.
> —Sonnet 94.7–8[1]

> . . . thou art made if thou desirest to be so; if not, let me see thee
> a steward still, the fellow of servants, and not worthy to touch For-
> tune's fingers.
> —*Twelfth Night*, 2.5.135–37

This essay hypothesizes a transgeneric afterlife for Malvolio in Webster's *Duchess of Malfi*.[2] If the scapegoated household manager and complex underling who provides a troubling residue to *Twelfth Night*'s concluding marriage festivities offered Webster material to mold into tragedy, he undergoes a striking transformation from which two figures emerge. Social-erotic fantasies foregrounded, Malvolio reappears as Antonio, the estate steward wooed by his aristocratic mistress. Sinister potential developed, he becomes Bosola, the brooding intelligencer delegated to manage Ferdinand's malevolent desires—that is, to steward information—in Webster's tragedy.

It may well be that, sparked by *Twelfth Night*'s grim potential, Webster pursued it by reinscribing Shakespeare's intriguing character in tragic events. But my hypothesis also suggests that Webster was attuned to the historical liminality of the steward, that he used Malvolio's erotically inflected relation to a female aristocrat to sharpen issues of social transition, service, class formation, and conflict introduced in Shakespeare's play. If Malvolio's parting words,

† Barbara Correll, "Malvolio at Malfi: Managing Desire in Shakespeare and Webster." *Shakespeare Quarterly* 58 (2007), 65–92. © 2009 The Folger Shakespeare Library. Reprinted with permission of Johns Hopkins University Press.

1. Quotations from Shakespeare are from *The Norton Shakespeare*, gen. ed. Stephen Greenblatt (New York: W. W. Norton, 1997).
2. Quotations from *The Duchess of Malfi* are from John Webster, *The Duchess of Malfi*, 3rd ed., ed. Elizabeth M. Brennan (New York: W. W. Norton, 1993), and are cited in the text.

"I'll be revenged on the whole pack of you" (5.1.365), stimulated Webster to write what amounts to a tragic sequel, then something significant may emerge from reading his play in light of the earlier work. That something may not only contribute to a reading of the two plays but also participate in the current reexamination of early modern service vis-à-vis the figure of the steward.[3] Bosola, of course, is not an estate steward in a great house; his official title is Provisor of the Horse for the duchess. However, his hypothetical link to the steward of *Twelfth Night* and the actual work that he performs for Ferdinand—certainly not for the duchess—give him a special place in Webster's play, in which stewardship and service are significant issues.

Cristina Malcolmson has argued that Malvolio's delusions of grandeur are socially damaging and contribute significantly to the crisis that *Twelfth Night* formally resolves with comic conventions. *The Duchess of Malfi*, however, strongly suggests that such putative delusions are also well motivated and certainly historically resonant—"misprisions" of degree.[4] The marriages of Olivia and Sebastian and of Viola and Orsino—couples appropriately matched by class, gender, and sobriety—are arguably one normative generic answer to the crisis of mobility represented by Malvolio (although Malvolio's heterosexual interest in a live and present Olivia stands out from the more complicated love interests in the play). For Malcolmson, *Twelfth Night* "links issues of gender and status in order to make marriage, with its inclusion of desire and its commitment to permanence, the model of all social bonds."[5] To the extent that we might partly agree with Malcolmson's claim that *Twelfth Night* achieves domestic and social stability, Webster's investment in the tragic dissolution of the beleaguered marriage, attended by deaths, mental disintegration, and dismemberment, constitutes an interesting response to the social and heteronormative stakes—or the homosexual panic—of *Twelfth Night*'s comic marriage festivity.

---

3. On the topic of service, see especially David Schalkwyk, "Love and Service in *Twelfth Night* and the Sonnets," *Shakespeare Quarterly* 56 (2005): 76–100; and "Love and Service in *The Taming of the Shrew* and *All's Well that Ends Well*," *Shakespearean International Yearbook* 5 (2005): 3–43; Michael Neill, "'A woman's service': Gender, Subordination, and the Erotics of Rank in the Drama of Shakespeare and his Contemporaries," *International Shakespearean Yearbook* 5 (2005): 127–46. See also David Evett, *Discourses of Service in Shakespeare's England* (New York: Palgrave Macmillan, 2005); Kate Mertes, *The English Noble Household 1250–1600: Good Governance and Politic Rule* (Oxford: Basil Blackwell, 1988); and Judith Weil, *Service and Dependency in Shakespeare's Plays* (Cambridge: Cambridge UP, 2005).
4. Cristina Malcolmson, "'What You Will': Social Mobility and Gender in *Twelfth Night*," in *The Matter of Difference: Materialist Feminist Criticism of Shakespeare*, ed. Valerie Wayne (Ithaca: Cornell UP, 1991), 29–57.
5. Malcolmson, 47. According to Malcolmson's idea of a socially conservative Shakespeare, Viola is rewarded for her feminine and social propriety; Malvolio is scapegoated for disorderly self-interest (49).

As some have noted, Malvolio is as serious a character as one might encounter in early modern dramas that offer a thematics of ambition and privilege, service and subordination.[6] Unlike Iago, who also entertains fantasies of social advancement and empowerment, Malvolio is not a playmaker. And since he never addresses the audience in speeches normally marked as asides, that audience lacks access to the reflections that threaten to make viewers complicit with Iago's destructive actions. Like Iago, however—and like Antonio and Bosola—Malvolio lives with "the curse of service" (*Othello*, 1.1.34) and the ressentiment of the tenuously positioned subordinate, delegated to serve his superior.[7] The subordinate reflects the success of the master or mistress whose interests he promotes and manages.[8] In many ways he shares in the life of the aristocrat, living in or upon the shadow of aristocratic desire, battening like a parasitic courtier on aristocratic status. Being the agent of his superiors' desires makes him the eyes and ears, arms and legs of aristocratic projects, the engine of aristocratic affects.[9] In addition to their specific administrative duties on estates and in households, stewards are factors of power, instrumental men tasked to concretize the desires of others, desires about which they may know very little. This is where Bosola's court position functionally approaches that of a steward. When, for example, the duke commissions Bosola to police the duchess in Act 1, he does so only with the vague explanation, "she's a young widow, / I would not have her marry again"

6. An argument for taking Malvolio seriously appears in Jonathan Crewe's excellent introduction to the play in *Twelfth Night, or What You Will* (New York: Penguin Books, 2000). Crewe notes that, like gender, issues of "entitlement and mobility [in the play and in England] . . . remain sufficiently undefined to cause anxiety" (xlv).

7. Michael Neill sees Bosola and Antonio as characters mirroring Iago and Cassio in "Servant Obedience and Master Sins: Shakespeare and the Bonds of Service," in *Putting History to the Question: Power, Politics, and Society in English Renaissance Drama* (New York: Columbia UP, 2000), 13–48.

8. *The Oxford English Dictionary* (OED), 2d ed., prep. J. A. Simpson and E.S.C. Weiner, 20 vols. (Oxford: Clarendon, 1989) explains that "manage" (noun) and "management" (noun) retained their equestrian meanings of taking the reins with the hands (from the Italian verb *maneggiare*, to "manage" or "train" horses), rather than the delegation of action to a substitute or, as my title anachronistically suggests, seeing to a superior's desire. But it seems clear that while stewards were not considered managers in the early modern sense, their job description amounted to what we now understand to be a management position. Interestingly, as provisor of the horse in the duchess's household, placed there by Ferdinand to gather and pass on secrets, Bosola is employed in a dual managerial position.

9. Katherine Rowe, *Dead Hands: Fictions of Agency, Renaissance to Modern* (Stanford: Stanford UP, 1999), takes up the issue of servitude and representative agency in *The Duchess of Malfi* and other texts. Her interest in Bosola as an extension or prosthetic hand of Ferdinand, an exemplar of the transition from status to contract society in the early modern period, is much in accord with my own reading of the play, although I interpret key scenes differently. D. R. Hainsworth, *Stewards, Lords and People: The Estate Steward and His World in Later Stuart England* (Cambridge: Cambridge UP, 1992), also speaks of the prosthetic function of the steward in an "'ambassadorial' role of serving as his master's voice, as well as his eyes and ears, in the affairs of the region or county in which the estate stood" (3).

(1.2.176–77). Bosola's response is a quizzical or discreet "No, sir?" (1. 177). But Ferdinand offers no more information than the opaque and unimpeachable authority of his wishes: "Do not you ask the reason: but be satisfied, / I say I would not" (11. 178–79). In Act 3, Ferdinand tells Bosola of his plan to extract a confession from the duchess without saying how he intends to get it, boasting of his inscrutability; Bosola disagrees by criticizing his employer's inflated self-image: "you / Are your own chronicle too much: and grossly / Flatter yourself" (3.1.87–89). Ferdinand's promise to reward him for his candor—"I thank thee. / I never gave pension but to flatterers, / Till I entertained thee" (11. 89–91)—clearly equivocates, given what he has already disclosed about his expectations for those around him ("Methinks you that are courtiers should be my touchwood, take fire when I give fire; that is, laugh when I laugh, were the subject never so witty" [1.2.43–46]). It also indicates the limits he would impose on his hireling's access to his interior life. As factor or steward of his master's malevolence, Bosola works within a division of labor that forecloses knowledge of Ferdinand's motives, even as he is tasked and entrusted to act upon them as the visual representative of what Ferdinand would himself conceal.

Triangulation

* * * Webster's tragedy takes up the culturally charged matter of Malvolio, the steward whose place is to be out of place. Webster enlarges and complicates Malvolio's role and then strategically positions a strong aristocratic female character in relation to two steward figures, heightening class issues and more strongly foregrounding historically embedded concerns about power relations, gender, and class in a period of challenges to the feudal political structure. But genre in this case is not merely a formal or restrictive category; rather, it is embedded in sociohistorical conflict and tensions that Webster so productively probed.[1]

Like Frank Whigham in an important reading of Duchess of Malfi, I am interested in historical issues of class mobility and conflict in the play, but this discussion takes issue with at least part of Whigham's reading and argues for the importance of what I'll call

1. Jean E. Howard argues that what she calls the "'comic city play'" is a dramatic innovation embedded in and reflecting changing urban social relations that also generate it as a distinctive form. Webster's tragedy also seems to partake of the activity of relinquishing the past, although in a traditional generic form. It has been quite productive for me to think about The Duchess of Malfi in light of reading Howard's essay; see "Competing Ideologies of Commerce in Thomas Heywood's If You Know Not Me You Know Nobody, Part II," in The Culture of Capital: Property, Cities, and Knowledge in Early Modern England, ed. Henry S. Turner (New York: Routledge, 2002), 163–82, esp. 164.

the play's social-erotic thematics.[2] Webster's play is remarkable for the ways in which desire and social-erotic energy collide and circulate, and I want to stress his sustained attention to mobility and social striving—most significantly, in Bosola and Antonio's concerns with "calling" and "falling." Webster represents the court hierarchy as a cultural political stock exchange of status, in which preferment, prestige, and pandering are operative terms in the social machinery and where the duchess's efforts to rechannel energy toward alternative domestic-political arrangements have a spectacularly violent outcome.[3] While Whigham's placement of her in an aristocratic triangle is helpful for its focus on the drama's special historical poignancy and class problematics, the duchess, considered in relation to the two servant figures, provokes other questions of agency that also figure in a critical reading of the play. This reading thus necessarily builds from the play's relationship to Shakespeare's *Twelfth Night*, whether that relationship is one of direct influence or of shared interest in the steward figure.[4]

Although Whigham's declared interest lies in delineating class "abrasions" and intersections in early modern drama, his familiar ambition-privilege model creates a kind of Checkpoint Charlie of class division and produces a strongly masculinizing reading of class conflicts, one that obscures gender issues and even the notion of masculinity itself. If agency in the drama flows from elite social status, legible in only one gender, Webster's play is about Ferdinand's crisis. For Whigham, that the duchess takes action makes her another case of noble (and masculine) "self-appropriation": "a refusal of the noblewoman's dynastic obligations in favor of personal marital autonomy . . . is itself one of the things that marks her unsentimentally as her brother's sibling, indifferent and reckless."[5] While

2. Frank Whigham, *Seizures of the Will in Early Modern Drama* (Cambridge: Cambridge UP, 1996). Ferdinand is "a threatened aristocrat, frightened by the contamination of his supposedly ascriptive social rank, and obsessively preoccupied with its defense," and he "construes Ferdinand's incestuous inclination toward his sister as a social posture" (191). Whigham desensationalizes the issue of incest by placing it in a political context of early modern social transition and struggles between the residual social formation of beleaguered aristocrats and that of emergent, ambitious agents of change. By viewing the duchess's character in relation to social conflict, he also challenges more idealizing views that tend to see her as an admirable person or even a protofeminist, not a character constructed by an author for thematic purposes.
3. By "circulation," I do not mean a closed, self-reproducing social circuit or structure but rather the movement, often indeterminate or threatening to ordered social energies, connected to conflicts and continually defiant of containment. This is quite different from Stephen Greenblatt's more functionalist "circulation of social energies" in *Shakespearean Negotiations: The Circulation of Social Energy in Renaissance England* (Berkeley: U of California P, 1988), 1–20.
4. For a quite different reading of the play that also recognizes the duchess's triangulated relationship to Antonio and Bosola, see Michael Neill, "'A woman's service,'" 131.
5. Whigham, 202.

her action "tends to undermine the ontology of clear social distinctions, whether of status or gender identity . . . it is her capacita-
tions as noblewoman that enable her ambiguous maneuvers," and
she woos Antonio "in the unmistakably masculine voice of the
Renaissance hero."[6] Whigham sees the duchess not as a class or gender transgressor but as a social and sexual predator who coerces a
markedly reticent Antonio into a relationship that dooms him precisely because it makes him a victim of the lethal triumvirate of
undifferentiated "masculine" figures of aristocratic power and privileged self-authorization: Ferdinand, the cardinal, the duchess.[7]
Making class an unbreakable mold that uniformly coins or casts
characters, however, means ignoring a more complicated reading of
the duchess offered through Antonio:

> But for their sister, the right noble Duchess,
> You never fix'd your eye on three fair medals,
> Cast in one figure, of so different temper. . . .
> All her particular worth grows to this sum:
> She stains the time past: lights the time to come.
>   (1.2.109–11, 130–31)

Antonio's admiration for the duchess acknowledges status and kinship while insisting on her substantial difference from her siblings.
Webster's duchess is an aristocratic "figure" like her brothers, yet tem-
pered to act outside the class mold in which she is cast. She not only
is different; in her abilities to eclipse and illuminate—"She stains
the time past, lights the time to come"—she also combines elements
of residual and emergent social formations.[8] Doubly triangulated,
strategically positioned in relation to her brothers and to Antonio
and Bosola, she occupies more than one historical location.[9]

For Whigham, class forecloses the very questions of female agency
and social erotics raised, although not happily resolved, in the
play. If the duchess transgresses aristocratic norms in choosing a
domestic companion like Antonio, her act does not provide an

---

6. Whigham, 202, 204.
7. Whigham, 206.
8. The line is a pointed borrowing from Webster's *A Monvmental Colvmne* (1613), a funeral
   elegy for Prince Henry: "VVhose beames shall breake forth from thy hollow Tombe, /
   Staine the time past, and light the time to come" (sig. Clr). In a quite different interpretation of Webster's play, "'Fame's best friend': The Endings of *The Duchess of Malfi*," in
   Issues of Death: Mortality and Identity in English Renaissance Tragedy (Oxford: Clarendon Press, 1997), 328–53, Michael Neill reads the play, especially its ending, in the
   context of the death of the young prince and sees echoes of Webster's elegy, as well as
   numerous references to mortality, making *The Duchess of Malfi* itself a kind of monument or dramatic memento mori.
9. Whigham's reading tacitly affirms versions of the popular story that treat the duchess
   as a lusty, appetitive widow who deserves what she suffers and not as a figure constructed
   in a historical fault line. For a summary of negative views of the duchess, see Laurie A.
   Finke, "Painting Women: Images of Femininity in Jacobean Tragedy," in *Performing
   Feminisms: Feminist Critical Theory and Theatre*, ed. Sue-Ellen Case (Baltimore: Johns
   Hopkins UP, 1990), 223–36, esp. 231.

adequate vision of an alternative.[1] The clandestine marriage is too brief, marked by adulterous shame, fertile but socially and affectively undeveloped, politically ungenerative, and always exploitative of Antonio, the alienated nocturnal sex worker who furtively exits before morning.[2]

To suggest *Twelfth Night* as another source for Webster is to take issue with Whigham's tragic genealogy of *The Spanish Tragedy, Hamlet,* and *King Lear,* a generic anchoring that undergirds his interest in intersecting conflicts of class and sexuality and their apparently inevitable tragic outcomes. But a critically more potent view of the duchess's historical character may emerge when we consider the links between administrative hirelings and women, who are marginally but instrumentally positioned in the power hierarchy, who are essential but threatening to official power. These transgressive negotiators of ambition and desire are cut off, contained by a threatened patriarchal structure and by powerful male figures who mark their own weaknesses and pathologies by controlling, disciplining, or executing those whom they expect to serve as the stewards of their desires. This power structure prevails in both plays, but the outcomes may be less important than appreciating how the plays may provoke the audience for whom the conflicts are staged.

A Case for Influence

That Webster knew and made use of many of Shakespeare's plays is well known, but that Shakespeare's *Twelfth Night* so strongly influenced Webster's tragedy might seem strained. * * *

Although there is lingering debate about whether *Twelfth Night* was performed first for the public, the queen, or members of the Middle Temple, a performance of *Twelfth Night* commissioned by the Middle Temple took place on 2 February 1602.[3] Thanks to the work of Muriel Bradbrook, we know that Webster had become a

1. Whigham notes, "for a female head of state such companionate marital selection for express and state-exclusive domesticity, unequivocally across status and dynastic imperatives (Antonio's as much as Ferdinand's), was dizzying" (207). Mary Beth Rose criticizes Whigham for emphasizing the Duchess's political dimension at the expense of the erotic in *The Expense of Spirit: Love and Sexuality in English Renaissance Drama* (Ithaca: Cornell UP, 1988), 162.

2. Theodora A. Jankowski, *Women in Power in the Early Modern Drama* (Urbana: U of Illinois P, 1992), 173–74, also finds the secret marriage politically reprehensible in light of what she considers to be the Duchess's obligations as a ruler.

3. Leslie Hotson, *The First Night of "Twelfth Night"* (London: Rupert Hart-Davis, 1954), argues that the play was first performed at Whitehall on 6 January 1601, as part of the Queen's entertainment of Virginio Orsino, duke of Bracciano, ambassador to the English court (13). Roslyn Lander Knutson, *The Repertory of Shakespeare's Company 1594–1613* (Fayetteville: U of Arkansas P, 1991), gives *Twelfth Night* a repertory date of 1601–2 (81); J. M. Lothian and T. W. Craik, eds., in their introduction to *Twelfth Night* (London: Methuen, 1975), find it more plausible that Shakespeare composed *Twelfth Night* in the wake of the duke's visit (xxvi-xxxv). Peter Thomson, *Shakespeare's Theatre* (London: Routledge, 1983), notes that "the performance in the Middle Temple on 2 February 1602 was a notable revival" (60).

member of the Middle Temple in 1598.[4] Even without the direct historical evidence to place him there, we can easily imagine Webster,
with his fellow Innsmen, in the audience of that 1602 performance.
We can even imagine that the talented and ambitious coachmaker's
son, pursuing his legal career and theatrical interests, was provoked
and impressed not only by the comedy's craft and its conflicts of
identity and misrecognition but also by Malvolio's humiliation and
scapegoating in a punitive spectacle, much like that of Shylock in
The Merchant of Venice, in which the social outcast's abrupt departure haunts an otherwise-celebratory conclusion.[5] Even if the cir-
cumstantial case for direct influence cannot be made convincing,
we should at least see the playwrights' common interests in class
transgression and female agency; we could hypothesize a conversation on power, class, gender, and genre arising from those interests;
and we should be impressed by how Webster further develops those
concerns in his treatment of the steward figure.

* * *

The Steward in History

"Art any more than a steward?" (2.3.102–3). Sir Toby's capsule insult
to Malvolio, when he tries to impose household order on cakes-and-
ale revelry, would reduce and fix the steward's social stature and
humble and silence him. Perhaps Shakespeare had a dim view of
the early modern steward as well, but the Oxford English Dictionary bears evidence of the complexity of the word "steward" as job
description, as social rank, and as signifier of mobility from the
medieval period until at least the end of the sixteenth century, when
the obligations of feudal service were being superseded by contractual and more overtly economic relations between masters and servants.[6] In the early modern lexicon, "steward" often overlaps with

---

4. M. C. Bradbrook, *John Webster: Citizen and Dramatist* (New York: Columbia UP, 1980),
   280. F. L. Lucas, ed., *The Complete Works of John Webster*, 4 vols. (New York: Oxford
   UP, 1937), states in his introduction to *The Duchess of Malfi* that "much more is known
   of the Duchess's life than of Webster's own" (2:6); this is probably a valid claim, even
   after Bradbrook.
5. It is tempting to see other links between Shakespeare and Webster suggested by the
   historical context of Elizabeth's courtly entertainment of Virginio Orsino, Shakespeare's
   Count Orsino, and the more notorious Duke Bracciano of Webster's *The White Devil*,
   the character who poisons the lips on his portrait and murders his virtuous wife when
   she kisses it in her nightly ritual.
6. On stewards, see especially Evett; Felicity Heal, "Reciprocity and Exchange in the Late
   Medieval Household," in *Bodies and Disciplines: Intersections of Literature and History
   in Fifteenth-Century England*, ed. Barbara A. Hanawalt and David Wallace (Minneapolis: U of Minnesota P, 1996), 179–98; Peter Laslett, *The World We Have Lost: Further
   Explored* (London: Methuen, 1983); Lynne Magnusson, *Shakespeare and Social Dialogue: Dramatic Language and Elizabethan Letters* (Cambridge: Cambridge UP, 1999);
   Eric S. Mallin, *Inscribing the Time: Shakespeare and the End of Elizabethan England*
   (Berkeley: U of California P, 1995), 167–219; Mertes, passim; and Neill, *Putting History to the Question*, 13–48.

"bailiff," "majordomo," and "seneschal," all of which, whatever the attendant rank or prestige, refer to administrative, secondary, and mediating positions in a large household. Thus, the steward could be "an official who controls the domestic affairs of a household, supervising the service of his master's table, directing the domestics, and regulating household expenditure; a major-domo"; or, like the bailiff, "one who manages the affairs of an estate on behalf of his employer," "one who transacts the financial and legal business of a manor on behalf of the lord . . . , holds the manor-court in the lord's absence, and keeps a copy of its rolls." The position could be limited to "merely nominal duties," but it could encompass judicial or diplomatic tasks, such as those associated with the Lord High Steward of royal courts.[7]

The bailiff could be "one charged with public administrative authority"; "an officer of justice under a sheriff, who executes writs and processes, distrains, and arrests; a warrant officer, pursuivant, or catchpoll"; "the agent of the lord of a manor, who collects his rents, etc.; the steward of a landholder, who manages his estate; one who superintends the husbandry of a farm for its owner or tenant"; or even "a royal envoy."[8] But whether administering, organizing, or representing a household, a rural estate, or a royal court, the bailiff or steward supported his superior and occupied a constitutively intermediate position.

Furthermore, according to D. R. Hainsworth, even the humbler sort of early modern steward's position covered a good deal more than Toby's terse and belittling remark would suggest:

> There can be no doubt that some men had found in steward-ship a career open to talent earlier than the early modern period. . . . Sir Thomas Thynne [d. 1580] . . . seems to have used his position as steward to the Earl of Hertford (subsequently Protector Somerset) to found the fortunes of a gentry family which subsequently entered the nobility. The fact that at least 190 Members of the Parliaments of Elizabeth I had been, still were or were destined to become stewards is an indication not simply that in the sixteenth century stewardship was a respectable calling, but that it could be a means of climbing the ladder of degree.[9]

Hainsworth describes the estate steward's mediating role:

> He was perfectly placed to act as the vital "broker" between the metropolitan society with which he was constantly in touch,

---

7. OED, s.v. "steward" (noun), 1, 5.
8. OED, s.v. "bailiff," 1–3.
9. Hainsworth, 7.

and the local community in which he lived. . . . [as] "mediator" between governors and governed, between capital and province, between the "great society" and the "popular" culture of the local community.[1]

Hainsworth's description of the steward as mediator, broker, conduit, ambassador, and, above all, social interface between an estate and the market environment of the local community makes such a servant a rather more slippery social and political entity at a time when property and social relations, as well as structures and valences of service, were changing.[2] As the very figure of mediation in a shifting agricultural economy with increasingly fluid market relations, the steward was something more than what Sir Toby implies and something more complex than Whigham's strict division between ambition and privilege allows. The steward functioned as a class hinge in the opening door of transition and social mobility.[3]

* * *

In the end, *Twelfth Night* leaves open the issue of counterfeit identity and the social issues of cross-class marriage that go with the unstable status of the early modern estate steward. Finding a place where fortune and fantasy meet is Malvolio's aspiration; being denied it or punished for having it leaves an embittered Malvolio, his complaint of abuse both acknowledged and quickly cast aside, to trouble the conclusion. But his promise of revenge, while unanswered in *Twelfth Night*, may have made its way toward the top of the thematic agenda in *The Duchess of Malfi*. As one reader of *Twelfth Night* says of Malvolio's musing about historical precedent for stewards marrying up: "Fourteen years later, he could have added, 'And the Duchess of Malfi married Antonio, her steward.'"[4] Actual Malvolios, of course, continued to move upward.

1. Hainsworth, 3.
2. See especially Robert Brenner, "Agrarian Class Structure and Economic Development in Pre-Industrial Europe" and "The Agrarian Roots of European Capitalism," in *The Brenner Debate: Agrarian Class Structure and Economic Development in Pre-Industrial Europe*, ed. T. H. Aston and C.H.E. Philpin (Cambridge: Cambridge UP, 1987), 10–63, 213–327; and Ellen Wood Meiksins, *The Origin of Capitalism: A Longer View* (London: Verso, 2002). On the status range of "higher servants" and "gentle servitors," see also Magnusson on "The Institution of Service and Its Ambiguities," 39–42; and Mertes, 52–74.
3. Although more concerned with attitudes toward and historical accounts of service, rather than the position of the steward, Weil (see n. 3 above) gives the most nuanced reading of class fluidity and self-representations. See especially "Introduction: Slippery People" (1–17) and her discussion (84–86) of I. M.'s nostalgia for master-servant friendship combined with his complaint of the historical change to contractual service, as found in *A Health to the Gentlemanly Profession of Servingmen*, Shakespeare Association Facsimiles 3 (1598; repr., Oxford: Oxford UP, 1931).
4. Ralph Berry, *Shakespeare and Social Class* (Atlantic Highlands, NJ: Humanities Press International, 1988), 71–72.

Calling, Falling, and the Social-Erotic

[In *The Duchess of Malfi* t]he courtship scene begins when the duchess summons [her steward] to "inquire / What's laid up for tomorrow" (1.2.285–86), and the two of them engage in an awkward but crucial communication struggle. Antonio understands her to ask for some accounting of her possessions, while the duchess speaks of a last will and testament as a pretext for the next, decisive step of communicating her desire (will) to marry him. The issue of the steward who serves the will of his employer is foregrounded here as a serious point of comparison with Ferdinand and the hirelings who unquestioningly serve his desires. The duchess underscores the boldness of her quest beforehand: "[W]ish me good speed," she says to Cariola before Antonio enters, "For I am going into a wilderness, / Where I shall find nor path, nor friendly clew / To be my guide" (11. 277–80). If the duchess is acting outside socially scripted roles, Cariola's remarks underscore her uncertain position: "Whether the spirit of greatness, or of woman / Reign most in her, I know not, but it shows / A fearful madness: I owe her much of pity" (11. 417–19). If she is moved by the spirit of greatness, she is acting out the traditional aristocratic-heroic script that Whigham finds in her actions; if she is moved by the spirit of "woman," something far less legible, far more awesome is taking place when she swears to make her "royal kindred" who pose obstacles "my low foot-steps" (11. 260, 262). It is significant that in the scene with Antonio Webster lets both motions collide, underscoring Cariola's indeterminate "I know not" (1. 418) and giving the duchess lines that reflect on her own dissembling and encoded performance:

> The misery of us, that are born great,
> We are forc'd to woo, because none dare woo us:
> And as a tyrant doubles with his words,
> And fearfully equivocates: so we
> Are forc'd to express our violent passions
> In riddles, and in dreams.   (11. 357–62)

The duchess's but-for-ceremony speech might first seem to align her with her tyrannical brother, an equivocating speaker of grim riddles, appearing to place her sexual passion close to his libidinally invested malice. But the marriage proposal also performs its own quite distinct and transgressive work.

The duchess's discursive maneuvering leaves the otherwise articulate Antonio in search of a script appropriate to his position and the unanticipated occasion. Like Malvolio, Antonio seems inclined to hear what he wants to hear, and he concedes that he has no small interest in their interview's outcome: "Conceive not, I am so stupid, but I aim / Whereto your favours tend" (11. 342–43). He is, however, a good deal more circumspect about the "saucy and ambitious devil" (11. 329) he sees at play in the duchess's words, and he is prudently suspicious of courtly speech. When Antonio responds somewhat evasively to the duchess's proposal—"I have long serv'd virtue, / And nev'r tane wages of her" (11. 355–56)—she is direct: "Now she pays it. / . . . here upon your lips / I sign your Quietus est" (11. 356, 379–80).[5] Although he speaks of his service to her as beyond remuneration and deploys the discourse of a more idealized feudal obligation, Antonio has been the duchess's employee. The duchess, however, has no investment in transcendental language; her insistence on unvarnished economic language has a metadiscursive and desentimentalizing effect that curiously echoes the anti-Petrarchan play enjoyed by Olivia and Viola/Cesario and that continues to characterize her relationship with Antonio.[6] Her candor, jarring to some of her critics, stems less from her use of sexual double entendres than from the language of the market. When she defends widowhood from her brothers' stereotypical notions of experienced and lascivious women—"Diamonds are of most value / They say, that have pass'd through most jewellers' hands" (11. 220–21)—she receives only a demeaning response: "Whores, by that rule, are precious" (1. 222). But at key moments in the play the duchess continues to turn to market discourse. The calling up and discharging of accounts puts the couple in a milieu first entirely worldly, circumscribed by the language of money and debt, and then otherworldly. The discharge of debt marks a knowing resistance to the social boundaries that would also confine or prohibit their desires, as well as an investment in an unrestricted economy of alternative, debt-free, affect-laden social arrangements, undetermined or at least not wholly bound by status or contract. It might seem at this moment that the duchess's valorization of the market as a way of defending her erotic prerogatives makes her the spokesperson for "emergent liberalism," as critiqued by Belsey, in which an "affective ideal" of private family life opposes the public and patriarchal political world.[7] Yet I would argue that the duchess uses the market in a demystifying way that serves not only to debunk the feudal valorization of honor and

---

5. Neill, " 'Fame's best friend,' " finds a "melancholy ambiguity" with an "ominous resonance" in "Quietus," which, echoing Webster's funeral elegy, circumscribes the courtship with "the language of epitaph" (335–36), rather than, as I argue, deploying the language of economy in a way that opens social-erotic possibility.

6. Rowe finds the combined amatory and economic speech "erotic and illogically vexed," discourse that "maintains their separation by rank," and claims that both the Duchess and Antonio are capable of turning on each other—the duchess as tyrant, Antonio as self-interested and dishonest servant (92). Such speculation, however, seems to wander from the text.

7. Catherine Belsey, *The Subject of Tragedy: Identity and Difference in Renaissance Drama* (London: Methuen, 1985), 199–200.

female chastity but to further destabilize it by unmasking the already interdependent relation between market and court, as well as its place in the private sphere.

What is so bold about the project, as Webster constructs it, is that the duchess demystifies economic language precisely even as she freely and playfully deploys it—"now the ground's broke, / You may discover what a wealthy mine / I make you lord of" (11. 345–47). By the same token, just as she openly acknowledges class difference, she raises Antonio to reciprocity, inscribing his lips with a receipt that resists status and contract. When Antonio bemoans his "unworthiness" (1. 347), the duchess invokes the market in an obstinately valorizing dis-analogy: "This dark'ning of your worth is not like that / Which tradesmen use i'th' city; their false lights / Are to rid bad wares off" (11. 349–51). As a "complete man" (1. 342), Antonio should look within himself for his worth, and he should do so in a rather radical parody of a nobleman making a state journey: "turn your eyes, / And progress through yourself" (11. 353–54). Threatened by her brother's violence in 2.3, the duchess is willing to fabricate a tawdry accusation against Antonio, the *magnanima mensogna* or "noble lie" of 3.2, in order to save her family. But her unrealized desire to erase difference outside the household realm, her violently aborted attempt at class leveling, may be the real *magnanima mensogna*, the utopian realm glimpsed in the courtship scene of the play. Canceling all "debts" (1. 103)—the mutual, if differentiated social obligations of steward-servants and masters—would not only level differences but magnanimously eliminate or socially eradicate them. Generically and socially, the project is as doomed as it is utopian; yet the careful staging of the duchess's failure to achieve her desire for life with Antonio because of the clearly unjust imposition of her brothers' cruel desires, through their intelligencer and henchman, seems designed to provoke the audience.[8]

While in Act 3 she defends herself against Ferdinand—"Why might not I marry? / I have not gone about, in this, to create / Any new world, or custom" (3.2.110–12)—it seems clear that Webster has been sufficiently innovative in creating or at least gesturing poignantly toward a clandestine micropolitical space: if not a new

8. I am in no way assuming a single, unified audience response here. For interpretations that differ from mine, see Whigham; Kathleen McLuskie, "Drama and Sexual Politics: The Case of Webster's Duchess," in *Themes in Drama 7: Drama, Sex, and Politics*, ed. James Redmond (Cambridge UP, 1985), 77–91; Belsey; Jankowski; and Lisa Jardine, "The Duchess of Malfi: A Case Study in the Literary Representation of Women," in *Teaching the Text*, ed. Susanne Kappeler and Norman Bryson (London: Routledge and Kegan Paul, 1983), 203–17. Belsey's reading of the play, as "a perfect fable of emergent liberalism" valorizing Antonio's merit and a private, strongly affective familial realm "separate from the turbulent world of politics, though vulnerable to it" (198), seems to neglect the strongly political valence of the duchess's economic language, as well as the political-erotic elements that inform the structure of her household.

world, then another, imagined one. Compared to the roles of actual early modern stewards, Antonio's job description is significantly changed by the duchess as she invites him not to be the alienated extension of her will, delegated to manage aristocratic desire, but to share her desire and act upon his own. If Antonio is a reliable voice (and his description of her as the medal stamped by a radically different temper is at least as historically significant), the duchess's actions mark a nearly world-historical moment, one conceived and scripted by Webster in adapting the novella of the duchess and quite possibly mediated by his exposure to *Twelfth Night*.

Cariola's reading of the courtship as great, womanly, or fearfully mad is strategically ambivalent and telling. To link the duchess's female desire to class leveling is to deliver a blow to the noble "greatness" in which her brothers are so invested and which Webster interrogates in his dedicatory epistle; it is also to redirect desire socially toward a realm of egalitarian reciprocity and power sharing.[9] The project will fail spectacularly; the courtship itself may be viewed as a utopian *magnanima mensogna*, but its radical audacity will leave its mark on all the play's social actors and on the audience that must weigh radical potential against tragic inevitability. When the duchess declares "I am Duchess of Malfi still" (4.2.139) to her delegated executioners, she seems to use the title as a shield rather than as an anchoring signifier of status, as a strategy rather than as a regression to her brothers' feudal framework. As duchess, she has hereditary rights, political responsibilities, and property; these should stand between her and the rope, should disarm her attackers. Such feudal signifiers invoke the masculine honor that Whigham sees as her fixed position, but the duchess always acts from a doubly triangulated place, between her brothers on the one hand and the two steward figures on the other. Her clandestine marriage challenges the traditional power that her brothers would preserve against the contamination that is already there; in effect, the play acknowledges that a mediating figure like the estate steward does much to contaminate putative aristocratic purity.

In the context of the early modern period, then, a steward is hardly just a steward. Webster's Antonio, the majordomo upon whom the duchess would thrust greatness, thus marks the reappearance of the Countess Olivia's self-deluded steward, gullible to the forgeries of Maria and Sir Toby because their letter offers him the legitimation of his own desires and the imagined gateway to fulfilling them, a gateway on the far side of the aristocratic desire he serves. Yet perhaps even closer to *Twelfth Night*'s steward is Bosola, who like

9. See Webster's "Dedication": "I do not altogether look up at your title: The ancientest nobility, being but a relic of time past, and the truest honour indeed being for a man to confer honour on himself, which your learning strives to propagate, and shall make you arrive at the dignity of a great example" (5, ll. 13–18).

Malvolio wears his ambition resentfully. The play opens with Antonio speaking to Delio first of the virtues of an uncorrupted French court, and then of Bosola, the malcontent in pursuit of advancement. Ferdinand economically negotiates the hire of Bosola, who, having returned from the galleys in punishment for some criminal service to the Cardinal, "haunts" Ferdinand's brother. To the duke's offer of gold, Bosola asks, "Whose throat must I cut?" (1.2.170) and weighs the ethical stakes against the material benefits—"these curs'd gifts would make / You a corrupter, me an impudent traitor, / And should I take these they'll'd take me to hell" (11. 185–87). He then commits himself fatalistically: "I am your creature" (1. 208). It is in Bosola that Malvolio's disciplinary fantasies, their violent potential unrealized in the conventional comic ending of *Twelfth Night*, are allowed to develop; as the creature of greatness, Bosola is suborned to concretize his master's malevolent desires, and his consent is contractual from the moment Ferdinand pays him: "For the good deed you have done me, I must do / All the ill man can invent" (11. 195–96). When his own complicated and disunified wishes are frustrated, his destructive agenda affects every character.[1] Bosola, it seems, eventually takes a clumsy sort of revenge on the whole lot of them, including the death blow he unintentionally delivers to Antonio.

Against Castruchio's advice in Act 1 to deputize a substitute for his own military presence, Ferdinand claims to be willing to go to war in his own aristocratic person, responding with caustic irony, "Why should [a noble] not as well sleep, or eat, by a deputy? This might take idle, offensive, and base office from him, whereas the other deprives him of honour" (11. 19–21). Yet in order to wage his campaign against the duchess, Ferdinand needs to hire someone to act for him; he depends upon Bosola's skills and labor to administer his will to control and punish her. Antonio is the object of the duchess's desire and her interlocutor in class reflexivity, while Bosola is Ferdinand's resentful hit man and hired hand. The duke makes him a steward of the family's libidinal economy, the figure delegated to manage his actively desiring sister and defend his birthright. As Whigham describes the Antonio–Bosola relationship, "the brothers, thinking to hire a spy, consider Antonio with Bosola: to noble eyes both are servants—men in the way of opportunity."[2] Toby sees Malvolio as no more than an ambitious crumb catcher in a

---

1. Cf. Francis Bacon, "Of Ambition": "So ambitious men, if they find the way open for their rising, and still get forward, they are rather busy than dangerous; but if they be checked in their desires, they become secretly discontent and look upon men and matters with an evil eye, and are best pleased when things go backward, which is the worst property in a servant of a prince or state," in *The Essays*, ed. John Pitcher (Harmondsworth: Penguin, 1985), 173. Rowe offers a critically rich discussion of the early modern agent and the history of agency, passim.
2. Whigham, 212.

noble household, just as Ferdinand considers Antonio to be Bosola's functional equivalent, although he knows Antonio's equestrian skills make him a better Provisor of the Horse for his sister. Significantly, when the duchess invents her accusation against Antonio in Act 3, one of Ferdinand's sycophantic underlings responds, "the chippings of the butt'ry fly after him, to scour his gold chain" (3.2.225–26).

Unlike Malvolio, however, Antonio and Bosola share more than the curse of service and a certain analytic distance from their superiors; they also have histories that testify to their intellectual credentials. In 3.3, Delio tells Antonio that Bosola was a student in Padua before being banished to galley service for the assassination suborned by the Cardinal. Antonio has served at the French court long enough to compare its monarch to the more corrupt territorial princes of Italy and is skilled at equestrian and jousting sports, the martial arts associated with nobility.[3] In Bandello's narrative, Antonio is from a "good" family, hardly the base-born "slave, that only smell'd of ink and counters, / And nev'r in's life look'd like a gentleman" (3.3.71–72), as Ferdinand derisively figures him. Nor is he a "base, low fellow," "[o]ne of no birth" (3.5.116, 118), as the vizarded Bosola, the duke's mouthpiece, insultingly calls him.

Significantly, in their shared intimate relationship to the duchess, Bosola and Antonio complete what is the critical constellation of Webster's drama, juxtaposing a mixed-class triangle to the noble one of Ferdinand, the cardinal, and the duchess. In the duchess's household their close, if not amicable, relationship suggests uncomfortable affinities between them, not least of which is a structure of inversion: Antonio's faithful benevolence against Bosola's self-interested malevolence, Antonio's fathering children against Bosola's killing children, Antonio's keeping secrets against Bosola's discovering and disclosing secrets. But the more analytical Antonio, who lacks Bosola's illusions about working for Ferdinand and who knows Ferdinand's reputation as a delegator who "Dooms men to death by information, / Rewards, by hearsay" (1.2.98–99), succinctly dissects Bosola at the play's beginning as "the only court-gall" (1.1.23) who "rails at those things which he wants, / Would be as lecherous, covetous, or proud, / Bloody, or envious, as any man, / If he had means to be so" (11. 25–28) and takes him apart directly: "Because you would not seem to appear to th' world / Puff'd up with your

3. See Baldesar Castiglione, *The Book of the Courtier,* trans. George Bull (Harmondsworth: Penguin Books, 1967), on the nobleman's profession: "'The first and true profession of the courtier must be that of arms; and this above everything else I wish him to pursue vigorously'" (57); and "'You know that in war what really spurs men on to bold deeds is the desire for glory, whereas anyone who acts for gain or from any other motive not only fails to accomplish anything worth while but deserves to be called a miserable merchant rather than a gentleman'" (89).

preferment, you continue / This out of fashion melancholy" (2.1.87–89). Until Bosola's remorse emerges in Act 4 and then only after he is denied the reward promised for overseeing the duchess's execution, his reflections are left to more private moments, except perhaps for an inadvertent comment on the fatal interdependence of the two stewards when the duchess first gives birth. When Antonio threatens to "pull thee up by the roots," Bosola suggests, "May be the ruin will crush you to pieces" (2.3.36–37). In fact, of course, it is Bosola who will dispatch a ruined Antonio and find himself crushed, stabbed by Ferdinand, his noble melancholic counterpart.

As a dramatic triangle, Antonio, Bosola, and the duchess are three figures pushing against social limits and compulsory service to the alienating desire of Ferdinand and the cardinal. Nowhere is their triangulated relationship (and its critical potential) clearer than in 3.2, the real turning point of the tragedy, in the duchess's private chambers. Webster's telescopic glimpse of quotidian life in the duchess's household abruptly ends with Ferdinand's menacing appearance, Antonio's orchestrated flight to Ancona, and Bosola's discovery that Antonio has fathered the duchess's children.[4] When the scene begins in the duchess's chambers, the conversation is ludic and erotic. It offers another glimpse at an alternative world of social-erotic arrangements, a place where, as with Olivia and Viola/Cesario in *Twelfth Night,* characters play with the constraints of language through equivocating puns, ironies, and double entendres that acknowledge the limits of the discourse that constructs them and the conditions of their desiring lives.

To the duchess's "[Y]ou are a lord of mis-rule," Antonio responds, "Indeed, my rule is only in the night" (3.2.7–8). But in the confined structure of their endangered relationship, the reference to a carnivalesque world turned upside down in which to rule is to misrule underscores the ways in which these characters offer a reconfiguring challenge to authority and its power to enforce meaning and value. One need only compare the sexy reciprocity of this lord of misrule's banter with Ferdinand's aggressive bawdry in Act 1 where he declares that "women like that part, which, like the lamprey, / Hath nev'r a bone in't" (1.2.255–56) or his intensely invested fantasies about his sister's imaginary lovers as strong-thighed bargemen, woodsmen throwing sledgehammers, or that "lovely squire / That carries coals up to her privy lodgings" (2.5.45–46).

Antonio and Cariola exit to eavesdrop, as the duchess continues her playful dialogue with Antonio and unwittingly discloses

---

4. I think (pace Whigham, 218) it important to view this scene as telescopic and deliberately condensed, rather than as evidence that the marriage is not sufficiently or all too briefly represented in the play.

incriminating information when her brother enters and abruptly aborts her pleasure with the menacing and overdetermined signifier of the patriarchal—phallic and aristocratic—poniard. When Antonio is with her next, they play a grimly serious game with more language play, as the duchess has Bosola summon officers and then concocts accusations in order to get Antonio and one child safely away to Ancona. Under the aegis of equivocating speech, in which she accuses Antonio of theft and faulty accounting, she counters Ferdinand's banal phallic threat with an equally banal representation of the ungrateful and dishonest servant.

When they are forced to separate, the duchess denounces Antonio with the magnanimous lie that "must shield our honours," as Antonio curses "the inconstant / And rotten ground of service" (3.2.181, 98–99) and disingenuously discloses a part of their intimate history: "You may see, gentlemen, what 'tis to serve / A prince with body and soul" (11. 207–8). As a desperate but residually erotic playfulness briefly reappears in their dialogue, Antonio produces his own equivocating self-defense and social critique. He curses the employment in which he serves a prince "body and soul" and suggestively tells the duchess, "I am all yours" (1. 208, 205). His ardor is clear sighted; at the same time that he sends a quite particular message to his spouse, he astutely reads class service as constitutively intimate and erotically inflected. To be in service is to belong to another. Antonio echoes Bosola's earlier "I am your creature" (1.2.208) at the same time that he marks the difference between the secret marriage and the court, communicating to the duchess what others can only misinterpret.

But when Antonio exits, Bosola's "most unvalu'd jewel" (3.2.248) speech to the duchess seems to top everything that precedes it in the way of equivocating discourse. Bosola defends Antonio in words that, as Whigham and others suggest, are invested with social conviction and offer a trenchant social critique, even as he traps the duchess into trusting him and making fatal disclosures. As Ferdinand's hired intelligencer, Bosola is delegated to learn the duchess's secret, a task he regards as his ticket to promotion and a sinecure: "I am certain to be rais'd" (1. 328). At least until after the murders of the duchess and her children, he honors dishonorable contracts, thinking to reach a goal that his patrons will absolutely withhold from him. He has already identified Antonio as the duchess's bawd in Act 2 when the first child is born, and he is generally suspicious when she accuses Antonio of theft. But the praise for Antonio the duchess elicits from Bosola in Act 3 seems calculated—the intelligencer's ploy flowing from his elastic principles—and also sedimented with another, more transgressive, desire. Calling Antonio a "most unvalu'd jewel" and a "trophy of a man" (1. 292)—compliments that entrap the duchess to confide her secret—Bosola, while disingenuous, makes a comment that resonates profoundly:

> Can this ambitious age
> Have so much goodness in't, as to prefer
> A man merely for worth: without these shadows
> Of wealth, and painted honours? possible?   (11. 276–79)

The collision between contractual commitment and social critique constitutes an amazing moment of tragic-historical anagnorisis. Bosola seizes the information that he has been hired to find in a moment of discovery that utterly contradicts his cynical beliefs about virtue, reward, and the very institution of service. Intensifying the violent ambivalence in these lines is what happens in Act 4 when, given his continued fidelity to contractual employment, he cannot or does not act upon his new knowledge until he has dutifully dispatched the duchess.

Each of these three embattled figures attempts to negotiate a desire that always expressed the power to which they answer. If we compare their rhetorical efforts to the tyrannical language of Ferdinand, then perhaps we can view the duchess, Antonio, and Bosola as agents radically reconfiguring their social and symbolic space. Ferdinand's gory figurative language in his letter to the duchess— "Send Antonio to me; I want his head in a business. / . . . I stand engaged for your husband for several debts at Naples: let not that trouble him, I had rather have his heart than his money" (3.5.27, 33–35)—is a grim form of wordplay that defaults to bloody-minded literalness. As the duchess parenthetically glosses it, it is "(A politic equivocation)" (1. 28). The duchess's *magnanima mensogna*, on the other hand, combines official and equivocating discourse; even as she reproduces aristocratic cant, she offers resistance to it.

This rhetorical difference between the duchess and her brother is shown most eloquently in their contrasting parables. After entering her chamber with the dagger, Ferdinand lectures the duchess on the family's honor and reputation through a sermonizing allegory in which Death, Love, and Reputation are about to part ways. Death and Love leave the usual forwarding addresses—for Death, battle and urban plagues; for Love, pastoral places uncompromised by venal interests or ambition. But while Death and Love may go their separate ways, Reputation can never be recovered: "'it is my nature / If once I part from any man I meet / I am never found again'" (3.2.132–34). As if the parable were not sufficiently tendentious, Ferdinand unpacks it further in his accusation: "And so, for you: / You have shook hands with Reputation, / And made him invisible" (11. 134–36).

Reputation signifies the honor Ferdinand sees as his noble entitlement; he has made his sister its keeper or steward, expecting her to bear it for him, unsullied, or suffer the violent consequences of his displeasure. In Act 3, however, the duchess offers a telling counter-parable, when the vizarded Bosola arrives at Ancona to take her prisoner. Bosola voices the aristocrat's order to renounce Antonio and the children whom her brothers deem illegitimate, but the duchess retorts, "I prithee, who is greatest, can you tell?" (3.5.122) and relates an ironic socioeconomic fable in which a scrappy and pretentious dogfish insults a passing salmon:

> "Why art thou so bold
> To mix thyself with our high state of floods
> Being no eminent courtier, but one
> That for the calmest and fresh time o'th' year
> Dost live in shallow rivers, rank'st thyself
> With silly Smelts and Shrimps? And darest thou
> Pass by our Dog-ship without reverence?"   (11. 126–32)

In this more encrypted lesson in value, added to the obvious irony that the salmon is the "greater" fish whose greatness is linked to the price she commands in a literally devouring market, is that the duchess's disennobling, reflexive response supersedes and ridicules an antiquated, ennobling notion of worth by assigning it to the mouth of a junk fish:

> "O", quoth the Salmon, "sister, be at peace:
> Thank Jupiter, we both have pass'd the Net,
> Our value never can be truly known,
> Till in the Fisher's basket we be shown;
> I'th' Market then my price may be the higher,
> Even when I am nearest to the Cook, and fire."   (11. 133–38)

The duchess's poignant counter-parable astutely contradicts Ferdinand's allegory of reputation not only by changing the soothsayer's gender but also by speaking a far more earthbound language of economics to his transcendental aristocratic discourse. Returning to the economic language of the courtship scene, the duchess crosses the language of status and market. She demonstrates that she knows the close relationship between patriarchal honor and a market that devours reputation, status, and ceremony. She shows, too, that she knows something about gender in a market where the subject evaluated is in a commodified and culturally feminized position. This is where, if sisterhood is not powerful, some sort of sisterly solidarity might well inaugurate the productive response from those subject

both to the market and to fraternal machinations and the status anxiety that fuels them. The less-than-sententious payoff of the
parable—"Men oft are valued high, when th'are most wretch'd"
(1. 140)—is not only the Salmon's putdown of the pretentious Dogfish and a richly ironic and oblique comparison between the wretched
nobleman Ferdinand and the ethically noble wretch Antonio, but
also the message that everyone, even or especially at court, is subject to the leveling forces that always already contaminate aristocratic households, especially in their dependence on delegation and
stewards. The duchess's defense of Antonio and prescient allusion
to Ferdinand's mental breakdown in 5.2 foreground the theme of
social mobility, of "calling" and "falling," that structures the play
from the beginning and that especially characterizes the actions and
speeches of the two stewards in the concluding events.

The duchess's parable sets the theme for the concluding cata-
strophic actions, and it constitutes a convincing, thematically relevant response to traditional criticism of the play's incoherence and
ungainly structure, dispatching the duchess in Act 4. But the parable is not the only sign of her afterlife in the play. Once the duchess
is physically removed, Antonio is left to try to salvage property and
safety for the "poor remainder" (3.5.3) of the family, while Bosola
fulfills his main commission even though he is shaken by Ferdinand's cruelty and shattered by the duke's refusal to pay what was
promised. Loss of the doubly triangulated duchess leaves the aristocratic brothers to oppose and ultimately to defend themselves
against Bosola and Antonio. Yet, acting always in the shadow of the
violence against the duchess, the four characters preserve the double triangulation. A crisis of responsibility for her death emerges
which precipitates their falling, as Ferdinand's structural dependency joins him to Bosola. His high rank and Bosola's ambition, it
seems, are both subject to a devouring energy, to the calling and falling of which the two steward figures speak. As he goes to confront
the cardinal, Antonio declares, "I'll go in mine own shape" (5.1.68),
hoping his guilelessness

> May draw the poison out of him, and work
> A friendly reconcilement: if it fail,
> Yet it shall rid me of this infamous calling,
> For better fall once, than be ever falling.   (11. 70–73)

Antonio's "infamous calling" as a secret husband inverts and ironically echoes his respectable calling as steward. While Antonio
fatalistically discards every strategic precaution and plunges into
hopeless, good faith action, Bosola clings to ambition and his own
infamous calling as intelligencer and executioner, until the last
illusion is shattered and the aristocratic brothers' guilt over the

duchess's death becomes unmistakably clear. The scene that marks the onset of Ferdinand's mental deterioration is one in which he disavows his connection to delegation and execution, that is, the politics of hire and desire on which his aristocratic status depends. Ferdinand first makes a claim of diminished capacity—"I bad thee, when I was distracted of my wits, / Go kill my dearest friend, and thou hast done't" (4.2.273–74). He then takes anachronistic refuge in civil authority and its juridical parameters:

> By what authority didst thou execute
> This bloody sentence? . . .
> Was I her judge?
> Did any ceremonial form of law
> Doom her to not-being? did a complete jury
> Deliver her conviction up i'th' court?   (11. 292–96)

Thus, just before lycanthropy and madness take over, Ferdinand categorically repudiates Bosola for following his own orders in the assassination of the duchess, refuses to honor his promise to promote him, and claims a higher ground of fraternal love and heartfelt grief. In that affective and morally superior realm, quite outside the space of aristocratic honor, Ferdinand would stand as sole defender of his sister. The cardinal, meanwhile, has his own social reality problem, believing that he can keep the intelligencer Bosola ignorant of his role in the killing and that he can suborn a now-quite-insubordinate Bosola to eliminate Antonio. In dedicating himself to help Antonio, Bosola makes his last contract with aristocratic superiors in bad faith (although, in mistakenly stabbing Antonio, with ironic and clumsy consequences).

Although the duchess's alternative world never materializes, her departure has a remarkable effect on the world and relations left behind. Without the living presence of the duchess between them, the male actors left in the opposing triangles are unmoored, affectively and socially; they proceed to fall, at times precipitously, from their positions. Aristocratic life hardly qualifies as a calling, yet Ferdinand and the cardinal's murderous project constitutes a horrific response to the call of noble duty, resulting in Ferdinand's mental disintegration and a collapsing house from which Bosola seeks escape. Bosola's appeal to Julia, the cardinal's mistress, for information on Ferdinand's melancholy, on the other hand, shows him trying to regain his footing:

> I have depended on him,
> And I hear that is fall'n in some disgrace
> With the Emperor: if he be, like the mice
> That forsake falling houses, I would shift
> To other dependence.   (5.2.201–5)

Bosola's acknowledgment of his dependence ("I cannot leave my calling" [1. 209]) leads him to solicit the cardinal: "That I might find a great man, like yourself, / Not out of his wits, as the Lord Ferdinand, / To remember my service" (11. 285–87). At the same time, he calls in a debt from past and present hire and reclaims some curiously equal footing with the cardinal, speaking plainly of his role in the duchess's death but alluding as well to the assassination antedating the play's events: "Now you know me for your fellow murderer" (1. 291).

The concluding bloodbath tacitly, perhaps sardonically, comments on the class structure that has informed the duchess's triangulated position. When the cardinal sets out to eliminate Bosola and his characteristic secrecy prohibits his sharing the plan with those who, like the Marquis of Pescara, are shocked by the duchess's murder, he suffers the triple indignity of an unassisted demise, which is observed as spectacle by those same peers, at the hands of a totally benighted Ferdinand performing a parodic spectacle of the embattled warrior aristocrat:

> Th'alarum? give me a fresh horse.
> Rally the vaunt-guard; or the day is lost.
> Yield, yield! I give you the honour of arms,
> Shake my sword over you, will you yield?   (5.5.46–49)

Ferdinand's hallucinatory thrashing about deals mortal wounds to both the cardinal and Bosola, but Bosola manages to kill Ferdinand as his last act, leaving Delio to "make noble use / Of this great ruin" (11. 109–10) and restore the duchess's remaining son to his property and title. This, we might argue, is Malvolio's revenge.

Generic expectations are certainly met in this concluding bloodbath—Bosola's "Revenge, for the Duchess of Malfi" (1. 80) signals that achievement—but it is the duchess who hovers over the play's conclusion, still seen in relation to her brothers and the two stewards. Following Malvolio's threat and dramatically developing its social-erotic dimension, Webster stages tragic consequences with a socially provocative potential. His concern is not only with amorous, aspiring stewards but with a self-privileging aristocracy blind to the mediating role of stewardship that, disregarding the more open historical perspective of the duchess, can do no more than fall back on the feudal. If my hypothesis of influence and adaptation holds, this is what Webster has extrapolated from the unfinished agenda of *Twelfth Night*.

Would Shakespeare have appreciated Webster's adaptive homage? Would Malvolio recognize himself in the tragic denouement? In Shakespeare's comedy, Malvolio is scapegoated in order to enable comedic resolution. In Webster, he is reincarnated as Antonio and

Bosola in a play where marriage is disabled and the resolution sees all the characters violently dispatched according to revenge-tragedy conventions. But Webster's adaptive move from comedy to tragedy says less about genre than about the social-erotic thematics of the two plays. The world of the hereditary aristocracy, preoccupied with a warrior-aristocratic imaginary, may seem blessedly stable and distant from the mobility of the market and the changing faces of service and servitude. But the early modern steward's place in these two dramatic texts goes a long way toward dispatching that nostalgia.

Afterlife

PASCALE AEBISCHER

From Shakespearean Heritage and the Preposterous "Contemporary Jacobean" Film: Mike Figgis's *Hotel*[†]

The turn of the millennium saw something of a boom in film versions of non-Shakespeare Jacobean drama. Marcus Thompson released *Middleton's Changeling* in 1998; Mike Figgis's *Hotel*, which features an adaptation of *The Duchess of Malfi*, was released in 2001; and Alex Cox's *Revengers Tragedy* appeared in 2002. Following, as they do, a wave of productivity in high-profile Shakespeare adaptations on screen, these films are striking for the way in which they pitch themselves against the nostalgic, spectacular mainstream Shakespeare productions mounted, most prominently, by the significantly named "Renaissance Films" and "Renaissance Theatre Company" associated with Kenneth Branagh's early career. Contrary to conservative Shakespeare films such as these, with their use of period costume, linear storytelling, and reverential attitude toward the Shakespearean text, the films by Thompson, Figgis, and Cox are deliberate in their use of anachronism, narrative disjunction, and irreverence toward their source texts. Adapting the terminology used by Susan Bennett in *Performing Nostalgia,* I would like to call the counter-cinematic and counter-Shakespearean aesthetic they cultivate "contemporary Jacobean."[1]

This essay is concerned with the ways in which one of these contemporary Jacobean films—Mike Figgis's *Hotel*—situates itself in the context of the late twentieth- and early twenty-first-century (not)Shakespeare industry. The film is arguably an example of what

---

[†] Pascale Aebischer, "Shakespearean Heritage and the Preposterous "Contemporary Jacobean' Film: Mike Figgis's *Hotel,*" *Shakespeare Quarterly* 60 (2009), 279–305. © 2009 The Folger Shakespeare Library. Reprinted with permission of Johns Hopkins University Press.

[1.] Susan Bennett, *Performing Nostalgia: Shifting Shakespeare and the Contemporary Past* (London: Routledge, 1996), 106. While Rosalind Galt has recently argued that the boundary between mainstream heritage and countercinema is more porous than my formulation suggests, I want to highlight the ways in which Figgis's *Hotel* tries to uphold that boundary and position itself as countercinematic and oppositional. See Rosalind Gait, *The New European Cinema: Redrawing the Map* (New York: Columbia UP, 2006), 7–11.

Douglas Lanier has termed "immanent theory"—"an artefact meditating on the theoretical grounds of its own existence."[2] The plot, which includes Jacobean excesses such as cannibalism, murder, usurpation, necrophilia, and revenge, self-reflexively centers on an international film crew following the rules set down in the Dogme95 manifesto of filmmaking to produce what Figgis has called a "sort of 'period punk'" adaptation of John Webster's *Duchess of Malfi* in Venice.[3] The metacinematic reflection is reinforced, often to the extent of self-parody, by the addition of a documentary film crew headed by the obnoxious Charlee Boux (Salma Hayek), who is filming a Dogme-inspired, MTV-style documentary of the making of *Malfi*.

Using Webster's *Duchess of Malfi* as a "preposterous" pre-text, *Hotel* takes issue with Shakespeare's canonical status, challenging his preeminence through an aggressive riposte to the disparagement of Webster in John Madden's *Shakespeare in Love* (1999), one of *Hotel*'s principal intertexts. Rather than offering *Shakespeare in Love*'s transparent correspondence between the plot of the frame narrative and the play–within–the–film, *Hotel*—much like Kristian Levring's contemporary Dogme reworking of *King Lear* in *The King Is Alive* (2000)—resists straightforward parallels and a "reliance on convention and the roots of culture."[4]

Hotel shows that filming Webster involves the exhumation of a forgotten author, the piecing together of a corpus / corpse for a modern audience gorged on processed Renaissance-as-heritage. For Figgis's film, this processing of *The Duchess of Malfi* into consumer goods is linked to the way the film industry treats its actresses. Through the insistent use of Doppelgänger figures who reflect aspects of the Duchess's character, the film problematizes the commodification and consumption of Renaissance culture and the female body alike; it establishes a link between the oppression of the Duchess by her brothers and the oppression of female creative expression by the apparatus of film. *Hotel* disrupts the preconceptions of the mainstream Shakespeare and heritage industries, with which it engages through intertextual references and allusive casting. Sidestepping Shakespeare and using Webster allows the film to question its own investment in cultural and textual authority and to oppose heritage with disinheritance, celebration of literary tradition with an insistence on obscurity, and nostalgia with a relish for seeing a Jacobean classic as something that is alien enough to be new—a preposterously contemporary Jacobean text.

* * *

2. Douglas Lanier, "Drowning the Book: Prospero's Books and the Textual Shakespeare," in *Shakespeare, Theory, and Performance*, ed. James C. Bulman (London: Routledge, 1996), 187–209, esp. 204; Lanier refers to *Prospero's Books*.
3. Mike Figgis, *Digital Film-Making* (London: Faber and Faber, 2007), 70.
4. Martha P. Nochimson, "The King Is Alive," *Film Quarterly* 55.2 (2001–2): 48–54, esp. 52.

Susan Bennett, describing Howard Barker's rewriting of Thomas Middleton's *Women Beware Women* as "contemporary Jacobean text,"[5] is concerned with the way "the Jacobean" has functioned "as a signifier bound to represent psychopathic violence and deviant desires." She notes, "Unlike the idealized authenticity and authority of Shakespeare's (great) texts, these Jacobean revivals point to a less than perfect past."[6] * * *

* * *

Putting the Cart before the Horse: The Preposterousness of the Contemporary Jacobean film

In view of the nostalgia that characterizes most Jacobean revivals in the late twentieth century, it is not surprising that it is only in a few cases, notably in Derek Jarman's films of *The Tempest* (1979) and *Edward II* (1991), that Bennett finds that "the 'Jacobean' provides one site where the contradictory impulses of nostalgia perform themselves in a disruptive and occasionally emancipatory mode."[7] * * *

Jarman's use of Shakespeare and Marlowe—to rewrite English history and to intimate that state terror and establishment power are contingent on the suppression of homosexuality and "the rigorous policing of desire and excess"[8]—opens up a contemporary Jacobean aesthetic that is deliberate in what George Puttenham would have called its "preposterousness." The "Histeron proteron" or the "preposterous," Puttenham explained in his *Arte of English Poesie*, is "disordered speech," a figure in which "ye misplace your words or clauses and set that before which should be behind & è conuerso." Most of Puttenham's examples of the trope are temporal as, for instance, "My dame that bred me up and bare me in her wombe."[9] It is in this sense that the term "contemporary Jacobean" is a preposterous anachronism, as it implies that the present is at the origin of the past, or that the past is located in the present.

* * *

Taking Jarman's lead, Mike Figgis's *Hotel*, which was filmed employing rigs of Figgis's own design (nicknamed "Fig-rigs"), night

5. Bennett, 106. On "neo-Jacobean" theatre of the 1980s, see also Richard Boon and Amanda Price, "Maps of the World: 'Neo-Jacobeanism' and Contemporary British Theatre," *Modern Drama* 41 (1998): 635–54.
6. Bennett, 93.
7. Bennett, 95.
8. Colin McCabe, "A Post-National European Cinema: A Consideration of Derek Jarman's *The Tempest* and *Edward II*," in *Screening Europe: Image of Identity in Contemporary European Cinema*, ed. Duncan Petrie (London: British Film Institute, 1992), 9–18, esp. 12.
9. George Puttenham, *The Arte of English Poesie. Contriued into Three Bookes: The First of Poets and Poesie, the Second of Proportion, the Third of Ornament*, 3 vols. (London, 1589), 3:141, 142.

vision, various split screens, and three frame sizes, almost program-
matically espouses the preposterous aesthetic of Jarman's contemporary Jacobean film. Rather than taking on the Shakespeare
industry from the inside, as an increasing number of alternative film-
makers are doing in what Thomas Cartelli and Katherine Rowe identify as a movement of New Wave Shakespeare,[1] Figgis follows Jarman
in jabbing at the industry from the marginal position of the "Jacobean" text. Figgis and Heathcote Williams, who helped him adapt
The Duchess of Malfi, capitalize on the transgressive connotations of
the Jacobean by focusing their script on "six scenes—the weirdest
bloodiest, sexiest scenes in John Websters extrordinary [sic] play."[2]

The choice of the "weirdest" scenes of a Jacobean play is comple-
mented by the use of unconventional methods and technology.
Because it was filmed with digital cameras, using digital video technology rather than a standard thirty-five millimeter print, Figgis's
screened film ended up being literally preposterous. As Figgis explains:

> In 2000 I shot a film called *Hotel* on four Sony PD100 digital
> cameras. But most people who saw it saw it projected as a 35mm
> print, and there were all kinds of problems in getting it on to
> 35mm—for instance, it had to project at a different speed from
> the speed I shot it [twenty-four frames per second instead of
> twenty-five]. And it had to have Dolby sound on it [Dolby being
> an older technology]. So at a certain point you have to ask: is
> the cart pulling the horse or the horse pulling the cart?[3]

Figgis's echo of Puttenham's "cart before the horse" to describe
the effect of using outdated technology to screen his material
highlights the preposterousness that seemingly affects every aspect
of his film, including the conception of both characters and plot.

Apart from the extracts from a heavily edited *Duchess of Malfi* and
the hotel maid's monologues, the film's dialogue was entirely impro-
vised by the actors. In the documentary that accompanies the film
on the DVD and which is a crucial component of *Hotel*, Mike Figgis explains to an understandably confused Burt Reynolds that the
plot, along with a sense of how the different characters and strands
of the emerging story relate to each other, was to be created through
editing after the completion of the shoot:

> REYNOLDS I would like for the relationship part to suddenly
> start coagulating, if you will, in the scenes, so that you, you know
> what these people's names are, and where they're going and . . .

1. Cartelli and Rowe (9–24, esp. 17) trace this "New Wave" tradition back to Akira Kuro-
   sawa's *Ran* (1985), Jarman's *Tempest*, and Jean-Luc Godard's *King Lear* and *Hamlet* (both
   1987).
2. Mike Figgis, *In the Dark: Images and Text by Mike Figgis* (London: Booth-Clibborn Editions, 2003), 158.
3. Mike Figgis, *Digital Film-Making*, 6 (emphasis added).

FIGGIS   As I said, that will come in an editing process.
REYNOLDS   . . . I'm just telling you that for the actors, you
need just a little bit of "what is my name, what is the relationship, how long does it last." Do, do we get together, and make
that up ourselves and bring that to you and show it to you?
FIGGIS   The idea is that, that unlike a regular film, I guess,
where people do come and say "my name is Pete and this is my
wife" and so on, erm, I would, obviously with an ensemble of
over thirty people, if everybody did that, then there wouldn't be
any time left to do anything else.[4]

From the position of mainstream ideas about cinema, represented
here by a reluctant Burt Reynolds, it is preposterous to act a scene
before the script is written, to be in a story which is yet to be created, to impersonate a character who will emerge only in post-
production through the director's editing. *Hotel* is insistently not a
"regular" film: it is as preposterous in its approach to plot and characterization as in its use of technology.

Figgis's film follows close on the heels of John Madden's *Shakespeare in Love*, itself a "novel, post-heritage kind of costume film"
centered on the performance of an early modern play.[5] While *Shakespeare in Love* has been praised for its "post-modern irreverence
toward canonical narratives," it has also been critiqued for its "safely
conventional sexual politics" and, crucially, for its reproduction of
"the Bard as the dominant popular cultural icon for our particular
sociohistorical moment."[6] The film, with its all-star cast, encompassing widely recognized RSC veterans Dame Judi Dench, Antony Sher,
and Joseph Fiennes and Hollywood draws such as Gwyneth Paltrow
and Ben Affleck, fuses high culture and popular culture to reinforce
the message of Shakespeare's "universality": "Shakespeare" becomes
the cultural glue that binds our society together in a moment of com-
munal understanding and rejoicing at the transhistorical power of
love, as transmitted by Shakespeare's immortal words.

In his answer to *Shakespeare in Love*, Figgis also employs an all-
star cast: apart from the actors already named, Saffron Burrows,
Lucy Liu, Danny Huston, and John Malkovich (a significant choice
in view of his mixed Hollywood, quirky indie film, and British stage
credentials) and an array of top-tier continental actors, including
Ornella Muti, Chiara Mastroianni, and Mía Maestro, all vie for

---

4. *Documentary, Hotel;* DVD, directed by Mike Figgis (MGM Home Entertainment LLC;
   Malibu, CA: Innovation Film Group, 2005). (Quotations from and references to the film
   are based on this DVD.)
5. Pidduck, 130. For the categorization of *Shakespeare in Love* as "post-heritage," see also
   Claire Monk, "The British heritage-film debate revisited," in *British Historical Cinema:
   the History, Heritage and Costume Film,* ed. Claire Monk and Amy Sargeant (London:
   Routledge, 2002), 176–98, esp. 181–82.
6. Pidduck, 131, 133; and Elizabeth Klett, "*Shakespeare in Love* and the End(s) of History," in *Retrovisions: Reinventing the Past in Film and Fiction,* ed. Deborah Cart-
   mell, I. Q. Hunter, and Imelda Whelehan (London: Pluto, 2001), 25–40, esp. 25.

attention. Notably absent from the list are established British actors with Shakespearean screen credentials or extensive RSC experience. The telling exception is Heathcote Williams, who scoffs at the "Ridiculous Shite Company" for which he never appears to have worked, but who played Prospero in Derek Jarman's *Tempest* and appeared as himself in Al Pacino's offbeat *Looking For Richard* (1996).[7] In *Hotel*, Williams plays Webster's Bosola and reprises his real-life role as the scriptwriter for the film-within-the-film. Williams's doubling as scriptwriter and the spy whose gaze surveys and directs the action makes him an author / director figure in whom Prospero-like control and Ariel-like spying are combined.

That Figgis's casting choices self-consciously eschew associations with Shakespeare is also made clear in one of the web shorts on the *Hotel* DVD. Entitled "Cliff's diary," it features the actor playing Ferdinand, "Clifford Beacham" (Mark Strong), recording a video diary in which he looks forward to working on the *Malfi* film with Alan Rickman, whom he remembers seeing in *Richard III*. The expectation is thwarted as he discovers that the Cardinal is to be played not by Rickman, but by Brian Bovell, who here has a Jamaican accent that marks him as distinctly "un-Shakespearean." Figgis's casting, which he has said is based on "very precise decisions, to be made after a lot of thought and observation,"[8] thus signposts *Hotel*'s position within the emergent alternative tradition of the preposterous contemporary Jacobean film.

Rejection of the Shakespearean performance tradition and challenge to Shakespeare's cultural hegemony are carried further within the film. There, at the beginning of the shoot of *Malfi*, Charlee Boux interviews Jonathan Danderfine (the producer of the film-within-the-film) about the project:

> DANDERFINE   The tentative title is *Malfi*. Ergh, from *The Duchess of Malfi*, which is a play written in, written by one . . .
> BOUX   What do you mean . . .
> DANDERFINE   . . . of Shakespeare's contemporaries. John, John Webster.
> BOUX   John Webster? Do we have a chance to interview him later on? Is he around?
> DANDERFINE   He's not around, unfortunately. You know what? I'll . . .
> BOUX   But are you happy with the script?

7. E-mail from Heathcote Williams to David Schwimmer; see Figgis, *In the Dark*, 202. The other exception is Danny Sapani, who played Bagot in Deborah Warner's television film of her National Theatre production of *Richard II* (1997). Like Jarman's *Tempest* and Pacino's *Looking for Richard*, this film, starring a cross-dressed Fiona Shaw as Richard, stands conspicuously outside the tradition of nostalgic mainstream screen Shakespeare.
8. Figgis, *Digital Film-Making*, 135.

Shakespeare, here, is no longer the stable point of reference that it was in Ingram's review of *The Changeling*. The scene is a striking reversal of the scene in *Shakespeare in Love,* where the sadistic urchin who loves *Titus Andronicus* for its gore, revels in torturing mice, and meanly betrays the cross-dressed heroine to the authorities is revealed to be John Webster. In *Shakespeare in Love,* this allusion is an obvious insider's joke directed at more knowledgeable viewers who will understand that Webster is in a conflictual relationship with his main influence, Shakespeare, and that his plays, unlike Shakespeare's *Romeo and Juliet,* are motivated not by love but by a relish of violence. In Paul Arthur's gloss on the scene, "Gratuitous violence, represented by the casual cruelties of an adolescent John Webster, is implied as inimical to humanistic values, and consequent social cohesion, imputed to Shakespeare's work."[9] In Figgis's riposte to *Shakespeare in Love,* Jonathan Danderfine's corresponding assumption that Webster can be understood in relation to Shakespeare falls spectacularly flat, as Charlee Boux's preposterous anachronism reveals her ignorance of that supposedly stable point of reference and its associated values. The butt of the joke is not so much Boux's ignorance as that of the Shakespeare industry which, by insisting that Shakespeare is our contemporary and universal, has succeeded in erasing his historical specificity.

Consuming the Renaissance: Authorship, Exhumation, and "Man's Control of Women's Sexuality" (I)

The joke evidently was crucial to Figgis's conception of the film, since it reappears, in a slightly different form, in the web short entitled "Charlee Boux." The victim of her physically aggressive interviewing style, this time, is Heathcote Williams's "John Charley," the scriptwriter of *Malfi:*

> BOUX You are the writer of *Duchess of Malfi.* Can you please tell us, what was your inspiration for this very tormentous [sic] piece?
> CHARLEY No, I'm not the writer of *The Duchess of Malfi.* It was written by John Webster, who was a contemporary of Shakespeare.
> BOUX Oh, I got confused with the Johns, same thing. Is he around?
> CHARLEY No I'm afraid he's not, no. He's died four hundred years ago.
> BOUX Well, I guess we can't interview that John . . .

9. Paul Arthur, "The Written Scene: Writers as Figures of Cinematic Redemption," in *Literature and Film: A Guide to the Theory and Practice of Film Adaptation,* ed. Robert Stam and Alessandra Raengo (Oxford: Blackwell, 2005), 331–42, esp. 338.

CHARLEY   But you're very resourceful, you could dig up the bones . . .

BOUX   . . . but we have this John, sweetie pie! [grabs Charley's face and squeezes it]

CHARLEY   Ooh!

BOUX   Okay, I would like to know . . . what's your character's name . . .

CHARLEY   My character is Bosola.

BOUX   Bosola.

CHARLEY   He's a spy, yes.

BOUX   He was a spyyyyyy, you dirty man. Who did you spied [sic] on?

CHARLEY   I spy on the Duchess. Would you like to know what the *Duchess of Malfi* is about?

BOUX   What was she doing, that little . . .

CHARLEY   [laughs] Trying to get married.

BOUX   Well, that's not so bad!

CHARLEY   No, not in this day and age. But it's a play really about man's control of women's sexuality. . . .

The scene touches on a number of crucial strands that run through the film. It challenges Shakespeare's status once again, it makes the production of Webster a re-membering of his bones, and it draws attention to what the play is "really about": "man's control of women's sexuality." On closer inspection, these apparently random strands can be woven together into a narrative that takes us back and forth between *Hotel*'s Jacobean pre-text, with its obsession with exhumation, cannibalism, and the policing of the Duchess's sexuality, and the film's own two governing obsessions. These are, on the one hand, the exhumation and cannibalistic consumption of Renaissance literature and, on the other, the exploitation, control, and consumption of actresses' bodies and sexualities in the medium of film.

While Charley's suggestion that Boux exhume Webster's bones for the purposes of an interview may seem like an offhand remark designed to put her in her place, it is thematically linked to *The Duchess of Malfi*. Ferdinand, suffering from the symptoms of lycanthropy, which causes men to "imagine / Themselves to be transformèd into wolves" so that they "Steal forth to church-yards in the dead of night / And dig dead bodies up," is seen walking around at midnight "with the leg of a man / Upon his shoulder" (5.2.9–15).[1] Earlier in the play, the guilt-ridden Ferdinand had warned Bosola: "The wolf shall find [the Duchess's] grave and scrape it up, / Not to devour the corpse but to discover / The horrid murder" (4.2.299–301).

---

1. John Webster, *The Duchess of Malfi*, 4th ed., ed. Brian Gibbons (London: A. and C. Black, 2001). All quotations from the play are taken from this edition.

The image of exhumation associated with Boux's desire to interview the author of *The Duchess of Malfi* is thus merged with the
desire, within Webster's play, to unearth the Duchess herself, to
discover her "horrid murder." Play and titular character become
one in that the unearthing and revival of the one will lead to the
discovery of the crime committed on the other.

Early in the film, a complex web of associations between the remembering of Renaissance drama and culture and the notions of
processing and consumption is spun. In the opening sequence, Omar
Johnsson (John Malkovich) registers at the hotel reception and is
next seen at a dinner table, conversing through bars with the hotel
staff and consuming what one of the diners calls an "international
agricultural harvest" of cured and smoked hotel guests, whose limbs
are suspended above a table bearing a platter of meat. There is a
nod, here, at the association of the Renaissance with cannibalism,
which began with the meat hooks in Peter Greenaway's deliberately
Jacobean *The Cook, The Thief, His Wife and Her Lover* (1989). The
motif was picked up, significantly, in Jarman's *Edward II*, in which
Gaveston's killer is hung onto a carcass before being butchered himself. It crossed into the mainstream as a conjunction of cannibalism and Renaissance connoisseurship in Thomas Harris's character
Hannibal Lecter, as popularized in the film *The Silence of the Lambs*
(1991) and the sequel novel *Hannibal* (2001), before finally returning, as a self-conscious cliché (signposted by the casting of Anthony
Hopkins), to the countertradition in Julie Taymor's *Titus* (1999),
where Lavinia's rapists are suspended from the ceiling like carcasses
before they, too, are "processed" and eaten.

In *Hotel*, the association of "the Renaissance" with cannibalism,
now both a cliché and a signifier of the oppositional stance of the
contemporary Jacobean, is reinforced by the inclusion at the dinner
table of a British tour guide who attempts, in the opening scenes, to
establish himself as the true authority on smoked meat, Renaissance
Venice, and cultural production. Played by Julian Sands, whose casting evokes the "heritage" values of *A Room with a View*, the guide
explains how Venetian citizens would find the dismembered entrails
of their friends and neighbors hanging from gibbets and describes
Venice as "the first police state," in which the quality of life was "as
magnificent as the patriarchy that ruled it." When his group of tour-
ists, whom he attempts to impress with his listing of "Tintoretto,
Titian, Tiepolo," encounters the *Malfi* film crew, it becomes clear
that the tour guide not only admires that patriarchy but also embodies its values. Advising his group to "bypass this display of not very
interesting street theatre," he shouts, "The Duchess of Malfi was a
slut!" He sets himself up as the ultimate judge of which bits of the
Renaissance and cultural production are worth remembering and
consuming and which are not: disembowelled Venetians alongside

Tintoretto and Titian are worthy of survival, while *Malfi*, with its portrayal of the Duchess's transgressive sexuality, is not. No wonder that, munching a particularly tasty bit of flesh in the opening sequence, he roundly condemns the film of *Malfi*, explaining to his fellow diners that "in this case, 'dogma' means unwatchable, unwatchable garbage. They've got a completely senseless interpretation of *The Duchess of Malfi*."

This reference to *The Duchess of Malfi* at the cannibalistic dinner table invites the viewer to realize the thematic link between the human limbs on meat hooks and the way in which Webster's play almost obsessively unearths, displays, and instrumentalizes various real and fake body parts or corpses. In the play, the Duchess is made to shake a dead man's hand and shown a macabre little exhibition of waxwork figures of Antonio and her children. Additionally, her own strangled (and not quite dead) body is presented for Ferdinand to view, as are her children's strangled bodies. Webster's physical tableaux are accompanied by recurring allusions to and metaphors of cannibalism. Ferdinand's desire to "boil [the Duchess's and Antonio's] bastard to a cullis / And give't his lecherous father to renew / The sin of his back" (2.5.71–73) is given particular prominence in the film, where the actor playing Ferdinand, memorizing his lines, addresses the camera directly with "updated" words: "Or boil his ill-born bastards into a broth and give it to their lecherous father and have him retch up his ungodly life with his own liquid offal." While Ferdinand's lines advertise the play's relationship to its generic predecessors and, in particular, the Ur-text of revenge tragedy, Seneca's *Thyestes*, the play's most coherent metaphors of cannibalism are applied to the Duchess-as-food. Her body, described as a "salvatory of green mummy" (4.2.118–19), is to be "hewed . . . to pieces" (2.5.31) and "fed upon" by "many hungry guests" (4.2.191), in particular by her brothers, as she specifies in her dying words: "Go tell my brothers when I am laid out, / They then may feed in quiet" (11. 226–27). Bosola's reference to the Duchess's brothers as "most cruel biters" (5.2.333–34) rounds off their representation as cannibalistic in their efforts to control the Duchess's body and sexuality. The play's obsession with corpses thus boils down to an obsession with one particular body, the Duchess's, which is to be investigated, carved up, and consumed by guests and brothers alike.

In *Hotel*'s opening sequence, the thematic association of the human limbs on meat hooks with the Duchess's body is complicated by the superimposition of the credit "Directed by / Mike Figgis" over the limbs. The body that is offered for consumption, it seems, is not simply that of the Duchess of Malfi, but that of the indigestible Jacobean text, which must be processed by the director into something more edible. This becomes apparent a few scenes later, when the entire film crew assembles and an actor complains that the script, as it now stands, has lost some of the poetry. In response, the script-writer explains that the group has decided to "cut the iambic pentameters, heptameters, archaisms in order to create a fast-food *McMalfi*, as it were, that would be very easily digestible and accessible even to aspiring Hollywood stars." Clearly, this is not what the updating of the text achieves. Certainly, the substitution of "broth" for "cullis" in Ferdinand's line quoted above is arguably more "digestible" (especially if the term "cullis," paired as it is with "the sin of his back," is understood to invoke Latin *culus* ["arse"] for a sodomitical pun). Nevertheless, while the pseudo-Jacobean "have him retch up his ungodly life with his own liquid offal," which replaces Webster's "to renew / The sin of his back," may be more "accessible," it also clearly signals indigestibility. *Hotel*'s fast-food *McMalfi* will not be so easy to swallow, nor will it dodge the question of how the text might relate to "aspiring Hollywood stars" and the industry they work in, whether in Hollywood or Europe.

Voyeurism, Fetishistic Scopophilia, and the Duchess As Function and Effect: "Man's Control of Women's Sexuality" (II)

One of the most impressive aspects of the film is how it uses *The Duchess of Malfi* as a pre-text for an examination of the control, oppression, and consumption of the female body and female sexuality both in Webster's play and in contemporary culture, as epitomized by the film industry. That is, Webster's *Duchess of Malfi* functions as a critique of twenty-first-century film, exposing the extent to which, through the direction of the gaze, "man's control of women's sexuality" is intrinsic to the medium.

The play's distinction between the idealizing, fetishizing gaze of Antonio and the inquisitive and punishing gaze of Ferdinand and his "creature" Bosola anticipates Laura Mulvey's influential analysis of conventional cinema.[2] Mulvey's "fetishistic scopophilia," where the male figure "builds up the physical beauty of the [female] object [of his gaze], transforming it into something satisfying in itself," is a feature that can be recognized in Antonio. Its nasty twin "voyeurism," which "has associations with sadism: pleasure lies in ascertaining guilt . . . asserting control and subjugating the guilty person through

---

2. For a detailed critique of Mulvey, see Judith Mayne's *Cinema and Spectatorship* (London: Routledge, 1993), 13–52. Mulvey's "Visual Pleasures and Narrative Cinema," first published in *Screen* 16.3 (1975): 6–18, was revised and criticized by Mulvey herself in *Visual and Other Pleasures* (Bloomington: Indiana UP, 1989), 21–22, which is the edition used here. The essay remains a very powerful hermeneutic tool, especially when applied to a film like *Hotel* that openly engages with the problem of the gaze in mainstream cinema.

punishment or forgiveness," fits Ferdinand's punitive scrutiny of his
sister. It is voyeurism which Figgis, as filmmaker, finds particularly
challenging: writing about *Hotel*, he admits to having "always had a
problem with cinema's essentially singular, voyeuristic eye," an eye
which puts the artist "suddenly in an area of perversity."[3] Figgis's
film translates the active desiring gaze of Webster's Duchess and
her quest for autonomy into a defiance of the film industry's dominant modes of representation of the female subject.

That this is partly what is at stake in *Hotel* becomes apparent early
on, when Isabella, the Italian actress playing Julia (Valeria Golino),
complains about the wholesale cutting of her and Cariola's lines.
Since she will appear naked in both her scenes, her concern that
she doesn't want to be "upstaged by [her] tits" exposes the way the
female actors' bodies are offered up for consumption by a male-
dominated industry that uses "the woman as icon, displayed for the
gaze and enjoyment of men, the active controllers of the look."[4] The
juxtaposition of the actress's complaint with the patriarchal tour
guide's appropriation of Ferdinand's lines—

> Foolish men,
> That e'er will trust their honour in a bark
> Made of so slight weak bullrush as is woman,
> Apt every minute to sink it!
> (*Duchess of Malfi*, 2.5.33–36)

—creates a link between early modern misogyny, the authority of
the cultural elite, and the cinematic exploitation and control of the
female body.

This association of early modern misogyny with film's exploitation
of women underlies a phenomenon where one female character after
another acts out aspects of the Duchess's oppression and rebellion,
until the film is crowded with Doppelgängers of Webster's defiant
heroine. Using the terminology suggested by Cartelli and Rowe
allows a distinction between Doppelgänger figures who embody a
"Duchess function" and those who embody a "Duchess effect." A
Duchess function is a Doppelgänger who "does things, performs
behaviours that are integral to the working out of a dramatic design."
By contrast, a Doppelgänger acting as a Duchess effect "suffers or
embodies the consequences"[5] of the Duchess's oppression. Isabella
/ Julia serves as a particularly clear example of such Duchess functions and Duchess effects. In the play, her initial sexual assertion,
marking her as a Duchess function, is quickly revealed to be but a
cover for her exploitation by the Cardinal, who poisons her and

3. Figgis, *In the Dark*, 68.
4. Mulvey, *Visual and Other Pleasures*, 21.
5. Cartelli and Rowe, 154.

makes her suffer as a Duchess effect. In Figgis's film, this trajectory is reversed. There, her role as a Duchess effect is made nastily obvious early on in her only scene in *Malfi*. Told by the director to "get down, suck his cock," Isabella crawls under the Cardinal's robes as he is warning the Duchess not to remarry. She reemerges only to wipe her mouth.

Although she is thus literally brought to her knees during filming, Isabella is offered an alternative to the domination of the male gaze in *Hotel,* enabling her to move from the position of Duchess effect to that of Duchess function. Storming out of the rehearsal room, she is accosted by Claude (Chiara Mastroianni). Claude, whose gender-neutral name and cigar smoking signal her appropriation of the phallus, compliments Isabella on her beauty and kisses her abruptly and passionately. In the underground passages of the hotel, the night vision camera—a significant inversion of the mode of viewing associated with what Figgis calls "regular film"—shows Claude's seduction of the blindfolded Isabella, who is as "stark blind" (1.1.402) as the Duchess makes Antonio through her revelation of her transgressive desire.

The preposterous class and gender transgression of the Duchess of Malfi's wooing of her steward is inverted and troped as lesbianism here as Claude, a member of the staff, seduces a hotel guest, introducing her to a hidden underground world of transgressive desire. If, as Bonnie Burns argues, classic Hollywood cinema consistently represents lesbianism as "at the limit of the visible, or indeed, as the limit of the visible,"[6] this perception is literalized in *Hotel*'s representation of lesbian desire as blinding and located in the underground space of the repressed and the dark—the space of cannibalism, another form of transgressive desire for "the same." The film, through this move from the Duchess effect's heterosexual subjugation to the Duchess function's lesbian eroticism, plots a trajectory of empowerment for this marginal figure (although this is tellingly qualified by her erotic subjection to the dominant Claude).

Lesbian sex might seem to be far removed from Webster's *Duchess of Malfi*. Nevertheless, a connection to the play is established in *Hotel*'s rendering of the Duchess's offer of marriage to Antonio, which is central to both Figgis's metacinematic reflection and his interpretation of Webster's play. The scene is pleonastic in that, like the joke about interviewing Webster, it occurs twice. The first time, *Malfi*'s director, Trent Stoken (a manic Rhys Ifans), surprises the

---

6. Bonnie Burns, "Dracula's Daughter: Cinema, Hypnosis, and the Erotics of Lesbianism," in *Lesbian Erotics,* ed. Karla Jay (New York: New York UP, 1995), 196–211, esp. 197. The attention given to lesbianism in this film is yet another way in which *Hotel* opposes "heritage" films, from which "lesbianism has generally been absent"; see John Hill, *British Cinema in the 1980s* (Oxford: Clarendon P, 1999), 98.

actors playing Antonio and the Duchess while they are rehearsing the wooing scene on their own as a "straight" love scene, with the Duchess set up as the object of Antonio's fetishizing desire. Trent's criticism of the actors' version of the scene amounts to a programmatic rejection of the "heritage" films of the Merchant-Ivory team that keep haunting *Hotel:* "But, of course, you must try all different ways, and I love the Merchant-Ivory version you're doing at the moment. Sweet, pungent smell of rose meadows, Earl Grey and a wet saddle on the back of a horse. That sort of thing. It's fucking shit!" Minutes later, having just instructed Antonio that he must "fuck [the Duchess] like a criminal" during the scene, Trent is shot by an assassin.

The "shagging scene," as Trent had called the wooing, is reprised in the second half of the film with film producer Jonathan Danderfine in charge. This time, the subject-object positions are reversed as the Duchess undresses Antonio in her bedchamber, turns him around, pulls up her dress, and energetically sodomizes him. The transgression of social boundaries in the play is here troped as doubly preposterous, female-on-male sodomy. The groans of the Duchess's orgasm mutate into the groans of labor as she collapses on her bed. She is told by Cariola, who has been there all along, to "push, push" and then gives birth to twin plastic babies. Lying on her bed after the delivery, the Duchess is framed by the figures of Antonio and Cariola, who kisses her on the mouth. At the margins of this scene of the Duchess's preposterous desire, this desire is associated with lesbianism.

The threesome on the bed embodies and sexualizes the implicit causal link in Webster's play between the mutual affection of mistress and maid, which creates "a secret space in the midst of male society" and "a haven where the normal modes of subjection are cancelled,"[7] and the Duchess's ability to express her autonomous identity and her desires. It is the homosocial (and potentially homoerotic) egalitarian intimacy between the Duchess and her female bedfellow that is exposed in *Hotel* as the unacknowledged origin of the Duchess's preposterous heterosexual transgression of class and gender boundaries. As Valerie Traub argues, this intimacy is "insignificant" in Renaissance culture in not being seen as a threat to order because it does not in itself challenge heterosexual marriage.[8] In Webster's Act 3, scene 2, the scene giving us the most intimate insight into the Duchess's and Antonio's marital life, it becomes clear that the Duchess's credentials as Cariola's "sprawling'st bedfellow"

---

7. Frank Whigham, "Sexual and Social Mobility in *The Duchess of Malfi*," *PMLA* 100 (1985): 167–86, esp. 172.
8. See Valerie Traub's discussion of female bedfellows in Renaissance drama in her chapter "The (in)significance of lesbian desire," in *The Renaissance of Lesbianism in Early Modern England* (Cambridge: Cambridge UP, 2002), 158–87.

give her yet greater piquancy for Antonio, who "shall like her the better for that" (3.2.13–14). Unlike the Shakespeare comedies that track the separation of female bedfellows as they move toward the heterosexual unions that lead to their "happy" dénouements,[9] Webster's tragedy of female "riot" insists, in this scene, on the compatibility and coexistence of female intimacy and heterosexual desire.[1] Cariola, the subordinate who preposterously presided over and authorized her mistress's marriage ceremony, is a constitutive part of the Duchess's preposterous sprawling family unit. By placing Cariola on the bed with the Duchess and Antonio, *Hotel* renders visible and significant the female-female bond that remains unremarkable in the play.

Hotel's scene of preposterous sex concludes with the camera panning away from the Duchess's widely spread legs, turning around to reveal Jonathan Danderfine filming the trio on the bed with a Figrig. Behind him, Bosola stands in the doorway, observing the scene. The line of vision of Danderfine's camera, which is focused on the Duchess's crotch, corresponds exactly to Bosola's, suggesting a precise equivalence between "man's control of women's sexuality" in Webster and in Figgis's film. If modern cinema is willing to put transgressive female desire center stage, the result is still a peculiarly "androcentric vision" of female desire, filmed by a man from the point of view of traditional patriarchal control, as embodied by Bosola.[2] The fetishizing gaze of Antonio's Merchant-Ivory take on the Duchess may be "fucking shit," but the alternative—an expression of polymorphous female desire which is monitored, recorded, and eventually punished by the voyeuristic gaze of Bosola—is no better.

Preposterous Doppelgängers: Fantastic Mutuality and Self-Violation

Since it is so self-consciously implicated in the very structures it is criticizing, Figgis's *Hotel* cannot—and does not even try to—provide a realistic answer to the problem of "man's control of women's sexuality." The resolution of the film hinges on the semi-supernatural figure of the anonymous hotel maid, played by Valentina Cervi, who Figgis wanted to be "very important" and "more exotic, strange, sexual as the film progresses."[3] Cervi is known principally for her performance of the title role in Merlet's *Artemisia*, a heritage biopic of the Renaissance painter Artemisia Gentileschi. Cervi's casting

9. Traub summarizes this trajectory: "In Shakespeare's and Fletcher's plays, an originary, prior homoerotic desire is crossed, abandoned, betrayed; correlatively, a desire for men or a marital imperative is produced and inserted into the narrative in order to create a formal, 'natural' mechanism of closure" (175).
1. See also Maurizio Calbi, *Approximate Bodies: Gender and Power in Early Modern Drama and Anatomy* (London: Routledge, 2005), 26–27.
2. Karla Jay, "On Slippery Ground: An Introduction" in *Lesbian Erotics*, 1–11, esp. 3.
3. Figgis, *In the Dark*, 71.

invokes a film which is insistently preoccupied with the dual issues of sexual violence and the ownership of the artistic gaze: as Rowland Wymer notes, Artemisia, while celebrating Gentileschi's creativity, makes it unclear to what degree "she achieves real agency and escapes being an object of the gaze of others."[4]

This ambivalence about the degree to which the female artist can avoid being the object of the gaze is fully exploited in *Hotel,* where Cervi's hotel maid delivers two elaborate erotic monologues spoken to the comatose Stoken and filmed with the night vision camera. In the first monologue, she tells him about a colleague of hers who is "willing to *play a role*" (emphasis added) to heighten the sexual excitement of the men who watch her and sleep with her. Cervi's hotel maid contrasts this sexual exploitation of the role-playing woman as object of the gaze with the way she herself has "perfected the art of being invisible as a woman. I can walk into a room full of men without exciting the slightest interest." Making herself "invisible as a woman" by refusing to act exempts the hotel maid from being trapped by the "to-be-looked-at-ness" Mulvey insists is characteristic of women in "normal narrative film." And indeed, although she is the most intriguing and alluring figure in the film and the character whose "visual presence" most conspicuously "freeze[s] the flow of action in moments of erotic contemplation" in a way typical of the exploitative cinematic gaze she objects to,[5] within the filmic narrative, the hotel maid remains unremarked in the upstairs world of the hotel's public areas, exciting no desire.

Whereas the hotel maid's first monologue focuses on the desiring gaze of others, her second monologue is concerned with her own desire. Figgis's editing places this monologue after the strangulation of the Duchess and her maid Cariola in the film-within-the-film. Using a split screen, Figgis shows us the faces of the two murdered women side by side (united in death), while on the soundtrack Franz Schubert's *Der Doppelgänger* is sung by Maestro, the actress playing Cariola, on whose dead face we gaze. Heinrich Heine's lyrics tell of the speaker's encounter with his uncanny, pale double, whose face is marked by the pain the speaker felt long ago.

> The night is quiet, the streets are resting,
> In this house my loved one used to live,
> She left the town long ago,

---

4. Rowland Wymer, "'The Audience Is Only Interested in Sex and Violence': Teaching the Renaissance on Film," *Working Papers on the Web* 4, online at http://extra.shu.ac.uk /wpw/renaissance/wymer.htm (accessed 6 July 2009). For an account of the film and the way in which it misrepresents its subject and her art, see Susan Felleman, "Dirty Pictures, Mud Lust and Abject Desire: Myths of Origin and the Cinematic Object," *Film Quarterly* 55.1 (2001): 27–40.
5. Mulvey, 19.

But the house still stands on the same spot.
There, also, stands a person who is staring upwards
And wringing his hands with the power of his pain,
I am horrified when I see his face—
The moon shows me my own shape.
You Doppelgänger! You pale fellow!
Why do you ape my woe of love,
Which used to torture me in this place,
So many a night, long ago?[6]

The lyrics thematically link this moment to the film's repeated use of the preposterous: the speaker's past is preposterously confronting his present, aping the pain he thought he had overcome. Doubling the self-recognition prompted by the perfect alignment of the gaze of camera and spy at the end of this scene of preposterous sodomy, the film's incorporation of Heine's lyrics draws attention to the way in which Webster's *Duchess of Malfi* functions as a hideous mirror held up to film, revealing the extent to which "man's control of women's sexuality" continues to govern this ideological apparatus through the direction of the gaze.

Der Doppelgänger continues on the soundtrack as the camera, using night vision, moves along a canal covered by a bridge, an image which is dissolved to reveal the hotel maid entering the room belonging to the wounded Trent, who remains unconscious. The sound bridge linking the modern maid to her early modern predecessor and her mistress makes her the ultimate Duchess function, a particularly uncanny Doppelgänger of these two victims of the male controlling gaze. As embodied by the comatose film director, that gaze is disabled. The gaze that dominates here belongs to the hotel maid, whose eyes are turned into two dots of light by the use of night vision. Asking, "Why should my body be interesting to him?" the maid slowly removes her shoes, apron, and underwear before climbing on top of the impassive Trent. As she languidly begins to make

---

6. The translation here is my own. In all of the published translations I have been able to identify, one or more nuances of the poem important to my argument are lost. The German text (below) is that of Heinrich Heine, "Still ist die Nacht," in *Heinrich Heine's Sämtliche Werke*, ed. Adolf Strodtmann, 21 vols. (Hamburg: Hoffmann und Campe, 1861–84), 1:105.

> Still ist die Nacht, es ruhen die Gassen,
> In diesem Hause wohnte mein Schatz;
> Sie hat schon längst die Stadt verlassen,
> Doch steht noch das Haus auf demselben Platz.
> Da steht auch ein Mensch und starrt in die Höhe,
> Und ringt die Hände, vor Schmerzensgewalt;
> Mir graust es, wenn ich sein Antlitz sehe—
> Der Mond zeigt mir meine eigne Gestalt.
> Du Doppelgänger! du bleicher Geselle!
> Was äffst du nach mein Liebesleid,
> Das mich gequält auf dieser Stelle,
> So manche Nacht, in alter Zeit?

love to him, she tells him of her seduction of a man who wanted to "make love to [her] in a conventional way" but whom she prevented by "clos[ing] his eyes, as if he had just died."

Once she achieves a position of total control over both the man in her narrative and Stoken, the maid, reaching her sexual and narrative climax, tells Trent how she relinquished some of her control over the man and "watched him all the time he watched [her]." At this moment, Stoken's eyes open, his face turns to the camera, and he slowly rises into her embrace. Evoking Antonio's assessment of the Duchess as capable of reviving someone "That lay in a dead palsy" with the sweet look "She throws upon a man" (1.1.192, 190), the hotel maid's desiring gaze and the reciprocity she allows magically raise and arouse the film director, a reformed, all-seeing character.[7] In the (otherworldly) world inhabited by the hotel maid, the problem of the male gaze is "solved" by a woman's desire to be watched as she is watching, her desire for the very gaze that she has identified as problematic.

The maid's monologues thus lead to a narrative and noticeably heterosexual and normative resolution of a film which works to erase its "queerness": the maid's initially polymorphous desires, evident from her cannibalism and connection with Claude, are no longer at the fore. Focusing the audience's attention firmly on the problem of the gaze, this ending once more uses The Duchess of Malfi to reflect on desire and power in film. Insofar as the resolution seems to hinge on the hotel maid's heterosexual desiring gaze (as Duchess function) rendering her acquiescent to her own objectification (as Duchess effect)—a point made self-consciously obvious in her assertion that she "violat[ed her]self the way [the man] would have violated [her]"— that resolution fails to satisfy. The allusion to the Duchess's ability to revive a man "That lay in a dead palsy" preposterously sends the viewer back to the beginning of The Duchess of Malfi, proposing that the Duchess's desiring look, for which she is punished, is the solution to the oppression she suffers.

Hotel seems ultimately unable to transcend the structures it attacks. Although Figgis privileges male over female nudity, it is still the female body that remains the erotic object of the gaze, above all in the lesbian scenes that are arguably meant to show a rebellion against such objectification. In fact, these scenes lead to a narrative dead end that cancels out their potential challenge to dominant structures. It is no coincidence, I think, that Hotel's most explicit critique of the cinematic gaze is contained in the words of the hotel maid, the only words in the film to have been scripted by Figgis

---

7. On Webster's sexual pun, see Celia R. Daileader, Eroticism on the Renaissance Stage: Transcendence, Desire, and the Limits of the Visible (Cambridge: Cambridge UP, 1998), 83.

himself.[8] The critique of the director's controlling male gaze ven-
triloquizes the director's own words: no female subject, whether
the Duchess or the maid, actually achieves sexual or artistic autonomy in this film.

Trespassers: The Preposterous Aesthetic of Hotel As a Contemporary Jacobean Film

At this point, I want to return to the beginning of my argument and
to my contention that, following in Jarman's footsteps, Figgis self-
consciously employs a contemporary Jacobean aesthetic that is
intrinsically preposterous, a mode of expression belonging to the
general category of "trespassers" and associated by Puttenham with
"vicious" and "undecent" modes of speaking signaling transgressive,
queer desire. In *The Tempest* and *Edward II*, Jarman used the preposterous contemporary Jacobean aesthetic to suggest that "the
modern English state [is founded] on a repressive security apparatus and a repressed homosexuality."[9] Figgis is similarly preoccupied
with the "patriarchy" running a "police state." But here, that state
is represented by the film industry, which polices female desire and
artistic expression and relies on the transformation of the (desiring)
female gaze into an erotic spectacle of heterosexual, bisexual, or lesbian desire for the benefit of a male director / viewer. As one reader
commented, "Mike Figgis seems to really like 'his' women and portrays them accordingly, maybe lovingly, who knows."[1] The difficulty,
for Figgis as for Jarman, is that both directors work within the structures and culture they seek to subvert. Bound within a mode of film
creation and projection which is preposterous in that it continually
imposes outdated technology on newer media and the conventional
narrative mode of montage on his preferred use of "collage,"[2] and
unable, it seems, to transcend the alternatives of fetishistic scopophilia and voyeurism, Figgis adopts a dual strategy of self-reflexivity
and self-vilification.

In view of the self-criticism embedded in *Hotel*, it is no wonder
that Figgis strays beyond the "tollerable inough" disorder of the preposterous to embrace the modes of presentation that Puttenham
condemns as "always intollerable and such as cannot be vsed with

---

8. Steve Erickson, "Cannibals in Venice and other Unanswered Questions: Mike Figgis'
'Hotel,'" *Indie Wire*, 28 July 2003; online at http://www.indiewire.com.ezproxy.auckland
.ac.nz/article/cannibals_in_venice_and_other_unanswered_questions_mike_figgis
_Hotel (accessed 7 July 2009). The uncut monologue is reproduced in Figgis, *In the
Dark*, 184–85.
9. McCabe, 14.
1. Reader comment by "Marco" to Jason Wood, review of *Hotel*, in *Kamera*, 30 August
2007, online at http://www.kamera.co.uk/reviews_extra/hotel.php (accessed 7 July 2009).
2. Peter Keough, "Leaving Montage: Mike Figgis Breaks Hollywood's Time Code," *Boston
Phoenix*, 23 October 2007; online at http://weeklywire.com/ww/05-15-00/boston
_movies_2.html (accessed 7 July 2009).

any decencie, but are euer undecent."[3] Unlike *Shakespeare in Love*, where the international cast all make an effort to speak "Shakespearean" English, or Received Pronunciation, *Hotel* makes no effort to harmonize even the strongest Italian and Spanish accents, resulting in what Puttenham terms "barbarousnesse."[4] Instead of the linear structure of Madden's film, Figgis's use of split screens juxtaposes different sequences that are not necessarily temporally related (Puttenham's "incongruitie"); his near-identical repetitions of scenes introduce pleonastic redundancy (Puttenham's "surplusage").[5] Figgis's film, as its reviewers insistently complain and Figgis himself highlights, is "an achingly pretentious slab of total nonsense" (Puttenham's "fonde affectation" and "extreme darknesse"), and its actors "shout and use the F-word as much as possible" (Puttenham's "unshamefast or figure of foule speech").[6]

Openly disenchanted with the conventional cinema Figgis lambastes, *Hotel* unearths Webster's *Duchess of Malfi* to expose the would-be elite's and mainstream's cultural consumption as a form of cannibalism and its efforts to make Renaissance literature more "digestible" as the creation of tasteless and indigestible fast food, to boot. The "Jacobean," as in Bennett's analysis of late twentieth-century revivals (quoted above), is coupled with everything Puttenham finds "vicious" and "undecent" in order to make it function "as a signifier bound to represent psychopathic violence and deviant desires."

Contrary to the revivals discussed by Bennett, however, Figgis's *Hotel* is not underpinned by latent nostalgia for a "gentle" Shakespeare, nor does he wish to deny the historical specificity of his Jacobean pre-text as does Baz Luhrmann, for example, in his anachronistic *Romeo+Juliet* (1996). To the cultural heritage that screen Shakespeares from Branagh to Luhrmann invoke and rely on, Figgis opposes cultural disinheritance: his actors are not familiar with Webster, read the play in three different editions (Penguin, Revels, film script), and are nervous about their interpretation of this unknown text. Employing the preposterous contemporary Jacobean aesthetic, Figgis makes Webster not only a contemporary, but a new author, an author who is not yet read, whom one would like to interview, whose script may not be satisfactory, but whose text has to be studied attentively. If *Hotel* is a film "about" how to produce a fast-food *McMalfi* for a contemporary audience, Figgis's use of the preposterous contemporary Jacobean aesthetic makes of *The Duchess of Malfi* a play "about" the making of *Hotel*, "about" man's control of transgressive female sexuality through the medium of film.

3. Puttenham, 3:141, 209.
4. Puttenham, 3:208.
5. Puttenham, 3:210, 215.
6. Puttenham, 3:210, 208, 212; for Figgis's quotations, see "Hollywood Reporter Review of 'Hotel' at the Toronto Film Festival," reprinted in Figgis, *In the Dark,* 205.

John Webster: A Chronology

ca. 1578–80	Born, St Sepulchre's parish, London. Parents: John Webster of the Merchant Taylors Company, coachbuilder, and Elizabeth Webster.
ca. 1587–89	Enters Merchant Taylors School.
1598, August 1	Admitted to Middle Temple.
ca. 1602	Begins work as a playwright, often working in collaboration with other playwrights, including Michael Drayton, Thomas Middleton, Anthony Munday, Thomas Dekker, John Ford.
ca. 1602	Writes *Sir Thomas Wyatt* (with Thomas Dekker), published 1607.
1604	Writes *Westward Ho!* (with Thomas Dekker), published 1607.
1604	Revises John Marston's *The Malcontent* for the King's Men.
1605	Writes *Northward Ho!* (with Thomas Dekker), published 1607.
1606, March 18	Marries Sara Peniall at St Mary's Church, Islington.
1612	*The White Devil* performed at the Red Bull; published 1612.
1613	Contributes verses on the death of Prince Henry to *A Monumental Column*.
1615	Contributes new additions to Sir Thomas Overbury's *New and Choice Characters*.
1614	Made a freeman of the Merchant Taylors.
ca. 1614	*The Duchess of Malfi* performed at the Blackfriars and at the Globe by the King's Men; published 1623.
?ca. 1615–c. 1623	Writes *The Guise* (lost tragedy).
ca. 1617–19	Writes *The Devil's Law-Case*.
ca. 1621	Writes *Anything for a Quiet Life* (with Thomas Middleton), published 1662.
ca. 1624	Writes *A Cure for a Cuckold* (with William Rowley and Thomas Heywood), published 1661.

1624	Writes *Keep the Widow Waking* (with John Ford, William Rowley and Thomas Dekker); lost play.
1624	Writes *Monuments of Honour*, Lord Mayor's show for John Gore, Merchant Taylor.
ca. 1608–c. 1625	Writes *Appius and Virginia* (with Thomas Heywood), published 1654.
1626	Writes *The Fair Maid of the Inn* for the King's Men (with John Fletcher, John Ford, and Philip Massinger).
before November 1634	Dies, London.

Selected Bibliography

• indicates works included or excerpted in this Norton Critical Edition.

Quartos

The Duchess of Malfi was printed in four quarto editions in the hundred years after its first performance: Q1 (1623), Q2 (1640), Q3 (1678), and Q4 (1708). Of these only Q1 has any claim to independent textual authority.

Later Editions

Bevington, David, et al., eds. *English Renaissance Drama*. New York: Norton, 2002.

Brennan, Elizabeth M., ed. *The Duchess of Malfi*, New Mermaids, 1st ed. London: A&C Black, 1964.

Brown, John Russell, ed. *The Duchess of Malfi*, Revels Plays, 2nd ed. Manchester, UK: Manchester University Press, 2009.

Dollimore, Jonathan, and Sinfield, Alan, eds. *The Selected Plays of John Webster*. Cambridge: Cambridge University Press, 1983.

Dyce, Alexander, ed. *The Works of John Webster*, 4 vols. 1830 (Dyce 1).

———. *The Works of John Webster*, 2nd ed., 4 vols. 1857 (Dyce 2).

Gibbons, Brian, ed. *The Duchess of Malfi*, New Mermaids, 4th ed. London: A&C Black, 2001.

Gunby, David, Jackson, Macdonald P., Hammond, Anthony, and Carnegie, David, eds. *Complete Works of John Webster*, 4 vols. Cambridge: Cambridge University Press, 1995–2012

Hazlitt, William, ed. *The Dramatic Works of John Webster*, 4 vols. London, 1857.

Lucas, F. L., ed. *The Complete Works of John Webster*, 4 vols. London: Chatto & Windus, 1927.

Marcus, Leah, ed. *The Duchess of Malfi*, Arden Early Modern Drama Edition. London: Methuen, 2009.

McLuskie, Kathleen, and Uglow, Jennifer, eds. *The Duchess of Malfi*, Plays in Performance. Bristol: Bristol Classical, 1989.

Rylands, George and Williams, Charles. *The Duchess of Malfi*. London: Sylvan Press, 1945.

Sampson, Martin W., ed. '*The White Devil' and 'The Duchess of Malfi.*' London, 1904.

Thorndike, Ashley H., ed. *Masterpieces of the English Drama: Webster and Tourneur*. New York, 1912.

Weis, René, ed. *The Duchess of Malfi and Other Plays*. Oxford: Oxford University Press, 1996.

General Studies of Webster

Berggren, P. S. "Spatial Imagery in Webster's Tragedies." *SEL: Studies in English Literature 1500–1900* 20 (1979): 287–303.

Berry, R. T. *The Art of John Webster.* Oxford: Clarendon Press, 1972.

• Bliss, Lee. *The World's Perspective: John Webster and the Jacobean Drama.* New Brunswick, N.J.: Rutgers University Press, 1983.

Bogard, Travis. *The Tragic Satire of John Webster.* Berkeley: University of California Press, 1955.

Bradbrook, M. C. *John Webster, Citizen and Dramatist.* New York: Columbia University Press, 1980.

Brooke, Rupert. *John Webster and Elizabethan Drama.* London, 1916.

Dent, R. W. *John Webster's Borrowing.* Berkeley: University of California Press, 1960.

Dollimore, Jonathan. *Radical Tragedy: Religion, Ideology and Power in the Drama of Shakespeare and His Contemporaries.* Brighton, UK: Harvester, 1984.

Ekeblad [Ewbank], Inga-Stina, 'The "Impure Art" of John Webster,' *RES* 9 (1958): 253–67.

Forker, C. R. *The Skull Beneath the Skin: The Achievement of John Webster.* Carbondale: Southern Illinois University Press, 1986.

Forker, C. R. "Love, Death and Fame: The Grotesque Tragedy of John Webster." *Anglia* 91 (1973): 192–218.

Forker, C. R. "'Wit's descant on any plain song': The Prose Characters of John Webster." *Modern Language Quarterly* 30 (1969): 33–52.

Goldberg, Dena. *Between Worlds: A Study of the Plays of John Webster.* Waterloo, Ont.: Wilfred Laurier University Press, 1987.

Holdsworth, R. V., ed. *Webster: "The White Devil" and "The Duchess of Malfi": A Casebook.* London: Macmillan Press, 1975.

Hunter, G. K., and S. K. Hunter, eds. *John Webster: A Critical Anthology.* Harmondsworth, UK: Penguin, 1969.

Jardine, Lisa. *Still Harping on Daughters: Women and Drama in the Age of Shakespeare.* Brighton, UK: Harvester, 1983.

Leech, Clifford. *John Webster: A Critical Study.* London: Hogarth Press, 1951.

Luckyj, Christina. *A Winter's Snake: Dramatic Form in the Tragedies of John Webster.* Athens: University of Georgia Press, 1989.

Morris, Brian, ed. *John Webster.* London: Ernest Benn, 1970.

Murray, P. B. *A Study of John Webster.* Studies in English Literature 50. The Hague: Mouton, 1969.

Orgel, Stephen. *Impersonations: The Performance of Gender in Shakespeare's England.* Cambridge: Cambridge University Press, 1996.

Ornstein, Robert. *The Moral Vision of Jacobean Tragedy,* Madison: University of Wisconsin Press, 1960.

Pearson, Jacqueline. *Tragedy and Tragicomedy in the Plays of John Webster.* Manchester, UK: Manchester University Press, 1980.

Price, Hereward T. "The Function of Imagery in Webster." *PMLA* 70 (1955): 717–39.

Ribner, Irving. *Jacobean Tragedy: The Quest for Moral Order.* New York, Barnes & Noble, 1962.

Schuman, S. "The Ring and the Jewel in Webster's Tragedies." *Texas Studies in Literature and Language* 14 (1972): 253–68.

Stoll, E. E. *John Webster: The Periods of His Work as Determined by His Relations to the Drama of His Time.* Boston: Harvard Cooperative Society, 1905.

• Wymer, Ronald. *Webster and Ford.* London: St. Martin's Press, 1995.

Studies of The Duchess of Malfi

Alexander, N. "Intelligence in *The Duchess of Malfi*." In *John Webster*. Ed. B. Morris (pp. 93–112). London: Benn, 1970.

Baker, C. B. "The Static Protagonist in *The Duchess of Malfi*." *Texas Studies in Literature and Language* 22 (1980): 343–57.

Balizet, A. M. "'Drowned in Blood': Honor, Bloodline, and Domestic Ideology in *The Duchess of Malfi* and *El Médico De Su Honra*." *Comparative Literature Studies* 49 (2012): 23–49.

Bartels, E. C. "Strategies of Submission: Desdemona, the Duchess, and the Assertion of Desire." *Studies in English Literature* 36 (1996): 417–435.

Behling, L. L. "'S/he Scandles our proceedings': The Anxiety of Alternative Sexualities in *The White Devil* and *The Duchess of Malfi*." *English Language Notes* 33 (1996), 24–44.

Belsey, Catherine. "Emblem and Antithesis in *The Duchess of Malfi*." *Renaissance Drama* 11 (1979): 115–34.

Belton, E. R. (1976). "The Function of Antonio in *The Duchess of Malfi*." *Texas Studies in Literature and Language* (18): 474–85.

Bergeron, D. M. "The Wax Figures in *The Duchess of Malfi*." *Studies in English Literature, 1500–1900* 18 (1978): 331–39.

Berlin, N. "*The Duchess of Malfi*: Act V and Genre." *Genre* 3 (1970): 351–63.

Best, M. R. "A Precarious Balance: Structure in *The Duchess of Malfi*." In *Shakespeare and Some Others: Essays on Shakespeare and Some of His Contemporaries*. Ed. Alan Brissenden (pp. 159–77). Adelaide, Australia: University of Adelaide, Department of English, 1976.

Bloom, Harold, ed. *John Webster's "The Duchess of Malfi."* Modern Critical Interpretations. New York: Chelsea House, 1987.

Boklund, Gunnar. "*The Duchess of Malfi*": *Sources, Themes, Characters*. Cambridge: Harvard University Press, 1962.

Calderwood, J. L. "*The Duchess of Malfi*: Styles of Ceremony." *Essays in Criticism* 2 (1972): 133–47.

Callaghan, Dympna. *The Duchess of Malfi: Contemporary Critical Essays*. New Casebooks. Basingstoke, UK: Macmillan, 2000.

Cave, Richard. "*The White Devil*" and "*The Duchess of Malfi*," Text and Performance. Basingstoke, UK: Macmillan, 1988.

• Chalk, B. "Webster's 'Worthyest Monument': The Problem of Posterity in *The Duchess of Malfi*." *Studies in Philology* 108 (2011): 379–402.

Cordner, Michael. "*The Duchess of Malfi* and the Tragedy of Service." *English Review* 21.4 (2011): 28–31.

• Correll, B. "Malvolio at Malfi: Managing Desire in Shakespeare and Webster." *Shakespeare Quarterly* 58 (2007): 65–92.

Doebler, B. A. "Continuity in the Art of Dying: *The Duchess of Malfi*." *Comparative Drama* 14 (1979): 203–15.

Dowd, M. M. "Delinquent Pedigrees: Revision, Lineage, and Spatial Rhetoric in *The Duchess of Malfi*." *English Literary Renaissance* 39 (2009): 499–526.

Driscoll, J. P. "Integrity of Life in *The Duchess of Malfi*." *Drama Survey* 6 (1967): 42–53.

Duer, L. "The Landscape of Imagination in *The Duchess of Malfi*." *Modern Language Studies* 10 (1979): 3–10.

Feinberg, A. "Observation and Theatricality in Webster's *The Duchess of Malfi*." *Theatre Research International* 6 (1979): 36–44.

Graves, R. B. "*The Duchess of Malfi* at the Globe and the Blackfriars." *Renaissance Drama* 9 (1978): 193–209.

Green, R. "'Ears Prejudicate' in *Mariam* and *The Duchess of Malfi*." *Studies in English Literature 1500–1900* 43 (2003): 459–74.

Greenhalgh, S. "The Jacobeans on Television: *The Duchess of Malfi* and *'Tis Pity She's a Whore* at Chastleton House." *Shakespeare Bulletin* 29 (2011): 573–89.

Haslem, L. S. "'Troubled with the Mother': Longings, Purgings, and the Maternal Body in *Bartholomew Fair* and *The Duchess of Malfi*." *Modern Philology* 92 (1995): 438–59.

Heering, H. "The Self and Madness: Marlowe's *Edward II* and Webster's *The Duchess of Malfi*." *Journal of Medieval and Renaissance Studies* 9 (1979): 307–23.

Henderson, A. "Death on the Stage, Death of the Stage: The Antitheatricality of *The Duchess of Malfi*." *Theatre Journal* 42 (1990): 194–207.

Jacqueline, P. "The Difficulty of *The White Devil* and *The Duchess* of *Malfi*." *Critical Quarterly* 22 (2007): 43–54.

• Jankowski, Theodora A. "Defining/Confining the Duchess: Negotiating the Female Body in John Webster's *The Duchess of Malfi*." *Studies in Philology* 87 (1990): 221–45.

Kerrigan, John C. "Action and Confession, Fate and Despair in the Violent Conclusion of *The Duchess of Malfi*." *Ben Jonson Journal* 8 (2001): 249–50.

Kerwin, W. "'Physicians are like kings': Medical Politics and *The Duchess of Malfi*." *English Literary Renaissance* 28 (1998): 95–117.

Kiefer, F. "The Dance of the Madmen in *The Duchess of Malfi*." *The Journal of Medieval and Renaissance Studies* 17 (1987): 211–233.

Kistner, A. L, and M. K. "The Big Sleep: Expectation and Delusion in *The Duchess of Malfi*." *Studia Neophilologica* 64 (1992): 159–70.

———. "Man's Will and Its Futility in *The Duchess of Malfi*." *Studia Neophilologica* 68 (2008): 49–60.

Leech, Clifford. *John Webster: "The Duchess of Malfi."* London: Edward Arnold, 1963.

Leinwand, T. B. "Coniugium Interruptum in Shakespeare and Webster." *ELH* 72 (2005): 239–57.

Lord, J. M. "*The Duchess of Malfi*: 'The Spirit of Greatness' and 'of Woman.'" *Studies in English Literature* 16 (1976): 305–17.

Loughnane, Rory. "The Artificial Figures and Staging Remembrance in Webster's *The Duchess of Malfi*." In *The Arts of Remembrance in Early Modern England: Memorial Cultures of the Post Reformation*. Ed. Andrew Gordon and Thomas Rist (pp. 211–28). Farnham, UK: Ashgate, 2013.

• Luckyj, Christina. "'Great Women of Pleasure': Main Plot and Subplot in *The Duchess of Malfi*." *Studies in English Literature* 27 (1987): 267–83.

Luecke, Jane Marie. "*The Duchess of Malfi*: Comic and Satiric Confusion in a Tragedy." *SEL* 4 (1964): 275–90.

Luisi, David. "The Function of Bosola in *The Duchess of Malfi*." *English Studies* 53 (1972): 509–13.

McLuskie, Kathleen. "Drama and Sexual Politics: The case of John Webster's Duchess." In *Drama, Sex and Politics*. Ed. James Redmond (pp. 77–91). Themes in Drama 7. Cambridge: Cambridge University Press, 1985.

Moore, Don. D. *John Webster and His Critics 1617–1964*. Baton Rouge: Louisiana State University Press, 1966.

• ———. *Webster: The Critical Heritage*. London: Routledge & Kegan Paul, 1982.

Mulryne, J. R. "*The White Devil* and *The Duchess of Malfi*." In *Jacobean Theatre*. Ed. John Russell Brown and Bernard Harris (pp. 201–26). Stratford-upon-Avon Studies 1. London: Edward Arnold, 1961.

Neill, Michael. "Fame's Best Friend: The Endings of *The Duchess of Malfi*." In *Issues of Death: Mortality and Identity in English Renaissance Tragedy* (pp. 320–53). Oxford: Clarendon Press, 1997.

———. "Monuments and Ruins as Symbols in *The Duchess of Malfi*." In *Drama and Symbolism*. Ed. James Redmond (pp. 71–87). Themes in Drama 4. Cambridge: Cambridge University Press, 1982.

Nordfors, M. "Science and Realism in John Webster's *The Duchess of Malfi*." *Studia Neophilologica* 49 (1977): 233–42.

Oakes, E. "*The Duchess of Malfi* as a Tragedy of Identity." *Studies in Philology* 96 (1999): 51–68.

Peterson, Joyce E. *Curs'd Example*: The Duchess of Malfi *and Commonweal Tragedy*. Columbia: University of Missouri Press, 1978.

Potter, Lois. "Realism Versus Nightmare: Problems of Staging *The Duchess of Malfi*." In Joseph G. Price (ed.), *The Triple Bond: Plays, Mainly Shakespearean, in Performance* (pp. 170–89). University Park: Pennsylvania State University Press, 1975.

Randall, Dale. "The Rank and Earthy Background of Certain Physical Symbols in *The Duchess of Malfi*." *Renaissance Drama* 18 (1987): 171–203.

Steen, S. J. "The Crime of Marriage: Arbella Stuart and *The Duchess of Malfi*." *Sixteenth Century Journal* 22 (1991): 61–76.

Thomson, L. "Fortune and Virtue in *The Duchess of Malfi*." *Comparative Drama* 33 (1999): 474–94.

Tricomi, A. H. "Historicizing the Imagery of the Demonic in *The Duchess of Malfi*." *Journal of Medieval and Early Modern Studies* 34 (2004): 345–72.

———. "The Severed Hand in Webster's *The Duchess of Malfi*." *SEL* 44 (2004): 347–58.

Wadsworth, F. W. "American Performances of *The Duchess of Malfi*." *Theatre Survey* 11 (1970): 151–66.

———. "Shorn and Abated: British Performances of *The Duchess of Malfi*." *Theatre Survey* 10 (1969): 89–104

———. "Some Nineteenth Century Revivals of *The Duchess of Malfi*." *Theatre Survey* 8 (1967): 67–83.

Whigham, Frank. "Sexual and Social Mobility in *The Duchess of Malfi*." *PMLA* 100 (1985): 167–86.